THE FOUNDATION OF PHENOMENOLOGY

EDMUND HUSSERL AND THE QUEST
FOR A RIGOROUS SCIENCE OF PHILOSOPHY

paine-whitman studies in social science and social theory

THE FOUNDATION OF PHENOMENOLOGY

PHENOMENOLOGY

Edmund Husserl and the Quest
for a Rigorous Science of Philosophy

BY

MARVIN FARBER

Professor of Philosophy, University of Pennsylvania

NEW YORK

PAINE-WHITMAN PUBLISHERS

1962

Paine-Whitman Publishers
1182 Broadway, New York (1) New York

142.7

F219f2

THE PUBLICATION OF THIS VOLUME HAS BEEN
AIDED BY A GRANT FROM THE AMERICAN COUNCIL OF
LEARNED SOCIETIES, FROM A FUND PROVIDED BY
THE CARNEGIE CORPORATION OF NEW YORK.

Second Edition

PRINTED GREGG ASSOCIATES, S.A. BRUSSELS, BELGIUM.

AFTER TWENTY-FIVE YEARS: BY WAY
OF AN INTRODUCTION

IT APPEARS APPROPRIATE to take another look at Edmund Husserl and phenomenology some twenty-five years after beginning the writing of the present volume.

In 1936 Husserl was near the end of his life, with his philosophy perpetually "unknown" — one might almost say, unknown as a matter of principle. That could not be said about his early thought. He had begun his career with studies on fundamental themes in mathematics, logic, and psychology. His first works were written clearly, with much attention to the literature, and they were entirely intelligible. The reception of his ideas would have been greatly facilitated had he proceeded along his early lines as a mathematical philosopher and logician. But he was affected by motives explainable in the light of the development of German philosophy deriving from Kant and Hegel. A justifiable feeling of independence became intensified by continued hostility and misunderstandings on the part of most of his contemporaries who reacted to his work. His independent development, allowing little personal discussion with dissenting thinkers, and his creation of a unique technical vocabulary, added to the difficulties in understanding his further studies. The legend that the real Husserl was "unknown" could easily become plausible. Scholars were admonished to look to the unpublished literary remains of Husserl for his "real" philosophy. Husserl's predecessor in Freiburg, Heinrich Rickert, who belonged to a rival idealistic tendency, was able to note with some truth that "Husserl held back" in the publication of his ideas. Furthermore, it was argued that Husserl's mode of inquiry could not be coordinated with other types of inquiry, and that it could not be subsumed under the genus of method. This could only become more confusing and discouraging to the student of philosophy.

Substantial progress has been made in the process of publishing the Husserl manuscripts. It is certainly true that a more complete knowledge of the nature and scope of Husserl's work is now possible. The present writer has taken account of some of Husserl's writings which were not available during his lifetime, in his *Naturalism and Subjectivism*. In this book, a thoroughgoing reconsideration of the first volume of the *Ideas* of 1913 is followed by an examination of the second and third volumes of that work. Positively, Husserl is viewed in the light of his attempt to construct a philosophy of pure subjectivism; and negatively, in his conspicuous historical function of opposing naturalism as a philosophical tendency. It has been generally supposed that he disposed of psychologism in all its forms, along with the admittedly faulty naturalism of his time. A reconsideration of his arguments, however, would lead one to qualify that judgment. Husserl's service to the philosophy of formal logic may be recognized,[1] without jumping to the conclusion that there are no points of contact between logic and psychology, biology, or social science.[2] It must be decided whether evidence of a faulty type of naturalism therewith disposes of all forms of naturalism, including a critical naturalism which is oriented to the progress of the sciences, and is constructed in strict conformity to the principles of methodology. The attempt at a radical refutation of naturalism, with the use of *ad hominem* charges, as illustrated by Husserl in his *Logos* essay on "Philosophy as a Rigorous Science," proves to be a hollow victory. The naturalist does not have to accept the purportedly damaging commitments in question, in order to be a naturalist. The convinced subjectivist may become so much accustomed to his stereotypes ("naturalism," "materialism," "empiricism," *et al.*) that he fails to do justice to the ranks of emerging science-oriented philosophers. It would have to be shown whether Dewey's *Logic* could be affected by the anti-naturalistic barrage of Husserl's *Logos* essay, or by any of the critical forays elsewhere in his writings. In short, Husserl's standing as a foe of naturalism must be reassessed.

On the other hand, his standing as a purely descriptive investigator in the subjectivistic sphere will not be challenged. Although much of his work still remains to be tested for its fruitfulness and possible results, there can be no doubt about his genius for painstaking descriptive inquiry. Ranking high in his work are his epistemological (phenomenological) studies of logical experience and reasoning; and also his descriptive studies of time-consciousness. It may be expected that psychologists will increasingly take account of his findings in the years to come.

---

1. Cf. the favorable judgment of Ernst Cassirer, for example, in his *Logic of the Humanities,* p. 130 (Yale University Press, New Haven, 1961).
2. Cf. John Dewey's significant attempt at a logic of inquiry, with due attention paid to the existential matrix of inquiry, in his *Logic, The Theory of Inquiry* (Henry Holt and Co., New York, 1938).

The merits of subjectivism as a specially devised type of procedure will not be denied. But it is only one type of procedure, and is not the sole *organon* of philosophy. Although one can approach problems of ontology on Husserl's premises (to begin with, the pure experiences of an individual knower, with all beliefs in transcendent existence extruded or suspended), major aspects of ontology are unavoidably shut out thereby. Husserl's discussion of wholes and parts in his *Logical Investigations*, and his treatment of fact and essence in his *Ideas*, are indications of his early mode of approach to ontology. He could not have been expected to bridge the gap between facts and essences or ideal forms, any more than any other thinkers deriving from Plato, all the way down to Whitehead. The concepts of essence, ideality, whole, part, etc., are devices for handling problems of experience. They cannot be self-sufficient for the purposes of a complete ontology, however. For the latter, *basic facts* must be taken over as the point of departure for philosophic inquiry. Existence cannot be derived from essence, or from any ideal constructions. It must be acknowledged in its prior status — prior to human experience in all its forms. The basic fact of the independent existence and reality of the physical world, antedating the emergence of mind (and philosophical systems) by an indefinitely great amount of time, and the dependence of mind upon cultural conditions, must be regarded as preconditions for all sound inquiry in philosophy. These are *factual* truths, conveyed to us by the course of ordinary experience, and by a host of scientific observations.

To retort that this is "naïve," or a "dogma," as Husserl insisted, is an indication of the astonishing length to which a philosopher long confined to his special "cave" could go. Surely it is not naïve or dogmatic to refer to Husserl's own parents as antedating his revered "phenomenological reduction." But that also applies to the ancestors of both of them, and the culture systems of which they were parts; but also the realm of physical nature, which must be accepted along with the culture systems; and therewith is granted the independence of infinite nature. It may appear disarming to allow that the natural view of the world has its "rights," but this admission may be merely a means of outflanking naturalism, while holding in reserve the epistemological principle of the limitation of reality to its place in experience. Without the basic truth concerning the independent natural world, there can be no talk of a phenomenological access to existence, and only a partial or an ancillary approach to an ontology would then be possible. The flesh and blood of ontology would be lacking without that truth. The real naïveté and dogmatism are shown by those who fail to recognize this truth, and who see only naïvetè and dogmatism in it. Let us guard against the error of "pseudo-ontology" — *i.e.*, seeking to find existence where it cannot be found on the available premises, because it has been extruded on principle by the "reduction." Only pure consciousness could come from pure consciousness; only spirit could come from spirit; and even the self-alienation of spirit remains what it was (let us do it the honor of allowing that it "was" in some sense), namely, spirit in disguise. The proof that the conditions of thought, or of experience, are also the conditions of the objects of thought, or of the objects of experience, remains to be established. The "conditions of thought" must first be shown to be effective conditions of all thought-experiences; and it must be proved that the same set of conditions applies to experience and to reality. Nowhere has Husserl done so.

What he has achieved will not be impugned, even by those who reject his arguments for idealism as inconclusive. Idealism reached its last, and its most ingenious, stronghold in transcendental phenomenology. Fortunately, that is a rationalistic type of philosophy, which makes an evaluation of it possible. The recently published volumes of Husserl's *First Philosophy* (*Erste Philosophie*) show how fully conscious he was of his idealistic mission.

The newer developments in the more general phenomenological tendency, known as "existential," are indebted to various aspects of Husserl's thought. But they are also indebted to other sources of influence, so that their appraisal presents a manysided problem, especially because of the elements of irrationalism that have appeared. Such mixed derivates of phenomenology tend to shine with the borrowed lustre of the terms "existence" and "being", which are more properly used in the naturalistic setting provided by the sciences and ordinary experience.

Husserl's critical view of the "existential" philosophy has been indicated by his marginal notes on some of Heidegger's writings, for example. It was his faith that transcendental, "constitutive" phenomenology was adequate for all philosophical purposes. In his last period, he introduced the concept of a "life-world" (a "pre-given" life-world), which was to bridge the gap between pure consciousness and the world of ordinary experience. It is important not to make excessive claims for this "life-world," lest it be as much abused as Husserl's *Wesensschau* ("essential seeing") was in its time. The world of natural existence was not accorded prior status with the conception of a pre-given life-world. The basic idealistic thesis of phenomenology was supposed to be further implemented, but not abandoned, with that conception.

The present writer never took the step toward acceptance of phenomenological idealism as a philosophy, even while studying with Husserl. He has always maintained an ontological position of physical monism which allows for a diversity of systems, depending upon the selective organization of the subject-matter of each system. This ontological monism goes along with logical pluralism, thus avoiding the error of over-simplification, which is so characteristic of a "reductionistic" ontology (the term "reductionistic" is obviously entirely different from the term as used in phenomenology, where it properly means restriction to the objects and contents of the experiences themselves).

One may accept the descriptive procedure of phenomenology without any idealistic commitments, and also do justice to the needs of a naturalistic ontology. That is made possible by means of a general conception of methods and their function for the solution of problems. A diversity of methods is required by the endless diversity of problems. If methods are instituted to solve problems, or to answer questions, we must be prepared to enlarge our conception of methods accordingly. The procedure of phenomenology is well suited to handle *one* set of problems. If used solely, it engenders new, artifical problems, which are "methogenic" in character — i.e., they follow from the use of the method in question. Thus, the problem of other minds, and the problem of existence, are methogenic for phenomenology. The methodological pluralism of the present writer has led him to urge the "cooperation of methods," insofar as they can be justified logically in connection with the solution of problems, and by the facts. In such cases it appears senseless to continue the stubborn warfare of the schools. The latter, while understandable historically, frequently turns out to be a mere survival of loyalty to a more or less vested tradition.

Despite the process of publication of Husserl's manuscripts by the Husserl Archives of Louvain University, the major outlines of his development, and the "foundation of phenomenology" itself, remain as presented in the present volume. The quarterly journal, *Philosophy and Phenomenological Research*, now published by the University of Pennsylvania, has continued to take account of the publication of Husserl's writings, and of the pertinent literature in the larger phenomenological tendency.

Of recent publications, mention may be made of Husserl's *Die Idee der Phänomenologie* (1950), which gives an early statement of his reflections leading to the formulation of a transcendental phenomenology; the second and third volumes of his *Ideen* (1952); the *Krisis der europäischen Wissenschaften und die transzendentale Phänomenologie* (1954); his *Erste Philosophie* (two volumes, 1956, 1959); the German original of the *Cartesian Meditations* (1950), of which an English translation by Dorion Cairns has appeared (1960) — all published by Martinus Nijhoff, The Hague, Holland, under the direction of Professor H. L. Van Breda — along with the present writer's recent critical work, *Naturalism and Subjectivism* (Charles C. Thomas, Springfield, Illinois, 1959).

Much still remains to be done for the understanding and critical evaluation of many aspects of Husserl's work, including its relationships and possible usefulness for other fields of inquiry. Before all, Husserl must be understood, and errors due to superficial impressions must be avoided. It is hoped that the present volume will continue to be an aid toward that end.

Philadelphia, Pa.   MARVIN FARBER.
February 24, 1962.

PREFACE

THE PRESENT WORK is the third in a planned series of Publications of the International Phenomenological Society, following the quarterly journal, *Philosophy and Phenomenological Research*, and *Philosophical Essays in Memory of Edmund Husserl*. Offering a detailed account of Husserl's philosophy as it developed from logical psychologism to transcendental phenomenology, in connection with its background and critics, it portrays him as historically conditioned, as well as in the role of a builder of a lasting scientific philosophy. The main content of his most famous work, the *Logische Untersuchungen*, is included, in essential fulfillment of a promise made to Husserl to render that work in English, the aim being to combine freedom of presentation with exactness of meaning. These investigations provide indispensable examples of phenomenological description. The writer's appraisals and critical comments are intended not only to evaluate particular ideas and principles, but also to determine the proper function of phenomenology as a methodological procedure. In keeping with the restricted scope of the book, the treatment of transcendental phenomenology is necessarily selective, a more detailed discussion being reserved for later publications.

It will be clear to the reader that an extensive literature is necessary for the complete assimilation of Husserl's contributions, and for independent investigations along phenomenological lines. The literature of the first phase of this movement, which included a number of excellent and significant studies, is being added to in the present period, in which there is sure to be greater interaction with other movements and thinkers. Of work now in preparation, mention may be made of publications undertaken by Dorion Cairns on transcendental phenomenology, Aron Gurwitsch on the phenomenology of perception, Fritz Kaufmann in the field of the philosophy of history and culture, and Herbert Spiegelberg on the theory of value.

All responsible, competent critical discussion is welcome, and should be encouraged wherever possible. But reactions which are not based upon adequate preliminary study are as absurd as they are in symbolic logic, or in mathematical physics. The professional hater of phenomenology is a product of the European warfare of "schools" who has no place on the American scene. It is to be hoped that all earnest readers will give this philosophy the attention required for its understanding. Such readers will not fail to recognize in it the spirit of a coöperative and genuinely philosophical enterprise.

In the course of his graduate study in Germany, which was made possible by Harvard traveling fellowships, the writer enjoyed the close association and personal guidance of Husserl, who remains one of the great influences upon his development. But the writer may not be credited with "orthodoxy" with respect to the later system of transcendental phenomenological idealism, where he has always differed with his honored master, and is compelled to reject the systematic attempts at its justification. A strict interpretation of phenomenology as a descriptive philosophy is possible, and is alone capable of winning general agreement.

Special acknowledgment is due to the University of Buffalo and its officers, Chancellor Samuel P. Capen and Dean Julian Park, for arranging for a sabbatical leave of absence and otherwise aiding in making this work possible; to the writer's colleagues in their common phenomenological enterprise — Fritz Kaufmann, Dorion Cairns, and Felix Kaufmann — for their careful reading of parts of the manuscript which appeared in the first volume of *Philosophy and Phenomenological Research* (included in the first and seventeenth chapters of the present work), and to these scholars, in addition to Alfred Schuetz, for suggestions as to terminology and discussions as to the direction to be taken by the phenomenological movement. Naturally, the writer bears sole responsibility for all decisions made in this work. Parts of the sixteenth chapter have appeared in *The Journal of Philosophy* (1930), *The Philosophical Review* (1935), and in the writer's monograph, *Phenomenology as a Method and as a Philosophical Discipline* (1928). Some details concerning Husserl's early life were provided by Mrs. Edmund Husserl. Finally, acknowledgment is due to the writer's wife for editorial aid and assistance in proofreading; and to the Harvard University Press for its excellent work.

M. F.

BUFFALO, NEW YORK
January 23, 1943

CONTENTS

CONTENTS

CONTENTS

CONTENTS

THE FOUNDATION OF PHENOMENOLOGY

CHAPTER I

EDMUND HUSSERL AND THE BACKGROUND OF HIS PHILOSOPHY

NOTHING in recent philosophy approaches the supreme confidence with which Husserl announced his triumphant beginning of a new science of philosophy, an "absolute" discipline achieved by means of an elaborately worked out method. It was advanced as the real positive outcome of the philosophical efforts of the centuries. In fact, all preceding philosophers were classified by him as either adumbrating or falling short of the ideals of phenomenology. There is something majestic and heroic about the tone of Husserl. His is not an opinion hastily advanced. More than fifty years of consecutive reflection and hard work, resulting in numerous superb examples of descriptive analysis, have made it necessary to greet his claim with respect and to give his contentions a hearing. The thought and contributions of one of the most penetrating and thorough of the philosophers of the last century deserve more widespread attention than they have received. A thoroughgoing consideration of his philosophy is now made all the more necessary in view of the insistent claim that his philosophy is still unknown,[1] and the philosopher's own repeated assertion that he had been misunderstood. The fact that Husserl rarely answered his critics has made it more difficult for the general philosophical public to grasp the significance of his work. For the most part he went steadfastly on his way, regardless of opposition, which was largely based upon misunderstanding. The important publications which appeared near the close of his life include two replies to critics, the only elaborate ones published since his answer to Palagyi in 1903. It is now possible to examine and appraise the phenomenological philosophy with far greater assurance than has hitherto been the case, despite the fact that numerous manuscripts have never been published. These manuscripts contain an enormous amount of valuable material which will enrich and no doubt modify the understanding of the phenomenological method. Thus the recent publication of Husserl's *Experience and Judgment* was revealing, and added much to the understanding of his philosophy of

---

[1] Cf. E. Fink, "Was will die Phänomenologie Edmund Husserls?" *Die Tatwelt* (1934), p. 15.

logic. It is nevertheless reasonable to assert that enough of Husserl's writings have been published to provide a basis for a just appreciation of his philosophy and a point of departure for further fruitful work along phenomenological lines.

It is necessary to conduct the examination of this philosophy objectively, i.e., free from "standpoint" narrowness and from personal attachments. This means that one must be prepared to recognize the positive advance made by Husserl in philosophy and in outlying sciences such as psychology; and also that one must endeavor to ascertain whether all elements in his thought are consonant with his avowed precepts. Of particular interest is the final form of idealism represented by the later system of transcendental phenomenology, which reveals the limits as well as the merits of the subjective mode of philosophical procedure. The renewed attention to method in philosophy makes the examination of phenomenology pertinent; and the great development of logical theory makes it desirable to bring phenomenology into connection with it for possible mutual reactions. Particular attention must be devoted to his logical contributions. Their significance for the present is great in view of doubts and difficulties which are analogous to the problems of the period of the *Logical Investigations*.

Inasmuch as the riddle presented by Husserl's thought can best be solved by close adherence to its development, some of the early influences upon it will be pointed out, and its various stages will be indicated. It will not be possible in the present account to do justice to all the influences: Husserl derived from the entire history of philosophy, and undoubtedly owed much indirectly to thinkers never explicitly mentioned by him. It will be sufficient for present purposes to call particular attention to that controversy for which Husserl has been most famous — the issue of the relationship of psychology and philosophy (in particular, logic) — and to indicate, in part by the mere mention of names, the most important effective influences upon his thought as acknowledged by himself.

A. PSYCHOLOGISM AND PHILOSOPHY IN THE 1880's

Prominent in philosophy at the close of the nineteenth century was a standpoint known as "psychologism." The philosophy of a given period has always been conditioned and influenced by the leading scientific ideas, particularly by those which were new. Thus rationalism in modern philosophy reflected the advances in the mathematical and physical sciences. In the period under consideration the rising science of psychology had a twofold significance for German philosophy: it suggested a sure way of solving perplexing problems of logic and the theory of knowledge, and it afforded either a substitute or a supplement to the idealistic standpoint in philosophy. Psychologism had already been prominent in English philosophy, J. S. Mill having been a recent representative. In Germany, Wundt, Sigwart, and Lipps may serve as examples. Natorp, Brentano, Stumpf, and later Frege are of particular importance, as providing the main historical background for Husserl. The reaction against psychologism was clearly illustrated in Natorp's early writings; and Schuppe and Volkelt, if only in a broad, programmatic manner, anticipated Husserl in the theory of knowledge, although they had no direct influence upon him. This is not to impugn Husserl's originality, for the systematic use to which he put the same motives resulted in their being recast radically; and in the course of the development of phenomenology problems were recognized of which his predecessors had no notion.

Psychologism was an extreme point of view, and a reaction was inevitable. Natorp's review of Theodor Lipps' *Basic Facts of Mental Life* [2] is an early indication of such a reaction. Lipps regarded psychology as constituting the basis of philosophy, but Natorp expressed doubt as to the possibility of "basing" logic and the theory of knowledge upon psychology. Lipps considered such topics as the psychological ground of the principle of contradiction and the general function of concepts in knowledge. In his view, the genetic derivation of the basic laws of knowledge out of original facts of psychical life was identical with their "epistemological" foundation; the theory of knowledge was a branch of psychology. Everyone will concede to Lipps, Natorp remarked, that psychical facts are represented in the laws of knowledge, and that these facts, as psychical, are also an object of investigation for psychology. Knowledge is admittedly only a psychical process, in the form of concepts and theories, or in general as consciousness. Even the truth as something objectively valid must be investigated by means of the consciousness which thinking beings have of it. The concepts and the truth of geometry are psychical facts in that sense, and yet Euclid's axioms are not regarded as psychological laws by anyone, nor does anyone suppose that its objective certainty depends upon the psychological understanding of geometrical presentation. Natorp merely emphasized the fact that the consciousness of truth is independent of all genetic explanation by means of general psychological connections, and called attention to the independence of an objective foundation of the principles of knowledge. The critique and the psychology of knowledge, in his view, require and condition each other. An indication of his point

---

[2] Cf. Paul Natorp, review of Lipps' *Grundthatsachen des Seelenlebens* (Bonn, 1883), in the *Göttingische gelehrte Anzeigen*, vol. IX (1885), pp. 190–232.

of view is given by his assertion that a law of knowledge is *a priori*, just as every law is *a priori* as opposed to that which is subject to the law.

Natorp's early reaction against psychologism is also expressed in a paper on the objective and the subjective foundation of knowledge,[3] in which he argued that there is either no logic, or it must build entirely on its own ground, and not borrow its foundations from any other science. Those that make logic to be a branch of psychology assume that psychology is the basic science, and that logic is at best an application of psychology. Natorp asserted that not only the meaning of logic but the meaning of all objective science is ignored and almost perverted into its opposite, if one makes the objective truth of knowledge to be dependent upon subjective experience. To base logic upon subjective grounds would be to annul it as an independent theory of the objective validity of knowledge. Hence Natorp was not only defending the rights of logic in the hitherto accepted sense of the term, but also the claim to objective validity that is made by all science, when he maintained that the objective validity must also be objectively founded. He formulated as a presupposition of objective science the precept that true scientific knowledge may depend only upon those laws which can be brought to certainty in the inner connection of science, and which are developed in a logical form, independently of all presuppositions that might be introduced from elsewhere. Thus all recourse to the knowing subject and its capacity for objective science is ruled out as completely foreign. Natorp was very clear in affirming that the objectivity of science requires the "overcoming" of subjectivity. His view of scientific truth is compatible, as far as it goes, with Husserl's later ideal of a rigorous science of philosophy, but it does not go so far as even to suggest the idea of a universal science, or of a "root-science" of philosophy. The object of Natorp's criticism was psychologism, however, and he succeeded in formulating the issue clearly. He pointed out that scientific truth, as illustrated in mathematical natural science, becomes certain for us on the basis of objective presuppositions, and he insisted upon the autonomy of such science. The mathematician and the physicist were not to look for the ground of the truth of their cognitions in psychology.

The expression "objective validity" was used to indicate independence of the subjective aspect of knowing. Its positive meaning was less clear to Natorp. The idea that there are objects outside of and independent of all subjectivity would be one answer; but Natorp believed that the "being-

---

[3] P. Natorp, "Über objektive und subjektive Begründung der Erkenntnis" (*Erster Aufsatz*), *Philosophische Monatshefte*, vol. XXIII (1887), pp. 257–286. Husserl refers to pp. 265 f. of this paper in the *Logical Investigations*, for a supplement to his discussion of psychologism.

in-itself" of the object was itself a riddle, in conformity no doubt to his unresolved Kantianism. He held that the object's independence of the subjectivity of knowing could only be understood by means of an abstraction, for objects really are given to us only in the cognition that we have of them. Thus it would be necessary to abstract from the content of subjective experience. In Natorp's view, the true beginnings and bases of knowledge are final objective unities. In mathematics it is not the phenomena that are basic, but rather the fundamental abstractions, which are expressions of the unity of the determination of possible phenomena, such as point, line, straightness, and equality of magnitude. All of these involve the fundamental function of "objectification," and the Kantian and Platonic "unity of the manifold." It is only in this way that the uniquely determined "phenomena" of science are possible. Natorp argued that there must be a determining and "positing" function, in order to make this positivity possible. In a later discussion [4] he undertook to see how the kind of foundation which he used was objective in the sense in which mathematical procedure is objective, and to show that formal logic must be based upon the logic of objective knowledge, or transcendental logic.

Another important idea of the time was the ideal of freedom from presuppositions in philosophical procedure. This ideal was taken by Husserl in the *Logical Investigations* as an obvious requirement that is to be imposed upon epistemological investigation.

It is possible to point out the direct influences upon his thought at the beginning of his career. They were derived from a few sources to begin with, although Husserl was later to approach philosophers who were at first avoided or neglected. Natorp, Volkelt, Schuppe, and Rehmke may be singled out as typical representatives of the rising generation of idealists whose works were to be prominent in the philosophical literature of the coming decades. Their published writings were either closely read by Husserl, as in the case of Natorp, or they may be regarded as developments parallel to Husserl's, which responded to similar motives. The orientation to Kant's philosophy, always prominent in Germany, was to be of great significance for Husserl. Brentano, who is not easily classified, combined Scholasticism and the philosophy of Aristotle with empiricism. He inaugurated a fruitful period of development in psychology, Stumpf being one of his earliest productive disciples. The modern development

---

[4] Cf. P. Natorp, "Quantität und Qualität in Begriff, Urteil, und gegenständlicher Erkenntnis," *Phil. Monatshefte*, vol. XXVII (1891), pp. 1–32, 129–160. In his *Einleitung in die Psychologie nach kritischer Methode* (Freiburg i. B., 1888), Natorp set himself the task of making secure the bases of psychology by a preliminary investigation of its object and method.

of symbolic logic, which was begun in England by Boole, was carried on in Germany by Schröder and Frege. These scholars may be cited particularly in reviewing the philosophical scene into which Husserl entered when he joined the faculty of the University of Halle in 1887. They represent a special section of the German philosophical world of the time, reflecting his early interests.

"My teacher Brentano" was an expression frequently heard in Husserl's classroom. Intellectually his debt to Brentano was considerable in the early period; but it was the moral element and the personal example of Brentano which led him to choose philosophy as a lifework, and which constituted a lasting influence upon him. Husserl was a grateful student of Brentano, whom he accompanied, along with Stumpf on occasion, during vacation trips. He was not at the time prepared, however, to profit fully by such contact. The effectiveness of Brentano as a teacher is sufficiently shown by the number of noted scholars owing their start to him, a group including Stumpf, Husserl, Meinong, Höfler, and Marty.

Among the men who exercised a lasting influence upon Husserl was Masaryk, whom he met during his first semester in Leipzig, in 1876. Husserl was seventeen years of age at the time, and Masaryk, his senior by eight years and already a doctor, guided his younger compatriot. Because of Husserl's dominant interest in astronomy, Masaryk's advice that he go to Brentano was not taken at the time. After three semesters he went to Berlin, where he found in Weierstrass a teacher who impressed upon him the ideal of the impersonal devotion to truth of the real scientist. Having taken his degree and completed the customary year of military service in Vienna, he renewed personal contact with Masaryk, who was then an instructor in the University of Vienna. It was then that he heard Brentano, and made the crucial decision to become a philosopher. His feeling of personal indebtedness to Brentano outlasted the inevitable philosophical break with the latter, a step which cost him much inner struggle.

Husserl has left a revealing tribute to Brentano in his contribution to a Brentano memorial volume.[5] He attended Brentano's lectures for two years, from 1884 to 1886, after having completed his formal university studies, in which philosophy had been a minor subject. Brentano lectured on practical philosophy, elementary logic and its necessary reforms, and

[5] Cf. Husserl's "Erinnerungen an Franz Brentano," Supplement II, pp. 153–167, in Oskar Kraus's *Franz Brentano, Zur Kenntnis seines Lebens und seiner Lehre* (München, 1919).

also on selected psychological and aesthetic questions. Husserl was then in doubt as to whether he would devote himself to philosophy or remain with mathematics, and Brentano's lectures decided his choice. Although he had been repeatedly advised by his friend Masaryk to study with Brentano, he relates that it was out of curiosity that he first attended the lectures, for Brentano was much discussed in Vienna at the time, admired by some, and reviled by others as a Jesuit in disguise. He was impressed from the beginning by the slender form with the mighty head. The expressive facial lines seemed not only to bespeak mental labor, but also deep mental struggles. Brentano impressed him as one who was always conscious of having a great mission. The language of the lectures was free from all artificiality and display of wit. The peculiar, soft, veiled tone of voice and the priestly gestures made him appear to be a seer of eternal truths and an announcer of another world. Husserl related that he did not long resist the power of his personality, despite all prejudices. It was from these lectures that he gained the conviction that philosophy is a field for earnest work which can be treated in the spirit of the most rigorous science, and this led him to choose philosophy as a lifework.

Brentano was most effective in the seminars, in which the following works were studied: Hume's *Enquiry Concerning Human Understanding* and *Principles of Morals*, Helmholtz's speech on "The Facts of Perception," and Du Bois-Reymond's "Limits of Natural Knowledge." He was at that time especially interested in questions of descriptive psychology, which he discussed with Husserl. In the lectures on elementary logic he treated the descriptive psychology of continua and took account of Bolzano's *Paradoxes of the Infinite*, and also the differences between "intuitive and non-intuitive," "clear and unclear," "distinct and indistinct," "real and unreal," and "concrete and abstract" ideas. Other topics included the investigation of judgment and descriptive problems of phantasy. How great an influence was due to Brentano is amply shown by Husserl's early writings as well as by later investigations in logic and the theory of knowledge. His indebtedness to Brentano was explicitly and gladly acknowledged. It is interesting to note that Brentano felt himself to be the creator of a *philosophia perennis*, although he did not remain fixed in his views and never really stood still. He required clarity and distinctness of fundamental concepts, and regarded the exact natural sciences as representing the ideal of an exact science of philosophy. This ideal was opposed to the tradition of German idealism, which was in his view a degeneration of philosophy.

Husserl carried on little correspondence with Brentano. In answer to a letter asking him to accept the dedication of the *Philosophy of Arithmetic*, Brentano expressed his warm thanks but warned against it, lest Husserl incur the animosity of his enemies. Husserl received no reply upon sending a copy of the book when it appeared. It was fourteen years later that Brentano first observed that the work had been dedicated to him, and he then heartily expressed his thanks. Husserl revered and understood his master too much to be sensitive to this incident. The independent development of the two men accounts for the small amount of correspondence between them.

Husserl saw Brentano in 1908 in Florence, when the latter was almost blind. He again felt like a timid beginner, and was inclined to listen rather than to speak. Once he was asked to speak, and was listened to without interruption. His account of the meaning of the phenomenological method of investigation and of his former conflict with psychologism did not lead to any agreement. Husserl stated that perhaps the fault was partly his own. He was inhibited by the inner conviction that Brentano, due to the firm structure of his concepts and arguments, was no longer adaptable enough to understand the need for the transformation of his fundamental ideas that Husserl had found himself compelled to make. Brentano continually lived in his world of ideas and in the completion of his philosophy, which he said had undergone a great development in the course of the decades. There lay about him an aura of transfiguration, as though he no longer belonged to this world, and as though he lived half in that higher world in which he believed so firmly. This last image sank most deeply into Husserl's mind.

This tribute from one great thinker to another reveals the degree of influence exerted personally upon Husserl by Brentano. The resemblance between the two men is striking. Husserl's acknowledgment that Brentano was a determining influence in his life is to be taken literally. He shared to a high degree the earnestness and lofty manner of Brentano, and also the disdain of humor and other lecture devices, which impressed him at the outset. Strongly characteristic also was his often expressed belief that he had created the foundation of the only valid philosophy. He, too, never stood still, and believed that his advances even in the last decade of his life were notable and far-reaching. The spirit of a "school" in which the master's beginnings would be developed further by young investigators was also illustrated in the phenomenological movement, although, to be sure, the elaborately developed method of the latter lifted it above the confines of a school in the usual sense. The portrait of Brentano is strangely familiar to those who have known Husserl personally; in depicting his teacher he has revealed himself.

C. BRENTANO AS A PRECURSOR OF HUSSERL

Brentano is best known for his *Psychology from an Empirical Standpoint* (*Psychologie vom empirischen Standpunkt*, 1874). The recent publication of his works by Kraus and Kastil [6] has made more clear the reasons for the extraordinary influence exercised by him. Husserl was indebted to Brentano for his interest in the concept of intentionality and the descriptive investigation of inner perception, and undoubtedly learned how to become a philosophical investigator by being shown concrete examples of descriptive analysis and how to recognize problems. It was inevitable that his development should run parallel to and overlap to some extent that of Brentano. Although it would also be easy to overdraw the amount of Husserl's indebtedness, it may be said that the study of the main elements of Brentano's thought is indispensable for the genetic understanding of phenomenology.

In Brentano's view the true method of philosophy is the method of the natural sciences.[7] He accordingly regarded philosophy as being scientific in character; and he thought that the possibility of basing knowledge upon immediate evidence would provide a presuppositionless beginning in philosophy. The following five propositions may serve to characterize Brentano's philosophy:[8] (1) The basic structure of human existence or of subjectivity is intentionality. (2) Every intentional act refers to something real, "real" meaning everything that comes from concrete intuition, or that can be presented. (3) Every cognition refers to an existing thing. (4) Every existent is a single or individual thing. (5) Every cognition apprehends the existent as something general. Brentano's belief that there is an "Archimedean point" in philosophy which assures it a permanent foundation represents a motive which becomes prominent in the philosophy of Husserl, beginning with his first programmatic discussion of a scientific philosophy in his essay on "Philosophy as a Rigorous Science."

The concept of intention is important both for Brentano and Husserl, although their use of the term was by no means the same. It means, broadly, a relationship to an object or objectivity of any kind, whether

[6] *Brentanos Gesammelte Philosophische Schriften*, ed. by O. Kraus and A. Kastil (Leipzig, 1922–1930), 10 volumes.
[7] Cf. Brentano, *Über die Zukunft der Philosophie*, ed. by O. Kraus (Leipzig, 1929), p. 317. This is one of the twenty-five "habilitation" theses added to this volume.
[8] Cf. O. F. Bollnow's review of Brentano's *Gesammelte Philosophische Schriften*, *Gött. gel. Anz.*, vol. LVII (1933), pp. 393 ff.

in purely cognitive experience, or in willing, wishing, etc. As used in phenomenology, it names a universal and essential characteristic of consciousness. The term intention is derived from medieval Scholasticism, but the phrase "intentional object" was used by Brentano, so that the suggestion of a Scholastic theory of knowledge was avoided.[9] This concept enabled Brentano to distinguish psychical and physical phenomena.[10] He held that everything psychical is characterized by that which the Scholastics called the intentional, or mental, "inexistence" of an object, and which he called the relation to an object or immanent objectivity. Each psychical phenomenon contains something as an object, although not in the same way. Thus in a presentation something is presented, in a judgment something is acknowledged or rejected, in love something is loved, and in desire something is desired. This "intentional inexistence" was regarded as exclusively peculiar to psychical phenomena, and hence they were defined as phenomena which intentionally contain an object in themselves. In a note written in 1911, Brentano corrected a misunderstanding resulting from the use of the expression "intentional inexistence."[11] Because this expression had been taken to involve purpose and the pursuit of a goal he proposed to avoid its use. He observed that the Scholastics used the expression "objective" more frequently than "intentional." What is in question, in his view, is that something is an object for a psychical being, and is to a certain extent present in his consciousness. He chose the term "intentional" because he thought the danger of a misunderstanding would have been still greater if he had described that which is thought, as it is thought, as "objectively existent."

In his *Psychology from an Empirical Standpoint* Brentano did not restrict objects to real things. He later changed his point of view, holding it to be erroneous to admit "irreal" objects [12] as Husserl and Meinong had done on the basis of his earlier view. Psychical phenomena are perceived only in inner consciousness, whereas only outer perception is possible for physical phenomena, a difference he believed to be sufficient for the characterization of psychical phenomena. Physical phenomena were regarded as existing merely phenomenally and intentionally, as distinguished from psychical phenomena, which exist actually as well as intentionally.[13] Thus

[9] Cf. Herbert Spiegelberg, "Der Begriff der Intentionalität in der Scholastik, bei Brentano und bei Husserl," *Philosophische Hefte*, vol. v (Prag-Dejvice, 1936), pp. 75–91.

[10] Cf. Brentano, *Psychologie vom empirischen Standpunkt*, vol. 1 (Leipzig, 1924), pp. 124 f., 137.

[11] *Ibid.*, vol. II (Leipzig, 1925), p. 8.   [12] *Ibid.*, vol. 1, p. 269, note by Kraus.

[13] *Ibid.*, p. 120. Cf. Husserl, *Logische Untersuchungen*, vol. II, part 2, p. 243 n.; and also chs. XII, B and XV, D herein.

knowledge, joy, and desire exist actually, but color and heat exist only phenomenally and intentionally. Examples of physical phenomena [14] are a figure or a landscape that I see, and heat, cold, and odor that I sense.

In a supplement to the "Classification of Psychical Phenomena," written in 1911,[15] Brentano stated that what is characteristic of every psychical activity is the relationship to something as an object. This is a more satisfactory expression of his meaning, which is merely the fact that one has something, whether a thing or an essence, as an object, or that one is related to it mentally. The misleading interpretation of "immanent objectivity" as a mode of being of a thing in consciousness is avoided thereby.

D. HUSSERL'S FINAL JUDGMENT OF BRENTANO

Brentano's judgment of Husserl's work a few years after the publication of the *Logical Investigations* has been made available by the publication of two letters written to Husserl in 1905,[16] in which he expressed his objections and misgivings concerning Husserl's work. He professed agreement with Husserl's criticism of psychologism, which he conceived to be essentially the Protagorean standpoint that man is the measure of all things. While admitting that Husserl's undertaking in pure logic was not sufficiently clear to him, he judged it to be impossible to assemble completely all truths following intuitively from concepts into a theoretical science of logic; and he was not disposed to give his approval to the attempt to delimit a theoretical science of truths which would exclude every empirical datum. Brentano's comments, although interesting in themselves, indicate his almost complete lack of understanding of Husserl's aim and work.

In the opinion of the editor, Professor O. Kraus, Husserl failed even to answer Brentano's "conclusive arguments," and Brentano's hope to turn him away from his errors was completely illusory. Kraus was particularly interested in undermining Husserl's claim to originality. Challenging the belief that the refutation of psychologism was due to the *Logical Investigations*, Kraus referred to Brentano's paper on evidence which he had incorporated in the text of the volume on *Truth and Evidence*. Brentano also opposed the conception of evidence as a feeling, an antipsychologistic point which had been credited to Husserl. By means of some passages from Brentano's *The Origin of the Knowledge of Right and Wrong*

---

[14] Brentano, *l.c.*, p. 104.

[15] *Ibid.*, vol. II, p. 133; also vol. I, p. 269.

[16] Cf. Brentano, *Wahrheit und Evidenz*, ed. by O. Kraus (Leipzig, 1930). The letters are in an appendix entitled "Concerning the Generality of Truth and the Fundamental Error of a So-called Phenomenology."

(*Ursprung sittlicher Erkenntnis*, 1889), Kraus attempted to establish Brentano's priority in opposing psychologism. Husserl's ideal objects and Meinong's "objectives" were traced by him to Brentano's introduction of the assumption of irreal "facts" (*Sachverhalte*, existents and non-existents).

All that this proves is that Brentano was a stimulating thinker who initiated many ideas which were developed further by gifted students. One can trace numerous ideas of phenomenology back to suggestions in Brentano's thought, but it would be absurd to overestimate such indebtedness to the extent of raising a claim of priority. From Kraus's point of view, the idea of irreal facts is hardly to the credit of Brentano, because the latter came to hold that only things, *realia*, or real essences can be thought, and *irrealia* such as being, non-being, fact, and truth are mere fictions.

In the *Logical Investigations*, Husserl called attention to defects in Brentano's theory of knowledge, pointing out the ambiguity of such expressions as "in consciousness" and "immanent in consciousness." [17] There can be no doubt about his indebtedness to Brentano for the concept of intentionality and the field for descriptive analysis opened up therewith. But it was his belief that Brentano nevertheless failed to grasp its real nature and to put it to philosophical use. As he expressed it near the close of his life, it was very late before he could correctly characterize reflectively the radically new kind of problems of intentionality which were discovered in the *Logical Investigations*, in their universal significance for a genuine psychology and transcendental philosophy. He finally came to the understanding that his honored teacher Brentano to be sure sought a psychology of the phenomena of consciousness (intentional experiences), but had no notion, in the sense of carrying it through, of the real meaning and method of such a task.

Kraus's criticism neither impressed nor detained Husserl. Looking back upon his early period from the perspective of his final maturity, he wondered at his attachment to Brentano for so many years. In a state of self-deception that he now found difficult to understand, he had believed himself to be a collaborator of Brentano's philosophy, and especially his psychology. But, he pointed out, in his first work (the habilitation thesis of 1887, in part more fully developed in the *Philosophy of Arithmetic*) his whole mode of thought was already entirely different from that of Brentano. Taken formally, Brentano sought a psychology whose entire theme is "psychical phenomena," which, among other things, was defined as consciousness "of" something. And yet his psychology was anything but

---

[17] *Log. Unt.*, vol. II, part 1, p. 375. Cf. also L. Landgrebe, "Husserls Phänomenologie und die Motive zu ihrer Umbildung," *Revue internationale de Philosophie*, vol. 1 (1939), pp. 280 ff.

a science of intentionality, the real problems of intentionality were never revealed to him, he did not even see that no given experience of consciousness is to be described without the statement of the pertinent intentional object "as such" (e.g., that this table-perception is only to be described exactly if I describe this table *as what* and *just as* it is perceived). Of intentional implication, intentional modifications, problems of evidence, problems of constitution, etc., he had no idea. Although Brentano had striven to go beyond Neo-Scholasticism, he was unsuccessful; the writings of his old age were regarded as "distilled Scholasticism" by Husserl. It was not possible that the latter could "borrow" ideas from a source in which they were not present. In a simple answer to such an extreme Brentanist as Kraus, one may readily grant every meaningful claim to Brentano's priority without in the least diminishing the stature of Husserl thereby. An unfortunate controversy will thus be reduced to its proper insignificance.

E. HUSSERL'S DEVELOPMENT

Husserl's own special preparation included mathematics and psychology. His doctor's degree was taken in mathematics, his studies under Weierstrass giving him a firm basis for later logical work. In psychology he was interested primarily in the pure descriptive type of investigation, "empirical" in Brentano's sense. The fusion of these two apparently diverse streams of scholarship determined the setting for his career. The important changes in his development are to be explained to a large extent by difficulties encountered in integrating these elements. His inner feeling of uncertainty, at times reaching distressing proportions of intensity, reflected the conflict between a formal, "realistic" point of view, according to which all logical propositions are determinate in themselves, and the psychologistic method of accounting for logical forms and principles by means of the process of experience. Shortly before his death, he spoke of having gone through a period of flagging, similar to experiences undergone periodically earlier in life, during which he was unable to undertake any work. Such periods were followed by intense work and productivity.

It is possible to distinguish a number of different periods in Husserl's development with respect to the determining elements in his early training. These are, broadly speaking, the periods of psychologism, simple descriptive phenomenology (phenomenology in a narrow sense), and transcendental phenomenology.[18] From the point of view of the later transcendental

[18] Cp. E. Fink's account in his introduction to Husserl's hitherto unpublished "Entwurf einer 'Vorrede' zu den 'Logischen Untersuchungen'" (1913), *Uit Tijdschrift Voor Philo-*

phenomenology, the first two periods are simply stages of progress toward the realm of philosophy which only the phenomenological reduction makes accessible. Thus the *Logical Investigations* was characterized as a "break-through" work by Husserl. Therefore one may speak of the two major periods in his development as being pre-transcendental and transcendental philosophy. The great progress recorded in the *Logical Investigations* was fully recognized shortly after the publication of that work, when he proclaimed phenomenology as an autonomous discipline. Being completely conscious of the important progress he had made, he was soon able to conceive the next step to be taken — the phenomenological reduction — which alone could provide adequate technique for the reflective descriptive analysis required for purposes of the theory of knowledge and philosophy in general.

Husserl himself believed that his development displayed an inner consistency despite the occurrence of epoch-making changes, which occasioned so much difficulty for his followers in the various periods. Those that failed to grasp or to endorse the periodical changes simply failed to participate in "the development." The epochal changes that occurred recall the philosophy of Schelling. The difference between the earlier and the later stages is striking; and yet Husserl could speak with right of the fundamental unity of his development. The early period was one of a gifted and well-trained young scholar with a penchant for the most fundamental problems. The extent of his psychologism may be questioned, although he did defend the psychologistic thesis concerning the fundamental concepts of mathematics and logic. But in logic he knew very well how to apply the formal method, as seen in his papers on the "Calculus of Inference" (1891). Although he reacted against his early position and continued to change periodically, the chief results of each stage were always retained in the later work. It may well be that the perspective of his development is distorted somewhat by the emphasis placed upon the issue of psychologism, so that one may be led to underestimate the element of continuity. It should be noted, e.g., that the *Logical Investigations* made use of the "Psychological Studies of Elementary Logic," belonging to his early period. Furthermore, although Frege has been credited with the demolition of the *Philosophy of Arithmetic* and with turning Husserl away from

sophie, vol. 1 (1939), p. 107. Fink divides the development of Husserl's phenomenology — taken externally — into three phases, approximately corresponding to Husserl's periods of teaching in Halle, Göttingen, and Freiburg. Accordingly, the *Logical Investigations* and the *Ideas* are the culminating works of the first two periods. This classification is useful in calling attention to the trend in each period toward the achievement of a deeper and more general level of analysis. Looking backward, one can discern the inner unity of each phase.

his early position, that contention cannot be sustained by the facts. Frege did indeed successfully point out inadequacies in that work, but he by no means discredited it as a whole; and the fact that Husserl's confidence in his work was not seriously shaken is shown by the frequent references to it in his later writings. Indeed, a close study of the *Philosophy of Arithmetic* brings to light some of Husserl's fundamental descriptive interests, and presents in a simple form types of problems which his later and more developed descriptive technique reveals in their actual complexity. If one reads all of Husserl's writings consecutively, one cannot but be impressed by the continuity of his development. But it would be absurd to disregard the great changes in Husserl's views (thus, e.g., the "phenomenological reduction" was not presented until 1913, in the *Ideas*, even though it was conceived and formulated some years earlier), or to discount his own repeated assertions concerning the important changes in his views.

Husserl made the following comments about his early period in a letter to the writer: "Concerning the inner connection of my writings, and consequently concerning my inner development, the new edition of the *Philosophen Lexikon* will give a correct account under my name in case the material prepared by Dr. Fink is accepted without change. External 'influences' are without significance. As a young beginner I naturally read much, including classics and contemporary literature of the 1870's to the 1890's. I liked the critical-skeptical point of view, since I myself did not see firm ground anywhere. I was always very far removed from Kantianism and German idealism. Only Natorp interested me, more for personal reasons, and I read thoroughly the first edition of his *Introduction to Psychology*, but not the enlarged second edition. I zealously read (especially as a student) Mill's *Logic* and later the work on Hamilton's philosophy. I have repeatedly studied the English empiricists and the principal writings of Leibniz (ed. by J. E. Erdmann), especially his mathematical-philosophical writings. I first got to know Schuppe *after* the *Logical Investigations* (1900–1901), when he could offer me nothing further. I never looked seriously at anything by Rehmke. Really, my course was already marked out by the *Philosophy of Arithmetic* (1891), and I could do nothing other than to proceed further." This statement is by no means complete, however. Husserl frequently spoke of James, whose *Principles of Psychology* was of lasting value for him, so much so that he credited James with aiding him in the abandonment of psychologism. Lotze and Bolzano were of great importance for him: to Lotze he was indebted for his interpretation of Plato's theory of Ideas, which determined all his further studies; and to Bolzano for the logical insights of his *Wissenschaftslehre*, which provided him with a first draft of a "pure logic" at a critical time in his development. Furthermore, no account of his intellectual relationships may omit mention of Twardowski, Marty and the other Brentanists, and also Avenarius and Dilthey.

It may well be true that no position held earlier was ever wholly wrong, so that the "correct" results of his investigations could always find their place in each successive systematic period. The genetic account of Husserl's thought is therefore the best way to explain the role of the various divisions and aspects of his philosophy. All through his intellectual life the main motives of his philosophy can be traced out, until the last period, when it was maintained that only the "difficult" medium of phenomenological reduction, now intricately elaborated, can reveal the "unmotivated" and unconditioned basis of all philosophy and science.

Bearing in mind the element of continuity, it is helpful to distinguish several groups of writings, which will describe more exactly the content of the three major periods already indicated. The arrangement will not be entirely chronological, in order to distinguish the psychological-epistemological writings from the formal. The content and method of the works are in question in this classification. Thus even though *Experience and Judgment* derives from an earlier period, as Landgrebe points out, it also derives from a later period, which is what is in question. It therefore belongs with the latest logical writings. (1) There is the work resulting from the first period of mathematical training, the dissertation on the calculus of variations, "Beiträge zur Variationsrechnung." [19]. (2) The attempt to establish a psychological foundation for logic and mathematics may be distinguished as a distinct stage in the early 1890's, although it runs parallel to investigations of a strictly logical nature. Husserl's studies from 1886 to 1895 were primarily in the field of mathematical and formal logic. This was the period of adherence to psychologism as a methodological position. It seemed to Husserl that the philosophy of mathematics was concerned with the psychological origin of the fundamental concepts of mathematics. In the course of his work on the *Philosophy of Arithmetic*, he devoted attention to what he called the "quasi-qualitative" or "figural" factors, which

[19] Cp. Illemann, *Husserls vor-phänomenologische Philosophie* (Leipzig, 1932), p. 70. Illemann is correct in pointing out the three periods of pure mathematics, pre-phenomenology, and pure or "epochistic" phenomenology, although it would be more in keeping with Husserl's own terminology to speak of phenomenology in two senses — simple descriptive and transcendental. Illemann makes the mistake of introducing criticism from the standpoint of the Driesch-Schingnitz school, while at the same time recognizing the incompleteness of the earlier periods. Cf. Becker's review of Illemann's book in the *Deutsche Literaturzeitung* (Feb. 4, 1934), in which Becker suggests the title of "perspectivistic phenomenology" for the fourth period.

were called "Gestalt qualities" by von Ehrenfels. (3) The *Logical Investigations* consists of the main results of Husserl's intellectual labors in the 1890's. The various portions of it were written at different times, so that they had to be revised fully in order to give them unity. The critical portion of the first volume, which has been most widely read, consists of a critique and repudiation of psychologism; it had already been presented in lectures in 1895. The content of the last chapter of that volume, on "The Idea of a Pure Logic," which derived from his earlier mathematical-logical studies, was essentially complete in 1894, and advanced the idea of a formal ontology. The six investigations themselves occupied Husserl up to the final preparation of the work in 1899. It is noteworthy that the *Logical Investigations* register a distinct advance in the understanding of formal science, as well as a landmark in the development of the theory of knowledge, the subject-matter of which predominates in the work. In it phenomenology is characterized as a *descriptive psychology* designed to provide the clarification of the fundamental ideas of formal reasoning. This was especially unfortunate in that it was a factor preventing the correct understanding of the investigations. It was, however, evident to the careful reader that they presented *essential analyses*. In his subsequent correction of this error, Husserl pointed out the fact that all psychological apperception is excluded, that experiences belonging to real thinking beings are not in question. In other words, "descriptive psychology" was not meant to be understood in the usual sense, but, as was clearly pointed out in the first edition of this work, the method of investigation was intended to be free from all assumptions of psychology and metaphysics. (4) The published writings after the first edition of the *Logical Investigations* and up to the publication of the *Ideas* in 1913 may be included in one group, comprising all known writings up to the first published formulation of the phenomenological reduction. The second *Logical Survey* (a critical discussion of German logical publications at the close of the century), while containing material largely belonging to the preceding period, contains a correction of the conception of phenomenology as descriptive psychology. The *Lectures on the Consciousness of Inner Time* (1905–1910) and the *Logos* essay, "Philosophy as a Rigorous Science" (1911), illustrate respectively the nature of phenomenological description and the programmatic ideal of phenomenology as the most rigorous of all the sciences. In this period the clarifying function of phenomenology is assigned to an autonomous discipline which serves as the prelude to all other knowledge. Although the descriptive analysis of time-consciousness includes elements of a "genetic" and "constitutive" character, and extends the field for analysis, the reduction of all knowledge to pure consciousness is not defined systematically, either there or in the *Logos* essay. Phenomenology is now, in short, an autonomous region for investigation that is free from the assumptions of psychology, in keeping with the requirements of a presuppositionless philosophy. (5) The *Ideas* ushers in a period of transcendental phenomenology, the method of phenomenological reduction being the way to philosophy. This work provides a systematic presentation of the new phenomenology. In it the phenomenological is distinguished from the natural "attitude." The latter assumes the existence of the world, along with other normally made assumptions. The phenomenological attitude requires the suspension of all assumptions. The existence of the world, and of everything that is "posited," is "bracketed." The phenomena that remain are the subject-matter of phenomenology, which is defined as the science of pure transcendental consciousness. The discussion of *noesis* and *noema* is especially important in bringing to light some fundamental structures of experience, and as indicating a fruitful field for research. The "reduction" opens up a universal field for philosophical investigation which is free from all prejudgments and assumptions, hence its crucial methodological importance. Husserl is careful to distinguish eidetic reduction (proceeding from fact to essence) from transcendental reduction, according to which the phenomena are characterized as "irreal," and are not ordered in the "actual world." The method of phenomenological reduction is applied in order to achieve the presuppositionless field of philosophy in the consciousness of an individual ego to begin with, which involves the suspension of all beliefs in transcendent realities. Phenomenology now becomes the most fundamental science and the "absolute" ground of all knowledge. Husserl's aim to bring the *Logical Investigations* up to the level of the *Ideas* in a revised edition (1913–1921) was not realized completely, although some portions of it were altered radically in conformity to the greater clarity which he had gained. The term "epochistic" aptly names this period. There need be no ambiguity in the use of this term. Other meanings of "epoché" than that of the *Ideas* must be pointed out explicitly. It signifies the way to the transcendental sphere, and its more detailed elaboration is provided by the *Cartesian Meditations*. This work deals with the problem of the experiencing of other minds through empathy, and introduces the concept of transcendental intersubjectivity, which is necessary for a complete constitutive phenomenology. (6) Although they properly come under the heading of transcendental phenomenology, it is desirable to list the latest logical writings separately. The *Formal and Transcendental Logic* (1929) is important not only in view of its marked excellence as a classic of logic, but also because it is the culmination of the lines of development of logic and transcendental phenomenology. The term "perspectivistic" calls attention to the attempt at a synthesis of the two traditionally divergent fields of interest with which Husserl's philosophical activity began, i.e., his original problem-statement, which involved psychology and epistemology as well as formal reasoning. The detailed examination of this work will enable the reader to judge the success of that synthesis. Included in it is a reinterpretation and evaluation of the *Logical Investigations* as viewed from the advanced level of transcendental phenomenology. The preparation and publication of Husserl's last logical studies, entitled *Experience and Judgment* (1939), finally makes possible the understanding of the phenomenological foundation of logic. It presents much needed material for his analysis of experience, and adds still more support to the claim to concrete investigations and results that has already been made with so much justification. This applies particularly to the analysis of "pre-predicative experience" and the "origin-analyses" of logical concepts and forms. Like the *Formal and Transcendental Logic*, this is a work of the greatest importance for logic, theory of knowledge, and psychology. It should be borne in mind that Husserl's opposition to psychologism by no means implied an opposition to psychology. On the contrary, not the least of his contributions has been to the field of psychology. (7) The last publications to appear, one before his death and the others posthumously, reveal his interest in extending the phenomenological method to an even greater scope than had heretofore been accomplished, to include reference to the history of science and philosophy, and to meet the problem of history confronting this method by means of the concept of "intentional history."

The seven groups listed above comprise the following writings: (1) *Mathematics.* Doctoral dissertation, "Beiträge zur Variationsrechnung," which was not published. (2) *Psychologism. Philosophie der Arithmetik* (Halle, 1891), volume 1 alone being published; "Psychologische Studien zur elementaren Logik" (1894). The habilitation thesis submitted to the University of Halle in order to qualify for an instructorship, "Ueber den Begriff der Zahl" (1887) was printed, but was not placed on sale. It was incorporated in the *Philosophie der Arithmetik.* (3) *Formal Logic and Phenomenology as Descriptive Psychology.* Review of Schröder's *Vorlesungen über die Algebra der Logik* (1891); "Der Folgerungscalcül und die Inhaltslogik" (1891); controversy with Voigt (1893); the first logical survey, "Bericht über deutsche Schriften zur Logik aus dem Jahre 1894" (1897); *Logische Untersuchungen*, first edition (Halle, 1900–1901). (4)

Pre-transcendental Phenomenology. Second logical survey, "Bericht über deutsche Schriften zur Logik in den Jahren 1895–99" (1903–1904); review of Palagyi's *Der Streit der Psychologisten und Formalisten in der modernen Logik* (1903); lectures on time-consciousness, *Vorlesungen zur Phänomenologie des inneren Zeitbewusstseins* (published in 1928, but written in the period from 1905–1910); the *Logos* essay on philosophy as a rigorous science, "Philosophie als strenge Wissenschaft" (1911). (5) *Transcendental Phenomenology.* The revised edition of the *Logische Untersuchungen*, together with the recently published preface of 1913, in which Husserl replied to critics (1913–1921); *Ideen zu einer reinen Phänomenologie* (Halle, 1913); author's preface to the English translation of the "Ideen" (1931); article on phenomenology in the *Encyclopaedia Britannica*, fourteenth edition (1929); *Méditations Cartésiennes* (Paris, 1931); Fink's essay in the *Kant-Studien*, "Die phänomenologische Philosophie Edmund Husserls in der gegenwärtigen Kritik," which Husserl endorsed as expressing his own views (1933). (6) *Synthesis of Formal Logic and Transcendental Phenomenology.* *Formale und Transzendentale Logik* (Halle, 1929); *Erfahrung und Urteil*, edited by Landgrebe (Prague, 1939). Husserl stated that he himself found the former difficult, but that it was by far his most mature work, apart from the fifth of the *Cartesian Meditations.* (7) *Phenomenology and History.* At the time of his death he was at work on his last book, *The Crisis of European Sciences and Philosophy: An Introduction to Transcendental Phenomenology*, the introductory portion of which ("Die Krisis der europäischen Wissenschaften und die transzendentale Phänomenologie") was published in the first volume of *Philosophia* (1936). This work was designed to introduce the student to the "radically new dimensions of knowledge" of transcendental phenomenology. The manuscript on the origin of geometry, "Die Frage nach dem Ursprung der Geometrie als intentional-historisches Problem," was published by Fink in the *Revue internationale de Philosophie* (1939). The literary remains of Husserl include a great deal of descriptive material on constitutive phenomenology, and reveal his many interests in the entire field of philosophy. One of his studies, on the origin of space, "Grundlegende Untersuchungen zum phänomenologischen Ursprung der Räumlichkeit der Natur," was published in *Philosophical Essays in Memory of Edmund Husserl*, edited by M. Farber (Harvard University Press, Cambridge, 1940); and a number of his manuscripts are being printed in *Philosophy and Phenomenological Research.*[20]

[20] The mathematical-philosophical publications of O. Becker in Husserl's *Jahrbuch* are of particular interest because of his use of Husserlian manuscripts as well as ideas. The phenom-

F. TOWARD THE FUTURE

Husserl believed that he had been making great progress until the last, and that he had finally achieved complete clarity of understanding. Declassed by official Germany and deserted or ignored by most of the outstanding "Aryan" scholars in Germany who were influenced by him, he faced the future with an appeal to the judgment of eternity, with the serene consciousness of one who had accomplished much that is permanent. He wrote: "And we old people remain here. A singular turn of the times: it gives the philosopher — if it does not take away his breath — much to think of. But now: *Cogito ergo sum*, i.e., I prove *sub specie aeterni* my right to live. And this, the *aeternitas* in general, cannot be touched by any earthly powers."

To be sure, Husserl had very few "followers" at the close of his life, from the point of view of the unreserved acceptance of his final philosophical efforts. But it would be a mistake to restrict the number of sincere representatives of the phenomenological philosophy to a few final adherents to it. The spirit of Husserl's work was one which forbade completion; his problems had a horizon that was forever open. If few students of philosophy could keep abreast of his progress, that was due largely to the paucity of his publications in relationship to the total output. But not only that, for it must be admitted that most students of philosophy did not devote the necessary time to the study of phenomenology. It was thoroughly understood by few, although it was discussed by many. Husserl could not but feel alone under the circumstances; and this was accentuated by his status in the new Germany.

The period of Husserl's international effectiveness on a large scale has now begun, as shown by the systematically organized interest of scholars all over the world in the understanding and development of his philosophy. Husserl is destined to be a subject of discussion for a long time. It is the intention of those organized in the International Phenomenological Society to make phenomenology effective for further philosophical progress.

The phenomenological method forbids all prejudgments and dogmas. Its ideal is the elaboration of a descriptive philosophy by means of a *radical* method, proceeding with the greatest possible freedom from presuppositions. It is a scientific tendency in philosophy, and its constructive program gives great promise of positive results. That the phenomenological method

enological writings of Becker maintain a high level of competence. All the more surprising, therefore, is his characterization (in the *Deutsche Literaturzeitung*) of the publication in French of Husserl's *Cartesian Meditations* as a "tragic symbol."

has a wide range of application to the various fields of scholarship has already been shown by numerous studies, which are concerned with art, mathematics, law, social science, psychology, and psychiatry. Admittedly only a beginning has been made. On the other hand, the nominal adoption and misuse of the phenomenological method has already illustrated the dangers of mysticism, one-sided and hence misleading description, dogmatism, and agnosticism. Its competent, critical mastery should keep the method free from such errors, and should provide a common basis for all scholars interested in the constructive program of philosophy as a rigorous science.[21]

[21] The new journal, *Philosophy and Phenomenological Research* (University of Buffalo, Buffalo, N. Y.), the historical successor of Husserl's famous *Jahrbuch für Philosophie und phänomenologische Forschung*, is dedicated to the promotion of this ideal. Taking the work of Edmund Husserl as its point of departure, it seeks the active participation of all scholars who are able to contribute toward the understanding and development of phenomenology in its now classical sense, and the further progress of philosophy in itself and in relationship to the other fields of learning.

CHAPTER II

THE PHILOSOPHY OF ARITHMETIC

A LEGEND has arisen concerning Husserl's first important publication, the first volume of his *Philosophy of Arithmetic: Psychological and Logical Investigations*.[1] It is commonly supposed that it was a thoroughly unfortunate attempt, ending in failure, so much so that Husserl was finally led to repudiate it completely. Nothing could be more wrong, however. The student of phenomenology would do well to look to this work for the rudimentary beginnings of phenomenological analysis, even though it must be regarded as pre-phenomenological. In fact, it may be said that this work contains the best key to the understanding of Husserl's philosophy.

The *Philosophy of Arithmetic* well repays reading, even at the present time. It is a well-organized and, in the main, a remarkably clear treatise. No claim was made in this work to construct a system of arithmetic, its aim being to prepare the scientific basis for a future construction by means of a series of "psychological and logical investigations." Both criticism and positive developments were included in the work. Husserl was not led exclusively by an interest in epistemological inquiry. Where the analysis of the elementary concepts of arithmetic and of its symbolic methods seemed significant for psychology or logic, detailed investigations were made. It was his belief that the treatment of the psychology of the concepts of plurality, unity, and number was not unfruitful. The investigation of the general logic of symbolic methods, or semiotic, was regarded as falling outside the scope of a philosophy of arithmetic, and was reserved for the supplement of the second volume, which would thus fill in an essential gap in the literature of logic. In it the arithmetic of numbers would appear as a member of a whole class of arithmetics. Husserl also planned to include a philosophy of Euclidean geometry in that volume, which he hoped to have ready for publication within a year. It is an indication of his rapid growth and enterprise that the second volume never appeared.

[1] Husserl, *Philosophie der Arithmetik: Psychologische und Logische Untersuchungen*, vol. I.

The *Philosophy of Arithmetic,* in its first part, treats of the main psychological questions connected with the analysis of the concepts of plurality, unity, and number, in so far as they are given to us really and not through indirect symbolization. The second part considers the symbolic ideas of plurality and number and attempts to show how the fact that we are almost entirely limited to symbolic concepts of number determines the meaning and purpose of the arithmetic of numbers.

Quoting Weierstrass to the effect that pure arithmetic requires no presuppositions for its basis apart from the concept of number, Husserl tentatively accepts the view that the concept of a cardinal number is fundamental and begins with an analysis of the concept of number. Because this presupposes the analysis of the concept of plurality, the general concept of plurality is first considered.

The basis for the abstraction of the concepts in question are totalities (*Inbegriffe*) or pluralities (*Vielheiten*) of definite objects. The concept of a plurality is perfectly distinct and its extension is precisely delimited. The extension may be regarded as given, even though we are still in the dark about the essence and origin of the concept; and the same holds for the concept of number. It is clear from such passages that Husserl means to name something objective when he speaks of totalities or pluralities. The discussion is first restricted to actually presented pluralities, symbolically presented pluralities being excluded. The domain thus consists of totalities of objects, whether given singly or taken together collectively. The origin and content of the genuine concepts of plurality and number are first considered, the analysis of the symbolic formations presupposing them being reserved for the second part of the volume.

The psychological analysis of abstraction leads to the concepts of plurality and number. The objects of the abstracting activity are totalities of definite objects of any kind whatsoever, as, e.g., a few definite trees, a feeling, an angel, etc. One can always speak, in such examples, of a totality, plurality, and definite number. It thus appears that Husserl means to construe these concepts objectively when introducing them. It will be seen that this interpretation is not adhered to consistently, a circumstance which was later pointed out by Frege. But Husserl's dual interest in the psychological and logical aspects of his subject-matter justifies the treatment of the psychological question of the origin of the ideas in question. A critical revision of the text would have prevented some of the confusion of statement which Frege later criticized. There need be no confusion on principle of the realms concerned.

In Husserl's view, the nature of the particular "contents"[2] that are compounded does not enter into consideration. His view is accordingly opposed to all theories of the origin of the concepts of number which restrict the concepts to certain kinds of content, such as physical contents. J. S. Mill is criticized for holding that numbers denote physical phenomena. The fact that psychical acts and states can be counted just as well as physical contents are counted is sufficient for the refutation of Mill's theory. But how is the relationship between the general concepts of plurality and number and the totalities of definite contents from which they are abstracted to be conceived? The process of abstraction by which they are obtained must be examined. It is not the individual contents entering into given totalities that are the bases of abstraction, but rather the concrete totalities as wholes. The totalities do not consist merely of particular contents. The additional factor of the connection of the individual elements into a whole must be present. Thus despite the greatest diversity of contents there can be homogeneity with respect to the connecting relations. Such homogeneous connections constitute the basis for the formation of the general concept of plurality. A totality is a whole in the same sense in which the points of a line and the instants of a duration of time are wholes. The presentation of a totality of given objects is a unity in which the presentations of the individual objects are contained as partial presentations. Husserl reasons that there must be a peculiar unification present, for otherwise the concept of a totality or plurality could not arise. The concept of plurality arises through reflection upon the particular type of union of contents which is exhibited by every concrete totality. The connection which characterizes a totality is called a "collective connection." Husserl's aim is not to define the concept of plurality, but to give a psychological analysis of the phenomena upon which the abstraction of this concept is based. The kind of unification that is present in a totality is established by direct reference to the phenomena.

In the second chapter, entitled "Critical Developments," a number of theories concerning collective unification, which are designed to explain the origin of the concepts of plurality and number, are examined. The discussion seems to shift from talking about totalities of objects to the question of the origin of the *concept* of a totality. It appears that Husserl is interested in the concepts rather than in the objects. One of the theories

---

[2] The ambiguous term "content" is an unfortunate one, and its adoption is a concession to the usage of the time. "Object" would be preferable.

that is considered is based upon time as a necessary psychological factor. In discussing this view, Husserl admits it to be a fact that temporal succession is an indispensable psychological requisite for the origin of presentations of aggregates, with the possible exception of a few, and of all presentations of numbers. Most if not all aggregates and numbers are regarded as results of processes, and where our will is involved, as results of the operations of collecting or counting. The element of succession in time is also a necessary psychological condition for most concrete pluralities, as well as for all complex concepts. Although they have a becoming in time, the temporal order does not therefore enter into their content. Time is really the basis for all higher thinking, but it cannot be said, e.g., that the relation between the premises and the conclusion is identical with that of its temporal succession. The concepts of plurality and succession are clearly different, for otherwise one could not speak of a plurality of simultaneous contents. The element of temporal succession does not enter into the idea of every totality, and hence it cannot enter into the general concept of plurality or number. Herbart is quoted with approval to the effect that number has no more in common with time than a hundred other kinds of idea that can only be produced gradually. In the course of this discussion a distinction is drawn between a phenomenon as such, and its function or meaning for us, and hence between the psychological description of a phenomenon and the statement of its meaning. The phenomenon is the basis for the meaning, and not the meaning itself. The concept of a logical content or meaning is also distinguished from the changing psychological contents which are actually experienced. In forming the presentation of the totality (A, B, C, D) we do not pay attention to the changes that occur to the contents in the process of collecting. The logical content of such a presentation is not D, C that is just past, etc., but is simply (A, B, C, D), without regard to any temporal differences. Husserl regards every conceivable attempt to clarify the concepts of plurality and number by reference to temporal succession as hopeless. In his view, time plays the role of a preliminary psychological condition for the concepts in question in two respects. In the first place it is essential that the partial presentations that are unified in the presentation of a plurality or number are present at the same time in our consciousness; and secondly, almost all plurality-presentations and all number-presentations are wholes which have arisen out of the elements by means of a temporal process. But he is careful to point out that neither simultaneity nor succession in time enter into the content of the presentations of plurality and number.

The popular theories of number, as illustrated by the writings of Kant,

Lange, Baumann, Jevons, Schuppe, and Sigwart, are examined critically. In his criticism of Kant, Husserl points out that "number" and "presentation of number" are not the same. Lange had reduced all mathematical and logical thought to the intuition of space, and he regarded everything psychical as being localized. Husserl observes that even if Lange's fundamental view were granted, no more would be proved concerning the idea of space than was the case for the idea of time. It would be an essential psychological condition for the origin of the concept of number, just as it would be necessary for the origin of any other concepts. Furthermore, there are infinitely many possible positions and orders of spatial objects, but a number remains unchanged. Hence number has nothing to do with spatial situation. Lange's doctrine of synthesis, which derives from Kant, is found to be untenable, and to be based upon misunderstandings. Baumann is found to have committed analogous errors. His view that numbers are purely mental creations involves him in difficulties when he maintains that number can again be found in the external world. Husserl observes that the contiguity of objects in space is not the same as the collective unification in our presentation, which is essential to number. It appears to him to be just as absurd to seek numbers in space as to search there for judgments and acts of will. Spatial objects are the contents of such acts, but are not the acts themselves; they are the objects that are counted, but are not the numbers. He then proceeds to consider a more scientific and plausible theory, according to which there can only be a plurality where there are objects that are different from one another. The differences must be observed, for otherwise there would appear to be an undifferentiated whole. Presentations of difference are therefore essential ingredients of every presentation of a totality. The same is true of the presentation of identity, which must be present in order to distinguish every individual object of the totality from the others. Each individual object must be thought as identical with itself. The presentations of difference and identity are common to all cases of plurality. The concept of plurality is regarded as the empty form of difference, and the concepts of number arise out of this empty form by means of a great many determinations. They are nothing but general forms of difference that are separated by classification. Views of this kind are found in the logical works of Jevons, Sigwart, and Schuppe. The analysis of plurality or number as an "empty form of difference" (Jevons) is not sufficient to characterize clearly the sharply separated number-concepts two, three, four, etc., in relation to one another. The unclearness concerning the concepts of distinction and difference is due to a number of equivocations, which are analyzed by Husserl. Distinction is found to be an entirely different mental activity from collecting and counting.

In the third chapter, which investigates the psychological nature of collective connection, Husserl first recapitulates the results of the discussion up to this point. In order to show the origin of the concepts of plurality and number, it was necessary to examine the concrete phenomena from which they are abstracted. These phenomena were seen to be concrete pluralities or totalities. The problem was to attain to general concepts by means of them. The nature of the individual objects of a plurality could not contribute to the content of the relevant general concept. One must therefore consider the connection of the objects in the unified presentation of their totality, in order to account for this concept. An exact account of this kind of connection is accordingly needed. That this is not easy was shown by the various theories about the origin of the concepts of plurality and number, all of which failed due to misunderstandings of the synthesis involved. One theory characterized the connection as a mere belonging to one consciousness. Although inadequate, it called attention to an important preliminary psychological condition. Other theories suggested that the basis of the concepts could be determined by means of the "intuitive forms" of time and space. Time was therewith recognized as a preliminary psychological condition of number. The last theory to be considered, the theory of difference, was the only really scientific one. It proceeded from certain psychical acts of distinction, which, however, could not be regarded as the synthetic acts determining the concepts in question.

The explanation of the psychological nature of collective connection is now undertaken. It cannot be reduced to any other kind of relation, such as time, difference, or equality. Collection does not presuppose the comparison of objects, for in order to compare any elements they must first be collected. Hence collective connection must be recognized as a distinct type of relation. This accords with the inner experience of "togetherness," for when single contents are thought together as a totality, the "together" cannot be reduced to any other relations.

This thesis is supported by a consideration of the theory of relations. Inasmuch as there is no theory of relations that is acceptable to him, Husserl devotes some attention to what he regards to be a very obscure chapter of descriptive psychology. He accepts J. S. Mill's interpretation of relations in terms of states of consciousness, i.e., any objects are related if they both enter a complex state of consciousness, but construes the latter in its widest sense, as agreeing in its meaning with the term "phenomenon." But Mill had only defined "standing in relation," and that leaves the question of the meaning of "relation" unanswered. By a relation Husserl understands the complex phenomenon which forms the basis for the formation of the relative attributes, and the "foundation of a relation" consists of every one of the related contents. The definition as here given is admittedly too narrow, because it considers only relations between two foundations. Relations are classified into two kinds, with respect to their own phenomenal character. (1) There are relations which have the character of "primary contents," or of "physical phenomena" in the sense defined by Brentano, although it appears to be better to avoid this expression. Such relations are, e.g., similarity, equality, the connection of the parts of a continuum, the connection of properties, as of color, with spatial extension, etc. Each of these relations represents a particular kind of primary content. It makes no difference, however, whether the foundations themselves are primary contents or any kind of psychical phenomena. The relations belonging to the primary contents are called primary relations. (2) In the second class of relations, the relational phenomenon is psychical. If a psychical act is directed upon more than one content, the contents are related to one another with respect to it. The presentation-content of such an act does not contain any relation, unless a primary relation is there besides. The contents are here united by the act, a fact which is observed by reflecting upon the act. Any act of presentation, judgment, feeling, or volition which involves more than one content will serve as an example. In agreement with Mill's definition, Husserl states that each of these psychical acts places the contents into relationship with one another. The two classes of relations can be distinguished by the fact that the primary relations belong to an idea-content of the same level as their foundations, whereas the psychical do not. In the case of the former, when a foundation is presented the relation is also given as an element of the same idea-content; but in the case of psychical relations an act of reflection upon the relating act is needed for the idea of the relation. Rejecting the usual distinction, according to which relations between two foundations are simple, and among more than two foundations are compound, Husserl proposes the following definition in its place: Relations which are themselves composed of relations are compound, whereas relations for which that is not the case are simple.

After this digression into the theory of relations, the psychological analysis of collective connection is continued. The question arises as to whether the relations which unite the objects of a totality, and which have been called collective connections, are primary or psychical in character. A rose, e.g., is composed of parts which are connected by relations, the primary connection being contained in the presentation-content. That is not the case with collective connections, however. There is an essential difference between collective connection and primary relations of content; in fact the former is not a primary relation at all. Relations are based upon foundations, which can only be varied within certain limits if the relations are to be maintained. In the case of a collective connection, however, every foundation can be varied arbitrarily and the relation remains nevertheless. The same holds for the relation of difference. Not every content can be conceived as similar to or as continuously connected with every other one, but they can always be conceived as different, or as collectively united. In these cases the relation does not lie directly in the phenomena themselves, but is in a sense external to them. That means that collective union is not given intuitively in the presentation-content, but only by means of certain psychical acts that embrace the contents. The elementary acts which are capable of comprising all contents, however disparate, are here in question. The collective connection can only be grasped in reflection upon the psychical act through which a totality arises. Inner experience is appealed to for the complete confirmation of this view. Thus if we ask wherein the connection consists when we think of a multiplicity of such disparate things as redness, the moon, and Napoleon, the answer is that it consists merely in the fact that we think these contents together, we think them in one act. A special act is needed for the apprehension of every one of the compounded contents, and their assemblage then requires a psychical act of a second order. If a plurality of six objects is presented in the form of 3 + 3, the formation of each sub-group requires a psychical act of a second order, and the entire collective unity is presented by means of a psychical act of a third order. Collective connection is held to be a simple relation, regardless of the number of foundations. Its prime importance in our mental life is shown by the fact that every complex phenomenon which presupposes parts and every higher mental activity and feeling require collective connections in order to arise. No presentation of a simple relation can occur, such as equality, similarity, etc., without an interested activity which selects the foundations and unites them. Hence this psychical relation is a necessary psychological condition of all relations and connections. The syncategorematic term "and" expresses in ordinary usage the elementary nature of collective connection.

In the fourth chapter Husserl brings to completion his analysis of the concept of number with respect to its origin and content. As has been seen, the abstract presentation of collective connection is obtained by reflection upon the psychical act which connects contents into a totality. By means of that presentation the concept of plurality is formed. It is the concept of a whole which connects parts in a merely collective manner. In other words, a presentation comes under the concept of plurality if it collectively connects contents that are perceived separately. In this Husserl believes that he has found the source out of which collective connection arises.

The concept of plurality is described as the concept of a something that possesses the abstract factor of collective connection. The concept of collective connection is thus the most essential constituent of the concept of plurality, without being identical with it. The process of abstraction which yields the concept of plurality is examined at this point. Husserl's comments about abstraction are of interest because they present a problem which is not clarified until the publication of the *Logical Investigations*, and also because of Frege's caustic criticism of them. Husserl maintains that no concept can be thought without being founded on a concrete intuition. Thus when we present the general concept of plurality, we have the intuition of a concrete plurality in consciousness, from which we abstract the general concept. Abstraction is made from the particular nature of the compounded contents, while their connection is retained as a conceptual extract. To look away or abstract from something merely means that one does not observe it, so that it is possible to abstract from the particular contents while attending to the collective connection. That is all that Husserl means. Frege makes sport of this view, but he does not do justice to Husserl's intention when he causes cats to disappear gradually by disregarding their various features until only the "bloodless ghost" of "something" remains. Plurality in general is finally defined as something and something and something, etc., or, more briefly, as one and one and one, etc.

The present investigation is constantly concerned with the origin as well as with the content or nature of the concepts in question. This dual interest remains a characteristic of phenomenological inquiry, although it is much later before the nature of "origin-analysis" is defined as an objective and essential procedure. Another characteristic feature that is never dropped is the concept of "something"; this is retained in the last logical writings of Husserl. As has been seen, the concept of plurality contains the concept of something in addition to the concept of collective connection. The term "something" is universal in its application, and can be applied to everything that is conceivable. Every real or thought thing is a something; and the same is true of a judgment, concept, impossibility, or contradiction. It cannot be obtained by any conceivable comparison of the content of all physical and psychical objects, for it is not a residue remaining after a process of abstraction. Husserl asserts (in a manner requiring clarification) that the one respect in which all objects — whether real or non-real, actual or possible, physical or psychical — agree is the circumstance that they are presentation-contents, or are represented in our consciousness by presentation-contents. The concept of something is due to reflection upon the psychical act of presentation. It is in this "external" and "figurative" (*uneigentlich*) manner that the factor of being "something" belongs to the content of every concrete object. Hence it is characterized as a relative determination. The concept of something cannot be thought without a content of some kind, but anything will do for that, if only the mere term "something." This concept ("something," or "one") is important for the origin of the concept of plurality because every single content which a concrete plurality-presentation comprises can only be attended to by means of it; and thus that most complete removal of content arises which imparts generality to the concept of plurality.

There is an element of indeterminateness that is essential to the concept of plurality in its general meaning. Its content can be expressed as "one and one and one, etc.," the "and so forth" indicating the indeterminateness. This does not mean that there is no limit to the collection of "ones," but only that no limit is found, or that a given limit does not matter. If this element of indeterminateness is removed, the concept of plurality breaks up into a manifold of sharply delimited concepts or numbers. Concepts such as "one and one," or "one and one and one" arise, and they have been named "two," "three," etc. But Husserl regards it as unnecessary to derive the number-concepts from the general concept of plurality. They can be obtained directly from concrete pluralities. Numbers can be abstracted by regarding the compounded single contents as "somethings" or as "ones." All concepts arising in that way are related, due to the similarity of the partial ideas which constitute them, as well as to the similarity of the psychical acts which connect them. Thus the number-concepts are delimited as a well-characterized class of concepts. In Husserl's view, the term "number" is a common name of the concepts two, three, etc., and not a name of the names two, three, etc., as James Mill held. There is no such thing, however, as a number in general. The relationship between number in general and a definite number is analogous to the relationship between a logical part and a logical whole. The concepts of number and plurality agree in their essential contents, but differ in one respect.

The former involves the distinction of the abstract forms of plurality from one another, whereas the latter does not. The generic concept of number arises out of the comparison of distinct forms of plurality or numbers, but the concept of plurality arises directly out of the comparison of concrete totalities. The indeterminate and vague concept of plurality is more deeply rooted in the experience of the race and in human development.

The relationship between the concepts "one" and "something" is finally elucidated. Because the term "one" came into use only in counting, it was correlated with a plurality. Thus "one" became synonymous with "counted thing" or "one thing" as contrasted with many things, whereas "a thing" in the sense of "something" remained free from this relation to the concept of plurality. The concepts of something, one, plurality, and number are the most general and emptiest in content of all concepts, and are designated form-concepts or categories by Husserl. They are not concepts of contents of a definite genus, but are concerned rather with all contents. Their all-comprehensiveness is explained by the fact that they are concepts of attributes which arise in reflection upon psychical acts that can be directed upon all contents. In opposition to Aristotle and Locke, Husserl maintains that the concepts of number and the "one" belong exclusively to the domain of reflection, even though the counted contents can be physical as well as psychical.

The fifth chapter is concerned with the psychological analysis of the relations of more and less. Husserl asserts it to be less easy to distinguish nineteen from twenty than nine from ten; and the latter is less easy than the distinction of three from four. Where immediate intuition either fails or could be in error, we resort to mechanical operations of counting and reckoning, whose real basis is the elementary relations of numbers. In accordance with a requirement which holds for all relations, the foundations of the relation of more and less must come together in one act of consciousness. That means that the totalities which are to be compared must be present in one act, which then appears as the "sum" of two totalities. We have the capacity to present several totalities together, and to unite them into one totality; and we can also present totalities of totalities of totalities, etc. The limits of actual presentation are soon reached, and everything else is figurative or symbolic presentation. As for the psychological basis for the more complex formations, there are psychical acts of a higher order, or acts which are directed upon psychical acts, and which thus indirectly refer to primary contents. The term "totality" is used here in preference to "plurality" because the psychical activities that are essential to the concept of plurality are in question, and this term expresses clearly the "grasping together as one" of the compounded contents.

The sixth chapter considers the definition of equality of number by the concept of one-to-one correspondence. Husserl observes that mathematicians have been overzealous at times in their desire to attain rigor in all definitions, even though some elementary ideas are not capable of definition or in need of it. This is the case with the so-called definitions of the equality and difference of numbers, with whose criticism he is concerned. Reference is first made to H. Grassmann, Leibniz, and Frege. In criticism of their definition of equality, it is pointed out that identity is defined instead of equality. The idea of more and less is contained in the definition of equality advanced by Stolz, whereas it cannot be conceived without the idea of equality. Hence there appears to be a circle.

In Husserl's view, one can only speak of the equality of two aggregates when there is equality with respect to all parts. In other words, they are compared by attempting to "match" or superpose their elements successively. If the aggregates to be compared are from the same genus, the process of comparison is much simpler. It is sufficient that there are corresponding elements, and there is no preliminary problem of ascertaining whether there are corresponding equal elements in the aggregates in question. That is the procedure for comparing concrete aggregates as such. The comparison of aggregates with respect to their number is also readily accomplished. Two aggregates have the same number if their units can be placed in one-to-one correspondence in thought. In order to determine equality of number both pluralities can simply be counted in a symbolic sense. Not only will their equality or inequality be determined, but the numbers themselves will be provided therewith.

Frege's concept of number, which is defined by means of the equality of number, is judged to be unacceptable. The unity of the concept of number is based for him upon the indefiniteness of a relation which mediates the coördination. Husserl argues that every other relation that is possible between the reciprocal elements can accomplish the same thing. What is essential, in his view, is that the corresponding elements are connected in our thinking, or that they are compounded. That is taken to be an absolutely certain sign that every unit of the one aggregate corresponds to every one of the second aggregate, hence its value for us. The discovery of an intensional connection which unites the elements of both aggregates by pairs is welcome for our connecting thought can then be represented symbolically. The importance which Husserl attaches to the present analysis is indicated by his reference to the thesis, regarded as important by

THE PHILOSOPHY OF ARITHMETIC

mathematicians, that the equality of number of two pluralities is independent of the mode of connection. That is to say, two pluralities which are shown to be equal in number by pairing every definite element of the one with a definite element of the other, also remain equal in number if the elements are paired differently. Schröder had referred the full explanation of this proposition to psychology. It is Husserl's belief that his analyses contribute the necessary psychological clarification.

This discussion is continued in the seventh chapter, entitled "Definitions of Number through Equivalence." The term "equivalent" is used instead of "equal in number" because the latter connotes the concept of number, whereas the definition is independent of it. Equivalence and equality of number have not the same content, although their extension is the same. Husserl maintains that what equivalent aggregates have in common is not merely equality of number or equivalence, but rather the same number in the true sense of the term. He opposes the view that numbers are relational concepts based upon equivalence, pointing out that every number-statement would then refer to its relations to other aggregates, instead of referring to a concrete given aggregate. To assign a definite number to an aggregate would be to classify it under a definite group of equivalent aggregates. But that is not the meaning of a statement about numbers, in Husserl's opinion. A given aggregate of nuts is not said to be four because it belongs to a certain class of infinitely many aggregates which can be placed in unique correspondence with one another. This view is judged to be as useless as it is involved, all the more so when large aggregates are in question. The situation is not improved for this theory by the use of such strokes as II, III, . . . which represent the classes, so that the aggregate to be counted can be subsumed under the class in question. In fact, the justification for the strokes themselves can only be found in the all-comprehensive concept of a "something," for that is all that can be denoted by each stroke. That is Husserl's reply to the theory of equivalence. He expresses strong opposition to what he describes as remote and artificial constructions which, in order to build up the elementary concepts of arithmetic out of ultimate definitional characters, reinterpret them in such a way that strange concepts, useless for practice and science, finally result.

Husserl then turns to Frege's attempt, in the latter's *Foundations of Arithmetic*,[3] which is devoted to the analysis and definition of the concept of number. His view is closely related to the theory of equivalence. Frege was opposed to the view that psychology can contribute anything to the

[3] G. Frege, *Die Grundlagen der Arithmetik* (Breslau, 1884).

foundation of arithmetic, so that he was not interested in making a psychological analysis of the concept of number. It would seem at first sight as though Frege stated a point of view which Husserl came later to endorse fully. That is not the case, however. Husserl later agreed with Frege in opposing psychologism, but he did not lose sight of his contention that there are ultimate concepts which must be clarified rather than defined, a task that falls to phenomenology. Husserl finally conceded the elimination of psychology from formal science, but he never gave up his program of epistemic clarification. What was really involved was the understanding of the role and nature of the "descriptive psychology" which is required.

As Frege expressed it, number is no more an object of psychology or a result of psychical occurrences than the North Sea is. In Husserl's opinion, the entire investigation up to this point presents arguments in refutation of Frege's position. In his view, one can only define that which is compounded logically. Such ultimate elementary concepts as quality, intensity, place, time, and the like are for him incapable of definition, and the same holds for the elementary relations and concepts based upon them. Equality, similarity, whole and part, plurality and unity, etc., are examples of concepts which are held to be incapable of a formal-logical definition. Accordingly, all that can be done is to exhibit the concrete phenomena from which they are abstracted and to make clear the nature of the process of abstraction. In opposition to Frege, Husserl does not find it objectionable for mathematicians to describe the way in which one comes to the concept of number, instead of beginning with a logical definition of number. He merely requires that the description be correct, and that it fulfill its purpose. It is his belief that he has shown clearly that the concepts of plurality and unity are directly based upon ultimate, elementary psychical data, and that they are consequently indefinable concepts; and that since the concept of number is so closely related to them it, too, cannot be defined. Hence he regards Frege's goal as chimerical.[4] A few of Frege's more important definitions are selected for examination. According to Frege, a number does not attach to a single object or to an aggregate of objects; it attaches to the concept of the counted objects. Thus if one judges that Jupiter has four satellites, the number four is ascribed to the concept "satellite of Jupiter." His view agrees fundamentally with the theory of equivalence, in that it also seeks to obtain the concept of num-

---

[4] This criticism of Frege is retracted in the *Log. Unt.*, vol. 1, p. 169 n., where Husserl states that he no longer approves of the criticism of Frege's antipsychologistic position, and where the *Grundlagen der Arithmetik* is referred to as a stimulating work. The reader is also referred to the preface of Frege's *Die Grundgesetze der Arithmetik*.

ber by proceeding from the definition of equality of number. The concept F is said to have the same number as the concept G if it is possible to coördinate uniquely all of the objects coming under each concept. This leads to the definition of the number which attaches to the concept F as the extension of the concept "having the same number as the concept F." Husserl professes inability to see how this method is a contribution to logic, and wonders that anyone could even temporarily hold its results to be true. Frege's method permits the definition of the extension of the concept of number and not its content. By the extension of a concept is meant the totality of all the objects coming under it. Hence "the number which attaches to the concept F" is defined as the extension of the concept "equal in number to the concept F." That means that the concept of this number is the sum total of the concepts with the same number as F, and hence a sum of infinitely many "equivalent" aggregates. Husserl deems further comment to be superfluous.

Following an analysis of Kerry's attempt to clarify the concept of number by means of unique coördination, which he regards as useless, Husserl concludes that he has shown that the concept of equivalence does not and cannot contribute anything to the definition of the concept of number.

All essential questions regarding the psychological origin and content of the concepts of plurality and unity, definite concepts of number, as well as the concepts of "just as much" and "more and less" have now been answered in Husserl's opinion. He now proceeds in the eighth chapter, on "Unity and Plurality," to the solution of difficulties which had been encountered in these concepts. The old definition of number as a plurality of unities serves as the point of departure.. In his view little is accomplished by the usual definitions of number because the difficulty lies in the phenomena, in their correct description, analysis, and interpretation, which alone will provide insight into the essence of the concept of number.

Of particular interest in this chapter is the discussion of a difficulty propounded by Frege. Frege is quoted to the effect that what does not apply to zero or one cannot be essential to the concept of number. This objection applies to Husserl's own theory of the concept of number, which does not provide for these concepts. Husserl is therefore led to deny that zero and one are concepts of number. According to his earlier investigations, numbers are regarded as all the conceivable determinations of the indeterminate concept of plurality. One object is not a collection of objects, and hence the statement that one is here is not a number-statement. The same holds for no object, which is also not a collection. "One" and "none" function linguistically as numbers and may be regarded as number-determinations by grammarians. There are also scientific reasons for such extended usage, for it would be involved and inconvenient to keep them apart; but in his opinion they are not numbers logically.

Frege had devoted much attention to the relationship of equality and difference to the concept of number, and he had formulated the following difficulty: If we try to account for the origin of number as arising by the compounding of different objects, we get an accumulation and not a number; but if the attempt is made to form a number by compounding equals, they continually flow together and we never get to plurality. Husserl attempts to meet this difficulty by means of his own theory. He points out that only things that are different can be connected into a totality, but that there are no relations of difference in the presentation of the totality. The process of counting requires only the difference of the objects to be counted, and not their distinction. In order to grasp the number of an aggregate, it is necessary to subsume every one of the objects to be counted under the concept of something. The numbers arise through abstraction from aggregates whose elements are presented as equal to one another in some respect. The unification of relational complexes is due to the fundamental relation of collective association and not to equality. The concept of number is constituted by the concepts of something and collective connection alone. If we proceed from concrete aggregates, abstraction is made from everything except the external character *that* they are contents. If we say that Jupiter, an angel, and a contradiction are three, they are alike in that each is a unit. But their equality is a result of the abstraction of numbers, and not their basis. Husserl concludes that presentations of equality contribute as little to the abstraction of numbers as do presentations of difference.

It appears to Husserl that Frege has confused equality with identity. But equality and difference are not contradictory. On the contrary, both may be illustrated by aggregates of equal objects, in which there is sameness in one respect and difference in another. Frege also stated that it is an error to denote the objects to be counted by 1, because different things would then receive the same sign. Husserl observes that this error is incurred, however, by every application of general names. If we call Hans or Kunz a man, the same kind of "error" is committed. The sign 1 is a general character which has its foundation in the concept of unity.

The term "unity" is found to be highly ambiguous. Eight meanings of it are selected and distinguished, although only the last two are relevant to the immediate discussion. According to the seventh definition, unity means a whole. That which is separated out as a whole because of its inner connection, in which we manifest an interest and which becomes an object for counting, is called "one." By extension, unity comes to denote as much as "whole." The eighth definition of unity shows it to mean wholeness or unitedness. This is also an extended meaning of the term. Thus the unity of the soul is spoken of as one of its properties.

In the ninth chapter Husserl considers the meaning of number-statements. That there is disagreement upon this point is an indication of the confusion concerning the concept of number. The great divergence of opinion among philosophers is especially striking. In the view of J. S. Mill, numbers are names of objects, so that two is a name of things that are two. For Sigwart two, three, four, . . . are predicates of number in general. Mill's view is quickly disposed of. Two cannot be the name of things that are two, for then each of them would be two. According to Herbart a number refers to a general concept of that which is counted, a view which Frege has defended. Frege endeavored to improve Herbart's undeveloped theory and to establish it positively, and his attempt is held to be worthy of full consideration. This discussion of Frege provides an excellent opportunity for appraising Husserl's own theory. Frege has commented upon the main points at issue in his review of the *Philosophy of Arithmetic*.

Frege's theory explains why one can with the same truth say "This is a group of trees" and "These are five trees." The name alone is changed, and that merely indicates that one concept has been substituted for another. Hence it appears to him to be clear that the citation of number contains a statement about a concept. Husserl agrees with Frege in holding that numbers are not attached to objects as characters; but he maintains that objects are bearers of numbers in another sense. That is because the origin of number is due to a certain psychical process that is connected with the objects of counting and is in this sense "borne" by them. A number is uniquely determined when the totality is determined, upon which the process of abstraction is performed. The objects by themselves do not determine the totality. The same objects can be presented in various totality-forms. We select one group or another in accordance with our interest. Thus the various numbers arise, each of which is uniquely determined by the totality-form at the basis of its counting. Common generic concepts guide our interest as a rule. It is not always the case, however, that there is a change of concept with a change of interest. We can arbitrarily select groups of two, three, etc., from an aggregate of homogeneous objects such as apples, e.g., without intending just those delimiting concepts. But even assuming that we only compounded and counted objects in so far as they come under a common concept, Husserl thinks that it follows from his discussion that a number cannot be regarded as a determination of a concept. He holds that the direct examination of the nature of number shows that number does not refer to a concept. Number is the general form of plurality under which the totality of the objects a, b, c comes. Therefore this totality, or plurality, or aggregate is the subject of a number-statement. Considered formally, number and concrete aggregate are related as concept and object of a concept. Hence number does not refer to the concept of the counted objects, but rather to their totality.

The relationship between number and the generic concept of what is counted thus in a sense appears to be the reverse of what was asserted by Herbart and Frege. It is only after the counting that a generic concept becomes a determining factor of a number. The at first empty idea of the counted something is determined by it as a something coming under the concept in question. A number does not state anything about the concept of what is counted; it is the latter that states something about number. The extension of a concept has a number and not the concept itself. Thus it can only be said indirectly: A concept has the property that its extension has the number four. But the usual number-statement does not mean this complex thought.

In a supplement to the first part of this work the nominalistic attempts of Helmholtz and Kronecker are presented and criticized. Numbers are regarded by Helmholtz as a series of arbitrarily chosen signs, for which only a definite kind of succession is held to be the "natural" one. According to Helmholtz, this is to begin with a pure game of acumen with imaginary objects; and by means of this system of signs we describe the relationships of real objects. Numbers are thus defined as arbitrary signs. Husserl observes that one will seek in vain in Helmholtz's text for the meaning of those signs. They can signify the most heterogeneous objects in different cases, and yet the meaning is not an arbitrary one. Husserl is interested in determining the concept which is involved in every application of the signs, and which makes up the unity of their meaning. He points out that at the basis of Helmholtz's view is the assumption of an unlimited supply of signs by means of which the elements of every thinkable aggregate can be signified. In conclusion he states that Helmholtz and Kronecker, like Berkeley before them, misinterpret the symbolic process of counting which we habitually practice. The names of numbers function to begin with as a fixed series of empty signs, for their conceptual content does not come into consciousness during the counting. It is only after the process that the genuine or symbolic number-concept comes into consciousness as the meaning of the resulting number-word. Holding to the external and blind process and misunderstanding its symbolic function, Helmholtz and Kronecker confused sign and thing. Helmholtz's belief that the conception of general arithmetic as a consistent system of signs could alone obviate all the great difficulties that beset this science led him to reinterpret the concept of number in a nominalistic sense.

B. THE SYMBOLIC CONCEPTS OF NUMBER AND THE LOGICAL SOURCES OF ARITHMETIC

The second part of the *Philosophy of Arithmetic* presents materials which have proved to be of real importance, and which indicate the promise of the author as an original investigator. In the tenth chapter, with which this part begins, Husserl attempts to give a psychological and logical account of our operations with numbers. The reader is reminded that the numbers in arithmetic are not concepts or *abstracta*. Although 2 and 3 make five, the concept 2 and the concept 3 remain the same and do not make the concept 5. That is because the arithmetician does not operate with number-concepts as such. Thus 5 does not mean the concept or *abstractum* five, but is a general name or an arithmtical sign for any aggregate which comes under the concept five. $5 + 5 = 10$ means that any aggregate coming under the concept five and any other aggregate coming under the same concept are together an aggregate coming under the concept ten.

Numbers arise directly through the counting of pluralities, and indirectly through operations of reckoning. The fundamental operations by which new numbers can alone be formed out of given numbers are addition and partition. With the exception of 0, 1, and 2, all numbers permit of further partitions into numbers. The psychological basis of the addition and partition of numbers has already been indicated. As has been seen, we are able to retain a number of presentations of totalities at the same time and to unite them collectively, thus forming totalities of totalities. We can also retain a given totality and at the same time unite its elements by means of particular totality-presentations, and in that way present a number of totalities within the given one. The same holds for the general presentations of totalities, or the numbers.

By addition is meant the formation of a new number by the collective connection of the units of two or more numbers. Viewed logically, the concept of a sum presupposes that of the collection of units, whereas from the mathematical point of view a collection of units functions as a special case of a summation of numbers. This is pointed out as an essential distinction. As for multiplication, the entire difference between it and addition appears to consist in a new kind of notation which is possible for special forms of addition. The abbreviated mode of notation is very convenient and useful, but there is no special operation of multiplication. It symbolizes briefly the way in which the number is to be found, and thus expresses a task and not a solution. In order to obtain the intended number the additions must be really carried out. Whereas addition connects a given plurality of numbers into a new number, partition separates a given number into a plurality of number-parts. Subtraction and division are the two special cases of partition. If the term operation is understood to mean an actual activity with the numbers themselves, there are no other operations than connection and partition. But what is called an operation in arithmetic does not correspond to this concept; numbers are characterized symbolically by relations instead of being constructed operationally. Arithmetic in short is not concerned with actual numbers. If it were, the evaluation of its symbolizations would require the performance of actual additions and partitions, which is not practiced in arithmetic. All presentations of number beyond the first few in the number series are only symbolic. That fact is of great importance in determining the nature of arithmetic, and its recognition is necessary for a deeper understanding of that discipline. If we had genuine presentations of all numbers there would be no arithmetic, for it would be superfluous. The most complicated relations between numbers which are now discovered by laborious calculations would be just as evident intuitively as are propositions such as $2 + 3 = 5$. But as a matter of fact we are very limited in our capacity for presentation. The actual presentation of all numbers could only be expected of an infinite understanding, which would have the ability to unite a real infinity of elements into an explicit presentation. Finite beings that could attain to the actual presentation of millions and trillions are also conceivable, and for them there would be no practical reason for developing an arithmetic. Arithmetic is in fact nothing other than a sum of technical means to overcome the imperfections of our intellect. Since it is only under especially favorable circumstances that we can actually present concrete pluralities of about a dozen elements, i.e., grasp each of the terms by itself and together with all the others, twelve or a somewhat smaller number is the ultimate limit for our conception of genuine (or "actual") number-concepts (reference is made to Wundt's *Physiologische Psychologie*). Despite that fact no one feels inhibited by these limits, which were first discovered by psychological analysis. Now the series of numbers is regarded as being infinite. But how can one speak of concepts which he does not have actually? The most certain of all sciences, arithmetic, is based upon such concepts. The answer is that if the concepts are not given actually, they are given in a symbolic manner. The discussion of this essential distinction and the psychological analysis of symbolic presentations of number constitute the task of the following chapters.

The eleventh chapter, on the symbolic ideas of plurality, is the most important and characteristic (with respect to the later Husserl) study in the volume. The difference between genuine and symbolic presentations is first elucidated because it is fundamental for all the subsequent discussion. If a content is presented to us indirectly through signs which characterize it uniquely, we have a symbolic and not a genuine presentation of it. Husserl refers to Brentano's emphasis upon the distinction between genuine and figurative or symbolic presentations in his lectures, and he acknowledges indebtedness to Brentano for a deeper understanding of the great significance of figurative presentation for our whole psychical life. But the above definition is not identical with the one given by Brentano. The uniqueness of the characterization is emphasized here, in order to separate figurative and general presentations. The general presentation "a man" is not even a symbolic presentation of a definite man Peter. More characters must be added if it is to function as a substitute for the genuine presentation of the definite man. We have a genuine presentation of the external appearance of a house when we really view it, and a symbolic presentation if someone characterizes it indirectly for us, such as "the corner house on such and such a street, etc." Every description of an intuitive object tends to replace the genuine presentation of it by a symbolic presentation which represents it. Symbolic presentations serve as provisional substitutes, and in cases where the real object is inaccessible, as lasting substitutes for genuine presentations. On the other hand, all judgments involving symbolic presentations can be carried over to the objects themselves. Abstract and general concepts can be symbolized as well as intuitive objects. For example, a certain species of redness is actually presented if we find it to be an abstract factor of an intuition. It can be presented figuratively by means of the symbolic determination of the physical properties of the color. A genuine presentation and a symbolic presentation appertaining to it are logically equivalent. Two concepts are logically equivalent if every object of the one is also an object of the other, and conversely. Thus symbolic presentations can be used as substitutes for corresponding genuine presentations, in accordance with our cognitive interests.

Husserl now proceeds to study the origin and meaning of symbolic presentations in the domain of number. To that end he first examines more closely the function of figurative presentation for the formation of presentations of plurality, restricting the discussion to pluralities of sensuous contents. The expression "sensuous aggregate" is used for convenience. A sensuous aggregate appears at first as a unified intuition, as a whole. How is such an aggregate distinguished from an individual sensuous thing? Analysis shows both to have a plurality of parts or of properties. In sensuous aggregates, however, the parts are not contained as properties, but as separate intuitive parts, and a unified interest is directed upon them which apprehends each intuitive part independently and unites it with the others. That is not possible for us in the case of larger aggregates, so that such aggregates or pluralities can only be spoken of in a symbolic sense. The successive apprehension of each element of the aggregate is possible, but not their comprehensive collection. A genuine presentation of an aggregate requires as many psychical acts as there are contents present, and these must be united by a psychical act of a second order. The terms aggregate, plurality, totality, etc., obtain their meaning only with respect to this form of psychical connection.

Let us consider the following examples. If we enter a hall full of people, one glance is sufficient for us to judge: an aggregate of people. We look at the starry sky and judge at once: many stars. The same is true for aggregates of entirely unknown objects. How are such judgments possible? In these examples there is not only an apprehension of the aggregate, but also a subsumption under the concept of the aggregate. If not more than a dozen elements can be apprehended under the most favorable circumstances, how can we account for cases in which hundreds of elements are involved immediately? Husserl regards the hypothesis of an "unconscious" activity that is immediately forgotten as being improbable. It is clear that the concrete presentation of a plurality is symbolic and not genuine in these cases. Neither can these experiences be explained as based upon the actual discernment of a small number of elements and the formation of a symbolic idea of the complete aggregate which would be engendered if the process of collection were to be continued to the end. The question to be answered is, how can the apprehension and uniting of a few elements serve as signs for the intended complete collection? In fact, it must be shown how we know that the process of collection can be continued even one step further. It must also be shown how we know that a "complete collection" is to be intended. Still another attempt to meet the problem proves to be of no aid. To regard the apprehension of an aggregate as being due to a series of successive apprehensions of all elements of the aggregate is unacceptable because the successive apprehensions cannot be kept together in one act. Only a small number of them remain sharply distinguished at a time, and the acts recede and finally vanish from consciousness. Nevertheless we have a definite concept of the unity of the whole process. The problem to be solved is how the aggregate-character could be recognized at a glance. The attempt to explain this by means of a successive process of apprehensions is even more objectionable when a greater number of elements are involved.

Only one solution appears to be conceivable. There must be marks in the intuition of sensuous aggregates which can be grasped immediately, and in which the aggregate-character can be recognized. These marks must indirectly guarantee the possibility of realizing the process described above. They could not attach to the individual elements, for the single elements do not acquire new positive characters through their connection with one another. There must therefore be an immediately discernible special character in the appearance of an aggregate, so to speak a sensuous quality of a second order. Those "quasi-qualitative characters" would in-directly warrant the existence of a complex of relations and of a plurality of points of reference founding them.

The difficulties involved in the understanding of the immediate appre-hension of large aggregates as aggregates leads Husserl to consider three hypotheses. Instead of a fusion of the relations contained in the unified aggregate-intuition, which is the first hypothesis, one might look to the fusion of the elements of the aggregate for the explanation. A third hypothesis would admit both kinds of fusion, and because of the close relationship between the first two types of fusion the third explanation is favored by Husserl. The term "fusion" is used in order to emphasize that the unified factors are not mere sums. Husserl's fusion of the relations into the unity of a "quasi-quality" is analogous to the fusion which Stumpf discovered in the case of simultaneous sense-qualities.

The testimony of experience is alone to be considered in making a decision. There are numerous examples to show that experience confirms the existence of quasi-qualitative factors (*Momente*) of the kind presup-posed by Husserl's hypotheses. Thus one speaks of a column of soldiers, a heap of apples, a swarm of birds, etc. In addition to naming such ob-jects generically, a certain characteristic property of the unified total in-tuition of the aggregate is expressed; that property can be grasped at a glance, and it makes up the most essential part of the meaning of the terms column, heap, swarm, etc. The element of sensuous similarity of the objects in each aggregate also belongs to these characteristic properties.

Some distributions of objects in the field of vision are first considered. We grasp a configuration at a glance just like a quality, without there being an analysis of the individual relations conditioning the figure. It is by a subsequent analysis that we learn that the factor of figure is conditioned by such relations as the variation of position, etc. The figural factor flashes up immediately, and it is by later reflection that we first note the conditioning relationships, which change from case to case. The expression "figural factor" means more than spatial properties or than the ordinary concept of the configuration of a spatial intuition as distinguished from its size or position. The general concept of configuration is the exact analogue of the concept of a genus of sense-qualities. Equality also means extreme similarity in the case of configurations. Two rows, swarms, etc., are never exactly equal. Qualitative equality, or in general the sensuous equality of all the elements of an aggregate, is one of the most prominent quasi-qualitative factors. For that reason it is not necessary that every single thing be compared with every other one in an aggregate. Besides relations, properties of the elements are also effective as fusing agencies. This is illustrated by the character of a chessboard pattern. The configuration of the black squares is exactly the same as that of the white. The squares of each kind are equal in form, size, and color, and thus found a figural factor of equality in each case. Despite that, the unified total character of both appearances is sharply distinguished by means of the different color of the squares.

All that has been said about aggregates within the field of vision can be applied to all kinds of sensuous aggregates, and also to aggregates in general, whether of sensuous objects presented in phantasy or in psychical acts. For the latter, e.g., temporal succession or temporal configuration forms such a factor. The various figural factors are fused in a variety of ways. The factor of temporal configuration, e.g., fuses with the factors of quality and intensity. The mixture has a unified figural character which is first divided into its components through analysis. A melody contains a complex mixture of that kind. A simple example is provided by a row of equal visual objects, where one can easily distinguish the factors of being in a row and of equality. When there is a plurality of distinct objects in an intuition, there is competition among the figural factors, which belong to all the conceivable sub-classes of the plurality. The one that has exercised the strongest stimulus upon our apprehension is victorious. This victory is only momentary, however, for we grasp now this and again that aggregate within the total intuition to which they all belong, depending upon whether the figural factor of the one or the other preponderates. It is thought appropriate to call these peculiarities of unified intuitions, which are analogous to sense-qualities, figural factors because of their most striking special case.[5]

An actual collection is impossible for larger aggregates, as has been seen. The question then arises as to how we can be certain that all elements have been apprehended. The correct answer to this question is of particular importance for the psychology of counting. If a series is limited, we begin with one of the extreme elements. The progress is uniquely determined, because two contiguous connections are always present at the same time as well as separated elements, so that a new one can be known as such. This uniqueness guarantees the completeness of the detailed individual apprehension. Even in the apprehension of small aggregates, where one can speak of an actual collection, figural factors often play a big role. The smallest group of visual objects, e.g., is characterized as an intuitive unity by a figural factor, which thus determines the frame for our successive individual apprehensions. Furthermore, there may be an arrangement in sub-groups such as $2 + 2$ or $2 + 3$, etc.

The supporting figural factors belong to the psychological but not to the logical contents of a presentation. Just as was done in the case of temporal succession, we can also abstract from the figural factors which distinguish either the whole aggregate or sub-groups of it, and attend to the mere togetherness of the elements in one presentation. This must be done if the real meaning of the presentation of an aggregate is in question. Any symbolically presented aggregates can be compared, and the concepts of equal, more, and less can be used symbolically. The logical contents are not affected by the changes which a presentation of a plurality undergoes through all the symbolizations.

The discussion of infinite aggregates is worth noting. Infinite aggregates are such that it is logically impossible to form them actually or to symbolize them through the successive enumeration of all the individuals concerned. The extensions of most general concepts are infinite. In every case of an infinite aggregate there is a symbolic presentation of a process of conceptual formation that can be continued without limit. A clear principle

[5] Husserl states that these investigations had been worked out nearly a year before the publication of the acute essay by von Ehrenfels on "Gestalt Qualities," in which the figural factors, which were introduced by Husserl in order to explain the indirect apprehension of aggregates, were submitted to a comprehensive investigation. Von Ehrenfels had been stimulated by Mach's *Analysis of Sensations*, and since Husserl had read that work soon after its appearance in 1886, he regards it as possible that he, too, had been influenced by it. Cf. v. Ehrenfels, "Gestaltqualitäten," *Vierteljahrsschrift für wissenschaftliche Philosophie*, vol. XIV (1890).

is given by which every concept already formed from a given genus can be transformed into a new one, distinct from it, so that there will be no return to the initial concept, or to the already generated concepts. What this continually extending aggregate can comprise, or what it cannot comprise, is determined *a priori* by means of precise concepts, i.e., it can be decided concerning every given object of thought whether it can be an element of this process or not. This can be regarded as an early adumbration of the concept of a "definite manifold," which is one of Husserl's important logical conceptions.[6]

In the case of an infinite aggregate the concept of a last step or element of the aggregate is meaningless, whereas in the finite case it is possible really to exhaust the process. That is an essential logical distinction. The absurd intention of forming an actual infinite aggregate is ruled out logically. But the presentation of a determinate unlimited process, as well as the concept of all that is included in its domain because of its conceptual unity, are logically acceptable. An essentially new concept is involved. It is not a concept of an aggregate in the true sense of the term, although it contains that concept, in the notion of a process, e.g., as an essential constituent.

This broad theoretical analysis is applied to the concept of number in the twelfth chapter, which is entitled "The Symbolic Presentations of Number." The symbolic presentations of aggregates form the foundation for the symbolic presentations of numbers. If we were restricted to actual presentations of aggregates, the number series would end at most with twelve, and we would not have the concept of a continuation beyond that point. The "limitlessness" that was seen in the symbolic enlargement of aggregates also applies to numbers, however. Numbers are the discriminated species of the general concept of plurality. A determinate plurality of units, or a number, corresponds to every concrete plurality, whether it be presented actually or symbolically. It can be said in a symbolic sense that every aggregate has a definite number before it is formed, even if we are not in a position to form it actually. Similarly it can be said that any two aggregates must either have the same or different numbers, whether they can be conceived or not. Proceeding from any presentation of an aggregate, we have at least ideally the capacity to enlarge it without limit by adding ever new elements. We cannot really

---

[6] Cf. *Phil. d. Arith.*, p. 247. In the *Ideas*, p. 205 n. (Eng. tr.), Husserl refers to the unpublished sequel to the *Philosophy of Arithmetic*, entitled *Studies in the Theory of Formal Mathematical Disciplines*, and states that he had already made use of the concept of a definite manifold near the beginning of 1890.

form the requisite repetitions *in infinitum*. Apart from the lack of time and energy for the continued mental activity, Husserl holds that there are not enough marks by which to distinguish them. By means of a process of idealization we can disregard our limitations and make use of symbolic concepts.

A rigorous systematic principle is needed for the formation of symbolic number-forms which supplement the narrow domain of numbers that can be presented actually. The process providing them must be determined uniquely, in such a way that for every genuine number not more than one symbolic number-form will result. The problem is to find a principle by which a system of signs can be constructed out of a few basic signs, and which confers a convenient, easily distinguishable sign upon every definite number and clearly indicates its place in the number-series. The problem concerns the concepts themselves, and is not one of mere nomenclature. If a system of number-notation based upon a few fundamental signs is to be constructed, there must be a corresponding parallel system of concepts, based upon certain fundamental concepts. A simple number-series can be thought as continued *in infinitum*, but it is really carried out and given to us only within the limits of naming. The question arises as to how the uniform steps of the unlimited formation of numbers can remain distinguished without the aid of names. The problem is to derive all numbers from the actually given numbers by means of a unified principle, in such a way that it is certain that every conceivable number will have a definite place in the system. In other words, every conceivable plurality must be denumerable by means of the system. That is the task to which Husserl addresses himself in this section of the work. He shows how a principle for the formation of numbers and number-signs can be obtained which meets the logical requirements.

The natural number series is not given first; only a small first part of it is given to us. The fact that we are mentally incapable of larger direct processes of counting led to the use of logical postulates and concepts. The number system obtained serves to construct new concepts. The so-called natural number-forms are in no way more natural than those that are systematic in a narrower sense, such as the decadic. In both cases there are symbolic formations for the number-concepts that are inaccessible to us. It is a matter of logical judgment as to what is suited to the purposes of the knowledge of the number-domain, or which method of symbolic formation is to be chosen.[7]

[7] In the *Log. Unt.*, vol. 1, p. 202 n., reference is made to the treatment of the natural number series in the twelfth chapter of the *Philosophy of Arithmetic*.

There is a strict parallelism between the method of continuation of the series of number-concepts and the method of continuation of number-signs, not only in general, but in the single steps as well. By abstracting from the meaning of the symbols 1, 2, . . . x, and from the meaning of all operations, an independent system of signs can be obtained which corresponds to the conceptual system. The system of signs can be developed independently according to rules, but every result obtained will have its correlate in the conceptual system. Although the rules of arithmetical operations arise out of conceptual sources, the sensuous signs are always necessary for practical activity. The explanation of this noteworthy fact is reserved for the last chapter.

Husserl states that the present discussion has called attention to a most significant logical distinction in the sensuous means of notation. The difference between word-signs and written signs is so essential for arithmetic that a restriction to the former would have made a larger development of arithmetic impossible. This he designates as a logical distinction. In the terminology of the *Philosophy of Arithmetic*, a distinction is logical if it influences the technical mastery of a domain of knowledge, and hence the kind of notation that conforms best to its purpose is superior logically. Lasting visual signs are therefore much superior to number-words. Another example is given to illustrate the influence of physical conditions upon the development of methods. Whether pen and ink be used on paper, or a slate pencil on a slate would influence essentially the course of arithmetical methods, in Husserl's opinion.[8]

An interesting section on the natural origin of the system of numbers is written from an anthropological perspective, the attempt being made to reconstruct *a posteriori* the psychological development of systems of number-signs. This is followed by a discussion of the estimate of numbers by means of figural factors. This problem is similar to the question of the immediate estimate of aggregates that had been raised in the preceding chapter, and its solution is accomplished also by means of figural factors. Every surface of a die, e.g., has a fixed configuration of points. But with every turn or change of position it receives a different figural character. No matter how three distinct objects may be distributed in the field of vision, they form a characteristic configuration, assuming that they can at all be blended into an intuitively unified aggregate. If there is an increase of the objects comprised by an aggregate, there is a greater number of figural types that can be distinguished intuitively.

The book closes with a discussion of the logical sources of arithmetic.

---

[8] Reference is made to this discussion in the *Log. Unt.*, vol. 1, p. 164 n.

Arithmetic is defined as the science of the relations of numbers, its essential task consisting in deriving numbers out of given numbers by means of certain known relations obtaining among them. This method of derivation is either essentially conceptual, the notations playing a subordinate role; or it is an essentially sensuous operation which derives signs from signs by means of rules, on the basis of a system of number-signs, the result being the notation for the desired concept. The latter method is more advantageous in arithmetic. The conceptual method is highly abstract, restricted, and difficult even with much practice, whereas the method of signs is concretely sensuous, all-comprehensive, and easy to handle with a little practice. In regarding it as all-comprehensive, Husserl holds that there is no conceivable problem which it could not solve. It therefore makes the conceptual method entirely superfluous. The method of sensuous signs is accordingly the logical method of arithmetic. The lack of a logic of the symbolic methods of knowledge, and especially of arithmetic, explains why this had not been recognized. The fact that one and the same system of symbolism can serve two or more conceptual systems which are formally similar while differing in content is pointed out as significant for the deeper understanding of mathematics. Such systems are dominated by the same system of calculation. This new concept of calculation is used by Husserl from this point on. If we attend only to the technical methods permitted by the system, disregarding the conceptual application, we have the pure mechanics of calculation which is basic to arithmetic and which makes up the technical side of its method. Then the art of calculation is no longer identical with the art of arithmetical knowledge.

The foundation of the arithmetical methods of calculation is provided by the number-concepts and their forms of connection. As has been seen, the system of numbers provides a method of continuing the domain of numbers beyond every limit. If every plurality is regarded as denumerable, there could be no actual number without a symbolic correlate in the system of numbers. There is only one symbolic correlate, for different systematic number-signs necessarily refer to different actual numbers. In Husserl's view, the systematic numbers can be regarded as representatives of the numbers in themselves (*Zahlen an sich*).

Renewing his discussion of addition, multiplication, subtraction, and division, Husserl designates these operations as arithmetical operations of calculation. They are operations of calculation because they deal with mere signs, and arithmetical because they serve the derivation of numbers. It is Husserl's belief that all difficulties and doubts encountered earlier in the understanding of the operations of calculation and the arithmetical treatment of them may be regarded as solved in this chapter.

The result of the discussion is expressed in a brief conclusion which closes the work, which calls attention once more to the central idea that it is necessary to elaborate the domain of numbers in the form of a system of numbers because we are restricted to the symbolic formation of numbers in the great majority of cases. From the totality of the symbolic formations that are equivalent to every actual number-concept, one is selected according to a fixed principle and is given a systematic place. The problem of evaluation arises then for all other thinkable number-forms, i.e., of the reduction to the number equivalent to them in the system. A survey of the thinkable kinds of number-formation shows, however, that the discovery of proper methods of evaluation is dependent upon the elaboration of a general arithmetic in the sense of a general theory of operations.

C. CRITICAL REACTION AND SIGNIFICANCE

The *Philosophy of Arithmetic* is a characteristic and important work in a number of respects. On the positive side there is first of all the significant recognition of the concept of configuration. Despite the endorsement of psychologism, there is much in the method of procedure that suggests the future method of phenomenology in its "realistic" or logical form. The largely gratuitous definitions of "unity" anticipate the subtle distinctions of the *Logical Investigations*, where the term "idea" or "presentation" is dissected similarly, for example. The discussion of Frege is one of the valuable parts of the book. The close student of phenomenology is sure to find the *Philosophy of Arithmetic* revealing and helpful in the understanding of the motives that have always been effective in Husserl's thought.

The *Philosophy of Arithmetic* was well received in some quarters. Hildebrand [9] reviewed it favorably, and after sketching its main contents merely expressed the wish for a more thoroughgoing analysis of the concept of collection and for the appearance of the second volume. Heinrich [10] wrote a reasonably favorable review of it, although he expressed the preference for a "genetic" investigation. In another favorable review [11] it was described as "a conscientious, thorough investigation."

Reference has already been made to the severe criticism by Frege.[12]

---

[9] Franz Hildebrand, *Gött. gel. Anz.*, vol. XVII (1893), pp. 175–180.

[10] W. Heinrich, *Viertelj. f. wiss. Phil.*, vol. XIX (1895), pp. 436–439.

[11] A. Elsas, *Phil. Monatshefte*, vol. XXX (1894), pp. 437–440.

[12] G. Frege, *Zeitschrift für Philosophie und philosophische Kritik*, vol. CIII (1894), pp. 313–332.

The importance of Frege's views as well as their influence upon Husserl make it desirable to include the essence of his criticism in the present context. Husserl's work is described by him as an attempt to justify a naive conception of number in scientific ways. A theory of number is "naive" in Frege's opinion if it does not regard a number-statement as a proposition about a concept or the extension of a concept. The view that number is something like a heap, or a swarm, in which the things are contained, is declared to be most naive of all. Next to that is the conception of number as a property of a heap or of an aggregate. It then becomes necessary to free the objects from their particularities. Husserl's attempt is characterized as one in which this process of purification is undertaken in a psychological wash-boiler. In Frege's opinion the mixture of psychology and logic, which was so highly favored at the time, was merely a means of avoiding difficulties. The process of abstraction by which the notion of "something" is obtained is submitted to ridicule because of Frege's assumption that a literal identification of presentations and objects had been made. Thus he states "First everything becomes a presentation . . . the objects are presentations." If that were the case, we could change objects by attending to them or disregarding them, and finally arrive at the "bloodless spectre" of "something." He observes that the something gained from one object is distinguished from the somethings of other objects, although it is not easy to see whereby. Frege is right in pointing out that the results of both the subjective and the objective are included under the word "idea," or "presentation." The term "totality" is, as has been seen, referred to as a presentation at times, and again as something objective. Emphasizing the danger of such confusion, Frege observes that it is an innocent pleasure to call the moon a presentation, so long as one does not come to think that it can be transformed or generated by psychological means. The ambiguous term "content" may readily be made to appear absurd, especially when applied to the moon. The possibility of doing so indicates that the usage is undesirable, even if consistency of statement and standpoint were otherwise achieved.

Husserl's treatment of definitions is also found to be objectionable. The psychological logicians and mathematicians differ, as Frege expresses it, in that the former are concerned with the meanings of words and with ideas, which they do not distinguish from the meanings, whereas the latter are concerned with the things themselves, with the indications of the words. Commenting upon the conception of number as referring to the totality of counted objects which are joined by the conjunctive "and," Frege points out that such number-propositions rarely occur in actual experience. We do not ask, "How many are Caesar and Pompeius and London and Edinburgh?" In reality we ask questions such as "How many satellites has Mars?" From the answer "The number of the Martian satellites is two" one learns something that is worth while asking about. A conceptual word appears in both question and answer, instead of the conjunctive "and." Husserl does indeed state that one can indirectly say that a concept has the property of having a number attributed to its extension. This is taken by Frege to be an admission that in a number-statement something is asserted about a concept.

Frege also criticizes the supposed origin of a totality, stating that he had never succeeded in forming one according to Husserl's directions; and he regards it as impossible to think or present together any contents without a relation or connection among them being presented.

Replying to Husserl's criticism, Frege declares that it is incorrect to ascribe to him (Frege) the view that a number-statement expresses the determination of a concept, for that is to misunderstand the distinction between a character (*Merkmal*) and a property (*Eigenschaft*). For the rest, Frege's review contains a reply to Husserl on the question of how the equality of units is to be reconciled with their distinguishableness, a criticism of Husserl's treatment of o and 1, and of large numbers. Frege points out that he had used the term "equal" in the sense of "not different," and hence the charge that he had confused equality and identity could not apply. Regarding Husserl's assertion that o and 1 are negative answers to the question "How many?" Frege observes that it is expecting a good deal to believe that the answer "one" to the question "How many moons has the earth?" is a negative one. As for Husserl's analysis of larger numbers, which are regarded as presentations or as the results of mental activities, Frege asks for the object of which a number is a presentation. That Husserl could not make that clear is ascribed to the confusion of the subjective with the objective, and to the circumstance that such expressions as "moon" and "presentation of the moon" are never clearly distinguished, which are declared to cause such an impenetrable fog that it is hopeless to attain clarity on this point. He concedes, however, that in the second part of the book there are indications of Husserl's recognition of the fact that the things themselves of which we seek to make presentations are primarily concerned, and not our presentations. The "numbers in themselves" are objective in character, and they are independent of our thinking. But, Frege argues, if my presentation of a number is not the number itself, then the ground is removed from under the psychological point of view, so far as the investigation of number is concerned. There is obviously a great difference between investigating a number-presentation itself and a presentation of a real object. Although Husserl's procedure appears to Frege to be suited only to the former, his later discussion of objective numbers suggests the latter. So great is the impression of confusion made upon him by the *Philosophy of Arithmetic* that he declares it to be as absurd as an attempt to explain the origin of the seas psychologically, which would surely be to miss the subject essentially. Even if the seas are real while numbers are not, he submits, the latter are something objective, which is what is in question.

In conclusion Frege states that in reading this book he has been able to estimate the damage caused by the intrusion of psychology into logic. The errors which he thought it his duty to expose are in his opinion due less to the author than to a widespread philosophical sickness. Ending his criticism with a note of caution, he admits that his fundamentally different standpoint makes it difficult for him to do justice to Husserl's merits, which he supposes to be in the domain of psychology, and in closing he calls the attention of the psychologists to the eleventh chapter, where the possibility of the immediate apprehension of aggregates is discussed. Being unable to claim competence in that field, he wisely refrains from passing judgment on what was indeed to prove most significant in the work.

Undoubtedly a critical revision of the text would have prevented some of the confusion criticized by Frege. Husserl's dual interest in the psychological and logical aspects of his subject-matter justifies the treatment of the psychological origin of the ideas in question. There need be no confusion on principle. As Frege recognized, Husserl also took account of the objective reference of his concepts; and it will be recalled that he took care to distinguish "number" and "presentation of number." But a complete emancipation from the standpoint of psychologism was necessary before consistency of statement could be achieved, to begin with, for only then could he be really aware of the importance of the distinction. There can be no doubt about the effectiveness of Frege's criticism, and its influence upon the course of Husserl's thought. It did not result in a wholesale repudiation of Husserl's early studies, and the final outcome of his development was by no means to be identical with Frege's position. Nevertheless, his vigorous reaction against psychologism and his admission in the preface to the *Logical Investigations* of his past errors may well be traced in large part to Frege. Husserl's retraction of his criticism of Frege's antipsychologism, referred to earlier, is one indication, among others, of the respect he had for the latter. But it should be noted that his retraction concerned a broad matter of principle, and that only pages 129–132 were mentioned. One infers then that the numerous other criticisms of Frege in the *Philosophy of Arithmetic* were still endorsed by him. The subsequent development of phenomenology was to supersede both Frege and the early Husserl.

In concluding this account of the *Philosophy of Arithmetic* the most significant points for the further development of Husserl's philosophy will be noted. (1) There is first of all the nature of the investigation itself. Although psychologistic, it is concerned with the origin and clarification of the basic ideas of arithmetic. It is evident from his introductory remarks, as well as from his own descriptive notice of the volume,[13] that Husserl was interested in making a beginning. It was his aim to "lay foundations" by means of an analysis of the fundamental concepts of arithmetic and a "logical elucidation" of its symbolic methods, and not to construct a closed system of a philosophy of arithmetic. (2) The tendency to reduce all knowledge to actual perception is modified later by the introduction of "general seeing." But in the present work direct perception is extended to include the immediate apprehension of aggregates, or aggregate-characters. (3) There is some degree of confusion of the objective and the subjective orders, including even an expression of a form of psychological idealism. Husserl's unguarded statement that every definite object is given as the content of a psychical act of presentation lends support to Frege's charge that he has transformed objects into subjective ideas. But taking the work as a whole into consideration, there is justification for regarding it as illustrating, even if inadequately and not always clearly, the "dual mode of analysis" so characteristic of the later phenomenology. Husserl himself preferred to speak of the "peculiar doubling of psychological and logical analyses" that is illustrated in the *Philosophy of Arithmetic*, and thus to credit his earlier work with what was to prove to be of fundamental importance when exactly defined by means of the phenomenological method. (4) Frege's criticism was only partial; not everything in the book was attacked or questioned by any means. In fact, even if every point made by Frege were admitted to be valid, most of the materials of the book, critical and original, might still remain. Nevertheless, Frege's criticism was important as a matter of principle, as well as in calling attention to details of inadequacy or incorrectness. In brief, he was dissatisfied with (a) the mixture of psychology and logic brought by psychologism; (b) Husserl's apparent confusion of the objective and subjective orders; and (c) Husserl's criticism of some of his own views. (5)

---

[13] Cf. Husserl, "Selbstanzeige" of the *Phil. d. Arith.*, *Viertelj. f. wiss. Phil.*, vol. xv (1891), pp. 360–361.

Despite Frege's criticism, which proved to be helpful and constructive, this first published work by Husserl was a promising beginning, already containing in a rudimentary form some of the most characteristic features of his later work, or at least those patterns of thought which eventuated in important ideas. Although Husserl always referred to it as his "youthful work," he retained some of its terms and concepts, such as the concept of "something," the distinction between genuine and symbolic presentations, etc., and later made numerous references to what he regarded as sound insights. Thus he pointed out [14] that in discussing the "origin" of the concepts of plurality, number, unity, etc., he came upon the basic form of synthetic "many-rayed" consciousness, which is one of the forms of "categorial" consciousness in the sense of the *Logical Investigations*; and in connection with the relationship of "collectiva" to these forms of unity, he came upon the distinction of sensuous and categorial unity. The question of the origin of "non-genuine" or "figurative" presentations of aggregates led to the recognition of "quasi-qualitative" or "figural" factors. There are, furthermore, a number of references to this work in the *Ideas*, as well as many references in the *Logical Investigations*. Attention is called to the fact that the concept of a "primary content" was already contained in the *Philosophy of Arithmetic* (pp. 72 ff.); that the distinction between the psychological description of a phenomenon and the statement of its meaning is drawn; and mention is made of a "logical content" as opposed to psychological contents (pp. 28 f.).[15] It is therefore certain that this work was never wholly abandoned. On the contrary, it provides strong evidence of the continuity of Husserl's development. For example, the further investigation of genuine and "figurative" presentations, was reserved for the second volume of the *Philosophy of Arithmetic*; but as a matter of fact it is not given until the sixth of the *Logical Investigations*. (6) There is also evidence of the recognition of the prescriptive nature of formal reasoning in the discussion of infinite aggregates, which suggests the later conception of a definite manifold. (7) The display of a capacity for searching analysis of fundamental concepts, and of undeniable ability to express his ideas clearly is evident in much of the work. (8) It is strange that Husserl, with all his mathematical training and competence in formal analysis, should hold so narrow a view of the possibility of formal definition. The explanation is not so much that he was an exponent of psychologism — which he was, to be sure — but that he did not at the time

---

[14] In his recently published "Preface" to the *Logical Investigations*. See also ch. x, B, 9, n. 11 herein.

[15] Cf. *Ideas* (Eng. tr.), p. 246 n. and p. 346 n.

realize the true and proper significance of "psychological" analysis as a preparatory or ancillary discipline for formal science, including mathematics. (9) It also appears that Husserl was unwilling to abandon "common-sense" objections in the realm of formal reasoning, when objecting to the extravagant "infinitely many equivalent aggregates" as an explanatory device. A simpler theory of number would of course be welcome; but the fact that a theory is complex does not make it absurd. (10) The first part of the work, which is primarily critical, is in itself sufficient to dispose of the long held belief that it is merely a repudiated psychologistic treatise; and it contains ideas and suggestions that are interesting and in part significant. The opposition to the unlimited use of formal devices could have been set forth in the name of intuitionism or "constructionalism," with no reference to the thesis of psychologism. In the name of a philosophy of experience and of actual construction Husserl could have protested against the assumption of "an unlimited supply of signs" and of infinite numbers of explanatory entities. The thesis of psychologism is combined with an unmistakable preference for intuitionism, which has come to mature expression in his later philosophy.

CHAPTER III

EARLY LOGICAL INTERESTS

A. SYMBOLIC LOGIC

IN THE YEARS from 1891 to 1893 Husserl was very much interested in problems concerning the nature of logic, not only from the psychological point of view as illustrated in the *Philosophy of Arithmetic*, but also from the formal point of view. Regardless of his periodical change of position with regard to the foundations of logic, his studies in formal logic represent an independent interest which continued from his first mathematical studies to the mature treatment of formal logic of his last period.

1. Critique of Schröder

The first volume of Schröder's *Lectures on the Algebra of Logic* [1] appeared in 1890, and Husserl took advantage of the event to define his own position in logical theory with respect to this representative work on symbolic logic. [2] He referred to this review with approval in his discussion of a work by Palagyi in 1903, [3] so that this publication does not belong to the repudiated part of his past work.

Schröder proposed in his work to present a completely reformed deductive logic in the form of an algebra of logic, the leading ideas being derived from the English extensional logic. This first comprehensive attempt at an extensional logic on German soil provided a welcome occasion to compare the old and the new logic. Inasmuch as Frege's *Fundamental Laws of Arithmetic* [4] appeared in 1893, this statement may be regarded as not unfair, even if instead of extensional logic "symbolic logic" were inserted. Schröder restricted his interest to logic in a narrow sense, or deductive logic, which deals with the laws of consistent thought, and which he wished to keep distinct from the logic of induction. Husserl states that

---

[1] Ernst Schröder, *Vorlesungen über die Algebra der Logik*, vol. 1 (Leipzig, 1890).

[2] Cf. Husserl's review of this work in the *Gött. gel. Anz.*, vol. xv (1891), pp. 243–278.

[3] Husserl's review of M. Palagyi's *Der Streit der Psychologisten und Formalisten in der modernen Logik* (Leipzig, 1902), was published in the *Zeitschrift für Psychologie und Physiologie der Sinnesorgane*, vol. xxxi (1903), pp. 287–294. Husserl states (p. 288) that he had made clear the absurdities of the "quantifying" logic twelve years before in a detailed critique, the reference being to the review of Schröder's work.

[4] G. Frege, *Grundgesetze der Arithmetik* (Jena, 1893).

one could hardly be more deceived concerning his own aims than Schröder was, and this deception he judges to be characteristic of the entire extensional logic. As conceived by Schröder, deductive logic comprises the "analytic truths" or "truisms," such as "All black crows are black," and also real deduction in the sense of necessary progress from already present convictions to new convictions. Husserl observes that the analytic truths do not include the totality of immediate evidences, but only a small part of them which belongs to the "formal" theory of inference. One might undertake to determine all the analytic judgments which can be constructed formally out of the given terms S, P, . . . Z, obtaining, for example, such judgments as "In so far as something is an S, it is not a non-S," and "In so far as something is both an S and a P, it is either an S or a P." Husserl points out that there are nevertheless countless evidences which, as dependent upon the particular nature of the judged terms, are not included here. Thus if S and P are numbers which really can be presented and do not have first to be defined through indirect symbolizations, say 2 and 3, then the immediate evidence $2 < 3$ exists, and that is not an "identical judgment" in the sense which the formal theory of inference presupposes. The domain of the calculus of symbolic logic comprises pure formal deductions, which as "pure" do not involve reference to the particular content of the judged terms. Only that which can be deduced from a given set of premises on the basis of their mere form is included in this domain. But this does not comprise the domain of deductive logic in general. Not one of the deductive sciences is included under it, for none is a consistent system of pure deductions from a totality of given premises, although each system often makes some use of such formal deductions.

Husserl contends that the "algorismic" logic errs, just as the traditional deductive logic had erred, in construing deduction too narrowly. The subject-matter of deductive logic is not made up of particular concepts, such as numbers and figures. It consists of the logical activities which are valid in all deductive disciplines, pure inference being only one of these activities. The deductive sciences also operate, construct, and reckon. Husserl denies that arithmetical operations and geometrical constructions are cases of inference. Similarly, reckoning is described as a blind procedure with symbols according to mechanically reproduced rules of the transformation and transposition of symbols. Neither is the interpretation of the final formula of a symbolic deduction a case of an inference. The theory of all such mental activities which serve the deduction of scientific truths while not being deductive themselves belongs to deductive logic. It does not, however, belong to the domain of the pure deductions. The traditional formal logic was in error in supposing that it had achieved the aims of logic by restricting itself to this narrow domain; and the algebraic logic took over this error.

With obvious lack of sympathy, the germ from which the proud structure of the calculus of logic has grown is traced to the Scholastic logic, with its technical rules whereby the conclusion could be constructed mechanically on the basis of any given premises, thus obviating the actual process of deduction. Far from being a theory of pure deduction, the calculus of logic is described as being rather an art which makes such deductions dispensable. It is a symbolic technique which makes it possible by means of a system of rules to determine the totality of the pure deductions contained in the premises. But this reckoning is declared to be only an external substitute for deducing. What Husserl demands and does not find in the algebra of logic is an adequate philosophical account of formal reasoning, which he believes a complete logic should be prepared to provide. He argues that if the algebra of logic were well founded theoretically as a special logical method, it could explain the essence and the logical justification of the method of calculation. But the logic of the algebraic calculus does not enter into the investigation, chiefly because the mental operations upon which it is based do not belong to the domain of pure deductions. The logical calculus of Schröder is held to be a mere calculus of pure deductions. It is not their logic any more than the *arithmetica universalis*, which comprises the entire domain of numbers, is a logic of that domain. The distinction at issue is one between logical systems and the system of logic, which Husserl was prepared to draw more clearly later in his development, when he could speak of a "theory" of logic in a well-defined sense. In the discussion of Schröder he emphasized the aspect of the activities of thought that are involved. The "laws" of the calculus are not rules which must be observed by all who infer correctly, but only which one can follow in every case, with complete confidence of a correct result. The question of a logical theory is not touched by the development of special algorismic methods. This explains, in Husserl's view, the striking fact that is seen in logic and mathematics, that one can be an excellent logical technician and a very mediocre philosopher of logic, and again that one can be an excellent mathematician and a very mediocre philosopher of mathematics. Boole is held up as an eminent example of both. He adds that it almost appears as though the mental activities necessary for the two types of investigation were too heterogeneous, since it is such an extraordinary rarity to find them united.

In his discussion of symbolism Schröder had asserted that the exact sciences have shown a tendency to refer difficulties encountered in the study of things as much as possible to the study of symbols. Husserl invites the reader to test this by means of Euclidean geometry, the symbols of which are figures, whether drawn on the board or in phantasy. A geometrical proposition does not arise through the mere study of these symbols. The symbols are mere supports for the conception of the really intended concepts, and similarly the sensuous operations on a figure are nothing more than sensuous aids. The activity of judgment is concerned not with the symbols, but with the objects that are symbolized through them. Since the symbols are not the only objects of consideration, it would appear, according to Schröder's criterion, that Euclidean geometry is still in its inductive stage of development. In algebraic systems, Husserl continues, one may speak of a transfer of the difficulties encountered in the study of things to the domain of symbols, but it would be incorrect even there to regard the symbols as being the only objects under consideration. In the process of reckoning with the symbols one is not concerned with the concepts which are basic to them, but deals exclusively with the rules of the symbols, or the laws of the calculus. That procedure is, however, only a part of deduction, and not the whole of it. The formation of an equation and the substitution of a problem by a corresponding algorismic problem equivalent to it are processes which precede it; and, as has been pointed out, the interpretation or the transposition of the final formulae into correct judgments follows it. These considerations are regarded as being sufficient to indicate the limitations of the calculus.

Schröder's discussion of the principles of denotation is designed to serve as the logical foundation of his symbolic method. Husserl observes that because of Schröder's equivocal use of the term "meaning," there is confusion of the two very different questions of whether names have a meaning, and whether corresponding to a name an object exists or not. Nonsensical names in an exact sense are names without meaning, as shown by the apparent name "abracadabra." But Schröder's example "round square" is a name to which nothing can correspond in truth.

Husserl proposes to refute Schröder's argument against a logic of intension (*Begriffsinhalt*) by showing that a logic of intension (or a "logic of ideal contents") can be built up, just as the so-called extensional logic is validly constructed, and that it can be done with the same technique and in response to the same problems. This attempt at a proof is the theme of a separate paper, and will be presented below. He regards it as certain that logic treats, among other things, of necessary truths, but asks whether a science of that which is necessary for thought is therefore itself necessary, or a deductive science. This is held to be the case only for that small part of logic which comprises the conditioning relations among judgments. Husserl argues that an independent extensional logic is impossible on principle, for every extensional judgment is really a judgment of content, or is intensional. In the judgment "Class A is contained in class B" it is recognized that the object of the concept "class A" is the object of the concept "being contained in class B." If these concepts were substituted by their extensions and the corresponding class-judgment were formed, the same would hold again, and so on. In his view, consequently, the logic of extension cannot be treated independently of the logic of intension, and the latter is presupposed by extensional logic. Husserl concludes that in so far as the logic of extension has meaning as a special logical method, and not as a new logic, it belongs entirely within intensional logic.

The presentation of logic in the form of an algebra has certain advantages, which Schröder points out. The use of a language free from the defects of ordinary language, with its ambiguity and inexactness, represents an advance. But Husserl denies that the "exact" logic is merely a logic based upon a new language, and insists that it is not a logic at all. Because it is a calculus serving special logical purposes, the talk of a "presentation of logic as an algebra" appears to him to be entirely inappropriate. There also appears to be a misunderstanding of the essential difference between language and algebraic symbolism, for Schröder seems to believe that when symbols replace natural words, the algebraic procedure is already given, an error which is found in the work of Descartes, Hobbes, and Leibniz. The two concepts are different basically, however, for language is not a method of systematic symbolic inference, and the calculus is not a method for the expression of psychical phenomena. As Husserl conceives language, its peculiar function consists in the symbolic expression of psychical phenomena, both for the purpose of communication and as a sensuous support for one's own thought-movement. Grammar is the art which shows us how to express judgments correctly in accordance with language; it does not teach us how we ought to judge, or give rules by which correct judgments can be derived indirectly by means of artificial symbolic devices. The peculiar function of the calculus consists in its being a method of symbolic inference for a certain region of knowledge and hence an art of substituting symbolic reckoning for real inference. Husserl does not deny that a judgment-language can be an inferential calculus at the same time, but he holds that the logical calculus is merely a calculus. He concludes that Schröder again deceives himself concerning his aims when he states his ideal as the discovery of the most rational system of

denotation for the naming of all objects and the expression of all occurrences of thought.

In thus rejecting the principles of the "exact logic" presented by
Schröder, Husserl has by no means rejected the logical calculus itself.
He observes that it is peculiar to all such disciplines that the application
and even the discovery of algebraic methods is independent of the insight
into their essence and the basis of their cognitive value. General arithmetic keeps growing, although even its most gifted representatives are far
removed from a deeper understanding of its bases. The meaning of its
fundamental concepts is still in question, and it thus remains a science
which does not know the nature of its subject-matter. The logical calculus
makes a contribution somewhat similar to that of arithmetic, in that it
provides ready methods to save very complicated and painstaking deductions in its limited domain, and to derive its results more rapidly and
easily. In Husserl's opinion it ought not to be too difficult to determine
the logical justification of this simple calculus, and so to understand the
inner necessity of its procedure.

Schröder's distinction between the logical and psychological content
of a judgment or statement is also criticized by Husserl. In the latter's
view, the truly logical content of a statement is its judgment-content, and
hence that which it asserts, and this does not express the corresponding
class-judgment. Husserl proposes that a distinction be made between the
logical and the algebraic content of a statement. If it is assumed that only
judgments about class-relations directly permit of algebraic treatment, and
if all other judgments can be transformed into equivalent class-judgments,
then the first problem is the transformation of all statements into equivalent
class-statements which express the algebraic content of the original statements. The fundamental principle of the "calculatory" theory of inference
is therefore the following: Every statement which is not already a class-
statement permits of being transformed into one and accordingly can
be expressed by the symbols of the calculus and be subject to its rules. Or
more briefly: Every statement has an algebraic content which is identical
with or equivalent to its logical content. The general applicability of the
calculus is based upon the fact of the "equivalence" of judgments, and
that should have been analyzed first of all. Two judgments are equivalent
if they can be deduced from one another. From the standpoint of the
cognitive interest, the one may be regarded as given when the other is
given. What can be proved for the one holds for the other, and that judgment with which it is more convenient to operate will therefore be chosen
in practice. This consideration is sufficient for the justification of the pro-

cedure required by the calculus, and Husserl holds it to be unnecessary to inquire beyond this simple fact of equivalence.

The new calculus is supposed to refer to any "domains" of any manifold, or to any manifolds. Husserl objects to this term (although he comes to use it later in his logical writings), and he proposes to replace it by the term "aggregates." The first question of the general calculus of aggregates would be: Which possible relations do any two aggregates a and b afford as such? There are five possible cases: a is a part of b; or b is a part of a; or both are identical; or they overlap; or they exclude one another. If one considers aggregates with respect to such relations, then it is to be expected that from the knowledge of certain relations that of others could also be derived. Thus the mere consideration of what lies in the concept of a general calculus of aggregates provides a broad basis for its construction. The various interpretations of the calculus which Schröder presents, including domains, classes, concepts, judgments, etc., are a part of the calculus of aggregates, in Husserl's view. The calculus, regarded as a symbolic technique, can be applied to all these cases, but Schröder errs when he supposes that the calculus, as "identical," includes all the applications in itself. Husserl denies that the fundamental concepts of the calculus of aggregates can found all the applications which the calculus as such permits; and he doubts whether there is a conceptual foundation of the calculus which really accomplishes that. It is interesting to note the early appearance of the problem of formal unity and diversity of interpretation in Husserl's development. The fact that in mathematics the algebraic calculus admits of heterogeneous conceptual applications is explained by the occurrence of analogous relationships in different conceptual domains, such as aggregates, continua, concepts, and judgments, which permit analogous forms of inference. Thus no matter how different the material domains may be, the same calculus may be developed on the basis of the analogous relationships. The dogma of the extensional logicians, that only an interpretation in terms of classes makes possible an algebraic deductive discipline, is refuted therewith.

It appears to Husserl, in view of these considerations, that two modes of procedure are available in the presentation of the calculus. It may either be founded as a mere technique, as a game of symbols, without regard to any applications; or one may proceed from a definite domain of application. In the former case, one knows that every domain whose relationships lead to the necessary and sufficient basic formulae of the system must also come under the entire calculus, and thus an inferential calculus is obtained. In the latter case, one derives the basic formulae and then the entire calculus from the nature of the concepts of the definite domain of application. The transfer to other domains follows according to analogy, by way of the basic formulae. In this procedure as little as possible should be inferred from the concepts and as much as possible through deduction from already known propositions, for relations which are clear in one domain may have to be apprehended indirectly in another domain. Schröder's presentation of the logical calculus can be well used as one of the second kind, Husserl admits, while maintaining that the fundamental insight upon which it is based is false.

It will be of interest to note certain specific criticisms of details in the logical calculus. The definition of equality as "If $a \subset b$ and at the same time $b \subset a$, then $a = b$" is judged to be circular, on the ground that the concept of equality is explicitly contained, not only externally in the symbol for subsumption, but also in the concept of the relationship itself. This is submitted as an evident proposition rather than a definition. Husserl also disagrees with the way in which the symbols o and 1 are introduced into the calculus. o is defined there as a domain which is subsumed under every domain a, and 1 as a domain under which every domain is subsumed; and these symbols are treated as though they were symbols of real domains. Challenging this procedure for its justification, Husserl holds that it illustrates the practice of those formalistic arithmeticians who "creatively introduce" definitions in the course of deductive reasoning, subject only to the condition of non-contradiction. But the avoidance of conflict (*Widerstreit*) is another condition to be observed, in his opinion. If the definitions of o and 1 contained incompatibilities, the calculus would cease to be a calculus of correct inference for classes. The principle of identity is taken by Schröder to hold not merely for manifolds, but for all that can possibly be thought, and hence for all names, whether meaningful or not. While agreeing with this, Husserl contends that $a \subset a$ is not the principle of identity, but rather a principle that applies only to aggregates. Instead of meaning a *is* a, it states that the aggregate a is subsumed under or equal to the aggregate a. In accordance with his tendency, which is strange for a trained mathematician, to challenge purely formal devices, Husserl refuses to regard the symbols o, 1, ab, and $a + b$ as belonging to the domains of the manifold as "unreal domains." He insists that the calculus is intended to be a calculus of real and not of "unreal" manifolds. The proof of existence appears to be successful everywhere except in the case of o; for there is no domain o which is included in every other domain, and there are actually disjunctive domains which have no domain in common. The o can therefore be added only as a fictitious domain. No domain can correspond to the concept of o because of the incompatibility of its determinations. The o of the logical calculus presents the same problem as the $\sqrt{-1}$ of the arithmetical calculus, its justification being a matter of algebraic technique.

The requirement that the elements of the manifold be compatible with one another is held by Husserl to be superfluous. The calculus deals with manifolds of all kinds, whether from the domain of reality, fiction, or absurdity, and is also applicable to aggregates of impossible and incompatible objects, in so far as such objects may be of interest. Such a unification of incompatibilities would be merely collective, and not, as Schröder holds, a unification of judgmental belief. Even explicit contradictions can be united in a collective meaning. They are only non-unitable in the sense of truth and conviction.

The interpretation of the formulae $o \subset a$ and $a \subset 1$ proves to be of importance in calling attention to a difficulty which besets the extensional logic. These formulae are translated as "Nothing is a" (e.g. gold), and "a (gold) is everything." Schröder recognizes that these statements are false, but instead of seeking the error in the translation he endeavors to find it in a defect of "word-language." Husserl finds that the misunderstanding lies in the interpretation, which he holds to be a point at which all attempts at an extensional logic since Boole had failed. If the distinction between real and imaginary classes is upheld, and it is seen that the o class belongs to the latter group, there is no way to avoid the absurdities to which the formulae $o \subset a$, $a \subset 1$, and $a \subset o$ lead, as the simple translation shows. The extensional logicians had overlooked the fact that all inference, in a formal theory of inference, is purely hypothetical in character, and consequently all the categorical judgments which appear in it are only apparently categorical. Judgments of the form "The class a is subsumed under the class b" are accordingly hypothetical in character. The existence of the subject-class is not asserted, the judgment meaning that if there is an extension belonging to a concept a, then it also belongs to the concept b under which it is subsumed. The talk of real and imaginary classes is therefore pointless for the present domain. The classes of round squares and of the non-existent enter into the pure theory of deduction just as do classes of gold objects or metals. Thus it can be asserted that the class of round squares belongs to the class of the non-existent. This leads Husserl to propose the following interpretation of the symbols o and 1: 1 is the symbol for the extension of the concept of existence, and o for the extension of the concept of non-existence. The formula $o \subset a$ accordingly means that if something is a non-existent, it also possesses any character a.

The formula $a \subset 1$ means on the other hand that if something is an a, it also possesses the character of existence. This is held to be obvious, for the categorical judgment "Something is an a" includes the existence of the subject. Husserl does not ask whether "existence" is used in the same sense here as in the foregoing. He believes that the consideration of the purely hypothetical character of all requirements of the domain is sufficient to eliminate all difficulties from the concepts o and 1, as well as from the interpretation of the formulae cited above.

In commenting upon Schröder's criticism of the Boolean concept of the 1 as the class of all that is conceivable, Husserl is led to make a distinction between a K whose elements are themselves classes and the subclasses that can be formed. The o is a subclass and not an element of K. Thus all elements of K are equal to 1, but the same does not hold for their subclasses. Hence o = 1 does not hold. The elements of the null class are also elements of K, and they are equal to 1, which is in accordance with their significance as objects of the class of the non-existent. In this way Schröder's objection to the Boolean concept of unity, to the effect that not only would 1 = 1 have to hold, but also o = 1, is found to be untenable. The only point that Husserl finds to be correct is that in cases where classes and classes of classes appear at the same time, the calculus may not be applied blindly. In the calculus of aggregates as such, every aggregate ceases to be valid as an aggregate as soon as it is regarded as an element of another aggregate. The latter is again only valid as an aggregate with reference to its primary and actual elements, but not with reference to the elements of these elements. Schröder has indicated that fallacies can arise if this is not observed, unfortunately by his own example. It would be asserting too much, however, to state that the calculus is not applicable to such "mixed" manifolds.

Concerning the theory of negation as a judgment-function, Husserl observes that psychological theories may be of fundamental significance for a logic, but that they are pointless for a logical calculus. That which is essential for the logical calculus can be expressed briefly. In order to apply to any judgments, what is required is that every negative judgment may be transformed into an equivalent affirmative judgment with negative matter. It is not necessary that the negation really belong to the content in the negative judgment. A negation in the strict sense of the term does not really occur in the calculus of classes.

If the symbol 1 may not signify the collective totality of everything conceivable, then in the formula $a + a_1 = 1$, a_1, which is the "negation" of a, cannot be the extension of the concept non-a. It follows that the formulae $aa_1 = 0$ and $a + a_1 = 1$ are not the class equivalents of the principles of contradiction and excluded middle, although Schröder regarded them as "the most concise expressions" of these principles. He believed that he had discovered an essential limit for the latter principle, with the limitation of the concept of 1. Husserl readily points out the weakness in Schröder's illustrations of difficulties which are alleged to follow from the assertion that everything must be a or non-a, and he argues that it is not necessary to restrict the 1 for the logical calculus. Consequently the definition of negation will also be unrestricted, in agreement with Boole, which would make the formulae of negation to be complete class equivalents of the two logical principles.[5]

Husserl concludes his discussion with an estimate of the value of the calculus, which is disappointing, even considering the comparatively undeveloped state of symbolic logic at the time. He recognizes that it is of value as a device for timesaving, and also because of the certainty realized by its means. But this fact is not sufficient, in his opinion, to accord the calculus a great practical value. If it really encompassed all deduction, then every philosopher, mathematician, and natural scientist would have to study it. The domain which is involved is, however, very small. Pure deductions occur everywhere in life and in science, but they are usually so simple that their calculatory solution would be a ridiculous detour. Pure deductions from complicated systems of premises have been so rare that scientists would not find it worth while to go to the trouble of learning and retaining mastery over the calculus. The future may bring fruitful regions of application, but as the matter now stands the representatives of the new discipline are faced with the peculiar difficulty of discovering problems to be solved by their methods. These objections are intended to apply only to the logical calculus of conceptual extensions, and not to the "identical" calculus of mere aggregates. While pointing out that it was still too soon to decide concerning the practical value of symbolic logic, Husserl recognizes the theoretical interest which attaches to the algorismic treatment of the theory of pure deduction and of set theory.

Although not drawn very clearly, Husserl endeavored to make a distinction between logical systems and the system of logic, for that was really the point of his denial that a particular logical system, such as the algebra of logic was, could function as logic itself. His conception of an intensional logic, based upon an analysis of meaning, seemed sharply opposed to the

[5] This should be compared with Husserl's later judgment, as expressed in the *Formal and Transcendental Logic*, according to which some restrictions are necessary. To be sure, these restrictions concern meaning primarily.

extensional type of logic for two reasons: (a) the excessive claims made for the extensional logic, more than was warranted; (b) the lack of understanding of formal logic, and of a philosophy of it. Husserl's talk of "logical activities," and of the significance of psychological theories for logic, is but a faint indication of the type of analysis he came to have in mind as he prepared the *Logical Investigations*; and it was not until he had completed the draft of a "pure" or formal logic in its universal form that he could claim to have made good his positive case against Schröder. His disparagement of symbolic logic went too far, in any case; it was unnecessary and unjustified for the most part. That was as bad in its way as was the claim that the class calculus *is* logic itself. He was right in challenging "the dogma of the extensional logicians," that only the class-interpretation makes possible a symbolic-deductive discipline, as the subsequent development of logic has amply shown. But as one deriving from a tradition which included Leibniz, Husserl might have been expected to see more in the potential usefulness and future possibilities of symbolic logic than his unsympathetic and even disdainful attitude allowed at the time. This attitude was to become to a large extent a part of the repudiated views of his earlier years. But not entirely, for until his last period he was inclined to disparage "mere technique" as compared with the "meaningful" procedure of phenomenology. Thus he maintained that it is only by a sound analysis "beginning at the beginning" that the technical difficulties and superficial patchwork on the higher cognitive level of symbolic logic are to be avoided. — For the rest, his recognition of the fact that the logical calculus deals collectively with manifolds of all kinds is a sound insight, for that allows for the play of possibilities in cognitive construction. In his discussion of Schröder, Husserl did not fail to point out the sense in which one can alone speak of unity in the sense of truth and conviction.[6]

2. *Husserl's Attempt at an Intensional Logic*

A paper entitled "The Deductive Calculus and Intensional Logic," which was published in the same year as the critique of Schröder, represents a systematic statement of Husserl's own views.[7] The contention that a calculus of deduction can be derived only by means of the "interpretation" of all judgments as class-judgments provides the point of departure. The

[6] Cp. Husserl's discussion of compatibility and unitableness in the *Logical Investigations*, for a similar judgment and position; cf. ch. xiv herein.

[7] Cf. Husserl, "Der Folgerungscalcül und die Inhaltslogik," *Viertelj. f. wiss. Phil.*, vol. xv (Leipzig, 1891), pp. 168–189; and also a later communication, in which certain changes and corrections were made, pp. 351–356.

attempts of Jevons and Wundt seem to be opposed to that view, for they prefer the point of view of intension to that of extension in the construction of their systems. But, Husserl points out, they are really extensional systems in essence. Jevons reduces all judgments to identities, and a statement containing a general term can only lead to an identity by means of the equivalent class-statement, as illustrated by the statement "A circle is a curve of least perimeter." [8] The same holds for Wundt, who begins with considerations of intensional logic, and then proceeds to extensional logic. Husserl concedes that hitherto only by means of the extensional logic had consistent developments of algebraic methods of deduction been achieved. He is careful to say "consistent" and not "logically unassailable" developments. The logic of the logical calculus had proved to be unsatisfactory because of the lack of clarity regarding the limits of this discipline, and also its relationships to deductive logic and to arithmetic. Just as the weakness of the logical foundation of arithmetic is not a sufficient ground for its rejection, so the logical algebra, despite its very limited practical applicability, must be of much interest to the logician. The possibility of its contributions is a serious problem here as in arithmetic.

The extensional logicians had argued that it could be shown that an intensional calculus is impossible as such, and that the detour of the class logic is unavoidable. Venn and Schröder are examples, the latter maintaining that extensional logic is not merely the method of deduction, but, as has been seen, that it is deductive logic itself. Husserl's answer is that the best argument against that contention is a *fait accompli*, and he proposes to show in more than one way how a calculus of pure deductions can be constructed on the basis of intensional logic. Schröder's extensional calculus is used in the interest of brevity of presentation, the procedure really being one of reinterpretation. In the "supplement" to this paper Husserl sets up definitions of 0 and 1, and he argues that if the intensional account is a failure, then so is the extensional theory.

In addition to applying the general calculus of aggregates to classes, Schröder had presented a number of other applications, including one to "conceptual contents." Husserl observes that conceptual contents can be regarded as character-totalities, and accordingly can be compared like aggregates. The collective totality of characters of the one can be included in that of a second, or be excluded by it, etc. In that way a system of relations of content can arise, although it would seem to be useless, for it would not comprise the whole domain of pure deductions. Only analytic judgments in Kant's sense would fall in its domain. Statements like "Gold

[8] Cf. Jevons, *The Principles of Science* (1883), p. 38.

is a metal" would be rendered in the form "The characters of the concept metal are contained in those of the concept gold." But it would not include synthetic statements such as "All equilateral triangles are equiangular," since the properties of equiangularity are not actually contained in those of the equilateral triangle. Schröder had distinguished between the factual and the ideal content of a concept, the latter comprising the totality of valid characters which attach to a conceptual object as such. Thus, e.g., the ideal content of the concept gold includes all the properties that can be validly attributed to gold. The ideal contents also permit of comparison like aggregates, and hence can be treated by means of the logical calculus. Schröder had tried to show that a "logic of ideal contents" involves circularity. He held such a logic to be impossible because he interpolated the necessity of actually operating with given ideal contents, the point being that of the infinity of characters of a conceptual object only a very small number can really be given. In rejecting this argument as erroneous, Husserl proposes to show that the logic of ideal contents can accomplish as much as an extensional logic, that it can solve the same problems with the same rules and formulae.

The intensional calculus is not regarded as having great value by Husserl, who accordingly contents himself with a brief statement of it. The first thesis to be established is that the ideal content of any concept is given to us, and that it is not given in the same way as the corresponding conceptual extension. Only a small part of the latter is generally given as a matter of fact. Such actual givenness is never required, however, in the sense of real knowledge of all conceptual objects. The symbolic idea of the "totality of objects which have the characters of the concept" is sufficient for us. Such symbolic ideas are at the basis of our operations with classes; and the same holds for ideal conceptual contents. That they are never actually given does not mean that they cannot be used logically for the construction of a "logic of ideal contents," for example. We possess uniquely determined symbolic ideas, such as "the totality of characters which are attached to a conceptual object as such," in the same sense as the corresponding class-ideas, and they are sufficient for us. For the construction of the calculus of ideal contents it is sufficient to regard such contents as totalities of their characters. They then permit comparison according to the relations of inclusion, being included in, exclusion, overlapping, and coincidence. The logical calculus can be applied directly by interpreting its symbols as some kind of ideal contents, instead of as some kind of classes. Every class-judgment can be transformed into an equivalent judgment about relations of ideal contents, which means that it is

HISTORY
BOOK CLUB
established 1947

PO Box 6417
Indianapolis IN 46206-6417

Please enroll me in History Book Club according to the no-risk terms outlined on right. Send me the 4 books whose numbers I have listed below. Bill me $1 for each book, plus shipping and handling. I agree to buy 1 more book in the next year.

(*For a 'Counts as two choices' book, write the 6-digit number in one box and 99-9999 in the next box.)

4 choices at \$1 each:

—	—	—	—	3-EH

H-1-008-03-0

Name

Address _____ (please print clearly) _____ Apt. #

City

State _____ Zip

www.joinhistorybookclub.com • AOL Keyword: History Book Club

Send no money now.

Guarantee of Satisfaction: You may examine your introductory books for 10 days, FREE. If you are not satisfied, for any reason whatsoever, simply return the books at our expense and you will be under no further obligation.

HISTORY
B O O K   C L U B ®
established 1947

BUSINESS REPLY MAIL
FIRST-CLASS MAIL   PERMIT NO. 447   Indianapolis IN

POSTAGE WILL BE PAID BY ADDRESSEE

HISTORY BOOK CLUB
PO BOX 6414
INDIANAPOLIS, IN 46209-8552

transformed to a certain extent into an analytic judgment. For the judgment "All men are mortal" there is substituted the equivalent judgment "The ideal concept of man includes that of mortality." In categorical judgments the ideal concept of the predicate is subsumed under that of the subject, or is excluded from it. Negative judgments are replaced by equivalent affirmative judgments with negative matter, and (as Husserl mistakenly supposes) particular judgments by equivalent universal judgments, just as in the extensional calculus. The only difference between this calculus and the old one is that one speaks of ideal contents instead of conceptual extensions. The same problems can be solved by means of the same formulae. Husserl maintains that this intensional calculus as well as the calculus of extension are superfluous reinterpretations, with respect to their logical purposes. He attempts to show that the same algebraic technique of the calculus of aggregates, which serves for the indirect solution of the problems of a pure theory of inference by means of its specializations as a calculus of classes and of ideal contents, can also serve these purposes directly, and without such detours involving extensions and ideal contents. What is proposed is to regard it from the outset as a calculus of the logic of content, i.e., of the usual intensional-logical deductions.

The choice of a logic of ideal contents and the recognition of the ideal nature of logical knowledge are of interest as representing themes which later gain prominence in Husserl's logical studies. The entire argument in the present paper is of little significance otherwise, for the demonstration that logic can be developed intensionally is a modest undertaking, at least as there advanced. It proves to be important as leading to a whole realm of epistemological questions that are preliminary to logic.

The various interpretations of the judgment-form "All S are p" are classified under the three headings of pure intensional interpretations, pure extensional interpretations, and mixed interpretations. The intensional interpretations are further subdivided into those without and those with quantification of content. Expressed hypothetically the former becomes "In so far as something has the characters of S it has the characters of p," or expressed negatively, "There is not an S that is not a p." The intensional interpretation with quantification of content reads "The ideal content of S comprises the ideal content of p," or "The totality of the characters attached to an S as such comprises the totality of characters attached to a p as such." This is presented as the basic form of the calculus of "ideal" contents. There could also be forms with incomplete quantity, referring to S alone or p alone, but they would not be of much interest. The extensional interpretations involve quantification of the concept of the subject as well as of the concept of the predicate by means of classes. Mixed interpretations occur when either the subject or the predicate is quantified in the sense of a class.

The exponents of the logic of classes maintain that a calculus can be founded only by means of classes, and hence all universal judgments are transformed into class-judgments. The "calculatory" logic often departs from the course of original thinking, when it makes use of the device of equivalent transformation. Husserl concedes that it is justified in so doing, but insists that it is a mere technique of deduction, and not a logic of deduction. While allowing the right to deviate from natural thought, he places restrictions upon that process, even if one remains within the limits of judgment-equivalence. Only those that do not result in unnecessary complication are to be approved for the construction and application of the calculus. The aim is to obtain a logical calculus with as little means as possible and with as close a connection as possible to natural thought. Thus Husserl does not observe a principle of psychological or practical irrelevance here, in his treatment of formal procedure, the ideal being to base the deductive calculus upon the simplest and easiest forms for natural thought. The majority of equivalent propositional forms are therewith excluded from the outset.

The intensional interpretations of "All S are p," given above, had not yet been used algebraically. The meaning of the form "All S are p" is more complicated in thought than "In so far as something has the characters of S, it has the characters of p." The attempt to utilize that simplest form for a deductive calculus is therefore of special logical interest. The calculus to be constructed is concerned with conceptual objects, and is therefore regarded as being truly logical. The particular natures of such objects are disregarded, the calculus being based upon the possible relationships which the objects of any kind of concepts can display. The point of view is thus purely "formal," and all deduction is essentially hypothetical.

Corresponding to the possible forms for conceptual extensions, there are five possible types of relationship between the objects of any two concepts A and B: (a) an object of the concept A is also an object of the concept B although the converse does not hold; (b) an object of the concept B is also an object of the concept A, but not conversely; (c) an object of the concept A is an object of the concept B, and conversely; (d) an object of the concept A is not an object of the concept B, and conversely; (e) an object of the concept A is also (or is not) an object of the concept B, but it is not, as an object of the concept A, also one (or not one) of B, so that none of the cases from (a) to (d) obtains.

Just as one speaks of the relations between the objects of the concepts A and B, one can also speak of the relations of these concepts to their objects. The same expressions are used as for classes, as illustrated by the pictorial statement that one concept includes another, or excludes another, etc. Expressions such as "The concept A 'conditions' the concept B" may also be used.

In order to make clear the relation of this calculus to the extensional calculus, the same symbols are used to signify relationships of objects (or of characters) as occur in Schröder's calculus for relationships of extension. The same order of definitions, axioms, and propositions is adhered to as much as possible. The procedure is to show that all the basic formulae which are known to be sufficient for the construction of the calculus of classes are also valid for his symbols, which have a different conceptual foundation. It then follows that the rest of the calculus is valid for Husserl's domain. The expression $A \subset B$ is defined by means of the linguistic expression "In so far as something is an A, it is a B." The principle of identity, or $A \subset A$, reads "In so far as something is an A, it is an A." The product $A.B$ is interpreted to mean "something that is at the same time an A and a B." It is not necessary to follow out in detail this interpretation of the logical system. The definitions of 1 and 0 occasioned some difficulty. The symbol 1 stands for the object of the concept of existence so that the axiom $A \subset 1$ holds, whatever A may signify. The formula is to be understood to mean "In so far as something is an object of the concept A, it is also an object of the concept of existence." The judgment "Something is an A" is taken to include the existence of the subject, as is the case with all categorical judgments. The symbol 0 signifies the object of the concept of non-existence. The axiom [9] $0 \subset A$ holds analogously, no matter what A represents. The formula means "In so far as something possesses the character of non-existence, it also possesses every other character." Negation is defined as not-A in the usual logical sense, as meaning that something has a character of which it can be asserted that it is not A. Negative judgments are replaced by affirmative judgments with negative matter. The formula $A.A_1 \subset 0$ means "That which is at the same time an A and a not-A does not exist"; and $1 \subset A + A_1$ states "In so far as something comes under the concept of existence it is either an A or a non-A."

These illustrations are sufficient to indicate how Husserl endeavors to prove that the formal bases of the calculus of classes are valid for the

[9] In a supplementary discussion Husserl regards this as a theorem, and not as an axiom.

relationships of conceptual objects, his aim being to transform the technique of the former at one stroke into a really logical calculus, thus proving the extensional logic to be superfluous.

If judgments take the place of concepts in the logical domain, analogous relationships are established. Husserl summarizes what is necessary for the independent foundation of the "propositional calculus" by means of the following analogues of the five basic relationships, already illustrated: (*a*) if the judgment *A* holds, the judgment *B* holds, but not conversely; (*b*) if the judgment *B* holds, the judgment *A* holds, but not conversely; (*c*) there is the case of the mutual conditioning or the logical equivalence of judgments; (*d*) mutual exclusion means that if the judgment *A* holds the judgment *B* does not hold, and conversely; (*e*) there is no relationship of conditioning between the judgments. The symbols $A \subset B$ mean "If the judgment *A* holds, the judgment *B* holds," or "The judgment *A* conditions the judgment *B*." The logical product *A.B* means the validity of the two judgments *A* and *B* at the same time. The symbol 1 stands for the validity of the proposition "Of two contradictory judgments, one is true and the other is false," which combines the principles of non-contradiction and excluded middle. The axiom that $A \subset 1$, whatever *A* may mean, is now seen to hold. The symbol o stands for the negation of this fundamental logical principle, so that $o \subset A$, whatever *A* may mean. If the opposite of the fundamental logical principle holds, then there is no difference between truth and error, and consequently any assertion can be set up. Husserl does not believe, in the present paper, that any other interpretation of the symbols o and 1 would be capable of founding the necessary formulae, $A \subset 1$ and $o \subset A$.[10] The negation of judgment *A*, or A_1, means that the judgment *A* does not hold. The axioms $A.A_1 \subset o$ and $1 \subset A + A_1$ are readily seen to hold. Husserl believes that he proves in this way all of the basic formulae which are sufficient for the construction of the entire symbolic technique of the calculus, and that he has founded the propositional calculus on its own basis.

In his supplementary comments, already referred to, Husserl asserts that the symbols o and 1 and the two formulae which depend upon them constitute the only essential difficulty in the construction of the calculus. But even if he were unsuccessful on these points, the intensional calculus would be no worse off than the extensional calculus, which faces the same difficulties. There is always the possibility of a direct transformation by

[10] Cp. Husserl's supplementary remarks on this, presented later in the same journal (1891), pp. 351–356, under the title "Der Folgerungscalcül und die Inhaltslogik," in which he makes changes and corrections of his paper.

which a correct interpretation of the symbols and formulae in the extensional calculus, for example, will provide for a correct interpretation in the intensional calculus, or in the calculus of objects. Husserl admits that he had serious doubts concerning the symbols o and 1, which led him to undertake a new and more satisfactory treatment of them. The interpretation of o and 1 is retained, but there is a change in the analysis and foundation of the two formulae (i.e., $A \subset 1$ and $o \subset A$), and he aims in particular to make clear the true meaning of the paradoxical formula $o \subset A$. The meaning of $A \subset B$ is "If something exists that possesses the property A, then it also possesses the property B." The formula $A \subset B$, which holds for every A, then means "If something exists that possesses the character A, then it exists," a proposition which is indubitable for every A.

The formula $o \subset A$ means "If something exists that possesses the property of non-existence, then it possesses the property A," no matter what A is. In other words, it possesses all properties. It is unnecessary to give the proof of this formula, to which Husserl evidently devoted much attention. If this formula is true for every A, the propositions $o \subset A$ and $o \subset A_1$ hold at the same time, although they seem to conflict. This paradox is explained by the absurdity of the hypostasis of the existence of a non-existent, which violates the fundamental principles of logic. It is a correct theorem about the relationship of two absurdities. The antecedent condition in which the existence of a non-existent is presupposed is absurd; and the consequent, according to which the entity in question must possess every property, including even contradictory properties, is also absurd. But the reasoning that if the one proposition were to hold then the other one would also have to hold is logically correct.

Husserl adds still another interpretation of o and 1. The symbol 1 signifies the property of possessing some property, and o stands for the property of possessing no property. The formula $A \subset 1$ then means "If something possesses the property A, then it possesses the property of possessing some property; i.e., then it possesses some property." The meaning of $o \subset A$ remains paradoxical. It is "If something possesses the property of possessing no property, then it possesses the property A, i.e., all properties." In his proof of this formula Husserl interprets A as meaning any property, and then speaks of non-A, which would have to be the negation of "any property." The term "property" is also used in so unrestricted a sense that it results in paradox. The proof is as follows: If something possesses the property of possessing no property, then it also does not possess the property non-A, where A signifies any property. But everything that possesses a property exists, and what exists is either A or non-A. As a result, if something possesses the property of possessing no property, then it possesses the property A, and hence all properties. The expression $A \subset o$ represents the proposition "A does not exist," for that which possesses no properties does not exist.

Husserl formally retracts his interpretation of the symbols o and 1 in the propositional calculus, and replaces it by the following: 1 signifies the judgment "There is a valid judgment," and o signifies "There is no valid judgment." The formula $A \subset 1$ then means "If the judgment A holds, there is a valid judgment," which requires no proof. The formula $o \subset A$, which is valid for every A, again contains a paradoxical proposition, "If the judgment holds, that there is no valid judgment, then the judgment A holds," and hence since A names any judgment, every ("beliebige") judgment holds. The proof of this formula involves the use of absurdities, but that is no objection in Husserl's view. He points out that in purely hypothetical reasoning the absurd may function as a hypothesis, which indicates his willingness to operate with purely formal devices.

3. Controversy with Voigt

Soon after the publication of these papers on symbolic logic Husserl became involved in an acrimonious controversy [11] with Andreas Voigt. The exchange of views with Voigt did not result in any change in Husserl's attitude, but it aids in making clear his early philosophy of logic. Voigt came to the defense of Schröder in a paper entitled "What is Logic?" It will be of interest to present the main critical points of Voigt, which contain some appropriate comments in reply to Husserl's doubts about the value and potentialities of the algebraic type of logic, comments which have been abundantly borne out by the subsequent history of that discipline. Unfortunately for his own case, however, he failed to stop at the right time and place. He distinguishes to begin with between the philosophical and the algebraic movements in logic. The former is represented by Kant, e.g., and holds to word-language in the main, whereas the algebra of logic uses its own symbolic language. But this difference in "method" is not sufficient to account for the opposition of philosophers to the algebra

[11] A. Voigt, "Was ist Logik?" *Viertelj. f. wiss. Phil.*, vol. XVI (1892), pp. 289–332; Husserl, "A. Voigt's 'elementare Logik' und meine Darlegungen zur Logik des logischen Calcüls," same journal, vol. XVII (1893), pp. 111–120; A. Voigt, "Zum Calcül der Inhaltslogik, Erwiderung auf Herrn Husserl's Artikel," the same, pp. 504–507; Husserl, "Antwort auf die vorstehende 'Erwiderung' des Herrn Voigt," the same, pp. 508–511; A. Voigt, "Berichtigung," same journal, vol. XVIII (1894), p. 135; R. Avenarius, "Erklärung des Herausgebers," the same, pp. 135–136.

of logic. Especially serious is Husserl's charge that the algebra of logic is not a logic at all, which seems to him to be striking in view of Schröder's aim to fill in the gap between the philosophical and the algebraic logic. Moreover, in view of Husserl's competence in formal science, his hostility could not be ascribed to fear of the special logical symbolism.

Despite the particular bearing of his discussion upon the writings of Schröder and Husserl that are in question, Voigt believes that his remarks have general significance, for they concern the issue between the algebraic and the philosophical types of logic. Voigt contends that the algebra of logic is in a position to solve the same problems which the philosophical logic raises. The algebra of logic wants to be a logic in a full sense, however, and it claims to have the same content as the older logic, although in a more exact form. Both types are held to deal with the laws of correct thinking. Husserl had distinguished between the rules that must be observed and those which can be observed, the latter being illustrated in the algebra of logic, whereas the real laws of thought remain foreign to it. To this Voigt replies that the inferential calculus of Husserl does not contain necessary rules, for it corresponds to the calculus of classes and differs from that calculus only by the interpretation of the formulae. Hence the intensional logic does not represent the real logic, according to whose laws one must think, but only shows that the formal laws may be derived from relations of conceptual objects. Voigt concludes that either the science which Husserl alone regards as logic does not yet exist, or that the latter has not justified his view that the algebra of logic does not contain the laws of logical thinking.

As to the advantages to be derived by means of the algebra of logic, which Husserl had questioned, the ability to handle problems too complicated for the old methods is cited, and Voigt predicts more significant applications at least of the method of the algebra of logic. Still more serious is the charge that the calculus lacks significant content, and Husserl's criticism amounts to a warning against this type of logic, despite the praise given to the mathematical side of Schröder's work. Husserl is in turn charged with ignoring the positive results of the new logic, and is criticized for his assertion that particular judgments are equivalent to certain universal judgments, in violation of the law of the algebra of logic that every particular judgment is the negation of a universal judgment, and can therefore never be equivalent to one. This encourages Voigt to state that Husserl is more indebted to his as yet not very detailed study of the algebra of logic than he thinks. The latter is accused of fighting windmills when he criticizes the formalistic arithmeticians who believe that freedom of definition gives them the right to introduce any concepts in the midst of a deductive discipline. Thus the symbol $\sqrt{-1}$ illustrates the hypothetical procedure of mathematical thought. The difficulties encountered by Husserl in the attempt to define the symbols 0 and 1 are not overlooked. Voigt then proceeds to give a positive presentation of elementary logic "as it may have occurred to Husserl," without his being able to give it. The parallelism between the extensional and the intensional interpretations of logic is held to be a fact easily ascertainable from the outset, rather than a striking fact. Voigt suggests that Husserl could have been still more brief in the presentation of "his" calculus by simply taking this parallelism as proved to begin with, and leaving the "mechanical" reinterpretation of the calculus of extension to the reader. He states that the opposition between the logic of intension and that of extension should not be confused with the difference between the philosophical and the algebraic logic; and he believes that a science which comprises the whole of logic may not neglect either one.

Voigt interprets 0 as an empty class, in accordance with the calculus of classes, and 1 as the class of all objects which come into consideration. In the logic of propositions 0 signifies a proposition that is not true, and 1 a proposition that is true, F and W in Voigt's calculus taking the place of 0 and 1. In the logic of concepts 0 signifies a concept which no object satisfies, and 1 a concept satisfied by every object entering into consideration. But these interpretations of the concepts 0 and 1 do not escape the difficulties encountered by Husserl.

Discussing the formal, analytic method of Schröder in conclusion, Voigt speaks of the need for a procedure which permits the derivation of the formal laws once and for all, without regard to the various domains of application. The formal method arranges its definitions so that they are applied to all domains, and new applications are only examined to determine whether the principles still hold and the postulates are fulfilled. In addition to this practical value of the formal method, there is also the philosophical interest attached to it, for it shows to what extent the laws of logic are formal. That is the case because they can be derived formally without bringing in the logical relations themselves. The formal principles are still not logical principles, nor are the formal definitions logical definitions. Voigt is willing to call them quasi-definitions with Husserl, without regarding them as being thereby undermined in their significance. He holds that they first become logical definitions through application or interpretation in accordance with the nature of the logical relations. Voigt's final remarks again raise the question of his fairness in depicting Husserl's attitude. He states that in opposition to Husserl he believes that he can recommend the study of the algebra of logic to the philosophers, and he predicts that logic and the philosophy connected with it will derive much stimulation from this most modern branch of science. He ends with the statement that the "philosophy of logic" which Husserl demands is in any case not possible without a thorough knowledge of all logical methods.

Husserl's answer to Voigt appeared the following year in the same journal. In it he points out that the algebra of logic was first invented and developed as a logic of classes, and that according to the prevailing view an algebraic formalism can only be built up in logic on the basis of classes and the relations of classes. According to Schröder, who represents this point of view, the algebra of logic is deductive logic, and the aim to construct an intensional logic from the outset (as a logic of "conceptual contents") may be compared to the attempt to build the roof before the house. Husserl states that never, so far as is known to him, has a consistent attempt been made to base logic directly upon the "intensional-logical" forms of judgment. While admitting that a considerable part of the literature in the English and American periodicals is inaccessible to him, he infers that if such attempts have appeared, they are not generally known, and neither have they been convincing. This inference seems to be justified by the artificialities resorted to by Boole and his successors in order to make possible the transformation of all judgments into class-judgments. Thus, for example, the judgment "If God is just, the evil will be punished" becomes "The class of points of time in which the judgment 'God is just' is true is subsumed under the class of points of time in which 'the evil will be punished' is true." Such procedures could have been avoided if it had been recognized that relations of properties and facts which can be judged, as they are, can be subjected to algebraic modes of treatment. Furthermore, Schröder makes no reference to the existence of such attempts in his work, although he discusses the question of the possibility of an intensional logic.

The purpose of Husserl's paper on the calculus of deduction was to break down this prejudice. He sought to show simply and clearly that the detour over classes is superfluous for judgments which are not concerned with class-relations to begin with, since any form of judgment can be taken as a point of departure for calculatory methods of deduction. It was convenient to show by means of the Schröder calculus that the basic formulae of the calculus can be given an intensional-logical interpretation from the outset. Voigt's correction of an error in the handling of particular judgments is acknowledged in a footnote; the belief that one could replace particular judgments by universal judgments for algebraic purposes was an obvious oversight. Another mistake pointed out by Voigt, to the effect that a calculus of "ideal" contents would not, as Husserl had asserted, possess the character of a "calculus of identity," but rather of a "calculus of groups," is acknowledged, but is held to be a matter of indifference so far as the content and the results of Husserl's work are concerned. The irony and open insults of Voigt are answered in kind. The reader learns that Voigt has abandoned his previously accepted standpoint of the logic of extension, and taken over Husserl's ideas, on the basis of which he has constructed an "elementary logic." Being sensitive to Husserl's criticism of the improper pretensions of the algebra of logic, however, he clothes the approval of the former's views in the paradoxical form of blunt rejection. Husserl finds it necessary to ask the reader to decide whether Voigt has at all times fulfilled the obligations of literary conscientiousness. Voigt's paper gives the reader the impression that Husserl's efforts result in falsity or in well-known trivialities. It also attributes views to Husserl which are directly opposed to what he actually maintains, in addition to attributing "modes of combat" to him of which he never approved.

Voigt maintains that Husserl's attempt is a failure, especially in the case of the interpretations of the symbols 0 and 1, but he never substantiates it. How seriously Husserl takes his own work is shown by his assertion that Voigt fails to recognize that he has contributed an entirely new idea for the foundation of the algebraic logic, and that the "elementary logic" is only a slightly modified statement of that idea. Changes in the order of Husserl's definitions and axioms, or the application of his idea in the domain of problematical or particular judgments are examples of the inessential changes introduced. The interpretation of $A \subset B$ as "If something is an A, it is also a B" readily suggested to Voigt the form "$X < Ax < B$," which Husserl had considered but not adopted because of his aim to retain Schröder's symbols, definitions, and axioms. As for the interpretations of 0 and 1, Husserl declares that he did not withdraw his first formulations because he held them to be false, but only because he had devised more suitable interpretations. He was not satisfied with the derivations of the basic formulae referring to them, but these also are not false. Husserl points out the equivalence of his "unsuccessful" and Voigt's correct interpretations of 0 and 1 in terms of F and W, or an unconditionally false proposition and an unconditionally true proposition. Voigt believes it to be an easily ascertainable fact that the formalism of the one logic agrees with that of the other completely, but he neglects to add that he was in ignorance of this fact one year before the appearance of Husserl's paper. The thought of the possibility of the "translation" of Schröder's system is something new and of fundamental importance for the logic of the calculus and is by no means a matter for amusement.

The criticism advanced by Husserl is not designed to frighten philosophers away from the algebra of logic; on the contrary, he states that it is of great interest to the logician. Husserl emphasized the view that the algebra of logic is a subordinate part of logic, which Voigt "quoted" in a manner indicative of his method of controversy, namely, "That one can regard the algebra of logic as a subordinate part of logic, Husserl will also admit." It is unnecessary to cite further illustrations. Husserl further charges Voigt with ascribing views to Schröder which were opposite to what he really maintained, in order to make the criticism of his work appear ridiculous. Thus Schröder proceeds from manifolds, and does not base his calculus upon a "formalistic standpoint." Had he constructed a purely formal calculus all of Husserl's objections would be ridiculous. Returning Voigt's imputation of ignorance, Husserl asserts that the former has no real understanding of the logic of symbolic methods, and that he has not even noted its essential difficulties and problems. The algebraic logicians see in an algebra of logic the salvation of logic, if not logic itself; but in his opinion they have no insight into the logic of this algebra, which cannot be deduced by means of any algebra of logic.

Voigt's reply, entitled "Concerning the Calculus of the Intensional Logic: An answer to Mr. Husserl's Article," was the second draft of an answer. The first, which had gone into the points under discussion in detail, was withdrawn after the editor had shown him Husserl's reply. In this brief article Voigt is concerned with challenging Husserl's originality, and with defending himself against what he takes to be a charge of plagiarism. He tries to answer the charge that he had no notion of the formal agreement of the "logic of content" and the logic of classes in his dissertation of 1890. Quoting at some length from his dissertation, he seeks to show that he holds the class logic not to be logic in general, but to be an extension of the older, purely conceptual logic. It therefore appears incomprehensible to him how it could be said that he had taken the idea of a logic that is independent of the relations of classes from Husserl, who cites his dissertation. To remove all doubt Voigt gives an authoritative quotation, attested to by Professor J. Lüroth of Freiburg, from his original manuscript, in which the relation between the two types of logic is discussed. This he had been advised to omit, in order to avoid all controversial philosophical discussions. In this passage there is mention of the two writers who had founded a logical calculus independently of the relations of classes, Frege and Peirce. Voigt suggests that Husserl should at least have known Frege, even if Peirce's main work had not been available.

Husserl's comments upon this reply call attention to the fact that it passes over all the points which had been made, and restricts itself to the disputing of the single question of the originality of Husserl's presentation. Voigt claims that in his dissertation he had knowledge of the formal identity of the calculus of "object-relations," of the calculus of "judgmental facts," and the like, with the calculus of classes; and he also asserted that Peirce and Frege had this knowledge long before Husserl. As for the first point, Husserl expresses his thanks for the quotations, for it is evident that they speak against Voigt, and not for him. They indicate that he had an unclear idea of the relationship between intensional and extensional logic, and also contain the error of denying the class calculus the right of operating with "indeterminate" or even empty classes. There is no indication of the knowledge Voigt claimed he possessed. Husserl reiterates his contention that the essential idea, which cuts at the root of an extensional logic on principle, is new, namely, that identically the same formulae which serve the extensional calculus can immediately serve as formulae of a calculus of property-relations or of object-relations, or of relations of judgmental facts, etc. Thus the logic of extension loses all support. Henceforth there may only be talk of a calculus which, according to circumstances, deals with classes or judgmental facts, etc., without any one of these "interpretations" holding as fundamental, to which all others must be reduced. As for the second point, Voigt fails to give references to the works of Frege and Peirce, and he did not attribute the knowledge in question to these men in his dissertation. Husserl states that the writings of Frege, whom he values very much, lie before him, and that he does not find any indication of the disputed ideas in them. It is also significant that Frege warns emphatically against a confusion of the efforts of Boole, Schröder, and others. Frege's *Begriffsschrift* is in Husserl's judgment not a calculus in the strict sense of the term, even if his formulae or types run parallel to certain formulae of the calculus. As a matter of fact, both Schröder and Frege dispute the formal parallelism of the *Begriffsschrift* with the calculus, the former emphasizing the almost entire absence of the analogue of calculation with "concepts." This appears to Husserl to be decisive. That Peirce had the idea of a system of intensional logic is not doubted; but that is not what is in question.

The controversy came to a close with the publication of brief statements by Voigt and the editor, R. Avenarius, from which it was evident that the former wished to avoid further discussion.

There can be no doubt about the controversy ending in a victory for Husserl, even though his own work had not been free from error. Some of his most distinctive traits and interests are manifested in this period. The spirit of being a reformer, and the consciousness of being on the track of profound and important discoveries pervade his endeavors. The criticism of Schröder's logic appears to be sharper than was necessary, even from the point of view of logical psychologism. The discussion of Schröder has historical importance as representing his own attempt to reconcile a psychologistic standpoint with formal reasoning, and also as being an acute criticism of Schröder's presentation of the algebra of logic. As such it deserves the attention of the historian of symbolic logic. Considerable skill in polemical discussion is shown, despite the occurrence of errors in his own efforts. In addition to the necessity of retracting obvious errors, his conception of the equivalence of intensional and extensional logics did not take account of all the problems involved.[12] His argument was based upon the fact of the multiple interpretation of the same set of formal structures. He was right in denying that the logical calculus must be extensional, and in pointing out the possibility of formally equivalent interpretations. The complete investigation of the problems involved would have led him along lines subsequently followed by Professor Henry M. Sheffer in his studies of the structure of logic as distinct from its various possible interpretations.

Most important was Husserl's interest in the clarification of the fundamental concepts of logic. The beginnings of his definition of pure logic, or of the logic of pure forms, as distinguished from interpreted forms of logic, run through the criticism of Schröder and underlie his discussion with Voigt of the limitations of the extensional logic. The need for clarify-

[12] On the possibility of the equivalence of intensional and extensional logic, cp. C. I. Lewis, *A Survey of Symbolic Logic* (Berkeley, 1918), pp. 35, 322 f. Lewis writes (p. 323): "The product and sum of classes are relations of extension, for which no analogous relations of intension exist." Cp. also J. Jørgensen, *A Treatise of Formal Logic*, vol. 1 (Copenhagen and London, 1931), p. 46 n. He writes: "Saint-Hilaire thought 'the relation between the intension and extension of concepts is often reversible.' This, however, is not correct, as the quantifications, which are of essential importance in extensional logic, cannot be introduced from the intensional point of view. See for instance J. Venn, *Symbolic Logic* (London, 1894), p. 463. There are also syllogisms which would not be valid from both points of view, but only from one of them. See, e.g., Couturat, *La Logique de Leibniz* (Paris, 1901), pp. 20–21." Venn regarded Husserl's attempt as occupying an intermediate place between "the true intensive and extensive renderings." While not objecting to the scheme of interpretation, which he admitted to be well worked out, Venn disputed its claim to rank as a truly intensional interpretation. Husserl was credited by him with showing how his interpretation could be

ing studies applies to symbolic logic in general. Such principles as identity and excluded middle are deduced in modern symbolic logic, to be sure. All such principles are supposed to be a part of logic in the sense of being deduced, thus making logic circular. Husserl proposed at this early time a kind of "epistemic" logic to take into account the "activities" employed. It has been seen that Husserl held that the logic of the algebraic calculus is not investigated by the algebra of logic, chiefly because the mental operations at its basis do not belong to the domain of pure deductions. He undoubtedly would have made the same point about the *Principia Mathematica* of Whitehead and Russell, despite the elaborate logical foundations undertaken in that work. He would have done so in the interest of an epistemic clarification of the fundamental concepts alone, which in his view constitutes another and necessary dimension of investigation. This pattern of thought was already present in his stage of logical psychologism. It was to be reinterpreted fundamentally, but remain in a sense, as reinterpreted, on the level of the *Logical Investigations*, and of his later logical studies. The activity of inference is distinguishable of course from the principle of inference. The crucial question, in the present context, is whether actual processes are to be meant, or abstract forms which are determined by definition and postulation, and with the use of the concept of possibility. That is a problem which had to be faced later in connection with the "ideal" nature of logical forms.

Husserl failed to recognize the irrelevance of psychological or practical considerations when he spoke of basing the deductive calculus upon the simplest and easiest forms for "natural thought." The preciseness of his handling of formal definitions shows him to be at home in this field, too much so to criticize it as a psychologistic "outsider" who makes protests in the only language he is able to speak, the language of "natural thought." It is evident that Husserl did not hesitate to justify the use of "the absurd" as a hypothesis when it suited his formal purposes. Judged from the later perspective of a more highly developed symbolic logic, he was clearly in error if he meant to deny that there is any set of principles which cannot be symbolized, and which consequently cannot function as postulates or theorems in a deductive system. On the other hand, the development of symbolic logic in the direction of a pragmatic relativism has not obviated, but rather has emphasized the need for a philosophy of logic which is designed to give a firm basis for formal thought.

---

carried through, although he differed with Husserl concerning some of his explanations, such as, e.g., of the symbols 1 and 0. Cf. J. Venn, *Symbolic Logic*, 2nd ed. (London and New York, 1894), pp. 438, 475 f., 503 f.

Husserl might well have become a leader in the development of symbolic logic. That he did not do so was due to his interest in pre-logical studies, and in large part because of his general philosophical position, which in challenging the autonomy of formal logic appeared to develop a spirit of antagonism toward it. A complete study of his logical contributions shows that there was really no antagonism toward formal logic as such, and that his work on the philosophy of logic is of great importance for formal logic, even in its most recent stage, in which it is supposedly completely emancipated from philosophy.

B. PSYCHOLOGICAL STUDIES IN LOGIC

An interesting indication of a growing interest in what was soon to become the phenomenological clarification of logic is provided by the "Psychological Studies in Logic." [13] These studies represent the last important expression of Husserl's psychologism. The fact that their main descriptive material was later incorporated in the *Logical Investigations* is evidence of Husserl's logical-philosophical interest in his period of psychologism, and of the continuity of his development. There was a change in the fundamental point of view rather than in the content of his work.[14] What appears to be a revolutionary change is an alteration in the theoretical framework; there is a steady, cumulative development throughout all of the years.

The first study is entitled "Concerning the Distinction of Abstract and Concrete," and includes a discussion of independent and dependent contents, a distinction already noted by Stumpf, and of abstract and concrete contents. The attempt is made to reduce the distinction between abstract and concrete contents to a difference between independent and dependent contents. Every instance of total consciousness is described as a unity in which everything is interrelated with everything else. There are nevertheless appreciable differences in the manner of connection, in their relative firmness, and in their mediateness or immediateness. The classification of contents into independent [15] ("separable," "presentable by themselves")

[13] Husserl, "Psychologische Studien zur elementaren Logik," *Phil. Monatshefte*, vol. xxx (Berlin, 1894), pp. 159–191. There are two studies, the first on pp. 159–167, and the second on pp. 168–191.
[14] Cp. W. Illemann, *op. cit.*, pp. 30 ff. Illemann draws a sharp contrast between the two publications. Pointing out that the fundamental attitude of Husserl in the "Psychological Studies in Logic" is in no way an advance beyond that of the *Philosophy of Arithmetic*, he asserts that the change undergone in the few years after 1894 is surprising, because of the complete abandonment of the psychologistic standpoint. This observation should be qualified, however, in view of the absorption of the main content of these studies in the later work.
[15] Husserl refers to Stumpf's *Ueber den psychologischen Ursprung der Raumvorstellung*

refers to such differences. The distinction is primarily psychological in character. Certain complex contents are noted separately with ease and appear to be natural unities, with a certain characteristic independence. This is the case with the intuitive content of perceptible things in comparison with the less complex contents which are called their inner characters, such as color and shape. It is not easy to say wherein this independence consists. Objective things affect one another and therewith condition relations of dependence between the perceived appearances, and thus between their intuitive contents. It is also often observed that the change of one appearance or intuition will occasion a corresponding change in the coordinated one. But there is nothing in the nature of the intuited contents themselves to place them in relations of dependence; nothing is found in them which makes the necessity of the connection evident. This concerns the objective things alone, and not the contents as such. It is possible by means of phantasy to think of the causal relations as suspended without changing the intuitive content of perception. One can in phantasy regard the head of a horse by itself and allow the remaining parts as well as the entire intuitive surroundings to disappear. A content is called *dependent* if we have the evidence that it will change or be annulled due to the change or annulment of at least one of the co-given contents. A content for which this is not the case is called *independent*, whereby it is not absurd to state that the annulment of all simultaneous contents would leave the content untouched. Husserl concludes that with regard to dependent contents we have the evidence that they are only thinkable as parts of more comprehensive wholes, whereas this evidence is lacking for independent contents. Husserl makes reference [16] to the paper "Concerning *Gestalt* Qualities" by von Ehrenfels, his own *Philosophy of Arithmetic*, and Meinong's paper on "The Psychology of Relations and Complexes." This is a note apropos of his remarks in the "Psychological Studies" con-

---

(Leipzig, 1873), p. 109, for comparison. Contents are divided by Stumpf into two main classes: *independent* contents and *partial* contents (*Theilinhalte*). The following distinction is determined as the definition and criterion: Independent contents are present where the elements of a presentational complex can also be presented separately; partial contents, where this is not the case. One cannot present a color-quality without intensity, or a movement without velocity, for that would contradict its nature. In such cases the connection is a necessary one, but not in cases of independent contents. Furthermore, it is not possible for us to present extension without color, or color without extension. By no means of phantasy or of outer experiment is it possible to make such a separation.

[16] Cf. Husserl, *op. cit.*, p. 162 n. Meinong's "Zur Psychologie der Relationen und Complexionen," which originally appeared in the *Zeit. f. Psych. u. Phys. d. Sinnesorgane* in 1891 as a discussion of von Ehrenfels' essay, is included in Meinong's *Abhandlungen zur Psychologie* (Leipzig, 1914), pp. 281–303. Reference is also made to von Ehrenfels in the *Log. Unt.*, vol. II (1901), p. 633 n.

cerning dependent contents, an example being extension in relation to quality, or figure in relation to both. Further examples are furnished in great numbers by the quasi-qualitative factors of intuitions (von Ehrenfels' *Gestalt* qualities, for which Meinong suggested the name "founded" contents), the quasi-quantitative factor in the domain of tone, etc. Finally, relative independence is distinguished from absolute independence, and relative from absolute dependence. In his first "Logical Survey" [17] Husserl adds a pertinent note in explanation. He does not mean that an accidental experience of evidence, which occurs only in subsequent reflection, makes the content to be dependent, and hence the determination must be applied objectively. It is an objective law that a content of the kind in question can only exist as a part of a whole when connected with other contents. This means that relatively independent contents can only exist in connection with one another. This important distinction is thus not limited to contents, but is held to be applicable to objects in general, whereby it gains metaphysical significance. The same holds also for the other distinctions connected with it in this study.

Husserl thinks it desirable to avoid such an equivocal term as "idea" or "presentation" (*Vorstellung*), and he avoids speaking of abstract and concrete presentations. It had been objected [18] that abstract and concrete are terms which could only be applied to presentations, and not to the presented things. Agreeing that they do not apply to the things, Husserl maintains that they refer to the contents of experience. The things are not the real contents of our presentations, but rather objective unities, and hence merely intended contents. Husserl points out that the distinction between abstract and concrete is not due to the mode of psychical activity; there is not a peculiar activity of "abstracting" which provides the positive character of abstract ideas.[19]

The second study, "Concerning Intuitions and Representations," is larger in scope than the first. It is a psychological study in the sense of pure descriptive psychology. After a preliminary analysis of examples, the concepts of intuition and representation are defined tentatively. Intuition is described as a particular concern with or a peculiar turning toward a content that is observed by itself. Only that which is observed by itself

---

[17] *Archiv für systematische Philosophie*, vol. III (Berlin, 1897), p. 225.

[18] Reference is made to Meinong, "Phantasievorstellung und Phantasie," *Zeit. f. Phil. u. phil. Kritik*, vol. xcv (1889), p. 202.

[19] In a note in his first "Logical Survey," Husserl states that since the appearance of this study he had become aware of the essential distinction between abstract contents (as intuitive parts) and abstract concepts. The occasional confusion of them will not disturb the results of the investigation if one thinks only of the abstract *contents*.

can be said to be "intuited" (*angeschaut*). If I look at the knife lying before me, only the knife is intuited, and not the unobserved background. I am only concerned with that which is selected, and I "look at" that alone. On the other hand, certain psychical experiences, which are generally called ideas, have the peculiarity of containing their "objects," not as immanent contents and hence as present in consciousness, but by "merely intending" them. That is, by means of certain contents given in consciousness they refer to them with understanding; they mean them without there being a conceptual knowledge of the relation between that which represents and the intended object. Such ideas are called representations by Husserl. Ideas in the sense of intuitions are directed toward an immanent content without its serving as a representative. The difference between intuition and representation is regarded as a difference in the "mode of consciousness," rather than as a difference of content. The function of representation is essential to thought. An example that is used again in the *Logical Investigations* will elucidate. At the moment that the arabesque becomes a sign, and hence gains the character of a representing content, the psychical situation has totally changed. We see the sign to be sure, but we have not intended to do so; we do not look at it. Thus heard words are only intuited when we hear without thought, attracted perhaps by a particular tonal quality of the voice. But if they exercise their natural effect they are not intuited, although they are heard.

It will be pertinent and sufficient for present purposes to single out the seventh and concluding section of the second study, which deals with the psychological and logical significance of both functions and the importance of their investigation. The investigation of the psychical function of representation is held to be of fundamental significance for all psychology, and in particular for the psychology of knowledge and logic. It is important for psychology because it is essential to a number of important acts, such as desire and will, to have ideas in the sense of representations as bases or presuppositions, whereas this is not the case for other acts. For logic its importance is due to the fact that concepts, judgments, and all other logical activities also belong to that significant group. In fact, no theory of judgment can do justice to the facts if it is not based upon a deeper study of the descriptive and genetic relationships of intuitions and representations. In his first "Logical Survey" Husserl speaks of the main task of every theory of apperception as being the descriptive and genetic investigation of these psychical phenomena, which are not dissolvable into mere complexes of content. This he holds to be the essential foundation of every theory of judgment. Every judgment has an "idea" as its "basis," whereby judgment is taken to mean the judging decision. The controversial question whether simple perception is a judgment or not is answered affirmatively or negatively, depending upon whether perception means apprehension (*Auffassung*), or mere intuition or observation. Husserl also points out the significance of the distinction for the wider field of psychology. If the distinction is made between primary contents and psychical acts, the latter being determined by the positive character of relationship to an immanent, and not an intentional object, then acts fall into two groups. There are those which are representations or have representations as a basis, thus gaining an intentional relation to objects, including affirmation, denial, supposition, doubt, question, love, hope, courage, desire, willing, etc.; and those for which this is not the case, as, e.g., sensuous enjoyment and unpleasantness. The latter are so to speak lower modes of consciousness, and are "genetically prior" and more primitive. The objection, that in a developed mental life representations are always attached to the contents that are present, would not destroy the value of the proposed distinctions.

Husserl regards representation as a very remarkable function and as causing wonder in various respects. It is remarkable in itself that a psychical act can point beyond its immanent content to something else of which one is not conscious in any way. Nevertheless it appears that we are conscious of it in a certain way, which Husserl finds striking, for we believe, while we are occupied with the representing contents, that we are concerned with the represented objects themselves. It is as though the meant objects themselves were basic to the series of words. Husserl ascribes the neglect of this fact by reputable psychologists and logicians to the circumstance that it is so far removed from the customary direction of attention; and he expresses the belief that there are great and unsolved problems in this obscure region of the theory of knowledge. He is not interested in the psychological explanation of this illusion and of the whole situation, although that is at the basis of all that follows, but rather in the possibility of knowledge in general. Scientific knowledge is based throughout upon the possibility of being expressed by means of merely symbolic or otherwise inadequate thought. But how is insight then possible; how does one come in such a way to empirically correct results? Although mathematics is regarded as the model of exact science, the meaning of its elementary concepts and the basis of the cogency of its methods are still not decided, and are in a strange conflict with the pretended evidence of the procedure. The theories change, but the procedure remains the same. Its evidence is, however, mere illusion. The question then arises, as to how it arrives at results which agree with experience and which are reliable practically. In view of the analogous doubts which concern all science and natural thinking, Husserl asks whether we ought to proceed from Hume's skepticism, and extend it to mathematics and all "a priori" science. He finds that the old and the new logic do not help to decide this question; they leave us in the lurch here. Husserl does not want to assert that one cannot aid the logical understanding of symbolic thinking without a more penetrating insight into the essence of the intuitive and representative elementary processes which mediate it everywhere. His own investigations concerning algorismic methods, of which only a small part devoted to special problems were published, were of this kind (reference is made to the twelfth chapter of the *Philosophy of Arithmetic*). A complete and satisfactory understanding of this, as of all logical processes, is not gained, however, without that insight.

In closing these studies Husserl points out the importance of the questions raised, but does not pretend to have the solution of the difficulties. His aim is to clarify the matter on some points, and to stimulate further investigation. This spirit is characteristic of his attitude through the years, and is illustrated again in the preface to the English edition of the *Ideas*, where he appears in the role of a founder and beginner.

The "Psychological Studies" are primarily of historical value, as providing an illustration of Husserl's use of psychological analysis in logic. These studies were never repudiated in every respect,[20] any more than the *Philosophy of Arithmetic* had to be cast into the discard. In pointing out that the theory of judgment requires a deeper study of descriptive and genetic relationships of "intuitions and representations," Husserl is really talking about the "foundation of logic" as he was soon to speak of it. His dissatisfaction with "the old and the new logic" becomes one of the opening themes in the *Logical Investigations*. The severe judgment of mathematical theory indicates his acute awareness of ultimate philosophical problems at the basis of formal procedures. He was right in seeing inescapable problems of a psychological, or "pure" psychological, nature in logic; and he also had a penetrating insight into the nature of formal logic. His failure in the former case was due to two reasons: the psychological "foundation" was made too broad, and the assumptions of psychology were not examined. The later "presuppositionless" program made it possi-

[20] Cf. *Log. Unt.*, vol. II (1901). On p. 227 Husserl states that he makes use of his essay on abstract and concrete contents. There are some omissions, but use is made of whole paragraphs. Cf. also pp. 238, 362, and 504 for further references to the "Psychological Studies." On p. 504 Husserl refers to the second study and states that he has given up the concept of intuition which is preferred there.

ble to clarify the fundamental concepts and principles of logic by means of a discipline lying "before" psychology, as well as "before" metaphysics and natural science. That discipline was taken to be methodologically prior to all other fields of knowledge. The reaction against psychologism was a reaction against a general method, particularly as regards logic and mathematics. The new method of phenomenology made it possible not only to overcome psychologism in its most general form, but also to appropriate and to delimit its truth. In this sense there has been continuity in Husserl's development. The descriptive material and positive findings always remain.

C. FIRST LOGICAL SURVEY

The survey of German publications on logic in the year 1894 may be regarded as bringing to a close the early period of Husserl's development,[21] even though it was published after the completion of the *Prolegomena*. In its content as well as emphasis upon principles it is of no phenomenological significance in contrast with the second survey of 1903–1904. There is a special merit in the "Logical Surveys," as in all of Husserl's polemical writings. He comes to grips directly with adversaries, and is forced not only to make his own views clear, but to orient them with respect to other points of view. The available literature of that kind is all too limited, and is doubly valuable in illuminating Husserl's views and motives. It therefore appears desirable to present them at some length.[22]

Husserl regarded the logical literature of 1894 as being unusually rich in valuable publications. The most discussed subject was the disputed domain of elementary logical theory, and there was a preference for questions belonging to the domain of the "theory of judgment," or for those closely related to it. In considering the revised edition of Wundt's *Logik*, he confines himself to the changes made in the new edition. As regards the treatment of the theory of number, he notes that much of what had been objected to in the *Philosophy of Arithmetic* had been eliminated or changed. Attention is called to the two meanings of the principle of identity which are distinguished by Wundt. It expresses on the one hand the requirement that in every given context of thought every concept must retain the properties assigned to it in thought. In its more important meaning it is the expression of the function of the recognition of agreement as

[21] Husserl, "Bericht über deutsche Schriften zur Logik aus dem Jahre 1894," *Archiv f. syst. Phil.*, vol. III (1897), pp. 216–244.
[22] The second logical survey was published in 1903–04, and thus belongs to the period following the published refutation of psychologism.

such. The principle of identity is accordingly a fundamental principle of positive judging.

After brief notices of works by Glogau [23] and Flügel,[24] Husserl proceeds to give a description of his own "Psychological Studies in Elementary Logic." This is followed by an estimate of W. Jerusalem's essay on "Belief and Judgment." [25] Husserl states that no benefit to the theory of judgment can be expected from such fictions. A. Marty's studies of propositions without subjects and the relationship of grammar to logic and psychology [26] are described as giving evidence of the acumen, clarity, and thoroughness of the author, who was also a disciple of Brentano. Because of the current disinclination to enter into critical discussion the author would not receive much love and gratitude. Of particular interest is Husserl's comment, that it is hard to understand how philosophy is to approach the ideal of unity and progress if the individual investigators philosophize past one another, unmindful of each other, and if instead of seeking a critical understanding they seek to avoid it.

The *Essay Concerning a Theory of Existential Judgments* by Hans Cornelius [27] is summarized and then criticized sharply. Lipps' "Subjective Categories in Objective Judgments" [28] is commended as an earnest piece of systematic-logical work. The central idea of the investigation is expressed by the principle that there are definite kinds of judgment that belong innerly to every subjective category. The review of Rickert's essay on "The Theory of the Concepts of Natural Science" [29] is of interest especially because of the later distinction of the author. In it Husserl takes a stand on the question of induction, as relating to particular facts; and he argues for a theory of science "from below." As Rickert views it, if we regard the task of knowledge to be the picturing of the world as it is through our ideas, which are then expressed in propositions, we encounter the extensive and intensive inexhaustibleness of things, or the infinite fullness of what is to be known in every single perception. The problem would therefore be insoluble. Hence if the finite human spirit is to have any knowledge of the material world the extensive and intensive manifold

[23] G. Glogau, *Die Hauptlehren der Logik und Wissenschaftslehre* (Kiel und Leipzig, 1894).

[24] O. Flügel, *Abriss der Logik und die Lehre von den Trugschlüssen* (Langensalze, 1894).

[25] W. Jerusalem, "Glaube und Urteil," *Viertelj. f. wiss. Phil.*, vol. xviii (1894), pp. 162–195.

[26] A. Marty, "Ueber subjektlose Sätze und das Verhältnis der Grammatik zur Logik und Psychologie," *Viertelj. f. wiss. Phil.*, vol. xviii (1894), pp. 320–356 and 421–471.

[27] Hans Cornelius, *Versuch einer Theorie der Existenzialurteile* (München, 1894).

[28] Th. Lipps, "Subjektive Kategorien in objektiven Urteilen," *Phil. Monatshefte*, vol. xxx (1894), pp. 97–128.

[29] H. Rickert, "Zur Theorie der naturwissenschaftlichen Begriffsbildung," *Viertelj. f. wiss. Phil.*, vol. xviii (1894), pp. 277–319.

of things must be obviated by means of general ideas. With the aid of word-meanings only a small part of the infinite intuitive content need be presented. The logical essence of the concepts of natural science is thus seen in their function of overcoming the extensive and intensive manifold of things. Husserl does not find this train of thought to be correct. The possibility of knowledge of the world could only depend upon the overcoming of the inexhaustibleness of things if its goal lay in the achievement of a single cognition. If this is not the aim of knowledge, or if it has other possible aims which are not touched by the inexhaustibleness of the individual, the conclusion is unfounded. That aim is judged by Husserl to be untenable. Even with the presupposition of the exhaustive experience of the world by a human spirit adapted to it, that aim would not be acceptable. The knowledge of that which is general and of the laws based upon it would retain its complete meaning and form the goal of theoretical striving, just as in the factual condition of the world. The problem of conceptual knowledge can therefore have no essential relation to the "extensive and intensive infinity" of the world. With regard to the nature of a theory of science, Husserl maintains that a fruitful theory of the formation of the concepts of natural science can only be a theory "from below," growing out of the work of natural sicence itself. He observes that Rickert's theory operates so much with general constructions, and is to such an extent a theory "from above," that in the whole paper not a single example is given — and none is missed.

Benno Erdmann's paper entitled "The Theory of the Classification of Types" [30] is judged to deal with an interesting but little treated domain of the doctrine of method, and is held to be stimulating. Husserl gives a summary of E. Mach's "brilliant" speech "Concerning the Principle of Equalization in Physics," [31] and he quotes Mach as speaking of the development of "a general physical phenomenology, comprising all domains." This is the ideal for a domain of facts. Description is all that an investigation can demand; it is a construction of facts in thoughts. Paul Biedermann's "The Scientific Significance of Hypothesis" and J. Henrici's "Introduction to Inductive Logic" are judged to be of no scientific significance. [32]

This is the end of the first logical survey. It has been seen that the whole story of the development of phenomenology is to be traced back to the

[30] Benno Erdmann, "Theorie der Typeneinteilungen," *Phil. Monatshefte*, vol. xxx (1894), pp. 15–49 and 159–191.

[31] E. Mach, "Ueber das Prinzip der Vergleichung in der Physik" (Leipzig, 1894).

[32] Paul Biedermann, *Die wissenschaftliche Bedeutung der Hypothese*; J. Henrici, *Einführung in die induktive Logik*.

motive of clarifying the basic ideas of mathematics and formal logic to begin with, and then of science and knowledge in general. The awareness of the existence of a region of problems concerning the non-formal foundation of logic at this early time provides the motivation for Husserl's most valuable and lasting investigations into the philosophy (or phenomenology) of logic. That this quest for presuppositions, whether of ideas or principles, was ultimately to lead to an idealistic theory of reality was due to the exploitation of the cognitive approach to philosophy. Husserl made little progress in method from the *Philosophy of Arithmetic* to the "Psychological Studies," with no change as far as the point of view of logical psychologism is concerned, thus making the progress that occurred in the few years, leading to the publication of the *Logical Investigations*, all the more striking. Frege's criticism and his own sound grasp of formal reasoning were the reasons for the change, which did not occur, however, before he had had an opportunity to test the possibilities of psychologistic analysis by means of concrete investigations. As has been seen, however, the descriptive findings are readily assimilable to a non-psychologistic point of view — only the general framework is changed. In his later development he did not abandon the aspect of the activity of thought, but merely reinterpreted it. Instead of psychologism there is the phenomenological clarification of logic and of essential structures of thought; and finally there are the constitutive activities of thought.

CHAPTER IV

THE REFUTATION OF PSYCHOLOGISM

A. THE "PROLEGOMENA TO PURE LOGIC"

HUSSERL'S TRANSITION in the 1890's to the strikingly new point of view of the *Logical Investigations* (1900–01) really gathered together all the results of his early studies, while correcting the general philosophical standpoint with which they had begun. The first volume, entitled *Prolegomena to Pure Logic*, contains a detailed statement and criticism of psychologism. It is characterized by thoroughness of treatment as well as by fairness to the writers examined. The numerous quotations and full expositions insure a fair hearing to all concerned. The criticism is especially incisive, and that it is also intended as a correction of his early point of view is indicated by a quotation of the words of Goethe, to the effect that one is never more severe with anything than with errors recently renounced.

The *Logical Investigations* developed out of Husserl's studies of the origin of the fundamental concepts of mathematics and of questions of mathematical theory. He had become convinced that neither the traditional nor the new logic was adequate to explain the rational nature of deductive science, with its formal unity and symbolic method. Difficulties were encountered particularly in the logical investigation of arithmetic and set theory, which led beyond the narrow sphere of mathematics to a general theory of formal deductive systems. The study of mathematical logic made him acquainted with a non-quantitative type of mathematics, thus bearing out his insight that the element of quantity does not belong to the most general essence of mathematics or to "formal" method. Problems of the relationship between quantitative and non-quantitative mathematics, and especially of the relationship between the formal structures of arithmetic and of logic, led to more fundamental questions regarding the essence of the form of knowledge as distinguished from the matter of knowledge, and regarding the meaning of the distinction between formal or pure and material determinations, truths, and laws. Some of the specific problems which necessarily involved epistemological inquiry have been reviewed. The clarification of the basis of mathematical logic constituted one of the motivating influences leading to logical studies of a phenomenological character.

Another line of thought leading to the same result was the unsatisfactoriness of logical psychologism. Husserl's point of departure had been the prevailing view that not only logic in general, but also the logic of the deductive sciences, must look to psychology for their philosophical elucidation. It was for that reason that psychological investigations occupied so much space in the *Philosophy of Arithmetic*. Psychological analysis seemed to be clear and instructive for questions of the origin of mathematical ideas or concerning practical methods. The situation was altered, however, with the transition from the psychological connections of thought to the logical unity of the content of thought, or the unity of theory. How the objectivity of mathematics and of science in general can be reconciled with a psychologistic foundation presented an acute problem. Losing confidence in the method of using psychological analyses for the logical explanation of science, Husserl was compelled to reflect upon the essence of logic and especially upon the relationship between the subjectivity of knowing and the objectivity of the content of knowledge. He set aside his studies in the philosophy of mathematics and devoted himself to the basic questions of the theory of knowledge and logic.

Husserl has emphasized the fact that the *Logical Investigations* was a pioneer work, representing a beginning (a "breakthrough") and not an end of his efforts. Referring to that work near the close of his life, he wrote of his "older, still entirely indispensable thoughts and writings," and stated: "To the world I am still the author of the *Logical Investigations*, and for the Anglo-American public this work is the necessary basis for the understanding of the new problems and modes of thought of phenomenology; and it is also necessary as a bridge of understanding to the writings of my period of final maturity. There are naturally some things to be said today which I was incapable of saying three and one-half decades ago." [1]

Numerous changes were introduced in the second edition of 1913–1921 in order to bring the work into line with the subsequent development of phenomenology, but the first volume was not revised radically. Although improvements in the presentation were made and errors were corrected, certain essential inadequacies were permitted to remain, such as the one-sided concept of "truth in itself," in order to maintain the unity of the work.

[1] From a letter to the writer.

Husserl's own descriptive notice [2] of the first part of the *Logical Investigations* is a helpful summary, and is worth quoting in full. "The *Prolegomena to Pure Logic,* which constitutes the introductory part of the *Logical Investigations,* aims to prepare the way for a new conception and treatment of logic. It endeavors to show that the exclusively psychological foundation of logic, to which our time attaches such great value, is based upon a confusion of essentially different levels of problems, upon presuppositions which are fundamentally incorrect concerning the character and the aims of two sciences participating here — empirical psychology and *pure logic.* The epistemological and especially the skeptical disadvantages which necessarily attach to the psychologistic logic are exposed in detailed analyses, and the proof is also provided therewith, that the inadequate method of treatment of the hitherto prevailing logic, its deficiency in clarity and theoretical rigor, is based upon the ignoring of the most essential fundamentals and problems. In opposition to the prevailing psychologism, the *Prolegomena* therefore seeks to revive the idea of a *pure* logic, and also to form it anew. It leads to the delimitation of a theoretical science, independent of all psychology and factual science, which comprises within its natural limits all of pure arithmetic and the theory of manifolds. Its relationship to *logic as methodology,* as the art of scientific knowing, whose justification naturally remains untouched, is construed as being analogous to the relationship of pure geometry to the art of field measurement. It is not in the psychology of knowledge, although that also enters into consideration, but in pure logic that the most essential foundations of the art of logic are found.

"This pure logic is anything but a mere renewal of the traditional formal logic, or of the pure logic of the Kantian and Herbartian schools. If the author approves of these last and not yet forgotten efforts as valuable first steps, it is his conviction that they nevertheless lack sufficient clarity regarding the aims and limits of the discipline in question; they still remain in a state of uncertain vacillation between theoretical and practical, psychologistic and purely ideal tendencies.

"Pure logic is the scientific system of ideal laws and theories which are grounded purely in the *sense* of the ideal categories of meaning, i.e., in the fundamental concepts which are the common estate of *all* sciences, because they determine in a most general manner that which makes sciences in an objective sense to be sciences at all, namely, unity of theory.

[2] Edmund Husserl, "Selbstanzeige" of the first volume of the *Log. Unt., Viertelj. f. wiss. Phil.,* vol. xxiv (1900), pp. 511 f. This volume had been printed by the end of November, 1899, and the second volume was already in print at that time.

In this sense pure logic is the science of the ideal 'conditions of the possibility' of science in general, or of the ideal constituents of the idea of theory.

"A *sufficient* clarification of pure logic, hence a clarification of its essential concepts and theories, of its relation to all other sciences and of the way in which it regulates them, requires very far-reaching phenomenological (i.e., purely descriptive-,[3] not genetic-psychological) and epistemological investigations. One can say that this task of an epistemological elucidation of logic coincides in the main with the critical elucidation of thinking and knowing in general, hence with epistemology itself. In the second part there then follow single phenomenological and epistemological investigations, which seek to solve the main problems of an elucidation of logic and logical thinking."

In characterizing the state of logic in his time, Husserl observed that the situation in logic had changed since Mill wrote of the great difference of opinion about the definition and treatment of logic. But the three principal tendencies in logic, the psychological, the formal, and the metaphysical, continued to illustrate the practice of using the same words to express different ideas. The psychological logicians, with the largest number of representatives, were only in agreement on the scope of their discipline, and its essential aims and methods. The fact that the expression *bellum omnium contra omnes* could be applied to the state of logic shows the necessity of a reconsideration of questions of principle.

This appears to Husserl to be very serious, in view of the fact that the definitions of a science mirror the stages of its development, so that the delimitation of its domain goes along with the progress of a science. On the other hand, the quality of the definitions may affect the course of the science itself, depending upon the degree of their truth. Husserl points out that the confused determination of a domain by the mixture of heterogeneous things into a supposed unity is the source of serious errors, as illustrated by the psychologically founded logic at the close of the nineteenth century. It leads to the use of methods not suited to the subject-matter of logic, and to the misinterpretation of the theoretical basis of logic, thus becoming a serious obstacle to progress.

The traditional questions at issue in the definition of logic are summarized as follows: (1) whether logic is a theoretical or a practical discipline (an "art"); (2) whether it is a science that is independent of other sciences, in particular of psychology or metaphysics; (3) whether it is a formal discipline, having to do with "the mere form of knowledge," or

[3] This passage indicates Husserl's early conception of phenomenology as descriptive psychology and theory of knowledge.

whether it must also take acount of its "matter"; (4) whether it has the character of an *a priori* and demonstrative or that of an empirical and inductive discipline. These controversial questions prove to be so closely connected that there are really only two parties. According to one point of view, logic is a theoretical discipline, independent of psychology, and it is also formal and demonstrative in character. Opposed to it is the second standpoint that logic is an art that is dependent upon psychology.

Husserl's aim is the clarification of the fundamental differences that are at issue, and of the essential aims of a pure logic. His procedure is first to examine the view that logic is an art. That leads to the question of the theoretical basis of this discipline, and its relationship to psychology. This question coincides largely with the central question of epistemology, regarding the objectivity of knowledge. The constructive aim of the investigation is the determination of the purely theoretical science which forms the foundation for every art of scientific knowledge and has the character of an *a priori* and purely demonstrative science. It is a science that had been sought by Kant and others interested in formal or pure logic, but without correctly determining its nature and extent.

B. LOGIC AS A NORMATIVE AND PRACTICAL DISCIPLINE

The critical investigation accordingly begins with the consideration of logic as a normative and practical discipline. The time-honored function of logic, to examine the methods and structure of the sciences, is accepted by Husserl. Logic is admittedly a normative discipline; and its practical value lies in the service it can render to science.

The various sciences are obviously incomplete, not only with respect to the truths which are sought, but also with respect to their inner clarity. That is no impediment to progress, however, for just as the practical artist can achieve results without being able to explain the principles of his art, so the mathematician and the natural scientist do not have to concern themselves with fundamental concepts and the ultimate justification or nature of their methods, or with the examination of presuppositions. The special sciences are, however, far removed from the clarity which can only follow the analysis of all presuppositions.

In order to attain to this theoretical goal, the special sciences need completion by means of investigations belonging to metaphysics. Presuppositions of a metaphysical kind, which are at the basis of at least all sciences dealing with reality, must be examined. They include the following, for example: that there is an external world which is extended in space and time, whereby space is three-dimensional Euclidean space and time has the character of a one-dimensional manifold; that all change is subject to the law of causality; etc. Such presuppositions are often incorrectly regarded as epistemological. This metaphysical foundation is not sufficient, however, to provide the theoretical completion of all the special sciences, because it does not apply to the pure mathematical sciences, whose ideal objects are independent of real being or non-being. This is undertaken by another class of investigations which apply to all sciences because they are interested in the nature of science as such, i.e., by the theory of science.

The justification of a theory of science is found in the need for general norms to govern the use of scientific methods. The aim of science is the establishment of knowledge. Since only a small part of our knowledge is immediately evident, methods of procedure must be developed in order to lead us away from that really trivial type of knowledge. Knowledge in its most rigorous or absolute sense is said to be evident if there is a "luminous certainty" regarding it, a certainty which must be distinguished from blind conviction, or from vague intention. By evidence is meant the immediate experience of the truth itself. There can be no reliance upon memory in that type of knowledge, although we do speak of an act of knowledge in cases in which there is a clear remembrance of an evident judgment. Every genuine cognition, and especially all scientific knowledge, ultimately is based upon evidence, and the knowledge reaches as far as the evidence. There is an ambiguity in the concept of knowledge which must be noted. In the narrowest sense, knowledge is the evidence that a certain fact obtains or does not obtain, e.g., that S is p, or not; and also the evidence that a fact in question is probable to this or that degree. With regard, however, to the existence of the fact itself, and not its probability, there is knowledge in a wider sense. One can accordingly speak of degrees of knowledge, corresponding to the degrees of probability, and the evidence that S is p becomes the absolute ideal limit of knowledge. Scientific knowledge is such that if all knowledge were immediately evident, science would be superfluous. In order to be scientific the single cognitions must be systematically connected and unified. The systematic connections are discovered and not invented. Because they are objectively real their investigation and presentation can be systematic, and the knowledge gained can be used as a basis for the achievement of further regions of truth.

The evidence upon which all knowledge ultimately is based does not simply turn up with the mere presentation of the facts, and without the use of any methodological devices. Countless propositions can only be grasped as truths after being "established." Not only are sciences therefore necessary, but also a theory of science, a logic. The consideration of the various methods and aids employed by the sciences can provide norms for such modes of procedure, and rules for construction.

Pointing out that combinations of grounds of knowledge, or of proofs, constitute theories which belong to the systematic unity of science, Husserl opposes the view that one may begin arbitrarily in setting up proofs. In his view, proofs have a firm structure, and he appeals to the case of mathematical proofs in substantiation of his position. Instead of arbitrariness and accident, the connections of proof are held to illustrate reason and order, and to be subject to a regulative law. For example, the proof of the proposition that a certain equilateral triangle is equiangular is provided by the syllogism "Every equilateral triangle is equiangular, the triangle *ABC* is equilateral, hence it is equiangular." This and countless other examples illustrate the same form "Every *A* is *B*, *X* is *A*, hence *X* is *B*." It is an "a priori" principle that every proposed proof of this form is actually correct, in so far as it proceeds from correct premises. The proof-forms can be conceived so "purely" that they are freed from all reference to a concrete domain of knowledge. These features of proofs have an obvious bearing upon the possibility of a science and of a theory of science.

There is a form inherent in every proof which is not peculiar to any individual case, and is typical of a whole class of proofs. There could be no science if this were not the case, for there could then be no systematic progress from cognition to cognition; there would be only accidental progress. The element of regulated form clearly makes possible the existence of sciences. On the other hand, the fact that form is independent of the domain of knowledge makes possible the existence of a theory of science. Without that independence there would be only a set of special sciences, each with its coresponding logic, but not a general logic. In reality there are investigations in the theory of science which concern all sciences uniformly, and in addition to that special investigations dealing with the theory and method of the single sciences. Both types must be provided for by logic as the theory of science.

In accordance with the conception of scientific knowledge that has been indicated, all scientific methods are declared to be either proofs or devices for establishing proofs. The proofs in turn may be employed by way of abbreviated substitute forms, which have been endowed with meaning and value once and for all. In the case of the algebraic methods, it becomes possible to perform mechanical operations with a minimum of mental effort; but in Husserl's view they obtain their meaning and justification from the essence of the thought providing the foundation. The auxiliary devices serve to prepare future proofs, and to make them possible. Thus it is important that the ideas be expressed by means of well-defined and unique signs; and it is desirable that short, characteristic symbols replace the more important and frequently used concepts, because cumbrous expressions inhibit the operations.

Individual proofs do not make a science, however. A certain unity of the connection and sequence of proofs is essential, and this ideal of unity has the function of promoting the investigation of the realm of truth. It is the task of the theory of science to treat of the sciences as types of systematic unity, to study their scope and the internal structure of theories. The systematic network of proofs can be ordered under the concept of method, so that the theory of science is seen to treat not only of the methods of knowledge employed in the sciences, but also of the sciences themselves. It has to distinguish valid and invalid theories and sciences, as well as valid and invalid proofs.

Logic as the theory of science is accordingly a normative discipline. That view is rendered all the more acceptable when one considers that sciences are mental creations that are directed toward a certain goal, and are therefore to be judged with respect to that goal. It is the business of logic to ascertain whether given sciences or methods fulfill their purpose. Logic as a normative science is thus different from the comparative point of view of historical science, which attempts to explain the sciences as concrete cultural occurrences of a given epoch. It does not attempt to furnish universal criteria; the theory of science can only give special criteria. Having regard to the highest aim of the sciences and the actual constitution of the human mind, various methods are defined, and propositions of the following form can be asserted: Every group of mental acts of the kinds $\alpha, \beta, \ldots$, which occur in the complex form M_1 (or $M_2, \ldots$) provides a case of correct method. If it were possible to set up all such valid propositions, the normative discipline would contain the rules for all methods, although only in the form of special criteria.

If the theory of science undertakes the further task of investigating the conditions upon which the realization of valid methods depends, and to set up rules for the construction of sciences, for the discovery or application of methods in them, and how we are to guard against errors, then it becomes an art of scientific knowledge. This contains the normative theory of science in itself, and because of its undoubted value it is appropriate thus to widen the concept of logic. This is pointed out despite the inadequacy of past definitions of logic as an art of thought, including Schleiermacher's definition of logic as the art of scientific knowledge.

The justification for logic as an art seems so obvious that the controversy that arose must appear strange. That a practical logic is indispensable to all sciences is shown by the fact that logic has developed historically in response to practical motives of scientific work. Logical rules can be of use in special sciences. It is also conceivable that practical rules could be derived with the aid of the ideal laws of pure logic. Although the ideal laws are independent of the human mind, the practical rules can take account of the particular nature of man. In this way a logic which is both general and practical can be obtained. A logic as a practical theory of science is justified sufficiently by the consideration that even a moderate degree of probability would make it worth while for the future advancement of science, apart from the fact that the derived rules are in themselves a valuable addition to knowledge.

C. THE THEORETICAL BASIS OF NORMATIVE DISCIPLINES

The real question at issue is, however, whether the definition of logic as an art expresses its essential character. Logicians like Beneke, J. S. Mill, and Sigwart held that logic is essentially an art, in opposition to the position of Kant, Herbart, and their followers, who maintained that a "pure" logic is basic to an art of logic. In Hamilton's opinion the question whether logic is an art or a science is futile and unimportant. But, Husserl argues, the controversy about definitions is really a controversy about the science itself, and it is important because its problems, methods, and doctrines are still in doubt. Drobisch and Bergmann are mentioned as excellent champions of the autonomy of a pure logic. The charge that the standpoint of pure logic involves the restoration of the Scholastic-Aristotelian logic is not serious, if one considers that the traditional logic was a very incomplete and unclear realization of a pure logic, but that it is nevertheless to be valued as a beginning.

Of deciding importance for the present analysis is the thesis that every normative or practical discipline is based upon one or more theoretical disciplines, inasmuch as its rules must have a theoretical content that is separable from the thought of being a norm. The understanding and determination of this question depends upon the clear analysis of the concept of normative science and its relationship to theoretical science. The laws of normative science purport to assert what should be the case. The proposition "A warrior should be brave" really means that a brave warrior is a "good" warrior, and hence that one who is not brave is a "bad" warrior. In general, the form "An A should be B" is equivalent to "An A that is not B is a bad A," or "Only an A that is B is a good A." The term "good"

is of course interpreted in diverse ways, as the useful, beautiful, etc. There
are as many kinds of "ought" as there are kinds of value, whether real or
supposed. The negative statements of "ought" are not to be interpreted
as negations of the corresponding affirmative statements. That a warrior
should not be cowardly does not mean that it is false that a warrior should
be cowardly, but rather, that a cowardly warrior is a bad one. Hence the
form "An A should not be B" is equivalent to "An A which is B is generally a bad A," or "Only an A which is not B is a good A." Every normative proposition presupposes a certain kind of valuation or approval,
through which the objects are classified into good and bad. Whether the
valuation is objectively valid or not does not enter into consideration here.
It is sufficient that something is held to be valuable or good. A proposition
is defined as normative if it expresses any necessary or sufficient, or necessary and sufficient conditions for the possession of a value-predicate. Once
we have made a difference between "good" and "bad" in a definite sense,
we are naturally interested to determine under which circumstances they
can be realized.

The totality of all norms constitutes a closed group that is determined
by the fundamental value. A normative proposition which requires of a
class of objects that they satisfy as much as possible the characters that
constitute the positive predicate of value is called a *basic norm*. The
categorical imperative is the basic norm in the group of normative propositions which make up Kant's ethics; and the same is true of the principle
of the greatest good of the greatest number in the ethics of the Utilitarians.
The relationship of the basic norm to the actual normative propositions is
analogous to the so-called definitions of the number series and the theorems
about numerical relations in arithmetic.

In a theoretical discipline there is no such central relation of all inquiries
to a fundamental value as the basis of normative judgment. The unity of
its inquiries and the order of its knowledge is determined exclusively by
the theoretical interest, which is concerned with the nature of the facts.

The sense in which every normative or practical discipline presupposes
one or more theoretical disciplines as its foundation has now been indicated. The important point to be noted is that it must have a separable
theoretical content that belongs to some theoretical science or sciences,
whether these are already defined or still remain to be constituted. In
short, theoretical sciences are at the basis of normative sciences. Every normative discipline requires the knowledge of certain non-normative truths,
which are either taken from theoretical sciences or are obtained by the
application of propositions taken from such sciences to cases determined

by the normative interest. This is even more true for the special case of an art, in which theoretical knowledge must provide a basis for the realization of a purpose. The concept of a normative discipline should not be identified, however, with that of a practical discipline, or art. Thus one may reject all practical moralizing, as Schopenhauer did because of his doctrine of an inborn character, and still hold ethics to be a normative science. An art is a particular case of a normative discipline, in which the basic norm consists in the attainment of a general practical purpose. In that way every art includes in itself a normative descipline. Its first task, disregarding all that refers to practical attainment, is to determine the norms by which its conformity to the goal is to be judged. On the other hand, when the fundamental valuation is transformed into the positing of a purpose, a normative discipline is enlarged to an art.

The basic norm, the basic value, or the ultimate purpose determines the unity of the discipline; and it also introduces the idea of being a norm into all the normative propositions. But in addition to their general normative character, these propositions possess their own theoretical character. Thus every normative proposition of the form "An A ought to be B" includes the theoretical proposition "Only an A that is B has the property C," whereby C means the value predicate "good" in any one of its interpretations. The new proposition is purely theoretical, and contains no normative element. That normative propositions can arise in a theoretical context is shown by the converse procedure. Thus if the proposition "Only an A that is B has the property C" is interpreted as "Only an A that is B is good," we obtain "An A ought to be B." Such propositions are, however, of secondary importance in theoretical science, because the primary object of interest is the theoretical consideration of the facts.

D. PSYCHOLOGISM AND ITS CONSEQUENCES

The point of these preliminary considerations is seen in their application to the question of the status of logic; for if logic is conceived as a normative discipline, the question arises as to which theoretical sciences provide the essential bases of the theory of science. According to one group of logicians, the essential theoretical bases are to be found in psychology, whose theoretical content contains the propositions which are characteristic of logic. Thus logic is related to psychology just as a branch of chemical technology is related to chemistry. J. S. Mill regarded logic as being a part of psychology, and in his view the art of logic obtained its theoretical basis from the science of psychology. Lipps also held that logic is a special branch of psychology. This point of view is called psychologism, in conformity to Stumpf's usage.[4] The expressions "psychologism" and "psychologistic logic" are intended to be purely descriptive. That psychologism was a well-considered point of view is shown by the effectiveness with which it met the attacks of its critics. The contention that psychology considers thought as it is, whereas logic investigates what it ought to be, was readily met by the psychologistic logicians with the reply that thinking as it should be is a special case of thinking as it is. According to Lipps, the rules of correct thought are identical with the natural laws of thought itself; and logic is either the physics of thought or nothing at all. Neither was it admitted that psychology is interested in determining causal laws, as distinguished from the interest of logic in the truth-content of mental acts, and in the conditions to be met in order that judgments may be true. On the contrary, it was argued that every "ought" is based upon an "is." The "ought" is interpreted in terms of what must be done in order to attain a certain goal, and that is equivalent to the question as to how the goal is actually to be reached. The following argument, advanced by such writers as Lotze and Natorp,[5] was no more successful. According to this argument, logic can no more be based upon psychology than upon any other science, for every science is possible only by conformity to the rules of logic, the validity of which is presupposed. Hence it would be circular to attempt to base logic upon psychology. In answer to this argument it was claimed that the impossibility of logic itself would result, for

[4] Stumpf, "Psychologie und Erkenntnistheorie," *Abhandlungen der K. bayerischen Akademie der Wissenschaften*, vol. xix, Section 2 (München, 1892), p. 468, Stumpf attributed the emancipation of the theory of knowledge from psychology, or the critique of knowledge, to Kant, even though that was not consistently adhered to by the latter. By "criticism" was meant the theory of knowledge which is designed to be free from all psychological bases; and the term "psychologism," which was first used by J. E. Erdmann, was defined as the reduction of all philosophical and especially all epistemological investigations to psychology. While praising Kant for maintaining the idea of necessity, not only in laws of thought but also in laws of nature, Stumpf regarded the tendency to reject psychological investigations as the point of departure and basis of the theory of knowledge as unfortunate. It was the function of psychology, in his view, to explain but not justify the general belief in an external world, no matter whether it be true or false, the external world being taken just as it appears to us. He concluded his discussion with the hope that both psychologism and criticism vanish from the scene, and that coöperative work take the place of the abstract and unfruitful standpoint-politics of the time. Although Stumpf protested against Mill's empirical foundation of the principle of contradiction, much more was required than he was prepared to offer for the refutation of the psychologistic theory of logic. Husserl later emphasized the fact that he was interested in combating a special kind of psychologism, namely, the "psychologizing" of the "irreal" meaning-structures which are the theme of logic. Psychologism as a universal epistemological error was not considered by him. Cf. *Formale und Transzendentale Logik*, § 56, pp. 135 f.

[5] Lotze, *Logik*, § 332 (German ed.), pp. 543–44; Natorp, "Ueber objektive und subjektive Begründung der Erkenntnis," *Phil. Monatshefte*, vol. xxiii (1887), p. 264.

logic as a science must itself proceed logically, and the same kind of circularity would be incurred. Logic must in short establish the rules which it presupposes. Examining the argument more closely, Husserl points out an equivocation in the concept of presupposition. The presupposition of certain rules by a science can mean that they are premises for its proofs; or rules can be meant to which the science must conform in order to be a science. Both meanings are thrown together in the argument, in that no distinction is drawn between inferring *according to* logical rules and inferring *from* them. The circularity would be incurred only if inferences were drawn from them. But an investigator can construct proofs without making use of logical laws as premises, just as artists can do creative work without a knowledge of aesthetics.

It appears from such arguments that the antipsychologistic logicians were at a disadvantage. Expressing surprise that there should be a controversy on this question at all, Husserl suggests that the truth lies between the two extreme positions. The dispute could continue only because each side had recognized a certain amount of truth and had failed to see that it is limited. In his opinion the more important part of the truth is on the antipsychologistic side, but the deciding ideas had not been worked out properly. The psychologistic logicians had merely proved that psychology participates in the foundation of logic, and not that it is alone or even primarily involved. The possibility remains open that another science contributes to its foundation in a much more significant manner. That would be the function of the science of "pure logic"; and it is in the delineation and development of this science, which includes the laws of pure mathematics, that Husserl is interested. The Kantians and Herbartians were not successful in the definition and construction of that science, although they recognized a region of truth in the traditional logic which belonged neither to psychology nor to other special sciences. They were thus able to sense an autonomous realm of truth. It is those truths to which all logical rules finally refer, so that they come to be regarded as the essence of logic, their theoretical unity being called "pure logic."

Husserl proposes that the thesis of psychologism be assumed for the sake of the argument, namely, that the essential bases of the logical precepts lie in pyschology, which is generally conceived as a factual science and hence as a science of experience. What would be the consequences for logic? The nature of psychological laws must be considered to answer that question. Husserl could say without prejudice that psychology was as yet lacking in exact laws, the propositions which it calls laws being valuable but vague generalizations of experience. They are statements about approximate regularities of coexistence or succession which do not claim to determine with unfailing precision what must occur under exactly defined conditions. Using the term "vague" in opposition to "exact," he explains that this fact is no more disparaging than the fact that meteorological laws are vague, while being important. The fact is, however, pertinent to the question at issue. It follows that only vague rules can be based upon vague theoretical foundations. If the laws of psychology are not exact, then the same must be true of the logical precepts. Even though it is true that some precepts have an element of empirical vagueness, the important logical laws, which as grounds make up the core of logic, are absolutely exact. Such are the logical "principles," the laws of syllogistic reasoning, the laws of the various kinds of inference, including probability, etc. These are genuine laws and not "merely empirical" or approximate rules. Any attempt to make them dependent upon empirical conditions would entirely alter their true meaning.

The situation would not be much improved even if the inexactness of the laws of psychology were denied, and the propositions of pure logic and mathematics were based upon the supposedly exact natural laws of thought. Natural laws cannot be known *a priori* or established by insight. They are established through induction from the facts of experience, which can only yield a greater or lesser degree of probability. Hence the logical laws would have the status of mere probabilities. But nothing appears more obvious, in Husserl's view, than that they are valid *a priori*, and that they are established through apodictic evidence and not inductively. The principle of contradiction does not state that it may be supposed that of two contradictory judgments one is true and one false; nor does one suppose that a true conclusion follows from two true premises in a valid syllogism. If they were inductively established, there would always be the possibility that future experience might not bear them out. Husserl maintains that we have insight into the truth and not the probability of the laws of logic and mathematics, so that it is absurd to speak of probability, approximation, etc., and that probability cannot dispute with truth, or supposition oppose insight. Because of its inability to yield more than empirical generalities, psychology cannot account for the apodictically evident, "superempirical," absolutely exact laws which make up the core of logic.

Laws of thought that are construed as causal laws could only be probable. Accordingly no assertion could be judged with certainty to be correct. The assertion that all knowledge is merely probable must then also be probable, and the same applies to this new assertion, and thus *in infinitum.* Since every step depresses the degree of probability of its predecessor, we must then be seriously concerned about the value of all knowledge. Husserl proposes to avoid such skeptical consequences by means of his view that the laws of thought are "evident."

The contention that the laws of thought are natural laws which, as such, cause our rational thought had never been proved. In the course of the controversy, the logical laws as "contents of judgment" had been confused with acts of judgment themselves. The latter are indeed real occurrences which have their causes and effects. By confusing a law with knowledge of the law, the ideal with the real, the law is made to appear as a determinative power in the course of our thought. A second confusion is then readily added, between a law as a causal element and a law as a rule of causation, as illustrated by the mythical talk about natural laws as powers of nature — as though the rules of causal connections could themselves function as causes. This is made clear by the following consideration. Suppose that we imagine an ideal being whose thought conforms entirely to the requirements of the logical laws. Such thinking must then be due to certain psychological laws which govern the course of the psychical experience of this being from certain first "collocations" on. Would these natural laws be identical with the logical laws in this case? Husserl's answer is in the negative: the causal laws to which thought must conform in order to satisfy the ideal norms of logic are not the same as the norms themselves. That a being is so constituted that it cannot assert contradictory judgments in any unified train of thought does not signify that the principle of contradiction is a natural law. The distinction is clearly illustrated by means of a calculating machine which is regulated according to the laws of arithmetic. No one would think of explaining the physical construction of the machine by means of arithmetical instead of mechanical laws. Analogously, the psychologistic logicians misunderstand the fundamental and essential differences between ideal and real laws, between normative and causal regulation, between logical and real necessity, between logical grounds and real grounds. In opposition to them it is maintained that there can be no conceivable gradations mediating between the ideal and the real.

There is still another result of the psychologistic doctrine that the source of the logical laws is to be found in psychological facts, which must be pointed out. If that were the case, they would have to have a psychological content; they would have to be laws of psychical facts as well as presuppose the existence of psychical facts. But no logical law implies a "matter of fact," or the existence of any cognitive phenomena. An analysis of the real meaning of logical laws shows that they are not laws of actual mental life. The psychologistic interpretation therefore does violence to the meaning of logical laws, which do not presuppose the facts of mental life, either in their content or in their establishment, any more than is the case in pure mathematics. The valid forms of inference refer generally to any terms or propositions, and do not involve the existence of any actual judgments or psychical phenomena.

Genuine laws, in the sense in which the term is here used, are a mere ideal in the domain of factual knowledge. The laws of the exact sciences referring to facts are genuine laws, but they are idealizing fictions, albeit fictions *cum fundamento in re*. The law of gravitation is truly founded only in the following form: according to our available knowledge it is a theoretically founded probability of the highest dignity that Newton's principle holds for the experience attainable by present means, or else one of the infinite manifold of mathematically conceivable laws which can only differ from Newton's law within the sphere of unavoidable errors of observation. "Absolute" knowledge is clearly not obtainable in empirical science; but it can be achieved in the domain of "purely conceptual" knowledge, which includes the laws of pure logic and of the *mathesis pura*. Their "origin," or more exactly, the proof that justifies them, is not obtained from induction, so that there is no element of probability. What they assert is founded with insight, and with absolute exactness. A pure law is not one of countless theoretical possibilities of a certain delimited sphere, as is the case with the law of gravitation. It is the one and only truth, which excludes all other possibilities.

As has been seen, such laws contain no existential assertions about mental facts. But neither can they be laws of those facts, for every law of matters of fact must be derived from experience and induction, which is not the case. Husserl speaks here of number-propositions as expressing generally valid relations on the basis of pure concepts. A pure number-proposition does not refer to things, but to numbers in pure generality, as in the case of "The number 3 is larger than the number 2"; and application can be made not merely to individual but also to "general" objects, e.g., to species of tone and color, to kinds of geometrical forms, and other non-temporal generalities. If these considerations are granted it is impossible to regard the pure logical laws as laws of mental acts or products.

To be sure, the knowledge of logical laws, as a mental activity, presupposes actual experience and has its basis in concrete intuition. But psychological "presuppositions" and "bases" of the *knowledge* of a logical law should not be confused with the logical presuppositions, grounds, or premises of the *law*. Our actual knowledge of the law is a psychologically conditioned event, whereas the logical proof is provided by insight into its objective nature. The intuitive apprehension of a law may require two steps psychologically, the consideration of the particulars of the intuition and the insight into the law relating to them. Logically there is only one thing there, however, for the content of the insight is not a conclusion from the particulars. All knowledge "begins with experience," but it does not therefore "arise" from experience. Every law of matters of fact arises from experience, and can be founded only by induction from particular experiences. It follows that laws which are known by insight cannot directly be laws of matters of fact.

A final argument is added in support of this thesis. If it is admitted that all pure logical laws are of the same type, and if it can be shown that it is impossible to conceive some of them as laws of matters of fact, then the same must hold for all of them. There are among them, however, laws which refer to truths in general, in which truths are the regulated "objects." Thus, e.g., the contradictory opposite of any truth *A* is not a truth. But, Husserl argues, it is absurd to regard laws which hold for truths as such to be laws of matters of fact. No truth is a matter of fact in the sense of being temporally determined. A truth may have the meaning that a thing exists, or that a change occurs, but the truth itself is above time, and it is meaningless to say that it arises or passes away. If that were the case, then the laws of coexistence and succession would, as truths, have to belong to the things that arise and pass away; the laws would change according to the laws, which is absurd. Such absurdities are unavoidable consequences of the failure to distinguish between the ideal and the real.

E. THE FUNDAMENTAL PRINCIPLES OF LOGIC

The attempts at the psychological interpretation of the fundamental principles of logic are of particular interest. Mill regarded the principle of contradiction as a generalization from experience, from the experience that such phenomena as light and dark, preceding and following, etc., exclude one another. But Mill did not show the connection between such empirical facts and the logical law. Not every pair of mutually exclusive propositions is contradictory. The impossibility that two contradictory propositions can be true together is interpreted by Mill as being the impossibility of believing them, in accordance with his view that acts of belief are the only objects that can be described as true and false. The defects of this point of view are readily exposed. Opposing judgments can exist not only in different individuals, but also in the same individual in a small duration of time; and opposites may even be held to be true at the same time. At the most, the method of establishing this principle inductively can only raise it to the rank of a plausible supposition, which is inadequate for purposes of science. When logicians assert that two contradictory propositions are not both true, they do not mean that under certain subjective conditions opposing acts of belief cannot coexist in the same consciousness. What they mean is the following normative principle: No matter which pair of contradictory acts of belief may be selected, whether in the same individual or in different individuals, whether at the same time or at different times, it is true with absolute rigor and without exception that both beliefs cannot be correct.

Because of the close relationship between empiricism and psychologism, Husserl pauses to point out the cardinal errors of empiricism. He hopes by the exposure of its main weaknesses to promote his idealistic aims in logic. Extreme empiricism proves to be no less absurd as a theory of knowledge than is skepticism. It makes impossible the rational justification of mediate knowledge, and therewith suspends its own possibility as a scientifically founded theory. If every proof is based upon principles according to which it proceeds, then either a circle or an infinite regress is incurred if the proof-principles themselves are to be proved. Circularity is incurred if the proof-principles that are used for the justification of the proof-principles are identical with the latter; and an infinite regress follows if they are always different. Husserl concludes that the requirement of a justification on principle of all mediate knowledge can only have a possible meaning if we are capable of immediate insight into certain final principles, upon which all proof ultimately is based. All basic principles of possible proofs must accordingly be reduced deductively to immediately evident principles, and the principles of this deduction itself must be included among these principles. Because complete reliance is placed only upon particular judgments by extreme empiricism, the possibility of justifying mediate knowledge rationally is abandoned.

Objections similar to those made to Mill's treatment of the laws of thought can be made with respect to every other psychological misinterpretation of them. Thus Heymans formulated the principle of contradiction as asserting that judgments which are at the same time known to be contradictory cannot exist together in one consciousness; and in Sigwart's version it is impossible consciously to affirm and to deny the same proposition. Husserl's criticism of the former interpretation is noteworthy. If it is to be kept free from all metaphysical hypostasis, such as the hypostasis of a "consciousness in general," then it merely turns out to be an equivalent statement of the logical principle and has nothing to do with psychology. The interpretation according to which it is impossible for a person to believe contradictory propositions mistakes the assertoric evidence of the existence of a single experience for the apodictic evidence of the existence of a general law. How can the feeling of impossibility be used to prove that we shall never be able to accept contradictories? The point is to obtain the evidence that the principle will hold universally and necessarily.

As Husserl sees it, the truth of the matter is that we do have the apodictic evidence or insight that contradictory propositions cannot be true, as well as that the opposing facts cannot coexist jointly. The law of this incompatibility is the genuine principle of contradiction. The apodictic evidence is then applied psychologically, so that we also have the insight that two judgments with contradictory contents cannot coexist in such a way that they both express what is really given in founding intuitions. We also have the more general insight that assertorically and apodictically evident judgments with contradictory contents can neither coexist in one consciousness nor occur in the consciousness of different knowers. What this means is that facts which are objectively incompatible because they are contradictory can never be found as actually coexisting in one's intuition and insight. But that does not preclude their being held to coexist. On the other hand we do not have apodictic evidence with regard to contradictory judgments in general. All that we have is the experiential knowledge that contradictory acts of judgment actually exclude one another in certain practically limited classes of cases.

Lange's attempt to provide the principle of contradiction with the double status of a natural law which governs actual judgment on the one hand, and of a standard which forms the foundation of all logical rules, also proves to be psychologistic in character. It is not shown to be a natural law. The "natural law of contradiction" reduces to a mere empirical generality, referring only to normal psychical individuals. The logical law, on the other hand, does not refer to real, temporal contradictory judgments; it expresses the incompatibility of non-temporal, ideal unities which are called contradictory propositions. The truth of that law does not contain the shadow of an empirical assertion about any consciousness and its acts of judgment.

Sigwart similarly regarded the principle of contradiction as a natural law which denies the possibility of saying consciously at the same time that "A is b and A is not b," as well as a law applying, as a standard, to the entire sphere of constant concepts. But the natural law deals with temporal things and the logical law, which is the genuine principle of contradiction, deals with the non-temporal, so that they are entirely different. They cannot be spoken of as one law if they are different in function and in their spheres of application. Furthermore, in order to show that they are one, it would be necessary to give a general formula which would apply both to the law about facts and to the law about ideal objects. The empirical application of the law presupposes that the concepts or propositions which function as the meanings of our expressions are really the same, as well as that the ideal extension of the law refers to all possible pairs of propositions with conflicting quality but identical matter. Just as it is a presupposition of the application of a law of numbers that determinate numbers are available, as designated by it, so it is a presupposition of the logical law that propositions with identical matter are before us. The consciousness in general that is depicted by Sigwart is not really helpful. All concepts and expressions would be used with an absolutely identical meaning in it, and there would be no changing meanings or equivocations. But in themselves the logical laws have no essential relation to this ideal, which was really formed for their sake. The appeal to an ideal consciousness suggests that the logical laws are strictly valid only for cases of ideal fictions, and not for empirically occurring particular cases. For the rest, as Husserl observed in connection with the views of the Kantian philosophers, transcendental psychology is also psychology.

The sense in which purely logical propositions "presuppose" identical concepts has been indicated. Concepts are "superempirical" unities; and their relationship to the conceptual ideas, whose "contents" they are, is like that of the identical species of color to the manifold of particular cases of color. The ability to apprehend ideationally the general in the particular, to discern a concept in an empirical idea, and to secure the identity of a conceptual intention in repeated experiences, is a presupposition of the possibility of knowledge. We can also obtain direct evidence of the logical laws which refer to the concepts, for the propositions of which the principle of contradiction speaks, e.g., and the meanings of the signs used in the propositions also belong to the order of "concepts" in the sense of ideal unities. Concepts occur whenever there is conceptual thinking, when the ideas have ideal meanings as their "contents," which can be treated in abstraction from thinking. The possibility of applying the logical laws is provided therewith. But the validity of these laws is unlimited, and does not depend upon the ability of anyone to apply them or to repeat them with the appropriate consciousness of sameness.

If the logical principles were psychological laws, then the syllogistic laws would also be psychological. The psychologistic explanation of the forms of inference faces the same difficulties, and incurs the same kind of fundamental confusion. It would seem that any fallacy would serve to refute this theory; but the contrary is the case, and the possibility of committing fallacies is regarded as a confirmation of the psychologistic view. The justification of the forms of inference must be provided on the basis of actual thought processes. The impossibility of thus establishing absolute generality has already been indicated. The best that psychologism can offer is the identification of insight into the laws of logic with an instinctive and supposedly immediate "sensation" of our psychological inability to execute contradictory acts of judgment at the same time. Evidence and blind conviction, exact and empirical generality, logical incompatibility of the facts and psychological incompatibility of the acts of belief, and hence the impossibility of joint truth and of joint belief are confounded by it.

Heymans' attempt to make plausible the doctrine that the formulae of inference are empirical laws of thought by comparing them with chemical formulae adds nothing but a new error to the argument. He appeals to an experience of an "unshakable necessity" which compels us to hold the conclusion to be true when the premises are given. But all conclusions, whether valid or invalid, are drawn with psychological necessity and the felt compulsion may be the same. That felt firmness is not a sign of real firmness is shown by the fact that it may even vary in cases of correct reasoning. It should not be confused with the genuine logical necessity that belongs to every correct inference and is known by insight. The fundamental fact for Husserl is that we have insight into the ideal nature of the law of inference, and also into the necessary validity of a special case of inference, on the basis of the law.

F. PSYCHOLOGISM AS SKEPTICAL RELATIVISM

The further consideration of the implications of psychologism shows that it leads to skeptical relativism.[6] Husserl argues that no charge could be more serious against a theory of logic than that it violates the conditions of the possibility of a theory as such, and psychologism is charged with violating both the subjective and the objective conditions of the possibility of a theory. A necessary subjective condition is provided by the evidence which distinguishes judgments from blind prejudices, and which gives

[6] Cf. John Wild, "Husserl's Critique of Psychologism: Its Historic Roots and Contemporary Relevance," in *Philosophical Essays in Memory of Edmund Husserl.*

one what Husserl calls the "luminous certainty" of having the truth. He declares that a theory which denies the precedence of evident to blind judgment removes the possibility of distinguishing it from an arbitrary, lawless assertion. The subjective conditions are not to be understood as real conditions which are rooted in the individual subject of judgment or in the changing species of judging beings, such as human beings. They are ideal conditions which are rooted in the form of subjectivity in general and in its relationship to knowledge. These are called *noetic* conditions, in order to distinguish them.

The objective conditions of the possibility of a theory do not concern the theory as a subjective unity of cognitions, but as an objective unity of truths or propositions, which are connected by the relation of ground and consequence. The objective conditions consist of all the laws which are based purely upon the concept of theory. The denial of these laws would be tantamount to depriving such terms as theory, truth, object, property, etc., of a consistent meaning. A theory suspends itself in this objective-logical respect if its content violates the laws without which a theory cannot have a "rational" consistent meaning.

The skepticism which follows from the thesis of psychologism is twofold in its reference, including noetic and logical skepticism. As Husserl understand the term, the very concept of a skeptical theory involves contradiction, or absurdity. The term "skepticism" is usually used somewhat vaguely. Thus a philosophical theory may be regarded as skeptical if it denies the possibility of ultimate metaphysical knowledge. But such views have nothing to do with the real epistemological skepticism which is here in question, and which involves noetic and logical contradiction.

For purposes of the criticism of psychologism it is necessary to examine the concept of subjectivism, or of relativism itself. The Protagorean dictum that man is the measure of all things expresses the standpoint of individual relativism, if by "man" an individual man is understood. Another type of relativism is obtained if one regards a *species* of judging being as the measure of truth, a point of view called "specific" relativism, or anthropologism when it is restricted to man as such. Individual relativism is at once refuted, but, Husserl points out, only for one who has insight into the objectivity of logic. The subjectivist cannot be convinced by pointing out that he presupposes the objectivity of truth in attempting to persuade others of his theory. It is sufficient for him that his theory expresses his own standpoint. But the point is to refute the subjectivist objectively and not to persuade him. The refutation depends upon the insight that the doctrine of skepticism is contradictory, because the content of its assertions denies what belongs to the meaning or content of every assertion.

Although it can be doubted that subjectivism has ever been seriously defended, "specific" relativism and anthropologism had so many adherents at the close of the nineteenth century that few thinkers could be said to be free from their errors. Husserl undertakes to show that they actually constitute a skeptical theory, involving the greatest absurdities that are conceivable for a theory. The criticism of this standpoint is formulated in six arguments.

(1) According to specific relativism, truth depends upon a species of judging beings, and may vary with different species. It follows that the same content of a judgment or proposition could be true for a member of the human species and false for a member of a differently constituted species. Husserl argues that the mere meaning of the words true and false rules this out, so that if the relativist uses these words in their proper sense, his thesis asserts something that violates its own meaning. He denies that the relativist may be merely talking about human truth and falsity, on the ground that an evident law cannot mean what is obviously contradictory, which is the case when one talks about different truths for different beings. The interpretation of the realm of truth as comprising all truths which are accessible or knowable to man as such, and as being the same for all types of being, is the counter-thesis to relativism.

(2) The contention that the relativist means something different by truth and falsity is considered in the second argument. The case against the relativist appears stronger when the principles of contradiction and of the excluded middle are introduced in connection with the meaning of truth. To hold that beings can exist who do not observe these principles means either that propositions could occur for them which do not accord with these principles, or that their actual judgments are not governed by them. The latter case is illustrated adequately by human thought, and is of psychological significance only. As for the former case, if all beings understood the words true and false in the sense that we do, it could not be said rationally that the principles do not apply, for they belong to the mere meaning of the words as we understand them. But if they mean something else, so that what we call "propositions" are "trees" for another type of being, the whole dispute becomes verbal. Thus relativism would involve changing the meaning of the word truth, while still claiming to speak of truth in the sense in which it is determined by the fundamental principles of logic.

(3) The constitution of a given species is a matter of fact, and hence

the truth that is based upon it must be factual, which is absurd. A matter of fact is individual and is determined temporally. One can, however, speak of the temporal reference of truth only with regard to a matter of fact that is posited by it, i.e., in case it is a factual truth, and not with regard to the truth itself. Truths cannot be thought of as causes and effects. That would be to confuse the ideal and the real, once more. The content of a judgment is an ideal unity, and should not be confused with an individual real act of judgment (the subsequent investigations bear this out amply). My judging that $2 \times 2 = 4$ is causally determined, but not the truth "$2 \times 2 = 4$." The content of the judgment "$2 \times 2 = 4$" is the same whenever it is asserted. Neither should a true judgment, in the sense of a correct act of judgment, be confused with the truth of the judgment or with the true content of the judgment.

(4) If the source of all truth is to be found in the general nature of man, as is maintained by anthropologism, then it follows that if there were no human beings there would also be no truth. The absurdity of this supposition is shown when one considers that the proposition "There is no truth" is equivalent to the proposition "It is true that there is no truth." If the thesis of anthropologism were factual in character, it could be false but not contradictory. A "logically impossible" or contradictory consequence is drawn from the "logically possible" or harmonious assumption of the eventual non-existence of man.

(5) According to relativism it might be "true" upon the basis of the constitution of a species that such a constitution does not exist at all, which is clearly contradictory. Does it not exist in reality, or is it only non-existent for us as human beings? The absurdity is not diminished greatly if one considers the human species instead of an imaginary species, which was possible in the relativistic view. By the relativity of truth is meant the dependence of what is called truth upon the constitution of the human species and the laws governing it. But this dependence can only be understood as causal. Therefore the truth that this constitution and these laws exist would have to derive its real explanation from the fact that they exist, whereby the principles according to which the explanation proceeded would be identical with just these laws, which is nothing but nonsense. The constitution would be *causa sui* on the basis of laws, which on the basis of themselves would cause themselves, etc.

(6) The relativity of truth involves the relativity of the existence of the world, for the world corresponds to the ideal system of all factual truths. The object of truth exists only if the truth exists, and hence it cannot exist independently if truth is made subjective. There would then be no

world in itself, but only a world for this or that accidental species of being, and there would be no world if none of the species of judging beings were so fortunately constituted as to have to acknowledge a world, and itself as well. Furthermore, the circumstance that a change in the constitution of an animal species must bring about a change of the world is strange when one considers that the animal species are supposed to be evolutionary products of the world. Thus there results a fine game: man is developed from the world, and the world from man.

The two forms of relativism are viewed by Husserl as special cases of relativism in the broad sense of the term; and the latter is defined as a doctrine which attempts to derive purely logical principles from matters of fact. It would follow that for different matters of fact there would be different laws. In opposition to that view Husserl relies upon the apodictic evidence of the logical laws, but he also makes a more significant point. By pure logical laws he understands all the ideal laws which are based solely upon the meaning of the concepts truth, proposition, object, property, relation, connection, law, matter of fact, etc. No theoretical assertion or theory may violate laws of this kind because they would not only be false but absurd. An assertion whose content conflicts with principles which are grounded in the meaning of truth as such "suspends itself."

The refutation of psychologism was really the goal in the critical analysis of relativism, for it is nothing other than relativism, even if that is not always recognized or admitted. It makes no difference whether it assumes the form of a formal idealism that is based upon "transcendental psychology" and claims to save the objectivity of knowledge, or whether it is based upon empirical psychology and accepts relativism as an unavoidable consequence. The reduction of the pure laws of logic to "primitive forms" or "functions" of the understanding, to "consciousness in general" as "generic reason" and the like is relativistic. Such terms as understanding, reason, and consciousness must be understood in their natural sense, as connected with the human species. It is the curse of the *a priori* theories that they do not use these terms consistently, but change from their real meaning to an ideal meaning, with the result that correct and incorrect propositions are confused. Those Kantians who allow for a few fundamental logical principles as principles of "analytic judgments" merely restrict the range of their relativism, but do not avoid its consequences. But of greater interest to Husserl here is the more extreme form of psychologism, as represented by Mill, Bain, Wundt, Sigwart, Erdmann, and Lipps. In particular, he examines Sigwart's anthropologism very carefully because of its great influence in promoting the movement of psychologism, and also the anthropologism in Erdmann's logic.

The fundamental conception of Sigwart's *Logic* is psychologistic. Pure logical principles are called functional laws or fundamental forms of the movement of our thought; and a judgment cannot be true without its being thought by some mind, so that the judgment expressing the formula of gravitation could not have been true before Newton. In Husserl's view, as has been seen, truth is "eternal"; it is an "Idea" and as such is supertemporal. We do indeed say of truth that it "comes to consciousness" and that it is "experienced" by us. But we do not "grasp" truth like an empirical content. Comparing truth, as an Idea, to redness, Husserl tells how it is experienced and thus explains what he means by "insight." It is experienced in an act of ideation that is founded upon intuition, i.e., an act of insight. It does not depend upon the existence of intelligent beings who have insight into it, and merely implies the possibility of such beings. If none should happen to exist, or if there are no beings capable of knowing certain classes of truths, they then remain ideal possibilities without fulfillment in reality. They nevertheless remain what they are, retaining their ideal meanings as valid unities in the non-temporal realm of Ideas. Husserl includes in that realm everything into whose validity we have insight or at least a founded supposition. It is the validity or truth that is unchangeable, and not the "certainty of a judgment" that is unchangeable, as maintained by Sigwart. If truth had an essential relationship to thinking beings, it would arise and pass away with them, with the species if not with the individual. Truth and being are both "categories" in the same sense, and they are correlative. Hence one cannot relativize truth while maintaining the objectivity of being. In presupposing an objective being as a point of reference, the relativist contradicts himself.

The question of the status of universals is also raised. Sigwart's view that universals as such exist only in our heads, or that concepts are purely internal and depend upon the inner power of our thought, applies to conceptual experience as a subjective act, with its particular psychological content. The concept as the "what" of such an act, however, cannot be regarded as an immanent part of the psychological content. It is not a "here and now" which comes and goes with the act. It can be meant but not created in thought.

The distinction between logical necessity and subjective necessity, which is the feeling of conviction attached to every judgment, is ignored by Sigwart. Apodictic necessity is defined as consisting of the peculiar consciousness in which the evident apprehension of a law or of something lawful is constituted. Husserl speaks of the fundamental equivocation which leads us to designate as necessary not only the apodictic *consciousness* of necessity, but its objective correlate, the law or the validity in accordance with the law. Thus the expressions "It is a necessity" and "It is a law" first obtain their objective equivalence. The same is true of the expressions "It is necessary that S is p" and "It is established according to laws that S is p." It is this purely objective and ideal concept which is basic to all apodictic judgments in the objective sense of pure logic; it constitutes all theoretical unity, and determines the conclusion as a "necessary" consequence of the premises.

Husserl sees in Leibniz's distinction between truths of reason and truths of fact an expression of the fundamental distinction which he wishes to point out. Leibniz's truths of reason are nothing other than laws in the sense of ideal truths based purely upon concepts; and his truths of fact are individual truths which involve existence. Corresponding to the fundamental objective-ideal difference between law and fact is a subjective difference in the mode of the experience. Husserl reasons that if we had never experienced the consciousness of rationality as characteristically different from that of factuality, we would not have the concept of a law, and could not distinguish it from a fact. Laws as ideal truths are known by us in an apodictically evident manner, as distinguished from the knowledge of matters of fact.

Erdmann's defense of relativism has the merit of showing clearly the consequences that follow from its conception of logical laws. It enables Husserl to contrast his own position more sharply and to deepen the understanding of his steadily growing conception of "logical absolutism." Erdmann had argued that the impossibility of denying the fundamental logical principles is due to the fact that these principles express the essence of our presentation and thought. Husserl points out that the denial of these laws contradicts their assertion, but that the denial as a real act can very well be compatible with the objective validity of the laws. Erdmann construes the impossibility of denying these laws as the impossibility of making the denial. Husserl, as a logical absolutist, as he refers to himself,[7] affirms the impossibility of their denial while rejecting the impossibility of making the denial. The ideal impossibility of the negative proposition does not conflict with the real possibility of the negative act of judgment. The laws express truths which are grounded in the mere meaning or content of certain concepts, such as truth, falsity, proposition, and the like. According to Erdmann they are "laws of thought" which express the

[7] Cf. *Log. Unt.*, vol. I, p. 141.

essence of our human thought and would therefore change along with human nature. But principles that merely formulate what is inherent in concepts make no statement about realities. It is accordingly misleading to designate the logical laws as laws of thought. They may be used as norms of thought as a practical matter, but that use is foreign to their content. The fundamental principles of logic are really trivial generalities which may not be denied by an assertion because that would be contradictory. On the other hand the agreement of thought with these norms merely shows that the thought is in itself formally harmonious. Husserl regards it as a rationalistic prejudice to speak of formal truth instead of formal harmony, holding it to be a highly objectionable use of the term truth. The two or three "laws of thought" in the traditional sense could not be sufficient for formally harmonious thought. Every case of formal absurdity can be reduced to a contradiction; but a number of other basic principles are needed, as seen in the case of syllogistic reasoning alone. The attempts to demonstrate them are only apparent proofs which either presuppose themselves or equivalent principles.

The laws of logic are said to be "eternal" in the sense that they are ideal norms for all judgments, regardless of time and circumstances. That they refer to psychical beings is no limitation because norms for judgments are binding on judging beings and not on stones. The proof of the logical absolutist is very simple. What he does is to appeal to his own insight. The fundamental principles are valid because they only develop what is grounded in the content of their concepts. Consequently every proposition, i.e., every possible content of judgment in an ideal sense, is absurd if it negates the fundamental laws or violates them indirectly. If such contents of judgment are absurd and false, then all actual judgments whose contents they are must be incorrect. A judgment is correct only when "that which it judges," i.e., its content, is true. The starting-point of the proof is my own insight. I cannot compel anyone to have the insight which I have. But I myself cannot doubt that I again have the insight that every doubt would be wrong when I have insight, i.e., grasp the truth itself. This is in Husserl's view the Archimedean point for reason and knowledge.

The difference between the ideal and the real is made more clear by the consideration of the question of whether laws may be variable. Husserl concedes that a mental life essentially different from our own may possibly exist. We have no choice but to take our thought as it is, so that it would be foolish to attempt to deduce its unchangeableness from the essence of our minds. It does not follow, however, that such changes in our specific constitution would affect the principles of logic, thus rendering them hypothetical in character. That would be absurd in the scientific sense in which the term is here used. The possibility of variable "laws of thought" in the sense of psychological laws of presentation and judgment is another matter and may be admitted; and the same holds for the normative laws of presentation and judgment which concern the rules and methods of practical logic. But it is absurd to speak of the possibility of variable laws of thought in the sense of the laws of pure logic, or of variable laws in the theory of numbers, or of set theory, etc. The vague expression "normative laws of thought" is apt to mislead one into confusing them with the psychologically founded rules of thought. Because of their very nature, the purely theoretical and ideal truths could not be affected by any real or imagined change in the world of matters of fact.

A threefold set of distinctions must be observed here. In addition to the distinction between a practical rule and a theoretical law, and between an ideal law and a real law, there is also the distinction between an exact and an "empirical" law. If we had insight into the exact laws of psychical occurrences, they would also be eternal and unchangeable, and they would hold even if there were no psychical occurrences. As soon as one has insight into the exact nature of logical laws, the possibility of their change through changes in the collocations of factual beings is precluded, and their "eternal" validity is guaranteed. No psychical occurrence can ever make the red that I see to be a tone instead of a color, or make the lower of two tones to be the higher, because everything that is inherent in the general nature of an experience is above any possible change. Change concerns the individual detail, and is simply meaningless with regard to the conceptual. The same applies to the "contents" of the acts of knowledge. Truth is implied by the very concept of knowledge. The character of truth belongs to the identical content of knowledge, and not to passing phenomena. It belongs to the ideal content that we have in view when we, and countless others, know that $a + b = b + a$. When errors occur, as in fallacies, the cognition has not become an error. The various elements have merely been arranged causally in such a way that an erroneous process is incurred. It could even happen that a certain species of beings capable of judgment were such that everything that it held to be true were false, and all that it held to be false were true. But truth and falsity would remain unchanged in themselves nevertheless.

G. THE PSYCHOLOGISTIC PREJUDICES

Up to this point in the discussion the consequences of psychologism have been considered primarily. In turning to the arguments themselves, Husserl now attempts to show that they are based upon deceptive prejudices, or prejudgments. According to the first prejudice it is self-evident that the directions for the regulation of psychical activities are founded psychologically, so that the normative laws of knowledge must be based upon the psychology of knowledge. Husserl points out that the logical laws in themselves are not normative propositions whose content states how judgments should be made. Laws which serve as norms for cognitive activities must be distinguished from rules which contain the thought of this normative process itself and state that it is binding generally. The syllogistic principle "All *A* are *B* and *S* is an *A,* therefore it is a *B*" is not normative. That it can be used as a norm does not make it to be a norm. In its normative form it becomes "All who judge that every *A* is also *B* and that a certain *S* is *A,* should judge that this *S* is also *B*." Every general theoretical truth can similarly serve as the basis of a general norm for correct judgment, so that this is not a distinguishing characteristic of logic. On the other hand the laws of logic do have a certain precedence in the matter of the regulation of thought. That does not mean, however, that the idea of regulation must lie in the content of the logical principles themselves. The antipsychologistic logicians had erred in regarding the regulation of knowledge as the essence of logical laws, thus failing to do justice to the purely theoretical character of formal logic in its relationship to formal mathematics. In Husserl's usage "pure" or "formal" mathematics comprises pure arithmetic and set theory, but not geometry. The theory of the Euclidean manifold of three dimensions corresponds to the latter in pure mathematics. The error of the psychologistic logicians is readily exposed by pointing out that every general truth, whether psychological or not, establishes a rule of correct judgment. This guarantees the existence of rules of judgment which are not based upon psychology.

The investigation of the concepts which determine the idea of systematic or theoretical unity, and of the theoretical connections which are based upon those concepts, belongs to the autonomous science of pure logic. Logic has the peculiarity of being subject to the content of its own laws. The elements and theoretical connections of which it consists, as a systematic unity of truths, are subject to the laws which belong to its theoretical content. The science that refers to all sciences with respect to their form *eo ipso* refers to itself. Thus the principle of contradiction regulates all truth, and since it is also a truth, it regulates itself. This is a "self-evidence" into which we have insight, in Husserl's view. The same applies to the regulation of pure logic with reference to itself. The present analysis attempts to establish pure logic as the first and most essential foundation of methodological logic. To be sure, the latter also has other foundations, provided by psychology. Every science can be considered from two points of view. It is a totality of human methods for the attainment and systematic presentation of knowledge on the one hand; and so its devices, instruments, etc., must be adapted to the human constitution. On the other hand, every science can be considered with respect to its theoretical content. The objective content of science, as objective truth, is independent of the subjectivity of the investigator and of the peculiarities of human nature in general. It is this ideal side of science with which pure logic deals, with respect to its form, and not its particular subject-matter. In keeping with the double aspect of science, there are two classes of norms: those that are purely ideal, although capable of application to human science; and those that are empirical in character. The latter group comprises aids for proofs, and refers to the specifically human side of the sciences. Such norms are based upon the psychical and even the physical constitution of man.[8]

Husserl accordingly takes a middle position in the controversy regarding the psychological or the objective grounding of logic. The antipsychologistic logicians consider chiefly the ideal laws of pure logic, whereas the psychologistic logicians are interested in the methodological rules, which are anthropological in character. The former group, represented by Drobisch, e.g., is wrong in holding that psychology deals with natural laws, in contrast to the normative laws of logic. The opposite of a natural law as an empirical rule of factual being is not a normative law as a prescription, but an ideal law in the sense of being based solely upon concepts. The psychologistic logicians on their side misconstrue the ideality of truth, just as they misunderstand the essence of the ideal in general.

In order to support his first prejudice, that rules of knowledge must be based upon the psychology of knowledge, the psychologistic logician refers to the actual content of logic, and reveals a second prejudice therewith. Ideas, judgments, inferences, truth, probability, necessity, and possibility are titles which indicate its subject-matter, and they are held to refer to psychical phenomena and structures. It would follow that pure mathematics also is a branch of psychology. Husserl states that the mathe-

---

[8] Husserl refers in this connection to his *Philosophy of Arithmetic* for the discussion of the influence of physical conditions upon the formation of methods.

matician would merely smile if one were to suggest that he engage in psychological studies for a better foundation of his theoretical constructions. He would say with right that the mathematical and the psychological are such foreign worlds that even the thought of mediating between them would be absurd. The pure mathematical theories are not branches of psychology, even though we would not have any numbers without counting, or any products without multiplication, etc. Despite the "psychological origin" of the concepts of arithmetic it would be a fallacious metabasis to hold that the mathematical laws are pyschological. For psychology, counting and the operations of arithmetic are temporal facts. It is entirely different with arithmetic, which deals with the non-temporal series of ideal species 1, 2, 3, . . . , and not with individual facts. The number five is a possible object of acts of presentation, but is not something real. The propositions of arithmetic and algebra do not assert anything about real things. A number as an ideal form-species is grasped directly. In the present context, the "abstraction" which is performed upon a collection is taken to mean "grasping of the idea," e.g., the number five as a species of form.

The same is true of pure logic. It can be admitted as an obvious fact that the logical concepts have a psychological origin. The methodology of scientific investigation and proof also requires the consideration of the nature of the psychical occurrences involved. Such logical terms as idea, concept, judgment, inference, proof, theory, necessity, truth, etc., thus can appear as class names for psychical experiences and structures. But the independent theoretical discipline of pure logic has nothing to do with psychical facts and laws. The concepts out of which its laws are constructed cannot have an empirical extension. They are genuine general concepts, whose extension is entirely ideal in character. The fact that the various terms in question are equivocal contributes to the general misunderstanding. Thus the term "judgment" is equivocal, meaning a certain kind of conscious experience in the psychological part of the art of logic, and "proposition" or an ideal unity of meaning in the pure logical part. Whoever asserts the principle of contradiction expresses a judgment; but neither the principle nor that about which one judges in this case are judgments. Judgment-contents or ideal meanings, which are called propositions, are alone in question in the context of logic proper.

The distinctions upon which the judgment of the psychologistic argument turns can be summarized briefly. There is, first, an essential difference between ideal and real sciences. In the second place, there is the fundamental difference between the order of cognitive experience, the order of things investigated and known theoretically in science, and the logical order of theoretical ideas. This holds for all science, the investigated things in logic and arithmetic being ideal species, and not real matters of fact as in physics. As has been noted, logic also has the peculiarity that the ideal connections which make up its theoretical unity are special cases of the laws which it itself sets up. The logical laws are at the same time parts and rules of these connections.

The third prejudice of psychologism relates to the locus of truth and the nature of evidence. The locus of truth is believed to be in judgment, and evidence is taken to mean a peculiar feeling which somehow guarantees the truth of the judgment to which it is connected. If logic deals with truth, then the laws of logic must be principles of psychology; they are principles which explain the conditions upon which the existence or lack of that "feeling of evidence" depends. Mill, Wundt, Höfler, and Meinong are cited as representatives of the tendency to interpret logic in this way.

Husserl does not concede that truth resides in judgment, although he holds that the knowledge and legitimate assertion of truth presupposes having insight into truth. He denies that pure logical propositions state anything at all about evidence and its conditions. Their relation to experiences of evidence is only possible by way of application. The evidential propositions arising thus retain their *a priori* character, and the conditions of evidence which they express are not psychological or real conditions. The pure conceptual propositions are transformed into statements about ideal incompatibilities or possibilities. The combined principle of contradiction and of the excluded middle illustrates how a pure logical law can be transformed into an evidential principle. It reads: Only one of a pair of contradictory judgments can be evident. The same procedure can be applied to all logical principles. The propositions "A is true" and "It is possible that some one will judge with evidence, that it is A" are equivalent. These evidential possibilities are ideal, and not real in the sense of psychological possibility. Although there are in actuality no numbers without counting, there are, in an ideal sense, numbers with a trillion places, and there are truths about them. No one can actually present such numbers or carry out operations with them. The evidence is here psychologically impossible, and yet it is, in an ideal sense, a possible psychical experience.

The turning of the concept of truth into that of the possibility of evident judgment is analogous to the relationship between the concepts of individual being and perceptual possibility. The equivalence of these concepts, in so far as perception is understood to be adequate perception, is held to be indisputable by Husserl. A perception is accordingly "possible" which apprehends the entire infinite world in one view. This possibility is ideal and not real, and could not be attained by any empirical subject.

Evidence is defined by Husserl as the experience in which a judger becomes aware of the correctness of his judgment, i.e., its conformity to the truth. The way in which formal laws are to be made useful psychologically is indicated by the statement that no empirical reckoning or geometrical construction is possible which would contradict the ideal laws of mathematics. It is possible at all times to derive from them possibilities and impossibilities which relate to certain kinds of psychical acts, such as counting, adding, etc. But that does not make them to be psychological laws. It is the task of psychology to examine the natural conditions in which evidence arises and disappears according to the testimony of our experience. Such natural conditions are concentration of interest, mental freshness,. practice, etc. The evidence of judgment is not only subject to such psychological conditions, but is subject to ideal conditions as well. Every truth is an ideal unity of an endless manifold of correct statements of the same form and matter. Every actual judgment belonging to this ideal manifold fulfills, either by its form or by its matter, the ideal conditions of the possibility of its evidence. The laws of pure logic are truths that are based upon the concept of truth and essentially related concepts, and they too are conditions of possible evidence. In application to possible acts of judgment they express ideal conditions of possibility or impossibility. In Husserl's view these conditions hold for every possible consciousness and are not limited by the particular constitution of psychical beings, as is the case with psychological conditions.

The clear understanding of the important epistemological distinction between the real and the ideal is again of deciding importance. It is necessary to understand what the ideal is in itself and in its relationship to the real, and how the ideal can be inherent in the real and thus be known. The basic question is whether ideal objects of thought are merely indications for "thought-economical," abbreviated modes of speech the content of which reduces to individual experiences, or whether the idealist is right in maintaining that every attempt to reduce these ideal unities to real particulars is absurd and unthinkable. The relationship between truth and evidence is misunderstood by empiricism, just as is the relationship between the ideal and the real in thought. Evidence is not an accessory feeling that is attached to certain judgments accidentally or according to natural law; it is not a psychical character at all. It is nothing other than the "experience" of truth.[9] Truth is experienced in the sense in which something ideal can be in a real act of experience; i.e., truth is an idea whose particular case is an actual experience in an evident judgment. An evident judgment is defined as a consciousness of "originary" givenness.[10] It is related to a non-evident judgment just as an adequate perception of an object is related to any presentation of it. That which is adequately perceived is given originarily in the act, just as it is meant; it is apprehended without residue. Similarly that which is judged evidently is not merely judged, but is given as present itself in the judgment-experience. Just as in the realm of perception not-seeing does not coincide with not-being, so a lack of evidence does not mean the same as untruth. Evidence is the experience of the agreement between the meaning and that which is present itself, which is meant by it; between the actual meaning of the statement and the self-given fact; and the idea of this agreement is truth. It is the ideality of truth that makes up its objectivity. According to this view, to assert a judgment *J* with insight, and to have the insight that the truth *J* exists, amount to the same thing. We also have the insight that no one's insight can conflict with our own, in so far as each of them is really insight. That merely means that what is experienced as true is simply true, and cannot be false. This follows from the essential connection between truth and the experience of truth. In this way Husserl attempts to avoid the skeptical difficulty that besets the conception of evidence as a feeling, the question, namely, whether the insights of different people could conflict with one another. As he has defined the terms "insight," "evidence," and "truth," the question is readily answered, for just as it is self-evident that where nothing is, nothing is to be seen, so it is not less self-evident that where there is no truth, there can be no evidence.

H. LOGIC AND THE PRINCIPLE OF THOUGHT-ECONOMY

The biological foundation of logic and the theory of knowledge by means of the principle of least force, as Avenarius called it, or by the principle of the economy of thought, as Mach called it, is closely related

[9] Evidence is also described in a later passage as the character of knowledge as such (*Log. Unt.*, vol. 1, p. 238 n.).

[10] The term "originär" is not used in the first edition of the *Log. Unt.* (cp. vol. 1, p. 190). For a later explanation of "originary" givenness, cf. *Ideas* (Gibson trans.), p. 51. To have something real originarily given is the same as to "become aware" of it and "perceive" it in simple intuition. In "outer perception" we have originary experience of physical things, but not in memory or in anticipatory expectation; and in inner perception we have originary experience of ourselves and our states of consciousness, but not of others and their experiences through "empathy." See also pp. 392 ff., where originary evidence is spoken of as immediate evidence more narrowly restricted.

to psychologism. When restricted appropriately, the thought-economical theories are regarded by Husserl as containing justifiable and very fruitful ideas, while maintaining that in their general form they would spell the ruin of all genuine logic and theory of knowledge, as well as of psychology. He first points out the nature of the Avenarius-Mach principle as a teleological principle of adaptation and considers its value for psychical anthropology and for the practical theory of science, after which he shows its unfitness to contribute toward the foundation of psychology, pure logic, and theory of knowledge.

The principle of thought-economy was formulated by Avenarius as stating that the change which the mind imparts to its ideas with the occurrence of new impressions is as small as possible. Instead of using the term "principle," Mach preferred to speak of the "economical nature" of scientific investigation, and of the "thought-economical function" of concepts, formulae, theories, and methods. Although this principle represents a valuable teleological point of view in the biological sciences, it is not a principle in the sense of rational theory. Its relationship to self-preservation and preservation of the species is obvious. The possibility of proving *a priori* that certain procedures are thought-economical, and of then showing that they are realized in our methods of thought, indicates an extensive sphere of instructive investigations. The thought-economical point of view is also able to illuminate the anthropological grounds of the various methods of investigation. By means of symbolic processes which take the place of intuition and actual evidence, the imperfections of our mental constitution can be overcome. Husserl's elaboration of this point is reminiscent of the *Philosophy of Arithmetic*. The idea of thought-economy plays an important part in logic in the practical sense of an art of scientific knowledge. Thoroughgoing analyses of symbolic methods and processes are needed for the theory of science, analyses which show the economical function of signs and of the various energy-saving mechanisms.

A certain adaptation to external nature is necessary for self-preservation. It requires the capacity to judge things correctly, to predict the course of events, and to estimate causal sequences correctly. But it is not possible to judge and infer correctly without insight, which science alone can provide generally. Even though some procedures, such as the decadic number system, developed naturally in response to the practical needs of the prescientific life, one must ask how they are possible, and how mechanical operations can coincide with that which is required by insight.

Although Mach's historical-methodological studies are instructive for logic, he did not consider the most fruitful problems of deductive thought-economy. That was due to the epistemological misunderstandings at the basis of his investigations. In common with Avenarius, his doctrine pertains to certain biological facts, and is therefore a branch of the theory of evolution. Such investigations throw light upon the methodology of scientific research, but not upon the pure theory of knowledge, and particularly the ideal laws of pure logic. The attempt to construct a thought-economical theory of knowledge meets with the entire arsenal of objections which have been directed against psychologism and relativism. It really reduces to the psychological foundation of the theory of knowledge. Husserl observes that a psychological or epistemological law that speaks of an endeavor to accomplish as much as possible is a nonentity. There is no "as much as possible" in the sphere of matters of fact, and there is no effort in the sphere of law. In a psychological respect something determinate occurs in every case, precisely so much and no more.

The question is not how experience, whether naive or scientific, arises, but what content it must have in order to be objectively valid experience. Husserl is interested in the ideal elements and laws which found the objective validity of real knowledge and of knowledge in general. He is interested, not in the becoming and change of the idea of the world, but in the objective right with which the world-idea of science is opposed to every other one, and with which it asserts its world to be the objectively true one. Psychology aims to explain with evidence how the world-ideas are formed. World-science, as the totality of the various real sciences, seeks to know with evidence what the true and actual world really is. The theory of knowledge, however, wants to understand with evidence what makes up the possibility of evident knowledge of the real, and the possibility of science and knowledge in general in an objective-ideal sense.

The aim to determine the most general laws is the goal of the rational sciences. In Husserl's view the principle involved is purely ideal, and not biological or merely thought-economical, and it is only secondarily a normative principle. He contends, furthermore, that it cannot be reduced to or transformed into the facts of the psychical life and of the social life of humanity in any way. To identify the tendency toward the greatest possible rationality with a biological tendency toward adaptation, or to derive it therefrom, and then to assign to it the function of a basic psychical force, are stigmatized as errors which are analogous to the psychologistic misinterpretations of the logical laws. It is incorrect to hold that our psychical life is actually governed by this principle. Our factual thinking does not proceed according to ideals, for ideals are not like natural forces. The ideal tendency of logical thought as such involves rationality. The thought-economist makes it to be a real tendency of human thought, and establishes it by means of the vague principle of the economy of force, and finally by the concept of adaptation. Thus he believes he has explained the norm that we *should* think rationally, as well as the objective value and meaning of science. Husserl argues that the principles of the thought-economists derive their justification only through the comparison of actual thought with the ideal norm that is known through insight. The ideal validity of the norm is therefore the presupposition of all meaningful talk about thought-economy. We can speak of a natural teleology of our mental organization, because our presentation and judgment in the main proceed as though they were logically regulated. But we must know the ideal before all thought-economy; we must know the ideal goal and structure of science before we can estimate the thought-economical function of its knowledge. In this sense, pure logic "precedes" and therefore cannot be based upon thought-economy. Husserl holds it to be an error to level out the difference between logical and natural thought, and to regard scientific activity as a mere "continuation" of natural and blind activity. A logical theory is essentially different from a "natural" theory. It has a goal, whereas we must introduce a goal into a "natural theory." A logical theory is a theory by virtue of the ideal connection of necessity which is inherent in it, whereas a natural theory is a process of accidental ideas or convictions, with average utility for practical purposes.

Because of their biological interest in the empirical aspect of science, the thought-economists failed to see that they had not touched the epistemological problem of science as an ideal unity of objective truth. Their growing prominence made all the more necessary the thoroughgoing analysis of the opposing views in the spheres of the real and the ideal, in order to aid in preparing the way for a final foundation of philosophy.

CHAPTER V

PURE LOGIC

A. HUSSERL'S HISTORICAL ANTECEDENTS

I N CONCLUDING the critical portion of the *Prolegomena*, Husserl maintains that he has shown the untenability of every kind of empirical or psychologistic logic, and that logic in the sense of a scientific methodology has its most important foundations outside psychology. The general discussion has been led by the thesis that "pure (formal) logic," as a theoretical science that is independent of all that is empirical and hence of psychology, first makes possible an art of scientific knowing, or logic in the usual theoretical-practical sense. Husserl speaks of his discussion as "idealistic criticism." The widespread view which Elsenhans expressed, when he attributed the growing success of logic to its use of psychological analysis, would have been endorsed by Husserl before the present investigations had been made; for he was not aware then of the insoluble difficulties in which the psychologistic conception in the philosophy of mathematics had involved him. The renunciation of this erroneous point of view did not imply hostility to psychology itself. Husserl makes it clear that he continued to take pleasure in the otherwise promising development of scientific psychology, even though he did not expect any genuine philosophical clarification from it. He hastens to add, however, in order to avoid misunderstanding, that empirical psychology is to be distinguished sharply from phenomenology; phenomenology "founds" empirical psychology, and is described as a pure doctrine of the essence of the experiences.

The most important historical antecedents of the theory of pure logic are Kant, Herbart, Lotze, Leibniz, and Bolzano. While agreeing in the main with Kant's distinction between pure and applied logic, Husserl rejects the confusing, mythical concepts of the understanding and reason, in the sense of mental faculties. In his view, understanding or reason as faculties of a certain normal attitude of thought presuppose pure logic, which defines the normal. Hence we would be no better off than were we in an analogous case to explain the art of dancing by the faculty of dancing, the art of painting by the faculty of painting, etc. Husserl takes the terms understanding and reason as mere indications of the direction to the "form of thought" and its ideal laws, which logic has to take in contrast to the empirical psychology of knowledge. Although the main tendency of Kant's logic appears to him to be sound, he points out that Kant did not clearly see the nature of the intended discipline.

Herbart is closer to the present view than Kant, chiefly because of his sharper distinction between pure logic and psychology, by means of his doctrine of the objectivity of the "concept," i.e., of presentation in the purely logical sense. Concepts were regarded by Herbart as non-temporal; and his emphasis upon the ideality of the concept was a great merit. But he did not discern the ambiguity of such expressions as "content," "that which is presented," and "that which is thought." These terms may denote the ideal, identical meaning-content, and, again, the object which happens to be presented. Neither did he clarify the nature of concepts. In Husserl's view a concept or presentation in the logical sense is simply the identical meaning of the corresponding expressions. Herbart also failed to recognize the seemingly deep problem of the harmony between the subjective process of logical thought and external reality for what it is, namely, as a pseudo-problem that has arisen out of unclearness. Husserl also expresses indebtedness to Lotze, who belongs to Herbart's sphere of influence, even though Lotze's great logical work proves to be an inharmonious cross between psychologistic and pure logic.

The relationship to Leibniz is closest of all. His position is fundamentally that of the pure logic defended by Husserl. In Leibniz's view the essential bases of a fruitful art of knowledge do not lie in psychology, but are entirely *a priori*. They constitute a discipline with a mathematical form, which as such includes the function of regulating knowledge practically, just as is the case with arithmetic. Bolzano is also lauded for his logical achievements. The *Wissenschaftslehre* is described as a work which surpasses all that the world-literature offers on the systematic treatment of the elements of logic. Although Bolzano did not explicitly define a pure logic in the present sense, he had done so *de facto* in the two first volumes of his work. Husserl's warm tribute to Bolzano leaves no doubt as to his indebtedness to that logician, while at the same time indicating his epistemological shortcomings.[1]

These historical references serve to connect the theory of pure logic with an illustrious and imposing past, and to show more clearly the nature of Husserl's point of departure and his specific contributions. Having defined his point of view negatively, with respect to the empirical logical theories,

[1] See § C, 2, this chapter, and ch. vii, B, 7 for Husserl's discussion and later judgment of Bolzano and Lotze.

and positively with respect to his own sources, he recognizes that his problem must now be the construction of logic upon a broad basis. By means of detailed investigations he proposes to remove the prejudice that pure logic is concerned with an unimportant domain of trivial propositions, and to show that its domain is very considerable, not only with respect to its content in systematic theories, but above all with respect to the difficult and important investigations which are required for its philosophical foundation. The present study has shown that a correct understanding of the essence of pure logic and its relationship to all other sciences is one of the most important questions of the theory of knowledge. It follows that it is of vital importance to that fundamental philosophical science that pure logic be really presented in its purity and autonomy. The theory of knowledge must not be understood to be a discipline that follows metaphysics, or coincides with it, but rather which precedes it, just as it precedes psychology and all other disciplines.

B. THE IDEA OF A PURE (FORMAL) LOGIC

The *Prolegomena* is concluded by a systematic account of the logical theory that was developed in the course of the criticism of psychologism, which indicates the goal of the six investigations that follow.

The "anthropological" unity of science, which means the unity of acts of thought, is not of interest here. It is the objective question of what makes science to be science that is under consideration. The ideal, objective connection which gives "unity" to science as such can be understood to be the connection of *things*, to which actual or possible thought-experiences refer intentionally, and also as the connection of *truths* in which the material unity comes to objective validity. The two orders belong together *a priori* and are inseparable from one another. On the one hand, nothing can be without being determined; and on the other hand, *that* it is determined is the "truth in itself," which is the necessary correlate of "being in itself." That holds not only for single truths and facts, but also for connections of truths and facts. But the order of truth is not identical with the order of the things which are "truly" in the former, as is shown by the fact that the truths holding for truths do not coincide with the truths holding for the things which are posited in those truths. The terms object and thing are here used in their widest sense, so that an object of knowledge may mean either real or ideal entities. The unity of the objectivity, as well as of the truth, which can only be thought separately by abstraction, are given to us in knowledge. When we perform a cognitive act, or live in it, as Husserl prefers to express it, we are "occupied with the object" that is meant and posited. We have knowledge in the most rigorous sense when we judge with evidence, in which case the object is itself given ("originarily"). Then the fact is actually before our eyes, and not merely supposedly. The truth becomes individualized in the experience of the evident judgment. If we reflect upon this and abstract ideationally, the truth itself becomes the grasped object. Truth is thus grasped as the ideal correlate of a transient subjective act of knowledge; it is *one* as opposed to the unlimited manifold of possible acts of knowledge and knowing individuals.

To the connections of knowledge there correspond ideally the connections of truths, to which the sciences, construed objectively, belong in the sense of unified truth. Corresponding to the unity of truth in a science is a unified objectivity, or the unity of the scientific domain.

As stated earlier, a certain fundamental unity is essential to science. That is not sufficient, however, for it does not specify the kind of unity of grounds that constitutes science. Scientific knowledge is as such knowledge "with grounds," and to know the ground of something is to have insight into its necessity. Necessity as an objective predicate of a truth signifies the lawfulness of the fact in question. Hence to have insight into a fact as lawful or into its truth as necessarily valid, and to have knowledge of the ground of the fact or of its truth, are equivalent expressions.

Truths are classified into individual and general, the former containing explicit or implicit assertions about the actual existence of particulars, whereas the latter are free from such reference and merely permit the inference from concepts of the possible existence of individual things. Individual truths are accidental as such. In order to explain them or to determine grounds for them, their necessity under certain presupposed circumstances must be established. For the proof of a general truth we are referred to certain general laws from which the proposition in question may be deduced. The proof of general propositions leads necessarily to certain laws which cannot be proved themselves because of their essential character, and which are called fundamental laws. The systematic unity of the ideally closed totality of laws that are based upon one fundamental law or set of homogeneous laws, and which arise therefrom by deduction, is the unity of a complete systematic theory. Theories in this rigorous sense are illustrated by general arithmetic, geometry, analytical mechanics, etc. General arithmetic provides the explanatory theory for concrete numerical propositions, analytical mechanics for the facts of mechanics, and so on. The possibility of assuming an explanatory function is a consequence of the essence of a theory in Husserl's "absolute" sense. The term theory is also used in a less rigorous sense as meaning a deductive system in which the final grounds are not fundamental laws. This type of theory constitutes a stage in the gradations of a closed theory. In other words, every explanatory nexus is deductive, but not every deductive nexus is explanatory.

Sciences which are unified as theories, and which ideally comprise all possible matters of fact and are based upon one fundamental law, are called, not very appropriately in Husserl's opinion, *abstract* sciences. It appears better to call them theoretical sciences, or *nomological* sciences, because the term "theoretical" is used in contrast to "practical" and "normative." The name *explanatory* sciences is apt if it signifies the unity of explanation and not the explaining itself. The unity of concrete science is not an essential unity, because it is possible that empirical explanation may lead to heterogeneous theories and theoretical sciences. The abstract or nomological sciences are the really fundamental sciences, from which the concrete sciences derive the theoretical element that makes them to be sciences. It is sufficient for the concrete sciences to connect the objectivity which they describe to the lower laws of the nomological sciences, and perhaps to indicate the main direction of ascending explanation. When the purely theoretical interest is in question, the individual matters of fact and empirical connections either do not count, or they serve as a methodological stage for the construction of the general theory. The normative sciences also depend upon the nomological sciences, deriving from them all that makes them scientific, which is their theoretical element.

The question regarding the "conditions of the possibility of science in general" is equivalent to the question of the conditions of the possibility of a theory in general. A theory as such consists of truths, and the form of their connection is deductive. The question thus involves the more general one of the conditions of the possibility of truth in general, or of deductive unity in general. This amounts to a generalization of the question of the "conditions of the possibility of an experience." The unity of experience was for Kant the unity of the laws of objects, and hence it comes under the concept of theoretical unity.

In its subjective interpretation, this is the general question of the possibility of theoretical knowledge for any human being. The conditions of that possibility are in part real and in part ideal. The psychological conditions are real causal factors upon which our thought depends. The ideal conditions can be of two kinds. Either they are noetic and are grounded *a priori* in the idea of knowledge as such, without regard to the empirical nature of human knowing; or they are purely logical, and are based solely upon the "content" of knowledge. Husserl holds it to be evident that truths and especially laws, grounds, and principles are what they are whether we have insight into them or not. They do not owe their status as truths, etc., to the fact that we have insight into them, but rather we can only have insight because they do have that status. Therefore they must be regarded as objective or ideal conditions of the possibility of knowledge of them. *A priori* laws which belong to truth as such and are grounded purely in the "content" of knowledge constitute the conditions of the possibility of theoretical knowledge in general. The *a priori* conditions of knowledge can be investigated apart from all relation to the thinking subject and to the idea of subjectivity in general. These laws can then be applied to the real possibilities of knowledge.

By theory is meant a certain ideal content of possible knowledge, just as is the case with truth, law, etc. The identical theory corresponds to the manifold of individual knowledge-complexes, in each of which the same theory is known, just as the one truth corresponds to the manifold of single cognitive acts, as the ideal, identical content.

The term "possibility," applied to theory in its objective sense, is defined as meaning the "validity" or "essentiality" of the concept in question. That has often been called the "reality" of the concept. The existence of objects which come under the concepts in question is said to be possible; and this possibility is guaranteed *a priori* through knowledge of the conceptual essence, which flashes up on the basis of the intuitive presentation of such an object. The possibility or essentiality of a theory is secured through "evident" knowledge of it. A further question to be answered is, then, what are the ideal conditions of the possibility of theory in general, or, what makes up the ideal "essence" of theory as such? The point is, to determine the primitive "possibilities" or essential concepts out of which the possibility or the concept of theory is constituted; and following this the pure laws that are based upon these concepts, giving unity to all theory as such, are to be determined. Such laws belong to the form of all theory as such.

The problems of pure logic are summarized under three headings. First, the pure categories of meaning must be determined and clarified. Those are the primitive concepts which "make possible" the objective nexus of knowledge. The concepts which constitute the idea of theoretical unity, as well as concepts which are connected with them by law, are investigated. Concepts of a second order, or concepts of concepts and other ideal unities appear here constitutively. A given theory is a certain deductive connection of given propositions, and these are themselves determinate connections of given concepts. The idea of the "form" belonging to the theory arises by substitution of indeterminates for the given concepts, and thus concepts of concepts and of other ideas come in the place of simple concepts. The concepts: concept, proposition, truth, etc., are of that kind. Correlative to the categories of meaning are the pure or formal categories of objects, such as object, fact, unity, plurality, number, relation, connection, etc. The "origin" of all these concepts must be investigated. It is not the psychological question of the genesis of conceptual ideas that is involved, but rather the phenomenological origin. Avoiding the inappropriate and unclear term "origin," what is in question is *insight* into the essence of the concepts, and as a matter of methodology, the determination of unique, sharply distinguished meanings of words. This goal is only attainable by the intuitive representation of the essence in adequate ideation; or in the case of complicated concepts, by the knowledge of the essential nature of the elementary concepts inherent in them, and of the concepts of their forms of connection. The problems of this first group are perhaps the most difficult of all.

The second group of problems consists of the formulation of the laws which are based upon both classes of categorial concepts. The truth or falsity of meanings in general must be determined purely on the basis of their categorial formation; and on the other hand the being and non-being of objects in general, facts in general, etc., must be considered, again on the basis of their pure categorial form. These laws, which apply to meanings and objects with the greatest conceivable generality, themselves constitute theories. On the side of the meanings are the theories of inference, e.g., syllogistic, which is only one such theory. On the side of the correlates, the pure theory of pluralities is based upon the concept of plurality, the pure theory of numbers upon the concept of number, etc., and each is a closed theory in itself. Thus all laws belonging here lead to a limited number of primitive or fundamental laws which are rooted directly in categorial concepts and, by virtue of their homogeneity, must found an all-comprehensive theory, which comprises the single theories as relatively closed parts. The categorial theories and laws constitute the source from which every valid theory derives its ideal, essential grounds. They are the laws to which theories must conform, and by which every valid theory can be justified fundamentally with respect to its "form."

The theory of possible forms of theories or the pure theory of manifolds represents the third task of pure logic. The science of the conditions of the possibility of theory in general involves a supplementary science which treats *a priori* of the essential kinds or forms of theories and the relational laws belonging thereto. Instead of investigating the possibility of theory as such, it is the possible theories that are to be determined *a priori*. The ordering of a theory in its form-class can be of great methodological significance. The solution of problems which occur within one theoretical discipline, or in one of its theories, may in some cases obtain very effective methodological aid by going back to the categorial type or, what is the same, to the form of the theory, and then perhaps to a more comprehensive form or form-class and its laws.

The objective correlate of the concept of a possible theory, determined only in its form, is the concept of a possible domain of knowledge in general. Such a domain is called a "manifold" by the mathematician. It is a domain that is determined alone by the fact that it is subject to a theory of such a form, or that certain relations are possible for its objects, which are subject to certain fundamental laws of a determinate form. The objects are completely undetermined materially; only their form is determined by the forms of the elementary laws assumed to hold for them. These determine not only the form of the domain, but also the theory-form that is to be constructed. In the theory of manifolds, e.g., $+$ is not the sign for the addition of numbers, but rather of a relation in general, for which laws of the form $a + b = b + a$ hold. The manifold is determined by the fact that its thought-objects render possible these and other operations. In its most general form a theory of manifolds is a science which elaborates the essential types of possible theories or domains, and investigates their relations to one another. All actual theories are then specializations or singularizations of the corresponding theory-forms, just as all theoretically constructed domains of knowledge are single manifolds. If the formal theory concerned is actually carried through in the theory of manifolds, then all deductive theoretical work for the construction of all actual theories with the same form is settled. This is emphasized as a point of view of the greatest methodological significance and as indispensable for the understanding of mathematical method.

Referring to the nature of geometrical knowledge as an example of his conception of theoretical knowledge, Husserl states his belief that all metaphysical fog and mysticism are banished by the understanding of the real intention of geometrical theories as pure categorial theory-forms, or formal deductive systems. Space conceived as the form of order of the world of appearance is distinguished from space in the sense of a formally defined manifold. If space is construed in the former sense, then it would indeed be absurd to speak of "spaces" for which the parallel axiom does not hold; and the same would be true for the various geometries, if geometry is called the science of the space of the world of appearance. But if by space is meant the categorial form of world space, and geometry means the theory-form of geometry in the usual sense, then space comes under the genus of pure (categorially determined) manifolds. The geometrical theory is similarly ordered under a corresponding genus of theoretically connected, pure theory-forms, which may be called in an extended sense "geometries" of these "spatial" manifolds. The theory of the Euclidean manifold of three dimensions is then seen to be an ideal limiting case in the series of formal ("a priori") systems. This manifold is the pure categorial form, or the ideal genus, of "our" space in the ordinary sense.

In commenting upon the respective contributions of the mathematicians and the philosophers, Husserl asserts that the philosopher goes beyond his proper sphere if he opposes the "mathematizing" theories of logic and is unwilling to hand over his temporary foster-children to their natural parents. The disparagement with which the philosophical logicians had been accustomed to speak about the mathematical theory of inference does not alter the fact that the mathematical form of treatment in this, as in all rigorously developed theories, is the only scientific one; it alone provides systematic completeness and a survey of all possible questions, as well as the possible forms of their solution. The role of the mathematician is that of a constructive technician, who does not have final insight into the nature and structure of theories. Fortunately it is not essential insight that makes science possible in the practical, fruitful sense, but rather scientific instinct and method. But for that reason the purely theoretical, "knowledge-critical" reflection of the philosopher is necessary. Philosophical investigation requires entirely different methods and has entirely different aims. It is not sufficient for the philosopher that we get on in the world, that our laws provide formulae according to which we predict the future course of things. He is interested in clarifying the essence of "thing," "event," "cause," "effect," "space," "time," and the like, and also in the wonderful affinity that this essence has to the essence of thinking, so that it can be thought; to the essence of knowing, which makes it possible to be known; to the essence of meaning, so that it can be meant, etc. Science constructs theories to meet its problems, whereas philosophy analyzes the essence of theory and the conditions of its possibility. Thus the *ars inventiva* of the special scientist and the critique of knowledge of the philosopher are supplementary scientific activities, by means of which the complete theoretical insight that encompasses all relations of essence is obtained.

The investigations for the preparation of this discipline on its philosophical side are designed to make clear what the mathematician will not and cannot contribute, and yet must be contributed. Inasmuch as no science is possible without explanation on the basis of grounds, and hence without theory, pure logic comprises in a most general manner the ideal conditions of the possibility of science in general. But logic thus conceived does not include the ideal conditions of experiential science as a special case. Experiential science is also science, and its theories are subject to the laws of logic. But it is not merely deductive in character. Theoretical optics, or the mathematical theory of optics, e.g., does not exhaust the science of optics. All theory in the sciences of experience is merely supposed theory. It provides explanation by means of laws which are merely probable, and not certain or evident. Hence the theories themselves are provisional, and not final. The same holds for the matters of fact that are to be explained theoretically. They are not unchanged in the process of setting up and verifying explanatory hypotheses, by which we penetrate ever more deeply into the "true essence" of real being. Matters of fact are only "given" to us originally in the sense of perception or remembrance. In the progress of knowledge, what we hold to be the "real" factual content of perceptual appearances is changed. The intuitively given things, the things with "secondary qualities," are held to be "mere appearances," and in order to determine them objectively, we need a method suited to this objectivity. All empirical procedure is dominated by an ideal norm, and not by psychological contingency. At each stage of scientific development there are appropriate changes in the determination of the real matters of fact. The probability value varies, but there is only one value that is correct at a given time, depending upon the stage of our knowledge. In the domain of empirical thought, or in the sphere of probabilities, there must also be ideal elements and laws, on which the possibility of empirical science in general, or the probable knowledge of the real, is based. Such ideal laws do not belong to the concept of theory and, more generally, to the concept of truth, but are related to the concept of the empirical unity of explanation, as well as to the concept of probability. This sphere of pure laws constitutes a second great foundation of the art of logic, and also belongs to the domain of pure logic in a wider sense. The *Logical Investigations* are restricted to the narrower domain, which is first in the essential order of the material.

With this brief and programmatic sketch of the structure of pure logic the survey of the early philosophy of Husserl is completed. The motives which led to the definition and construction of an autonomous philosophical science have now been made clear.

The immediate critical reaction to the *Logical Investigations* will now be considered because it referred primarily to the *Prolegomena*, which was the most controversial part of the work. In this way the summary presentation of the six investigations will be allowed to stand by itself, as descriptive-analytic material. The six investigations generally have been referred to with respect (with a few exceptions to be noted), although rarely on the basis of the required careful study. It was the first volume which stirred up protest and aroused opposition; but it succeeded in emancipating some philosophers from psychologism. It will be helpful for the understanding of Husserl's historical significance to see him through the eyes of some of his contemporaries; and his response to criticism also aids in defining his own intentions.

1. Some Critics of the "Prolegomena"

Paul Natorp, the weightiest of Husserl's early critics, was held in great respect and personal esteem by Husserl. Natorp discussed the first volume of the *Logical Investigations* in an article entitled "On the Question of Logical Method." [2] In this article he acknowledges that the question of logical method has received a new, thorough discussion in Husserl's work; and he points out that the task which is assigned to "pure logic" is basically the one which the Kantian school designates as the critique of knowledge. Interpreting Husserl's distinction between logic as a theoretical science and as a practical, empirical science as being absolute, Natorp maintains that logic of the first type need not be formal alone, but may also be material (as though Husserl had not allowed for a correlative "material" realm). Schuppe and the "transcendental" logic of Kant are cited as examples. Obviously unimpressed by the dismissal of the "pseudo-problem" of the metaphysical significance of logic — which is discussed more fully in the second volume — he observes that the question of the relationship of logic to metaphysics was neglected in the consideration of the rival standpoints. With a clear discernment of the inevitable drift of Husserl's analysis (without, however, being able to appreciate the possibilities latent in that analysis), Natorp states that he who holds it possible to found a logic of objective truth purely theoretically will not allow metaphysics to hold besides, but will regard it as dissolved in logic — in the words of Kant, the old "ontology" is dissolved in the "analytic of the pure understanding."

---

[2] Paul Natorp, "Zur Frage der logischen Methode," *Kant-Studien*, vol. VI (Berlin, 1901), pp. 270–283.

But he credits Husserl with a successful critique of psychologism, one in which all its defenses are cut off after an all-sided examination.

Husserl had defined skepticism as the denial of the logical or noetic conditions of the possibility of a theory in general, which makes it to be contradictory. But does not this depend upon one's wanting rigorously valid theory at all costs? The skeptic could even say that he also wants that, but that he finds it to be an unattainable ideal. Natorp also asks how subjectivity could be overcome without one's positing the object. Husserl refutes skepticism in its individualistic form for one who has insight into the objectivity of logical knowledge. But, Natorp contends, that is just what is disputed.

Husserl is criticized for lack of smoothness in disposing of the question of the independence of logical propositions from psychological conditions, and for obscurity of expression, which makes him seem to incur the very error he had so energetically and correctly exposed — that logical, ideal laws could ever enter into causation. We could not know anything about the supertemporal truths of theoretical logic if there were not the temporal experience of "insight," in which, in Husserl's language, the "ideal" is "realized" for us. Husserl would agree with Natorp's assertion that nothing of the time-character of this experience goes into the content of that into which we thus have insight in time. Natorp is right in pointing out that Husserl's statement, that "Truth is an idea whose individual case is an evident judgment in an actual experience," needs explanation, if it is not to be misunderstood as metaphysics. Similarly, when Husserl tries to show that the truth of the judgment-content is the essential preliminary condition even of the "feeling" of evidence, the logical law appears to go over into causation. (Thus Husserl had stated: Where nothing is, one cannot see anything; where no truth "is," one cannot have insight into anything as true.) For Natorp the term "condition" can only be construed causally.

The formulation of the fundamental question of logic as the question concerning the conditions of the possibility of science, theory, truth, and deductive unity, is recognized by Natorp as the necessary generalization of the Kantian question of the conditions of the possibility of experience. The sought-for conditions are ideal, and not subjective. But Husserl's conception of Kant and the Neo-Kantians is challenged by Natorp. The former had stated that transcendental psychology is also psychology. Natorp replies that if one *wants* to find psychological elements he can find them everywhere, even in Husserl, for the use of the words "insight," "insightful," and even "reasonable" is not a whit less free from the suspicion of being psychological than the "confusing, mythical concepts" of Kant, the concepts of the understanding and reason. That he at all maintains an "a priori" is sufficient in Natorp's opinion to place him in the same position as the transcendental philosophy. He has extended his little finger to this devil; and Natorp predicts that he will have to give the whole hand.

In Natorp's view, the problem of the relationship between the formal and the material, the *a priori* and the empirical, the logical and the psychological is not solved by Husserl; or, in the latter's terminology, between the ideal and the real. The material, empirical, psychological, i.e., the "real" seems to remain as an incomprehensible, irrational residue. The critical discussion of psychologism impresses Natorp as taking the form of a dramatic struggle between two opponents; and what really compels them to fight for life and death is not clear to him. The author of the drama takes the side of the "ideal" and adheres to idealism, in the Platonic sense; and the "real" remains standing as a strange, rejected residue which cannot be eliminated. Natorp expresses the belief that Husserl, when the continuation of his logical investigations places him before this unsolved (and, indeed, hardly recognized) problem of the *Prolegomena*, will be forced along Kantian lines. It seems to him that a logical connection must be provided between the supertemporal nature of the logical and its temporal factuality in experience, if the talk of the "realization of the ideal" is not to remain an enigma, a metaphysical turn of speech of the worst kind.

In broad outline, Natorp really indicated the course of Husserl's further development. His discussion is at once an admonition to greater precision of statement, and a reminder that the idealistic stand that had been taken must face the problem of the relationship to reality. In the later period of constitutive phenomenology, the program of Kant is deepened and enlarged. So far as the *Prolegomena* is concerned, it may be said that Natorp discerned its merits and shortcomings more clearly than anyone else at the time.[3] As will be seen, however, the contents of the second volume of the *Logical Investigations* are a partial reply to Natorp, whose remarks were restricted to the first volume.

In an article submitted as a "supplement" to the *Prolegomena*, Schuppe [4] expresses approval of Husserl's acknowledgment of his previous error.

---

[3] This judgment is borne out by Husserl's own comments. Cf. ch. VII, B, 1 herein.

[4] Wilhelm Schuppe, "Zum Psychologismus und zum Normcharakter der Logik; Eine Ergänzung zu Husserl's *Logische Untersuchungen*," *Archiv f. syst. Phil.*, vol. VII (1901), pp. 1–22.

Schuppe confines himself in the main to details, and to careful references to his own earlier writings, in order to establish his priority and to instate himself as one whose ideas had been adopted and developed. His efforts in this respect miss the larger aspects of the questions at issue. Thus he claimed priority in the view that epistemology precedes metaphysics, as well as psychology and all other disciplines. Operating as he did within the traditional frame of idealism, Schuppe was incapable of understanding the freedom from all standpoints toward which Husserl's analysis was tending at this time.

Schuppe appears to take the idea of "founding" logic literally. Thus he asks: If the foundation of logic on consciousness in general still appears too psychologistic, upon what should it be based? On nothing? Or should we simply proclaim the principle of identity? His inability to follow Husserl's apagogic reasoning is indicated by his question: If you show a person that the denial of the principle of identity incurs contradiction, and that he contradicts himself in so doing, how does it hurt him if he can endure it? Furthermore, the intolerableness of a contradiction would be meaningless if we were to disregard consciousness. Schuppe regards such knowledge as being not merely logical, but also ontological; for if that were not so, the concept of truth as knowledge or the having-in-consciousness of the real would disappear.

Another note of disapproval was sounded by Husserl's junior Göttingen colleague, Leonard Nelson. In his book *On the So-called Problem of Knowledge*, Nelson [5] makes much of what he believes to be the confusion of "grounding" (*Begründung*) and "ground" (*Grund*) on the part of the antipsychologistic thinkers. He holds that Husserl misses this distinction in his polemic against psychologism, and that it hurts the rigor of his proofs. According to Husserl, the "psychological grounding" of logic is absurd, because the propositions of psychology are empirical and those of logic are apodictic; and propositions referring to mere form cannot be inferred from propositions of entirely heterogeneous content. But, Nelson argues, this argument would apply only to one who wanted to *prove* logical propositions on the basis of psychological propositions; for then such an attempt would have to take psychological propositions as grounds of the logical, and would fail due to the modal inequality of the supposed premises and conclusions. It seems to him that the possibility of a psychological grounding of the fundamental logical principles is by no means precluded therewith. Fundamental principles cannot be proved, in his

[5] Leonard Nelson, *Ueber das sogenannte Erkenntnis-problem* (Göttingen, 1908). Chapter xi includes examples of "dogmatic premises" in the antipsychologistic argumentation of

opinion, either psychologically or otherwise. What Nelson proposes is a critical "deduction" of the fundamental logical principles; and since this does not contain the ground of the propositions to be established, he holds that it can be accomplished psychologically.

Nelson contends, furthermore, that when Husserl criticizes the attempt to establish purely categorial laws with the aid of sensibility as being a case of the fallacy of metabasis, he makes the tacit assumption that the grounding of a cognition must be homogeneous with the cognition, a proposition which is not established by him. Disregarding the main force of the extensive arguments of the *Prolegomena*, Nelson finds that Husserl merely states that truths which are based solely upon the content of certain concepts cannot be located in sciences of matters of fact, and therefore not in psychology. If by "location" the ground were understood, Nelson would find the statement unobjectionable; but it cannot be construed in that case as an argument against the possibility of a psychological grounding of logic. It would simply be dogmatic, in Nelson's view, to dispute the possibility of a psychological grounding of logic.

There can bo no doubt that Husserl would have paid full tribute to the value of the psychological approach to logic, were he to have commented upon Nelson's argument, as shown by numerous passages in his writings. He was moreover vitally concerned with separating the process of proof from logical proof, or the process of establishing propositions from the independent validity of propositions. Instead of attempting to find an elementary confusion which was not present, Nelson should have faced the argument more squarely by considering the difference between the presuppositions, methods, and subject-matter of psychology on the one hand, and the pure theory of knowledge and logic on the other hand. The easily accomplished dialectical *coup* sought by Nelson did not occur, and for good reasons, sufficiently clear to the careful reader of the *Prolegomena*.

It will be sufficient to refer, finally, to the criticism advanced by Maier and Sigwart. Heinrich Maier [6] protested against what he termed the revival of Fichte's "pure ego." There are in his opinion no facts of a superindividual consciousness, and there is therefore no knowledge "of the ideal essence of science as such." In his view, this whole ideal world exists only as the object of human-empirical desire; and it is not "known" in theoretical investigation, but rather in normative reflection. He remarks

---

Natorp, Frege, and Husserl; and Husserl's phenomenological method and intellectual intuition are considered in chapter XII.

[6] Heinrich Maier, *Psychologie des emotionalen Denkens* (Tübingen, 1908), pp. 50 ff.

that Sigwart is not entirely wrong when he states, in his *Logic*,[7] that the propositions of Husserl lead necessarily to a double consciousness, an empirically real one, and an ideal one entirely different from it that apprehends the non-temporal truth. Sigwart adds that this is only to be attained through a state of ecstasy,[8] in which we are removed from our temporal course of thought, so that we are confronted with mysticism.

In Sigwart's opinion, Husserl has prepared a concept of psychology according to which the empirical mental life is subject to causal laws of "vague generality." Sigwart argues that the proper theme of psychology is the analysis of self-consciousness, an analysis which leads to the discovery of logical necessity. Husserl is quoted as maintaining that the certainty of the logical laws is an "experience," and as appealing to the evidence in which the truth is revealed. But is not an experience an empirical, psychical matter of fact, and evidence a condition of the mind which we experience in time? If basing one's assertions upon the experienced evidence is empiricism and psychologism, then it seems to Sigwart that Husserl himself has been guilty of them; and in that case, why the dispute?

Sigwart's attempt to defend himself against Husserl's criticism of his anthropologism is unsuccessful, despite Maier's willing help. Sigwart declares it to be mythology, to hypostatize "propositions" as independent essences. To state, as Husserl does, that the judgment expressing the formula for gravitation would be false before Newton, if the truth of a judgment depends upon an intelligence asserting it, would be tantamount to saying of an unborn person that he is sick, merely because it is not true that he is healthy. In other words, Husserl is accused of confusing mere negation with the assertion of the contrary opposite, just as he confuses reality and truth. It appears that Sigwart found it impossible to rise above his anthropologism, and to appreciate the need for a theory of objective truth as a fundamental requirement of scientific knowledge. He was not clear regarding the consequences of his point of view for the theory of reality.

In his supplementary comments Maier argues that one cannot infer the existence of a truth from its conceptual possibility; and in his view, the talk of the "supertemporal" nature of the existence of conceptual objects

---

[7] Cf. C. Sigwart, *Logik*, vol. 1 (Tübingen, 1924), ed. by H. Maier, pp. 23 f. Cf. also Maier's notes, pp. 502 ff., 510 ff., and 524 ff.

[8] The term "ecstasy" was as a matter of fact subsequently used, but with no thought of mysticism, by Husserl's son, Gerhart Husserl, in an essay entitled "Recht und Welt," in the *Ergänzungsband zum Jahrbuch für Philosophie und phänomenologische Forschung* (Halle, 1929), p. 114. Ecstasy is there contrasted with all natural attitudes; the non-naive attitude which makes possible the attainment of a region of indubitable certainty is described as

belongs in the realm of fable. The capacity for actualization which the conceptual possibilities presuppose is held by him to be a *present* capacity. Denying that Sigwart was an exponent of psychologism, if one takes into account the whole course of thought and structure of the *Logic,* and not "misleading details," Maier agrees with him in rejecting the "absolutistic-antipsychologistic demands of Husserl."

2. *Husserl's Defense of His Position*

Neither Sigwart nor Maier gives any evidence of having really understood Husserl's position, and it was reactions of this kind that weighed heavily with Husserl in his decision that it was not worth while to enter into polemical discussions. Moreover, it was impossible to enter into controversy with all interested parties, in view of his ambitious constructive program in philosophy. Apart from the second "Logical Survey," in which several important contemporary works are discussed, his review of Palagyi's *The Controversy between the Psychologistic and the Formal Logicians* [9] was his only answer to critics in this period.

Palagyi's misunderstanding of the *Prolegomena* was typical. Husserl treats him very severely in his review, charging that he intended in advance to read every kind of absurdity out of the text, so that he could not read it in accordance with its meaning and connection. In his book he attributes to Husserl the inclination to "let logic be submerged in mathematics," and to "tear" logic away from psychology. Husserl points out that he ignores the distinction, which had been made carefully, between logic in the comprehensive sense of a practical discipline, and pure logic as the theoretical system of purely formal or categorial truths. He also ignores the fact that Husserl completely approves of a logic of the methodological tendency of such logicians as Mill, Sigwart, and Wundt; that Husserl in no way disputes the basing of this logic in the usual sense upon empirical psychology; and that he even requires it to a large extent. "Pure" or formal logic is a title which names an independent *a priori* discipline comprising the so-called logical propositions. This discipline is independent of psychology; and in a natural extension it also comprises formal mathematics, and is finally identical with the *mathesis universalis* in the generalized sense of Leibniz. The fact is also ignored that Husserl distinguishes between the mere technique of formal logical theories, which

---

"ecstatic." This term is intended to indicate that one is lifted out of his natural setting and in fact gets "outside himself."

[9] Review of *Der Streit der Psychologisten und Formalisten in der modernen Logik* (Leipzig, 1902), in the *Zeit. f. Psych. u. Phys. d. Sinnesorgane,* vol. XXXI (1903), pp. 287–294.

is assigned to mathematicians, and the sphere of real philosophical investigation. The latter is described as the epistemological elucidation of the basic concepts and principles of pure logic by means of descriptive-psychological ("phenomenological") analyses. The phenomenological method is thus restricted to descriptive psychology, in its first formulation. This method is illustrated in the second volume of the *Logical Investigations*, in which the descriptive phenomenology of thought-experiences is investigated to a greater extent than had ever occurred before. Husserl denies that his critique of psychologism is in any way an opposition to the psychological foundation of logical methodology, or to the descriptive-psychological explanation of the origin of logical concepts; it is rather an opposition to an epistemological position that has unfavorably influenced the mode of treatment of logic.

In answer to the charge that he had used Bolzano, but had ignored his dependence on him, Husserl points out that he had designated Bolzano as the one from whom, besides Lotze, he had received his "deciding influences." The concepts of "ideal" meanings, ideal presentation- and judgment-contents are derived from Lotze's *Logic*, as the expression "ideal" indicates. The latter's interpretation of the Platonic theory of Ideas made a deep impression upon Husserl. It was the inner elaboration of these not completely clarified thoughts of Lotze that gave him the key to the strange conceptions of Bolzano, which were at first incomprehensible in their phenomenological naïveté, and to the treasures of the *Wissenschaftslehre*. If before that the "propositions in themselves" had appeared to be mythical entities hovering between being and non-being, it was now clear at one stroke that what was conceived was an obvious conception that had not been properly recognized in the traditional logic. A "proposition in itself" was now seen to be merely that which is called the "sense" of a statement. It is that which is declared to be the same, when one says that different persons assert the same thing; or it is that which is simply called a proposition in science, e.g., a proposition in geometry. In such cases one does not think of the judgment-experiences.[10] This identical meaning was seen to be identical with the general, the species, which is a certain factor present in all statements with the same meaning, and which makes identification possible with otherwise changing descriptive contents of the experiences. As Husserl had pointed out, a proposition is related to every one of the

---

[10] By "truth in itself," or what is in ordinary speech regarded as the truth of a proposition as distinguished from the act of judgment, Bolzano meant something objective. The being judged or known is extra-essential to it. That does not mean, however, that not being known is essential to it.

acts of judgment, to which it belongs as their identical meaning, just as, e.g., the species of redness does to the single cases of "the same" red. With this interpretation, Bolzano's doctrine that propositions are objects which nevertheless do not "exist" is readily understood. They have the "ideal" being or validity of "general objects," or the kind of being that is established in the "existence-proofs" of mathematics, e.g.; but not the real being of temporal things. Bolzano himself did not indicate in any way that the phenomenological relations between meaning, meaning-factor, and complete act of meaning had been observed by him; on the contrary, everything indicates that he had taken over his conception in an unclarified form.

The doctrine of the identical ideal meaning is misunderstood if one makes an identical *factor* of an experience out of it. In so doing, Palagyi overlooks the distinction that had been emphasized, between a species and an individual case, or between the meaning as the idea becoming objective through "specific" abstraction, and the descriptive-psychological factor of meaning. Husserl distinguishes conceptually between the identical meaning and the act, in the sense in which the quality-species of redness is different from a red thing; but that does not imply that the concrete psychical experience of judging consists of two factors, the supertemporal meaning-factor and the act. It therefore does not follow that Husserl and Bolzano wanted "to tear loose the meaning-factor from the act." It would be simply nonsensical to characterize a factor of an experience as supertemporal; and that is not at all what is meant by a "proposition in itself" or a meaning as a species.

Husserl's distinction between real and ideal laws, which is carried over to logic, also comes in for criticism. For how can extra-temporal, ideal laws be effective in the real world, which is separated from them by an "infinite abyss"? Such a bifurcation would seem to involve the complete impossibility of all knowledge. But Palagyi must have read too selectively; for otherwise he would not have construed the *opposition* between the ideal and the real as *unrelatedness*. Since the ideal meanings are individualized in acts of meaning, every purely logical proposition expresses a generality, which *eo ipso* permits of being related to the ideal extensions of the meaning-species in question, and hence to possible real acts of thought. General truths about ideally possible or impossible psychical connections can thus be read out of every ideal law, e.g., from every arithmetical law; its character as a *vérité du raison*, which is carried over to such derivations, is not touched thereby. Ideal and real laws differ essentially, and there is a difference in the mode of knowledge of the lawful facts in each type. In the critical context of the *Prolegomena*, "real law" does not mean any general proposition referring to the real, but a general matter of fact, or at least a proposition which is loaded with factual content in the manner of our assertions of natural laws. What this amounts to essentially is the distinction between truths of matters of fact and purely conceptual truths, or ideal laws. If the world were so constituted that all spheres in it were red, then we would come inductively to speak of a "law of nature." In itself it would, however, be no real law; it would not be a proposition which is grounded in the conceptual essence of "sphere" and "red," but a general matter of fact. The objective distinction in question, which is logically and epistemologically fundamental, is the distinction between what Hume calls "relations of ideas" and "matters of fact." The truths of the former class are rooted in the ideas, which means, in the concepts involved, and therefore cannot be denied without contradiction; whereas negations of factual truths are indeed false, but are not contradictory in themselves.

D. THE OUTCOME OF THE "PROLEGOMENA"

The failure of so many reviewers to do justice to their tasks presents a curious problem, especially in the field of philosophy. Nothing appears more clear today than Husserl's aims; and nothing more quaint than the reactions of some of his well-known contemporaries. It may well be due in part to the habit of many philosophers of entering a discussion with weapons ready for an expected battle, calm and coöperative inquiry being the last thing to be looked for.

Although most of the critical attacks upon the *Prolegomena* missed the mark, something was gained from them nevertheless, for Husserl was made aware of the need for greater exactness in exposition. But it was also true that he had not achieved complete clarity on all the issues in question. In the *Formal and Transcendental Logic* he gives evidence of more mature reflection upon the problems and program of the *Prolegomena*. Before proceeding to the second volume of the *Logical Investigations*, it will be well to consider a number of critical questions that have been raised in connection with the issue of psychologism and pure logic, including reference to some recent literature.

The first question to be considered is that of the significance of the sharp antithesis drawn between empirical and pure logic. Husserl's reference to the naive, uncritical, everyday experience of the empiricist seems to reflect an excessive opposition to empirical method. The motive of adding to empirical method was unfortunately accompanied by remarks which suggested a tendency to disparage it. The contention that the failure of empiricism to grant ultimate principles based upon insight would make its own theory to be an arbitrary assumption is not and could not be proved. Too much experience speaks for empiricism to call it "arbitrary." Husserl's readiness to qualify this opposition, and to avow his recognition of all empirical methods in their proper sphere, has already been noted. His acceptance of the methodological logic as an indispensable discipline was pointed out sufficiently in the *Prolegomena*. He is not concerned with the process or art of acquiring knowledge, or of actual persuasion. The level on which he operates is ideal and objective, and presupposes its own actual, cognitive attainment. Then why the attack on psychologism, it may be asked? It is enough to point out that psychologism restricted the field of logic, so that it had to be refuted as a self-sufficient theory of logic. If the criticism in the *Prolegomena* appeared to go too far, that was corrected in subsequent discussion. It was never intended to deprive natural experience of any of its methods. But it was argued that the structure and validity of the forms of knowledge are not identical with the content of natural experience and its empirical generalizations; and that justified the independent development of a science of pure forms.

There is particular merit in Husserl's treatment of the relationship between the normative and the theoretical, and of the function of logic as an art. His position is well balanced: logic has psychological, normative, and practical aspects, and also a pure structure. Recognizing all phases of logic as legitimate when properly understood, he emphasizes the fundamental status of pure logic. The latter is really fundamental by definition. Although the psychological approach to logic begins with what is first for one as an individual knower, the discovery of objectively binding principles discloses a realm that is "first in itself." There is truth in the view that logic is an art, and also that it is normative. But underlying both functions is the theoretical science of logic. Husserl is careful to point out explicitly that his conception of a pure logic does not affect the question of the justification of logic conceived as a methodology, and declares its relationship to the art of logic to be analogous to the relationship of pure geometry to the art of field measurement. He makes clear his acceptance of the time-honored function of logic, to examine the methods and structure of the sciences. There can be no doubt about his full recognition of the use of methodological devices, and of the procedures of "practical logic," a fact which is frequently forgotten in the characterization of his philosophy of logic. It is noteworthy that logic is portrayed as the theory of science in the *Formal and Transcendental Logic*. Furthermore, logic is clearly distinguished, *qua* theory of science, from the historical investigation of sciences as cultural products of a given period. Such passages may be adduced in support of the view that phenomenology has its peculiar problems and procedures, which must be used in coöperation with other types of method.

The demonstration of the possibility and necessity of the reduction of normative to theoretical propositions is of far-reaching significance; it makes possible a universal theory of science which applies to all scientific knowledge, whether normative or theoretical. This may be illustrated by reference to some recent (and really post-Husserlian) philosophical literature.

It is not necessary to regard ethical propositions as asserting nothing, as logical positivists do.[11] Carnap reduces the rule "Do not kill" to the value statement "Killing is evil," the latter being regarded as the expression of a wish. A value statement is in his view merely a command in a misleading grammatical form; it does not assert anything and is neither true nor false. Carnap does not consider the possibility of formalizing the value propositions, so that they may be arranged in a deductive order. When interpreted in terms of ethical concepts, the concrete (although to be sure incomplete) system of ethics results. A variety of interpretations of the same formal system would be possible, in accordance with a well-established principle of postulational theory, namely, the principle of multiple interpretation. On the other hand, one may begin *concretely* with a given historical situation more or less restricted in time and space, and arrange the accepted ethical code in terms of basic principles and derived propositions. There is at least no essential obstacle in the way of such procedure. In terms of such a system the proposition "Killing is evil" could be true or false in the formal sense. In other words, formal ethical propositions may be claimed to have as much significance as mathematical propositions; and the problem of making material application to real situations admits of solution much more readily in the case of ethical systems.

Schlick has argued [12] that if value propositions are conceived as being similar to logical or mathematical propositions, they then become tautologies, which is not what is wanted in ethics. But there are ethical-logical propositions, just as there are mathematical-logical propositions, and they are meaningful in their particular domains. It is important to distinguish

---

[11] Cf. R. Carnap, *Philosophy and Logical Syntax* (London, 1935), pp. 22 ff.; and also A. J. Ayer, *Language, Truth, and Logic* (New York, 1936), ch. VI, and the present writer's review of the latter, *Philosophical Review* (1938), pp. 88 f.

[12] M. Schlick, *Problems of Ethics* (New York, 1939), pp. 107 ff.

the pure logic of ethics from its empirical applications. Not only can systems of ethics that are limited to particular periods and conditions be constructed; but also the ideal system of ethical propositions which must hold if a group life is to be possible, and if certain defined values are to be realized.

The transformation of normative propositions into theoretical propositions makes possible the formulation of a system of ethics with independent validity, and with the potentiality of application to concrete situations. No science can be exhaustively described as normative; and the natural sciences, on the other hand, may themselves be regarded as normative in relation to practical projects. It is one of the results of Husserl's analysis that it is not necessary to assign value statements to the realm of metaphysics, which in Carnap's language spells nonsense. To be sure, when Husserl introduces the idea of a "basic norm" and illustrates it by means of the Kantian categorical imperative and the quantitative standard of the Utilitarians, the reader receives little indication of the way in which the normative system may be constructed. It would have been pertinent to point out more explicitly the ideal of a deductive ordering of the propositions of the ethical system. Reinterpreted according to the method shown by Husserl, the propositions would be seen to be valid in their own system; and the difference between two systems would be determined by the choice of basic values and principles. Just as in the case of pure geometry, the question of application to real conditions would be an additional one, which would of course determine the worth (and in its way the "truth") of the formal value-system. The formal validity of the latter is another matter, and is unaffected by its application or realization in actual conditions.

These remarks would fit very well with Husserl's draft of a pure logic, and would agree with his view of the parallelism of the valuational and the theoretical as judgment-structures. In the present context, however, he does point out an important difference between the normative and the theoretical, which indicates that he might not go the full length suggested here. The fundamental value at the basis of a normative judgment has no analogue, in his view, in a theoretical discipline, the unity of which is determined by the theoretical interest and the nature of the facts. But that should not preclude a deductive ordering, allowing for changing historical content.

Husserl correctly shows that psychologism cannot be a theory in the sense in which he conceives theories; and in so far as that is desired by psychologistic logicians, the result is conclusive. Psychologism is charged

with violating the subjective and objective conditions of the possibility of
a theory. A theory would suspend itself if its content were to violate the
laws which are necessary to make theories meaningful. In other words,
the requirement of non-contradiction is final. But is there any other way
to construct theories? The answer must be in the negative if "pure"
theories, patterned after deductive mathematical systems, are meant, for
all other types of theory would be limited by particular conditions of
reality, or by the state of our knowledge. That would be the case for a
theory constructed with a restricted conception of truth. If one speaks of
different conceptions of truth, that can only mean the introduction of
modalities, which Husserl admitted later; or differences in the range of
truth, meaning by that the restriction of "truth" to actually verified judgments, or its extension to apply to all possible propositions, whether real
or ideal in reference. In the latter sense there would be human conceptions of truth with different degrees of generality, ranging in the extent
of their application from the set of actual judgments of one person to the
possible judgments of all human beings, either actual or possible. Inasmuch as he is interested at this time in achieving a theory of knowledge
which would meet the needs of formal science, Husserl chooses to treat
all judgments from the point of view of their ideal content or meaning.
A theory of knowledge with universal application would have to allow
for the modalities of judgment and truth. To speak of a restricted conception of truth, such as truth for a certain individual or species, is to
consider only those judgments which happen to be asserted by the individual or species. Such "constructional" theories (i.e., built up on the basis
of actual knowledge, or by means of an actual method of construction)
need not be self-contradictory or absurd. A theory in the constructional
sense should not be criticized upon the basis of a theory in the ideal, formal
sense. An infinite number of kinds of theory would be possible in the
constructional sense. But a logic of formal thought can only be constructed along the lines sketched by Husserl, which requires abstracting
from all subjectivity, as well as from all concrete meanings. It is distinguished by its exclusive use of abstractions, and its peculiarly fundamental
nature as the presupposition of all concrete systems of propositions; and
its structure is such that it is capable of deductive representation.

That Husserl does not consider different constructional interpretations
of truth, such as truth for the formal thinker or for the intuitionist, for the
infinitist or for the finitist, is shown by his illustration of different meanings
of the words true and false. He suggests that if other beings were to regard
what we call "propositions" to be "trees," then the whole dispute of the rela-

tivist becomes verbal. This applies to the relativistic argument in question. But it does not dispose of the possibility of alternative conceptions of truth, in the sense here indicated. It is not necessary to deny that there is a "world in itself," meaning by that a world apart from actual knowledge, e.g., if one speaks of restricted conceptions of truth. The limitation can be imposed as a matter of knowledge, and without the dogma that reality depends upon the verification of judgments.[13] Perhaps Husserl would state today that he had been talking about "pre-logical" concepts and principles which are necessary for all theories, and for all empirical systems of knowledge. His version of objective truth would accordingly apply to all the more restricted conceptions of truth; the latter would be but a specialization of the former.

The contention of the skeptical relativist, that truth depends upon a species of judging beings and that it may vary with different species, is criticized with right; the mere meaning of the words true and false rules that out. The argument, that if the relativist were to use the words true and false with their proper meanings his thesis would assert something that violates its own meaning, assumes one conception of truth as final. This argument would be a cogent objection if the objective definition of truth were really assumed by the relativist, or if it were demonstrated that there can be only one conception of truth. The refusal to grant that the relativist may be merely talking about human truth and falsity, on the ground that an evident law cannot mean what is obviously absurd, assumes the concept of one compelling evidence as well. The relativist's contention is only absurd on the basis of an objective theory of truth and evidence. It must be admitted, however, that even a consistently worked out relativistic theory could not provide for all regions of knowledge. The interpretation of truth as consisting of all truths that are knowable and as being the same for all types of being is the proper counter-thesis to relativism. Unfortunately Husserl appeals to a "luminous certainty" which guarantees truth, and which exposes his otherwise objectively formulated position to attack. Such an appeal is hardly an aid in meeting skepticism or relativism. Although he points out that different versions of truth were due to equivocations, he does not satisfactorily show that only one conception of truth is possible.

The attempt to force relativism into contradictions must be examined carefully. Does relativism allow it to be "true" upon the basis of the constitution of a given species that such a constitution may not exist at all? Such a possibility could not exist as far as the species in question is con-

---

[13] This observation is made in connection with argument (6), § F of the preceding chapter.

cerned. To allow the possibility of other kinds of truth for different species does not mean that it would be possible truly to declare the non-existence of a given species. To do so would be to incur either falsity or self-contradiction: falsity if judged by some other species, and self-contradiction if judged by the given species itself. Although relativism is neither complete nor adequate, it need not be self-contradictory. Husserl's criticism of the attempt to derive purely logical principles from matters of fact assumes that such facts are "accidental" and that they could have been otherwise, or that they could also not be at all. It is impossible to derive logical laws from matters of fact if they are so conceived that there is an insuperable gap between them. This distinction is at the basis of the criticism of relativism. Even if it be granted that to assert something is to state that a certain content "is in truth," that is not to state that the term "truth" can only be used in the ideal sense of Husserl. It appears that relativism has not been disposed of in all its possible forms, although the criticism does refute the arguments of its then existing representatives.

Husserl relies upon insight to found the laws of pure logic and mathematics, and he credits such a foundation with "absolute exactness." The objection has been frequently made that one can never be quite sure whether he has the insight, as a matter of fact; and that different people may have different views of the same laws, or deny that insight justifies one or the other of them; etc. In the course of the present discussion, as well as elsewhere, Husserl endeavors to dispose of such objections. He tries to meet the general line of thought which prompts them by arguing, in effect, that they are based upon a confusion of realms, that considerations pertinent for matters of fact are not therefore pertinent for ideal relationships. As maintained in the *Logical Investigations*, ideal laws would be valid even if no one ever knew them, or actually had insight into them. One may fail to have the insight when it might be expected to be present, as every student of mathematics knows. It is therefore clear that what is in question is a logical insight which validates ideal relationships. It must be admitted that the objections here referred to should have been discussed more fully and pointedly than was the case in the several passages that are available in Husserl's published works. There is no attempt to establish criteria for the guarantee of insight, for there is no interest here in what we experience as a matter of fact. In order to avoid any possible confusion between the ideal and the real, Husserl hastens to deny that real thinking is in question when subjective conditions are spoken of. If it is said that facts which are objectively incompatible cannot actually coexist in one's experience, then the insight is the correlate of an objective state of affairs, and the principle expressing that state of affairs is a condition of the possibility of our experience.

Finally, it will be asked how one is to *persuade* an individualistic relativist of the falsity of his position. The point is to *refute* his point of view objectively, and not to persuade him. Persuasion pertains to the realm of matters of fact, whereas the refutation may be valid on principle, regardless of how a given individual may react. It is possible to deny the fundamental logical principles in fact, as a real experience; that can go along with their independent objective validity. The troublesome problem of giving criteria, which pertain to the real order, is avoided by speaking hypothetically: *If or when* I have the insight, then that cannot be doubted. The certainty or apodictic evidence of which he had spoken thus appears to be a part of a hypothetical situation. Care must be taken in understanding the term "evidence" to name an objective relationship. It is unfortunately an ambiguous term, so that it is easy for disputants to argue past one another if different interpretations are selected. While placing firm reliance upon insight, which means possessing the truth itself, Husserl does not show why the "eternal" truth may not be a changing truth in all cases. He merely restricts its range of application, arguing that we never really had "the" truth if it "changes." [14]

Husserl admits that his concept of "truth in itself" was one-sided, while explaining why he permitted it to remain in the revised edition, i.e., in order to maintain the unity of the original work. An absolute, "realistic" theory of truth was advanced as the answer to relativism. Truth does not depend upon the existence of intelligent beings who have insight into it, although its fulfillment in reality requires that it be known. As ideal possibilities, truths are assigned a place in a non-temporal realm of "Ideas." If one's own insight is the final test of the apprehension of truth, the practically important problem is to find a way to compel the assent of other knowers, i.e., if truth is to be regarded as objective in the sense of holding for all thinkers. All that Husserl is certain of is his own insight, "the Archimedean point for reason and knowledge." Viewed empirically, this basis of certainty can be shown to be very thin by reducing it to insight of the immediate present, which makes it to be unsatisfactory for the purpose of establishing rigorous knowledge. It is a further problem to provide grounds by which one can compel the acceptance of a truth if such insight is the final court of appeal. Because this problem involves actual thought

---

[14] This question is raised in another form in *Experience and Judgment*, where Husserl points out that a given proposition may cease to be true for given conditions, while retaining its "timeless" identity.

processes and is proper to the empirical logic of persuasion, it is neglected in the analysis of pure logic. The problem of making the transition from the indubitable sphere of a single ego to the intersubjective world, which is a crucial problem in the later development of the phenomenological method, is not affected by such difficulties, for it is not concerned with actual knowers.

In closing his discussion of Erdmann, Husserl asks a number of questions which should also be considered in the light of his own position. Objective truth is identified with general validity, or validity for all, by Erdmann; but how one can attain to justified objective truth in a particular case has not been made clear by him. According to him the judgments which we assert in agreement with others are certain, but not this agreement itself. But what is this subjective certainty? Our assertion would only be justified if we knew about this agreement and were aware of its truth. Husserl asks how we are to achieve the subjective certainty of the agreement of *all* people; and he questions the requirement of general certainty, which implies that truth is to be found by all instead of by a few select people. Must the justification of "insight" face the same kind of challenge, and is it, too, restricted to a few select knowers? The reply which Husserl offers is the argument that one has the insight that no one's insight can conflict with his own, *in so far as each of them is really insight.* This is correct enough in itself, for the concept of genuine insight rules out the possibility of conflict. The question of validity is distinct from the question of actual knowledge; hence the question of the testing and the actual achievement of genuine insight is not considered. It is sufficient for the purposes of pure logic to establish the necessity of insight, and to trace out the consequences that follow from its possession.

Although it is necessary to distinguish the ideal and the real, and there is great merit in Husserl's thoroughgoing attempt to elaborate a theory of ideal meanings and forms, the autonomy of the ideal order must be regarded as being only partial. The complete separation of the two orders is necessary in order to develop ideal sciences, which are not only of interest in themselves, but serve the order of reality as well. When Husserl states that our factual thinking does not proceed according to ideals, for ideals are not like natural forces, he separates the real and the ideal essentially. Although he denies that such an opposition implies unrelatedness, he does not satisfactorily explain how the two orders are related. The necessity of operating with disengaged pure forms by no means implies that they must assume an independent metaphysical status, which Husserl is careful to avoid, and which his descriptive method strictly forbids. The interpretation of the ideal meanings of formal science in terms of approximations to ideal limits would assign to them a place in experience and reality. Husserl does not consider this possibility because of his overwhelming interest in making a place for the ideal construction of knowledge, in itself a necessary undertaking. The thought-economists, on the other hand, had failed to show the proper connection between the ideal and the real orders. In opposition to them Husserl argues that pure logic precedes thought-economy, and cannot be based upon it, for we must know the ideal goal and structure of science before we can estimate its thought-economical function. That is to regard explanatory devices as prior to the facts, which would be the case if pure logic were proved true, with reference to reality. The disparagement of natural theories is unnecessary. The designation of a natural theory as "blind" and accidental, in contrast to the binding power of a logical theory, is not necessary for the independent development of ideal knowledge.

If one speaks of the conditions of the possibility of theoretical knowledge, construed subjectively, and proceeds to point out ideal conditions as well as real, causal factors, it may be asked how he can be sure that the ideal conditions will not vary. If the temporal order is irrelevant, then the conditions cannot be effective, especially since "pure logic" only "applies" to the real. Unfortunately, Husserl leaves much to be discussed in this context. Precisely how the ideal conditions determine the real realm is not explained. Although they can be "applied," the question of alternative applications is left open. Natorp was right in maintaining that the problem of the relationship between the ideal and the real is not solved by Husserl, at this point at least.

If pure logic is the theoretical system of purely formal truths, it must be basic to all concrete systems of propositions. It should not appear to be a mystery that pure logical propositions apply to reality, inasmuch as our original nucleus of logical knowledge was abstracted from concrete propositions. There is no essential difficulty in connection with the application of pure propositions to reality. The only issue which arises is one that has become prominent in recent years. That is the problem of maintaining logical absolutism — or the doctrine that there is one kind of logic, with its necessary principles, just as there is one interpretation or conception of truth — in the face of *logical* relativism, or the view that there are alternative logics (or, rather, logical systems). Husserl's later logical writings do not consider this problem, and go no further than the more explicit definition of the "logic of consistency," so that this newest and most formidable type of relativism was probably unknown to him. Had he been informed about it, he would no doubt have admitted its partial truth and justification. Some of his statements should be amended in view of recent progress in formal science. This applies to his rationalistic ideal of a unified structure of scientific knowledge, the collective nature of which must be pointed out. The conception of a pure law as "the one and only truth" which excludes all other possibilities is also in need of enlargement, to take account of "alternative" formal systems. Husserl speaks of general propositions which cannot be proved themselves because of their "essential character" as fundamental laws. The subsequent development of formal logic has shown this rationalistic principle to be untenable. If the rationalist replies that the proofs of the "relativistic" formalist who deduces the law of non-contradiction, e.g., are merely "apparent" proofs (as Husserl has referred to them), he must nevertheless admit that the alleged fundamental principles can be deduced formally, at any rate; and that is precisely what is here in question. Husserl distinguishes between a deductive system in this rigorous sense, and a deductive system in which the "final grounds" are not fundamental laws, but this distinction is not sufficiently clarified.

The thesis that pure logic, as a theoretical science that is independent of all empirical conditions, makes logic possible in the usual theoretical-practical sense, must be recognized as sound on principle. It represents a point of view which has been justified amply by the subsequent development of logic. The way in which it is related to the actual procedures of "practical" logic has been shown by such logicians as C. I. Lewis,[15] whose conception of a "pragmatic a priori" bridges the gap between the purely theoretical and the practical. Having argued for the general thesis of the primacy of pure logic, Husserl devotes his full attention to the elaboration of pure logic by itself. His judgment that the problem of the harmony between the subjective process of logical thought and external reality is a mere pseudo-problem that is due to unclearness indicates the extent to which this separation reaches.

The references to Kant show that Husserl's thought may in an important respect be considered to be a generalization of the Kantian philosophy. This becomes increasingly clear in his later development. The question of the conditions of the possibility of experience is generalized to be the question of the possibility of truth in general, and of deductive unity in general. If truths are regarded as objective conditions of the possibility of our knowledge of them, as Husserl holds at this time, the range of the concept of unity is greatly extended. But the traditional problem

---

[15] Cf. C. I. Lewis, *Mind and the World-Order* (New York, 1929).

of monism is not formulated therewith in its most general form, for it involves not only the conditions of experience and of truth, but also the conditions of physical reality.

In occasional passages reference is made to the problem of error in so far as that has meaning with respect to phenomenological analysis. Husserl observes that when errors occur, as in fallacies, the *cognition* has not become an error. The entire discussion of the distinction of the ideal from the real explains why this is the case. The interest in *essential* determinations and distinctions does not mean the denial that even a phenomenologist may record falsely. That may indeed happen! If the phenomenologist himself is brought into the picture for any reason, then every phenomenological finding must be expressed hypothetically, in the form "If one has the insight, then. . . ."

It is of interest to note the use of the term "constitution" as meaning the construction of the complex out of the simple. It is a logical procedure that is involved. The peculiar meaning of the term "origin" ("Ursprung") should be noted. The phenomenological and not the psychological origin of such concepts as unity, relation, etc., is to be investigated. The term "origin" is used in a systematic sense, and involves insight into the essence of the fundamental concepts in question, and the clear determination of meanings of words.[16] Speaking of the laws of pure logic and mathematics, Husserl uses the term "origin" in the sense of the proof which justifies them. The term "proof" is perhaps not well chosen, for what is meant is "justification in experience," or "evidential justification."

Husserl's conception of a theory of possible forms of theories, or of the pure theory of manifolds, is one of his most promising insights, and is evidence of his power of clear generalization. His aim is the *a priori* de-

---

[16] Cf. Husserl, *Erfahrung und Urteil*, §§ 5, 11, and 12 for the significance of the concept of "origin" or of "genesis" as conceived later in the phenomenological method. Husserl's genetic statement of the problem of origins, as relating to logic, is not psychological in the usual sense. The term "genetic" refers to the production by which knowledge arises in its "origin-form" of self-givenness, a production which repeatedly yields the same cognition. The factual, historical process of meanings arising out of a definite historical subjectivity is not at all in question. Our world becomes an example for us, by means of which we study the structure and the origin of a possible world in general. The clarification of the origin of the predicative judgment is a fundamental task of the genealogy of logic in a transcendental sense. The aim is to investigate the contributions of the knowing reason to the construction of the world. In order to attain to the ultimate, original experiences, it is necessary to go back to the simplest units and to regard the world purely as the world of perception, abstracting from everything else. In this way the realm of nature as perceived by me is first obtained. Thus we may come to the most primitive building-stones of logical contribution, out of which our world is built up. The systematic line of "transcendental" inquiry of these important logical studies is an illustration of such "origin-analysis."

termination of possible theories. Whether this is a possible program is a question on which logicians are divided now as in the past. The names and various techniques have changed, but, fundamentally, the parties of empirical and of pure logic are replaced by positivism and intuitionism on the one hand, and by a "realistic" formal logic on the other hand. Husserl is right in regarding his analysis as having great methodological significance, and as being necessary for the understanding of mathematical method. Finally, he corrects the impression of hostility toward the mathematical tendency in logic, which he had given in the Schröder-Voigt controversy, when he asserts that the mathematical form of treatment in all rigorously developed theories alone provides systematic completeness.

Mention has already been made of Husserl's judgment of the *Prolegomena*, as viewed from his later perspective. His early efforts were viewed in the light of his later achievements, in the interest of establishing the unity of his development.[17] While maintaining the soundness of the essential content of his early work, it is portrayed as being on the way to something more mature and more complete. The account given in the *Formal and Transcendental Logic* calls attention to the importance and originality of the *Prolegomena* (thus the claim is made that the idea of a formal ontology is first given literary expression in that work), and also points out some of its defects. The most serious defect to be pointed out is the failure to mention the modalities of truth along with the concept of truth. Probability was not introduced as one of the modalities. It was now clear to him that formal logic must be enlarged in such a way that modal inflections of judgments may enter into the logic of certainty or truth as formal possibilities. Not only the forms judged with certainty, but also those judged as possibilities, pertain to the "something-in-general." There are also feeling-modalities of the "something-in-general," and these are involved in the doxic (belief) sphere. In addition to this, the *Prolegomena* did not distinguish between the different kinds of irreality; the ideality of meanings and the ideality of general essences or species are special cases of the "irreal." Husserl also came to recognize that it was wrong to regard "theoretical" or "nomological" explanatory science as the ideal of all science. Sciences such as psychology, phenomenology, or history differ fundamentally in their theoretical type from the nomological; their system-form is not that of a definite deductive theory. These critical remarks are indications of the broader theory of science achieved in the later

[17] Cf. *Formale und transzendentale Logik*, §§ 27, 28, 31, 35, 36, 57; and also Hauer, Ziegenfuss, and Jung, *Philosophen Lexikon* (Berlin, 1937), pp. 447 ff. for Husserl's own account of the development of his thought.

logical studies. The determination of the three basic strata of logic, as well as the clear distinction between the formal "logic of non-contradiction" and the formal "logic of truth" are among the indications of Husserl's progress beyond the *Prolegomena*.

The latter work was really designed as an introduction to the phenomenological investigations of the second volume of the *Logical Investigations*. It had been said that these phenomenological investigations, which were required for the clarification of the fundamental concepts of logic, signified a return to psychologism. That was because the first volume had been erroneously regarded as a mere refutation of psychologism in general, whereas it was the psychologistic theory of logic which was examined. This particular problem of psychologism is given a more searching treatment in the *Formal and Transcendental Logic*.

Husserl's last published writing, on "The Crisis of European Science and Transcendental Phenomenology," recalls the concluding discussion of the *Prolegomena*. The principle that all empirical procedure is dominated by an ideal norm, and the emphasis upon ideal elements and laws in the domain of empirical thought, remain central motives in his thought until the end.

In considering the arguments of such representative philosophers as Schuppe, Sigwart, and other members of the reigning philosophical schools, one becomes aware of the great need for a reform in philosophy, a reform which could only be accomplished by means of a rigorously defined method designed to penetrate to the final grounds of knowledge. The complete emancipation from all traditional schools of philosophy was a necessary condition for such an undertaking. It was the historical mission of Husserl to give philosophy that new impetus. The six logical investigations provide actual illustrative material for the proposed new philosophical discipline, by means of concrete descriptive studies.

CHAPTER VI

GERMAN LOGIC AT THE CLOSE OF THE CENTURY

ALTHOUGH the second logical survey [1] was published after the *Logical Investigations*, it provides a good introduction to the second volume of that work. The logical literature that is discussed in it was published while the *Logical Investigations* was being written. The reader will thus become acquainted with some of the outstanding logical problems of the time. In the second survey the refutation of psychologism is regarded as an accomplished fact. Husserl's hope to avoid fundamental misunderstandings of his logical aims by means of his repeated attempts at a clear formulation of the province and function of pure logic was destined to be disappointed for the most part. Persuasion was difficult in the face of the school alignments and fixed points of view of most philosophers.

A. FUNDAMENTAL PROBLEMS OF LOGIC

1. *The Nature of Logic*

Husserl speaks with high praise of Bergmann's *Fundamental Problems of Logic*.[2] The empirical tendency so prominent in the logic of the time, with empirical psychology used for the foundation of logic, is foreign to Bergmann, and Husserl regards it as no mean merit that Bergmann holds to the idea of a pure logic as an *a priori* discipline. But, Husserl adds, that kind of psychological foundation which is in fact indispensable for the explanation of the meaning of purely logical concepts and laws is inadequately treated in Bergmann's work. Husserl gives therewith an early version of the restricted field and function of phenomenology, his point being the necessity of those purely descriptive analyses of thought-experiences which are "prior" to all empirical, explanatory, genetic psychology and which he designates as *phenomenological analyses*.

Commenting upon the Kantian distinction between pure and applied logic which is taken over by Bergmann, Husserl allows that the Kantian

---

[1] "Bericht über deutsche Schriften zur Logik in den Jahren 1895–99," *Archiv f. syst. Phil.*, vol. IX (Berlin, 1903), pp. 113–132, 237–259, 393–408, 523–543. The concluding article follows in vol. X (1904), pp. 101–125.

[2] J. Bergmann, *Die Grundprobleme der Logik*, 2nd ed. (Berlin, 1895).

distinctions are justified in themselves (just as had been done in the *Prolegomena*), but holds that they do not bring to complete clarity the various distinctions and types of logic. The contrast between pure and applied logic is synonymous with the difference between *theoretical* and *practical* logic. But if "pure" is taken to mean "a priori" there is a second distinction between *a priori* and *a posteriori* logic, which can be made to coincide with the first distinction. Husserl asserts once more that he gives full recognition to the old concept of a practical logic, or of logic conceived as an art; as an empirical art of thought it is clearly founded upon empirical psychology. Not only is psychology basic to it, however, but also the science of pure logic for which he had argued — a theoretical and *a priori* discipline whose pure laws are applied and made practically fruitful under the empirical conditions of human and scientific thinking. This pure logic has nothing to do with thinking and knowing, or with their direction and guidance, but is concerned rather with the unities of thought and knowledge, with the meanings and validities to be realized in thinking and knowing, with ideas and ideal laws constituting the idea of the "understanding." Hence instead of dealing with ideas, judgments, inferences, and insights as psychical experiences, it treats of concepts, propositions, inferences, etc., as "specific singularities" which are derived from such acts by real abstraction, and the general logical laws refer to these specific singularities. To have brought to clarity the fact that the essential content of every normative and practical logic is formed by propositions and theories which do not lie in the acts of thought, but rather in ideas which are individualized in certain of their factors, appears to Husserl to be one of the most important logical insights. It is latent in the *Wissenschaftslehre* of Bolzano, who unfortunately detracted from the understanding of his discovery by the way in which he introduced his fundamental conceptions of "presentation in itself" and of "proposition in itself" and in which he left them without any investigation of their phenomenological origin. Bolzano's work was not used by Bergmann, just as was the case with almost all logicians of the time, and so he lacked that essential idea of formal logic which was anticipated by Bolzano.

Husserl concurs with Bergmann's refusal to restrict logic to mere noncontradiction or "formal truth" to the exclusion of material and real truth, involving agreement with the object. But he finds a valuable idea in the views of the formalists, despite all traditional unclearness. The question turns upon the manner in which the concept of logic is construed. If it is to be pure logic, its theoretical character must be considered more closely than usual. When the cognitive purpose is placed first in logic, and rules and norms are expected from it to further this purpose, the standpoint of logic as an art has been adopted. Then we ought to be consistent and make this practical logic as practical as possible, in order to promote our cognitive purpose. But if we restrict ourselves to the general and pure logic, conceived as a theoretical discipline, there should be no talk of purposes and norms. The situation is similar to the case of pure and theoretical arithmetic, which contains laws for number-relations but does not provide norms for calculation. Naturally such laws permit of being transformed at any time by conceiving them as practical rules, which was originally foreign to them. The same holds for pure logic and the rules that can be formed directly out of its laws by reference to the cognitive purpose. That which the formalists were accustomed to teach about logic now holds for this pure and theoretical logic, but not for logic in general. Pure logic is "formal" logic, as the science of the forms of thought. The "matter of knowledge" does not enter its domain; it only follows the laws which are grounded in the categorial "forms" and which therefore yield truths, no matter how the forms are filled out with sensory "substances." These derived truths no longer belong to the content of pure logic itself, but to the field of its possible "applications." No "material" truth, i.e., no truth containing "sensory" concepts is to be found in the sphere of the purely logical or mathematical, all matter being left indeterminate in the manner of the indeterminate symbols $a, b, c, \ldots$ of algebra. The difference between the material and the formal is thus identical with the distinction between the *sensory* (whether "inner" or "outer") and the *categorial*. The sphere of formal logic in its broadest conception, or of the most broadly construed pure *mathesis*, is one of mere non-contradiction; it does not include a single real existential proposition or a single assertion about "facts," but only the propositions which belong to the meaning of thought as such, i.e., to the categorial forms. A thought which conforms to these laws as norms is assured of "formal" truth, but it is not assured therewith of "material" truth. That is because the only material truth that is warranted by it is based upon the form and not the matter of things, and it therefore remains valid despite arbitrary variation of the matter. Not every error is a "logical absurdity," or a violation of the laws of logic. It appears to Husserl that this interpretation, which is freed from inadmissible restrictions and confusions, does justice to the real tendency of the formalists.

Husserl criticizes Bergmann for regarding the laws of formal logic as essentially normative. According to Husserl's conception, as already indicated, the idea of norms is originally foreign to the laws of logic. The extension of the normative and practical logic beyond the sphere of its "applications" to definite cognitive contents ("matters"), its extension to scientific methodology, e.g., necessarily suspends its exclusively *a priori* character. The consideration of empirical human nature also introduces rules which cannot be founded upon the basis of pure logic alone. Husserl speaks of his essential agreement with Bergmann on the view that logic may not be conceived as a mere formal theory of purely categorial laws. But, apart from its use for practical purposes, as philosophical logic it needs epistemological elucidation. In Husserl's terminology this means phenomenological elucidation. By means of the latter we are not merely certain of the validity of the concepts and theories, but also "understand" them. That the much reviled "dreary formalism" does not satisfy the philosophical interest does not prove anything against its inner worth, for it satisfies the mathematical interest instead. The critique of knowledge clarifies the objective meaning of the "dreary" forms, which is a specifically philosophical task.

2. *Logic and Metaphysics*

Bergmann's discussion of the relations of logic and metaphysics leads Husserl to give an interesting statement of his own views. According to Bergmann metaphysics precedes logic in the system of philosophy, its function being to make clear the concept of being and to solve the problems attaching thereto. Husserl agrees only in a very qualified manner, pointing out that everything depends upon the conception of logic and metaphysics that is accepted. If one restricts himself to pure logic as a theoretical system of purely categorial truths, then that may be regarded as "preceding" all sciences, for it leaves knowledge completely indeterminate so far as "matter" is concerned. Thus pure arithmetic does not need any basic principle from another science, especially from metaphysics. But pure mathematics in the broadest sense, as well as in the usual sense, requires a supplementary philosophical investigation which elucidates the difficulties concerning the meaning and objective validity of its fundamental concepts and laws. What is involved is not a gap in the connection of the theories or in their foundation through basic principles, for the filling in of such gaps is a matter of mathematics and not of philosophy; but rather the satisfaction of cognitive needs which even an ideally complete mathematical theory leaves unsatisfied, and which do not relate primarily to the meaning and construction of the single mathematical theories, but to thought in general and the elementary forms and laws belonging to its logical content. In short, it needs the critique of knowledge. If the concept of pure logic is construed so widely that it also comprises the critique of knowledge elucidating it philosophically, then the answer to the question of how logic and metaphysics are related depends upon the question of the relationship between metaphysics and the theory of knowledge. In Husserl's view one would hardly be able to separate the elucidation of the concept of being from the other epistemological investigations. Metaphysics in the sense in which Bergmann uses it (as the science of being as such) therefore passes over into that which Husserl calls the critique of knowledge. It, along with pure logic, would precede practical logic and all sciences. As Husserl sees it, the usual meaning of the term metaphysics is, however, entirely different. It falls to metaphysics to work out the final, absolutely valid determinations of true being from the confusion of that which is merely tentatively and relatively valid in the empirical sciences. If these are concerned more with laws and formulae for orientation in the world of appearance, and if the assumptions about existence have the value of mere aids for this purpose, then the theoretical interest of metaphysics deals primarily with existence itself. It aims to trace out the final meaning of the world, and does not rest content with the merely economical formulae which are of aid in making predictions; it does not aim at practical mastery over nature, but simply wants to know what is true and real. Metaphysics, in this sense, follows all the sciences, i.e., as the science of that which can be definitively said about true reality, on the basis of all the special sciences and with the continual use of the elucidations gained in the critique of knowledge. It is the task of the latter to provide elucidations of the concept of being, the forms of being and thought, the meaning and possibility of objectively valid knowledge, etc. The same holds for logic as an art, for it is based upon pure logic and the critique of knowledge, upon empirical psychology and, because it is concerned with the methodology of the special sciences, upon all of the special sciences.

Husserl expresses opposition to Bergmann's view that the meaning of the "existence" of a thing is that the world contains it, and that to present a thing as existing, one must have already presented his ego as existing. He holds that an unprejudiced answer to the question as to what we present when we present the number π must be: just the number π, the well-known transcendental number, which is neither a thing nor a class of things; and one cannot bring in the reference to the world and the ego without changing the meaning of the idea. The notion of an existing ego is beset by further difficulties. The statement "Socrates exists" means according to Bergmann "Socrates is contained in the world of my ego."

If another person makes the same assertion, he must mean accordingly that Socrates is contained in the world of his ego. Even if the world of the two egos were identical, both statements would differ in meaning, and it follows that an existential proposition would have as many meanings as there are persons to assert it.

3. Problems of the Theory of Judgment

The discussion of Bergmann's theory of judgment contains interesting material in connection with the phenomenological foundation of logic. According to Bergmann there are no "tautological" and no "enantiological" judgments. Forms like *S is (or is not) S* are not judgments, or they are not exact expressions of what the speaker means. All judgments are heterological in his view. Expressing disagreement on this question, Husserl admits that tautological expressions such as "Napoleon is Napoleon" usually have a modified meaning, but denies that that must be the case. He denies that tautologies, and especially partially tautological statements, cannot be understood in the sense in which they are indicated by the form of the expression. One can really assert tautological statements as often as one wishes to do so. Husserl suggests that a broad concept of inference be retained, allowing for the distinction between tautological and heterological inferences, the term "heterological" being interpreted as signifying the extension of knowledge.

According to Bergmann's analysis, every judgment in a narrower sense contains the following elements: (*a*) a presentation, i.e., the positing of an object, (*b*) a predication, and (*c*) a critical attitude toward this predication, a corroboration or rejection of the predication. As a collaborator in this domain Husserl states his objection to Bergmann's treatment of negative judgments. The interpretation of the general negative statement "*S* is not *p*" by means of the expression "that *S* is *p* is incorrect" is subject to an objection raised by Bolzano. The one expression can be true and the other false, hence they are not even equivalent in meaning, let alone identical. If one rejects the judgment "Prime numbers are even numbers," one does not therefore assert that prime numbers are not even numbers, which is not the case with regard to the number two. According to Bergmann, in judgments of the form "that *S* is *p* is incorrect" what is concerned is a conflict of the object with the judgment or, as Husserl states it, of the actual fact (to be given in a possible evidence) with the judgment. But, Husserl reasons, if we examine the consciousness of conflict and what it presupposes, we must consider actual cases in which the conflict becomes evident. The judgment-intention must in part agree with the given or believed circumstances; a part of its content must correctly "express" a part of the circumstances, but it has still other parts which conflict with correlative parts of the meant circumstances. Thus the presupposition of the possibility of a conflict between a judgment and a fact consists of conflicts between some parts of a judgment which are not judgments themselves, and parts of the fact which are no longer facts themselves. These conflicts are expressed by means of simple negative predications, in which some determination is denied of the given (posited) object. If someone says, e.g., that this surface is green, whereas I perceive it to be red, then a consciousness of conflict attaches to the "is green," and I assert that it is not green. The form "S is not p" is primitive, and is regarded by Husserl as coördinate with the affirmative form, "S is p." The negative proposition does not mean an affirmation of the determination "conflict with p" of the S. It expresses the conflict in the same sense in which the "S is p" expresses an agreement, namely, that the p attaches to the S. In the original and simple judgment, S is first posited, and on the basis of this the supplementary and dependent act "is p" is performed. In a precise sense, this dependent act may be called an act of "predication"; but in a wider sense the predication is taken to be the complete act "S is p." In an evident judgment, the fact or what the judgment intends is "perceived." Husserl here makes use of a very broad concept of perception, which should not be confused with the ordinary concept of sense-perception. That S is p is perceived, and in this perceived unity there lies the basis for the abstraction of the relational concept of attribution or "attaching to," for example. In reflection upon it the "subject" S is conceived as "having" the "predicate" p, and p as "attaching to" the subject S. This is the origin of circumscriptive concepts and expressions (Husserl uses Marty's term "zirkumskriptive" to name expressions which in an indirect way refer to a thought, thus warning against taking them to be identical in meaning with the thought). The situation is exactly the same for a negative judgment and its negative fact. If that is evidently given, or imagined exactly, the circumscriptive concept of conflict can arise and then function as a predicate.

Without giving up the view that a negative predication is on a par with a positive, Husserl adds that a negative predication "refers back" to the affirmative in a certain manner, and thus presupposes it. This enables him to embrace the interpretation of negative judgment to a theory of the modalities of judgment, as he discusses it elsewhere, beginning with the "number one" case of positive assertion. While conflicting with the S, the p nevertheless makes the claim as it were of belonging to it. However one may construe this "claim," the meaning-forms are essentially different in the two cases. It would be entirely wrong to say that the negative judgment contains the affirmative, for whoever asserts the former cannot in the same breath assert the latter. Even in abstraction from the character of belief and with sole regard to the meaning-content of the judgments the negative judgment cannot be said actually to contain the affirmative.

This analysis also aims to do justice to what is sound in the doctrines that negation affects the copula, and that it belong to the predicate, and in effect it reconciles them with each other. The "not" belongs together with the "is," but the "is" is not a "copula"; it is not a connection between S and p. The "is p," as a dependent but unified act, is founded upon the subject-positing S. The S is connected with the unified "is p," and not with an independent p. "Is p," or "is not p," is the predicate. The doctrine according to which the "not" is in the predicate had this in view, but it confused predicate-meaning (the "is p") and predicate-concept ("p"), due to the ambiguity of the word predicate. It made the fundamentally incorrect interpretation of "S is not p" as "S is not-p," or as an affirmative judgment with a changed predicate-concept. The "not" really belongs, as is the case with the "is," in the predicate, or in its meaning-content.

The present discussion leads Husserl to complete his analysis of judgment in relation to the other elements of knowing. If it be asked, what must be added to a "mere" presentation in order that it become a judgment, then the term "presentation" must refer to the whole meaning-content of the judgment, and not, as Brentano and Bergmann hold, to the nominal presentation of the object, even if it be with a content that comprises the predicated determinations. The only factor that must be excluded is the "belief," or the character of certainty. One can express a whole meaning such as "S is p," "S is not p" and the like while not believing what one hears, and hence not judging. To every judgment "S is p" there thus corresponds the mere presentation "S is p," not as a presentation of the judgment, but rather of the judged fact. Husserl calls the sense of this presentation, which comprises all that the judgment believes, the "matter" of the judgment, and thus he comes to the same distinction between content and quality in every judgment that Brentano had advocated. But for Husserl the content is not the presentation as it existed say before the predicative analysis, and is not a presentation that can be expressed nominally; and the quality is not a recognition or a rejection referring to such a presentation. The thought of a reduction of every judgment to the supposed normal form of the existential proposition is remote from his conception. Not only the content in the traditional sense, or S and *p*, but also all the categorial forms, such as "one" and "some," "if and then," and especially the "is" and "not," belong to the "content." The "is" is therefore not an expression of "belief," and neither is the "is-not" an expression of a coördinated "disbelief." The character of positing or of certainty belongs rather to the whole content, regardless of how its parts may be articulated. The usual expressions for this character, such as "to hold to be true," "belief," "consciousness of validity," and the like, lead to the erroneous conception that what is involved is a predication of truth, validity, or correctness referring to the content, and that two coördinated qualities, "holding to be true" and "holding to be false," are to be distinguished. But Husserl also questions this last. Every normal statement expresses a judgment, but every judgment also finds its expression in a possible statement. There are statements which express a disbelief, a rejection, or a declaration of invalidity. But they only do so in the manner of predications which either state about the judging subject, "I or some one else does not believe it, or denies it," or which objectively say about the proposition or matter in question that it is untrue or incorrect. In every case the expression of rejection, of disbelief, or of untruth belongs to the content of these statements, and what makes them themselves to be statements is not this predicated disbelief, but the character of conviction that so to speak animates this content. Every statement is a "belief." Whether this conception, to which Husserl inclines after much vacillation, is final or not, he holds it to be founded in any case upon actual facts which need attention and a clarifying investigation.

Finally, Husserl regards the view as not proved that all judgments can be reduced to predications. From the circumstance that judgments as such can be classified as true or false it does not follow that they are either affirmative or negative, and hence that they state something about something. The question regarding the fundamental forms of judgment, or rather of the matters of judgment, does not appear to Husserl to be treated adequately. That one can bring all propositions equivalently into the categorical form does not prove that the categorical form is essential to every judgment, and is only concealed by grammatical forms. Objectionable also is the view that in every judgment the existence of the subject is asserted, for that does not hold for all cases. Let us suppose that as we are engrossed in looking at a picture, we bring its subject to consciousness. Do we not judge about the painted objects as we judge about real things, while not holding them to be real for one moment? The same holds for appearing objects, if we are undecided whether they are hallucinatory or real objects. Husserl expresses doubt about the attempt to achieve simplicity by means of the reduction of all judgments, such as the disjunctive, etc., to the supposed fundamental form of the categorical proposition. That may lead to transformations of language and of the original thoughts. He therefore holds the attempt to treat immediate and evident equivalent forms as identical to be a danger in the formal doctrine of meaning.

Bergmann's discussion of analytic and synthetic judgments, which is described as important and fruitful by Husserl, provides the latter with an occasion for a more pointed analysis of his own. To begin with, he considers the two essentially different ways in which a judgment can be known to be true "through immediate comparison with its object." Either (*a*) the object must be given in perception, and only thus can its existence (in case individual existence is also asserted in the judgment) be known, as well as the belonging of the predicate to it; or (*b*) the intuition does not need the character of a perception in order to make this "belonging to" known. In the latter case two possibilities again exist. Either that which is predicated of the object is "contained" in the subject-determinations, i.e., the predicate does not bring in anything "materially" new; or there is the possibility that the predicated determinations are not "contained" in those of the subject, but are necessarily connected with them and are knowable as dependent. In the first case, which is described by Bergmann, all the partial meanings of the proposition are unrestrictedly variable; in the second, the judgments are grounded in the generic nature of the determinations in question. They are therefore not unlimited, but are variable only within their genera. If unlimited variables are introduced into the propositions of the first class which are analytic in character, universal and "pure" propositions, free from all individual, existential content are obtained. Thus the proposition "These 7 apples and these 5 apples together are 12 apples" becomes "$7 + 5 = 12$." They are propositions which are exclusively constructed out of categorial concepts and forms, such as unity, number, plurality, relation, object, determination, inference, etc., and contain no concepts obtained through sensory abstraction, such as color, sensation, or house. Furthermore, they do not admit any individual positing of existence, as illustrated by "this," "a certain thing," etc. Such pure, analytic propositions are entirely *a priori*. Husserl construes the concept of the analytic so widely that it comprises the entire sphere of that which is valid purely categorially. The propositions of the second class are also *a priori*, if the possible cases of the positing of existence are excepted, but they are *a priori* synthetic judgments. If they are purified of all that is empirical and of all individual positing, then synthetic *a priori* laws arise. They are laws of real syntheses, regulating the necessary connection of the dependent factors in the unity of sensory objects and based upon the genera of those factors. The following will serve as examples of this type: There can be no color without extension, no extension without a qualitative covering, no tone-quality without tone-intensity, and the like. Bergmann had omitted this latter class of *a priori* propositions and laws. The tone-intensity does not lie analytically in the tone-quality, and yet it is sufficient to think of an object as merely determined as a tone-quality, in order to think of it as also being the possessor of tone-intensity. Since these determinations are connected by means of the generic essences of quality and intensity, the necessity is an *a priori* one. Husserl holds it to be indubitable that these are laws belonging to the general essence of all real factors, without which no real unity would be thinkable, and that these laws, in so far as they belong to the genera given in our sensibility, provide unquestionable examples of *a priori* synthetic propositions. This discussion of analytic and synthetic judgments is instructive in the light of Husserl's later treatment of logical forms and the concept of essence, and also in connection with the analysis of Kant.

The reader of Husserl's logical writings, particularly in his last period, is familiar with the frequently used concept of a "fact" or *Sachverhalt*. It is of interest to note that in the present context Husserl uses "the important auxiliary concept" of "judgment-content" as synonymous with "Sachverhalt." The term "fact" is by no means ideal to name what is intended; but the cumbrous expression "judgment-content" is still less acceptable.

A few remaining points will be selected finally as worthy of mention. In commenting upon such logical principles as the law of the excluded middle, Husserl commits himself explicitly to the standpoint that there are immediate axioms at the basis of logic. Such principles must, in his view, serve as irreducible, fundamental principles, so that one should not speak of "deducing" them. The opposition of Berkeley to the infinitesimal calculus is held up as an admonition to trust the mathematical instinct, which is at first uncritical, but is in the main a sure guide. He adds that the technical elaboration of a purely logical theory and its philosophical explanation are two different things.

In discussing the relations of subordination Bergmann seeks to renew the old doctrine of the reciprocity of extension and intension, interpreting the intension as constitutive and the extension as ideal. But old objections are not avoided thereby, as Husserl points out. The enrichment of the constitutive content will not decrease the extension if it is enriched by a predicate that is necessarily connected with one of the original predicates and is nevertheless not contained in it.

Bergmann's inadequate treatment of the concept of "presentation," in which he fails to distinguish the narrower and wider concepts of presentations and their essential modifications, leads Husserl to state briefly the most important pertinent distinctions, which his more extended analysis in the *Logical Investigations* had made clear. It is apparent that the expression "content of a presentation" can be interpreted in various important ways. If the term "presentation" is taken to mean the act or the experience of presentation, the content in a psychological sense, which comprehends everything psychologically constituting the experience, is distinguished from content in a logical sense. But logical content may mean several things, as follows: (*a*) It may refer to the object of the presentation, or (*b*) the meaning of the presentation, e.g., the identical meaning of the nominal expression. The same object can be meant by various meanings. The usual term for this "sense" or this "meaning" is, however, not the "content" of the presentation, but the "presentation" itself. (*c*) It may mean the content as distinguished from the categorial form. The content is the totality of the partial presentations (partial meanings), whether it be to bring the object itself to direct expression, or objects, characters, and forms of complexes related to it. Thus in the two presentations, "Socrates the teacher of Plato" and "the teacher of Plato or Socrates," the content in the present sense would be the same, namely, the sum of the presentations (meanings) Socrates, Plato, and teacher. The difference lies in the logical "form." (*d*) If the "content" of a presentation refers to the content of the object, the entire totality of the parts and factors of the object which find their explicit or implicit expression in the presentation (meaning) can be meant.

B. PHENOMENOLOGY AND PSYCHOLOGY

A paper by Theodor Elsenhans on "The Relationship of Logic to Psychology"[3] gives Husserl an opportunity to characterize phenomenology more pointedly than had been done in the past. This serves as a correction of the definition of phenomenology (already noted) as "descriptive psychology" which had also been given in the introduction to the first investigation, in the second volume of the *Logical Investigations*. That led

---

[3] Theodor Elsenhans, "Das Verhältnis der Logik zur Psychologie," *Zeit. f. Phil. u. phil. Kritik*, vol. CIX (1896), pp. 195–212.

to the misunderstanding of phenomenology as a revival of self-observa-tion.[4] The standpoint of Elsenhans was the familiar thesis of psychologism as the way to solve the problems of logic; for, he reasoned, since logic elaborates certain mental occurrences, its subject-matter is a part of the subject-matter of psychology. In order to dispose of this controversial question, Husserl points out once more the need of separating logic into various realms, and emphasizes the part played by pure logic as an essential foundation of logic. It would be nonsense to think of ordering the realm of pure logic, or of formal thought (including set theory and the pure mathematical theory of probability), under psychology. The task of the "critique of knowledge" refers to just this realm; it aims to make comprehensible the possibility of knowledge by an investigation of the "origin" of the pure-logical concepts and laws and in this way to solve the problems involved in the opposition between the subjectivity of the act of knowledge and the objectivity of the cognitive content and object, or between truth and being. This task does not fall to pure logic as such. The critical (in the sense of the critique of knowledge) elucida-tion of pure arithmetic is not a task of arithmetic, and neither is the cri-tique of pure syllogistic a syllogistic task. It is also not a task of psychology, at least as it is usually understood. Just as physics, or natural science in the usual sense, is an empirical science of corporeal facts, so psychology is the empirical or natural science of mental facts. Both sciences proceed from the world in the usual "pre-critical" sense, with its separation of facts into bodily and mental; and both remain uncritical, no matter how they may reinterpret the original idea of the world. As explanatory sci-ences they presuppose "pre-given objectivations"[5] whose meaning and elucidation can be dispensed with, as the great success of these sciences without the aid of the critique of knowledge shows. These pre-critical objectivations contain distinctions between egos and non-egos, between the "ego itself" and a "strange ego," and interpret the immediate givenness of consciousness as being "psychical activities and conditions" in one's own ego, whereas physical things and "strange" persons are located outside of the ego. Husserl maintains that such pre-critical objectivations give rise to the metaphysical problem of the possibility of knowledge, which on its side presupposes an explanation of knowledge in general, apart from all metaphysical considerations. This explanatory elucidation requires a phe-nomenology of knowledge, which analyzes the cognitive experiences in

[4] Cf. *Logos*, vol. 1 (1910–1911), p. 318 n., where Husserl refers to pp. 397–400 of the present logical survey for the correction in question.

[5] For the concepts "objectivation" and "objectivating act," see chs. XII–XIII herein.

which logical concepts originate, an analysis which is confined to the immanent content of these experiences, and which brings to evidence the genuine meaning of the logical concepts, or their general essences. The necessity of making himself understood leads the phenomenologist to use objectivating expressions, as when he says that "we find" something present in an immediate experience. But in reality the natural world and all metaphysical objectivations are completely eliminated. It would therefore be wrong to designate phenomenology as descriptive psychology, for its descriptions do not refer to the experiences of empirical persons. It knows nothing and presumes nothing about persons; it raises no questions about myself or other human beings, and makes no hypotheses. A phenomenological description deals with the given in the strictest sense, with experiences just as they are in themselves. The thing-appearance is analyzed, e.g., and not that which appears in it; and all apperceptions by means of which the appearance and that which appears enter into correlation with the ego, to which something appears, are rejected. The elucidation of knowledge that results from this analysis is simply adequate intuitive abstraction, which brings the general essence of that which is fixated phenomenologically to evident consciousness. The true content of the concepts and laws of logic are thus brought to clear and distinct understanding. The thoughts which before the critique were confused and permeated with symbolic and pictorial elements now pass over into clear and fully realized thoughts, whose possibility and validity are directly seen and grasped. The psychological apperceptions here eliminated may be brought in at any time and thus make the results of phenomenology and of the critique of knowledge directly useful. The phenomenological analyses then take on the character of descriptive psychological analyses, and they function as bases for the theoretical explanations of psychology as the natural science of mental appearances. The elucidation of the logical laws is also of fundamental significance in relationship to psychology. Corresponding to the ideal laws and connections of the conceptual essences are laws of coexistence and non-coexistence in the sphere of the particular psychical contents. Husserl holds it to be of deciding importance for a consistent theory of knowledge and for philosophy in general, however, that a distinction be made on principle between the purely immanent phenomenology and critique of knowledge, which is kept free from all suppositions going beyond the content of the given, and empirical psychology, which makes such suppositions even when it describes. Accordingly, the question of epistemological origins from the point of view of the critique of knowledge should not be confused with the question of psychological origins.

As a result of this confusion the critique of knowledge is led over into psychology and biology, and is involved in the absurdities of skeptical empiricism and relativism. Husserl charges Elsenhans with these mistakes, especially as seen in his parallelism of the feeling of evidence and the feeling of language, as well as in his reduction of logic to a psychology of evidence. This reduction, which was indicated by Mill and carried through by Höfler and Meinong in their logic, has no more value than a reduction of arithmetic to a psychology of "correct" counting. Every mathematical law has a meaning to be interpreted psychologically, and yet none has a psychological meaning itself. With regard to the fuller analysis of the theory of evidence and of the psychologistic misinterpretation of ideal laws or laws of essence in general, Husserl refers to the *Logical Investigations*. He tried to show in that work that the idea of a normal, mentally healthy person presupposes the idea of reason, and hence is not at all suited to define it or the realm of logic.

C. THE IDEAL OF INFINITE THOUGHT

Heinrich Gomperz's *Psychology of the Fundamental Facts of Logic* [6] is characterized by Husserl as an extreme example of nominalism and sensationalism. In the introduction to his work Gomperz sketches the intellectual ideal of "divine" thought. It is for him, as for Rickert, a thought that could survey the entire fullness of the world of appearance, distinguish all particulars, and grasp the infinite number of relations obtaining among them; and man uses general concepts and inferences for the practical purpose of lessening his imperfections. Husserl observes that in the depiction of the intellectual ideal a small matter has been overlooked — the intellect. This godly thinking is no longer thinking, but is an all-comprehensive, all-discriminating intuition. It is a blind intuition, since without concepts "intuition" is "blind." According to Gomperz, it is only for the finite consciousness of man that concepts and laws are needed, as a linguistic aid. Husserl asks whether the finite consciousness ought not to be preferable to the godly, because of its knowledge of eternal necessities and possibilities, as well as the relating of particulars to a law. He suggests that the depicted ideal of infinite wisdom is rather one of infinite stupidity, which sees all and nevertheless conceives and knows nothing. These errors are ascribed to a defective descriptive analysis of intellectual experience, in which there is no proper distinction between the intuitive and the symbolic function on the one hand, and between the sensory and the categorial function on the other hand. As a result the old equivoca-

[6] H. Gomperz, *Zur Psychologie der logischen Grundtatsachen* (Leipzig und Wien, 1897).

tions attached to the concepts of intuition and thinking cannot be avoided, i.e., intuition as sensory, and as intellectual, expressing insight and evidence; and thinking by means of symbolic substitutes, and by means of categorial functions.[7]

An illustration of the nature of phenomenological questions and the degree of analysis that is required is provided by Husserl's comments upon Gomperz's analysis of five psychical factors in a speaker, namely, the idea occasioning the expression, the feelings connected therewith, the sensation of innervation, the sound, and the written character. Phenomenologically viewed, there are also the "meaning" and the "object." Furthermore, which types of the relation of meaning an object are to be distinguished? There is also the question concerning the place of the "forms" of which not only logic treats, but by which thinking is actually permeated. That Gomperz did not see the essential problems is shown by his treatment of the fundamental difficulty of nominalism, which is to explain how a thought occurring in mere individual ideas can attain general meaning and validity. This question was transformed by him into the question of how one can think on the basis of individual ideas without having erred because of their individual peculiarities. He is criticized for his failure to understand the task of the pure descriptive analysis of judgment, which is the foundation of the theory of knowledge, and to distinguish between it and genetic analysis (in the naturalistic sense), which is irrelevant epistemologically. The important problems of phenomenology and the theory of proof which were not recognized include the determination of the conditions under which the experience of motivation appears, what it presupposes necessarily, what elucidates the difference between supposed and real proof, what are the further differences between ground and consequence, between empirical and rational grounds, etc.

D. THE CRITIQUE OF KNOWLEDGE

Wilhelm Jerusalem's *Function of Judgment*[8] is criticized sharply. This discussion illustrates again the problem of reconciling psychological and logical analysis. The psychology of judgment was for Jerusalem the basis of all theoretical philosophy, and he believed that the investigation of the judgment-form solves the epistemological problem and leads closer to the solution of ultimate metaphysical problems, such as pertain to God, the soul, etc. Husserl again calls attention to the distinction between the psychology of knowledge and the critique of knowledge. There is a funda-

[7] Cp. *Log. Unt.*, vol. II, part 2, chs. VI ff.
[8] W. Jerusalem, *Die Urteilsfunktion* (Wien und Leipzig, 1895).

mental essential difference between the objective and theoretical analysis of occurrences of thought and the elucidation of the unities of thought, or the analysis of meaning and validity. The former places us in an objective context and speaks of human beings as psychophysical individuals, of their relations of life and social organizations and the psychical structures arising therein. It goes back to the elementary psychical conditions of these individuals and investigates their causal connections and natural laws. The critical elucidation on the other hand does not theorize, it does not ask about mental or physical things and explains nothing on the basis of natural laws. It clarifies instead of explaining, and asks wherein the idea of a theory as a valid unity and all the ideas and ideal laws constituting it arise, what validity and being really mean, and what makes them understandable. The adequate description of judgment must include a pure descriptive analysis of all the experiences out of which the various essentially different types of descriptive judgment are built up. The task of a theory of judgment requires that one take account of linguistic experiences and investigate the difficulties involved in meaning and its relation to what is meant. This leads to the more general question of what endows certain experiences, which we call presentations and which are taken to include judgment-intending, with the relation to "objects," and also the question as to which essentially different types of this relation are to be distinguished. Further questions include the following: which functional relationships and possible complex forms are based upon the essence of the different kinds of presentation, and how the fundamental logical and noetic concepts arise and are freed from elements of confusion and ambiguity. In Husserl's opinion there can be no systematic theory of judgment without such investigations. The psychology of judgment presupposes the clarification of such concepts as sign, mark, expression, meaning, concept, proposition, object, fact, perception, presentation, and intuition.

The present discussion contains a statement of Husserl's views on anthropomorphism and the use of the genetic method which will aid in understanding his non-natural point of view. Jerusalem is accused of introducing an anthropomorphic element into the function of judgment because of his view of judgment as the most primitive kind of apperception and orientation in our environment. Husserl remarks that no one will deny the anthropomorphism which dominates the childish conception of the world, and which we more developed people "never entirely get rid of." Language everywhere shows traces of this anthropomorphism, and a biological and cultural-historical account of the human intellect will proceed from these well-known facts. But he regards it as perverse to make them the foundation and beginning of an elementary psychological analysis, and to want to base a theory of knowledge and a system of philosophy upon them. His line of argument is indicated by the question of how a theory can undertake to clarify the essence of apperception *in general* through the genetic reduction of all materially determined apperceptions to a *single* one of them, which arises naturally among the factual, biological relationships of man. Is there not a *proton pseudos* in such a theory? It appears obvious to him that even if such a reduction were successful, the problem would still remain untouched. The factual account would not make clear the nature of apperceiving, conceiving, and interpreting, nor what makes their correct or false relation to objects possible and comprehensible.

Husserl is not satisfied with a mere anatomy of judgment, i.e., with a purely descriptive phenomenology of the general characteristics that are essential to judgment, and with a purely descriptive determination of its essential varieties and the essentially different forms in which it combines to make more comprehensive psychical structures. He also wants a physiology of judgment, which would provide knowledge of the elementary laws of the coming and going of these descriptively determined experiences, or of their formation and transformation. In illustration of his meaning Husserl asks whether the problem of the anatomy and physiology of man would be solved, or even attacked, if one were to determine that all men are descended from Adam, or from a certain human race, or a known natural-historical species, the monkey or the like. He distinguishes between abstract, nomological natural science arriving at elementary laws, and concrete, ontological natural science, which undertakes the explanation of the concrete formations of nature. The latter is based upon the former, its theoretical explanation being accomplished by the application of the elementary nomology gained in the abstract sciences. Husserl holds it to be an absurd undertaking to reverse this order and to base abstract science upon concrete science. That would be just as perverse in his opinion as it would be to base genetic psychology, as an elementary, nomological science, upon child-psychology, racial psychology, cultural psychology, anthropology, and concrete biology. That does not, however, preclude deriving from these concrete spheres stimulating suggestions or indirect evidence of something that can only be established finally and decisively through direct elementary, analytic investigation. Husserl admits that there are works with a psychologistic tendency which, despite extreme errors, have made even immortal achievements for psychology and philosophy. Thus Hume's *Treatise*, although wrong in principle, is nevertheless invaluable for the phenomenology and critique of knowledge. But Jerusalem's work does not belong to that class.

E.   THE LOGIC AND PSYCHOLOGY OF JUDGMENT

The essay on "The Psychology of Judgments" [9] by J. v. Kries is praised as an extraordinarily stimulating and fine work. In connection with the discussion under consideration, Husserl speaks of evidence as being the greatest problem and the real goal of the clarification of knowledge. Expressing disagreement with von Kries, Husserl argues that logic does not deal with idealizing fictions, and not merely with select cases of actual thinking, or with judgments of a preferred "character of validity." Logic as an art aims to provide norms for actual thought, just as it is; but pure logic, from whose principles the norms are obtained, has nothing to do with actual thought, or with select cases or idealizations of it. It therefore does not presuppose clarity, constancy, and determinateness of concepts or word-meanings, or the evidence of judgments. Husserl asserts that it does not presuppose anything at all. Such factors as clearness and determinateness, or rather the capacity for clarity and determinateness, are requirements of practical and not presuppositions of pure logic. They are requirements derived from pure logic and do not establish it. Pure logic does not make requirements any more than pure arithmetic does. Acts of presentation and of judgment are subject to the norms of logic, just as acts of counting and of calculation are subject to the norms of arithmetic. But pure logic and pure arithmetic do not deal with such psychical things. The former deals rather with concepts, propositions, objects, and facts according to validity and invalidity or being and non-being, and that in "formal" generality; and the latter with pure numbers and relations of numbers. A concept such as the concept of an angle, or a proposition such as the proposition concerning the sum of the angles of a triangle, is not a psychical experience. In common with most psychologistic logicians von Kries fails to ditsinguish between pure and practical normative logic. In Husserl's opinion the general analysis of judgment must accomplish much more than logicians such as von Kries are inclined to admit. To establish definitely what gives unity to the manifold intentions of thought and judgment, and what belongs to their general essence, requires the most comprehensive phenomenological investigations, whose results are not to be compressed in any formulae. The situation in the realm of thought is

---

[9] J. v. Kries, "Zur Psychologie der Urteile," *Viertelj. f. wiss. Phil.*, vol. XXIII (1899).

not as simple as had been hitherto assumed. Husserl submits that at least this may well have been made clear by the *Logical Investigations*.

F. MARTY'S LOGICAL STUDIES

The closing part of the present logical survey is devoted to the sixth and seventh articles making up Marty's logical studies,[10] of which notice was taken in the first logical survey. Husserl begins by summarizing the earlier articles of the work, because of its exceptional significance for the logic and psychology of knowledge. The first three articles had been based upon the simpler form of the theory of judgment of Brentano, as presented in the latter's *Psychology* of 1874. Marty distinguishes three classes of predicates: real predicates, such as red or two feet long; non-real predicates, such as not existing, past, merely possible, or merely presented; and aoristic predicates, as illustrated by non-red and non-man. Aoristic predicates can attach both to the real and the non-real. The predicate "existence" belongs to the aoristic class. Husserl observes that this distinction is in need of a phenomenological investigation, and calls attention to the more important epistemological distinction between the real and the categorial. By real is meant that which can be experienced in simple intuition, whereas the categorial can only be intuited in categorial or founded intuition. Examples of purely categorial concepts are being, identity, difference, relation, totality, and number. Existence is also a concept in this sense; it does not enrich its subject by any "real character." Purely categorial or "purely logical" transformations of a concept and proposition do not bring in any "real" content. Closely connected therewith is the relative and absolute difference between substance and form. Husserl refers to the *Logical Investigations*, especially the fifth and sixth investigations, as showing how many more fundamental distinctions there are in the domains of "presentation" and "judgment" than had hitherto been assumed, and also that we are still at the beginning of such knowledge.

Husserl states that there are very weighty logical grounds for regarding the identical meaning which is judged in the "judgment" as a proposition. If that is accepted, then one must exclude nominal positings from the sphere of judgment. "The Kaiser," "this house" and the like are not existential propositions because they are not propositions at all; they are neither grammatical nor logical propositions. They posit objects by naming, and not facts by assertion. To every positing name there corresponds

[10] Anton Marty, "Ueber subjektlose Sätze und das Verhältnis der Grammatik zur Logik und Psychologie," sixth and seventh articles, *Viertelj. f. wiss. Phil.*, vol. XIX (1895), pp. 19–87, 263–334.

ideally a possible equivalent existential proposition, which must contain the same name or another positing name.

The discussion of belief is also of interest. An act of belief is not a judgment in the logical sense. Although it means a being in a certain manner, it is not as though it were contained in its content or meaning. Husserl states that the deep core of Brentano's idea is seen here. If a belief is correct, then a verification is ideally possible. Its correctness, or the identity of the meant and the given, would be an experience. By means of such experiences, something meant is viewed, conceived, and designated as "being," as something identical with itself. The concept of being is lacking in a case of simple nominal positing; it first appears in an existential proposition, the self-identity that was viewed in the experience of evident "correctness" being ascribed to the meant object as a categorial predicate. Corresponding to this predicate of the presented object is the predicate of the presentation, namely, that it is capable of adequation. Therefore the proposition "The presentation A has objectivity" is not, as Bolzano holds, identical in meaning with "A is, or exists," but is only its immediately evident equivalent. The relationship of this "is" of the predicate in an existential proposition to the "is" of the copula is seen. The latter also expresses identity, not of self-apprehension, but that which belongs to every case of subject and predicate. Therefore a "belief" is not expressed in either case. It could not do so, because everything in the expression belongs to the fact, which is not a psychical experience, but an "intentional unity" (i.e., meant or intended as the same). Thus the "is not" does not express a disbelief, but rather a predicative conflict, an objective relationship. In agreement with Hume and in opposition to Marty and Brentano, Husserl does not assume an opposite to belief in general. A "belief" is no affirmation, recognition, or assent, to which a denial, rejection, or refusal is opposed. The word is deceptive. If one holds to the experience itself, to the simple intending in the statement, he finds within the class of "objectivating acts" the coördinated but not opposed phenomenon of "mere" presentation. While engrossed in the act of viewing a picture, we judge about the objects without taking them to be actualities. Furthermore, yielding to the play of phantasy, we may judge about the forms that enchant us. Husserl asks whether we are to explain away all of these modified judgments on the basis of mere presentations, through reinterpretations. The subject-presentations do not function in them as positings, but rather as presuppositions. The case is similar in the sphere of the conditional judgment, where actual judgments function at one time and propositional assumptions at another time as foundations for judgments that are built upon them, and are accordingly characterized differently.

In his critical remarks about Brentano and Marty, Husserl recognizes the irreducibility of the categorical judgment to simple existential judgments, or mere sums of such judgments. A categorical judgment is not only a "double" judgment, i.e., a peculiar interweaving of elementary judgments. It is at the same time *a* judgment; it believes as a whole, and it believes something. Hence the separation of quality and matter, of acknowledgment and content of acknowledgment, must find a place here, as well as anywhere else. Marty fails to distinguish the fundamentally different concepts of matter. There is matter as the correlate of belief, as the unity of the believed "what," e.g., as the sense of an asserted proposition, and, on the other hand, matter as the totality of the "terms" as opposed to the unity-giving categorial forms of the proposition, such as one, some, all, is, not, etc. The situation is similar for the two fundamentally different concepts of quality. Quality may be understood in the traditional sense of formal logic, as referring to a proposition, and also in the descriptive psychological sense, as referring to a judgment, namely, as the character of belief.

The remainder of the discussion contains comments upon the nature of the universal affirmative judgment, negation, mathematical existence, hypothetical judgments, and a logical paradox which had occurred to Husserl some years earlier. Husserl expresses agreement with B. Erdmann on the interpretation of "All *S* are *p*" as a purely affirmative judgment, and also on the interpretation of hypothetical and particular forms of propositions. The being-*p* is asserted about all *S*, and the "all" belongs to the subject. In opposition to Marty, Husserl holds that particular judgments, indeterminate-singular or indeterminate-plural, are categorical and not existential, just as are the closely related determinate-singular and determinate-plural judgments, as, e.g., "S_0 and S_1 are *p*." The negative judgments of these forms cause no difficulty if one distinguishes between the negative predicate-concept and negative predication. The negation belongs to the predicate; it is asserted about all or a few that they are not *p*, but it is not asserted that they are not-*p*. To say of people that they are not smokers is not to say that they are non-smokers. The former does not need the negative concept, which may never have been formed by the judger. In any case, the origin of the negative concept presupposes the negative predication.

Husserl states, in criticism of Marty, that a transcription of mathematics into negative existential propositions would not only be impossible on linguistic grounds, but also essentially. The mathematician does not assert a universal proposition without first establishing the objects postulationally at the beginning of the deductive system by means of existential assumptions. Mathematical existence is of the lowest species, e.g., that of definite numbers of the number-series, of definite space-figures, and the like, or of any kind of character indicated in the set of concepts determined by the postulates and definitions. There are so to speak mathematical individuals, whose existence, as defined in a certain way, is deductively proved at every step. Mathematics does not refer to real individuals, so that its negative existential propositions exclude mathematical existence and not real existence.

Marty as well as Brentano believed that they had reduced hypothetical and disjunctive judgments to existential judgments. For example, "If A then B" $\cong$ "A does not hold without B." Husserl states that there is reason to dispute the congruence, for they are not equivalent or equipollent. The test of negation, which would have to yield an equivalent, fails. The negation of the left side is "A can hold without B holding," and that of the right side is "A holds without B holding." Husserl adds a note about a logical paradox which had occurred to him about ten years before and which had stimulated him to make extensive investigations concerning the hypothetical judgment. From the proposition "If A then B" it follows evidently that "A does not hold without B"; and it is also evident that the first proposition follows from the second. Hence the propositions are equivalent. The negation of both sides proves, however, and again with evidence, that the two propositions are not equivalent, which is a contradiction. A and B can signify propositions and also concepts, so that it is to be read more completely: "If proposition A holds, proposition B holds," or "If something is A, then it is B," or "If A exists, then B exists," etc. The problem receives no further treatment at this time, however.

Marty's interpretation of causal judgments is finally considered. Whereas the hypothetical judgment "If A exists, B exists" simply rejects the matter "existence of A and non-existence of B," in the causal judgment "Because A exists, B exists" the fact that A exists establishes the fact that B exists. Husserl submits that an unprejudiced analysis would find that both assume the same thought, that if A is presupposed, then B is also to be posited; but the presupposition in the one case is characterized as a mere "assumption" or "hypothesis," and in the other case as the positing of an established matter of fact. The function of a proposition as a "presupposition," as a "grounding" proposition, is realized phenomenologically in a definite character of the propositional act in question. This act carries in itself either the character of "belief" or that of "mere" presentation, and thus the difference between the "If *A* exists" and "Because *A* exists" results; and analogously for the consequents.

Husserl states in conclusion that a real decision, as regards the issue between Marty and his opponents, can only be arrived at through an extensive and penetrating phenomenology of thought-experiences, especially of the linguistic, and that only the beginnings of such work are as yet present.[11]

G. RESULTS OF THE SECOND LOGICAL SURVEY

In the second logical survey Husserl appears as a severe but just critic. Having arrived at adequate clarity on the status of German logic and theory of knowledge at the close of the century, he was prepared to devote all his efforts to the fundamental reform of philosophy. With few exceptions, little notice is henceforth taken of living and recent philosophers.

Although nothing of deciding importance is advanced in the survey, there are a number of reasons for calling attention to it. It contains a statement of the nature of phenomenology in what will later be seen to be a narrow sense, in which the difference between phenomenology and psychology is drawn clearly. The kind of psychological foundation that is necessary for the explanation of the purely logical concepts and laws of which Husserl speaks is not empirical in character; such phenomenological analyses "lie before" empirical, genetic psychology. Because of the misunderstanding which may arise if the same terms are used in different senses, phenomenology is no longer called descriptive psychology. Psychology is a natural science of mental facts, and, like physics, it is an "uncritical" science. The important point to be noted is that phenomenology is a purely immanent critique of knowledge, and that it is concerned only with essential forms and structures. If no suppositions are made which go beyond the content of the given, phenomenology differs fundamentally from empirical psychology, which makes such assumptions. Phenomenology must in short operate without presuppositions, at least in the usual sense of the term. The same is said to be true of pure logic, which is conceived as presupposing nothing at all. If the concept of pure

[11] Of the minor works reviewed, only R. Heilner's *System der Logik* (Leipzig, 1897) need be mentioned. In commenting upon it Husserl refers to a publication which appears to be unknown to the author, and which he holds to be incomparably more valuable than the latter's own work, namely, to the "Function und Begriff" of the acute mathematician G. Frege, which unfortunately had not received the attention it deserved from the professional logicians. This indicates the high esteem in which he had come to hold Frege.

logic is extended to include the critique of knowledge, as Husserl suggests, it provides for the clarification of its own basic ideas and principles. As such it is a self-founding discipline.

The discussion of the logic and psychology of judgment completes the account of the distinction between psychological and logical analysis in relation to the phenomenological critique of knowledge. The psychological description of judgment presupposes the clarification of all the basic concepts that are used on its (higher) level, namely, meaning, concept, proposition, presentation, etc. Although the phenomenological method is, strictly speaking, non-natural, it is intended to serve both psychology and logic.

When Husserl speaks of the absurdity of "basing" the abstract on the concrete, the meaning of the term "base" forbids that procedure. The abstract is derived from the concrete by a process of abstraction; or it is constructed, in the wider sense of abstractions in general which are not originally bound to concrete situations. If "basing" as a formal process is so interpreted that the general is presupposed by the particular, then the abstract cannot be based upon the concrete. But, apart from such a view, the way remains open for a possible construction which proceeds from concrete objectivities.

The reason for the almost total neglect of all mention of metaphysics in the context of phenomenology is now made clear. The methodological reason for eliminating metaphysics in the usual sense is explained herein. The value of the traditional metaphysics is not denied; but it is pointed out that it follows the sciences, and therefore cannot be regarded as the first science. It must make use of the findings, provided by the critique of knowledge, regarding the concept of being. The elucidation of the concept of being falls to phenomenology, along with its other tasks. Phenomenology is thus prior to metaphysics, as well as to all other disciplines. In commenting upon the meaning of "existence," Husserl is careful to avoid the pitfalls of idealism as well as what he holds to be the philosophically naive view of independent, natural existence.

It is noteworthy that the terms "clarification" and "elucidation" are not defined here, or elsewhere in this period. Undoubtedly it was Husserl's intention to illustrate rather than to define the processes involved by concrete descriptive studies. The clarifying descriptions of the *Logical Investigations* lead to the method of constitutive analysis of transcendental phenomenology, where an attempt is made to define the nature of the phenomenological method.

The term "Sachverhalt" or fact, which is here called judgment-content, is wider in its scope than matters of fact, inasmuch as mathematical facts and all kinds of non-natural facts may be included. Other points to be noted in the "survey" include the interesting discussion of negation, the important conception of analytic propositions as comprising all that is valid purely categorially, and the analysis of *a priori* knowledge. Touching upon various concepts more adequately treated in the *Logical Investigations*, including, in addition to some already mentioned, the concepts of matter and quality, Husserl makes clear the reasons for the detailed investigations of meaning, judgment, etc. He also reaffirms his conception of the absoluteness of logic when he states that the principles of logic, such as the principle of the excluded middle, cannot be deduced. Such principles are at the basis of purely logical theories, and must in his view be regarded as immediately evident. His remarks about formal logic, in which he designates its sphere as one of mere non-contradiction, indicate that he had arrived essentially at a final understanding of that discipline so far as his later work was concerned. The next step in the development of his logical theory was to be in the direction of transcendental logic.

CHAPTER VII

THE "BREAKTHROUGH" TO PHENOMENOLOGY

UNLIKE the first volume of the *Logical Investigations*, which proved to be effective immediately, the second volume, which presented detailed studies in logic and the theory of knowledge and made more difficult reading, required a longer period of years before its nature was understood by the philosophical world. This work, which is judged with right to be one of the important direction-giving works of modern philosophy, was at once the culmination of a decade of work and a dividing-line in Husserl's development.

In the preface to the revised edition of the first two volumes of the *Logical Investigations* (1913) there is a brief account of the author's development after the appearance of the first edition. He at once continued his studies, and sought to do greater justice to the meaning, method, and philosophical extent of phenomenology, and also to investigate the parallel problems in all ontic and phenomenological domains. The conception of phenomenology illustrated by the first edition of the *Logical Investigations* was a narrow one, for Husserl was still thinking in terms of descriptive psychology, and did not yet have the consciousness of having taken a very radical step in philosophical inquiry. But by 1913 much had happened in his development. The *Lectures on Time-Consciousness* and the essay on "Philosophy as a Rigorous Science" are evidence of his steady tendency toward the transcendental philosophy of the *Ideas*. It was clearly necessary to introduce numerous changes into the new edition of the work if it was to be of use in the more systematic philosophy represented by the *Ideas*. In revising the work it was possible to make numerous improvements. Thus obscure points could be clarified and ambiguities removed. The changes introduced were not mere additions, but were frequently revaluations, and were believed by Husserl to represent a deeper as well as a broader knowledge of the subject. They show his wish to infuse the original logical and epistemological discussion with the spirit of the later *Ideas*. Some of the original directness of statement is lost thereby, and in the place of a work with a restricted subject-matter there appears — and this has become characteristic of the literature of phenomenology — the promise of unexplored and hitherto inaccessible depths.

The *Ideas* shows clearly the nature and extent of his development. Instead of waiting until he could write a new set of investigations in the place of the original work, which would have taken many years, Husserl decided to publish the *Ideas* first. This book was designed to give a general idea of the method and problems of the new phenomenology, and to show how it makes possible a rigorously scientific philosophy, as well as a rational theory of empirical psychology. After that the *Logical Investigations* was to be made to conform to the standpoint of the *Ideas*, so that the student could be introduced to actual phenomenological work. The *Logical Investigations* is not devoted to programmatic considerations or to discussions of the relative merits of conflicting standpoints, but always makes appeal to the immediate data of experience. The *Ideas* was to be regarded as based upon this work, and was intended to clarify the method by recourse to the final sources of knowledge, to trace out the main structures and problems of pure consciousness.

The first part of the plan proved relatively easy to accomplish. Although two volumes of the *Ideas* were ready for publication, it was found desirable to publish the first volume by itself, which was sufficient at the time; but as a result of the delay the second volume was never published. It soon became evident that it was impossible to bring the old work up to the level of the *Ideas*. On the other hand, it could not be reprinted simply, with all its errors and vacillations. A middle course had to be adopted, of improving all that could be improved without undermining the old work, which meant that some errors and inadequacies had to be allowed to remain. The fact that the *Logical Investigations* is a systematically connected chain of investigations rather than a book in a literary sense gave promise to this plan. They are intended to represent a continuous ascent from a lower to a higher level of logical and phenomenological insights, in which process the growth is cumulative. This character of the old work made it seem possible to reach the level of the *Ideas* in the last investigation, a plan which was not to be realized completely, however.

In keeping with these considerations the *Prolegomena* and the first part of the second volume, consisting of the first five investigations, were revised.[1] As for the *Prolegomena,* it did not seem desirable to introduce

---

[1] Because Husserl calls attention to the nature of the changes in the second edition, Illemann cannot be right in stating that the fact of the changes is little known, unless one is to assume that the author's preface to the second edition is ignored by all who read the work. Cf. W. Illemann, *op. cit.*, p. 75. But he is right in pointing out that Husserl does not refer ex-

new material on the issue of psychologism, for there was nothing fundamentally new to be added. Since the publication of that volume some writers, such as Lipps, who had been exponents of logical psychologism, had changed their point of view essentially, while others endeavored to establish their psychologistic position in a different manner. But no notice was taken of such cases in the revised edition.

The introduction to the second volume was revised radically. It will be sufficient to quote briefly from the first edition, in order to indicate the general nature of the changes introduced. Husserl speaks (p. 4) of "discussions of that most general kind, which belong to the wider sphere of an objective *theory of knowledge,* and what is most intimately connected therewith, to a *purely descriptive phenomenology of thought- and knowledge-experiences.* It is this entire sphere which must be investigated for an epistemological preparation and clarification of pure logic." Inserted before the last sentence, in the second edition (p. 2) are the following statements which reflect the language and emphasis of the *Ideas,* with its systematic doctrines of essence and general seeing: "This (discipline), like the *pure phenomenology of experiences in general* which includes it, has to do with the experiences that can be grasped and analyzed in intuition in their essential generality, but not with empirically apperceived experiences as real matters of fact, as experiences of experiencing people or animals in the appearing world, posited as a matter of fact of natural experience. The essences directly grasped in essential intuition, and the connections based solely upon the essences, are brought to expression *descriptively* in concepts of essence and lawful statements of essence. Every such statement is an *a priori* one in the best sense of the term." It was also necessary to distinguish phenomenology from descriptive psychology more sharply, in order to make clear the need for an autonomous discipline at the basis of all the sciences, including psychology. The role assigned to phenomenology in the first edition is a modest one (p. 18): "It is not psychology as a complete science that is a foundation of pure logic; certain classes of descriptions constitute a preliminary stage for the theoretical investigations of psychology (namely, in so far as they describe empirical objects, whose genetic connections this science aims to trace out), and form at the same time the basis for those fundamental abstractions, in which the logician grasps the essence of his ideal objects and connections with evidence. Since it is epistemologically of very great significance, to separate the purely de-

plicitly to the significant changes that were made, and in emphasizing the importance of taking account of the difference between the first and the later editions of the *Logical Investigations* in all studies of Husserl's philosophy.

scriptive investigation of knowledge-experiences, which is not concerned with any theoretical-psychological interests, from the the really psychological investigation, aiming at empirical explanation and genesis, we shall do well to speak of *phenomenology* rather than of descriptive psychology."

Husserl felt the defects of the introduction immediately upon its publication, and soon found an opportunity [2] to correct his misleading characterization of phenomenology as descriptive psychology. Phenomenological description is distinguished sharply from the psychological description of inner experience and the description of external events of nature. The phenomenological method requires the elimination of all transcendent interpretations of immanent data, including the "psychical activities and conditions" of real egos, and of physical things and the experiences of other persons. In revising the introduction to the second volume and the text of the investigations that followed, Husserl proceeded from the conception of phenomenology illustrated by the *Ideas,* in which the technique of phenomenological reduction is developed to a high degree.[3]

As in the *Prolegomena* Husserl did not, with the exception of the notice taken of Marty in the fourth investigation, discuss the many criticisms of his work, which he held to be based almost entirely upon misunderstandings of the meaning of his presentation. He regarded it as being more useful to discuss in a general way the typical misunderstandings of his philosophical efforts at the close of the second volume. The reader is advised to turn to that supplement first, in the hope that errors would be avoided thereby.

B. AGAINST THE MISUNDERSTANDING OF PHENOMENOLOGY

For some unexplained reason the promised discussion was not included in the second part of the second volume when it finally appeared in 1921,

[2] In the discussion of Elsenhans, "Das Verhältnis der Logik zur Psychologie," in the second logical survey.

[3] Thus in revising the fifth investigation (first edition, pp. 324 f.) the words "in accordance with its phenomenological essence" are added to the passage, "to delimit the concept of the psychical act." The term "reelles" is substituted for "reales," and "phenomenological" for "psychological" (p. 326). A new paragraph is introduced into the discussion of "consciousness as the phenomenological unity of ego-experiences" (second edition, pp. 347 f.), in order to bring it up to the level of the *Ideas,* beginning as follows: "Let it now be pointed out that this concept of experience may be understood *purely* phenomenologically, i.e., in such a way that *all reference to empirically real existence* (to people or animals of nature) *remains eliminated*: an experience in the descriptive-psychological sense (in the empirical-phenomenological) then becomes an experience in the sense of *pure* phenomenology." He goes on to speak of the *a priori* essential insights which are to be obtained into the "descriptive-psychological" material, and refers to the *Ideas,* second section. The revised edition is referred to unless otherwise mentioned.

possibly because of the distraction of the period of war which had inter-
vened. What appears to be a first draft of such a discussion was found
among his papers and published posthumously.[4] It is a brilliantly formulated document, and is of great value for the understanding of his
philosophical development, as well as of the nature and program of
phenomenology.

Looking back upon his philosophical position at the close of the century,
Husserl states that it was very difficult to bring himself to publish a work
which was, for him, a beginning and not an end. As he had pointed out
in his own notice of the second volume,[5] the investigations were not really
written for publication, but were intended to serve as the basis for a more
systematic theory of knowledge as well as for the elucidation of pure logic,
which explains the easily seen imperfections. He did not expect to receive
serious attention from a contemporary literature which was almost entirely
historical in its reference or dominated by physiological and experimental
psychology. Despite that fact, however, the *Logical Investigations* received
a prompt hearing (if not understanding), and gradually reached a wider
circle of readers. The influence of the work was not entirely to Husserl's
satisfaction, for there were misinterpretations of it on the part of those
who valued it as the beginning of a methodological reform of philosophy,
as well as of those who saw in it a Scholastic ruin of modern philosophy.
Even professional philosophers could not but feel hostile toward the un-
usual and hence difficult-appearing phenomenological attitude and method,
especially because they believed the same subjects could be treated in a
more simple manner. Thus the analyses of the *Logical Investigations* were

---

[4] Cf. Husserl's "Preface," already referred to, *l. c.*, pp. 106–133, 319–339. In his introduction Dr. Fink characterizes this writing as a "self-interpretation" of the first phase of Husserl's
phenomenology on the basis of its second phase, which is facilitated by its polemical orientation. He points out, however, that it was only in the third and last developmental period of
phenomenology that the motives of the *Logical Investigations* were clarified and realized,
and he calls attention to the inner unity of the "three phases," as the history of the "rad-
icalization" of a problem. The fact that the "Preface" belongs to the second phase is shown
by the conception of phenomenology as a theory of knowledge; by the program of a "philosophical reform of the positive sciences" as an epistemological clarification of their fundamental
concepts; by the emphasis upon the eidetic character of the analysis of consciousness; and by
the criticism of the transcendentalists, particularly of the Neo-Kantian type. — In the third
phase the conception of phenomenology is no longer restricted to a theory of knowledge,
and Husserl endeavors to realize the aims of the great transcendentalists by means of the
more elaborately developed method of phenomenological analysis. An interpretation of the
Logical Investigations on the basis of the third phase is given in the *Formale und Transzendentale Logik* (§§ 55 f.).

[5] Husserl, "Selbstanzeige" of the second volume of the *Log. Unt.*, *Viertelj. f. wiss. Phil.*,
vol. xxv (1901), p. 263.

judged by one reviewer [6] (in the only complete review, referring to both volumes of the work, to appear) to be "hair-splitting," "cumbrous," "involved," and "opaque," and to be merely psychological analyses after all. This attitude was reflected by the scholarly periodicals, most of which failed to review the work. Of the very few reviews of the *Prolegomena*, the instructive discussion by Natorp [7] was the only favorable one, despite its author's critical reservations.

1. On the Significance of the "Prolegomena"

Some misunderstandings of the *Logical Investigations* occurred because the *Prolegomena* alone was read, or only its discussion of psychologism. It was never Husserl's aim to bring together "accidentally" the psychological and the pure-logical, for the act of thought on the one hand and the meaning or thought object on the other hand belong together necessarily. They are separated, however, in that "the purely logical" is shown to be something "ideal" which is independent of the psychical acts of empirical, real persons. The logical-ideal sphere is defined in the *Prolegomena* by means of the concept of the *mathesis universalis*.

Acknowledging the "masterful manner" in which Natorp handles his discussion, Husserl is careful to point out that Natorp is not to be included among the critics who misunderstand his work. As already seen, Natorp had declared the "opposition" of the *a priori* and the empirical, the logical and the psychological, the objective and the subjective, to be unresolved

---

[6] Review of Husserl's *Log. Unt.*, by L. Busse, *Zeit. f. Psych. u. Phys. d. Sinnesorgane*, vol. xxxiii (1903), pp. 153–157. Although holding Husserl's standpoint to be correct in principle, the reviewer charges him with inconsistency, maintaining that he frequently falls back into the rejected psychologism. The terms "arise" and "origin," as applied to the laws and concepts of pure logic, are singled out as evidence of Husserl's defection. The reviewer argues that all truths and laws must then at first appear in the stream of psychical occurrences, as individual, psychologically conditioned experiences; and he does not believe Husserl succeeds in attaining to the level of objective truths and laws on that basis. Despite Husserl's example of a geometrical proposition, as expressing an objective truth and not a subjective, momentary judgment, and all that he had to say on that point, the reviewer contends that it is not yet established that Husserl's own judgment is such a truth, and that everything that is said about ideal meanings, etc., is to begin with a thought or conviction in an individual mind, in a causal context, to be explained by psychology. How the reviewer read the work on which he pronounced judgment with so much finality (this applies to so much "reviewing" of the present as well!) is shown by his statement that it cannot be denied that the knowledge of truth and its validity is a psychical occurrence — as though this obvious fact were not understood by the writer, or ignored in the text. As a matter of fact, the problem of justifying ideal, objective validity despite subjective change appears as a prominent initial motive in the *Logical Investigations*.

[7] Already referred to in ch. v.

by Husserl; and he described the empirically real as an irrational residue, which somehow cannot be gotten rid of. Natorp had not been able to reconcile the apparent opposition between the two opponents in the drama unfolded for the reader, with their gradually appearing mutual relationship and inseparable connection.

Husserl neither denies nor apologizes for the sharpness of the opposition between the purely logical and the psychological in the first volume. On the contrary, the function of the discussion of psychologism for the work as a whole made a sharp delimitation of the sphere of pure logic unavoidable. There are admittedly serious problems to be met in considering the relationship between the ideal realm and consciousness, and the phenomenological investigations which are provided by the second volume are intended to solve these problems. It is necessary to understand the difference between the "naive" *mathesis universalis,* with its natural, objective direction of view, which is the concern of the mathematician, and the genuinely philosophical, "clarified" logic.

Most readers ignored the second volume, or glanced hastily at it, the psychologists regarding it as a Scholastic, falsified psychology, in view of its talk of the ideal and the *a priori,* and the idealists being disappointed at not finding in its transcendental constructions "from above," of the usual type. Finding, instead of that, analyses of experience, acts, intentions, fulfillments, etc., they concluded that Husserl had lapsed back into psychologism.

2. *The Appeal to the "Things Themselves"*

In contrast to the familiar appeal to a principle of supposedly pure thought, Husserl proposed to view the at first vague and ambiguous problems in the light of intuition by means of painstaking, clarifying work. His aim was to inspect thinking and knowing themselves, and to make clear their reference to objectivity by means of an examination of their immanent relationships and structures. The "principle of principles" for the philosopher who seeks "absolute knowledge" (this is defined by Husserl as knowledge which is "radical" and "evident" in all dimensions of possible questions) forbids the pursuit of irrelevant constructions — as though one could not reach the "things themselves" — and it requires that all knowledge be derived from "self-seen" principles or sources. Required also is that there be no prejudgments, so that even the "exact sciences" cannot be simply taken over if that which is "original" and which "lies before" all theories is to be the goal. The difficult appeal to final "seeing" and its illustration by means of descriptive analyses is undertaken by phenomenology; and because of its method this new science cannot be identified with psychology, even though it is a science of "experiences."

This intuitive method, appealing to the "things themselves" that are here in question, i.e., to the inspection of knowledge "itself" as directly given, is emphasized in the second volume of the *Logical Investigations.* The method of the intentional analysis of the correlates, consciousness and objectivity, is developed, and the general style of the solution of the problem of pure logic with reference to the categorial, "analytic" sphere is seen in the last investigation.

3. No Platonic Hypostasis

It is wholly unjustified to charge Husserl with "Platonic hypostasis" and with the revival of "Scholastic Realism," as was done by superficial readers who could not free themselves from fixed prejudgments. To advocate a doctrine of ideal objects in the present sense is not to set up a metaphysical theory, or any other type of construction. As a matter of everyday experience one can see that the object of his judgment is in countless cases something objective that is nevertheless not real. It is sufficient to cite judgments about numbers, and to realize that logic would be impossible if "Ideas" could not be regarded as objects.

For Husserl, the "final measure" of all theory is that which is "originally" given in simple seeing. The term "original" applies to that which can be experienced in direct observation; the "originally given" is something that is "naively" meant and possibly given as existent. That which can be "grasped" by simply looking is prior to all theory, including the "theory of knowledge." The phenomenologist is not disturbed by doubts as to the reality of the objects of experience, or by epistemological theories which try to prove that we are restricted to the immanent contents of consciousness. If I judge about the table before me, the object is something transcendent of all "immanent" data. The judgment itself may be false, but it is certain that what is "perceived" and "judged" here is a table, and a transcendent thing. The phenomenologist is interested in *that which is meant as such*, and that can be "grasped absolutely." That which is seen cannot be explained away, and is the final standard in all truly philosophical thought.

4. The Mathesis Universalis and Philosophical Logic

The *mathesis universalis*, as it was founded with a "natural-objective direction of view," has nothing in common with phenomenology. But if its phenomenological elucidation is undertaken, then the problems may be solved which arise from the correlation between being and consciousness; and that, along with the clarification of its fundamental concepts and principles, transforms the *mathesis universalis* as a naive logic into a really philosophical logic. Similarly, physics becomes a "philosophy of nature" with the phenomenological treatment of its epistemological problems, in which the contributions of subjectivity are considered in order to begin with thoroughly justified and exact concepts.

A parallelism had been drawn by Husserl between the idea of a "pure" or formal logic and the related rational ontologies. Just as formal logic refers to the formal idea of an object, to "something in general," and hence can be designated as formal ontology, so the "regional" ontologies refer to uppermost material genera of objects in general, which are called "regions" in the *Ideas*. Geometry, as a logic of pure, idealized space, is an ontological discipline that is naive, being constructed with the "natural-objective" attitude. Hence, corresponding to every such naive logic would be a "philosophical" logic which is phenomenologically clarified, or else one thus clarified to begin with. It should be noted that in Husserl's restricted use of the term "ontology" merely refers to the eidetic structure of regions of objects, as viewed in a naive ("natural-objective") manner.

Although only certain very general cognitive forms have to be considered in the *Logical Investigations*, the material ontologies require more for their clarification. Thus, for the ontology or logic of a possible (or merely physical) nature, the basic forms of the subjectivity which "constitute" nature must be investigated, and similarly for the ontology of the mind or spirit, etc. This is stated in order to meet Natorp's objection, which, Husserl concedes, was justified in its way because there was no mention of this point in the text, the discussion having been limited in its reference to pure logic.

5. *The "Logical Investigations" as Achieving a "Breakthrough"*

The "breakthrough" to phenomenology as achieved in the *Logical Investigations* may be traced back to motives impelling Husserl very early in his mathematical-philosophical studies. It appeared to him to be obvious, as a result of his training, that a philosophy of mathematics must be interested in the "psychological origin" of the fundamental concepts of mathematics. In this way he came to recognize a number of concepts and distinctions later developed and incorporated in the *Logical Investigations*, to which reference has already been made (at the close of the second chapter).

Husserl was disturbed at this time by the distinction between that which a presentation "means" and that which it itself contains. The presentation of an "aggregate" was supposed to arise out of collective connection (the unified consciousness of meaning-together), and that appeared to be correct. A "collectivum" is not a "material" unity, and could not be held to be physical. It would seem, then, that the concept of a collection must arise through psychological reflection upon the act of collecting, and similarly the concept of unity through reflection upon the act of positing something. But is not the concept of number something essentially different than the concept of collecting, which is all that the reflection can yield? Such doubts were very disquieting to Husserl, and they were extended to all categorial concepts, finally to all kinds of objectivities. He was disturbed, furthermore, by the general question of how "the mathematical" that is "given" in the medium of "the psychical" can be valid in itself, and the question of how the objective relations of logic and mathematics are "constituted" in subjectivity.

The emancipation from psychologism was first accomplished in the limited field of Husserl's studies from 1886 to 1895, which were primarily in mathematics and formal logic, but this reaction was soon extended. Of aid in this change of view was Husserl's renewed study of Leibniz; he was interested in the distinction between truths of reason and of matters of fact, and also in Hume's analysis of knowledge and his distinction between relations of ideas and matters of fact. The contrast of the latter distinction to the Kantian distinction between analytic and synthetic judgments was striking to Husserl and became important for his later position.

The relationship between formal-ontological propositions, or propositions about objects, facts, series, etc., as such, on the one hand, and propositions about meanings (about propositions and possible parts of propositions as such) on the other hand, required much reflection, and led to the fundamental division of logical categories into meaning categories and formal-ontological categories, and to the reference of logic as a *mathesis universalis* to all the *a priori* truths that are based upon them. It also led to the definition of a lower level of logic as the formal theory of meaning, as represented by the theory of wholes and parts in the third investigation, and the account of pure-logical grammar in the fourth investigation.

6. Ontology and the Theory of Objects

The relationship between Husserl's conception of ontology and the "theory of objects" of Meinong has long been misunderstood. As conceived in the *Logical Investigations*, the idea of ontology is not related to the elaborate ontologies of the tradition, but signifies a purely rational, eidetic science of objects. The *mathesis universalis* is accordingly an ontology (only the word is avoided in the first edition). It is characterized as the *a priori* science of objects in general, and correlatively of meanings in general, i.e., of meanings which refer to objects in general. Inasmuch as that is brought out clearly in both volumes, Husserl observes that no one is justified in trying to instruct him with regard to the "object-theoretical" character of formal logic and mathematics. Indeed, the third investigation is explicitly declared to belong to the "*a priori* theory of objects as such," and Husserl suggests that it is this passage that led to the formation of the undesirable expression "Gegenstandstheorie." Ontology, or the theory of objects in the present sense, not only comprises all that relates to the field of the pure *mathesis universalis*, but includes the first volume as well as the third and fourth investigations of the second volume.

The expression "object-theoretical knowledge" is really only a synonym for "essential knowledge." As a matter of fact, Husserl had covered the ground referred to by the "theory of objects," in so far as it is well defined, when he adopted the general standpoint of essential analysis early in his development, and ascribed an essence to every kind of objectivity. But he never assumed "ontology" to mean the correlate of the vague collection of all *a priori* cognitions and sciences. It was Husserl's aim through the years to determine the genuine concept of the analytic, as distinguished from Kant's unclear concept of it, and to distinguish the genuine analytic ontology from the essentially different material (synthetic–*a priori*) ontology. After the appearance of the *Logical Investigations* he planned a systematic theory of categories, or of the possible regions of being; and he was careful to distinguish the phenomenological *a priori* from the ontological *a priori*. It finally became clear to him that all essential knowledge has an essential context. Holding that the expression "theory of objects" as the title for a vague collection of all "homeless" objects does not add to these conceptions, Husserl is led not only to deny that Meinong's work is parallel or supplementary to his own, but to suggest that the latter's work might have been more acceptable had he actually carried through an investigation in the theory of objects, or had he studied the *Logical Investigations* more carefully.

7. *Relationship to Lotze and Bolzano*

In view of the persistent misunderstanding of Husserl's relationship to Lotze and Bolzano, it appeared necessary to make a final statement of the facts. Although it is true that Husserl was indebted to Lotze's and Bolzano's writings, it must be borne in mind that the result of his endeavors was a new theory of knowledge. The way in which Lotze's doctrine of validity and the Platonic theory of ideas as interpreted by him were worked over by Husserl led to a fundamentally different theory of knowledge. How different that is may be seen when one considers that Lotze, despite his opposition to a psychological foundation of logic, is nevertheless an exponent of psychologism, anthropologism, and naturalistic relativism, as defined in the *Prolegomena*. Thus Lotze abandons his apparently pure theory of Ideas when he speaks of our thinking in an actual, anthropologistic sense.[8] Lotze's fundamentally incorrect problem of "the real and formal meaning of logic," which is so severely criticized in the sixth investigation, arises because he presupposes an independent metaphysical world of things, and opposed to it a world of presentation that is supposed to copy it — and then tries in vain to explain the ground of their correspondence in knowledge. The postulated "reality in itself" must somehow be made an object of knowledge. Although Lotze had no notion of the real problem and procedure of phenomenology, so that Husserl could not acknowledge himself to be his follower in any important sense, he nevertheless pays tribute to Lotze as one of the most significant contributors to the nineteenth century literature of the theory of knowledge, and expresses indebtedness to him in connection with the *Logical Investigations*.

Husserl was no more a continuator of Bolzano's work than he was a follower of Lotze, for Bolzano did not have the concept of a *mathesis universalis*, or the concept of a pure form-theory of meanings and the other ontological concepts of the *Logical Investigations*; and his propositions or truths "in themselves" are not to be identified with Husserl's "ideal unities." He would certainly have opposed pure logic in Husserl's sense, and also the program for its epistemological elucidation. For the rest, Husserl observes that apparently no one noticed that Bolzano's theory of knowledge is extremely empirical.[9] Thus Bolzano declared that logic, arithmetic, geometry, and pure physics are certain because they can readily be tested by experience; and we are so certain of the correctness of syllogistic procedures because they have been tried out countless times. Bolzano, far from being the founder of phenomenology, was really as remote from it as Hume or Mill. That he was able to accomplish much with his "naive" manner of investigation (naive in the sense in which the mathematician's view may be called that when he deals with numbers) is shown by his original theory of inference and in his beginnings of a scientific theory of

[8] Reference is made to Lotze's *Logik* of 1874, p. 155.
[9] Reference is made to Bolzano's *Wissenschaftslehre*, vol. III, pp. 244 f.

probability, to which Husserl calls particular attention. That Bolzano's draft of formal logic was incomplete, that he failed to see its inner unity with pure mathematics, that he did not distinguish propositions as logical judgments and facts — such deficiencies show why it would be absurd to try to trace Husserl's work back to Bolzano, despite the great merit of the latter.

8. *Phenomenology Not an Analysis of Word-Meanings*

A rather strange misunderstanding of the nature of phenomenology, as illustrated in the *Logical Investigations*, was the belief that it is the analysis of meanings, or of word-meanings. The investigations are to be sure concerned with meanings to a large extent. But phenomenology could no more be said to be a theory of meaning, or an essential analysis of meaning, than geometry could be said to be a science of straight lines and triangles. The second volume was not intended to found phenomenology, but, as has been pointed out, merely to present a set of preliminary investigations which are indispensable for the epistemological elucidation of the *mathesis universalis*; and the analysis of logical phenomena requires that one begin with meaning. But the larger scope of phenomenology is clearly indicated in the work, in which analyses of perception, phantasy, and other kinds of experience are undertaken.

9. *Phenomenology Not Descriptive Psychology*

Husserl admits freely that he was unable, at the time of writing the *Logical Investigations*, to avoid old habits of thought and to carry certain distinctions through consistently. The investigations had been written at various times, and it was difficult to unite all the material from one point of view. The relationship between descriptive psychology and phenomenology was perhaps the most serious point of unclearness. In addition to making the published correction in 1903 of the designation of phenomenology as descriptive psychology, the more positive character of phenomenological analysis should have been discussed more fully. To begin with, all empirically real elements, or all psychological "positings" of being, are excluded; and the phenomenological investigations are *a priori*, essential descriptive analyses.

10. *The Charge of "Logicism" and the Nature of Phenomenological Description*

The surprising charge of "logicism" had been made by no less a scholar than Wilhelm Wundt, in his "Psychologismus und Logizismus," [10] his aim being to show the incorrectness of logicism, which he regarded as culminating in Husserl's work. Although Wundt declared psychologism to be just as objectionable in its way, it was the critique of logicism that interested him primarily. Logicism was defined by him as the attempt, by means of logical reflection to give an account of the connection of appearances, and especially of those which are given in our own consciousness; and again, as the attempt to gain an understanding of positive life by interpreting it logically or "dissolving" it in dialectical, conceptual constructions.

Husserl observes that Wundt was the only one among the older scholars, apart from Dilthey, who recognized the significance of the second volume for psychology. Although Husserl himself said nothing in the work about a reform of psychology, and did not mention it until 1911 (in his *Logos* essay), Wundt saw its significance, even if wrongly, and he thought it necessary to save psychology from the errors of logicism and the "invasion of logic." In Husserl's view, new modes of treatment of psychological problems are prepared by his work, and, indeed, as Wundt stated it, a "reform of psychology" is involved. The latter was not able to understand the essence-theory of phenomena because he failed to realize that the phenomenological method is intuitive in an extended sense, so that he did not see the fundamental difference between the rationalism and idealism of Husserl and of the tradition, as well as between his work and all Scholastic ontologies. How wide of the mark Wundt's understanding of the *Logical Investigations* was is shown by his belief that it tends to transform psychology into a reflective analysis of concepts and words, thus making it to be an inferior part of general logic.[11]

The careful reader of the second volume can only agree with Husserl in expressing surprise at such an impression of his aims and procedures. As the very title of the work indicates, he is interested in *logical* phenomena. Hence, beginning with the empirical-psychological attitude, the point of departure is the fact that I think or state "This paper is white," that I understand the words, or that they occur to me without my "stating" them, etc. Is it Scholasticism, Husserl asks, if one *looks at* these phenomena in reflection; and is it an invention, if a certain relationship of unity and transition is established between experiences, and if one chooses the term "fulfillment"? Husserl accuses Wundt of ignorance of entire domains of experience, of never having investigated them in reflection, and of not seeing whole worlds of immanent distinctions in them.

---

[11] As Wundt puts it (*op. cit.*, pp. 603 f.), the "phenomenology" which is "substituted for psychology," and which is no psychology at all, is a conceptual analysis which continues grammatical and especially word-analysis.

In reply to Wundt's "a priori" denial of phenomenological intuition,[12] Husserl contends that he is able to see phenomenological differences, especially differences of intentionality, just as well as he sees the difference of this white and that red. One who cannot see differences of the latter kind is said to be blind; and if one cannot see differences of the former type, then he, too, is blind, even if in an extended sense. Seeing is really no easy matter in any case, even in the case of the perception of the external world; and if a person has *a priori* grounds against the possibility of perceiving the world of nature, no mechanical instruments could persuade him. Admitting (as Husserl does) that there are errors due to interpretations in the case of phenomenological "seeing," it is no different in that respect from ordinary external perception. Description is surely not valueless because of the occurrence of errors in either case.

The reader of the *Logical Investigations* is invited to read every finding therein described just as he reads a zoölogical or a botanical description, with reference to the object itself, and consequently as an expression of something seen which can only be understood by means of direct intuition. It is the "evidence" of "inner intuition" that is required, in short. Errors which arise despite this evidence are, e.g., illicit generalization, or the imperfect process of distinction which fails to separate different phenomenological strata, just as an explorer may fail to recognize two rivers as different and therefore interpret them as parts of the same river. Scientific confirmation is always necessary, but that is not to deny that intuition is the only possible authority; for, obviously, all indirect methods merely presuppose intuition in the last analysis.

There is no room for "dialectical constructions" in phenomenology, for it is restricted throughout to that which is given intuitively. They are excluded by the "philosophical epoché" which Husserl explicitly carries over from his *Ideas* to the present work. Although some valuable descriptive contributions had been made before the *Logical Investigations*, no explicitly formulated, "radical," and systematic approach to the phenomena had been achieved. With its interest in description on a universal scale, phenomenology appears as a new science, "within the frame of the phenomenological reduction and of ideation," whose findings are all matters of essential insight.

Phenomenology was first conceived by Husserl (although he avoided

---

[12] Cf. *op. cit.*, p. 623, for Wundt's criticism of the "immediate intuition" of logicism, in which he goes so far as to suggest that Mill is even more moderate as an empiricist than Husserl. In his extended polemic Wundt falsifies the latter's position in a manner that is difficult to explain.

using the expression) as a new kind of "rational psychology," as having the same relationship to empirical psychology as "rational" physics (comprising the pure theories of space, time, motion, and mechanics) has to empirical physics. The analogy has its limits, of course, for phenomenology is not a deductive system of phenomenal formation. Husserl recognizes, however, that this difference presents a far-reaching problem, if one is to explain why there can be no color-geometry, bio-geometry, etc. It was much later, about in 1908, before Husserl saw that a distinction must be drawn between transcendental phenomenology and rational psychology, a distinction which does not affect the psychologist in his particular empirical procedures, but is of the greatest significance for phenomenology in its role of the true "first" philosophy. Only then did it become possible to overcome psychologism in its most universal form.

As viewed from the later perspective of transcendental phenomenology, the *Logical Investigations* signifies a necessary first stage of philosophical analysis. The reader is admonished to withhold all judgments during the study which have not been obtained from his own active seeing and describing. In that way, no doubt, some errors may have to be corrected in the work, just as a later explorer may have to correct the observations of his predecessors.

C. THE NATURE AND ROLE OF PHENOMENOLOGICAL INVESTIGATIONS

To begin with, linguistic analyses are indispensable for the philosophical preparation of pure logic.[13] It is only with the aid of such analyses that the real objects of logical investigation can be defined. This does not mean the grammatical treatment of any particular historical language. What is needed is something more general, an investigation belonging to the objective theory of knowledge and to the pure phenomenology of experiences of thought and knowledge. As already pointed out, the subject-matter of this discipline consists of experiences that can be analyzed in intuition in their essential generality and not of experiences as real occurrences in the natural world. The essences which are apprehended in essential intuition and the connections based upon the essences are described by means of concepts and laws. All laws of essence are *a priori* in character. It is this sphere that must be investigated for the critical preparation and clarification of logic.

Pure phenomenology is described at this time as representing a domain of neutral investigations in which various sciences have their roots. Accord-

---

[13] Cf. *Log. Unt.*, introduction to vol. II, part 2.

ing to the program of the middle period of Husserl's development, phenomenology has a twofold function. On the one hand, it serves to prepare psychology as an empirical science. The phenomenology of thinking and knowing is concerned with the essential structure of the experiences of presentation, judgment, and knowledge, which psychology conceives empirically and investigates as real occurrences in the natural world. On the other hand, phenomenology aims to reveal the "sources" out of which the fundamental concepts and the ideal laws of pure logic "arise," and to which they must be traced back in order to provide the "clarity and distinctness" that is necessary for a critical understanding of pure logic. The terms "phenomenological" and "epistemological" are here used synonymously, and this indicates the restricted program undertaken by Husserl in his early investigations.[14] As pointed out in the *Prolegomena*, in connection with the problems of pure logic, what is intended is the clarification of the concepts and laws which provide all knowledge with objective meaning and theoretical unity.

The objects investigated by pure logic are given to begin with in a grammatical form. They are embedded in concrete psychical experiences of meaning-intention or meaning-fulfillment, and form a phenomenological union with the linguistic expressions. The logician has first to study descriptively the act-characters of these unities, in which logical presentation and judgment occur, to the extent that this is desirable for his real logical problems. But the pure logician is not really interested in psychological judgments, which are concrete psychical phenomena; he is interested in logical judgments. A logical judgment is an identical statement-meaning, and is *one* as opposed to the multiplicity of diverse judgment-experiences. The single experiences have a common feature which corresponds to this ideal unity. It is the generality that is apprehended in abstraction which interests the pure logician. Even though the phenomenological analysis of concrete thought-experiences does not belong to the proper domain of pure logic, it cannot be dispensed with as an aid to pure logical investigation. All that is logical must be given in concrete

---

[14] Cf. M. Farber, *Phenomenology as a Method and as a Philosophical Discipline*, University of Buffalo Studies in Philosophy, No. I (Buffalo, 1928), pp. 10 f., on "Phenomenology in Two Senses." From the perspective of transcendental phenomenology, the early phenomenology represented a realm which had been sought under the title of "Empirical Psychology"; this takes the place of traditional epistemology. In its wider sense, as "First Philosophy," it is the first approach to a system of philosophy and must be universal in scope. It must not only found the natural and strictly formal sciences, but the "cultural sciences" as well. This requires a theory of value and philosophy of history, the latter presenting a real difficulty, for which Husserl sought a solution in his last period.

intuitive fullness, in order to make possible the evidence of the *a priori* laws based thereon. At first, concepts are given as more or less fluctuating word-meanings, and the laws that are built up out of concepts are given as fluctuating assertions. There are equivocations in the words and propositions.

The aim of phenomenological analysis is to bring the logical concepts and laws to epistemological clarity and distinctness. The logical concepts as valid thought-unities must originate in intuition, and must arise through "ideating abstraction" on the basis of certain experiences. In repeated performances of this abstraction the logical concepts must be always confirmed anew, and must be grasped in their self-identity. Expressed otherwise: Husserl is not content with "mere words," or with a merely symbolic understanding of words, such as we have to begin with in our reflections about the meaning of the laws set up in pure logic regarding "concepts," "judgments," "truths," etc. Meanings which are only animated by remote, confused, figurative intuitions — if by any at all — cannot satisfy him. He proposes to return to the "things themselves." By means of fully developed intuitions we are to see with evidence that what is given here in actually performed abstraction is really and truly that which the word-meanings of the law mean.

The phenomenology of logical experiences has the purpose of providing us with as extensive a descriptive understanding of these psychical experiences and of the meaning inherent in them as is necessary to give all fundamental logical concepts firm meanings. The fundamental logical and noetic concepts had been insufficiently clarified, so that numerous equivocations were allowed to remain, which was the main reason for the backward state of pure logic and the theory of knowledge. The phenomenological theory of the essence of experiences of thought and knowledge, always having regard to that which is meant by them, was intended to give the necessary clarification. To identify this descriptive study with empirical psychology, which is the experiential science of the psychical properties of animal realities, would be to misunderstand its nature entirely. Pure phenomenology was advanced as the only means of overcoming psychologism, and of providing all the presuppositions for a satisfactory determination of pure logical distinctions and insights.

The epistemological questions of objectivity and form are inseparable from the problem of the elucidation of the concepts of pure logic. The clarification of logical ideas, such as concept and object, truth and proposition, matter of fact and law, etc., leads to the central questions of the theory of knowledge.

The reader of phenomenological literature is reminded frequently of the difficulties of pure phenomenological analysis. The source of the difficulties is held to be the unnatural direction of intuition and thought that is required in phenomenological analysis. The attitude of reflection is held to be unnatural and difficult. Instead of living in the performance of the various acts of knowledge, in which one naively posits objects as existent or draws hypothetical conclusions, etc., one must reflect upon these acts and their immanent meanings. The essence of these acts is described and analyzed in new acts of intuition and thought, without positing any objects as realities. Because it is opposed to our oldest habits of thinking, Husserl believes that there is an almost ineradicable inclination to drop the phenomenological attitude (*Denkhaltung*) and to assume the simple-objective attitude again.

There are undeniably difficulties in the way of a phenomenological theory of essence. There is first of all the much discussed objection that in turning from the naive performance of an act to the attitude of reflection, the former necessarily changes. How is one to know the nature and extent of this change? There is also the difficulty of the communication of one's results to others.[15] The available expressions for the essential findings are adapted to the natural world, and such terms as sensation, perception, and presentation are ambiguous. It is not possible to describe the acts of meaning without referring to the meant things. There is also the need for acquiring the great skill required for phenomenological description. But these difficulties are by no means insurmountable. The coöperative work of a generation of investigators, Husserl ventures to predict, will decide fully the most important questions of the discussion. We have to do here with a sphere of attainable discoveries that are necessary for the construction of a scientific philosophy.

The "analytical phenomenology" which is needed for the preparation and foundation of logic includes an account of the grammatical side of logical experiences. A certain parallelism between thinking and speaking is readily seen. Because of the concomitance of word-forms and thought-forms there is a natural inclination to seek a logical distinction behind every grammatical distinction. It is therefore of importance to logic to clarify analytically the relation between expression and meaning, so that it can always be decided whether a distinction is logical or grammatical. This can only be accomplished by means of a complete analysis of the essential phenomenological relation between expression, meaning, meaning-intention, and meaning-fulfillment.

[15] Many years later Husserl came back to these difficulties and rendered them as "paradoxes." See ch. xvii, B herein.

The *Logical Investigations* aims to clarify the ideas that are constitutive of pure or formal logic, and of the pure theory of logical forms to begin with. Proceeding from the empirical setting of experiences of meaning, the equivocal terms "expression" and "meaning" are examined, and the essential phenomenological or logical distinctions belonging *a priori* to expressions are established. Furthermore, to consider first the phenomenological side of expressions, the experiences are described essentially, and the pure genera under which they are to be ordered are determined. The analysis is also concerned with the way in which "presentation" and "judgment" are related to the corresponding "intuition," how they are "fulfilled" in it and find their "evidence" in it, and the like. Such investigations must precede the clarification of the fundamental concepts or categories of logic. The discussion of "presentations" includes the consideration of "acts" and ideal meanings. Because the ambiguity of the term "presentation" has been confusing to psychology and the theory of knowledge as well as to logic, its clarification is an important matter. The same is true of the concept of judgment, for the so-called "theory of judgment" is essentially the "theory of presentation." What is undertaken is not psychology, but the phenomenology of experiences of presentation and judgment. This includes the question of the unity of the meaning of expressions and the unity of the object, and, in general, the question of truth in relation to intention.

It is clear that these investigations are not intended to offer a system of logic, but only preliminary studies for a philosophical logic, clarified by reference to the "primal sources" of phenomenology. The phenomenological foundation of logic encounters the difficulty of having to use in the presentation almost all the concepts which it seeks to clarify. It also proves to be necessary to depart from the systematic order of procedure in order to take account of unclear concepts. The investigation therefore seems at times to follow a zigzag course.

Husserl is careful to point out again (obviously in the hope of making clear one of the first distinctions to be grasped if he was to be understood at all) the difference between the "pure" description or the essential intuition of phenomenology, and the empirical description of natural science. The subject-matter of psychology, the perceptions, judgments, feelings, etc., refer to real conditions of animal beings, and its propositions apply to the natural world. But phenomenology is not interested in the conditions of animal beings, or even in those of a possible natural world. It is interested in perceptions, judgments, feelings, etc., *as such*, in their *a priori* nature, in their *essences*. The procedure is analogous to the way in which numbers are treated in pure arithmetic, or spatial forms in geometry. At the same time, however, phenomenology functions as the necessary foundation of scientific psychology, just as pure mathematics is the necessary foundation of every exact natural science. Essential insights into perceptions, volitions, etc., naturally apply to the corresponding empirical conditions of animal beings, just as geometrical insights apply to the spatial forms of nature.

Finally, it is made clear that the investigations satisfy the requirement of freedom from presuppositions in the sense of freedom from metaphysical, psychological, and natural scientific assumptions.[16]

D. THE STYLE OF THE "LOGICAL INVESTIGATIONS"

Judging by the *Logical Investigations*, one important aspect of phenomenology might well be defined as the art of making, or finding, distinctions. That Husserl regarded his teaching as extending "seeing" in philosophy and psychology may be illustrated by an incident which occurred in his Freiburg period. Upon asking the wife of a visiting scholar what she got out of listening to his technical lectures, he was told that the lessons in phenomenology gave her so many new eyes. In Husserl's opinion this aptly expressed the spirit of his undertaking. Where we are accustomed to finding simplicity, a very complex situation is shown to exist; and after numerous distinctions have been drawn carefully, the reader is made to feel that only a beginning has been made.

Not only were the distinctions a matter of descriptive analysis; they were also a badge of virtuosity at the turn of the century. Following Brentano, an entire generation of writers had practiced the art of subtle distinction. In comparison with the achievement of Husserl, their efforts appear to be modest. There can be no doubt that a high point in descriptive analysis is reached in his writings. The only question to be answered is, are the distinctions actually founded on the facts of experience? Their practical importance is a secondary matter on this level of investigation. It is a proper testimonial to his unrelenting grasp of reality that his analyses are invariably founded on experience.

The patient and plodding process of establishing distinctions is an indication of the preparatory nature of the investigations. As in the dialogues of Plato, fundamental concepts are to be fixed and clarified, and definitions are to be framed satisfactorily, in order to make objective and systematic knowledge possible. More exact perhaps would be the designation of the

[16] Cf. M. Farber, "The Ideal of a Presuppositionless Philosophy," in *Philosophical Essays in Memory of Edmund Husserl*.

investigations as the Socratic stage of Husserl's development, the *Ideas* representing his Platonic period. Certain it is that it was his firm intention in the former exploratory work to remain on the neutral ground of descriptive analysis, in contrast to the idealistic turn which his thought took in the later work.

Due largely to the revision of the text and the interdigitation of new sentences and paragraphs, the literary quality of the investigations is uneven. The unity and completeness of the *Prolegomena* are not possessed by the investigations that follow. The sometimes long and ponderous sentences give evidence of breadth of vision and meticulous care not to be misunderstood; and the large amount of repeated emphasis of the basic ideas is indicative of the spirit of the prophet and crusader. The primary aim is to break new ground, and to illustrate the phenomenological method of analysis. The numerous points of contact with traditional philosophy, particularly British empiricism, are a great help in showing how the standpoint of phenomenology was achieved. Despite the fact that the complete "purity" of concepts that was to be attained in later writings is not realized in this work, and in fact because of its very imperfections as judged from the perspective of the later point of view, it remains the best introduction to the phenomenological philosophy. The reader is slowly introduced to the searching method of reflective analysis that is so peculiar to Husserl, with its large and in part specially invented technical vocabulary.

Not that a special vocabulary is as such objectionable. In this case it is justified by its function and performance. Subtlety of analysis requires ingenuity in the coining and adaptation of all available terms. Nowhere is this seen to better advantage than in the analysis of meaning. It may well be that too much time is consumed in justifying distinctions which are fairly obvious to one as soon as they are pointed out. There are two reasons which may explain the otherwise unpardonable prolixity. First, the distinctions had either been drawn inadequately, or had not been recognized at all; and second, preconceived (and hence pre-descriptive) philosophical theories frequently vitiated correct or partially correct analyses, just as they also made impossible the very recognition of the first facts of experience. In the effort to avoid all possible misunderstandings and to anticipate all objections that might be raised, the content of the work is increased greatly.

It is a work which unquestionably marks the beginning of a new movement in philosophy. The wealth of insights and of descriptive material, and the gradually developed double thesis of the ideality of meanings and of the peculiar kind of intuition by which they are known, the "general seeing," are features which decisively outweigh all practical, linguistic, and aesthetic defects, including the obvious lack of completeness. With respect to the inherent value of its content as well as to the influence it has exerted, the *Logical Investigations* must be accorded a place among the most important works in the history of logic and the theory of knowledge.

Commenting upon his development near the close of his life,[17] Husserl emphasized the importance of the "correlative mode of procedure" that is illustrated in the *Logical Investigations.* This is traced back to the *Philosophy of Arithmetic*, with its "peculiar doubling in psychological and logical analyses," which were now seen to have an inner relationship. The unity of the *Prolegomena* and the six investigations, which was missed by contemporary critics, was due to the realization of the correlative nature of the descriptive analysis. It was first necessary to defend the objectivity of logical structures against all subjectivizing attempts, before proceeding to the epistemological preparation of the science of pure logic. Although a great advance over the *Philosophy of Arithmetic* had been made, the analysis of consciousness is mainly "noetic," which means that it was concerned more with the experiencing than with the "noematic" stratum of meaning belonging to each experience. The necessity and technique for a thoroughgoing two-sided analysis of consciousness was first made clear by the *Ideas.*

The "phenomenology" represented by the *Logical Investigations* makes use of immanent intuition alone, and does not pass beyond the sphere of the intuitively given. That is the meaning of the precept "Back to the things themselves": it meant the appeal to intuitive givenness. The second volume of the work illustrates this methodological principle by means of actual analyses. All the insights of this work are apodictic insights of essence. The realm of ideas which is thus disclosed is finally referred back to the subjectivity of consciousness, which is "the primal field of everything *a priori.*" Of deciding importance in the universal investigation of consciousness is the insight that the immanent sphere is governed by essential laws.

E. THE SIX LOGICAL INVESTIGATIONS

As originally conceived by Husserl,[18] the six investigations are connected studies for the phenomenological elucidation of the unities of thought and

---

[17] Cf. *Philosophen Lexikon*, by E. Hauer, W. Ziegenfuss, and G. Jung (Berlin, 1937), pp. 447 ff.

[18] Cf. Husserl, "Selbstanzeige" of the second volume of the *Log. Unt., l. c.,* pp. 260–263.

knowledge arising in logical acts. Since theoretical thinking and knowing occur by means of statements, the analysis begins with the nature of expression and meaning. Following the preliminary account of the ideality of meanings, as well as of the knowledge-unities going along with them, of the first investigation, the second investigation begins with the more general question of the ideality of species or of "general objects." The discussion of the leading modern theories of abstraction includes a consideration of Locke's psychological hypostasis of the general, the attention-theory of abstraction, the doctrine of general representation, Hume's doctrine of the *distinctio rationis*, and a review of the various concepts of "abstraction" and "abstract."

One of the concepts of the abstract concerns abstract factors (Stumpf's "partial contents," or "dependent contents"). In connection therewith the third investigation discusses the general distinction of independent and dependent contents. It attempts to show that to every case of dependence there corresponds a law of connection based upon the specific nature of the contents concerned, whereby the distinction between the material and the "analytic" or categorial laws appears. Developing these ideas, the investigation contains a draft of a systematic theory of real wholes and parts with respect to their pure or categorial types, by which a contribution is made to an important but almost unnoticed part of the theory of knowledge.

The results of this investigation are applied in the fourth investigation to the clarification of the grammatical distinction between categorematic and syncategorematic expressions, or between independent and dependent meanings. The question regarding the laws belonging to this particular class of dependences leads to a hitherto hardly touched group of laws, in its content rather trivial, but most important for the understanding of logical reason. It excludes formal nonsense, as distinguished from the purely logical laws in the usual sense, which exclude formal absurdity (contradiction); it prescribes which meanings can be connected, on the basis of their form, to *one* meaning, regardless of whether it be true or false, harmonious or conflicting. It is these "pure-grammatical laws," which give to the old idea of a general, *a priori* grammar a secure, although very limited sphere of justification.

The two main phenomenological investigations now follow. Their goal is the analytical determination of phenomenological distinctions, in which the most primitive logical distinctions have their origin. The fifth investigation begins with a consideration of three relevant concepts of consciousness — consciousness as the phenomenological unity of ego-experiences, as inner perception, and as "intentional experience" or "psychical act," the last of which is particularly in question. The analysis of the equivocal expression "content of an act" leads among other things to the fundamental distinction between quality and matter ("apprehension-sense"). This occasions a difficult discussion of the well-known principle that every psychical act is either a presentation or has a presentation at its basis. The principle is seen to be unclear and incorrect if taken in its usual sense, its unclearness being due to the ambiguity of the term "presentation." The investigation also contributes to the phenomenology of presentation and judgment, and closes with a review of the most important meanings of the terms "presentation" and "presentation-content."

The sixth investigation is the most comprehensive and fruitful of all. Proceeding from a special problem — whether non-objectivating acts, such as questions, wishes, commands, and the like, can have an "expression" in the same sense as do presentations and judgments — it begins with a discussion of the essence of objectivating intentions and fulfillments, and elucidates recognition as the synthesis of objectivating fulfillment. The basic relationships of meaning-intention and meaning-fulfillment are first made clear; and this is followed by an indirect characterization of the essential kinds of objectivating intentions through the phenomenological distinction of fulfillment-syntheses. The distinction of significative (symbolic) and intuitive presentations is involved, and within the latter, the distinction of imaginative and perceptual presentations. A number of fundamental concepts is introduced in the subsequent discussion of the phenomenology of knowledge-levels, including the concept of the "intuitive content" of a presentation or of its "fullness"; the concepts of pure signification and pure intuition, pure imagination and pure perception, and representation or apprehension; the distinction between apprehension-sense, apprehension-form, and apprehended content; the distinction between complete and incomplete intuitions, between conformable and objectively complete envisagements, etc. This is followed by an inquiry concerning the phenomenological and ideal relationships of compatibility and incompatibility, the ideal of adequation, and the origin of the concepts of evidence and truth, or being in the sense of truth.

The second part of the investigation, entitled "Sensibility and Understanding," is advanced as a foundation-stone for all future phenomenology and theory of knowledge through its extension of the concepts of perception and intuition to include categorial acts. There is not only perception of "real" objects, but also of categorial or ideal objects, e.g., of collections, of facts, of general objects, etc. Making use of preceding analyses, the *a priori* laws of "genuine" and "figurative" thinking are contrasted, the former referring to categorial intuitions, and the latter to categorial significations, or to acts of signitively obscure presentation. The investigation closes with a brief elucidation of its introductory problem. Appended to it is a critical discussion, oriented to Brentano's doctrines, of the distinctions between outer and inner perception, physical and psychical phenomena, and inadequate and adequate perception.

It will now be in order to present the leading theses and main content of the investigations, taking them in their original order. In order to appraise them and to estimate their philosophical significance in detail, they should be read with the following questions in mind: (1) What did each investigation really aim to establish? (2) Which questions were raised? (3) Are they real questions? (4) Were they answered? (5) Are the answers true to the precepts of the descriptive phenomenological method? (6) Could they be appropriated in any other way than idealistically for purposes of a constructive logical philosophy?

CHAPTER VIII

EXPRESSION AND MEANING

THE FIRST INVESTIGATION, entitled *Expression and Meaning*,[1] is an example of phenomenological descriptive analysis at its best. This material, along with the analyses of meaning in later investigations and writings, is one of the chief reasons that can be given for the lasting value of Husserl's work.

The investigation begins with the total, unanalyzed *cognitive situation*, in which actual psychical processes and physical events are involved. In ordinary discourse the terms "meaning" and "expression" are equivocal; and the same is true of "mental" and "real" (or the "subjective" and the "objective"). Beginning with the psychology of meaning, with its dependence upon signs, and with their function of manifestation and communication, the problem is to account for the sameness of meanings and their reference to an objectivity, whether real or fictive in character. This investigation is of fundamental importance because it concerns all knowledge, including logic. Expression and meaning are essential to all knowing in a significant sense. The theory of knowledge, and of science, therefore properly begins with their analysis.

The central theme of the analysis of meaning, or its chief positive outcome, is the determination of the sameness of signs and meanings. The sounds which are emitted in speaking, as in asserting the proposition "The tree is green," may be in the neighborhood of the tone *d* for one person, and tone *e* for another; and yet we say that the same sign has been used. There are also physical variations for the same person, if the statement is repeated by him. Therefore when we speak of the *same* signs we are not describing what really occurs; we are referring to something unreal or

---

[1] The first investigation retains its "merely preparatory" character in the revised edition. Its purpose is to draw the attention of the beginner in phenomenology to the first problems of meaning without attempting to do full justice to them. Husserl states that the treatment of "occasional" (*okkasionellen*) meanings, to which all empirical meanings belong, is arbitrary, and is the result of the unsatisfactory conception of the essence of "truth in itself" in the *Prolegomena*. Another defect of this investigation which is not corrected until the close of the volume is the failure to recognize the distinction and the parallelism of the "noetic" and the "noematic," a distinction which is of fundamental importance in the *Ideas*. The noetic concept of meaning is overemphasized, although the noematic concept is considered to some extent.

"ideal," as we may express it. Thought and experience in general have the peculiarity of such ideal identifications. The propositional expression "The tree is green" (or "the greenness of the tree") is alive with a meaning, which is "the same" in an ideal sense. This holds not only for meaningful propositions referring to the real world, but also for "nonsensical" propositions. It would not be proper or meaningful to ask whether such ideal meanings are "real" in the sense of having a locus in space and time, for they are precisely non-real. They are meant, and are inexpugnable features of our mental life, without which ordered experience and scientific knowledge would be impossible. To ask what they *are* would be to raise a false question. The words of Kant[2] may be applied here: "To know what questions may reasonably be asked is already a great and necessary proof of sagacity and insight. For if a question is absurd in itself and calls for an answer where none is required, it not only brings shame on the propounder of the question, but may betray an incautious listener into absurd answers, thus presenting, as the ancients said, the ludicrous spectacle of one man milking a he-goat and the other holding a sieve underneath." This also applies to the hypostasis of universals. Only the experience of ideal meanings can be said to be real. The point is to proceed descriptively as far as possible, endeavoring to do full justice to the complexity of the subject-matter, and extruding all metaphysical questions from the investigation. The realm of facts is not restricted to physical facts.

The meaning-situation is tripartite and comprises: (1) meaning-endowing acts, together with the meaning-fulfilling acts which may blend with the former; the fulfillment may be accomplished by means of a real experience of intuition, or by means of a phantasy-image; (2) the "contents" of these acts, or their meanings; (3) the reference to an objectivity that is meant.[3] The more detailed analysis of this situation, which represents

---

[2] Kant, *Critique of Pure Reason* (Smith trans.), p. 97.

[3] It would be of particular interest to compare in detail the present analysis with that by Professor Lewis in *Mind and the World-Order*, but a brief comment will suffice here. The three elements distinguished by Lewis are (1) concepts, (2) qualia, and (3) objects. Concepts are logical in character and are contributed by the mind; qualia are universals, and are ultimate given elements; and objects are the things of experience, which are partly given and partly interpreted by us. While in essential agreement with this analysis, Husserl undertakes an almost never-ending process of separating out all the elements which are given and contributed by the mind. The two accounts differ with regard to logic, which Husserl construes as absolute after the fashion of rationalism, as distinguished from the pragmatic relativism set forth by Lewis. The latter is contented with a brief systematic analysis and classification of the elements of the cognitive situation, and merely describes enough to achieve that end. The dimension of descriptive analysis that is opened up by the clarification of concepts and qualia has the function of preparing the ground for logical reason. The general question whether a pre-categorial description is at all possible is one which must be faced. This is an

the first stage of the phenomenological description of cognitive experience, will now be given.

A. THE ESSENTIAL DISTINCTIONS

The descriptive analysis of expression and meaning must provide for a number of essential distinctions, and thus avoid ambiguities. To begin with, the term "sign" (*Zeichen*) is ambiguous. Every sign is a sign of something, but not every one has a "meaning" (*Bedeutung*) or "sense" which is "expressed" by the sign. Signs in the sense of marks (*Anzeichen*) do not express anything, unless they also fulfill a meaning-function besides the function of being a mark. If we restrict ourselves to expressions which function in communicative speech, the concept of a mark appears to be wider in extension than that of an expression. But it is by no means the genus of the latter. The function of meaning can also occur in a solitary mental life, in which expressions do not function as marks. Hence the two concepts of a sign do not stand in the relationship of a wider and narrower concept. This requires a more detailed discussion.

Consider first the concept of a mark. The relation obtaining here is called *indication* (*Anzeige*). In this sense the stigma is a sign of the slave, the flag a sign of the nation. In the same way, characteristic properties make known the objects to which they are attached. But the concept of a mark is wider still, and includes such examples as fossil bones, the button that is placed in the pocket as an aid to the memory, etc. In brief, something is a mark if and when it actually serves some one as a mark of something.

If a fact *A* is regarded as a mark of the fact *B*, the being of the one refers to the being of the other, and we really expect to find the latter. The mark *A refers* to the fact *B*, but that does not mean that there is an objective, necessary connection between *A* and *B*. Thus the concept of *reference* (*Hinweis*) is different from the concept of *proof*. The subjective processes of inference and proof involve correspondence to objective inference and proof, which are ideal unities; they are the ideal "contents" (the propositions) of the corresponding experiences of judgment.

The "origin" of the concept of a mark is ascribed to the association of ideas. If *A* calls *B* into consciousness, a perceptible connection usually

---

epistemic-centric predicament, just as there is a logic-centric predicament. Although Lewis speaks of qualia as universals, descriptive analysis shows them to be contents that are presumptive of sameness. They are presumed universals, the recognition of which is natural to human thinking. The phenomenological description of the perceptual process, and of knowing in general, is thus intended to supply the assumed dimension of cognitive description.

arises such that one refers to the other. It is by means of the associative function that intentional unities appearing to belong together are formed from merely contiguous things. This holds for all unity of experience. The empirical unity of a thing or occurrence is a phenomenal unity by virtue of the fact that the parts and sides of the appearing objectivity appear to belong together. One thing refers to another in a definite order in the appearance. That which appears, whether as an object or as a part, has a new phenomenological character, in that it is not self-sufficient, but delineates an object different from itself.

Husserl distinguishes *significant* signs, or expressions, from signs in the sense of marks. The term "expression" is construed more narrowly than is the case in ordinary usage. All language, and every part of language, as well as every essentially homogeneous sign, is an expression, regardless of whether the language is actually communicated to anyone. The play of features and gestures are to be excluded, because they are not expressions in the sense of language, and they lack the intention of presenting "thoughts" in an explicit manner. Hence such "expressions" really have no meaning. If another person interprets them, they only have meaning for him in the sense of marks, and not in the significant sense of linguistic signs.

According to the traditional analysis, a distinction is drawn between the physical side of the sign, or the sign as written, as a sound-complex, etc., and the psychical experiences which make it to be an expression of something. The latter are usually regarded as the sense or meaning of the expression. Husserl undertakes to show that this conception is incorrect, and that the mere distinction between the physical sign and the meaning-endowing experiences is not adequate, especially for logical purposes.

In the case of names, the distinction has long been noted between that which a name manifests, or the psychical experiences, and that which it signifies (*bedeutet*); and also between that which it signifies, or the "content" of the nominal presentation, and that which it names, or the object of the presentation. Similar distinctions apply to all expressions, and it is necessary to investigate their essence; and still other important distinctions are to be noted in the course of the investigation. In this way due account will be taken of the fundamental oppositon between the symbolic function of meanings and their cognitive function.

In order to work out the essential logical distinctions, expression is first considered in its communicative function, which is its original purpose. All expressions in communicative speech function as marks; they serve the hearer as signs of the "thoughts" of the speaker. This function of linguistic expressions is called their *manifesting* (*kundgebende*) function by Husserl. The manifesting psychical experiences make up the content of the manifestation.

When functioning for communication, expressions are effective as marks. But expressions also play a big role in one's own mental life, in which the same meanings are retained. Hence the meaning of an expression cannot be identical with that which it manifests. In a certain sense one can also *speak* alone, as when one says to himself, "You have done that badly." This is not speaking in the real communicative sense, however, for one does not communicate anything to himself. In a monologue the words cannot serve as marks of the existence of psychical acts, for such an indication would be pointless. The acts in question are experienced by us at the same time.

If an expression is considered with respect to distinctions that obtain whether it functions in solitary speech or in conversation, two things are seen to remain: the expression itself, and that which it expresses as its meaning or sense. There is an ambiguity to be noted in speaking of expression and meaning. As seen descriptively, the concrete phenomenon of an expression that is animated with meaning divides into the physical phenomenon, in which the expression is constituted on its physical side, and into the acts which give it meaning and possibly intuitive fullness (*Fülle*), and in which the relation to an expressed objectivity is constituted. Because of these acts the expression is more than a mere word-sound. It means something, and in so doing it refers to something objective. This objectivity can either be present actually or at least appear as represented, as in a phantasy-image, and where this occurs the relation to the objectivity is realized. If that is not the case, and the expression functions meaningfully, it is more than an empty word-sound, although it does not have the founding intuition which gives the object to it. The relation of the expression to the object is now unrealized inasmuch as it is merely contained in the meaning-intention. Thus a name names its object under all circumstances in so far as it means it. It has its use in mere intention if the object is not there intuitively. When the at first empty meaning-intention is fulfilled the naming becomes an actual conscious relation between the name and that which is named.

On the basis of this fundamental distinction between intuitively empty and fulfilled (*erfüllten*) meaning-intentions, and after separating out the sensory acts in which the expression as a word-sound appears, two kinds of acts are to be distinguished. There are, first, those that are *essential* to the expression if it is to be a word-sound animated with meaning. These acts are called *meaning-endowing acts* or *meaning-intentions*. Second, there are also acts which are extra-essential to an expression, but which have the fundamental logical relation to it of fulfilling its meaning-intention with greater or lesser conformity, thus actualizing its objective reference. These acts, which are blended with the meaning-endowing acts in the unity of knowledge or of fulfillment, are called *meaning-fulfilling* acts. The meaning-animated expression is united with the acts of meaning-fulfillment in the realized reference of an expression to its objectivity. Husserl often chooses the more indeterminate term objectivity (*Gegenständlichkeit*) because objects in the narrower sense are not concerned alone, but also facts, properties, "dependent" real or categorial forms, and the like. The term expression is usually taken to mean a meaning-animated expression, and hence one ought not to say that an expression expresses its meaning (the intention). It is more appropriate to regard the fulfilling act as that which is expressed by the complete expression, as when one says of a statement, e.g., that it gives expression to a perception or imagination.

The acts of expression-appearance, of meaning-intention, and, as may be, of meaning-fulfillment, that have been distinguished form an innerly blended unity in consciousness, of a peculiar kind. Both the word-presentation and the meaning-giving act are experienced. We do not live in the presenting of the word, however, but rather in the performing of its meaning. Our whole interest belongs to the object intended in the meaning-intention and named by it. The function of the word, or rather of the intuitive word-presentation, is to excite the meaning-endowing act, and to point to what is intended "in" it and perhaps given through fulfilling intuition.

Being an *expression* is not to be explained associatively; it is a descriptive factor in the unity of experience between a sign and that which is signified. In purely phenomenological language, the intuitive presentation in which the physical word-appearance is constituted undergoes an essential phenomenal modification when its object assumes the status of an expression. The intentional character of the experience is changed. An act of meaning is constituted which is based upon the intuitive content of the word-presentation but is essentially different from the intuitive intention directed upon the word itself, and this act is often blended with fulfilling acts. Much is involved in describing the phenomenological situation. That is unavoidable when it has been made clear that all objects and relations of objects are what they are for us only through acts of meaning that are essentially different from them, in which they become known to us and in which they stand opposite us as meant unities. From the purely phenomenological point of view there is nothing but a network of such intentional acts.

Until now expressions have been considered as concrete experiences. It is now pertinent to consider what is given "in" them, the expressions themselves, their sense, and the objectivity belonging to them. This involves turning from the real reference of the acts to the ideal reference of their objects or contents. The subjective view therewith yields to the objective view. The ideality of the relationship between expression and meaning is shown by the fact that, when asking about the meaning of an expression, e.g., *quadratic remainder*, we do not mean the *hic et nunc* sound-structure that is uttered, the transient sound which never returns as identically the same. We mean the expression *in specie*. The expression *quadratic remainder* is identically the same, whoever may utter it. This essential distinction is shown by every example. Take, e.g., the statement *The three altitudes of a triangle intersect in one point*. Essentially "the same" statement may be repeated because it is the form of expression for the identity that is called its meaning. The actual act of judging and the person who asserts the judgment have no place in this identical meaning, which can be brought to evident consciousness by repetition of the statement at all times. By means of this statement we gave expression to a fact of whose validity we felt assured. The fact itself is what it is whether we assert its validity or not; it is a valid unity in itself. My act of judgment is a transient experience which arises and passes away; but not that which the statement asserts, the content *that the three altitudes of a triangle intersect in one point*. That does not arise and pass away. That which is asserted in a statement is not something subjective, but is always the same. In the present illustration it is the one and the same geometrical truth.

The same holds for all statements, no matter if they are false or even absurd. The meaning of a statement is also a unity in the manifold of experiences. We discern it to be an identity of intention in the evident acts of reflection. We do not arbitrarily put it into the statement; we find it therein.

What holds for complete statements can be applied readily to real or possible parts of statements. In the judgment, *If the sum of the angles of a triangle is not equal to two right angles, then the parallel axiom does not hold*, the hypothetical antecedent condition is not a statement by itself. It expresses something nevertheless, and what it expresses is not a psychical act of hypothetical presupposition, but something objective and ideal. It is the hypothesis with its conceptual content, which can appear as the same intentional unity in manifold possible thought-experiences. The same is also true of those parts of statements that do not have the form of propositions.

The statement that an expression *expresses* something may mean three things. (1) It may refer to the aspect of manifestation, especially to meaning-giving acts, but also to meaning-fulfilling acts if they are present. Thus we give expression to a judgment in a statement, or manifest it, but perceptions and other meaning-fulfilling acts are also expressed. (2) It may refer to the "contents" of these acts, or, to begin with, to their meanings. (3) There is finally a third sense of "being expressed" which refers to the *objectivity* meant in the meaning and expressed by means of it. Not only does every expression say something, but it is also *about* something. It not only has a meaning, but it also refers to objects. This relation may be different at times for the same expression. But the object never coincides with the meaning. Both belong to the expression only because of the meaning-giving acts.

The necessity of the distinction between meaning (content) and object is made clear by the fact that divers expressions can have the same meaning but different objects, and that different meanings can have the same object. It is possible that they differ in both respects, and also that they agree in both. The latter is the case for tautological expressions, or expressions which mean and name the same thing, e.g., in various languages, such as London and *Londres*, or two, *zwei*, *deux*, etc. The clearest examples of the separation of meaning and objective reference are provided by names. Two names can have different meanings while naming the same thing. Thus, e.g., the victor of Jena and the one who was defeated at Waterloo, or equilateral triangle and equiangular triangle. These illustrations show how the expressed meaning may be different while the same object is meant. Two expressions can also have the same meaning but different objective reference. In the statements "Bucephalus is a horse" and "This cart-horse is a horse," the "content" or meaning of the expression "a horse" remains unchanged, but the objective reference is different. Similarly "one" is a name that always has an identical meaning; but the different "ones" in a computation may not therefore be regarded as identical. They all mean the same, but they differ in their objective reference.

It is otherwise with proper names, whether of individual or general objects. A word like *Socrates* can name different things only by signifying different things; in other words, by becoming equivocal. When a word has one meaning, it names one object; and this is also true of expressions such as *the two*, *the redness*, etc. Names with different meanings (equivocal names) are to be distinguished from names with many "values" (universal names).

The same holds for all other forms of expression, although there may be some difficulties in the way of conceiving their objective reference. In the case of statements of the form *S is p*, the subject becomes the object of the statement as a rule, and is regarded as that "about" which something is asserted. But another view is also possible, which regards the whole state of affairs pertaining to the statement as an analogue of the object named by a name, and distinguishes it from the meaning of the statement. Pairs of propositions, such as *A is larger than b* and *B is smaller than a*, can then be adduced as examples. The two propositions obviously state different things. They are not only different grammatically, but also "in thought," or in their meaning-contents. But they express the same state of affairs; the same "thing" is conceived and stated in a twofold manner. Whether we define the object of the statement in one way or the other (and each has its own justification) it is always possible that statements which differ in meaning may relate to the same "object."

The distinction between the meaning of an expression and its property of naming this or that objectivity is now clear, as is also the distinction between the meaning and the object itself. There is of course a close connection between them. It is only by signifying something that an expression can refer to something objective, so that the expression signifies or names the object by means of its meaning. The essence of an expression consists exclusively in the meaning, and hence the talk of the "two sides" of an expression, or the aspects of meaning and of objective reference, should not be taken too seriously.

The factors of manifestation, meaning, and object nevertheless belong essentially to every expression. All of these are equivocally spoken of as "expressed." When a meaning-intention is fulfilled by means of a corresponding intuition, the object is constituted as a "given" object in certain acts, and is given in the same way in which the meaning means it. In this "unity of coincidence" (*Deckungseinheit*) between the meaning and the meaning-fulfillment, the essence of the meaning-fulfillment corresponds to the essence of the meaning. The *content* of a fulfilling act, or the meaning of a categorially formed perception, is distinguished furthermore from the perceived object.

Just as the ideal conception of the intentional essence of a meaning-endowing act yields the intending meaning as an idea, so the ideal conception of the correlative essence of a meaning-fulfilling act also yields the fulfilling meaning as an idea. In perception this is the *identical con-*

tent, which belongs to the totality of possible perceptual acts which mean the same object. This content is the ideal correlate of the one object, which can also be fictive in character.

The many equivocations that occur in the discussion of that which an expression expresses can be summarized by distinguishing between content in a subjective and in an objective sense. The latter involves the distinction between (1) the content as an intending meaning, or as a meaning simply, (2) the content as a fulfilling meaning, and (3) the content as an object.

The application of the terms meaning and sense not only to the content of the meaning-intention but also to the content of the meaning-fulfillment results in an unpleasant equivocation. The acts in which the intending and the fulfilling meaning are constituted are in no way the same. What leads to the use of the same terms for fulfillment as for intention is the peculiar nature of the unity of fulfillment, as a unity of identification or of coincidence. By meaning Husserl understands the identity of intention that is essential to an expression as such.

Meaning and sense are used synonymously by Husserl. Frege [4] distinguishes sense and meaning, the one being used for meaning in Husserl's sense, and the other for the expressed objects. But this is held to be objectionable, in view of the firm habit of using the two terms as synonyms.

These terms are used equivocally in scientific as well as in ordinary discourse. The manifesting acts may be meant, or the ideal meaning, or the expressed objectivity, as the sense or meaning of the expression in question. Because of their harmful consequences it is important to analyze the equivocations, not only of meaning and sense, but also of *meaningless* or *senseless* expressions.

Husserl separates out the various concepts that are mixed up and presents them as follows: (1) An expression must have a meaning, for a meaningless expression is no expression at all. For example, *Abracadabra* and *Green is or* are not expressions and only appear to be such. (2) The reference to an object is constituted in the meaning. To use an expression with meaning, and to refer to or to present an object, are one and the same thing. It does not matter if the object exists or is fictive in character. Meanings are often construed in the sense of meaning the meant objects, but such usage is due to confusion with the real concept of meaning. (3) If meaning is identified with the objectivity of an expression, then a name like "golden mountain" is meaningless. But "objectlessness" is generally

---

[4] Cp. B. Russell, *The Principles of Mathematics* (London, 1937), p. 502.

distinguished from "meaninglessness." To say that expressions like "round square" are senseless, as Sigwart does, is to confuse meaninglessness in the first sense (above) with the *a priori* impossibility of a fulfilling meaning. Meaning is taken here to depend upon the possible fulfillment of an intention. This possibility is regarded as ideal, and as involving the ideal contents of acts of fulfillment. (4) It is also necessary to consider those cases in which the meaning-intention of an expression is fulfilled intuitively. In this way the "conceptual presentation," or the meaning-intention, gains "clarity and distinctness" and is confirmed as "correct." Since the intention corresponds to the fulfilling act and is blended with it, it appears as though the expression first derived meaning from the fulfilling act, and the fulfilling intuitions thus come to be regarded as the meanings. If the significance of expressions is removed to the accompanying intuitive images, it naturally follows that absurd expressions must be denied meaning. This new concept of meaning thus results from the confusion of meaning and fulfilling intuition. According to it, an expression only has meaning if its meaning-intention actually is fulfilled, even if partially or remotely; in short, if its comprehension is animated by "meaning-presentations," or by illustrative images.

A fifth conception of meaning is due to J. S. Mill, who held the essence of the significance of names to consist in their connotation, and who accordingly regarded non-connotative names as meaningless. The distinction between signs and expressions was, however, confused by Mill. A proper name is an expression, and not a sign like a chalk-mark. In its manifesting function, like all expressions, it also acts as a sign. But that is only an aid for the meaning function. In relation to the object a proper name is not a sign, for the named object does not have to exist. The distinction between connotative and non-connotative names has nothing to do with the difference between the significant and the meaningless. Mill's distinction between that which a name denotes and that which it connotes should not be confused with the merely related difference between that which a name *names* and that which it *means*. This confusion appears to be promoted by Mill's presentation.

The analysis of the logical concepts of presentation and judgment is clearly impossible without the clarification of these distinctions.

B. MEANING–ENDOWING ACTS

The essential phenomenological character of an expression as such has now been considered, and the concept of meaning has been distinguished from a mere word-sound. This character may be real without functioning as knowledge, or being related to sensory intuition. Husserl now turns to the view that the contribution of a significant expression consists in the awakening of phantasy-images constantly coördinated with it. To understand an expression would thus be to find the phantasy-images belonging to it, and where they are not forthcoming the expression would be senseless.

The fact that such theories are possible indicates the backward state of descriptive psychology. It is true that in many cases linguistic expressions are accompanied by phantasy-ideas which are related to their meaning, but such accompanying factors are not always necessary for understanding. Take, e.g., algebraic signs or any mathematical proposition. What one finds is an open book, the sign $\sqrt{}$, etc., and not any accompanying images. This holds for expressions like culture, religion, science, and art, and also for names of individual objects, persons, cities, etc. Although the capacity for intuitive representation may be present in a given case, it need not be realized.

A number of objections that arise at this point must be met. To the objection that phantasy also operates in such cases, although with great rapidity, that an inner image arises and disappears forthwith, Husserl answers that the complete understanding of the expressions, their complete, living meaning continues after the image dwindles away, and accordingly could not lie in just this image. If it is argued furthermore that the phantasy-image has perhaps become imperceptible or was imperceptible from the outset, but that, whether perceptible or not, it is there and makes continued understanding possible, there is no doubt about the answer. Whether such an assumption is necessary or desirable for purposes of genetic psychology does not have to be determined here. It is obviously useless for the present descriptive question. That a phantasy-image is frequently imperceptible may be admitted; and it will also not be denied that the understanding of the expression can nevertheless exist and even be very perceptible. But is it not wrong to assume that an abstract factor of an experience is perceptible, namely, a factor in the phantasy-presentation which is supposed to make up the meaning, and that the whole experience, or the complete, concrete phantasy-presentation, is imperceptible? Cases in which the meaning is an absurdity would also have to be considered. Here the imperceptibleness cannot be based upon accidents of psychical powers; the image cannot exist at all in such cases, for otherwise it would provide an evidential support of the possibility of the thought concerned, or the harmony of the meaning.

Husserl admits that one could indeed refer to the fact that we do render "absurdities" perceptible in a certain manner, such as closed straight lines, or triangles the sum of whose angles is greater than or less than two right angles (he does not state whether this refers to Euclidean plane geometry; but, in any case, it is not deductive validity that is in question). But, he contends, no one will seriously regard intuitions of that kind as really making concrete the concepts in question and as the possessors of the word-meanings. Only when the phantasy-image of a meant thing really conforms to it as its image does it seem plausible to seek the meaning of the expression in this image. But such conformity is not the rule, even for absurd expressions. In such examples as a chiliagon there is only a partial representation of that which is thought; we think of such a figure, and imagine a polygon with "many" sides.

Geometrical examples do not have to be selected particularly in order to show the incommensurateness of the concrete representation. Strictly speaking, no geometrical concept can be rendered adequately perceptible. The sensory images merely serve as aids to the understanding, and not as meanings or bearers of meaning. The geometrical structures are idealizations.

It would be incorrect to charge Husserl with an extreme nominalism which identifies words and thoughts, for he is far removed from such a view. He does not regard a mere sign as there when we understand signs without the support of accompanying phantasy-images. There is rather comprehension, an experiential act that is related to the expression, investing it with meaning and objective reference. The meaning lies in the sense-giving act-character, and this is different if the interest is directed upon the sensory sign, or upon the object, even if there is no phantasy-image.

An expression may be meaningful and yet function without an illustrative intuition. There can be comprehension without intuition. Even the "senselessness" characterized as absurdity is constituted in sense; it belongs to the sense of a nonsensical expression to mean something that is objectively incompatible. If the significance does not reside in the intuition, non-intuitive speaking does not have to be thoughtless. Should the intuition be dropped, there remains attached to the expression an act of the same kind as that which is otherwise related to the intuition and mediates the knowledge of its object. Thus the act in which the meaning occurs is present in both cases.

Concrete intuitive images play a small role, or no role at all, in wide regions of everyday as well as scientific thought. We can judge, infer, consider, and refute on the basis of "merely symbolic" ideas. It would be inappropriate to speak here of a "substitutive" function of the signs, as though the signs themselves substituted for anything, and as though the thought-interest were turned to the signs themselves in symbolic thought. They are not in any way the objects of thought. We live entirely in the consciousness of meaning and of comprehension, which is not lacking in the absence of an accompanying intuition. Symbolic thought is only thought for the sake of the new "intentional" or act-character which makes up that which is distinctive of a significant sign, as opposed to the "mere" sign or word-sound, which is constituted as a physical object in merely sensory presentations. This act-character can be established descriptively as a feature of the experience. This is Husserl's interpretation of symbolic thought.

That the mere signs substitute for concepts in arithmetical thought (Husserl refers here to his analysis in the *Philosophy of Arithmetic*) is no argument against this interpretation. Besides their original meaning the arithmetical signs have their formal meaning, which is oriented with respect to the rules of reckoning operations. If the signs of arithmetic are taken purely as counters in the sense of these rules, the solution of the problems of the reckoning game of arithmetic involves number-signs, or number-formulae. One does not operate with meaningless signs in arithmetic. It is not the merely physical signs, deprived of all meaning, which substitute for the original signs that are animated with arithmetical meanings. The same signs, taken in a certain operation-meaning or game-meaning, substitute for the arithmetically significant signs. The greater mental work required by the original series of concepts is saved by the easier "symbolic" operations, which are performed in the parallel series of game-concepts. Thus a system of natural and so to speak unconscious equivocations becomes infinitely fruitful. The reference to the substitutive function of arithmetical signs does not touch the question whether explicit thought is possible without an accompanying illustrative, exemplifying, or "evident-making" intuition. Symbolic thought in the sense of such non-intuitive thought and symbolic thought in the sense of thought involving substitutive operational concepts are different things.

The understanding [5] apprehension in which the meaning of a sign occurs is related by means of an experienced sense-complex to the objectivating experiences in which the intuitive idea of an object arises. If we imagine a consciousness before all experience, we must ascribe to it the

[5] The term understanding need not be used in the narrow sense of referring to a speaker and a hearer. A monological thinker "understands" his words, and this understanding is simply the actual meaning.

same possibility for sensation that we have. But it does not intuit any things; it does not perceive houses and trees. To such a consciousness the sensations do not *mean* anything; they are not signs of the properties of an object and have no objectivating interpretation. The sensations are not perceived except in psychological reflection. A perceptual idea arises by animating the sense-complex with a certain act-character or meaning. The difference between sensation and perception is readily seen, and may be illustrated by the uniform color of a sphere which we see but have not sensed.

Such an "interpretation" is basic for signs in the sense of expressions, but only as a first conception. In the more simple case of an expression without an illustrative intuition, the mere sign appears as a given physical object, such as a word-sound. This first conception founds a second, which proceeds beyond the experienced sensory material and no longer finds in it the analogous building material for the new objectivity that is now meant. The latter is meant in the new act of meaning, and is not presented in sensation. The signifying, or the character of the expressive sign, presupposes the sign. Or, stated purely phenomenologically: the signifying is an act-character that presupposes an act of intuitive presentation as a necessary foundation. In the latter the expression is constituted as a physical object. But it first becomes an expression in the complete and genuine sense by means of the founded act.

That which holds in the simplest case of the non-intuitively understood expression must also hold in the complicated case, in which the expression is interwoven with a *corresponding* intuition. One and the same expression, significantly used now with and again without illustrative intuition, cannot derive the source of its significance from different kinds of acts.

It is not easy to analyze the descriptive situation without taking account of more refined gradations and ramifications. There are difficulties in correctly conceiving the function of intuitive presentations — the strengthening or even the making evident of the meaning-intention, which they contribute, their relationship to the understanding- or meaning-character, which already serves in the non-intuitive expression as a meaning-endowing experience. This is a large field for phenomenological analysis, a field which no logician can avoid, if he wishes to bring to clarity the relation between meaning and object, judgment and truth, unclear intending and confirming evidence. These analyses are undertaken in the sixth investigation.

The preceding section was concerned with the act of meaning. The analysis of the first section has shown that the meaning itself must be distinguished from the act of meaning; there is an ideal unity as opposed to the manifold of possible acts. Clear distinctions were also drawn between an expressed content in a subjective and in an objective sense; and in the latter respect, between content as meaning and content as naming. Although there can be no misunderstanding of them in the context of science, e.g., there are cases which require special attention because they tend to confuse the distinctions that have been made. Such are expressions that fluctuate in meaning, and especially expressions that are essentially "occasional" (i.e., referring to a particular occasion, or to the occasion of judgment) and vague. The solution of these difficulties by the distinction between fluctuating acts of meaning and ideal-unified meanings, among which they fluctuate, is the theme of this section.

Expressions can have reference to the present psychical experiences of a person, as well as to other objects. They are accordingly classified as those which at the same manifest the objectivity that they name or denote, and those for which the named and the manifested content are distinct. The former are, e.g., questions, wishes, and commands; and the latter are illustrated by statements that refer to external things, or by one's own past psychical experiences. If one expresses the wish, "I wish a glass of water," that is for the hearer a mark of the wish of the speaker. But this wish is also the object of the statement. That which is manifested and that which is named coincide partially — partially, because the judgment also belongs to the manifestation.

Essentially subjective and occasional expressions are distinguished from objective expressions. An expression is *objective* if it binds its meaning merely by its appearance-content of sound, and can be understood without regard to the person uttering it, or to the circumstances of its utterance. An objective expression can be equivocal. A *subjective* and *occasional* expression is such that its occasional actual meaning must be oriented with respect to the speaking person and his condition. All principles and theories of the "abstract" sciences belong to the order of objective expressions. No expression containing a personal pronoun has an objective sense. The word "I" names a different person from case to case. Its general meaning-function is to denote the person happening to speak; but the concept by which we express this function is not the concept which directly makes up its meaning. The word "I" has an *indicating* function, which as it were says to the hearer: the person opposite you means himself. Husserl distinguishes here between the indicating and the indicated meaning.

The further distinction between exact and vague expressions is one which relates to the ambiguity of expressions. Most expressions of ordinary life are vague, such as tree and bush, animal and plant, and the like, whereas all expressions that are constituents of pure theories and laws are exact. Vague expressions do not have a meaning-content that is identical in every case of their use. Their meanings relate to typical but only partially clear examples, which usually change frequently.

The question arises, whether the fluctuation of meanings undermines or restricts Husserl's conception of meanings as ideal and hence fixed unities. It would be wrong to conclude that meanings are divided into objective and subjective varieties. The content which is meant by a subjective expression, whose meaning is related to a particular occasion, is an ideally unified meaning in just the same sense as the content of a fixed expression. This is shown clearly by the circumstance that it is ideally possible to replace every subjective expression, with the identical retention of the meaning-intention belonging to it at the moment, by objective expressions. This substitution is not made in fact because of practical difficulties. Husserl's assertion that every subjective expression can be replaced by an objective one implies the boundlessness of objective reason. Everything that is, is knowable "in itself" and is documented in "truths in themselves." Corresponding to being in itself are the truths in themselves, and to these there correspond the fixed and unique statements in themselves. In order really to assert them everywhere, there must be not only the necessary number of well-distinguished word-signs, but especially the corresponding number of exact significant expressions.

The fluctuation of meanings is really a fluctuation of the acts of meaning, i.e., there are changes in the subjective acts which invest the expressions with meaning; and they not only change individually, but particularly with respect to the specific characters in which their meaning lies. But the meanings themselves do not change. To say that would be absurd, assuming that we continue to regard meanings as ideal unities in the case of equivocal and subjectively unclear expressions, just as is the case with univocal and objectively fixed expressions.

D. PURE LOGIC AND THE IDEAL MEANINGS

When pure logic treats of concepts, judgments, and inferences it deals exclusively with these ideal unities, which are here called meanings. In endeavoring to obtain the ideal essence of meanings from psychological and grammatical structures, and in aiming to clarify the *a priori* relations of adequation by means of the meant objectivity based upon this essence, we are in the field of pure logic.

By logic is meant the nomological science which deals with the ideal essence of science as such; or, what is the same, the nomological science of scientific thought in general, with respect to its theoretical content and structure. The theoretical content of a science consists of the meaning-content of its theoretical statements, which are independent of all accidents of the judger and the occasions of judgment. The statements are unified in the form of a theory and the theory owes its objective validity to the ideal-lawful conformity of its unity as a unity of meaning to the meant objectivity that is "given" to us in evident knowledge. That which is called *meaning* in this sense comprises only ideal unities which are expressed in a diversity of expressions and are thought in various acts of experience, and yet must be distinguished from the accidental expressions and experiences of a thinker. If all given theoretical unity is essentially unity of meaning, and if logic is the science of theoretical unity in general, then logic must be the science of meanings as such, of their essential kinds and distinctions, as well as of the ideal laws based upon them. These distinctions include the difference between meanings with objects and without objects, and between true and false meanings; and among the ideal laws are the pure "laws of thought," which express the *a priori* nexus of the categorial form of meanings and their objectivity or truth.

The scientist judges when he sets up propositions. He does not want to speak of his or of any one's judgments, but rather of the facts referred to; and when he refers to the propositions in a critical discussion he means ideal statement-meanings. He designates the propositions and not the judgments as true or false. Propositions are building stones of inferences. Here again there is a distinction between the acts of inference and their unified contents, the inferences, i.e., the identical meanings of certain complex statements. The element of necessity in an inference is not based upon an empirical connection of experiences, but is an ideal relation of possible statement-meanings, of propositions. The expression "It exists" means "It holds, or is valid"; and validity has no essential relationship to an empirical judger. The scientist knows very well that an expression is something accidental and that the thought, the ideal-identical meaning, is the essential thing. He also knows that he does not make the objective validity of the concepts and truths, but that he discovers them and has insight into them. He knows that their ideal being is not a psychical "being in our minds," since the genuine objectivity of truth and of the ideal requires that all real being, including subjective being, be suspended. With respect to its objective content, all science, as a theory, is constituted out of one homogeneous "substance"; it is an ideal complex of meanings. The entire network of meanings which is called the theoretical unity of science belongs under the category that encompasses all its constituent parts, for it itself constitutes a unity of meaning.

All that is logical falls under the correlative categories of *meaning* and *object*. If logical categories are spoken of in the plural, they can only be pure species which are distinguished *a priori* within this genus of meaning, or correlative forms of the categorially conceived objectivity as such. The laws to be formulated by logic are grounded in these categories. On the one hand, disregarding the ideal relations between meaning-intention and meaning-fulfillment, and hence the possible cognitive function of the meanings, there are the laws which concern the mere complication of meanings to new meanings, whether "real" or "imaginary." On the other hand, there are the logical laws in a pregnant sense, which deal with the meanings with respect to their reference to an objectivity, their truth and falsity, or their harmoniousness and absurdity, in so far as they are determined by the mere categorial form of the meanings. To the latter laws there correspond equivalent and correlative laws of objects in general, in so far as they are thought as determined through mere categories. All valid statements about existence and truth which can be set up on the basis of the forms of meaning and by abstracting from all cognitive matter are contained in these laws.

E. THE PHENOMENOLOGICAL AND IDEAL CONTENT OF EXPERIENCES OF MEANING

Husserl sees the essence of meaning not in the experience which endows the meaning, but in its "content," which presents an identical intentional unity as opposed to the scattered manifold of real or possible experiences of speakers and theories. The term "intentional" is understood to permit application to meaning as well as to the object of the "intentio." Hence intentional unity does not necessarily mean the intended unity of the object. The "content" of a meaning-experience in this ideal sense is by no means what psychology means by content, namely, a real part of an experience. The psychological content changes from individual to individual, and for the same individual at different times, even with respect to "the same" word. My individual peculiarities belong only to the psychological content of my presentational experiences.

That which is the same from case to case belongs to the psychological content, as well as that which changes. Hence Husserl does not hold that the act-character that remains the same everywhere is the meaning. What the proposition π *is a transcendental number* states, and what we understand by it, is not an individual feature of our thought-experience which always returns. From case to case this feature is individually different, whereas the sense of the proposition is supposed to be identical. If other persons repeat the same proposition with the same intention, each has his phenomena, his words, and factors of comprehension. But opposed to this unlimited manifold of individual experiences is that which is expressed in them, which is identical everywhere and is the same in the strictest sense of the term. The proposition-meaning does not multiply according to the number of persons and acts; the judgment in the ideal logical sense is *one*.

The insistence upon the strict identity of the meaning and upon distinguishing it from the constant psychical character of the act of meaning is due not to a preference for subtle distinctions, but to the theoretical conviction that only in this way can one do justice to the understanding of logic. This is directly apprehended in evidence, which is the final authority on questions of knowledge. I have the insight that what I mean in the proposition, or conceive to be its meaning, is identically what it is whether I think and am, and whether any thinking persons and acts are, or not. That also holds for the ideal determinations which belong primarily to meanings alone, e.g., the predicates true and false, possible and impossible, general and singular, determinate and indeterminate, etc.

This true identity, which Husserl maintains here, is none other than the identity of species. Thus, and only thus, can it as an ideal unity encompass the scattered manifold of individualities. A meaning is related to the occasional acts of meaning, a logical idea to the acts of presentation, a logical judgment to the acts of judgment, or a logical inference to the acts of inference, as say redness *in specie* is to the slips of paper which all "have" this same redness. Every slip of paper has, besides other constitutive characters, such as extension, form, etc., its individual redness, i.e., its particular case of this species of color, whereas the redness itself does not really exist, either in this slip or anywhere else in the world, and especially not "in our thought," in so far as that also belongs to the domain of real being, or to the temporal sphere.

It can also be said that the meanings form a class of concepts in the sense of "general objects." These are not to be thought of as objects existing in the mind of God. Such metaphysical hypostasis would be absurd. The talk of general objects merely refers to the validity of certain judgments, such as those in which numbers, propositions, geometrical structures, etc., are judged about. Here, as usual, the correlate of judgmental validity can be spoken of as an "object that truly is." Viewed logically, the proposition about the parallelogram of forces is an object just as well as the city of Paris.

The ideality of meanings is a particular case of the ideality of species in general. It has not the sense of normative ideality at all, as though it were an ideal of perfection, or an ideal limiting value, as contrasted with the particulars. The meanings "in themselves" are specific unities, no matter how the acts of meaning fluctuate; they are not ideals. Ideality in the usual normative sense does not preclude reality. An ideal is a concrete prototype that can even exist as a real thing and be seen, such as a work of art by a great master. But even if the ideal cannot be realized it is an individual, at least in the intention of presentation. The ideality of species is opposed, however, to reality and individuality. It is not the goal of possible striving. Its ideality is that of "unity in a manifold." Not the species itself, but the particular thing falling under it may be a practical ideal.

The meanings form a class of general objects, or species. To be sure, every species, if we want to speak about it, presupposes a meaning in which it is presented, and this meaning is itself a species. But the meaning in which the species is thought and its object, the species itself, are not one and the same thing. Just as in the domain of the individual, e.g., we distinguish between Kant himself and the ideas of him, say *Kant — the foremost German philosopher*, and the like, so we distinguish in the domain of the specific; e.g., between the number 4 itself and the ideas or meanings which have 4 as their object, such as *the number 4, the second even number in the number series*, etc. Hence the generality *which* we think is not dissolved in the generality of meanings *in* which we think them. The concepts of "meaning" and "concept" in the sense of species do not coincide.

If we make a statement, we judge about the thing in question and not about the meaning of the proposition, about the judgment in a logical sense. This first becomes an object for us in a reflective act of thought in which we do not merely look back at the statement asserted, but perform the necessary abstraction or ideation. What characterizes logical reflection is the theoretical context and the process of theoretical reflection upon the contents of the acts of thought just performed. We could not express a "therefore" in a process of reasoning without regard to the meaning-content of the premises. In judging the premises we do not only live in the judgments, but reflect upon the judgment-contents. Only with respect to them does the conclusion appear motivated. Thus alone can the logical form of the premises determine insightfully the deduction of the conclusion.

There is no necessary connection in themselves between the ideal unities which actually function as meanings and the signs to which they are bound, i.e., by means of which they are realized in the human mind. Just as numbers, in the ideal sense that is presupposed in arithmetic, do not arise and pass away with the act of counting, and as the infinite number series therefore represents an objectively fixed totality of general objects that are sharply delimited by ideal laws and which no one can increase or diminish; so with the ideal, purely logical unities, the concepts, propositions, and truths, in short the logical meanings. They form an ideal, closed totality of general objects to which being thought is non-essential. There are countless meanings which are merely possible meanings in the usual relative sense of the term, because they never come to expression and due to the limits of human powers of knowledge can never come to expression.

CHAPTER IX

UNIVERSALS AND ABSTRACTION

THE ESSENTIAL DISTINCTIONS that are necessary for establishing the locus of ideal meanings were made in the first investigation. The psychological, physical, and epistemological factors were separated out, and the basic distinctions for a general theory of signs were outlined. Because identity or sameness is necessary for all knowledge, and for logic in particular, the description of the experience and factor of sameness was of primary interest. Logic was treated as a science whose subject-matter consists of ideal meanings.

This study is deepened in the second investigation,[1] the central theme of which is the problem of the status of universals. The preceding investigation had established the fact that ideal meanings are necessary for thought. But the question of the status of such ideal entities remained to be determined. The problem was to avoid the extremes of Platonic realism and nominalism, as well as the psychological hypostasis of the general; and that meant settling accounts with the empirical-psychological theories of modern philosophy. In the course of an extended polemic against Locke, Berkeley, Hume, and Mill, Husserl gradually makes clear his fundamental insight into the role of universals in knowledge, and his view concerning the immediate apprehension of meanings. He exposes the harmful confusions of British empiricism, and refuses to commit its initial errors of the analysis of experience and its objects. It is apparent in the course of the investigation that phenomenology in its narrow sense is the true heir of British empiricism, and that it is more successful in doing justice to the analysis of experience.

Husserl is right in pointing out that without universals no significant statement could be asserted. That we "grasp" universals immediately can be taken as a matter of fact. How we do so is a theme for descriptive analysis, concerning which there should be no dispute. The process of the abstraction of universals can be accounted for descriptively.

---

[1] The second investigation possessed a certain completeness which made it undesirable to make extensive changes. In the second edition the essentially different types of "Ideas," to which essentially different "ideations" correspond, remain undiscussed. The point of this investigation is merely to see Ideas such as are represented by the Idea "red," and to make clear the essence of such "seeing."

The large amount of disagreement in explaining our knowledge of universals gives cause for wonder. The explanation is perhaps to be found in the complex of factors which influence and complicate philosophical thought — the influence of the traditional metaphysics and theory of knowledge, and the prevailing motives, conscious or unconscious, of the times. Thus sensationalism, with its atomistic theory of experience as consisting of simple ideas in the last analysis, belongs to the social pattern of individualism in social and political theory, and physical atomism in the theory of matter. The theory was disposed of in epistemology long after the original historical motivation had disappeared. In this sense ideas may be said to survive themselves, for they tend to live a life of their own. But such historical explanation is foreign to Husserl's line of interest, which is confined entirely to systematic analysis.

Reference is first made to the act-character of meaning, as discussed in the first investigation. This possesses a definite characteristic (or "tinction") which distinguishes the consciousness of the meaning of one expression from that of another which is different in meaning. That is not to say, however, that this act-character is the concrete basis on which the meaning is constituted for us as a species. The concrete basis involved is rather the whole experience of the understood expression, in which that character inheres as an animating "tinction." The relationship between a meaning and a meaningful expression is the same as the relationship between the species red and a red object of intuition. While the red object and the character of red in it appears, we mean the one identical word, and we mean it in a new kind of consciousness, the object of which is a species and not an individual.

The meaning as a species arises through abstraction. It is necessary to understand this process in its proper sense, and not after the fashion of empirical psychology and theory of knowledge. The question of abstraction is important for a philosophical foundation of pure logic for two reasons. In the first place, corresponding to the opposition between individual and general objects there is a categorial distinction of meanings which must be observed by pure logic. In the second place, meanings in general, in the sense of specific unities, form the domain of pure logic, and consequently every misconstruction of the essence of species must affect its own essence. It is therefore necessary to consider the problem of abstraction, and to safeguard the main foundation of pure logic and the theory of knowledge by a justification of specific (or ideal) objects in addition to individual (or real) objects. This is the point at which a relativistic and empirical psychologism is distinguished from that idealism which in Husserl's view alone presents the possibility of a consistent theory of knowledge. No metaphysical doctrine is meant by the term idealism; it signifies the form of the theory of knowledge which regards the ideal as a condition of the possibility of objective knowledge in general, and does not explain it away psychologistically.

A. GENERAL OBJECTS AND THE CONSCIOUSNESS OF GENERALITY

Husserl maintains that the validity of the distinction between specific and individual objects, and the different kinds of presentation in which the two types of objects come to clear consciousness, are matters of direct evidence. This evidence is given along with the clarification of the presentations (or ideas) in question. We need only to go back to the cases in which individual or specific presentations are fulfilled intuitively, and we obtain the most luminous clarity about the kind of objects they really mean. Reflection upon acts of both types enables us to determine whether essential distinctions exist or not.

Comparison shows that an act in which we mean something specific is in fact essentially different from one in which we mean something individual. To be sure both kinds have a certain phenomenal element in common. The same *concretum* appears to both, and so the same sensory contents are given to both in the same manner of apprehension, i.e., the same amount of actually given sense- and phantasy-contents underlies the same "apprehension" or "interpretation," in which the appearance of the object is constituted for us with the properties presented through those contents. But there are different acts for the same appearance in the two cases. On the one hand, the appearance is the presentation-basis for an act of individual meaning, in which we simply mean the appearing thing itself, or a character of it. On the other hand, it is the presentation-basis for an act of specific meaning, i.e., while the thing or the character of the thing appears, we do not mean this objective character, this here and now, but rather its content, its "Idea." We do not mean this character of red in the house, but the red (*das Rot*). This meaning is founded (*fundiert*) in so far as a new kind of apprehension is built upon the "intuition" of the individual house, or of its red, which apprehension is constitutive of the Idea *red*. Just as a species is there as a general object because of the nature of this apprehension, so there arise formations such as red, the red of this house, and the like. The primitive relation between species and particular cases comes to the fore, and the possibility arises of surveying a manifold of particular cases and of judging with evidence that in all cases the individual character is different, but "in" every one the same species is realized. It is evident that this red is the same as that red, viewed specifically, and yet is different if viewed individually. This is a categorial distinction, like all fundamental logical distinctions. It belongs to the pure form of possible objectivities of consciousness as such.

The excesses of conceptual realism brought about a reaction in which not only the reality but the objectivity of species was disputed. This was certainly wrong in Husserl's view. The question whether it is possible to regard species as objects can only be answered by going back to the meaning of the names of species, and to the meaning of the statements which are held to be true of species. If these names and statements can be so interpreted that the actual objects of the intention are individual, then the opposing doctrine must be admitted. But if that is not the case, if the analysis of the meaning of such expressions shows that their direct and actual intention cannot be directed upon any individual objects, then the opposing doctrine is evidently false. That would be the case if it were shown that their relation to individual objects is merely indirect, indicating logical connections whose content is first developed in new thoughts and experiences. It is necessary to distinguish between individual singularities such as empirical things, and specific singularities such as numbers and sets in mathematics, or concepts and propositions in pure logic. *Number* is a concept which comprises the singularities 1, 2, 3, . . . ; and the number 2, e.g., is not any group of two individual objects.

Corresponding to the difference between individual and specific singularities is the equally essential difference between individual and specific generalities. These distinctions apply to the domain of judgment and pervade logic. Singular judgments are divided into those that are individually singular, such as *Socrates is a man*, and those that are specifically singular, such as *2 is an even number*, *Round square is an absurd concept*. Universal judgments are also divided into those that are individually universal, and those that are specifically universal. The former may be illustrated by *All men are mortal*, and the latter by *All analytic functions can be differentiated*, *All propositions of pure logic are a priori*.

Such distinctions are unavoidable. It is easy to see how a species becomes an object of knowledge. Logical presentations, or unified meanings in general, are ideal objects, whether they present something individual or general. This may be illustrated by *the city of Berlin* as the identical sense in repeated expressions and acts of meaning, and by the direct presentation of the Pythagorean proposition. Every such meaning is a unity and may be judged about with evidence; it can be compared with other meanings and distinguished from them; it can be the identical subject of many predicates; and it can be collected with other meanings and counted as a unit. These features are just like those of other objects which are not meanings, such as horses, stones, psychical acts, etc. Only because a meaning is something identical can it be treated as something identical. This appears to Husserl to be an indisputable argument, and to hold for all specific unities, including those which are non-meanings.

The question arises as to whether the unity of species is a genuine unity or not. We say of like things that they are *the same*. For example, we speak of the same coat, the same hat, etc., of products which are made according to the same pattern and are alike in all ways that interest us in such things. In this sense one speaks of the same conviction, the same question, and the same wish. Such figurative talk of the identity of like things refers back to a corresponding genuine identity. Wherever likeness exists we actually find an identity in the strict sense. We cannot denote two things as like one another without giving the *respect* in which they are alike; and there is the identity. Every likeness has reference to a species under which the compared things are comprehended. This species is not, however, something that is again merely similar, and cannot be, for otherwise a *regressus in infinitum* would be incurred. If two things are alike with respect to their form, then the form-species concerned is the identical element; if they are alike in color, it is the color-species, etc. It would be wrong to define identity as the limiting case of likeness. Likeness is the relation of objects which are comprehended under one and the same species. If one is not allowed to speak of the identity of species, of the respect in which likeness obtains, then the talk of likeness is also groundless.

In opposition to the view that ideal unity can be reduced to a manifold of particulars, or that the one attribute can be reduced to certain relations of likeness, Husserl submits the following distinction. He proposes to compare (1) our intention when we apprehend a group of objects as being alike, or when we recognize their likeness as such at one stroke; or also, when we discern in single acts of comparison the likeness of a definite object to other particular objects, and finally to all objects of the group; [2] and (2) our intention when we, perhaps even on the same intuitive basis, grasp the attribute which makes up the respect of the likeness, or of the comparison. It is evident that in the two cases the goal of our intention, the objectivity which is meant and is named as the subject of our statement is totally different. No matter how many like objects may appear to us in intuition or in comparison, they and their likenesses are

[2] Reference is here made to the discussion of the intuitive apprehension of collections and of the intuitive knowledge of likeness in the *Phil. d. Arith.*, p. 233.

not meant in the second case. What is meant is something "general," the ideal unity, and not these individuals and pluralities.

The two intentional situations also differ psychologically. In the second case no intuition of likeness or comparison is necessary. I recognize this paper as paper and as white, and bring the general sense of the expressions "paper" and "white in general" to clarity without having to make use of any intuitions of likeness or comparison. One might say that the conceptual presentations would never have arisen psychologically without the joint appearance of like objects. But, Husserl answers, this psychological fact is entirely irrelevant here; that which is in question is the role of the attribute in knowledge as a matter of evidence.

Every attempt to reinterpret the being of the ideal as a possible being of a real must clearly be shattered by the fact that possibilities are themselves ideal objects. Possibilities cannot be found in the real world any more than numbers in general or triangles in general. The empiricist conception which endeavors to obviate the assumption of specific objects by means of their extension therefore fails. It is unable to tell us what gives unity to the extension. Husserl adds a characteristic argument in support of his position. The empiricist conception operates with "spheres of similarity," but takes too lightly the difficulty that every object belongs to a plurality of spheres of similarity, and that the question must be answered as to what separates these spheres from one another. Without the already given unity of species an infinite regress would be unavoidable. An object A is similar to other objects, to some with respect to point of view a, and to others with respect to point of view b, etc. But the point of view itself is not to mean that a species is there which provides unity. What is it then that makes, e.g., the sphere of similarity determined by redness to be unified as distinguished from the one determined by triangularity? The only answer that can be given from the empiricist point of view is that they are different kinds of similarity. The similarities are themselves compared and form genera and species, like their own elements. It would be necessary to go back to the similarities of these similarities, and so on *in infinitum*.

That the psychologistic conception which splits up the unity of a species into the manifold of objects comprehended under it incurs difficulties has been recognized, but their solution has been accepted too easily. J. S. Mill, in conflict with his own psychologistic doctrine, sought to maintain the identity of the attribute and to justify it against Spencer, who with greater consistency would only admit exactly like attributes.

In Husserl's view it is sufficient to ask what is to establish the unified

homogeneousness of all the similarities, in order to recognize the incorrectness of the relativistic conception. Like Mill and Spencer, he does not
advocate the reality of attributes, i.e., that an attribute is a real thing possessing objective existence; but he demands a sharper analysis. Mill overlooked the fact that the unified sense of a name and of every expression
is also a specific unity, and that the problem is only pushed back if one
reduces a species to the unity of a word-meaning.

Husserl regards it as indispensable to proceed to further criticism, in
order to make his conception of the essence of general objects useful for
the examination and analysis of the main forms of the modern theories
of abstraction. The critical demonstration of the errors of other views
provides an opportunity to supplement the elaboration of his own conception, and also to test its reliableness.

It does not appear to be appropriate to describe the empiricist treatment
of abstraction as a "theory," because according to that view there is nothing to be explained. That view confuses two essentially different scientific
interests, of which the one deals with the psychological explanation of
experiences, and the other with the "logical" elucidation of their thought-
content or sense and the critique of their possible contribution to knowledge. The latter is an investigation of the "origin of the concepts" that
belong to words, which provides a clarification of their "real meaning."
That is accomplished by the evidential confirmation of their intention by
means of a process of fulfillment requiring the appropriate intuition. The
study of the essence of these phenomenological connections provides indispensable foundations for the critical elucidation of the "possibility" of
knowledge. In the present case this means the clarification of the possibility of valid assertions about general objects, or about single objects as
objects of the corresponding general concepts, and also the evidential
determination of the proper sense in which the general can be said to be
existent, or something particular to be comprehended under general predicates. A doctrine of abstraction which seeks to be epistemological, i.e.,
to clarify knowledge, should deal with the immediate descriptive situation
in which the specific comes to our consciousness; it must clarify the meaning of attribute-names, and also take account of the many misinterpretations which the essence of species has undergone. It misses its goal from
from the outset if, instead of so doing, it loses itself in empirical-psychological analyses of the process of abstraction according to causes and effects,
and, going beyond the descriptive contents of the consciousness of abstraction, turns its interest mainly to unconscious dispositions and hypothetical connections of association. But even if a theory of abstraction

avoids the confusion of essential analysis and empirical analysis, or of knowledge-critical elucidation and psychological explanation, it also misses its goal if it confuses phenomenological and objective analysis, i.e., if that which the acts of meaning merely ascribe to the objects is regarded as a real constituent of the acts themselves. The sphere of consciousness and its immanent essence are again abandoned and everything results in confusion.

In the analyses that follow, Husserl shows that this characterization applies to the most influential modern theories of abstraction.

B. THE PSYCHOLOGICAL HYPOSTASIS OF THE GENERAL

Two misinterpretations have dominated the development of the doctrines of general objects: (1) the metaphysical hypostasis of the general, the assumption of the real existence of species *outside of* thought; and (2) the psychological hypostasis of the general, the assumption of the real existence of species *in* thought. A third misinterpretation is that of nominalism, which in its various forms attempts to reinterpret the general in terms of individuals, with respect to the object and act of thought.

The first misinterpretation, which is at the basis of Platonic realism in the traditional conception, has long been disposed of. The older nominalism, both extreme and conceptual, opposed it. The opposition to the second misinterpretation, especially in the form of Locke's abstract ideas, determined the development of the modern theory of abstraction since Berkeley and showed a decided inclination toward extreme nominalism, which at present is simply called nominalism and is contrasted with conceptualism. In order to avoid the absurdity of Locke's abstract ideas it was thought necessary to deny general objects as peculiar thought-unities and general presentations as peculiar acts of thought.

Questions regarding the essence of general objects cannot be separated from questions pertaining to the essence of general ideas. For present purposes it is necessary to remove all doubts as to how such objects can be presented, and also to refute the theories which appear to prove by scientific psychological analyses that they are only individual ideas, that consequently only individual objects can be known to us, and that therefore the talk of general objects must be regarded as only fictive or figurative.

In view of the continued influence of psychological realism, Husserl undertakes to consider it more closely.

In order to show apagogically the untenability of the doctrine of species as general objects, the following line of thought might be advanced in opposition to Husserl's view. If species are not something real, and if they are also not something in thought, then they are nothing at all. How can we talk about something without its being at least in our thought? The being of the ideal is therefore obviously a being in consciousness, and hence it is properly called a content of consciousness. In contrast to that, real being is not mere being in consciousness or the being of a content, but is being-in-itself, transcendent being, being outside of consciousness.

To this type of metaphysics Husserl answers that for him "real" applies to what is "in" consciousness just as it does to that which is "outside." The individual with all its constituents is real; it is something here and now. Temporality is sufficient for us as a characteristic feature of reality. Real being and temporal being are not identical concepts, but their extensions are equal. Husserl does not mean that psychical experiences are things in the sense of metaphysics. If metaphysics is excluded, reality may be defined by temporality; for what is alone in question is the opposition to the non-temporal "being" of the ideal.

It is furthermore certain that the general is something that is thought by us, as often as we speak of it. But it is not therefore a thought-content in the sense of a real constituent of a thought-experience, or in the sense of a meaning-content, but is rather an *object* that has been thought. Husserl does not place the being of the ideal upon the same level as the being thought of the fictive or the absurd. The latter does not exist at all, and nothing can be stated categorically about it in a real sense. To speak of them as having their own kind of being, the "merely intentional" kind, is really to use figurative language. There are only certain lawfully valid connections among "presentations without objects," which by virtue of their analogy with truths referring to presentations with objects, suggest the idea of merely presented objects which do not truly exist. Ideal objects exist truly, on the contrary. It is not only meaningful to speak of such objects as the number 2, the quality redness, the principle of contradiction, and the like, and to present them as having predicates, but we also grasp with insight certain categorical truths which refer to such ideal objects. If these truths are valid, everything which their validity presupposes objectively must exist. If I have the insight that 4 is an even number, that the stated predicate really belongs to the ideal object 4, then this object cannot be a mere fiction, or a mere nothing.

This is not to deny that the sense of this being and of this predication is not entirely the same as in the cases in which a real subject and a real predicate, its property, are involved. On the contrary, Husserl attaches

weight to the fundamental categorial distinction within the field of existence, or of objects in general — the distinction between ideal being and
real being, being as species and being as something individual. Similarly
predication is divided into two essentially different kinds, depending upon
whether its properties are attributed to or denied of an individual, or
whether its general determinations are attributed to or denied of a species.
But this distinction does not undermine the highest unity in the concept of
an object, or, correlatively, categorical propositional unity. In every case
an object (or a subject) has or has not something (or a predicate), and
the meaning of this most general attribution, with its laws, determines
the general sense of being, or of an object in general; just as the more
special sense of general predication with its coördinated laws determines
the sense of an ideal object, or presupposes it. Assuming that everything
that exists is valid as existent by virtue of the evidence with which it is
grasped in thought as being, Husserl concludes that there can be no
ground for the denial of ideal being. In fact, no art of interpretation can
eliminate ideal objects from our speaking and thinking.

Locke's psychological hypostasis of the general was especially influential
historically. It arose due to the following line of thought: In actual reality
no such thing as a universal exists; only individual things exist, and they
are ordered in species and genera with respect to similarities. The appearances of things are seen to be complexes of "simple ideas," if we keep to
the sphere of what is immediately given and experienced. The fact that
we can name many things uniquely by means of one and the same general name proves that a general meaning, a "general idea" must correspond
to that. A general name refers to the objects of the class in question by
means of a quality or quality-complex that is common to all the objects.
The general thinking that occurs in general meanings therefore presupposes that we have the capacity for abstraction, i.e., the capacity to separate partial ideas or ideas of single characters from the phenomenal
things which are given to us as complexes of qualities, and to connect
them with words as their general meanings. The formation of "abstract"
or "general" ideas is admittedly not without difficulty.

Maintaining that the cardinal error of the Lockean as well as of the
British theory of knowledge in general, the unclear conception of an idea,
is illustrated here, Husserl points out several fundamental errors in Locke's
reasoning. (1) The term idea was taken by Locke to mean any object of
inner perception. This was extended to include every possible object
of inner perception, and finally every content in an immanent-psycholog-
ical sense, or every psychical experience in general, was included under the

title idea. (2) But it also had the narrower meaning of presentation in the sense of an intentional experience, so that an idea is an idea *of something*. (3) Locke confused idea with that which is presented, appearance with that which appears, and the act, i.e., the act-phenomenon as a real immanent constituent of the stream of consciousness, with the intended object. Thus the appearing object becomes an idea, and its qualities become partial ideas. (4) This error is connected with the circumstance that Locke confused the qualities which are attached to an object with the immanent contents which make up the sensuous core of the act of presentation. (5) Furthermore, under the title "general idea" the qualities as specific attributes were confused with qualities as factors of objects. (6) Finally, Locke failed to make the distinction between idea in the sense of intuitive idea (or appearance) and idea in the sense of idea of meaning. One can understand by the idea of meaning the intention of meaning as well as the fulfillment of meaning, for these two were also never separated by Locke.

Only these confusions, from which, Husserl adds, the theory of knowledge suffered up to the time of his writing, gave to Locke's doctrine of abstract general ideas the semblance of self-evident clarity which could deceive its author. Husserl expresses opposition to the view that the objects of intuitive ideas, the animals, trees, etc., just as they appear to us, are complexes of "ideas." They are not objects of possible "inner perception," as though they formed a complex phenomenological content in consciousness and could be found therein as real data. A fundamental distinction must be drawn between "color," "smoothness," and "form" in the sense of objective properties and in the sense of sensations. The sensations represent the objective determinations in the thing-perceptions in question by means of the apprehensions animating them, but they are never the objective determinations themselves. The appearing object, just as it appears there, is transcendent of the appearance as a phenomenon. The appearing objects of outer intuitions are *meant* unities, but not ideas or complexes of ideas in Locke's sense. Naming by means of general names, Husserl concludes, does not consist in selecting single common ideas from such complexes of ideas, and in connecting them to words as their "meanings." Naming may refer to a single quality, but that is an act of meaning in an analogous sense to the way in which the reference to the concrete object itself is an act of meaning. This act of meaning means something by itself, which is co-meant in a certain manner in meaning the *concretum*. But that is not to say that a separation is made between them.

Anything upon which an intention is directed thereby becomes an object of the act. That it becomes the act's *own* object, and that it becomes an object *separated* from all other objects, are two fundamentally different assertions. The characters, provided that they are understood to be attributive factors, are inseparable from their concrete basis. Contents of this kind cannot be by themselves. An intention does not separate; it means, and what it means it circumscribes. That holds for all kinds of meaning or intending; and it should be noted that not every meaning is intuition, and not every intuition is adequate, completely and perfectly comprising its object.

An individual factor of an object is not the same as an attribute *in specie.* If the former is meant, then the act of meaning is individual; and if something specific is meant, it has the character of specific meaning. If the intuitive basis is the same, the difference between them can only be due to the character of the act. Similar distinctions are to be observed between a generic idea in the usual sense, such as tree, horse, and the like, and direct ideas of things. The distinction must be drawn generally between the total and partial intuitions which form the basis, and the changing act-characters which are built thereupon cognitively, without anything having to be changed sensuously and intuitively.

For a more exact analysis many more distinctions of acts would enter into consideration than are needed for purposes of the critique of Locke. A single intuitive thing may be meant directly as *this* here, or as *the bearer of something general*, as subject of an attribute, as a single member of an empirical genus; or, again, the general itself may be meant, e.g., the species of a character that is discerned in a partial intuition; or furthermore, such a species may be meant as a species of an ideal genus, etc. In all these modes of apprehension, the same sense-perception may serve as a basis.

To the distinctions of "real" thought, in which the diverse categorial forms are actually constituted, the *symbolic intentions* of expressions must be added. Statements are made which mean something that is perhaps not at all actualized in a real, intuitively fulfilled manner. The "thinking" is now "merely symbolic" or "figurative."

Locke was not able to do justice to this phenomenological fact. The sensory intuitive image by means of which the meaning-intention is fulfilled was taken by Locke to be the meaning itself, as already pointed out. This identification is not correct if by meaning we understand either intentional or fulfilling meaning. The former belongs to an expression as such. A meaning-intention makes up general presentation in the sense of general signification, and such presentation is possible without any actual intuitive basis. But if there is a fulfillment, the sensory intuitive image is not the meaning-fulfillment itself; it is rather the mere basis of the fulfilling act. To a merely "symbolic" general thought, i.e., to the mere meaning of a general word, there corresponds a "really" executed thought which is founded on an act of sensory intuition, but is not identical with it.

This suffices to show the deceptive confusions in Locke's reasoning. The obvious fact that every general name has its own general meaning led him to assert that a general idea belongs to every general name, and this idea was for him nothing other than a separate intuitive idea or a separate appearance of a quality. Since Locke did not keep apart the appearance of a quality and the appearing quality, any more than a quality as a factor and a quality as a specific attribute were distinguished, his notion of a "general idea" incurred a psychological hypostasis of the general; the general became a real datum of consciousness.

Husserl finally observes that in any case the "difficulties" of general meanings provide no cause for serious complaints about the "imperfections" of the human mind.

C. ABSTRACTION AND ATTENTION

Husserl now proceeds to the analysis of an influential theory of abstraction which was first elaborated by J. S. Mill in his work on Hamilton, according to which abstraction is merely a function of attention. There are, it is said, neither general ideas nor general objects; but while we intuitively present individual concrete things we can turn our exclusive attention or our exclusive interest to the various parts and sides of an object. An attribute that can neither be real nor be presented by itself becomes the object of an exclusive interest which neglects the other attributes with which it is combined.

Husserl's positive answer to the nominalists consists in his painstaking analysis of that which is descriptively given in cognitive experience. As has been seen, the distinction between names that name something individual and those that name something specific is fundamental. If we restrict ourselves for simplicity to direct names, or proper names in a broad sense, then names such as *Socrates* or *Athens* on the one hand are contrasted with names such as the number *four* and the tone *c* on the other hand. Certain meanings correspond to the names, and by means of them we refer to objects. In the one case it is the person Socrates, the city of Athens, or some other individual object; in the other case it is the number four, the pitch of the note *c*, the color red or some other ideal (*ideeller*) object. What we intend in the meaningful use of the words, what the objects are that we name, and what they mean for us therewith, no one can dispute with us. It is therefore evident that when I say *four* in a general sense, as, e.g., in the proposition *Four and seven are relatively prime numbers*, that I mean the species four, that I have it in my logical view as an object; that is to say, I judge about it as an object, and not about something individual. Therefore I do not judge about any individual group of four things or about any constitutive factor, about any part or side of such a group; for every part of something individual is itself individual. To make something to be an object, to be the subject of predications or attributions, is, however, only another expression for *presentation* in the logical sense. Hence our evidence states that there are "general ideas," or ideas of something specific, just as well as there are ideas of something individual.

Evidence has been spoken of. Evidence with respect to objective distinctions of meanings presupposes that we go beyond the sphere of the merely symbolic use of expressions and turn to the corresponding intuition for final information. On the basis of intuitive presentation we execute the meaning-fulfillments corresponding to the mere meaning-intentions, we realize their "real" intention. If we do this in the present case, one single group of four is to be sure present to our minds; but we do not judge about it, and do not mean it in this illustration. It is not the image-group, but the number four, the specific unity, that is the subject, of which we say that it is relatively prime to seven. What is meant is the four, the ideal, timeless unity.

Phenomenological descriptions would have to be made in reflection upon the experiences of individual and specific meaning — experiences of purely intuitive meaning and of purely symbolic meaning, and of experiences which are both symbolic and fulfill the meaning-intention. They would have the task of showing the fundamental relations, which are important for the clarification of knowledge, between blind or purely symbolic and intuitive or real meaning; and in the domain of the intuitive they would aim to make clear the various ways in which an individual image functions in consciousness, if one's attention is occupied with something individual or with something specific. We would thus be placed in a position to answer the question as to how and in what sense the general can come to subjective consciousness and perhaps to evident givenness in a single act of thought, and how it can attain relationship to an unlimited sphere of particular objects that are subordinated to it.

Mill says nothing in the way of recognition of that which is given with evidence, and accordingly nothing about the line of thought just sketched. What his theory states may be instructive with respect to certain preliminary psychological conditions or components of the intuitively realized consciousness of generality, or with respect to the psychological function of symbols in the directing of a unified train of thought and the like. But this does not directly concern the objective sense of general meanings and the truth of the doctrine of general objects and of the predications related to them; and the indirect relationship would first have to be made clear. Certainly the expressions *general object* and *general idea* remind one of old errors. But no matter how many misinterpretations they may have undergone historically, there must be a normal interpretation which justifies them. This normal interpretation cannot be provided by empirical psychology, but only by going back to the evident sense of the propositions which are constructed by means of general ideas and relate to general objects as the subjects of their predications.

The criticism of "abstract ideas" went too far in the hands of Berkeley, Hume, and Mill. The ambiguity of the term "idea" was responsible for absurd errors. The new nominalism, not content with rejecting realism, also criticized conceptualism. Not only the absurd general ideas of Locke were rejected, but also general concepts in the genuine sense of the term.

This point of view was arrived at because of misunderstandings of psychological analysis. The natural inclination to direct one's view only upon the primary intuitive and "tangible" element leads to the belief that the inner images which are found are the meanings of the names. If one realizes, however, that the meaning is nothing but what is meant by the expression, or what it is understood to be, he cannot remain with this view. For if the meaning resided in the single intuitive ideas which make "clear" to us the sense of the general name, the objects of these ideas, just as they are intuitively presented, would be meant, and every name would be an equivocal proper name. In order to do justice to the distinction it is said that the single intuitive ideas, where they appear in connection with general names, are bearers of new psychological functions which determine different kinds of ideational processes.

Nevertheless, nothing is said thereby which would belong in any way to the phenomenological situation. We mean something general here and now, the moment that we meaningfully express a general name, and this intention is different than in the case in which we mean something individual. This distinction must be shown in the descriptive content of a single experience, in the single actual assertion of a general statement. That which is causally connected therewith, or the psychological results which an actual experience may entail, are not of interest here. They are matters for the psychology of abstraction, but not its phenomenology.

It is an important defect of nominalism, that it overlooks the peculiar consciousness which is manifested in the actual understanding of signs, on the one hand, and in the correlative acts of fulfillment which make up the "real" presentation of the general, on the other hand; in other words, it ignores the "evident ideation" in which the general "itself" is given to us. This consciousness means to us what it means whether we know anything about psychology or not. If the nominalist wanted to explain empirically this consciousness of generality as a fact of human nature, if he wanted to say that it is dependent causally upon certain factors, such as preceding experiences, unconscious dispositions, and the like, Husserl would have no fundamental objection to make. He would only observe that these empirical-psychological facts are not of interest for pure logic and the theory of knowledge. As opposed to this the nominalist holds that there is no distinction between general and individual ideas, and that there is no abstraction in the sense of a consciousness of generality.

Every thought-experience, like every psychical experience, has, viewed empirically, its descriptive content and its causes and effects; it enters into the bustle of life and exercises its genetic functions. But only essence and meaning belong in the sphere of phenomenology, and above all in the theory of knowledge as the phenomenological clarification of ideal unities of thought or knowledge: what we intend in general when we make a statement; what constitutes the intending as such, with respect to its sense; how it is essentially constructed out of partial intentions; which essential forms are exhibited by it; and so on. What interests the theory of knowledge must be shown exclusively in the content of the experience of meaning and fulfillment itself, as something essential. If the distinction between general and individual intuitive ideas can be found in that way, then no talk of genetic functions and connections can alter anything about it, or even contribute to its explanation. The generality of the psychological function, consisting in the psychological connection of "the same sign" to "the same" objective factor, is anything but the generality which belongs to the intentional content of the logical experiences themselves; or, objectively and ideally stated, which belongs to the meanings and fulfillments of meanings. The latter generality is entirely lost to nominalism.

In order to make clear the important distinction between the generality of the psychological function and the generality which belongs to the meaning-content itself, it is necessary to consider the various logical functions of general names and meanings, and the different sense in which they are said to be general, or in which they refer to a sphere of particular objects.

Husserl juxtaposes the following three forms: an *A*, all *A*, and *A* in general; e.g., a triangle, all triangles, and the triangle, the latter interpreted according to the proposition *The triangle is a species of figure.* The expression *an A* can serve as a predicate in an unlimited number of categorical statements, and the totality of the true or possible statements of this kind determines all possible subjects which can truly be *an A*, or can be *an A* without incompatibility; in short, the true or possible "extension" of "the concept" *A*. This general concept *A*, or the general predicate *an A*, refers to all objects of the extension, i.e., the propositions of the designated totality hold; and, expressed phenomenologically, the judgments of corresponding content are possible as evident judgments. This generality belongs therefore to the logical function of the predicate. The article *an* expresses a form that belongs to the meaning-intention as well as to the meaning-fulfillment, with respect to *what* it means. It is an irreducible factor, whose peculiarity one can only recognize but cannot explain away by any considerations of genetic psychology. To put it ideally, the *an* expresses a primitive logical form.

The generality in this case belongs to the *logical* function of the predicates, as has been stated; it exists as a logical possibility of propositions of a certain kind. The emphasis upon the logical character of this possibility signifies that what is in question is an *a priori* possibility belonging to the meanings as specific unities, but not to the psychologically accidental acts. If we have the insight that *red* is a general predicate, i.e., one that is to be attached to many possible subjects, then the intention is not directed upon that which can regulate the occurrence of temporal experiences according to natural laws. There is no talk here of experiences, but rather of the same predicate *red*, and of the possibility of certain propositions in which it appears.

In the form *all A* the generality belongs to the form of the act itself. We mean explicitly *all A*, and our presentation and predication refer to them in the universal judgment, although we perhaps do not present a single *A* "itself" or "directly." This presentation of the extension is not a complex of presentations of the terms of the extension; the single presentations do not belong at all to the meaning-intention of the *all A*. The *all* here, too, refers to a peculiar meaning-form, whereby the question may be left undecided as to whether it is analyzable into simpler forms or not.

Finally, in the case of the form *the A* (*in specie*) the generality again belongs to the meaning-content itself. But this is an entirely different kind of generality; it is a case of specific generality, which is closely related logically to the generality of the extension, but is evidently distinguished from it. The forms *the A* and *all A* are logically different forms, giving expression to essential differences of meaning. The consciousness of specific generality must be valid as an essentially new mode of "presentation" which brings "specific singularities" to consciousness. What kind of singularities these are, and how they are related *a priori* to the individual singularities, or are distinguished from them, must be gathered from the logical truths. The latter, which are based upon the pure forms, are valid *a priori* (or essentially) for both types of singularities and their mutual relations. There is here no unclearness and no possibility of error, if one holds to the simple sense of these truths, or what is the same, to the simple sense of the meaning-forms involved, the evident interpretations of which are called logical truths. It is the erroneous metabasis to psychologistic and metaphysical lines of thought that first causes unclearness; it creates pseudo-problems, and pseudo-theories for their solution.

The nominalistic theory of abstraction errs above all in overlooking the forms of consciousness (the forms of intention and the forms of fulfillment correlative to them) in their irreducible peculiarities. Because of the defectiveness of its descriptive analysis it lacks the insight that the logical forms are nothing other than these forms of meaning-intention raised to a consciousness of unity, and objectivated to ideal species. Generality also belongs to these forms. Nominalism furthermore confuses the different concepts of generality which were distinguished above. It prefers onesidedly the generality which belongs to concepts in their predicative function, as the possibility of attaching the same concept to divers subjects predicatively. Since it fails to recognize the logical-ideal character of this possibility, it interpolates psychological connections into it which are foreign to the sense of the predicates and propositions concerned, and are incommensurable with it. It claims to clarify the essence of general meanings by means of such psychical analyses. That which belongs phenomenologically to the immanent essence of a single act is reinterpreted as a psychological play of events which have nothing to say about the single act in which the entire consciousness of generality is alive, except in the manner of effects or causes.

After quoting Berkeley [3] on the theory of attention as a generalizing power, according to which abstraction is an exclusive interest involving

[3] Cf. Berkeley, *A Treatise Concerning the Principles of Human Knowledge*, Introduction, § 16, in which he concludes "And here it must be acknowledged that a man may consider a figure merely as triangular, without attending to the particular qualities of the angles, or relations of the sides. So far he may abstract; but this will never prove that he can frame an

generalization, Husserl proceeds to state his objections. That he must reject such a view becomes clear at once if one considers the aim of a theory of abstraction, which is to clarify the distinction between general and individual meanings, i.e., to point out its intuitive essence. The intuitive acts in which the mere word-intentions (the symbolic meanings) are fulfilled with intuition are supposed to be pictured in such a way that we can see what is "really meant" by the expressions and meanings. Hence abstraction is supposed here to be the act in which the consciousness of generality occurs as the fulfillment of the intention of general names. Is attention capable of performing this function? And what about the presupposition of this theory, that the content which distinguishes abstractive attention is a constitutive factor of the concrete object of intuition, a character that is inherent in it?

Attention is a function which shows a preference for objects of consciousness and, aside from certain gradual differences, is distinguished from case to case only by means of the objects to which it gives this preference. Consequently, according to the theory which identifies abstraction with attention, there can be no essential difference between meaning an individual, such as belongs to the intention of proper names, e.g., and meaning the generalities that are attached to the names of attributes. It consists precisely in the fact that an entire individual object is fixed as it were by a mental glance, on the one hand, and an attribute, on the other hand. Since according to the theory an attribute is supposed to be a constitutive factor of the object, it may be asked whether it would not have to be something individual just as much as the entire object. Suppose that we concentrate our attention upon the green of the tree before us; and if possible, let us entirely disregard all other factors of the tree. If another object with an exactly similar color were suddenly substituted for it, we would not notice any difference, the green would be one and the same for us. All of this may be allowed. But would the one green really be the same as the other? Would not that which is objectively different remain different, and is not the objective character to which we pay attention something that exists here and now and nothing else?

It cannot be doubted that the difference really exists. The comparison of two concrete, separate appearances of "the same" quality, say of "the same" green, teaches with evidence that each has its green. The green of the one is just as distinct from that of the other as are the concrete wholes

abstract, general, inconsistent idea of a triangle. In like manner we may consider Peter so far forth as man, or so far forth as animal, without framing the forementioned abstract idea, either of man or of animal, inasmuch as all that is perceived is not considered."

in which they inhere. How could there otherwise be unified qualitative configurations in which the same quality can appear repeatedly, and what meaning would it have to speak of the spread of a color over an entire surface? To every geometrical division of the surface there evidently corresponds a division of the homogeneous coloring, although we say that "the" color is "the same" everywhere.

The theory accordingly gives no explanation of what is meant by the identically *one* attribute, of the species as a unity in a manifold. It is evident that what is meant is something other than the objective character that appears sensuously as a single case of a species. Statements that have meaning and truth for a single case become false and even absurd for species. The coloring has its place and its time; it arises and passes away. Applied to color as a species, however, these predicates are absurd. If a house burns down, all its parts are burned; all the individual forms and qualities are destroyed. Are the geometrical, qualitative, and other species in question burned, or is it absurd to speak of that? Since it cannot be denied that we speak of species in a distinct sense, that in countless cases we mean and name, not a single thing but its Idea, and that we can make statements about this ideal *one* as a subject just as we can about an individual thing, it follows that the theory fails to attain its goal. It seeks to explain the consciousness of generality and abandons it in the content of its explanation.

Husserl agrees with Berkeley that one can get on without the assumption of general ideas in the sense of Locke's theory. But he thinks it incorrect to do this by means of a nominalistic doctrine. While approving of Berkeley's reasoning in the main, he rejects the interpretation which is introduced. Berkeley confused the basis of abstraction with what is abstracted; the concrete single case from which the consciousness of generality derives its intuitive fullness was confused with the object of thought-intention. He spoke as though a geometrical proof referred to an ink-triangle on the paper or a chalk-triangle on the board, and as though in general thinking the single objects accidentally occurring to us were the objects of thought, instead of mere supports of our thought-intention. No geometrical proposition holds for that which is drawn in the physical sense, because in reality there can never be a straight or geometrical figure. The ideal geometrical determinations are not present in it, as is color in the case of the intuition of something colored. In no act of thought does the mathematician mean the drawing; he means rather "a straight line in general." This thought is the subject-term of his theoretical proof.

That to which we attend is neither the concrete object of intuition nor an "abstract partial content," i.e., a dependent factor of it, but is rather an idea in the sense of a specific unity. It is an abstract idea in the logical sense; and accordingly a logical and epistemological abstraction is not the mere selection of a partial content, but is the peculiar consciousness that directly apprehends the specific unity on an intuitive basis.

If any individual feature of the object, say its peculiar color, strikes us, we attend especially to this feature, and still we do not have a general idea. The same question applies to whole concrete things that applies to individual factors: Wherein does the difference lie between the exclusive attention to the individually appearing statue, and the intuitive apprehension of the corresponding idea, which is to be realized in countless real statues? The assumption that the individualizing determinations are observed incidentally is of little help. Much is observed incidentally, but is not therefore meant. Where the consciousness of generality occurs intuitively as a genuine abstraction, the individual object of the founding intuition is also known, although by no means meant. Mill's talk of unconsciousness with respect to abstractively excluded determinations is a useless and even absurd fiction. That which is not "conscious" cannot differentiate the conscious.

The sorest point in the theory lies in the question: What is attention? The theory does not clarify the essence of attention in a way that is necessary for its purpose. The mistake is made of taking the experienced contents to be the normal objects to which we attend; and the contents are construed as sensations. Husserl observes that if, e.g., we present or make a statement about a horse, we present or talk about the horse and not about our sensations. From his standpoint, he distinguishes in the sphere of sensory abstraction between the acts in which an attributive factor is intuitively "given," and the acts constructed thereupon. The latter are not acts of mere attention to this factor, but are new kinds of acts which generalize and thus mean the pertinent species. Whether the intuition gives the attributive factor in an adequate manner or not does not matter here. Husserl distinguishes furthermore between cases of sensory abstraction, i.e., abstraction adapted simply and perhaps adequately to sensory intuition, and cases of non-sensory or at most partly sensory abstraction, i.e., where the realized consciousness of generality is constructed in part upon acts of sensory intuition and in part upon non-sensory acts, and is consequently related to categorial thought-forms which cannot be fulfilled in any sensory way. Examples of the former are provided by the unmixed concepts of outer or inner sensibility, such as color, noise, pain, judgment, and will; and of the latter, concepts such as series, sum, identity, being, and the like. This distinction is considered seriously in the following investigations.

Attention is not restricted to "contents" in a psychological sense, but applies beyond the sphere of intuition and comprises the whole sphere of thought, whether intuitively founded or purely symbolic. If our judgment has the form *All A are B*, our attention appertains to this universal fact; we are concerned with universality and not with this or that singularity. Every thought, or at least every one that is consistent in itself, can indeed become intuitive by being built up in a certain manner upon "corresponding" intuition. But attention on the basis of inner or outer sensibility is not attention to its phenomenological content, or to the object appearing in it. The *all* or *every*, the *if* and *then*, the *and, or, not*, and the like are nothing that can be shown in an object of founding sensory intuition; they cannot be sensed or represented and painted externally. Naturally certain acts correspond to them; the words have their meaning, and by understanding them we use certain forms which belong to the objective intention. These acts are, however, not the objectivity that we mean; they are the intending (the presenting) itself; they only become objective in psychological reflection. The objective of the intention is accordingly the universal fact *All A are B*, the general *A (in specie) is B*, the indeterminate singular *Any A is B*, etc. That to which we attend is neither the individual intuition which accompanies thought-presentations for the founding of evidence, nor the act-characters which form the intuition or are fulfilled intuitively in the formed intuition, but rather the thought objects that have become "evident" in the performance of the acts on such a basis, the objects and facts conceived by thought as this or that. Naturally the "abstraction" in which we grasp something of the nature of thought or meaning, instead of an individual intuitive thing, means nothing other than that we live in this insightful performance of intellectual acts, which are formed in various ways.

The extension of the unified concept of attention is therefore so wide that it comprises the whole realm of meaning, including intuition and thinking. It extends as far as the concept of consciousness *of* something. The view that attention involves a certain preference within the sphere of consciousness therefore relates to a distinction which is independent of the species or kind of consciousness. We execute certain "presentations" while we "concentrate" upon the objects of other presentations.

Because of the confusion of object and psychical content the fact is overlooked that the objects of which we become "conscious" are not simply in consciousness as though in a box, so that one could simply find them there and reach for them; but that they are rather first *constituted* as that which they are for us in various forms of objective intention. The fact is overlooked, that from the finding present of a psychical content, i.e., from the purely immanent intuition as such, up to the outer perception and imagination of objects that can never be found immanently, and from there up to the highest formations of thought with its manifold categorial forms and forms of meaning adapted to them, that an essentially unified concept continues on, that there is always an intention that aims at an object, a consciousness that is consciousness of an object. The mere existence of a content in a psychical context is, however, not its being meant. This first arises in the "noting" or presenting of this content. To define the mere being experienced of a content as its being presented, and then to call all experienced contents presentations (or "ideas") is declared by Husserl to be one of the worst conceptual falsifications that is known to philosophy. The number of epistemological and psychological errors that it has caused is legion. If the *intentional* concept of presentation which alone holds for logic and the theory of knowledge is accepted, then the differences between presentations cannot be reduced to the differences of the presented "contents." On the contrary, it is evident, especially in the domain of pure logic, that to every primitive logical form there corresponds a particular "mode of consciousness," or a particular "mode of presentation." Inasmuch as every new mode of intentional relationship also involves the objects in a certain way, i.e., in that it constitutes the new forms by which the objectivity is known, it can also be said that all differences of presentation are to be found in the presented objectivity. Inspection shows that the latter differences (of the presented objectivities) are of two kinds — differences of categorial form, and of the "thing itself," which can be known as identical in a number of forms. This is considered further in the later investigations.

D. ABSTRACTION AND REPRESENTATION

It is an error deriving from medieval nominalism, to regard general concepts and names as mere devices of a thought-economy, which devices are supposed to save us the task of the separate observation and naming of all individual things. By means of the conceptual function, it is said, the thinking mind is able to overcome the limits that are due to the immense number of individual things. General concepts make it possible to discourse of things in bundles, as Locke expressed it. This view is seen to be absurd, Husserl argues, when one reflects that without general meanings no statement at all, and hence no individual statement, can be asserted, and that in no logically relevant sense of thinking, judging, or knowing can there be any statements merely on the basis of direct individual ideas. The most ideal adaptation of the human mind to the manifold of individual things would not make thinking superfluous, for the achievements thus attainable are not the achievements of thinking.

There are no laws along the route of intuition. It may be granted that the knowledge of laws is of value for the preservation of thinking beings, that it regulates the formation of intuitive ideas of expectation and does so in a much more useful way than the natural train of association does it. But the relation of the thought-function to the preservation of thinking beings, and in our case of humanity, belongs in psychical anthropology and not in the critique of knowledge. What a law accomplishes as an ideal unity, namely, to comprehend logically an immense number of possible single cases in the manner of a general statement-meaning, cannot be accomplished by any intuition, even if it were a universal, divine intuition. Intuition is simply not thought. Not mere intuition, but adequate, categorially formed intuition, which thus conforms perfectly to thinking, is the goal; or conversely, the thinking which derives evidence from experience is true knowing. Only within the sphere of thinking does "thought-economy," or knowledge-economy, have a meaning and proper application.

The view that general concepts are thought-saving devices is developed in greater detail by means of the theory of *representation*. In truth there are only single intuitive ideas, it is said, and all thinking occurs by means of them. Due to need or to convenience, however, we substitute certain ideas for the ideas to be really experienced, to act as their representatives.

This doctrine is met by Husserl's objections, which have already been presented. The word "representation" is ambiguous. Undoubtedly the expression can be used in the sense that a general name or a single founding intuition is the "representative" of a class. The various meanings of the word may lead to confusion instead of to clarity. It is, however, not necessary to criticize the theory of representation which regards representation as a psychological function and does not touch the fundamental phenomenological fact, the new kinds of consciousness which distinguish the single experience of general expression and thinking. The essential fact must not be overlooked that it is the immanent essence of the act-characters involved to be consciousness of something general, and that all modes of meant generality which are dealt with in logic according to form and law only come to givenness by means of corresponding modes of such intentional characters.

That which is intuited is not merely meant just as it appears; the species in its ideal unity is now meant, e.g., *the tone c, the number 3*; and again, a class as a totality of the particulars partaking of the general, such as *all tones of this pitch*, or *all A*; or again, a determinate particular of this kind (*an A*) or of this class (*some one among the A's*), and again, this intuited particular, but thought as the bearer of the attribute (*this A here*), etc. Every such modification changes the "content" or "sense" of the intention; in other words, that which is called the "presentation" in the sense of logic is changed at every step, i.e., that which is presented, just as it is logically conceived and meant. Whether the accompanying individual intuition remains the same or always changes is a matter of indifference; the logical idea is changed when the intention (the sense of the expression) is changed, and it remains identically the same so long as its intention remains the same. It is unnecessary to emphasize the fact, Husserl asserts, that the founding appearance can be entirely omitted.

The difference between intellectual and sensory "apprehension" is an essential one; it is not as though we, e.g., apprehend "the same object" once as a wax doll and again, in an illusion, as a living person, as though we had only confused two individual intuitive apprehensions with each other. The character of the intention, and consequently the meaning-content, is totally different from that of any sensory presentations. To mean *an A* is different than to simply present an *A* intuitively without the thought *an A*, and it is again different to refer to it in direct meaning and naming by means of proper names. The idea *a man* is different from the idea *Socrates*, and the idea *the man Socrates* is different from both of them. The idea *some A* is not a sum of intuitions, and is also not a collective act which unites given single intuitions. What we mean is "some" *A* and not the appearing particulars or their totality, and this cannot be perceived either in inner or outer perception. The same holds for other general meaning-forms, such as the number-forms *two* or *three*, and again for the universal form, such as *all A*. The universality is presented in a logical sense as soon as we understand the expression *all A* and apply it meaningfully. It is then presented in the manner of a unified thought, and only thus or in a corresponding "real" form can it come to consciousness as a universality. We can only intuit this and that. No matter how many cases we may go over, in the best possible case all *A* would be presented if the extension of the concept were really covered, and still *all A* would not be presented, so that there would be no logical presentation. If there is a logical presentation, on the other hand, it may be clarified by intuition. An intellectual intention must, in the way that its form and its content require it, relate to intuition and be fulfilled in it, and thus a complex act arises which achieves clarity and evidence, but does not set aside the thought and substitute a mere image for it.

Husserl points out finally that these are but provisional indications of his analysis. The last investigation clarifies the difference between thinking and intuition, and discusses a new concept of intuition which is different from the usual concept of sensory intuition.

In view of these considerations, Husserl is not inclined to endorse the theory of the representative function of general signs and intuitive images. The generality of the presentation is supposed to lie in the generality of the representation. That would be acceptable if by the latter that new mode of consciousness were understood which functions on the basis of intuition. That a name is a representative merely means that its physical appearance is the bearer of the meaning-intention in which the conceptual object is intended.

Nominalism would be ruled out by this conception. Thinking is not reduced to any external operations with names and single ideas, or even to unconscious associative mechanisms which allow the particulars to come into their places like the ciphers of a calculating machine. There is rather a conceptual presentation that differs descriptively from the intuitive presentation. As distinguished from the intending that is related directly to the appearing object, this intention is of a fundamentally new kind, to which the forms of the *one* and the *many*, of *two* and *three*, of *anything in general*, of the *all*, etc., belong essentially. Among them is also the form in which a species is constituted in the manner of a *presented* object, so that it can function as the subject of possible attributions or predications.

In the historical theory of abstraction "general representation" has not the meaning that has just been given, and which alone is justified, so that the term representation is not appropriate. What is meant is rather the substitution of a sign for that which is signified. According to Locke, the general and the universal are inventions of the understanding and concern signs only, whether words or ideas; words are general when used as signs of general ideas, and ideas are general when they are set up as the representatives of many particular things. For Berkeley, particular ideas and general names have the same representative function assigned by Locke to abstract ideas.

Two essentially different things are confused by Berkeley: (1) the sign (name or particular idea) as a representative of every particular of the conceptual extension, whose idea it suggests according to Berkeley; (2) the sign as having the signification, the sense, *all A* or *an A, whatever it may be*. In the latter respect there is no talk of representation in the sense of substitution. One or more A's may be presented, but the particular one that I have in view does not refer to anything else for which it is a substitute. All A or any A are presented in an entirely different sense, namely, intellectually presented. The consciousness *all A* occurs in a homogeneous and special kind of act, an act that has no components which could refer to all of the single A's, and which could not be produced or replaced by any sum or interweaving of single acts. Through its "content," its ideal sense, this act relates to every term of the extension, not in a real, but rather in an ideal, i.e., logical manner. What we assert about all A, as in a unified proposition of the form *All A are B*, holds self-evidently for every A_0 that is definitely present. The inference from the general to the particular is to be drawn in every given case and B is to be logically predicated of the A_0. But the general judgment does not therefore include the particular, or the general presentation the particular presentation coming under it, in any psychological or phenomenological sense; and hence not in the manner of a bundle of representations. The infinitude of the extension of all "pure" general concepts, unmixed with the empirical positing of existence, such as number, spatial form, color, and intensity, shows such an interpretation to be absurd.

Commenting upon the errors of Locke and Berkeley, Husserl states that what "meaning" is can be just as immediately given to us as is the case with color and tone. It cannot be defined further, and is descriptively ultimate. As often as we use or understand an expression it means something to us; we are actually aware of its sense. This understanding or meaning is not the hearing of the word-sound or the experiencing of any simultaneous phantasm. Just as phenomenological differences between appearing sounds are evidently given, so are differences between meanings. The phenomenology of meanings has not reached its end therewith, but rather begins at that point. One can, on the one hand, establish the fundamental epistemological difference between symbolic-empty meanings and those that are intuitively fulfilled, and, on the other hand, one must study the essential kinds and forms of the connection of meanings. This is the domain of the actual analysis of meaning. Its problems can be solved by the representation of the acts concerned and of what is given through them. The essential kinds and forms of meaning are obtained in purely phenomenological identification and discrimination, by means of processes of connection and separation, as well as by generalizing abstraction. In other words, the elementary logical concepts are thus obtained, which are nothing other than ideal expressions of the primitive distinctions of meaning.

Instead of analyzing meanings phenomenologically, however, in order to determine the basic logical forms, or conversely, instead of making it clear that the basic logical forms are nothing other than the typical characters of acts and their forms of connection, logical analysis in the usual sense is pursued; and after considering what is intended in the meanings in an objective respect, that which is intended is sought as something immanent in the acts. It is a fundamental source of error to think *in* the meanings instead of *about* them, and to be occupied with presented and judged facts, instead of with presentations and judgments, i.e., nominal and propositional meanings. A descriptive analysis of acts cannot be accomplished if one has left the ground of reflection and has inserted an objective analysis in the place of phenomenological analysis. The purely logical analysis which investigates "what lies in mere concepts or meanings," or what is to be attributed *a priori* to objects in general, as thought in these forms, is also objective. In this sense the axioms of pure logic and pure mathematics arise "by the mere analysis of concepts." In an entirely different sense the actual analysis of meaning investigates "what lies in the meanings." Here alone can it be said that the meanings are reflectively made to be *objects* of investigation; their actual parts and forms are investigated, and not that which applies to their objects. The way in which Locke comes to his doctrine of general ideas and among other things also to his doctrine of representation; and similarly the way in which Berkeley treats this doctrine and defends it, and especially the way in which he treats the meaning of general propositions, provide illustrations of what has been said.

E. A PHENOMENOLOGICAL STUDY OF HUME'S THEORY OF ABSTRACTION

Hume's conception of abstraction is by no means identical with that of Berkeley, although he adopts what he takes to be Berkeley's view, namely, that "general ideas are nothing but particular ones, annexed to a certain term, which gives them a more extensive signification, and makes them recall upon occasion other individuals, which are similar to them." [4] This is not entirely the view of Berkeley, who does not assign to general names the power of making the accompanying particular ideas to be representatives of the other particular ideas of the same class, as Hume does. According to Berkeley general names can function representatively by themselves without corresponding particular ideas, particular ideas can also function without names, and, finally, both can occur. The main point is retained nevertheless: the generality lies in the representation;

---

[4] Cf. Hume, *A Treatise of Human Nature*, Book I, Part I, § VII.

and this is regarded by Hume as the substitution of the appearing particular for other particulars, which are "suggested to the mind" by the former, in the words of Berkeley, or are "recalled" as Hume expresses it.

Because of the greater clarity of his formulation Hume's theory meets with all of Husserl's objections even more than was the case with Berkeley. Although he endorses Berkeley's theory, Hume does not merely reproduce it; he seeks to develop it in greater detail and to deepen it psychologically. In this respect the arguments which Hume directs against the theory of abstract ideas do not enter into the discussion as much as the considerations of association psychology which are introduced in connection with them.

The "ideological" psychology and theory of knowledge, which attempts to reduce everything to "impressions" (sensations) and associative connections of "ideas" (to phantasms, as pale shadows of "impressions"), must find modes of consciousness, or acts in the sense of *intentional* experiences, to be inconvenient. Husserl recalls here Hume's futile use of the concept of belief, and how he attempts to locate this act-character in ideas as intensity or as something analogous to intensity. Then "representation" must also be reduced to something tangible; and this is to be accomplished by genetic psychology, which must show how we come to use the mere particular image that we experience in our judgments "as though it were universal."

What Hume endeavors to accomplish by his psychological analysis can be expressed by means of the following two questions: (1) How does a particular idea come to have a representative function; how does it acquire the capacity to function psychologically as a representative of other similar ideas, and finally of all possible ideas of the same class? (2) The same particular idea is ordered under many spheres of similarity, whereas in every definite context of thoughts it represents only ideas of one such sphere. Why is it that precisely this sphere of representation is distinguished in this context; what restricts the representative function of the particular idea in this manner and thus first makes possible the unity of the meaning?

Husserl observes that these psychological questions have their good sense if one drops the concept of representation that is used and substitutes for it the genuine concept of general presentation as an act of general meaning, or of meaning-fulfillment (of general intuition in the sense of the sixth investigation, § 52). That general ideas have arisen genetically out of individual intuitive ideas is generally assumed. But if the consciousness of the general derives clarity and evidence from individual intuition, it has not therefore arisen directly out of particular intuition. Then how have we come to go beyond individual intuition and to mean something general? And how have all the forms arisen which give a changing objective relation to the general and determine the differences of the logical kinds of presentation? As soon as associative connections are adduced for explanation we encounter similarity-groups and the signs externally connected with them. The second question arises therewith, as to how it is possible that the spheres of similarity retain their independent unity and are not confused in thinking.

In view of this it is no contradiction if Husserl characterizes Hume's treatment of abstraction as an extreme error and nevertheless gives it credit for showing the way for the psychological theory of abstraction. It is an extreme error in a logical and epistemological respect, for the point is to investigate cognitive experiences purely phenomenologically, to regard the acts of thought as that which they are by themselves, in order to provide clarity for the fundamental concepts of knowledge. But as for Hume's genetic analysis, it cannot claim to be theoretically adequate or final, since it lacks an adequate descriptive analysis as a basis. Because Hume really undertakes an empirical-psychological investigation instead of an epistemological inquiry, he arrives at a conception of thinking as a knowledge-economical function, as a point of view for its epistemological clarification. In that respect Hume is a genuine disciple of the Lockean philosophy. The objections to that point of view have already been indicated.

Although Husserl is not interested in psychological investigation here, he regards it as necessary to consider it to a certain extent because of a paradoxical thought which appears to be in Hume's presentation, and which has been advanced more explicitly by modern Humeans. This thought is as follows: Characters or inner properties are nothing to the objects which "have" them. Or, expressed psychologically: The different, mutually inseparable sides or factors of an intuitive content, such as the color, form, etc., which we believe are grasped as something present in it, are really not at all in it. There is only one kind of real parts, namely, parts which can also appear separately by themselves, and these are called portions (*Stücke*) by Husserl. The so-called abstract partial contents — of which it is said that although they cannot be or be observed by themselves, they can be considered by themselves — are to a certain extent mere fictions *cum fundamento in re*. The color is not in the colored thing, or the form in that which is formed; there are in truth only those spheres of similarity under which the object in question is comprehended, and certain habits belonging to its intuition, unconscious dispositions or imperceptible psychical occurrences which are stimulated by the intuition.

More precisely, the doubt would be a double one, an objective and a subjective one. In an objective respect it refers to the *objects* of the appearance in relation to their inner properties; in a subjective respect, to *the appearance itself*, understood as the immanent experience, in relation to its sensory contents, i.e., those contents which experience an objectivating "apprehension" (apperception) in the act of intuition. The appearance of the corresponding objective characters or qualities occurs in this apprehension. On the one hand, the sphere and its inner properties are in question; on the other hand, it is the appearance of the sphere and the complex of sensations inherent in it, including, e.g., the continually "adumbrating" (*abschattende*) sensation of white — the subjective correlate of the objective white appearing uniformly in the perception. But Hume failed to take account of this distinction; the appearance and that which appears flow together for him.

In the course of this discussion Husserl states that one can deceive himself as to the existence of the object of perception, but not regarding the fact that he perceives it as determinate in this or that respect. The *intended object of this perception* could not be totally different, e.g., a tree instead of a cockchafer. This evidence in the determining description, or identification and mutual distinction of the intentional objects as such has its limits, but it is true and genuine evidence. Without it the much extolled evidence of *inner perception*, with which it is usually confused — where "inner" perception is understood as the perception of *intentional* experiences — is simply useless; when the descriptive distinction of the innerly perceived experiences is made, this evidence is already presupposed, inasmuch as the distinction and description of intentional experiences is impossible without reference to their intentional objects.

This evidence is of value to us here. It is evidently something different, to intuit the red of this object and to intuit a relation of similarity. If one transfers the latter intuition into the unperceived or the unconscious, the inconvenience is only increased, since one gives up the evidently given intention in favor of something imperceptible.

The preceding discussion enters into the present consideration of appearing *objects*, in so far as the *contents* in reflective phenomenological analysis become *objects* of perception. Although we do not call the appearance of the sphere (the experience) a thing and the abstract contents inherent in it are not and may not be called properties or characters, the descriptive situation with regard to the points in question is the same as in the foregoing. The differences between thing and property are ontological and are not characters of inner experience. They are not anything that can be shown as being in a phenomenon as an immanent factor, but refer back to connections of conscious experiences in which they appear and are scientifically determined.

The evidence that the sensory factors, the color-factor, configuration-factor, and other immanent determinations actually belong to the unity of an intuition as factors constituting it is in no way to be explained away. One may perhaps explain them as the results of some kind of fusion or as products which contain their factors immanently although in an imperceptible manner; but interesting though this be psychologically, nothing is changed thereby in the immediate descriptive situation, in that which alone enters into consideration for the clarification of concepts and cognitions. To theorize away the abstract contents and with them the abstract concepts is to want to prove something to be fictive which is in reality the presupposition of all insightful thinking and proof.

To the skepticism regarding abstract partial contents there corresponds a possible skepticism with regard to the concrete, the "portions." A homogeneous white surface is for us a divisible object, and all the parts that can be distinguished in actual division are ascribed to it from the outset as parts of it. This is also applied to sensation. The content which is actually experienced in the view of the whole surface contains portions that are related to the collective content, analogously to the way in which the objective surface-portions are to the entire surface.

But whence do we know that the content is really a compound? If we phantasy divisions into the unified white surface, the corresponding sense-content may really exhibit a connection of parts; but the original content does not remain unchanged during that procedure. The discontinuous complex content that is now given is not identical with the original unified content. We exercise certain activities of phantasy and judgment on the basis of the inseparable content of consciousness, and what they engender we put into the original content itself.

The doubt is increased further if we turn to the case in which the intuitive content already exhibits divisions. Does not the experience offer us a certain unified content to begin with, which we later designate as a content composed of parts? We attend now to one part of the content, and again to another part. But the experience is different at each step. Because of the inclination to confuse the sensed contents with the perceived or phantasied objects, strongly different contents are introduced step by step into the original content.

If we proceed further in this skeptical direction we must doubt whether there are at all parts of any kind; and further, whether there are at all pluralities of concrete contents, since the contents appearing in coexistence and succession are always unified in a certain manner. The skepticism would finally culminate in the assertion that consciousness is something absolutely unified, of which we at least cannot know if it has partial contents at all, or if it develops into any experiences, either arranged simultaneously or in temporal succession.

It is clear that such skepticism would make psychology impossible.[5] The foregoing discussion shows how it may be met. The flux of immanent appearances does not make it impossible to conceive them to begin with by means of indefinite concepts which are, however, fully clear, being formed directly on the basis of intuition; and then by means of these concepts, to make many evident distinctions, which are entirely sufficient to make possible a psychological investigation.

As regards the case of the white surface, we note the changes very well in examining the content "white surface" (the white surface itself viewed as a thing is not meant here), but along with the changes we also note the same thing, or the identical thing. The limits that are due to phantasy do not make the portions, but merely circumscribe them. It is evident that these portions were really present in the unity of the content "white surface." The content that is held fast in an identical intention coincides with the same content which is only changed by the process of phantasy; it coincides with the latter in respect to the circumscribed parts. The parts were and are always in the whole, only not as unities that are separated out by themselves. A certain fluctuation and flow of the contents, the uncertainty and even impossibility of their completely identical fixation does not annul the evidence of these judgments. They are valid, as are all purely descriptive judgments which are asserted in the manner of an accurate "expression" about something intuitively given as such, within a certain sphere of possible fluctuation, and hence with a certain index of vagueness.

If we transform empirical concepts and relationships into exact ones, if we form ideal concepts of extension, surface, qualitative equality, continuity, etc., then *a priori*, exact laws arise, which explain that which is grounded in the intentions of the rigorous concepts. In comparison with them the purely descriptive statements are inexact approximations. But

---

[5] Reference is made to Schumann's attempt to achieve the greatest possible rigor and freedom from presuppositions by means of such skepticism. Cf. F. Schumann, "Zur Psychologie der Zeitanschauung," *Zeit. f. Psych. u. Phys. d. Sinnesorgane*, vol. XVII (1898), pp. 106–148.

although that which is vague, the sphere of phenomenal particulars, does not belong to the sphere of exact knowledge, which operates only with the ideal, it is by no means excluded therefore from the sphere of knowledge in general.

Husserl's view of the doubts leading to the denial of all parts and distinctions is accordingly clear. Doubt is quite possible in a single case of the flux of experience; but it is not possible in all cases. Where the differences are large, an evidence is attainable which removes the justification of any doubt.

Cornelius is among the writers to be influenced by Hume. His "Psychology" attempts to carry through a psychologistic theory of knowledge on the basis of modern psychology. As a theory of knowledge it confuses that which belongs to the *intentional content* of knowledge (to its ideal sense, to that which it means, and which is necessarily posited therewith) with that which belongs to the *intentional object* of knowledge; and both of these are confused again with that which belongs more or less to the psychological constitution of a cognitive experience. These confusions, Husserl states, have hardly been made to such an extent in the literature as is the case with Cornelius. Although the latter was influenced by William James, he failed to take over his epistemological standpoint; for James does not modernize the Humean philosophy, as may be said of Cornelius. Husserl speaks with praise of James' brilliant observations in the province of the descriptive psychology of presentational experience, which not only did not lead to psychologism, but aided him in breaking away from the psychologistic point of view.

F. THE DISTINCTION OF VARIOUS CONCEPTS OF ABSTRACTION AND ABSTRACT

The theory of abstraction through attention presupposes what the theory of the *distinctio rationis* denies, namely, that there is a certain difference in the contents themselves which corresponds to the difference between the abstract and the concrete. According to this theory there is only one kind of parts, here called portions, which are separable or which can be presented as separated. In the contrary view, however, dependent "partial contents" are distinguished from these "independent" parts (in Stumpf's terminology), and included in the former are the inner determinations of a content, with the exception of portions, and among them are also the forms of unity that are perceptible in it (expressed objectively, the forms of unity that are present in it), through which its parts are connected into the unity of the whole. With regard to this same distinction one also speaks of *concrete* and *abstract* contents, or parts of contents. (The further investigation of this distinction, extended to objects and parts of objects in general, is the theme of the third investigation.)

In the theory of abstraction since Locke, the problem of abstraction in the sense of the lifting out of "abstract contents" is confused with the problem of abstraction in the sense of the formation of concepts. The latter involves a descriptive analysis of the essence of the act in which a species comes to evident consciousness, or the clarification of the meaning of a general name by means of the fulfilling intuition; but in an empirical-psychological respect what is aimed at is the investigation of the corresponding psychological facts in the context of human consciousness, the genetic origin of the general ideas of man in the natural process of naive living, or in the artificial process of arbitrary and logical conception. The abstract ideas which come in question herewith are ideas whose intention is directed toward species and the dependent or abstract contents. If these intentions are intuitively fulfilled, they are based upon concrete intuitions with abstract content-parts that are accepted as it were; but the intended species are not these content-parts themselves, which are not intended themselves, or objects of their own acts of attention. The abstract or dependent factors in the object are nevertheless continually being confused with *species*, the corresponding *objectively experienced* abstract contents with *abstract concepts* (the meanings of certain names), and again the acts of attending to these abstract contents are confused with acts of *general presentation*. For Locke, e.g., abstract ideas are general meanings; but they are described as properties and construed psychologically as abstract sense-contents which are separated from the concrete intuitions. Similarly the theory of attention shows the possibility of one's own attending to such abstract contents without their separation, and it is believed that the origin of general concepts, as meanings, has been clarified therewith. In a similar way it is denied that abstract contents can be intuited, as in the case of Höfler and Meinong, although they are also intuited as factors of concrete intuitions; and this occurs because such writers are deceived by the fact that general concepts cannot be objects of sensory experience. To be sure they cannot be set up as images. If it is absurd to paint tones or to portray colors by odors, it would be doubly absurd to represent sensuously something that is essentially non-sensory.

Continuing to use the popular term "contents," which was a term favored by the recent abstraction theories, Husserl proceeds to distinguish various conceptions of "abstract" and "abstraction," as follows:

(1) "Abstract" contents are *dependent* contents, and "concrete" contents

are *independent*. We think of this distinction as objectively determined, such that the concrete contents can be by and for themselves with respect to their own nature, whereas the abstract ones are only possible in or with concrete contents.

Contents must be construed more broadly here than in the phenomenological sense of immanent elements of consciousness. The external phenomenal object which appears but is not an immanent datum of consciousness (at least if one does not falsely interpret the "intentional," i.e., merely *intended* object as an immanent constituent of the experience in which the intention occurs), is concrete as a whole; the determinations that are inherent in it, such as color, form, etc., understood as constitutive factors of its unity, are abstract. This *objective* distinction between abstract and concrete is the more general one, for immanent contents are only a special class of objects (whereby it is not said: of things). The difference in question would therefore really be more appropriately designated as a difference between abstract and concrete *objects*, or object-parts. If Husserl nevertheless continues to speak of contents, that is because he does not wish to offend the majority of the readers. But he points out clearly that the term "contents" is in no way restricted to the sphere of the contents of consciousness in an immanent sense, and that it also comprises all individual objects and parts of objects. Even the sphere of objects which become intuitive for us does not limit us. The distinction also has ontological value: objects are possible which factually lie beyond all appearances that are accessible to human consciousness. In short, the distinction refers to individual objects in general, in unrestricted generality, and as such it belongs in the frame of *a priori* formal ontology.

(2) If the objective (ontological) concept of "abstract contents" is now made basic, *abstraction* will mean the act by which an abstract content is "distinguished," i.e., by which it is to be sure not separated, but still becomes the object of an intuitive presentation that is directed toward it. It appears in and with the *concretum* from which it is abstracted. Although it is specially meant, it is not merely meant as in an "indirect," merely symbolic presentation, but is also intuitively given as that which is meant.

(3) An important and already frequently emphasized distinction must still be taken into account.[6] If we attend to one of the surfaces of a die "coming into appearance," this is the "abstract content" of our intuitive presentation. The truly *experienced* content which corresponds to this *appearing* surface is itself different from this appearing surface, however; it is only the basis of an "apprehension" by means of which, while it is

---

[6] Cp. also the sixth investigation, § 15; and ch. XIII, B, 3 herein.

sensed, the die-surface (which is different from it) comes to appearance. The sensed content is not the object of an intuitive presentation; it first becomes the object in psychological or in phenomenological "reflection." Yet descriptive analysis teaches that it is not merely contained in the whole of the concrete appearance of the die, but that it, as opposed to all the other contents not functioning representatively in *this* presenting of the surface in question, is lifted out in a certain manner. This is also the case if it itself becomes the object of a presenting intention that is specially directed toward it; but then, and hence in reflection, this intention is also added. This lifting of the content, which is itself *not an act* (in the strict sense to be established in the fifth investigation), but is a descriptive peculiarity of the appearance-side of those acts in which the content becomes the bearer of a peculiar intention, could also be designated as *abstraction*. A new concept of abstraction would, however, be determined therewith.

(4) If one assumes that the abstracting is a peculiar act or in general a descriptively peculiar experience, to which the lifting out of the abstract content from its concrete basis is due, or if one sees in the manner of the lifting that which is essential in the abstract content as such, then a new concept of the abstract arises. The difference from the concrete is not sought in the peculiar nature of the contents, but in the manner in which it is given; a content is called abstract in so far as it is abstracted, and concrete in so far as it is not abstracted.

It will be noted readily that the inclination to refer to the acts for the characterization of the difference of content is due to the confusion with the following concepts of abstract and concrete, according to which the essence of the matter lies in the acts.

(5) If one understand by abstracting in a positive sense the preferential attending to a content, and by abstracting in a negative sense the disregarding of simultaneously given contents, then the word loses its exclusive reference to abstract contents in the sense of dependent contents. In the case of concrete contents abstraction is also spoken of, although only in a negative sense; one attends to them, e.g., "in abstraction from the background."

The concepts which are grouped about the concept of species will now be distinguished.

(1) Abstract and concrete concepts are distinguished, and concepts are understood to be the significations of names. Corresponding to this difference there is a difference of names, and in the nominalistic logic only this grammatical distinction is usually introduced. Names can name in-

dividuals, such as *man, Socrates*; or also attributes such as *virtue, whiteness, similarity*. The former are called concrete, the latter abstract names. The predicative expressions corresponding to the latter, such as *virtuous, white*, and *similar*, are included among the concrete names. More exactly, it should be said that they are concrete if the possible subjects to which they relate are concrete subjects. This is not always the case: names such as *attribute, color, number*, and the like refer predicatively to attributes (as specific particulars) and not to individuals, or at least to individuals only indirectly and with a change of the predicative sense.

Back of this grammatical distinction there obviously lies a logical one, namely, the difference between the nominal meanings which refer to attributes and those which refer to objects, in so far as they partake of attributes. If one calls all logical ideas concepts, and that means all nominal meanings, as Herbart does, then the concepts of this kind are divided into abstract and concrete ones. But if one prefers a different interpretation of concepts, according to which a concept is an attribute, then the difference is one between the meanings which present concepts and those which present conceptual objects as such. This difference is relative, inasmuch as conceptual objects themselves can again have the character of concepts, namely, in relation to certain new objects. This cannot go on *in infinitum*, however, and we necessarily come finally to the absolute difference between concepts and conceptual objects which can no longer function as concepts; hence attributes, on the one hand, and objects, on the other hand, which "have" attributes but which are not themselves attributes. A distinction in the objective domain thus corresponds to the distinction of meanings; it is, in other words, the difference between individual and specific or "general" objects. But the general objects as well as the general ideas (general meanings) are also called equivocal; or more exactly, the *direct* ideas of general objects, or "concepts." The concept redness is either the redness itself — as when one opposes to this concept its manifold objects, the red things — or the meaning of the name redness. They are in the same relationship as the meaning *Socrates* and Socrates himself. To be sure the word *meaning* (or signification) also becomes equivocal as a result of the confusion of these distinctions, so that sometimes the object of the presentation and sometimes its "content" (the sense of the name) is called the meaning. Inasmuch as meaning is also called concept, to speak of connecting concepts and conceptual objects is ambiguous: in the one case, what is in question is the relationship between an attribute (redness) and the object to which it is attached (the red house); in the other case, it is the totally different relationship between a

282 THE FOUNDATION OF PHENOMENOLOGY

logical presentation (e.g., the meaning of the word *redness*, or of the proper name *Thetis*) and the presented object (the attribute redness, the goddess Thetis).

(2) The difference between concrete and abstract ideas, however, can also be conceived in another manner, namely, an idea is called concrete if it presents an individual object directly, without the mediation of conceptual (attributive) ideas; and abstract in the opposite case. On the one side, there are the meanings of proper names, and, on the other side, are all other nominal meanings.

(3) Corresponding to the meanings of the word abstract that were characterized above is a new sphere of meaning for the term abstraction. It comprises the acts through which abstract "concepts" arise. More exactly, what are involved are the acts in which general names obtain their direct relationship to specific unities; and again, the acts which belong to these names in their attributive or predicative function, and in which forms such as *an A, all A, some A, S which is A*, and the like are constituted; and finally the acts in which the objects conceived in these manifold thought-forms are evidently "given" to us as thus conceived, in other words the acts in which the conceptual intentions are fulfilled and gain their evidence and clarity. Thus we grasp the specific unity *redness* directly, "itself," on the basis of a particular intuition of something red. We look at the factor of red, but perform a peculiar act whose intention is directed toward the "Idea," toward the "general." The abstraction in the sense of this act is entirely different from the mere attending to or lifting out of the factor of red. To indicate the difference, Husserl speaks of *ideating (ideirender)* or *generalizing abstraction.* The traditional talk of abstraction refers to this act; in that sense not individual features, but general concepts (direct ideas of attributes as thought-unities) are obtained through "abstraction." In any case the same view also applies to the conceptual ideas (or presentations) of the more complicated forms that have been indicated; in the ideas *an A, many A's,* etc., abstraction is made from all other properties; the abstract idea *A* takes on new "forms," but no new "matter."

CHAPTER X

THE ANALYSIS OF WHOLES AND PARTS

HUSSERL expresses the belief that the third investigation,[1] "The Theory of Wholes and Parts," had been read all too little. It had been a great help to him, and it is essential for the complete understanding of the investigations that follow. The investigation of wholes and parts contributes toward the foundation of an *a priori* theory of objects. The determination of the essential laws which constitute wholes leads to the distinction between analytic and synthetic laws, and between the formal and the material in the theory of objects. Husserl pointed out in the preceding investigation that this distinction, which first appeared in the domain of the descriptive psychology of sense-data, can be regarded as a special case of a general distinction. It then reaches beyond the sphere of the contents of consciousness and becomes a most significant theoretical distinction in the domain of objects in general. Consequently the systematic place of its discussion would be in the pure (*a priori*) theory of objects as such, in which the concepts belonging to the category of *object*, such as whole and part, subject and property, individual and species, genus and species, relation and collection, unity, number, series, ordinal number, magnitude, etc., as well as the *a priori* truths relating to these ideas are treated.[2] The analytical investigation cannot be determined by the systematic nature of the objects. The difficult concepts with which we operate in the knowledge-clarifying investigation, and which must so to speak serve as a lever in it, may not be left unexamined, in order to wait until they appear in the systematic context of the logical domain itself. Husserl's aim here is not a systematic exposition of logic, but its epistemological ("knowledge-critical") clarification, and at the same time a preparation for every future presentation of this kind.

A deeper exploration of the difference between independent and dependent contents leads directly to the fundamental questions of the pure doctrine of wholes and parts, belonging to formal ontology, so that it is necessary to go into these questions in some detail.

---

[1] The third investigation was revised thoroughly, the aim being to make its meaning more effective and to remove numerous imperfections.

[2] Cp. the last chapter of the *Prolegomena*, pp. 244–46, regarding these "formal categories of objects" and the formal-ontological essential truths pertaining to them. See ch. v, B herein.

Since part-relationships are of central importance in the present investigation, Husserl begins with a general discussion of them.

Objects can be related to one another as wholes and parts, or can be in the relationship of coördinated parts of a whole. Such relationships are grounded *a priori* in the idea of an object. Every object is an actual or possible part, i.e., there are actual or possible wholes which include it. On the other hand, perhaps not every object has to have parts, and thus there follows the ideal division of objects into *simple* and *compound*.

The terms compound and simple are defined through the determinations: having parts, and having no parts. They can be understood, however, in a second and perhaps more natural sense, in which the being compounded, as the etymology of the word also suggests, refers to a plurality of disjunct parts of the whole, so that that which does not permit of being "analyzed" into a plurality of parts, i.e., in which at least two disjunct parts are not to be distinguished, would have to be designated as simple. In the unity of a sensuously appearing thing we find (say) a determinate red color as a factor, and again the generic color as a factor. Color and determinate red are not disjunct factors; but that is the case with the red color and the extension which it covers, since these have nothing in common with respect to their content. They are connected with one another in the widest sense of the term. It might appear appropriate to call the connected parts *elements* (*Glieder*) of the connection, but with so wide a conception of elements of a whole, color and configuration would have to be regarded as elements connected in the unity of a colored, extended thing. Linguistic usage is opposed to that. For such wholes the elements are "dependent" upon one another, and we find them so innerly united that we can even speak of a "penetration." It is otherwise with the wholes that are divided or that can be divided, to which the terms elements and analysis apply naturally. The parts are here not only disjunct, but are "independent" of one another; they have the character of "portions" that are connected with one another.

It is seen at once that part-relationships have characteristically different forms, and that these forms are based upon the cardinal distinction of independent and dependent objectivities.

The concept *part* is construed so widely that everything may be called a part which is distinguishable "in" an object, or to put it objectively, is "present" in it. Everything is a part which the object "has" in a "real" sense, in the sense of a something really making it up, the object being taken as it is by itself, in abstraction from all contexts in which it is inter-woven. Thus the factor of spatial configuration is a proper part of the table.

In the usual interpretation, parts are taken to be independent. These are called "portions" in Husserl's terminology. Objects are similarly un-derstood to be independent objects, in the usual account. In this respect the term *content* is less restricted. Abstract contents are also spoken of generally. On the other hand, the term content usually is restricted to the merely psychological sphere, a restriction with which we begin in the distinction now to be investigated, but with which we shall not remain. The confusion between the presented content in the sense of any presented object (in the psychological sphere: of every psychological datum) and the presented content in the sense of the meaningful "what" of presenta-tion is not a danger in the present investigation.

The distinction between independent and dependent contents has arisen historically in the domain of psychology, or more exactly, in the domain of the phenomenology of inner experience. Following Stumpf,[3] Husserl formulates the essence of Berkeley's distinction as follows: The contents that are presented together, or that are together in consciousness, are divided into two classes, the independent and the dependent. Independent contents are said to be present when the elements of an idea-complex or content-complex can be presented separately; dependent contents, when that is not the case.

For the closer characterization of this "possibility of presenting sepa-rately," or the impossibility of so doing, the following considerations[4] are advanced, making use of Stumpf's pertinent observations.

We have the evidence with regard to certain contents, that the change or elimination of at least one of the contents given together with it (but not included in it) must change or eliminate the content in question. In the case of other contents this evidence is lacking. Contents of the first kind are only thinkable as *parts* of more comprehensive wholes, whereas the latter appear to be possible even if nothing were there besides them which would connect them into a whole.

Every phenomenal thing and every portion of one can be presented separately in this sense. We can present to ourselves the head of a horse "separately" or "by itself," i.e., we can hold it fast in phantasy while we allow the other parts to change or to disappear. Husserl cites such exam-

---

[3] Cf. C. Stumpf, *Ueber den psychologischen Ursprung der Raumvorstellung* (1873), p. 109.
[4] Husserl's paper, "Ueber abstrakte und konkrete Inhalte," the first of the "Psychologische Studien zur elementaren Logik," is used in the following discussion.

ples as appearances of sounds and sound-structures, of odors, and other experiences which can be thought as freed from any relationship to real existence.

Let us now consider examples of inseparable contents. The relationship between visual quality and extension, or the relationship of both of them to the delimiting figure can serve as an example. In a certain way these factors can be varied independently of one another. The extension can remain the same while the color changes, and the color can remain the same while the extension and the figure change. Taken exactly, however, this independent variability applies only to the species of the factors in their genera. While the color-factor remains unchanged with respect to the species of color, the spread and form can change specifically, and conversely. The same (specifically the same) quality and qualitative "adumbration" is to be "extended" or "spread out" over every extension, and conversely the same extension is to be "covered" by every quality. But there still remains a place for functional dependences in the change of the factors, which are not exhausted by that which the species ideally comprise. The color-factor, as an immediate content-part of the intuited concrete object, is not the same for two concrete intuitions, if the quality, the lowest difference of the genus, is the same. Husserl observes that quality must be regarded as an abstraction of a second order, just as are figure and magnitude of extension. But just because of the element of law which is here under discussion, the factor in question can only be named by means of the concepts determined by the genera quality and extension. That which differentiates the quality to the present factor of quality is no longer limited by the genus color, and therefore the quality, e.g., a definite nuance of red, is designated with right as the *lowest* difference within this genus. Similarly a definite figure is the last difference of the genus figure, although the corresponding immediate factor of intuition is differentiated still further. But the connection of any one of the last differences within the genera figure and color fully determines the factors; it determines lawfully what can be alike and unlike in a given case. The dependence of the immediate factors is therefore a matter of lawful relationship among them, which is determined by the next higher order of the *abstracta* of these factors.

As Stumpf pointed out, it follows from the functional dependence of the factors of quality and extension that they are inseparable in their very nature and that they form a whole content of which they are only content-parts; and they cannot exist separately and independently of one another in a presentation. Husserl states that the same could be said for the relationship between intensity and quality. The intensity of a tone is not something indifferent to its quality, something so to speak foreign to it. We cannot retain the intensity by itself, as that which it is, and change or eliminate the quality. With the elimination of the quality the intensity is necessarily lost, and the same holds conversely. This is not a mere empirical fact, but an *a priori* necessity based upon the pure essences.

Further examples are provided by the unity-factors of intuitive contents, factors which are built upon the elements that can be primarily discriminated, and make up their homogeneous or heterogeneous connection into sensory-intuitive wholes. We obtain the first and narrower concepts of whole, connection, etc., with respect to them, and also the distinguishing concepts of different genera and species of external or internal sensory wholes.

The factors of unity are nothing other than those contents which have been designated as "Gestalt" qualities by von Ehrenfels, by Husserl himself as "figural factors," and by Meinong as "founded contents." A supplementary distinction is, however, necessary here, between the *phenomenological* factors of unity, which give unity to the experiences or experience-parts themselves (to the immanent phenomenological data), and the *objective* factors of unity, which belong to the intentional and in general to the experiential sphere of transcendent objects and object-parts. The expression *unity-factor*, suggested to Husserl by Riehl, has the advantage of immediate understandableness, so that its general acceptance would seem to be desirable.

Whereas Stumpf engages in considerations of this kind in order to *prove* the mutual inseparableness of extension and quality, and hence their dependence, Husserl wants to use them to *define* the inseparableness or dependence, and on the other hand the separableness or independence. To say that a content can be presented "by itself," "separately," does not mean that it can be torn out of consciousness, apart from all coexisting contents. In this sense all contents are inseparable. The same holds for the appearing thing-contents with respect to the entire unity of that which appears as such. If we imagine the head of a horse by itself, we necessarily picture it in a context; the content is necessarily given with numerous other contents and is united with them in a certain manner. What does the separableness of this content through the presentation therefore mean? The answer is as follows:

By separableness we mean that we can hold this content identical in the presentation, despite unlimited variation of the contents that are connected and co-given. This evidently implies that this content, so far as its essence is concerned, is not at all conditioned by the existence of other contents, that it, just as it is, i.e., with respect to its essence, could have *a priori* status even if nothing were there besides itself, or if everything about it changed arbitrarily. Or, what is obviously equivalent: No dependence upon other contents is based upon the "nature" of the content itself; it is essentially unconcerned about all others. It may be the case, as a matter of fact, that along with the existence of this content other contents are given according to empirical rules; but in its essence the content is independent, and does not require any interweaving with other essences.

In the case of dependence, the content is essentially bound to other contents; it cannot be if other contents are not given at the same time with it. That they are one with it does not have to be emphasized, for can there be essential coexistence without at least some degree of connection or "fusion"? Hence dependent contents can only be as content-parts.

It is only necessary to say object and object-part instead of content and content-part (provided that the term "content" is regarded as restricted to the phenomenological sphere), and we have gained an objective distinction which is freed from all relationship to the apprehending act on the one hand and to any phenomenological contents to be apprehended on the other hand. No referring back to consciousness is therefore needed, say to differences in the "manner of presenting," in order to determine the difference in question between the "abstract" and the "concrete." All determinations which use such a relationship are either (through confusion with other concepts of abstract) incorrect or mistaken, or they are nothing more than subjectively turned expressions of the purely objective and ideal situation.

We cannot *think* of a character or a form of connection as being by itself and as separated from everything else (here the term "think" is used instead of "present"); that can be done only in the case of real contents. Differences such as these, that an object [5] can be by and for itself, or can be only in and with another object, do not apply factually to our subjective thinking. They are material differences which are based upon the pure essence of the things, which, however, because they exist and we know of them, lead us to assert that any judgment deviating therefrom is absurd. In Husserl's view, that which we cannot think, cannot be, and what cannot be, we cannot think. This equivalence determines the difference between the truly significant concept of thinking, and presenting and thinking in the usual subjective sense.

[5] The term object is understood in its widest sense, as comprising the experienceable intuitive contents.

When the word "can" appears in connection with the term "thinking" in its significant sense, subjective necessity, or subjective inability to present otherwise, is not meant, but rather the objective-ideal necessity of not being able to *be* otherwise.[6] This is essentially given in the consciousness of apodictic evidence. It is now seen, on this basis, that correlative to the essence of such objective necessity is a definite pure law. In general, objective necessity is equivalent to *being on the basis of objective law*. A particular "by itself" is accidental in its being. That it is *necessary* means that it is in a context that is determined by law, which prevents its being otherwise. It must be noted, however, that just as the necessity that is involved in the discussion of dependent factors is an ideal or *a priori* necessity which is based upon material essences, so correlatively the law is an essential (non-empirical) law which is unconditionally valid. There is no relation to existence, or positing existence, in the case of such laws, as distinguished from general empirical rules and laws. "Natural laws," laws in the sense of the empirical sciences, are not laws of essence (ideal laws, *a priori* laws), and empirical necessity is not necessity of essence.

The not-able-to-exist-by-itself of a dependent part is determined by a law of essence; in short, dependent objects are objects which can exist only as parts of more comprehensive wholes. In other words, they are parts which only exist as parts, and which cannot be thought as being by themselves. The color of this paper is a dependent factor of it; it is not only a part factually, but is essentially, with respect to its pure species, predestined to being a part; for a color in general and purely as such can exist only as a factor in something colored. In the case of independent objects such an essential law is lacking; they can, but do not have to be ordered under more comprehensive wholes.

Husserl's distinctions referred, to begin with, to the being of individual particulars conceived "in ideal generality," i.e., those that were conceived purely as particulars. They also apply to "Ideas" themselves, which therefore can be designated as independent and dependent, even if in a somewhat changed sense. A lowest difference of a highest pure genus can, e.g., be called relatively independent with respect to the series of levels of pure species up to the highest genus; and every lower species is again relatively independent as contrasted with the higher. Genera which are such that corresponding individual particulars cannot be without belonging at the same time to the extension of other genera, would be dependent

---

[6] Husserl calls attention to the fact that the decisive ontological transformation of the notion of evidence into that of a pure law of essence, which begins with this statement, was already accomplished in full sharpness in the first logical survey. Cf. *l. c.*, p. 225, note 1; and also ch. III, B herein.

with respect to the latter, and so *mutatis mutandis* in other spheres of examples.

Still another distinction must be made in the present phenomenological analysis. The difference between independent and dependent contents is to be distinguished from the difference between intuitively discernible and fused contents.

The dependent factors of intuitions are not merely parts, but we must also grasp them as parts in a certain manner. We cannot observe a figure or a color by itself without the entire object that has this figure or color standing out. Sometimes a "striking" color or form seems to appear alone; nevertheless it is the whole object that "stands out" phenomenally, although that occurs by virtue of the particular feature that strikes us, and which is alone objective in the real sense. The lifting out of a sensory unity-factor is similarly related to the grasping of the unified sensory whole itself, e.g., the factor of spatial configuration, which along with other unity-factors founds the inner nature of the sensory aggregate appearing as a unity.[7] In this manner the standing-out of a content is sometimes the foundation for the noting of something else related to it innerly.[8]

The difference between independent and dependent contents in the phenomenological domain (the intuitively given as such) is crossed by a second, which is confused with it, namely, the difference between intuitively "separated" contents and those that are fused with the connected contents. This is an essentially new distinction. If we think of independent contents in the former sense, which are what they are no matter what happens to their surroundings, they do not have to have the entirely different kind of "separation." The parts of an intuitive surface of uniform or continuously "adumbrating" whiteness are independent, but they are not separated. Although one thinks first of the case of continuous gradations of contents when one speaks of intuitive separation, the latter is frequently based upon discontinuity.

The following theorem is asserted by Husserl: Two simultaneous sensuous *concreta* necessarily form a "unity without distinctions," if all immediately constitutive factors of the one pass over "continuously" into corresponding constitutive factors of the other. The case of the sameness of any corresponding factors is to be regarded as an admissible limiting case of continuity, namely, as continuously "passing over into itself." This can be applied readily to the majority of *concreta*.

These propositions are to be sure idealized expressions of the facts.

[7] Cp. Husserl, *Phil. d. Arith.*, ch. xi, p. 228 (a "row" of trees, etc.).
[8] From Husserl's "Psychologische Studien zur elementaren Logik," *l. c.*, p. 162.

Continuity and discontinuity are not to be taken with mathematical exactness. The places of discontinuity are not mathematical limits, and the interval must not be "too small."

It would be somewhat better to distinguish between sharp and confused separation or delimitation, in the vague empirical sense in which one speaks in ordinary life of sharp points and corners as opposed to blunt or rounded corners. The essential formations of all that is intuitively given cannot on principle be brought under "exact" or "ideal" concepts, as is the case in mathematics. The spatial form of the perceived tree as such, taken exactly as it is found in a given perception, as a factor in its intentional object, is not a geometrical structure, and is nothing ideal or exact in the sense of exact geometry; and similarly the intuitive color as such is not an ideal color. The essences grasped in that which is intuitively given are "inexact" essences and should not be confused with the "exact" essences, which are "Ideas" in the Kantian sense, and which (as "ideal" point, plane, etc., or "ideal" color-species in the "ideal" colored body) arise through a peculiar "idealization." The descriptive concepts of all pure description, and hence also of all phenomenological description, are accordingly fundamentally different from the determinative concepts of objective science. To clarify this situation is a phenomenological task which has hitherto not been undertaken seriously and has not been solved with reference to the present distinction.

Husserl goes far enough in his analysis to see that one moves in the sphere of "subjective" intuitions in considering the difference between contents that are presentable by themselves and those that are not presentable by themselves; and that one does not at all attain with this distinction to the general *ontological* distinction between abstract and concrete contents, or, as expressed above, between independent and dependent contents. In the former case what are in question are facts of analysis and blending, whereby the contents that are separated out can be independent as well as dependent. But the two distinctions may not be confused, as is done, e.g., if the dependence of the *unseparated* parts of a uniformly colored surface is placed on the same level as the descriptively entirely different dependence of the *abstract* factors. There is confusion similarly if one attempts to establish the essence of the ontological distinction between *concrete* and *abstract* by the phenomenological fact (belonging to the act-sphere) that the act of presentation of a *concretum* is immediate and is independent if it does not need any other presentation as a basis, whereas the act of grasping an abstract content is indirect and dependent, if the presentation of a related *concretum* must constitute its basis. The present analysis relates to entirely different things, and in any case does not throw light upon the essence of the ontological distinction.

There is an *a priori* law of dependence which has its conceptual basis in that which is general in the part and whole in question. It is sufficient to say for the determination of the concept of dependence that a dependent object can only be what it is in a more comprehensive whole. The kind of completion that is necessary is different in different cases. For example, if we state that the factor of sense-quality, say the factor of sensory color, is dependent, that it requires a whole in which it is embodied, then the law prevailing here is only determined in one respect, namely, with reference to a part whose general character as a sense-quality is specified. The kind of whole remains undetermined, and hence also the way in which such a "quality" is a part, and the kind of completion which it needs in order to exist. It is entirely different if we say: A sense-quality can only be in a "sensory field," e.g., a sensed color in a visual sensory field; or that it can only be as a "qualification" of an "expansion." The structure of law is here also determined in other respects, for the concept of a visual sensory field is given, and it denotes a definite and particular kind of whole among the possible kinds of wholes. Similarly the concept of "qualification" and that of "expansion" denote particular ways among the various possibilities, of how something dependent is lawfully inherent in a whole. The particular is determined generally by the essence of the sense-quality, or the essence of the expansion, but each is in *its* way contained in the essential unity of the visual sensation, or of the visual field, under which all such unities are comprehended. This way cannot be described any further. For no further answer could be given, e.g., to the question as to what differentiates *being a sensory factor* from *being a sensory factor in the mode of a "quality"*; no determination could be cited which would not include the concept of quality — just as we could only answer *red* to the question as to what must be added to *color* in order that the species *red* might result.

The concept of dependence is equivalent to that of an ideal structure of law in unified contexts. If a part is in such a context (and not a merely factual context), it is dependent; for such a context means that a part of a certain essential species can exist only in connection with certain other parts of related species. Also where a law speaks of the impossibility of a connection, instead of the necessity, where it says, e.g., that the existence of a part *A* excludes that of a part *B* as incompatible with it, there too we are led back to dependence. For an *A* can only exclude a *B* in that both demand the same thing exclusively. One color excludes another in the same surface-portion that they are both supposed to cover. Corresponding to every case of exclusion involving essential law is a postive demand of corresponding extent, and this also holds conversely.

These "material" laws will now be distinguished from the "formal" or "analytic" laws. The necessities or laws which define any classes of dependences are based upon the essential peculiarity of the contents; or more exactly, they are grounded in the pure genera, species, or differences under which the dependent and supplementary contents in question come, as accidental particulars. The totality of such ideal objects is the totality of pure "essences," of the essences of all ideally possible individual objects (existences). Corresponding to these essences are "material concepts," or propositions, which are to be sharply distinguished from "merely formal concepts" and propositions, which are free from all "substantive matter." To the latter concepts there belong the formal-logical and the essentially related formal-ontological categories, which were discussed in the last chapter of the *Prolegomena*, and the syntactic formations deriving from them. Concepts such as something or one, object, property, relation, connection, plurality, number, order, ordinal number, whole, part, magnitude, etc., differ fundamentally from concepts such as house, tree, color, tone, space, sensation, feeling, etc., which bring something substantive to expression. Whereas the former are grouped about the empty idea of something or object in general, and are connected with it through the formal ontological axioms, the latter are ordered with respect to various highest substantive genera (material categories), in which material ontologies are rooted. This cardinal separation of the "formal" from the "substantive" or material sphere of essence provides the real distinction between analytic-*a priori* and synthetic-*a priori* disciplines, as well as laws and necessities.

It is now clear that all the laws belonging to the various kinds of dependences or necessities are ordered in the spheres of the synthetic *a priori*, and what separates them from the merely formal is now understood thoroughly. Such laws as the law of causality, which determines the dependence of real changes of things, or laws (as a rule not sufficiently formulated) which determine the dependence of mere qualities, intensities, extensions, limits, forms of relations, and the like, are not to be placed upon the same level as pure "analytic" generalities such as: *A whole cannot exist without parts*; or with analytic necessities such as *A king, a master, a father cannot be, if there are not subjects, servants, children*, and the like. Generally speaking: correlatives require one another mutually; they cannot be thought without one another, or be without one another. But if we juxtapose such a proposition as, e.g., *A color cannot be without something that has color*, or *A color cannot be without a certain extension covered by it*, etc., then the difference is obvious. *Color* is not a relative expression whose meaning contains the idea of a relation to something else. Although color is not "thinkable" without something colored, the existence of something colored, or of an extension, is not "analytically" founded on the concept of color.

The essence of the distinction is made clear by the following consideration. A part as such cannot exist without a whole of which it is a part. But on the other hand we say (with regard to independent parts): A part *can* often exist without a whole of which it is a part. There is no contradiction in that, for what is meant is the following: If we consider a part with regard to its *inner* content, with regard to its own essence, then that which possesses this same content can also be without being a part of a whole; it can be by itself, without connection with something else, and it is then not a part. Only its relation of being a part is dropped in that case, and the content of the part is not touched. The reverse is the case with other kinds of parts; without their relations they are unthinkable as non-parts, by virtue of the peculiarity of their content. These possibilities or impossibilities are based upon the essential peculiarity of the contents. The case is entirely different with the "analytical" triviality that a part as such cannot be without a whole of which it is a part. It would be a "contradiction," i.e., a "formal," "analytic" absurdity, to regard something as a part where there is no related whole. The inner content of the part is not at all concerned here; the "formal" law in this case has nothing in common with the foregoing material one, and therefore cannot affect it.

1. Analytic and Synthetic Propositions

Analytic laws are unconditionally general (and consequently free from all explicit or implicit existential positing of something individual) propositions, which contain only formal concepts, and consequently if we go back to the primitive ones, nothing but formal categories. Opposed to the analytic laws are their particularizations, which arise by the introduction of material concepts or the individual existence of positing thoughts (e.g., *this, the Kaiser*). Just as in general the particularizations of laws yield necessities, so the particularizations of analytic laws yield analytic necessities. What are called "analytic propositions" are as a rule analytic necessities. If they involve the positing of existence (e.g., *If this house is red, then redness is attached to this house*), then the analytic necessity refers to the content of the proposition which makes it to be an empirical particularization of the analytic law, and hence not to the empirical positing of existence.

Analytically necessary propositions are defined by Husserl as propositions whose truth is completely independent of the material peculiarity of their objectivity and of anything factual or existential, and hence as propositions which can be "formalized" completely and can be conceived as special cases or empirical applications of the formal or analytic laws validly arising through such formalization. In an analytic proposition it must be possible to replace all substantive matter by the empty form *something* while retaining the logical form of the proposition, and to eliminate every positing of existence by means of the corresponding judgment-form of "unconditional generality" or law.

The existence of this house includes that of its roof, walls, and other parts is an analytic proposition. For the analytic formula holds that the existence of a whole $G (\alpha, \beta, \gamma, \ldots)$ in general includes that of its parts α, β, γ. The pure law is analytic, and is constructed out of formal-logical categories and categorial forms.

The concept of an *a priori synthetic law* and of *synthetic-a priori necessity* is now really determined. Every pure law that includes material concepts in a manner that does not permit a formalization of these concepts *salva veritate* (in other words, every such law that is not an analytic necessity) is an *a priori* synthetic law. Particularizations of such laws are synthetic necessities; and this also includes empirical particularizations, such as, e.g., *This red is different from this green.*

This suffices to make clear the essential distinction between laws based upon the specific nature of the contents with which the dependences are connected, and analytic and formal laws, which are based upon the formal "categories" and are indifferent to all "matter of knowledge."

The present analysis should be compared with the Kantian, which in Husserl's view does not at all deserve to be called "classical." It appears to Husserl that by means of his analysis one of the most important problems of the theory of science has reached a satisfactory solution, and that at the same time a first decisive step toward the systematic separation of the *a priori* ontologies has been accomplished.

It is readily seen that the main concepts treated in this discussion — whole and part, independence and dependence, necessity and law — undergo an essential change of meaning if they are not understood to refer to essences or pure concepts, and are interpreted as empirical. For purposes of the following investigations it is not necessary, however, to discuss in detail these empirical concepts and their relationship to the pure concepts.

2. Relative Independence and Dependence

Independence has until now been regarded as something absolute, as independent of all connection with contents; and dependence as dependent upon at least one content. But it is important also to define the concepts as *relative*, such that the absolute distinction is characterized as a limiting case of the relative one. The reason for this lies in the things themselves. *Within the sphere of mere sense-data* (and thus not of the things represented or appearing in them, as such), the factor of visual expansion (the representing factor for the *spatial extension* of the appearing, colored, spatial form) with all its parts is for us dependent; but within the expansion regarded *in abstracto*, every one of its portions is relatively independent; each of its factors, e.g., the form to be distinguished from "position" and "magnitude," is relatively dependent.

Relative dependence may be defined as follows: Every content-part which can only exist as a part of a whole G is said to be dependent in and relative to the whole G. Every content-part for which this does not hold is said to be independent in and relative to the whole G. In brief we also speak of dependent or independent parts of the whole, and in a corresponding sense of dependent and independent parts of parts of the whole.

The determination can be generalized still more. The definition can be so conceived that not only a content-part is placed in relation to a more comprehensive whole, but that in general one content is related to another content, even if disjunctively. The following may accordingly be defined: A content a is relatively dependent with respect to a content β, or to the collective totality of contents determined through β and all its parts, if a pure law based upon the peculiarity of the content-genera concerned exists, according to which a content of the pure genus a can only exist *a priori* in or connected with other contents from the collective totality of pure content-genera determined through β. If such a law is lacking, then we call a relatively independent with respect to β.

More simply it can be said: A content a is relatively dependent with respect to a content β, if a law grounding in the generic essences a, β exists, according to which a content of the pure genus a can only exist in or connected with a content of the genus β. The case is left open, in which the genera a and β are also genera of complexes.

In the sphere of the phenomenological occurrences of the "stream of consciousness" an illustration of dependence is provided by the essential law that every actual, fulfilled, present consciousness necessarily and continuously passes into a just past; hence that the present consciousness places continuous demands upon the future consciousness; and connected therewith is the retentional consciousness of the just past, which has the immanent character of the actual now, and requires the being just past of the phenomenon known as just having been. Naturally the time to which reference is here made is the immanent time-form belonging to the phenomenological stream of consciousness itself.[9]

In the sense of Husserl's definition, every portion is independent in and relative to the concrete whole of a visual factor in intuition, i.e., of every concretely fulfilled section of the visual field; every color of such a portion, the color-configuration of the whole and the like, is dependent. Again, in and relative to the whole of the total, momentary sensory intuition, the fulfilled visual field, the fulfilled tactual field and the like are independent, whereas the qualities, forms, etc., regardless of whether they attach to the whole or to single elements, are dependent. The following general truth holds: That which is independent or dependent in relation to a β retains this property in relation to a whole β', in relation to which β is independent or dependent, a proposition which does not, however, admit of conversion.

B. THE THEORY OF PURE FORMS OF WHOLES AND PARTS

1. The Concept of Foundation (Fundierung) and Relevant Theorems

Nothing can place the value of rigorous determinations in a brighter light than the possibility of establishing deductively propositions made known to us in another form. Because of the great scientific interest which the constitution of a deductive theory claims in every domain, Husserl pauses a little here in order to introduce the basic definitions and some theorems.

Definitions. If in accordance with essential law an α can only exist in a comprehensive unity which connects it with a μ, then we say, an α as such needs foundation through a μ, or also, an α as such is in need of completion by means of a μ. If accordingly α_0, μ_0 are definite particular cases of the pure genera α, or μ, which stand in the cited relationship, and if they are members of one whole, then we say that α_0 is *founded* by μ_0; and it is *exclusively* founded by μ_0 if the need of the completion of α_0 is alone satisfied by μ_0. This terminology can be applied to the species themselves; the equivocation is harmless. The indefinite expressions: α_0 is in need of a supplement, or it is based upon a certain factor, are synonymous with the expression: α_0 *is dependent.*

[9] See ch. xvi, A herein.

Theorem I. If an a as such requires foundation through a μ, then just such a foundation is required by every whole which has an a, but not a μ, as a part.

The theorem is axiomatically evident. If an a cannot be without being completed by μ, then a whole of a that does not include any μ in itself also cannot satisfy the requirement of completion of the a.

As a corollary, with regard to the definition of the preceding paragraph, it may now be asserted:

Theorem II. A whole which includes a dependent factor without the completion required by it as a part, is also dependent, and it is dependent relative to every more comprehensive independent whole in which that dependent factor is also contained.

Theorem III. If G is an independent part of Γ, then every independent part g of G is also an independent part of Γ.

If g, viewed relatively to Γ, would need a completion μ, and thus possess a foundation μ_0 in the domain of Γ, then it would also have to be contained in G. For otherwise, according to Theorem I, G would be in need of completion with respect to μ; and since μ_0 is a part of Γ, according to Theorem II it would be dependent relative to Γ; which contradicts the presupposition. But in accordance with it g is an independent part of G, and hence also relative to G; therefore nothing can exist in the domain of G which could serve for the foundation of g; and consequently also not in the entire domain of Γ.

This theorem can also be expressed as follows: If a is an independent part of β, β an independent part of γ, then a is also an independent part of γ. Or, more briefly: An independent part of an independent part is an independent part of the whole.

Theorem IV. If γ is a dependent part of the whole G, then it is also a dependent part of every other whole of which G is a part.

γ is dependent relative to G, i.e., it possesses a foundation in a μ_0 belonging to the domain of G. Naturally this same μ_0 must also occur in the domain of every whole containing G as a part; therefore γ must also be dependent relative to every one of these wholes. (On the other hand γ can very well be independent with respect to a subordinated whole; we merely have to draw its boundaries in such a way that the necessary completion remains excluded from it. Thus a portion of an appearing extension, taken as a factor, is *in abstracto* dependent relative to the concrete wholes of the fulfilled extension.)

This theorem can also read: If a is a dependent part of β, β a dependent part of γ, then a is also a dependent part of γ. In other words, a dependent part of a dependent part is a dependent part of the whole.

Theorem V. A relatively dependent object is also absolutely dependent, but on the other hand a relatively independent object can be dependent in an absolute sense.

For the proof compare the preceding paragraph.

Theorem VI. If α and β are independent parts of any whole G, then they are also independent relatively to one another.

For if α were in need of completion through β or through any part of β, then there would be in the totality of the parts determined through G those (namely, those of β) on which α would be founded; therefore α would not be independent relatively to its whole G.

2. *Transition to the More Important Part-Relations*

There are differences in the *a priori* relationships between whole and part, as well as between the parts of one and the same whole. The generality of these relationships allows ample room for the most varied differences. Not every part is contained in a whole in the same way, and not every part is interwoven with every other in the unity of a whole in the same way. In the comparison of the part-relationships in different wholes, or in the comparison of the part-relationships in one and the same whole, striking differences are found, which are at the basis of the usual distinctions between different kinds of wholes and parts. A hand is, e.g., a part of a man in an entirely different way than the color of the hand, or than the total extension of the body, or than the psychical acts or the inner factors of these phenomena. The parts of the extension are united with one another in a different way than they themselves are with their colors, etc. It is seen at once that these differences belong in the sphere of the present investigations.

3. *Reciprocal and One-Sided, Mediate and Immediate Foundation*

If any pair of parts is brought into view, the following possibilities exist: (*a*) There is a relationship of foundation between the parts, or (*b*) There is not this relationship. In the former case the foundation can be (1) a *reciprocal* one, or (2) a *one-sided* one, depending upon whether the law in question can be converted or not. Thus color and extension are mutually founded on a unified intuition (more exactly: on the unity of something intuited visually as such), since no color is thinkable without a certain extension, and no extension without a certain color. On the other hand, a judgment-character is one-sidedly founded on the presentations at its basis.

Of interest is the question regarding the relative independence or dependence of the parts, relative to the whole in which they are viewed.

If between two parts there exists a mutual relationship of founding, then their relative dependence is beyond question; thus, e.g., in the unity of quality and place. But if it is merely one-sided, the founding (and not the founded) content can be independent. Thus in an extension the figure of a portion is founded on the portion, and hence something relatively dependent with respect to the whole of this extension is founded on something independent of it.

The founding of one part on another can further be: (a) an *immediate* one, or (β) a *mediate* one, depending upon whether both parts stand in immediate or mediate connection. This relationship is, just as in the case of the preceding one, not bound to the individual factors present, but concerns the founding-relationship with respect to its essential nature. If a_0 is immediately founded on β_0, but mediately on γ_0 (in so far as β_0 is immediately founded on γ_0), then it holds generally and essentially that an a in general is immediately founded on a β, and mediately founded on a γ. The order of mediateness and immediateness is based upon the pure genera as a matter of law. For example, the generic factor of color, and in an entirely different manner again the factor of brightness, can only be realized in and with such a factor as red, blue, etc.; and the latter again only in connection with a certain determinateness of extension. These immediate connections and foundations condition the mediate ones between the factor *color*, or *brightness*, and *determinateness of extension*. The laws of connection belonging to the mediate foundations are analytic, deductive consequences of those that belong to the immediate foundations.

4. Definition of Portion, Factor, Physical Part, Abstractum, Concretum

A number of fundamental concepts can be reduced to the concepts defined above, and thus gain determinateness. There is first a fundamental division of the concept *part* into *portions* or parts in the narrowest sense, and *factors* or *abstract parts* of the whole. Every independent part relative to a whole G is called a portion, and every dependent part relative to it is called a factor (an abstract part) of this same whole G. It is indifferent whether the whole itself, viewed absolutely or relatively to a higher whole, is independent or not. Abstract parts can accordingly again have portions, and portions again abstract parts. We speak of portions of a time-duration, although this is something abstract, and similarly of portions of an extension. The forms of these portions are abstract parts inherent in them.

Portions which have no portion in common are called mutually exclusive (disjunct) portions. The division of a whole into a plurality of exclusive portions is called a *partition* (*Zerstückung*) of it. Two such portions can still have an identical element in common. Thus the common boundary is shared by the adjacent portions of a divided continuum. Portions are said to be *separated* if they are disjunct in a rigorous sense, and hence have no identical factor.

Since an abstract part is also abstract in relation to every more comprehensive whole and in general to every totality of objects comprising this whole, it follows that something that is abstract when viewed relatively is *eo ipso* abstract when viewed absolutely. The latter can be defined as the limiting case of the relative view, in which the relation is determined through the entire totality of objects in general; so that it does not therefore need a previous definition of the abstract or dependent in an absolute sense. An *abstractum* is accordingly an object for which there is a whole with respect to which it is a dependent part.

If a whole permits such a partition that the portions are essentially from the lowest genus as determined by the undivided whole, it is called an *extensive whole*, and its portions are called *extensive parts*. The division of an extension into extensions, e.g., belongs here; or more particularly of an extension of space into spatial extensions, an extension of time into temporal extensions, and the like.

The following definitions can be added: With reference to its abstract factors an object is called a *relative concretum*, and with reference to its nearest factors, it is their *nearest concretum*. A *concretum* that is not abstract in any direction can be called an *absolute concretum*. Since the theorem holds that every absolutely independent content possesses abstract parts, every one can also be regarded as an absolute *concretum*. Both concepts therefore have the same extension. For the same reason the expression "concrete part" can be used instead of "portion." Where the word *concretum* is used simply, the absolute *concretum* is meant as a rule.

5. *The Difference between Mediate and Immediate Parts of a Whole*

Closely connected with the difference between portions and abstract parts is the difference between mediate and immediate parts, or expressed more distinctly, between nearer and more remote parts. For the terms immediateness and mediateness can be understood in two senses, each of which will be considered.

If $\theta(G)$ is a part of the whole G, then a part of this part, say $\theta(\theta(G))$, is again a part of the whole, but it is a mediate part. $\theta(G)$ may then be called an immediate part of the whole. The distinction is a relative one, since $\theta(G)$ can itself again be a mediate part with reference to another part of the whole in which it is contained as a part. The relative distinction is transformed into an absolute one, if we understand by absolutely mediate parts those which inhere in parts of the whole; and by absolutely immediate parts, those which are not parts of any part of the same whole. Every geometrical part of an extension is mediate in this sense, for the latter always has parts which comprise it. It is more difficult to find suitable examples of absolutely immediate parts, but the following may be cited. If we select, in a visual intuition, the unified complex of all inner factors which remain identical through mere change of place, then it is a part of a whole for which there is no more comprehensive part. If the distinction is restricted to parts of one and the same kind, the factor of unified color is an absolutely immediate part, in so far as there is no homogeneous factor of the whole under which it could be ordered as a part. On the other hand, the color which is attached to a portion of the whole is to be regarded as mediate, in so far as it contributes to the total color of the whole.

6. *Nearer and More Remote Parts of a Whole*

The distinction between immediate and mediate parts gets a new meaning if we consider certain striking distinctions which come up in the comparison of the relationships between wholes and mediate parts.[10] If we think of an extensive whole as partitioned, then the portions again admit of partitions, and again the portions of the portions, etc. Here the parts of the parts are parts of the whole in exactly the same way as the original parts; and we observe not only the similarity with respect to the kind of the part-relationship — the portions of the portions are again portions of the whole — but there is also a similarity of these relationships between the whole and the mediate parts on the one hand, and the (relatively) immediate parts on the other hand, so that there can be no way of making an absolute preference of the one or the other. Not as though the talk about mediate and immediate parts were entirely arbitrary, lacking an objective basis. A physical whole has really those parts that were first considered, and these again really have the parts distinguished in them, which are mediate with respect to the whole; and thus with every step of continued division. But in themselves the furthest of these parts are not further from the whole than the nearest. In any case the parts also owe their gradation to the gradation of the divisions, and the latter lacks an objective basis. In an extensive whole, there is no division that is first in itself, and also no firmly delimited group of divisions as a first stage of division. Every mediate part can, according to the favored mode of division, also be viewed as an immediate one, and every immediate one as a mediate one.

It is different with other examples. An intuitively unified succession of tones, say a melody, is a whole in which single tones are parts. Every one of these tones has parts, a factor of quality, a factor of intensity, etc., which as parts of parts are also parts of the melody; but it is clear here that the mediateness in which say the factor of quality of the single tone is inherent in the whole is not to be ascribed to our subjective process of division or other subjective motives. If the factor of the quality of the single tone is to be noted by itself, the tone must indeed be "lifted out" itself. The particular grasping of the mediate part presupposes the particular lifting out of the immediate one. But this phenomenological relationship is not to be confused with the objective situation under consideration here. It is evident that the quality in itself is only a part of the melody in so far as it is a part of the single tone; it belongs immediately to the latter, and only mediately to the whole tone-structure. This "mediate" refers here not to an arbitrary preference or a preference of a certain course of division conditioned by psychological compulsion, with which we would first have to come upon the tone and then upon its factor of quality; but *in itself*, in the whole of the melody, the tone is the earlier, and its quality the later, mediate part. It is similar with the intensity of the tone; indeed it might almost appear here as though it took us a step further from the whole of the melody, as though it were not an immediate factor of the tone but were nearer to its quality, and hence a secondary part with reference to it (a conception which would be in need of further consideration, however). If we are justified in assuming a part in the quality, say *c*, of the tone considered, which is common to it and all tones and thus represents their generic factor, then this part inheres in the quality primarily, in the tone secondarily, in the entire tone-structure tertiarily, etc. Precisely in this way the color-factor or configuration-factor which inheres in an extensive part of a visual object (as such) fits into this part first of all, and secondarily into the whole of the intuition.

The new and significant sense of the distinction between mediate and immediate parts should now be clear. But the distinction is not a merely relative one, inasmuch as there are parts in every whole which belong directly to it itself and not primarily to one of its parts. It is definite for the single part whether it is mediate in the present sense or not, and in the former case whether it is mediate on a first, second, or further level. In order to distinguish terminologically one could speak here of *nearer* and *more remote* parts, and more exactly of primary, secondary, etc., parts of a whole. The terms mediate and immediate part are retained in a general sense, and are applicable to any parts.

Primary parts can be and are in general absolutely mediate ones. There are, however, also primary parts which are absolutely immediate, i.e., which are not contained as parts in any part of their whole. Every portion of an extension is primarily contained in it, although it can always be conceived as a mediate part of the same extension. Objectively there are always parts whose part it is. On the other hand the form of an extension is not contained as a part in any one of its parts.

Mediate and immediate, nearer and more remote parts have been considered in relation to the whole to which they belong. But these terms are also used where parts are considered in relation to one another, although in an entirely different sense; we speak of an immediate and mediate connection of parts, and in the latter case further distinctions are made. Two connections form a *chain* if they have some but not all terms in common. Every chain is accordingly a complex connection.

7. *The Concepts of Whole and Part Defined by Means of the Concept of Foundation*

In the above definitions and descriptions the concept of a whole was presupposed. This concept can be dispensed with, and the simple coexistence of the contents which were denoted as parts can be substituted for it. Thus one could define, e.g.: A content of the species a is founded on a content of the species β, if an a cannot exist with respect to its essence (i.e., as a matter of law, on the basis of its specific peculiarity), without a β also existing: whereby it remains open whether certain γ, δ must also exist, or not.

The other definitions follow similarly. The significant concept of a whole can be defined by means of the concept of foundation, as follows: By a *whole* is meant a totality of contents which are comprised by a unified foundation, and that without the aid of further contents. The contents of such a totality are called parts. The expression "unity of the foundation" means that every content is connected with every one, whether directly or indirectly, through foundation. This can so occur, that without outer aid all these contents are founded on one another immediately or mediately; or also in such a way that all together found a new content, and that again without outer aid. In the latter case, this unified content may be built up out of content-parts, which in their turn are founded in a similar manner on partial groups of the presupposed totality, as the total content in the entire totality. Finally, mediating cases are also possible where the unity of the foundation, e.g., comes about in such a way that α founds a new content with β, β again with γ, γ with δ, etc., in short in the manner of a chain.

One notes at once how essential separations of wholes are determined through such distinctions. In the first cases pointed out, the "parts" "penetrate" one another (the parts being defined as the members of the totality in question); in the other cases the parts are "outside of one another," but whether all together or chained in pairs, they determine real forms of connection. Where one speaks of connection and the like in a narrower sense, one means wholes of the second species; i.e., relatively to one another independent contents found new contents as "forms connecting" them.

The same whole can be a penetration with respect to certain parts, and a connection with respect to others: thus the sensuously appearing thing, the intuitively given space-form covered with sensory quality (just as it appears there) with respect to its mutually founding factors such as color and extension, and the same with regard to its portions.

8. Sensory Forms of Unity and Wholes

According to Husserl's definition, not every whole has to have its own form, in the sense of a particular *factor of unity* connecting all parts. If, e.g., the unity arises through concatenation in such a way that every pair of neighboring elements founds a new content, then the requirement of the definition is met, without there being a peculiar factor of unity founded on all parts together. According to Husserl's concept of a whole it is not required that the parts be connected even as groups or as pairs by their own factors of unity. Only when the whole is an "extensive" one and is dissectible into portions are such factors indispensable on *a priori* grounds.

It is an obvious fact that wherever connecting forms can really be shown in intuition to be peculiar factors of unity, that which is connected consists of parts that are independent relatively to one another; e.g., tones in the unity of a melody, or partial figures in the unity of a complex figure, and the like. Besides the form-contents, which give unity to the portions, we are not able, on the other hand, to find anything in the unity of a visual appearance that connects the dependent factors, e.g., color and extension, with one another; or within the former, hue and brightness, within the latter the factors of form and magnitude, and the like. But that is not to argue that the non-finding implies a non-being. In any case it is of great importance to consider the *possibility of sensory unities without a sensory form that can be abstracted*.

It may appear to be strange that mere necessities of coexistence or requirements of completion should function as unifying agencies. It will be objected at once: Could not the contents lie side by side in complete separation? The answer is clear. The talk of separation implies the thought of the relative independence of the separated contents; and just this has been excluded. The image of the "side by side" presupposes relatively independent contents which, because they are that, are able to found this sensory form of the "side by side." What recommends this unsuitable (unsuitable because it aims to illustrate sensory formlessness by a case of sensory form) image so much is the indifference toward one another of the contents given in merely spatial togetherness. But, it will be objected, it is absurd to want to unite contents without a bond; and it is argued that where there is no form to unite, the contents have nothing to do with one another, and must remain isolated. — This is correct for the contents which the image presupposes. But those which are here under consideration have very much to do with one another; they are founded on one another, and for that reason they do not need any chains and bonds in order to be chained or connected with one another. These expressions have really no meaning for them. Where there is no sense to speak of separation, there the problem of how the separation is to be overcome is meaningless.

This view holds not only in the domain of intuitive objects (especially of phenomenological contents), which served as examples, but for the domain of objects in general. *The relationships of foundation*, it may be said in plain words, *are all that truly unify*. Consequently the unity of independent objects also occurs only through foundation. Since they, as independent, are not founded on one another, it follows that they themselves together found new contents which are called unifying contents with respect to the founding "elements." Unity is a *categorial predicate*.

Husserl's conception avoids any infinite regresses of parts splitting up in ever new series. Nothing real (perceivable in a possible sensory experience) exists beyond the totality of the portions of the whole, as well as the sensory forms of unity which are based upon the togetherness of the portions. But what gives unity to the factors within the portions, as well as to the factors of unity *with* the portions, are the foundations as defined herein.

Finally, as regards the *concept* of the *factor of unity*, which Husserl distinguishes from that of the "form" which gives unity to a whole, that has already been defined in passing. By that is meant *a content which is founded by a plurality of contents* — by all together and not merely by single ones among them. (Husserl obviously presupposes *his* concept of foundation therewith.) Limited to the phenomenal sphere, this content, according to the nature of its foundations, can be a content of outer or of inner sensory experience.

The factors of unity are ordered, like all other abstract contents, in pure genera and species.[11] Thus the genus *spatial figure* is differentiated to *triangular figure*, and this again to the lowest species *definite triangular figure*. It can be seen by such examples that the genus of factors of unity is determined through the genus of the contents founding them, and that similarly the lowest difference of the former is uniquely determined by that of the latter.

9. *Categorial Forms of Unity and Wholes*

In the sense of the determination, here attempted, of the concept of a whole, a mere totality of any contents (a mere being-together) is not to be called a whole, any more than a likeness (as a being of the same kind) or difference (being of a different kind or in another sense: not identical being) is to be called a whole.[12] "Totality" is the expression for a "categorial" unity corresponding to the mere "form" of thinking; it denotes the correlate of a certain *unity of meaning*, related to all the objects concerned. The objects themselves, in so far as they are taken together in thought, do not found a new content, either by groups or all together; no unified form of connection accrues to them through the unified intention; they are perhaps "in themselves unconnected and relationless." This is shown in that the form of totality is completely indifferent with respect to its matter, i.e., with completely arbitrary variation of the contents it can continue to exist. But a founded content adheres to the particular

---

[11] Cp. *Phil. d. Arith.*, p. 232.

[12] The sensory factor of likeness is to be distinguished from likeness as categorial unity, the former being related to the latter as the sensory aggregate-characters, which serve us as indirect signs for plurality and non-identity, are related to plurality or non-identity themselves. Cp. *Phil. d. Arith.*, p. 233. Husserl states that his first work is to be compared for all discussions of the present work concerning totalities, factors of unity, complexes, wholes, and objects of a higher order. He expresses his regret that in the many new treatments of the doctrine of "Gestalt Qualities" this publication has remained mostly unnoticed, although a not inconsiderable part of the later writings of Cornelius, Meinong, and others on the questions of analysis, apprehension of plurality, and "Komplexion" is already found in its essence in the *Philosophy of Arithmetic*, even if in other terminology. It appears to Husserl that it would still be useful today to look through that work for the phenomenological and ontological themes in question, especially since it was the first publication which thoroughly investigated and evaluated acts and objects of a higher order.

"nature" of the founding contents; there is a pure law that makes the genus of the founded content dependent upon the definitely denoted genera of the founding contents. In general a whole, in a full and real sense, is a connection determined through the lowest genera of the "parts." To every material unity there belongs a law. According to the various laws, in other words according to the different species of contents which are to function as parts, different species of wholes are determined. The same content therefore cannot arbitrarily function as a part now of this, and again as a part of that species of whole. The being-a-part, and more exactly, the being-a-part-of-this-determinate-species (a metaphysical, physical, logical part, and whatever may also be distinguished) is based upon the pure generic determination of the contents in question according to laws which in Husserl's sense are *a priori* or "essential laws." This is a fundamental insight which must be treated and formulated in accordance with its significance. With it the basis is given at the same time for a systematic theory of the relationship of wholes and parts with respect to their pure forms, or with respect to their categorially definable types, abstracting from the "sensory" matter of the wholes.

Before considering this thought further, a doubt must be met. The totality-form is purely categorial, and in opposition to it, the form of the whole, of the unity of foundation, has appeared to be material. But in the preceding discussion, was not unity (and it was the unity of foundation that was spoken of) called a categorial predicate? In the sense of Husserl's doctrine, the idea of unity or of a whole is based upon that of foundation and this again upon that of a pure law; furthermore the form of a law in general is categorial (law is not something material, and hence is nothing perceivable), and thus the concept of a foundation-whole is also a categorial concept. But the *content* of the law belonging to every such whole is determined through the material peculiarity of the founding and of the founded species of content, and it is this law, which is determined with respect to its content, that gives unity to the whole. Therefore every ideally possible particularization of the idea of such unity may be called a material or a real unity.

According to Husserl's earlier discussion, the laws constitutive of the different kinds of wholes are *a priori* synthetic, as opposed to the *a priori* analytic laws which belong to the categorial forms, as, e.g., to the form-idea of a whole in general and to all mere formal particularizations of this idea.

10. The Pure Formal Types of Wholes and Parts, and the Postulate of an A Priori Theory

The pure forms of wholes and parts are determined according to the pure form of the laws. Only that which is formally general in the relationship of foundation as it is expressed in the definition comes in question therewith, as well as the *a priori* complexes which it makes possible. We attain to the pure form of a whole, to its categorial type, by "abstracting" from the peculiarity of the kinds of content involved. More clearly expressed, this *formalizing* "abstraction" is entirely different from the usual kind of abstraction, as when, e.g., the general "red" is taken out of a concrete visual datum, or the generic factor "color" is taken out of the already abstracted red. Formalizing, we put indeterminate expressions in the place of the names denoting the kinds of content concerned, such as *a certain kind of content, a certain other kind of content*, etc.; and the corresponding substitutions of pure categorial thoughts for the material ones occur therewith, on the side of meaning.[13]

After formulating some theorems in prose, Husserl states that these thoughts are only an indication of the future treatment of the theory of wholes and parts. The theory should of course be formulated mathematically.

11. On the Partition of Wholes through the Partition of Their Factors

That portions, viewed relatively to the whole whose portions they are, cannot be founded on one another, either one-sidedly or reciprocally, either as wholes or with respect to their parts, is an analytical proposition. On the other hand, it does not follow from the content of the definitions in question, that it is impossible that portions establish a relationship of foundation with regard to a more comprehensive whole, in which they all are dependent factors. *De facto*, however, we find no example in the domain of pure intuition and evidence that is accessible to us; and in connection therewith noteworthy part-relationships may be pointed out. The following proposition, which is phenomenological in a broader sense, can be asserted: To every portion in a relative *abstractum* there corresponds a portion in each of its relative *concreta*, such that the excluding portions of the former establish excluding portions in each of the latter. In other

---

[13] On the role of foundation for the constitution of the idea of a pure logic as a *mathesis universalis*, cp. *Log. Unt.*, vol. I, §§ 67–72; and also ch. v, B herein. Husserl emphasizes the fact that where he speaks simply of abstraction, the selection of a dependent factor of content is meant; and by the title ideating abstraction, the corresponding ideation is meant, and hence not formalization.

words, the partition of a dependent factor conditions a partition of the concrete whole, in that the portions which exclude themselves, without themselves entering into a relationship of foundation to one another, attract new factors, by which they are supplemented singly to become portions of the whole.

A few examples will elucidate. The partition of the quasi-spatial expansion of a visual content which endures unchanged, but is viewed in abstraction from the temporal factor, also determines a partition of this content itself. The same holds for spatial intuitive data in relation to spatial partition. The separated spatial portions found factors of completion which are independent of one another. The color of one portion is not founded by the color of any other one, for example. The colors of the portions stand in the same relationships of division (exclusion, inclusion, intersection) as the portions themselves. This peculiar situation, that the partition of a factor here also involves a partition of the whole, is obviously based upon the fact that the portions of the factor also do not found one another in the more comprehensive whole, but require new factors for their foundation; and also upon the fact that these new factors themselves find their required foundation only in those portions, and not mutually in one another.

The case is similar with temporal wholes of intuition. If we partition the duration of a concrete process of time, then we have partitioned it itself; corresponding to the sections of time are sections of movement (whereby this term is understood in the broadest Aristotelian sense). The same holds in the case of rest; it too has its sections, which are portions in the sense of the present analysis, since rest during a partial duration and rest during any other partial duration do not stand in an evident relationship of foundation in any respect.

If, instead of restricting ourselves to the sphere of the essential data of intuition, we consider the empirical-real connections of nature, the situation is different. But this transition requires an enlargement of concepts. In the present context, all conceptions have been related to the pure sphere of essence; the laws of foundation have been found to be subject to pure laws of essence. As for what on the other hand concerns nature with all its things, it also has its *a priori*, whose systematic elaboration is the still unsolved problem of an ontology of nature. From the outset it is indubitable that natural laws in the usual sense do not belong to this *a priori*, to this pure and general "form" of nature, that they do not have the character of essential truths, but of factual truths. Their generality is therefore not "pure" or "unconditioned," and similarly the "necessity" of all occurrences of things ordered under them is "accidental." Nature with all its physical laws is a matter of fact that could also be otherwise. If we now treat the laws of nature as real laws, disregarding this element of the accidental, if we relate to it all pure concepts formed by us, then we obtain modified ideas: of *empirical* foundation, empirical wholes, empirical independences and dependences. But if we think of the idea of a factual nature in general, whose particularization our given nature is, we obtain general ideas which are not bound to *our* nature, of empirical wholes, of empirical independence, etc., ideas which are obviously constitutive of the idea of a nature in general and which must, with the essential relations belonging to them, be classified under a general ontology of nature.

Presupposing this, let us return to our particular question. Whereas in the material sphere of essence there were no examples in which a partition of a dependent factor, e.g., of a spatial and temporal factor, did not involve such a partition of the concrete whole, it is different in the domain of all empirical-real connections in coexistence and succession. That becomes clear if we consider the meaning of the empirical relations of necessity, which connect things that are spatially and temporally separated from one another. If, according to a definite causal law, to the concrete change occurring in a time-segment t_1–t_0, there is attached with necessity a certain new change in the adjacent time-segment t_2–t_1, then the former thereby loses its independence with regard to the latter. If there belong ontologically (hence included in the idea of nature in general) to *every* concrete process of change laws that can only be known empirically, and which assign to the processes of change certain necessary, temporally adjacent consequences; and if every process must itself be a necessary consequence of antecedents: then every concrete process of change of nature is dependent with regard to the more comprehensive time-wholes in which it is realized, and therefore no partition of a time-interval conditions a partition of the *concrete* time-whole belonging thereto. But the restriction to processes of change is unnecessary. The fictive case of "rest" may be allowed as a limiting case. With respect to the causal connections from which no temporal being is exempt, it may be asserted that a partition of the time-factor never involves a partition of the concrete time-whole. The supplementary factors belonging to the time-portions are indeed separated according to the time-portions, but this separation does not suffice to bring about a partition in the temporal *concretum*; that is prevented by the mutual causal foundation of the temporally separated contents.

It is similar with spatial partition, at least in the wholes in which spatial and temporal extension are brought to coincide, such that with every partition of the one factor, a partition of the other is given, and vice versa. The partition of a spatial factor of a movement does not bring about a partition of the movement itself, any more than that of its temporal factor.

It also follows from these considerations that within the objective time of nature the time-stretches (which with regard to a time-extension comprehending every one of them, possess the character of portions *in abstracto*) also lose mutual independence with this character, if we regard it in relation to a concretely fulfilled temporal unity, in which they are inherent as dependent factors. The theorem that every objective time-duration is a mere time-part, which does not merely permit the two-sided extension *in infinitum*, but also requires it, is a mere consequence of causality and hence refers to time-fulfillment. Through it the time-part becomes dependent not only with regard to *its* fulfillment by itself, but also with regard to adjacent time-parts and their fulfillments. This dependence of the time-parts and their mutual foundation are subject to laws which connect not only time-intervals with time-intervals, but concretely fulfilled time-wholes with just such time-wholes. Since in these laws, besides the other variables which represent factors of the fulfilling time-content, the times, or time-intervals, also function as mutually influencing variables, these time-intervals also gain a relationship of foundation with reference to the more comprehensive concrete unity. It is similar with space-portions in relation to more comprehensive space-unities and finally to the entire infinite space of nature. The theorem that every space-portion requires all-sided extension, or as one must here say more exactly, the *real* possibility of all-sided extension, up to the infinity of the *One* space, is a consequence of certain causal laws, more exactly, of certain natural laws. The fact that we extend spatial as well as temporal intervals at will in phantasy, that we can place ourselves in phantasy at any imagined limit of space or time, whereby ever new spaces and times appear before our view — all that does not prove the relative foundation of space- and time-portions; it does not prove the necessity that space and time must be infinite in reality, or even that they *can* only be infinite in reality. Only a causal law which presupposes and consequently requires the possibility of continuation beyond every given limit can prove this.

CHAPTER XI

PURE GRAMMAR AND THE ANALYSIS OF MEANING

THE FOURTH INVESTIGATION,[1] entitled "The Distinction of Independent and Dependent Meanings and the Idea of Pure Grammar," is a continuation of the analysis of meaning that was begun in the first investigation. In addition to the renewed analysis of meaning, it advances the idea of a pure-logical grammar as an *a priori* form-theory of categorial meanings.

In this investigation Husserl proposes to consider a fundamental distinction in the domain of meanings which is concealed behind insignificant-looking grammatical distinctions, namely, between categorematic and syncategorematic, complete (*geschlossen*) and incomplete expressions. The clarification of such distinctions leads to an application of the general distinction between independent and dependent objects in the domain of meaning, so that the distinction intended in the present investigation is to be characterized as one between independent and dependent meanings. It is the necessary basis for the establishment of the essential categories of meaning, in which, as will be shown shortly, a manifold of *a priori laws of meaning*, disregarding the objective validity (real or formal truth, as well as objectivity) of the meanings, is rooted. These laws, which obtain in the sphere of meaning-complexes and have the function of separating sense from nonsense in it, are not the logical laws, so-called in a significant sense; they give to pure logic *the possible forms of meaning*, i.e., the *a priori* forms of complex, unified, significant meanings, whose "formal" truth or "objectivity" then regulate the "logical laws." Whereas the former laws prevent nonsense, the latter prevent formal or analytic absurdity. If these pure-logical laws say what the possible unity of the object requires *a priori* and on the basis of the pure form, then the laws of meaning say what the mere unity of the sense requires, i.e., indicate the *a priori* forms by which meanings of the various categories of meaning are united to *one meaning*, instead of resulting in chaotic nonsense.

The old idea of a general, or of an *a priori* grammar, receives a sound

---

[1] Husserl's standpoint on the subject-matter of the fourth investigation did not change after the publication of the first edition. The second edition contains improvements in the text and some enrichment of the content, which indicates the direction of his future publications on logic.

basis through the demonstration of *a priori* laws determining the possible forms of meaning. To what extent still other spheres of an *a priori* belonging to grammar are to be shown lies outside the frame of the present interests. Within pure logic there is a sphere of laws abstracting from all objectivity which, in distinction from logical laws in the usual sense, could be designated as pure-logical, grammatical laws. In contrast to the pure form-theory of meanings is the pure theory of their validity which presupposes it.

A. SIMPLE AND COMPOUND MEANINGS

Husserl takes his departure from the at first self-evident division of meanings into *simple* and *compound*. It corresponds to the grammatical distinction of simple and compound expressions. A compound expression is an expression, in so far as it has a meaning; as a compound expression it is built up out of parts which are themselves parts, and which as such have their own meanings. Thus, e.g., "a man of iron" has the partial meanings man and iron. Even if the partial meanings themselves have partial meanings, we must come finally to simple meanings as elements. That there are really simple meanings is shown by the example of "something." The experience of presentation that occurs in the understanding of the word is certainly compounded, but that is not true of the meaning.

B. COMPLEXITY OF MEANINGS AND OF OBJECTS

Husserl considers the question whether the complexity or simplicity of meanings [2] is a mere reflex of the complexity or simplicity of the objects "presented" in them. But it would be incorrect to regard the presentation as the mental image of the object. The presupposed parallelism does not exist in any aspect. First, compound meanings can "present" simple objects. A clear example is provided by the expression *simple object* itself. It is a matter of indifference, whether there is such an object or not.[3] But it may also be that simple meanings can "present" compound objects, or can refer to them in the manner of meaning. Even if one were to doubt (regardless of whether it be right) that such simple names as man, iron, etc., really express simple meanings, names such as *something* and *one*

---

[2] "Presentations" could be inserted just as well in the place of "meanings"; for with the more special question the more general one, referring to presentations in general, or objectivating acts in general, is also answered.

[3] Husserl follows Bolzano here. In objection to Bolzano, Twardowski maintained that there are no simple objects. But Twardowski spoke of presented objects, and meant objects *as such* are here in question.

would have to be admitted. The latter can in their indeterminateness refer to everything possible, hence to every compound object, although in the most indeterminate manner.

It is furthermore clear, that where a compound meaning refers to a compound object, not every part of the meaning has a part of the object appertaining to it, let alone the converse. Bolzano's pertinent example, "land without mountains," was to be sure contested by Twardowski; but this is explained by the fact that he identified meaning and direct, intuitive presentation of the meant object, while missing the fundamental logical concept of meaning. Therefore he came to regard constituents of the meaning ("without mountains") as "auxiliary presentations."

C. COMPLEXITY OF MEANINGS AND OF THE CONCRETE ACT OF MEANING

There are other questions — e.g., to decide whether a given meaning may be regarded as compound or as simple. Consider proper names such as *Schultze* (as the name of a person known to us). Two senses of *simplicity* and *complexity* are to be distinguished here, such that simplicity in the one sense does not exclude simplicity in the other. The meaning of the proper name, or the "proper meaning," is undoubtedly simple. Besides, it is clear that the content of presentation, with which this *Schultze* is presented along with the proper name, can change in many ways, while the proper name still functions in identical meaning, always naming the same *Schultze* "directly." Through its own essence, the actual meaning-consciousness establishes possibilities of fulfilling coincidence with intuitions of certain groups and of no others. Consequently it is clear that this consciousness, as also the completely non-intuitive one, necessarily carries with itself a certain intentional content, through which the individual is presented, if not meant, not as a completely empty something, but as somehow determinate and as determinable according to certain types (as a physical thing, as an animal, as a man, etc.).

A certain double-sidedness is accordingly seen in connection with the meaning-consciousness belonging to proper names, a double direction in which one can speak of complexity or of simplicity. The one side determines the simplicity or complexity of the meaning itself. It is therefore the side on which the pure essence of the act of meaning as such lies; but belonging to it is that intentional essence of the concrete, complete meaning-consciousness, which, conceived specifically, is the meaning. In our case of the proper meaning, this side is simple. But it necessarily presupposes a further intentional content as a basis, in keeping with the circumstance that the same thing that is meant, in an identical sense (or that which is named uniquely by the same proper name), can be "presented" in very different ways, with a changing content of determining characters — whereas this change and the complex of this content does not concern the meaning itself.

The essence of the distinction treated here must be made clear first of all. Concrete meaning-giving experiences, which are compounded purely as meaning, are distinguished from those which are compounded only with respect to the content of presentation by which the meant object is known. The proper name E names (or the proper meaning E means) the object so to speak in one ray (*Strahl*). Explicative meanings such as E *is a*; (*Ea*), *which is b*; (*Eb*), *which is a*; and the like are "many-rayed," and in any case are constituted in divers stages and in various forms, so that they can refer with different contents to the same object. The fact that there are many stages does not prevent their unity: they are unified, compounded meanings. The corresponding consciousness of meaning is *an* act of meaning, but a compounded one.

Husserl states further that logical definition, in which a limit is set to the difficulties of systematic analysis, and above all to the fluctuation of word-meaning, is merely a practical logical device by which the meaning is not restricted in a real sense and innerly arranged. Opposed to the meaning, just as it is, there is a new meaning of organized content, namely, as the norm according to which we are to be directed in the judgments based upon the meaning concerned. To avoid logical deceptions, we exclude judgments in which the meanings in question are not replaceable by their normal equivalents; and at the same time we recommend the rule, to use these normal word-meanings as much as possible in the activity of knowledge, or to regulate the given ones by frequent comparison with the normal ones.[4]

D. "SYNCATEGOREMATIC" CONSTITUENTS OF COMPLEX EXPRESSIONS

The consideration of compound meanings leads at once to a new and fundamental distinction. Such meanings are given to us as a rule as meanings of articulated word-complexes. The question arises, whether a separate meaning is to be coördinated with every word of the complex, and whether in general all arrangement and form of a linguistic expression is to be recognized as the impression of a corresponding arrangement or

---

[4] The double-sidedness of the meaning-intentions treated in this paragraph, and already contained in the first draft of it, received a clearer and phenomenologically deeper formulation in the revised treatment. In the original conception, Husserl did not exhaust the complete sense and the extent of the distinction; and the sixth investigation does not take due account of it.

form of a meaning. Bolzano held that every word in language serves to denote its own presentation.[5] On the other hand, some words are regarded frequently as "merely connotative," i.e., as not having meaning by themselves, but only in a context with others.

The distinction between categorematic and syncategorematic expressions has its justification; but Husserl is led, with regard to syncategorematic words, to a view which opposes that of Bolzano, mentioned above. Since the distinction between categorematic and syncategorematic is a grammatical one, it might appear that the situation that is basic to it is also "merely grammatical."

But the grammatical distinction admits of still another interpretation, if one decides to conceive the completeness or incompleteness of the expressions as the mark of a certain completeness or incompleteness of the meanings, and hence the grammatical distinction as the mark of certain essential meaning-distinctions. It is clear that if the presentations are to be truly mirrored in the sphere of meaning-intentions, then to every form on the side of the presentation there must correspond a form on the side of the meaning. And if, further, language is to mirror truly, in its verbal material, the *a priori* possible meanings, then it must have control over the grammatical forms which permit the endowing of a sensuously distinguishable "expression" to all distinguishable forms of the meanings.

E. INDEPENDENT AND DEPENDENT MEANINGS:
THE DEPENDENCE OF SENSUOUS AND OF EXPRESSIVE WORD–PARTS

This conception is obviously the only correct one. Not only must categorematic and syncategorematic *expressions* be distinguished, but also categorematic and syncategorematic *meanings*;[6] but Husserl speaks more characteristically of *independent* and *dependent* meanings. Only significant signs are called expressions, and expressions are called compound only if they are composed of expressions. Thus the word *king* is not called a compound expression. On the other hand expressions with several words are regarded as compound, because it belongs to the concept of a word to express something; only the meaning of the word does not have to be independent. Just as dependent meanings can only be factors of certain independent ones, so linguistic expressions of dependent meanings can only function as form-constituents of expressions of independent mean-

[5] Bolzano's "presentation" means as much as "presentation in itself," which corresponds to Husserl's concept of meaning.
[6] Marty speaks of "autosemantic" and "synsemantic" signs, in his *Grundlegung der allgemeinen Grammatik und Sprachphilosophie* (Halle, 1908), pp. 205 ff.

ings, and they therefore become *linguistically* dependent, "incomplete" expressions.

F. THE CONCEPTION OF DEPENDENT MEANINGS AS FOUNDED CONTENTS

The apparently indifferent distinction of expressions into categorematic and syncategorematic corresponds to a fundamental difference in the domain of meanings. Although the former was taken as the point of departure, the latter was shown to be the original one, as first founding the grammatical distinction.

Even the concept of an expression, and the distinction of merely audible and in general sensuous expression-parts from partial expressions in the genuine sense of the word, or as one could say more significantly, from the *syntactic parts* (root-syllables, prefixes, suffixes, words, cohering word-complexes), can only be determined by recourse to a distinction of the meanings. If these divide into simple and compound ones, then the expressions conforming to them must be either simple or compound, and this complexity leads back necessarily to final significant parts, to syntactic ones, and consequently again to expressions. As for the distinction of categorematic and syncategorematic expressions, the one type can serve alone as complete expressions, can stand alone as closed language, and the other not; hence one must go back to the domain of meaning and in it show that need of supplementation which attaches to certain meanings as "dependent."

In denoting the syncategorematic meanings as dependent, the essence of these meanings is indicated. In considering dependent contents in general, Husserl had determined the concept of dependence, and it is this same dependence which he believes must be assumed in the domain of meaning. He had stated in the third investigation that dependent contents can only be as parts of more comprehensive wholes, which has its *a priori* ground of law in the kind of essence of the contents in question.

Only the meanings are of interest here. Husserl had conceived them as ideal unities; but obviously his distinction was carried over from the real to the ideal domain (in the third investigation). Corresponding to the meaning in a concrete act of meaning is a certain factor that makes up the essential character of this act, i.e., necessarily belongs to every concrete act in which this same meaning is "realized." But with regard to the division of acts into simple and compound, a concrete act can contain several partial acts, and such partial acts can inhere in the whole now as independent, and again as dependent parts. In particular an act of meaning as such can be compound, namely, compounded out of acts of meaning.

A total meaning then belongs to the whole, and a partial meaning (meaning-part, which is itself again a meaning) to every partial act. Accordingly, Husserl calls a meaning *independent* if it can make up the complete and whole meaning of a concrete act of meaning, and *dependent* if this is not the case. It can then only be realized in a dependent partial act of a concrete act of meaning, only in connection with certain other meanings supplementing it can it obtain concretion, only in a meaning-whole can it "be." The dependence of meaning as meaning thus defined determines the essence of the syncategorematic according to Husserl's conception.

G. DIFFICULTIES OF THIS CONCEPTION

It might appear that the distinction between the independence and dependence of meanings reduces to the distinction between the independence and dependence of the meant objects. Thus it might seem to be self-evident that categorematic expressions refer to independent, and syncategorematic to dependent objects. But it can be seen at once that such a view would be false. The expression *dependent factor* provides a contrary case, for it is a categorematic expression and nevertheless presents something dependent. In general, everything dependent can be made to be the object of an independent meaning, e.g., *redness, figure, equality, magnitude, unity,* and *being*. From these examples it is seen that independent meanings correspond not only to the *material* objective factors, but also to the *categorial* forms, and are especially directed upon these forms, to that extent making them to be objects by themselves; whereas the latter are not therefore "by themselves" in the sense of independence. The possibility of independent meanings directed upon dependent factors is not strange, if one considers that although the meaning "presents" something objective, it has not for that reason the character of an image; but rather that its essence lies in a certain intention which can be "directed" upon everything and anything, whether independent or dependent. Thus everything and anything can become objective in the manner of meaning, i.e., become an intentional object.

A further difficulty is presented by the understanding of *syncategorematica* detached from every connection. If Husserl's conception is correct, such cases cannot occur, for the dependent elements of a language cannot be detached. How could it therefore be possible to regard these elements, as Aristotle did, apart from all connection?

Husserl answers this objection by pointing to the difference of "real" and "unreal" presentations, or, which means the same, to the distinction of merely intending and fulfilling meanings. Detached *syncategorematica,*

such as *equals*, *in connection with*, *and*, *or*, cannot achieve intuitive understanding, or any fulfillment of meaning, except in the context of a more
comprehensive meaning-whole. If we want to "make clear" to ourselves
what the word "equals" means, we must look to an intuitive equality, we
must actually perform a comparison ("really") and on that basis bring a
proposition of the form $a = b$ to a "fulfilling understanding." If we want
to make clear to ourselves the meaning of the word *and*, we must actually
perform an act of collection, and in the totality thus coming to real presentation, bring a meaning of the form *a and b* to fulfillment; and thus
everywhere. The dependence of the fulfilling meaning, which necessarily
functions in every performed fulfillment as a constituent of a fulfilling
meaning of a more comprehensive content, is at the basis of the *extended*
notion of the dependence of the intending meaning.[7]

The valuable thought here indicated can be expressed as follows: No
syncategorematic meaning, namely, no act of dependent meaning-intention, can have the function of knowledge, if not in the context of a categorematic meaning. And instead of *meaning*, we could also say *expression*,
normally understood as the unity of word-sound and meaning or sense.

But how is it that individual *syncategorematica*, e.g., the individual word
and, are understood? They are dependent with respect to their meaning-
intention, which means that such intentions can only exist in categorematic
contexts; hence the detached particle, the isolated *and*, would have to be
an empty sound.

The difficulty can only be solved in the following manner: The detached *syncategorematicum* has either not at all the same meaning as in
a categorematic context, or it has, but undergoes a supplementation of
meaning (even if materially indeterminate), so that it then becomes an incomplete expression of the momentarily lively and completed meaning.
The isolated *and* is either understood by means of a thought of *a certain
particle well known to us*; or, with the aid of vague material presentations
and without any verbal supplement there is a thought of the type *A and B*.
In the latter case the word *and* functions normally.

In this manner the difficulties are met, and it may be assumed that
the distinction of independent and dependent meanings concerns the domain of meaning-intention just as it does that of fulfillment, and that
consequently the situation really exists which is required for the possibility
of adequation between intention and fulfillment.

---

[7] The counterpart of fulfillment, or "disappointment," must also be allowed for, i.e., the
way in which absurdly connected meanings in a meaning-whole are seen as "incompatible"
in the process of intuitive clarification, whereby the intended unity is "disappointed" in the
intuitive disunion.

H.   A PRIORI LAWS IN MEANING COMPLEXES

If the distinction of independent and dependent meanings is connected with the more general distinction of independent and dependent objects, then one of the most fundamental facts of the domain of meaning is really included, namely, that *the meanings are subject to a priori laws which regulate their connection into new meanings.* In every case of a dependent meaning there is a certain essential law which regulates its need of supplementation by new meanings, and hence shows the kinds and forms of contexts in which it must be ordered. Since there is no compounding of meanings into new meanings without connecting forms, which themselves have the character of dependent meanings, it is evident that *a priori* laws of essence are effective in the connection of meaning. Of course, the important fact present here is not peculiar to the domain of meaning alone, but plays its role wherever there is connection.

In the domain of meaning, we are not free in the connection of meanings to meanings. The meanings belong together and constitute unified meanings only in certain ways that are determined in advance, whereas the remaining combinatorial possibilities are excluded by law: they yield only a heap of meanings instead of *one* meaning. The impossibility of connection is one of essential law, and is not merely subjective. In the cases here in question, the impossibility is objective, ideal, grounding in the "nature" or in the pure essence of the domain of meaning, and as such it is to be apprehended with apodictic evidence. This impossibility attaches to the essential genera under which the single uniting meetings fall, i.e., to the categories of meaning. To be sure, the single meaning is already something specific, but relative to the category of meaning it is only a single particular. Thus in arithmetic the numerically determined number is a single particular relative to the number-forms and number-laws. Hence wherever we have the insight, with given meanings, into the impossibility of their connection, this impossibility refers to an unconditionally general law. The same holds for the *possibility* of connections of meaning.

Consider an example. The expression *This tree is green* is unified and meaningful. By formalizing the given meaning (the independent logical proposition) we obtain the corresponding pure meaning-form, the proposition-form, *This S is p,* a form-idea which applies only to independent meanings. The materialization of this form, its particularization to determinate propositions, is possible in infinitely many ways, but we are not completely free in that process, being bound to firm limits. Not every meaning may be substituted for the variables *S* and *p*. While keeping to the category in question, false or ridiculous meanings may result, but there are always unified meanings or grammatical expressions, whose sense can be unifiedly expressed. Thus "this gold" or "this algebraic number" may replace "this tree." But when we pass beyond the categories, that is no longer the case. We can juxtapose the words, *This frivolous is green, More intensive is round, This house is equal* — and we get a word-series in which every word as such has a sense, or refers to a complete connection of sense, but in such cases we do not have a unifiedly closed sense.

We can order together the words: *a tree is and*, etc., but the word-series is not understandable as *one* meaning. It is an analytic proposition, that in a whole, forms cannot function as matters nor matters as forms; and that also holds for the sphere of meaning.

It must be recognized that every concrete meaning is an into-one-another of matters (or "substances," *Stoffen*) and forms, that every one stands under a form-idea that can be derived by formalization, and that, furthermore, an *a priori* law of meaning corresponds to every such idea. It is a law of the formation of unified meanings out of syntactic matters, which come under firm categories belonging *a priori* to the domain of meaning, and according to syntactic forms which likewise are determined *a priori* and compose a firm system of forms. From this there arises the great task, equally fundamental for logic and grammar, to determine this *a priori* constitution comprising the realm of meanings, to investigate the *a priori* system of formal structures in a "form-theory of meanings."

I. MODIFICATIONS OF MEANING WHICH ARE ROOTED IN THE ESSENCE OF EXPRESSIONS, OR OF MEANINGS

In such cases as *"If" is a particle*, or *"And" is a dependent meaning*, the meaning of the words used as subject is not the same as in a normal context. What is here in question is not the composition of the words, but that of the meanings; in any case that of the words with the same meaning retained. Logically viewed, all change of meaning is to be judged as an abnormality. The logical interest which is concerned with identical, unified meanings requires constancy of the function of meaning. But it turns out that certain changes of meaning even belong to the normal grammatical features of every language.

If we say *"The earth is round" is a statement*, then the meaning of the statement does not function as the subject-presentation, but a presentation of the statement as such; it is not the fact that the earth is round that is judged, but rather the proposition, and this proposition itself functions in this case as its own name. If we say *"And" is a conjunction*, we do not have the factor of meaning that normally corresponds to the word *and* brought to the subject-place, but the independent meaning is here directed toward the word *and*. In this case the *and* is really not a syncategorematic but a categorematic expression; it names itself as a word.

There is an exact analogue of the *suppositio materialis* here, where the expression carries, instead of its normal meaning, a presentation of this meaning (i.e., a meaning which is directed toward this meaning as its object). That is the case, e.g., if we say: *"And," "but," "greater" are dependent meanings*. As a rule it will be said here that the meanings of the words *and, but, greater* are dependent. Similarly in the expression *"Man," "table," "horse" are thing-concepts*, presentations of these concepts, and not the concepts themselves function as the subject-presentations. In such cases the change of meaning is indicated as a rule at least in the written expression, say by quotation marks or other heterogrammatical means of expression, as Husserl suggests that they be named. All expressions with "modifying" instead of "determining" predicates function anomalously in the last designated manner; or, similarly, in a more or less complicated manner, the normal sense of the whole expression is to be replaced by another, involving a presentation, either logical-ideal in character, or empirical-psychological, or purely phenomenological. For example, *The centaur is a fiction of poets*. Rewriting this we can say: Our presentations of centaurs (our subjective ideas of the meaning-content "centaur") are fictions of poets. The predicates *is, is not, is true* or *false*, and the like are modifying predicates. They do not express properties of the apparent subjects, but those of the corresponding subject-meanings. For example, *That* $2 \times 2 = 5$, *is false*; that means the thought is a false thought, the proposition is a false proposition.

If we eliminate in the examples of the last paragraph those in which the modifying presentation is subjective, or more exactly, a presentation in the psychological or phenomenological sense, and if we understand the analogue of the *suppositio materialis* in the restriction noted above, then we observe that what are here in question are changes of meaning, or more exactly, changes of the act of meaning which are rooted in the ideal nature of the domain of meaning. There are *a priori* laws in the domain of meaning, according to which meanings, with retention of an essential core, are to be transformed in various ways into new meanings. Also belonging there is the transformation, which every meaning can undergo, into the "direct presentation" relating to it, i.e., into the "proper" meaning *of* the original meaning. Accordingly the linguistic expression functions in the modified meaning as a "proper name" of its original meaning. Because of its *a priori* generality, this modification is at the basis of a large class of *general grammatical* equivocations, as modifications of verbal meaning reaching beyond empirical languages.

Husserl also refers to the cases of nominalization of adjectival predicates, or attributes, in order to dissipate possible doubts about the material of the preceding section. The adjective is so to speak predestined to a predicative, and further to an attributive function; it functions normally, in an "original," unmodified meaning, as in the example *This tree is green*. It remains unchanged in itself — apart from its syntactic function — if we say *this green tree*. This manner of change of the syntactic form as opposed to the syntactic matter is first of all to be ascertained, and is a main theme of the description of general structures of the domain of meaning. That which is adjectival, in the sense of the identical syntactic matter along with change of predicative into attributive functions, undergoes a further modification if the adjective does not merely function as an attributive factor of a nominal meaning, but is itself nominalized, i.e., becomes a *nomen*. For example, *Green is a color* and *Greenness is a difference of being colored*. Both do not say the same thing, inasmuch as in the one case the dependent factor can be derived from the content of a concrete object, and in the other case it may be the nominalization of the being. The same word "green" changes its meaning in the nominalizations; in the written expression at least something general of this modification is indicated by the large initial letters (which is therefore not logically and grammatically worthless). The original and nominalized meaning (*green* and *Green*, *is green* and *being Green* or greenness) have an essential factor in common, an identical "core" ("Kern"), which is something common that has different core-forms in the two cases, forms which are to be distinguished from the *syntactic forms* (which as such already presuppose core-contents in and with core-forms as syntactic matters). If the modification of the core-form of the adjectival core-content (of the core itself) has yielded a syntactic matter of the type *nomen*, then this *nomen*, built in itself determinately, can enter into all the syntactic functions which require *nomina* as syntactic matters, in accordance with the formal laws of meaning. This suffices for present purposes.

J. NONSENSE AND ABSURDITY

The lawful incompatibilities to which the study of *syncategorematica* led must be well distinguished from those others which the example *a round square* illustrates. As emphasized in the first investigation, the senseless (the nonsensical) must not be confused with the absurd (the "countersensical"), which is a part of the domain of the significant. The connection *a round square* provides a unified meaning which has its manner of "existence," of being in the "world" of ideal meanings; but it is an apodictic evidence, that no existent object can correspond to the existent meaning. If, however, we say *a round or, a man and is,* and the like, then no meanings exist which could correspond to these connections as their expressed sense. We have the apodictic evidence that such a meaning cannot exist, that such meaning-parts are incompatible in a unified meaning.

The difference between the two incompatibilities is therefore clear: In the one case, certain partial meanings are not compatible in the unity of the meaning, in so far as the objectivity or truth of the entire meanings is concerned. An object, e.g., a thing, a fact, in which everything is united which the unified meaning, by virtue of the "incompatible" meanings, presents as unifiedly attached to it, does not exist and cannot at all exist; but the meaning itself exists. Names such as *wooden iron* and *round square*, or propositions such as *All squares have 5 corners*, are surely also names, or propositions. In the other case it is incompatible with the possibility of the unified meaning itself that certain partial meanings coexist in it. We then have only an indirect idea, aiming at the synthesis of such partial meanings to *one meaning*, and therewith the insight that an object can never correspond to such a presentation, i.e., that a meaning of the kind that is here intended cannot exist. The incompatibility-judgment pertains here to presentations, and in the former case to objects; whereas here presentations of presentations enter in, there simple presentations enter into the unity of judgment.

If we ask for the reasons, why in our language certain connections are permitted and others prohibited, then we are referred to a large extent to accidental habits of language and to matters of fact of the development of language. But on the other hand we come upon the essential difference of independent and dependent meanings, as well as upon the *a priori* laws of the connection and transformation of meaning that are intimately connected therewith, laws which in every developed language must be manifested more or less distinctly in a grammatical form-theory and in a pertinent class of grammatical incompatibilities.

The task of a science of meanings would now be to investigate the structure of essential laws of meanings and the laws of the connection and modification of meanings based thereupon, and to reduce them to a minimum number of independent elementary laws. For that it would be necessary first of all to trace out the primitive forms of meaning and their inner structures, and in connection therewith to establish the pure categories of meaning which delimit in the laws the meaning and extension of the indeterminates (or variables). Formal laws of connection may be illustrated by an arithmetical "operation" such as $a + b$, etc. In the domain of meaning there are laws relating to the existence or non-existence of *meanings*, and in these laws the meanings are not free variables, but are restricted to the extension of the categories grounding in the nature of the domain of meaning.

In the pure logic of meanings, whose higher goal lies in laws of the objective validity of the meanings, in so far as such validity is conditioned by the pure form of meaning, the doctrine of the essential structure of the meanings and of the laws of their form-constructions constitutes the necessary foundation. The traditional logic provides isolated pertinent beginnings in the doctrines of the concept and judgment, but without consciousness of the goals to be placed under the point of view of the pure idea of meaning. In pure logic as such, the "matter of knowledge" is eliminated, i.e., all that which could give to the forms of meaning (types, structures) a determinate relationship to material spheres of being, remains eliminated. Instead of even the highest concepts, such as physical thing, the spatial, the psychical, etc., there are indeterminate general presentations of materialities, although these are of a firmly determinate category of meaning (e.g., nominal, adjectival, propositional meaning).

What is concerned first of all in a pure logical form-theory of meanings is the establishment of primitive forms in the purity just indicated. More fully, the primitive forms of independent meanings, of complete propositions with their immanent arrangements and structures in the arrangements would have to be ascertained; and, furthermore, the primitive forms of complication and modification, which the various categories of possible terms essentially permit (whereby it is to be noted that whole propositions can also become terms in other propositions). Then what is involved is a systematic survey of the unlimited manifold of further forms, which are to be derived through continued complication or modification.

Naturally the forms to be established are "valid"; that is to say here, they are forms which provide actually existent meanings — existent as meanings — in arbitrary particularization. A certain *a priori* existential law therefore belongs, to begin with, to every primitive form, and it states that every connection of meaning which conforms to such a form also actually yields a unified meaning, in so far as the terms (the indeterminates, the variables of the form) belong to certain categories of meaning. But the deduction of the derived forms must at the same time be the deduction of their validity; hence existential laws must also belong to them, and they must be deduced from the laws of the primitive forms.

For example, to every two nominal meanings M and N there belongs the primitive form of connection M *and* N, with the law that the result of connection is again a meaning of the same category. The same law obtains if for the nominal meanings we take those of other categories, e.g., propositional or adjectival meanings. Any two propositions connected in the form M *and* N again yield a proposition, two adjectives again an adjective (again *one* meaning, which can stand as a complex but unified attribute or predicate). Again there belong to any two propositions M, N the primitive forms of connection *if* M *then* N, M *or* N, such that the result is again a proposition. To any nominal meaning S and to any adjectival p there belongs the primitive form Sp (e.g., *red house*); as a matter of law the result is a new meaning of the category of nominal meaning. Etc. For all the statements of law belonging here it is to be noted that in the conception of the categorial ideas *proposition, nominal, adjectival presentation*, etc., which determine the variables of the laws, we abstract from the changing syntactic forms which necessarily belong to such meanings. We speak of the same name, whether it stands in the place of the subject or in the function of a relative object; of the same adjective, whether it functions in the predicate or attributively; of the same proposition, whether it be a free proposition, or a conjunctive, disjunctive, or hypothetical antecedent or consequent. The much used but not scientifically clarified talk of *terms* in the traditional logic is defined therewith. In the formal-logical laws falling in its province, and also in our laws of structure, such "terms" function as variables, and the categories delimiting the domain of variability are categories of terms. The examination of these categories is one of the first tasks of the theory of forms.[8]

If one substitutes step by step, in the primitive forms presented, a connection of these forms for a simple term, and applies the primitive existen-

[8] With respect to what it offers in really pure-logical doctrines, the entire syllogistic is comprehended under the logic of statement-meanings (the "apophantic" logic).

tial law, there result new forms of deductively assured validity; thus, e.g., (M and N) and P, (M and N) and (P and Q), {(M and N) and P} and Q, etc. The complication can progress *in infinitum*, every new form remaining bound to the same category of meaning, as the sphere of variability for its terms; and as long as this sphere is retained, all connections of meaning to be formed necessarily *exist*, i.e., must represent a unified sense. One also sees that the pertinent existential propositions are direct consequences of propositions referring to the primitive forms. Instead of always applying the same form of connection, various forms of connection can, within the limits that can be permitted lawfully, be used combinatorially for the constructions, and so infinities of complex forms can be thought as generated. There thus arises the insight into the *a priori* constitution of the domain of meaning with respect to all those forms which have their *a priori* origin in the basic forms.

This insight, and finally the all-comprehensive insight into the formal constitution of the entire domain of meaning, is the only purpose of such investigations. It is not intended to obtain practically valuable rules of the complication of meaning, or of the grammatical complication of expressions, in addition to the formulation of the types of meaning and of the existential laws belonging thereto. What is in question is the insight that all possible meanings are subject to a firm type of categorial structures, marked out *a priori* in the general idea of meaning, and that an *a priori* structure of law reigns in the domain of meaning, according to which all possible cases of concrete formations are systematically dependent upon a small number of primitive forms laid down through existential laws, from which they can therefore be derived through pure construction. The fact that this structure of law is *a priori* and purely categorial brings us to a basic portion of the constitution of the "theoretical reason."

L. THE AVOIDANCE OF NONSENSE AND ABSURDITY AND THE IDEA OF PURE–LOGICAL GRAMMAR

The discussed formal laws of meaning, which provide for the mere separation of the domains of the meaningful and the meaningless, will certainly have to be valid as formal logical laws. One would be more likely to understand by logical laws those other laws which are much nearer to our practical cognitive interests, which, limited to significant meanings, relate to their objective possibility and truth. Consider more closely the two kinds of laws.

The *a priori* laws which belong to the constitution of the essential forms of meaning leave it entirely open, whether the meanings to be formed have objects or not, or whether they (if proposition-forms are involved) yield possible truth or not. These laws have, in accordance with what has been said, the mere function of separating sense from nonsense. The word nonsense is to be taken strictly; a word-heap, such as *king but or similar and*, is not at all to be understood as a unit; every word has a meaning by itself, but not the compound. These laws (normatively applied) of the nonsense to be avoided assign to logic the possible forms of meaning in general, whose objective value it has to determine first of all. And it does this by setting up entirely different laws, which separate the formally harmonious sense from the formally disharmonious, from *formal absurdity*.

The harmoniousness or absurdity of meanings means objective and therewith *a priori* possibility (harmoniousness, compatibility) as opposed to objective impossibility (incompatibility); in other words, it means the possibility or impossibility of the *being of meant objects* (compatibility of being and incompatibility of being of meant objective determinations), in so far as it is conditioned by the *essence* of the meanings and can consequently be intuited with apodictic evidence. This opposition between objective harmonious sense and absurdity is distinguished sharply by Husserl from the opposition of sense and nonsense. The distinction is also needed here between *material (synthetic) absurdity*, for which material concepts (material final cores of meaning) have to come up, as that is the case, e.g., in the proposition *A square is round* and in every pure geometrical proposition which is false; and *formal* or *analytic absurdity*, under which is included merely formal objective incompatibility, based upon the pure essence of the categories of meaning, disregarding all substantive "matter of knowledge." (An analogous separation naturally goes through the opposite concept of harmonious sense.) Laws such as the principle of contradiction, or of double negation, or of *modus ponens*, are, normatively applied, laws to avoid formal absurdity. They show us what holds for objectivity in general by virtue of the pure "thought-form," i.e., what can be stated for the objective validity of the meanings independently of all matter of the meant objectivity on the basis of the pure form of the meaning, in which they are thought. These laws may not be violated if falsity is not to result, before we have taken account of the objectivity with respect to its material nature. They are, in the sense of the third investigation, "analytic" laws, in opposition to the synthetic "a priori" laws, which contain material concepts and are bound to them in their validity. In the sphere of analytic laws in general, these formal laws, i.e., the laws based upon the pure categories of meaning, are separated from the objective validity of *ontological-analytic laws*, which are based upon the formal-logical categories (such as object, property, plurality, etc.), and determine sharply a second, narrower concept of the analytic. The latter may be designated as the *apophantic-analytic*, in the sense of the apophantic logic. In part only do relationships of equivalence obtain between both kinds of laws.

If we restrict ourselves now, disregarding all questions of objective validity, to the *a priori* that is rooted purely in the generic essence of the meaning as such, namely, to the discipline shown in the present investigation, which investigates primitive types of arrangement and connection, as well as the laws of operation of the complication and modification of meaning, then we recognize the merit of the idea of a *universal grammar*, conceived by the rationalism of the seventeenth and eighteenth centuries. In the grammatical sphere there is also an *a priori* norm which may not be overstepped. Just as the *a priori* as "pure logic" is separated from the empirically and practically logical, so in the grammatical sphere is the "purely" grammatical, i.e., the *a priori* (the "ideal form" of language), separated from the empirical. In both cases the empirical is partly determined by the general and nevertheless merely factual features of human nature, and partly by accidental particulars pertaining to the race, or to the people and their history, to the individual and his individual life-experience. But the *a priori* is, at least in its primitive formations, "self-evident," even trivial; and still its systematic demonstration, theoretical examination, and phenomenological clarification is scientifically and philosophically of the very greatest interest and of no little difficulty.

Husserl points out that the thought of a universal grammar can be extended beyond the *a priori* sphere, in that the (in one respect vague) sphere of the generally human in an empirical sense is included. There can and must be a universal grammar in this widest sense, and Husserl does not doubt (as Marty erroneously charged) that this extended sphere is "rich in important and sufficiently definite knowledge." But here, as everywhere where philosophical interests are in play, it is a matter of the greatest importance to separate sharply the *a priori* and the empirical. A universal grammar in the widest sense is a concrete science. In our age of natural science, empirical researches are not neglected in the study of grammar. It is otherwise with the *a priori,* although all fundamental insights lead back to it. Therefore Husserl defends the old doctrine of a "grammaire générale et raisonnée," of a "philosophical" grammar which deals with the *a priori* of the form of meaning.

It is therefore of primary significance for the investigation of language to gain the insight that language not only has its physiological, psychological, and cultural-historical, but also its *a priori* foundations. The latter include the essential forms of meaning and the *a priori* laws of their complication or modification, and no language is thinkable which would not also be essentially determined by this *a priori*. Every investigator of language operates with concepts derived from this domain, whether he is clear about it or not.

The pure form-theory of meanings is accordingly delimited as a first and fundamental sphere within pure logic. Regarded from the standpoint of grammar, it reveals an ideal structure which every factual language, following in part general human motives, in part changing empirical motives, fills out and invests with empirical material in a different way. All historical languages are bound to this ideal framework; and thus the theoretical investigation of it must make up one of the foundations for the final scientific clarification of all language in general. One must have the "ideal framework" in view, in order to ask meaningfully: How does the German, the Latin, the Chinese, etc., express "the" existential proposition, "the" categorical proposition, "the" hypothetical antecedent, "the" plural, "the" modalities of the "possible" and "probable," the "not," etc.?

With regard to the fact that in this lower logical domain the questions concerning truth, objectivity, and objective possibility still remain out of play, and with regard to the function of this domain for the understanding of the ideal essence of all language as such, one could designate this founding domain of pure logic as *pure-logical grammar*.

M. PURE–LOGICAL GRAMMAR AND ITS PHILOSOPHIC SIGNIFICANCE

In the first edition Husserl spoke of "pure grammar," a name which was conceived as an analogue of Kant's "pure natural science." But inasmuch as the pure form-theory of meanings does not comprise the entire grammatical *a priori* — e.g., a peculiar *a priori* belongs to the grammatically so influential relationships of the mutual understanding of psychical subjects — the expression *pure-logical grammar* is to be preferred.

Nothing has harmed the discussion of the question of the correct relationship between logic and grammar as much as the continual confusion of the two logical spheres, which have been distinguished as the lower and upper, and have been characterized through their negative counterparts — the spheres of nonsense and of formal absurdity. Logic, in the sense of the upper sphere dealing with formal truth or objectivity, is certainly a matter of indifference for grammar. But not so logic in general. If one wanted, however, to discredit the lower sphere because of its supposed narrowness and obviousness, as well as of its *practical* uselessness, then one could answer that it would ill become the philosopher, the one who is called to represent the interests of pure theory, to be determined by the question of practical utility. He ought to know that precisely back of the "obvious" the most difficult questions are concealed, and this so much so that one could paradoxically, but not at all without deeper meaning, characterize philosophy as the science of trivialities. What appears trivial here becomes a source of deepseated problems. The previous logic, including that of Bolzano, did not even come to a scientific formulation of these problems, or to a conception of the idea of a pure-logical form-theory. In this way logic lacks a first foundation, it lacks a scientifically rigorous and phenomenologically clarified distinction of the primitive elements and structures of meaning, and the knowledge of the pertinent laws of essence. Thus it can also be explained why the many theories of "concepts" and of "judgment," which reach into this domain in an essential aspect, have had so few tenable results. This is due to a large extent to the lack of correct points of view and goals, to the confusion of problem-strata that should be separated radically, and to the presence of psychologism.

CHAPTER XII

INTENTIONAL EXPERIENCES AND THEIR "CONTENTS"

THE PHENOMENOLOGICAL mode of investigation first comes to complete expression in the last two of the *Logical Investigations*, which abound in subjective-descriptive analyses, and also in painstaking terminological distinctions. In the fifth investigation, "Concerning Intentional Experiences and their 'Contents,'" [1] the subjective sources of logical structures are examined, and a contribution is made to the theory of judgment. This is undertaken on the basis of a general discussion of the nature of conscious experience.

In the second investigation, Husserl had made clear the meaning of the ideality of species in general, and had pointed out the sense in which the ideality of meanings comes in question for pure logic. Just as is the case for all ideal unities, corresponding to the meanings are real possibilities and perhaps actualities. The acts of meaning correspond to the meanings construed *in specie*, and the latter are nothing but ideally conceived factors of the former. The question now arises regarding the origin of the concept of meaning and its essential varieties, which requires an examination of the psychical experiences involved. Furthermore, the meanings are supposed to lie in meaning-intentions which can enter into relationship with intuition. Husserl had spoken frequently of the *fulfillment* of the meaning-intention through corresponding intuition, and also of the highest form of this fulfillment as being given in evidence. This phenomenological relationship must be described and its role determined, i.e., the cognitive concepts grounding in it must be clarified.

The present investigation does not undertake these tasks, for a much more general phenomenological investigation is needed first of all. "Acts" are supposed to be the experiences of meaning, and the element of meaning in each single act is supposed to lie in the act-experience, in that which makes it to be an "intentional" experience that is "directed" upon ob-

[1] Far-reaching changes were introduced in the fifth investigation in the second edition. It was not possible to achieve greater clarity without changing the form and content of the investigation. The much quoted but unclear seventh section, "On the Mutual Delimitation of Psychology and Natural Science," which was unnecessary in this context, was eliminated. Husserl states that he was perhaps too conservative in retaining the entirely unsuitable expression "nominal idea," in keeping with his general hesitancy in changing the terminology of the work.

jects. Similarly the essence of the fulfilling intuition lies in certain acts: thinking and intuition are supposed to be different as acts. Nothing is more disputed in descriptive psychology than the notion of "acts." It is therefore an important preliminary condition for the solution of the problems indicated that the concept of an act (in the sense of an intentional experience) be clarified.

The investigation of the phenomenological essence of acts as such requires the clarification of the distinction between act-character and act-content, and the examination of the various meanings of the "content" of an act. The discussion of the essence of acts also requires the consideration of the phenomenology of "presentations." Husserl refers to the well-known thesis, that every act is either a presentation or has a presentation as its basis; and he points out that it is necessary to determine which of the very different concepts of presentation is to be used.

The treatment of these problems is connected with the descriptive-psychological distinction of several concepts of consciousness. Psychical acts are often characterized as "activities of consciousness," as "relations of consciousness to a content (object)," and sometimes "consciousness" is even defined as a comprehensive expression for psychical acts of every kind.

A. CONCERNING THE NATURE OF CONSCIOUSNESS

Husserl discusses three concepts of consciousness which come in question for his interests: (1) consciousness as the total immanent (*reelle*) phenomenological existence (*Bestand*) of the empirical ego, as an interweaving of psychical experiences in the unity of the stream of experience; (2) consciousness as an inner becoming aware of one's own psychical experiences; (3) consciousness as a comprehensive designation for all kinds of "psychical acts" or "intentional experiences." This list is not intended to be exhaustive.

1. Consciousness as the Immanent Phenomenological Unity of Ego-Experiences

Consider first the concept of consciousness as the immanent phenomenological unity of ego-experiences. If psychology is defined as the science of the conscious experiences of experiencing individuals, or as the science of their contents of consciousness, then a certain concept of consciousness, and certain concepts of experience (*Erlebnis*) and content are determined therewith. By "experience" and "content" the modern psychologist means the real occurrences (or events, as Wundt puts it), which, changing from moment to moment, make up the immanent unity of consciousness of a psychical individual. In this sense, perceptions, phantasy-presentations, acts of conceptual thinking, joys and pains, hopes and fears, and the like, as soon as they occur in our consciousness, are said to be experiences or contents of consciousness. The parts and abstract factors composing these experiences are also experienced; they are immanent contents of consciousness.

Husserl points out that this concept of an experience can be conceived purely phenomenologically, i.e., such that all relation to empirical-real existence (to the men or animals of nature) is eliminated: an experience in the descriptive-psychological sense (in the empirical-phenomenological sense) then becomes an experience in the sense of pure phenomenology. The required elimination is at all times a matter of our freedom, and the "descriptive-psychological" findings which are first of all obtained are to be taken "purely," and then are to be understood as pure essential insights (as *a priori*).

For example, in the case of an outer perception the sensory factor of color is just as much an "experienced" or "known content," as the character of the perceiving and as the complete perceptual appearance of the colored object. On the other hand, this object itself, although it is perceived, is not experienced or known; and the same holds for the color perceived in it. If the object does not exist, and if the perception is therefore to be critically judged as a deception, hallucination, illusion, etc., then the perceived, seen color of the object also does not exist. These distinctions between normal and abnormal, correct and deceptive perception, do not concern the inner, purely descriptive or phenomenological character of perception. Whereas the seen color, i.e., the color posited in the visual perception as existing in the appearing object, certainly does not exist as an experience, there is something *corresponding* to it in this experience, i.e., in the perceptual appearance. The color-sensation corresponds to it, the qualitatively determinate phenomenological color-factor, which undergoes an objectivating "apprehension" in the perception.

Color-sensation and objective color of the object are often confused. In Husserl's time, a view was very much favored according to which the two were regarded as being the same, only regarded from different "points of view and interests": psychologically or subjectively regarded, it is called sensation; physically or objectively regarded, a property of the external thing. It is sufficient to refer here to the distinction between the red of a sphere which is seen as objectively uniform, and the perceptually indubitable and even necessary "adumbration" of the subjective color-sensations

—a distinction which is repeated in relation to all kinds of objective properties and the sensation-complexes corresponding to them.

What has been said of single determinations may be applied to concrete wholes. Hence the view in question, according to which the same appearance occurs on the one hand in a subjective context (in the context of the appearances related to the ego) and again in an objective context (in the context of the things themselves), is false phenomenologically. The equivocation which permits the term "experience" to denote not only that in which the appearing of the object consists (e.g., the concrete perceptual experience, in which the object itself it supposedly presented to us), but also *the appearing object as such*, cannot be emphasized sharply enough. The thing-appearance (the experience) is not the appearing thing (that "which stands opposite" to us, supposedly bodily). As belonging to the context of consciousness, we experience the appearances; as belonging to the phenomenal world, the things appear to us. The appearances themselves do not appear; they are experienced.

If we appear to ourselves as members of the phenomenal world,[2] then the physical and psychical things (bodies and persons) appear in physical and psychical relations to our phenomenal ego. This relation of the phenomenal object (which is also called "content of consciousness" by many) to the phenomenal subject (I as an empirical person, as a thing) must be distinguished from the relation of a content of consciousness, in Husserl's sense of an experience, to consciousness in the sense of the unity of the contents of consciousness (the phenomenological existence of the empirical ego). There what is in question is the relationship of the appearing things; here it is the relationship of a single experience to the experience-complex. Similarly, the relation of the appearing person "I" to the externally appearing thing must be distinguished from the relation between a thing-appearance as an experience and the appearing thing. If we examine the latter relation, we see that the predicates of the appearance are not at the same time the predicates of that which appears in it. Another relation to be noted is the *objectivating* relation which we ascribe to the sensation-complex experienced in the appearance, to the appearing object. That occurs when the sensation-complex is "apprehended" or "apperceived" in a certain manner: due to the animating apprehension of the sensations the so-called appearing of the object (or appearance in the phenomenological sense of an experience already referred to) is made possible.

That which immanently composes perception must clearly be distin-

[2] That which appears as such is in question here, whereas all questions concerning the existence or non-existence of that which appears — including the empirical ego appearing

guished from that which is "in it" in a figurative (the "intentional") sense. Such essential distinctions must be made in the case of other "acts" as well.

Husserl's concept of an experience does not agree with the popular one, whereby the distinction which he draws between the immanent and the intentional content plays a role. The experiencing consciousness, in the phenomenological sense, does not have such occurrences as events of the war of 1870 in itself as its "psychical experiences," as its immanent constituent parts or contents. What it finds in itself as immanently present are the acts of perceiving, judging, etc., that are involved, with their changing sensory material, their content of apprehension, their positing-characters, etc. To experience outer occurrences means: to have certain acts of perception directed upon them, etc. In the phenomenological sense it means that certain contents are constituent parts of a unity of consciousness, in the phenomenologically unified stream of consciousness of an empirical ego. This itself is an immanent whole that is immanently composed of diverse parts, and every such part is said to be "experienced." There is no difference between the experienced or known content and the experience itself. That which is sensed, e.g., is nothing other than the sensation. But if an experience "refers" to an object that is distinct from it, as, e.g., an external perception to the perceived object, a nominal presentation to the named object, and the like, then this object is not experienced or known in the present sense, but is just perceived, named, etc.

This situation justifies the use of the term "content." This term refers generally to a whole, to a comprehensive unity comprising a totality of parts as its content. In the usual descriptive-psychological talk of contents the concealed point of reference, i.e., the corresponding whole, is the immanent unity of consciousness. Its content is the collective totality of present "experiences," and the term "contents" then refers to these experiences themselves, i.e., all that which immanently makes up the actual phenomenological stream of consciousness.

Although Husserl later stated that he no longer approved his opposition to the doctrine of the "pure" ego,[3] it will be of interest to include it here.

---

in it — are eliminated. That must be done if the procedure is to be purely phenomenological, and not descriptive-psychological. Every psychological analysis admits of that "purification."

[3] Cp. *Ideen*, § 57, p. 109; § 80, p. 159. In a note added to the second edition of the *Log. Unt.*, he states that his earlier position on the question of the pure ego is irrelevant for the investigations of this volume. The passages in question were retained in an abbreviated form because of Natorp's polemical discussion of it in his *Allgemeine Psychologie*, vol. 1 (1913). Although this question is important phenomenologically, he points out that much can be done in phenomenology on intentional experiences, etc., without taking a stand on the question of the ego. — For a recent discussion, cf. A. Gurwitsch, "A Non-Egological Conception of Consciousness," *Phil. and Phen. Research*, vol. 1, pp. 325–338; and also A.

His point was that the phenomenologically reduced ego, or the purely psychical ego restricted to its phenomenological content, is nothing peculiar that hovers over the various experiences, but is simply identical with its own unity of connection. The forms of connection which are based upon the nature of the contents and their laws finally constitute a totality of content which is nothing other than the phenomenologically "reduced" ego itself. The contents have their lawfully determined manner of going together to blend into more comprehensive unities, and in thus becoming unified, the phenomenological ego or the unity of consciousness is constituted, without needing an ego-principle bearing all contents and uniting them once more. Husserl concluded (at this time) that here, as elsewhere, the contribution of such a principle would be incomprehensible.

2. "Inner" Consciousness as Inner Perception

The preceding discussion has made clear the sense in which the terms consciousness, experience, and content are to be understood in the present context, unless other concepts are explicitly indicated. It is a descriptive-psychological sense; and with appropriate "purification" it is phenomenological.

A second concept of consciousness is indicated by the expression *inner consciousness*. This is the "inner perception" which is supposed to accompany experiences that are actually present and to refer to them as their objects. Inner perception is said to be *adequate* if it does not attribute anything to its objects which is not intuitively presented in the perceptual experience itself and immanently given. Now every perception is characterized by the intention to grasp its object as something present "bodily." A perception is adequate if the object is really present in it, and is grasped completely just as it is. It follows, therefore, from the very essence of perception, that only "inner" perception can be adequate. One cannot say, however, that every perception directed upon one's own experiences must be adequate. Husserl suggests the desirability of a terminological distinction between inner perception (as the perception of one's own experiences) and adequate (evident) perception. The false epistemological opposition between inner and outer perception would then disappear, as distinguished from the genuine opposition between *adequate* and *non-adequate* perception, based upon the pure phenomenological essence of such experiences.

Schuetz, "Scheler's Theory of Intersubjectivity and the General Thesis of the Alter Ego," same journal, vol. ii, pp. 323-347.

In Husserl's view, the second and narrower concept of consciousness is "more original" than the first, and is "first in itself."

3. Acts or Intentional Experiences

The third concept of consciousness, which embraces acts or intentional experiences, will be analyzed in the next section. If one does not recognize — what is for Husserl the most certain of all things — that being-an-object, phenomenologically expressed, lies in certain acts in which something appears as an object or is thought, then he will not be able to understand how the being-an-object can itself become objective. For Husserl the matter appears to be clear: Acts are "directed" upon the peculiarity of acts in which something appears; or acts are directed upon the empirical ego and upon its reference to an object. The phenomenological core of the ego (of the empirical ego) is formed by acts which "bring to consciousness" objects for it; "in them" the ego is "directed" upon the object concerned.

The self-perception of the empirical ego is an everyday matter which presents no difficulties to the understanding, for the ego is perceived just as well as any external thing. That the object is not perceived completely does not matter in either case, for it is essential to perceiving to be a supposed grasping of the object, and not an adequate intuition.

The analysis of the third concept of consciousness requires a more detailed discussion, which will now be presented.

B. CONSCIOUSNESS AS INTENTIONAL EXPERIENCE

1. Acts as "Intentional" Experiences

As already pointed out, according to Brentano every psychical phenomenon is characterized by what the medieval Scholastics called the intentional (or also mental) "inexistence" of an object. This is called by Brentano the reference to a content, the direction upon an object (whereby something real is not to be understood here) or immanent objectivity. Every psychical phenomenon is supposed to contain something in itself as an object, although not in the same manner in all cases. Thus the "mode of relation of consciousness to a content" is different in presentation and judgment; and Brentano's classification of psychical phenomena into presentations, judgments, and feelings ("phenomena of love and hate") is based upon this mode of designation.

What is in question here is not the adequacy of Brentano's classification. Only one thing is held up as important by Husserl — that there are essential, specific differences of intentional relation, which make up the descriptive generic character of the "act." The way in which a "mere presentation" of a fact means the latter as its "object" is different from the way in which the fact is held to be true or false by a judgment. Also distinct as types of experience are supposition or doubt, hope or fear, pleasing or displeasing. Most, if not all, acts are complex experiences, and very often the intentions themselves are complex. Affective intentions are built up upon presentation- or judgment-intentions, and the like. But in the analysis of those complexes we always come to primitive intentional characters, which, with respect to their descriptive essence, cannot be reduced to other kinds of psychical experiences. It is also certain, in Husserl's view, that the unity of the descriptive genus "intention" ("act-character") displays specific differences which are grounded in the pure essence of this genus, and consequently precede the empirical, psychological matters of fact as something *a priori*. There are essentially different species and sub-species of intention. Thus, aesthetic approval or disapproval is a mode of intentional relation which is irreducibly and essentially distinct from a mere presentation or a theoretical judgment about the aesthetic object. To be sure, the aesthetic approval and the aesthetic predicate can be stated, and the statement is a judgment which as such includes presentations. But then the aesthetic intention, as well as its object, is the *object* of presentations and judgments, whereas it itself remains essentially different from these theoretical acts. To evaluate a judgment as valid, an affective experience as lofty, etc., presupposes analogous and related, but not specifically identical intentions. The situation is similar in the comparison of judgment-decisions and will-decisions, etc.

The intentional relation, understood purely descriptively as an inner peculiarity of certain experiences, is regarded by Husserl as an essential determination of "psychical phenomena" or "acts."[4] As he expresses it phenomenologically: The ideation performed on single cases of such experiences — and so performed that every empirical-psychological conception and positing of existence is avoided and only the immanent phenomenological content of these experiences comes into consideration — gives us the purely phenomenological generic idea *intentional experience* or *act*, and also its pure species.[5] That not all experiences are intentional is shown by sensations and sensation-complexes.

[4] For Husserl there are no controversial questions, such as whether all psychical phenomena, e.g., the phenomena of feeling, really have the designated peculiarity. Instead, one ought to ask whether the phenomena in question are "psychical phenomena."

[5] If we remain within the framework of psychological apperception, then the phenomenologically pure concept of an experience is modified to become the concept of the *psychical condition* of an animal being (whether of a factual nature, or of an ideally possible one with an ideally possible "animal" essence — hence in the latter case with the exclusion of any

The following discussion will make more clear the essential difference between the two uses of the term "contents." All phenomenological findings sought here are to be understood as determinations of essence.

2. Prevention of Terminological Misinterpretations

a. The "mental" or "immanent" object

Husserl rejects Brentano's terminology, while retaining his essential analysis. For Brentano, every intentional experience is a phenomenon; and, for him, the term "phenomenon" denotes an appearing object as such. But Husserl prefers not to speak of psychical phenomena or of phenomena at all in this connection.

In Husserl's view, it is very doubtful, and often misleading, to say that the perceived, phantasied, wished, etc., objects "enter into consciousness," or that "consciousness" (or "the ego") "enters into relationship" with them in this or that way, etc.; and it is also questionable to say that the intentional experiences "contain something in themselves as an object," and the like (reference to Brentano is made here). Such expressions may incur two misinterpretations: (1) that there is a real relation between consciousness or the ego and the "known" thing; (2) that there is a relationship between two things found as immanent in consciousness — act and intentional object — or that one psychical content is included in another.

Consider the second misinterpretation. The expression *immanent objectivity* is used to denote the essential peculiarity of intentional experiences, and so are the synonymous Scholastic expressions *intentional* or *mental inexistence* of an object. An object is "meant" in an intentional experience; it is "aimed at," in an experience of presentation or judgment, etc. It is essential to such experiences that there be a "reference to an object," that an object be "intentionally present." Such an intentional experience may occur without the object existing (in fact, it may be impossible that the object exist). In that case, meaning the object is an experience; but the object is merely meant, and is really nothing.

If I present the God Jupiter, then this God is a presented object, it is "immanently present" in my act. Of course the descriptive analysis of this intentional experience will not disclose the God Jupiter as being in it. Hence the "immanent," "mental" object does not belong to the descriptive, immanent nature of the experience, and is not at all immanent or mental.

---

positing of existence). The purely phenomenological, generic idea of intentional experience is furthermore modified to be the parallel and closely related *psychological*, generic idea. Depending upon the exclusion or inclusion of the psychological apperception, the same analysis takes on either purely phenomenological or psychological significance.

But it is also not *extra mentem*, so that it really *is* not at all. That does not, however, prevent the presenting-the-God-Jupiter from being real. If, on the other hand, the intended object does exist, then nothing needs to be changed phenomenologically. For consciousness the given is essentially the same, whether the presented object exists, or whether it is imaginary and even absurd. *Jupiter* and *Bismarck* are presented in the same manner, and the same is true of the *Babylonian Tower* and the *Cologne Cathedral*.[6]

If the so-called "immanent contents" are merely intentional (intended), then the truly immanent contents which belong to intentional experiences themselves are not intentional: they build up the act and make possible the intention, but they are not themselves intended; they are not the objects which are presented in the act. I do not see color-sensations, but colored things; I do not hear tone-sensations, but the song of the singer, etc.

What holds for presentations also holds for the other intentional experiences built upon them. To judge *about* the *Berlin Palace*, to enjoy its architectural beauty, or to cherish the *wish* to do so, and the like, are new experiences, characterized phenomenologically in a new manner.

In view of what has been pointed out, it will be well to avoid speaking of "immanent objects" and to us the expression *intentional object*, which is not open to similar objections.

The expression that an object is "known in consciousness" or is "immanent in consciousness," is also equivocal, for "consciousness" here means something entirely different from what it did in the foregoing analysis. Because the first concept of consciousness showed a tendency to penetrate into psychology, Husserl decided to prefer this concept, construed phenomenologically. When he speaks of "consciousness" in the sense of inner perception, or in the sense of an intentional relation, such expressions are used with caution, in keeping with his carefully defined concepts.

b. *The act and the relation of consciousness or of the ego to the object*

According to the first mentioned misinterpretation, consciousness (or "the ego") on the one hand, and the known thing on the other hand, enter into relationship to one another in a real sense. In Husserl's view, the proposition "The ego presents an object, or the ego has an object as an intentional object of its presentation" means the same as the proposition "In the phenomenological ego, in this concrete complex of experiences, a certain experience named according to its specific peculiarity 'presenta-

---

[6] Husserl suggests that one again convince himself that the presupposition of a natural reality with people and other living animals can be eliminated here, so that these considerations may be understood as concerned with *ideal* possibilities. All elements of transcendent

tion of the object referred to,' is immanently present." Similarly the proposition "The ego judges about the object" means "An experience of judgment determined in a certain way is present in it," etc. In the *description*,
the relation to the experiencing ego is not to be avoided; but the actual
experience itself does not consist of a complex which contains the ego-
presentation as a partial experience.

c. Choice of terminology

Husserl chooses his own terminology in such a way that disputable presuppositions and ambiguities are excluded as much as possible. The expression "psychical phenomenon" is therefore avoided, and wherever
exactness is required, he speaks of *intentional experiences*. "Experience"
is to be taken in the above phenomenological sense. The term "intentional" names the peculiarity of *intention*, the reference to something
objective. As a briefer expression the word *act* is used.

These expressions are to be sure not without objections, because of other
prevalent meanings of the term "intention," for example. As this term
is understood here, the image of "aiming at" is made use of, which is
applicable to acts of theoretical and practical aiming. This image, however, does not apply equally well to all acts, so that Husserl is led to distinguish a narrower and a wider concept of intention. Corresponding to
the activity of aiming at (*Abzielen*), as a correlate, is the activity of
obtaining (*Erzielen*). Similarly, corresponding to certain acts called "intentions" (e.g., intentions of judgment, or of desire), are other acts called
"attainments" or "fulfillments." The fulfillments are also acts, and hence
are also "intentions," although, in general, they are not intentions in the
narrower sense of reference to a corresponding fulfillment. Once recognized, the equivocation is not dangerous. Where the narrower concept
is in question, that must be stated explicitly. For the rest, the parallel
expression *act-character* helps to avoid possible misunderstandings.

The term "act" is not to be understood in the original sense of *actus*;
the idea of activity must be excluded. Like Natorp, Husserl also rejects
the "mythology of activities"; he defines "acts," not as psychical activities,
but as intentional experiences.[7]

---

apperception and positing are separated out, in order to establish what belongs to the experience
itself, to its immanent, essential nature.

[7] Thus Husserl, like Russell (*Analysis of Mind*), rejects "acts" in the outmoded traditional
sense, while retaining the term, in the present sense of intentional experience, in order to do
justice to the descriptive nature of experience.

3. Acts as a Descriptively Founded Class of Experiences

In view of the objections raised by such investigators as Natorp, Husserl proceeds to examine more carefully the notion of an "act." He agrees with Natorp in saying of the heard tone: "Its existence for me, that is my consciousness of it. . . ." But, Husserl states, the "existence of a content for me" is a matter requiring a further phenomenological analysis. In the first place, the content may be "there" for me in different ways. Thus I may note it as something merely implied, without special selection, in a whole; or, again, as selected. Furthermore, I may note it by the way, or deliberately hold it in view. More important here is the distinction between the existence of a content in the sense of a *sensation* of which we are conscious but which has not itself become a perceptual object, and of a content in the sense of a *perceptual object*. The distinction is somewhat concealed in the example of a tone. In ordinary speech "I hear" does not mean experiencing a sensation, but "I perceive" — I hear the *Adagio of the violinist*, the *twittering of the birds*, etc. Different acts can perceive the same thing and still sense something entirely different. We hear the same tone spatially near, and again far away. The converse holds similarly: we "apprehend" the same sense-contents in different ways at different times. On the basis of the same experienced contents of consciousness (sensation-contents), different objects may be perceived. The apprehension itself can never be reduced to a conflux of new sensations; it is an act-character, a "mode of consciousness." The experiencing of the sensations in this mode of consciousness is called the perception of the object. Not only does this hold from the natural scientific-psychological point of view within the framework of natural existence; but this may be viewed in its pure phenomenological nature with the elimination of everything empirically real. If we view the pure experiences and their essential content, then we apprehend ideationally the pure species of sensation, apprehension, or perception with regard to what is perceived, as well as the essential relationships belonging thereto. We then have the essential insight that the being of the sensed content is entirely different from the being of the perceived object, which is presented through the content but is not immanently known.

An example in the sphere of visual perception will make this clearer. I see a thing, e.g., this box; I do not see my sensations. I continually see this *one and the same* box, no matter how it may be turned. I continually have *the same* "content of consciousness" — if the perceived *object* is called a content of consciousness. With every turn I have a new "content of consciousness," (meaning by this expression, more appropriately, the *experienced contents*). Hence very different contents are experienced, and still the same object is perceived. Therefore, generally speaking, the experienced content itself is not the perceived object. It is to be noted therewith that the real being or non-being of the object is irrelevant to the essence of the perceptual experience, and consequently to its being a perception of the thus and thus appearing object, or of the meant object. Our belief that we grasp one and the same object perceptually, in the change of the experienced contents, is again something belonging to the domain of experience. We experience the "consciousness of identity," i.e., this supposition that identity is grasped.[8] Husserl now asks, what is at the basis of this consciousness? His answer is that the different sensation-contents that are given are apprehended, apperceived in "the same sense," and that the apprehension is an experience-character which first makes up the "existence of the object for me." Furthermore, the consciousness of identity occurs on the basis of these experience-characters, as the immediate consciousness of their both *meaning the same*. This consciousness is an *act* as here defined, and its objective correlate lies in the denoted identity. In Husserl's view nothing is more evident than the distinction between contents and acts, and more particularly between perceptual contents in the sense of representing sensations and acts of perception in the sense of the apprehending intention, which has still other characters. This intention, in unity with the apprehended sensation, makes up the full, concrete *act* of perception.

The intentional characters as well as the complete acts are contents of consciousness, in the widest descriptive sense of experiences, inasmuch as all differences which we can ascertain are *eo ipso* differences of content. But within this widest sphere of that which can be experienced, the distinction is drawn between intentional experiences in which *objective intentions* are constituted through *immanent characters* of the actual experience, and those for which that is not the case, hence contents which can function as building-stones of acts but are *not themselves acts*.[9]

The modern theory of apperception had failed to do justice to the *phenomenological* fact; it did not enter into its analysis and description. But the differences of apprehension are above all descriptive differences.

[8] Cf. Aron Gurwitsch, "On the Intentionality of Consciousness," in *Philosophical Essays in Memory of Edmund Husserl*.

[9] Husserl refers here to his "Psychological Studies" for illustrations. All logical distinctions and especially all distinctions of categorial form are found to be constituted in logical acts in the sense of intentions.

Only such data concern the epistemologist, and not any hidden and hypothetically assumed occurrences in the unconscious depths of the mind or
in the sphere of physiological happening. The critique of knowledge
requires a purely phenomenological view which eliminates all transcendent
positings and operates exclusively with such descriptive data. Apperception is for Husserl the surplus which exists in the experience itself, in its
descriptive content as distinguished from the "raw" existence of the sensation; it is the act-character which as it were animates the sensation and
makes it possible for us to perceive this or that *objectivity*, e.g., see this
tree, hear that ringing, smell the perfume of flowers, etc. The sensations
and also the acts "apprehending" or "apperceiving" them are *experienced*
therewith, but they do not appear objectively; *they* are not seen, heard, or
perceived with any "sense." The *objects*, on the other hand, appear, and
are perceived; but they are not experienced. Obviously the case of adequate
perception is excluded herewith.

That which is called a presentation (a perceiving, remembering, imagining, copying, denoting *intention* toward it) in relation to the intentional
object, is called an apprehension, interpretation, or apperception in relation to the sensations immanently belonging to the act.

It appears to be evident that there are essentially different "kinds of
consciousness," namely, of the intentional relation to something objective.
The character of intention is specifically different in the case of perception,
of sheerly "reproductive" representation, of image-representation in the
usual sense of the apprehension of statues, pictures, etc., and again in the
case of the presentation of signs and of presentation in the sense of pure
logic. Corresponding to every logically distinguished manner of mentally
presenting an object is a difference in the intention. Husserl holds it to
be indisputable that we only know of all these differences because we
intuit them in a single case (i.e., adequately grasp them immediately),
bring them under concepts by comparison, and thus in various acts make
them to be objects of intuition and thought. By means of ideating abstraction we can at all times adequately grasp the pure species and the accompanying specific, essential connections. In holding that the consciousness
of a simple sensation is not distinguished in kind, as consciousness, from
the consciousness of a world, Natorp had failed to hold apart the different
concepts of consciousness and content, and had even elevated their identification to an epistemological principle. The "content" is the experience
immanently constituting the consciousness; and the consciousness itself is
the complex of the experiences. But the world is by no means the experience of the thinker. The experience is the meaning-the-world; the world

itself is the intended object. This distinction is not affected by meta-physical considerations as to the nature of objective being and its rela-tionship to the subjective process of thought, etc. It is an epistemological distinction which precedes metaphysics, and hence presupposes no answers to questions which epistemology must answer first of all.

4. The Question of Intentional Feelings

In Husserl's opinion many experiences, which are generally designated feelings, really have an intentional relation to something objective. That is the case, e.g., with being pleased by a melody, with being displeased by a shrill whistle, etc. The opponents of the intentionality of feelings regard feelings as mere conditions; and where they relate to objects, they are held to owe this relation to an added presentational element.

Brentano, who defended the intentionality of feelings, held that feel-ings, like all acts which are not mere presentations, have presentations as a basis. The phenomenological view of the situation appears to support Brentano's position. A case of being pleased without something pleasing is not thinkable. The specific essence of the being pleased requires a rela-tionship to something pleasing. Similarly, there is no desire without that which is desired, etc. These are all intentions, genuine acts in Husserl's sense. They all "owe" their intentional relation to certain presentations underlying them.

The intentional relation should not be construed as a causal relation, i.e., as an empirical, substantial-causal context of necessity. The intentional object comes in question only as intentional, and not as something actually existent outside of me and determining my mental life psychophysically. A combat of centaurs which I present to myself in phantasy "stimulates" my pleasure just as does a beautiful, real landscape.

The question whether there are non-intentional feelings is answered by Husserl in the affirmative to begin with. The sensuous feelings, such as sensuous pain when we burn ourselves, may not be placed on the same level with a conviction, or a volition, etc., but are classified with roughness, red, etc. Sensations are not acts, but enter into the constitution of acts. A burning, stinging pain, e.g., appears to function like other sensations, as a support for an empirical, objective apprehension. In his discussion of the intentionality of feelings, Brentano had distinguished between *sen-sations* of pain and pleasure (sensations of feeling), and pain and pleasure in the sense of *feelings*. The contents of the former (or, as Husserl pro-poses, the former, for he identifies the sensation of pain and the "content" of the pain sensation) are for Brentano "physical" and the latter are "psychical phenomena," so that they belong to essentially different genera. Expressing agreement with this view, Husserl also holds that there is no community of genus between intentional and non-intentional drives or desires.

5. Distinction between Descriptive and Intentional Content

Husserl now introduces the important phenomenological distinction between the *immanent* content of an act and its *intentional* content.[10] By the immanent phenomenological content of an act is meant the totality of its parts, whether concrete or abstract; in other words, the totality of the partial experiences building it up immanently.

As already made clear, in changing from the psychological-experiential-scientific attitude to the phenomenological-ideal-scientific attitude, all experiential-scientific apperceptions and positings of existence are eliminated. General "ideative" essences and essential connections are read out of the experiences — ideal experience-species of various stages of generality and ideally valid, essential cognitions which hold *a priori* for ideally possible experiences of the species in question. In this way the insights of pure phenomenology are obtained.

By content in an immanent sense is meant the simple application of the most general concept of content, which holds for all domains, to the intentional experiences. The expression "intentional content"[11] refers to the peculiarity of intentional experiences (or acts) as such. Three concepts of an intentional content are to be distinguished: the *intentional object* of the act, its *intentional matter* (as distinguished from its *intentional quality*), and finally its *intentional essence*. These distinctions are presented in a series of general analyses, which are necessary for an essential clarification of knowledge.

[10] In the first edition this reads "real *or phenomenological* content." In fact, the word "phenomenological," as also the word "descriptive," was used in the first edition exclusively with regard to immanent constituents of experience, and in the revised edition also it was used mainly in this sense until now. That corresponds to the natural departure from the psychological attitude. It will become increasingly clear that the description of the intentional objectivity as such (taken as it is known in the concrete act-experience itself) represents a different direction of purely intuitive descriptions than those of the immanent act-constituents, and that it too must be designated as phenomenological. It is important consciously to separate the descriptive levels. The reader is referred to the discussion of *Noesis* and *Noema* in the *Ideen*.

[11] "Real" ("Real," instead of "reell") would sound much better in connection with "intentional," but it suggests the thought of thing-transcendence, which should be eliminated through the "reduction" to immanent (*reelle*) experience. Husserl suggests that a relationship to things be associated with the word "real."

6. *Intentional Content in the Sense of Intentional Object*

Consider first the concept of the intentional object. Suppose, e.g., that we present a house, say this house. As has been shown, the intentional object differs entirely from the immanent content of the act in question. This holds not only for acts which relate to "outer" things, but in part also for acts which relate intentionally to their own present experiences which belong to the background of consciousness. There is a partial coincidence only in those cases in which the intention is concerned with something that is experienced in the intentional act itself, as in acts of adequate perception.

The object, just as it is intended, must be distinguished from *the object which is intended.* In every act an object is "presented" as determined in a certain way, and as such it may be the goal of changing intentions, of judging, feeling, desiring, etc. Objective properties may be attributed to the same object by means of real or possible connections of knowledge that are not comprehended by a given intention. In all of them, the object which is intended is the same, although the intention is different in each case, and the object is meant in a different manner. Thus, e.g., the presentation *Germany's* (last) *Kaiser* presents its object as a Kaiser, and as belonging to Germany. The same person is the son of Kaiser Friedrich III, the grandson of Queen Victoria, and has other properties not named or presented here. Accordingly one could speak of an intentional and an extra-intentional content of the object of a presentation.

In this context there is another and more important distinction, namely, between the *objectivity* upon which an act, taken completely, is directed, and the *objects* upon which the various partial acts are directed, which build up the same act. Every act, whether simple or compound, relates intentionally to an objectivity belonging to it. No matter how an act may be compounded out of partial acts, it is one act; it has its correlate in one objectivity, to which it is related in a *primary* sense. The partial acts also relate to objects which are in general not identical with the object of the entire act. That the whole act relates to these objects is true only in a *secondary* sense; its intention can only refer to them in so far as it (the act) is constructed out of acts which primarily intend them. They are its objects only in so far as they help to constitute its actual object in the manner in which it is intended. They function as points of reference of relations, by means of which the primary object is presented as a correlative point of reference. For example, the act that corresponds to the name *the knife on the table* is compounded. The object of the entire act is a knife; the table is the object of a partial act. But inasmuch as the entire act means the knife as being on the table, one can also say in a secondary sense, that the table is an intentional object of the total act. In the proposition *The knife lies on the table*, the knife is again the object, "about" which a statement is made; but it is not the primary or complete object of the judgment. Corresponding to the entire judgment as a complete object is the judged *fact*, which is identically the same and can be presented in a mere presentation, wished in a wish, questioned in a question, doubted in a doubt, etc. The wish, *The knife ought to be on the table*, does indeed refer to the knife, but in it I do not wish the knife; I wish that the knife lie on the table, that this be the state of affairs (*dass sich die Sache so verhalte*). This fact (*Sachverhalt*) should not be confused with the judgment in question or with the presentation of the judgment; I do not wish the judgment or any presentation.

7. Simple and Compound, Founding and Founded Acts

The object of a total act could not appear as such, if the partial acts did not present their objects in their way: they must have the function to present parts of the object, or relational terms external to it, or relational forms, and the like.

The unity of a categorical judgment can serve as an example. The subject-term of a categorical statement is a basic act of subject-positing, upon which the predicate-positing, the affirmation or denial, is built. But the total experience is one act; it is one judgment, with one total objectivity (the "fact"). Just as the judgment is the unity pervading the subject- and predicate-acts, and is not something between or beside them, so the judged fact is the objective unity which appears here, and is built up out of the subject and predicate.

The situation can also be more complicated, as in the case of joy in determining a fact, which is therefore joy about the fact. The judgment is the founding act for the joy; it determines its content, and realizes its abstract possibility, for without such founding joy cannot be at all. Again, judgments can found presumptions, or doubts, questions, wishes, acts of will, etc.; and the same holds conversely, for acts of the latter kind can serve as foundations.

8. The Function of Attention in Complex Acts

The whole which comprises expression and meaning will serve as an example. Expression and meaning are two objective unities which are represented for us in certain acts. As seen in the first investigation, an expression in itself is a physical object, and is "given" just like any other physical object; there is an experience in which certain sensory experiences are "apperceived." The acts here in question are presentations of perception or of phantasy, and the expression in a physical sense is constituted in them.

The acts involved are what make the expression to be an expression. These acts are one with it, and by the term expression is really meant the act-unity presenting it. Thus in the case of a statement there is a unified judgment-experience. There is one act of experience and not a sum of acts, and we so to speak distinguish a bodily and a mental side of the act. The analysis shows that there is an intentional connection between word and thing, because when a word names a thing, it appears as united with it in a certain way, as belonging to it, only of course not as a material part or as a material determination. Hence material unrelatedness does not exclude a certain intentional unity, which corresponds to the connection of the corresponding acts to a single act.

It has already been stated that if we express something *as such*, we do not live in the acts which constitute the expression as a physical object; we live in the meaning-endowing acts, we attend exclusively to the objectivity that appears in them, we intend or "mean" it. It has also been pointed out how a turning to the physical expression is possible, and how it changes the essential character of the experience; it ceases to be an "expression" in the normal sense of the word.

Obviously we have to do here with a case of *attention* which has not yet been sufficiently explained. It is important to recognize that attention is a distinguishing function which belongs to acts in the sense of intentional experiences, and consequently there can be no talk of its descriptive understanding so long as one confuses the being-experienced, in the sense of the sheer existence of a content in consciousness, with the intentional objectivity. Acts must be there in order that we may "live" in them, or that we may be engrossed in their performance, and in doing this (in modes of performance which must be described more closely), we attend to the *objects* of these acts, we are devoted to them incidentally or primarily, or are thematically occupied with them.

Husserl does not dispute the possibility of our attending to experienced contents. But when we do, they are objects of an "inner" perception; and perception is here not the mere existence of the content in the context of consciousness, but is an act in which the content becomes *objective* for us. Thus it is only intentional objects to which we can attend. At the basis of attention there must be an act in which that to which we are to attend becomes objective or presented, in the widest sense of the term. This presentation can be non-intuitive as well as intuitive; it can be inadequate as well as adequate.

9. The Distinction of the Quality and the Matter of an Act

In an entirely different direction from the distinction between acts in which we live, and acts which are incidental, is the very important distinction between the general character of an act which characterizes it as merely presentational, or as judgmental, feeling, desiring, etc., and its "content," which characterizes it as a presentation of *this* presented thing, as a judgment of *this* that is judged, etc. Thus, e.g., the two assertions $2 \times 2 = 4$ and *Ibsen is the main founder of modern realism in the dramatic art* are both qualified as assertions. That which they have in common is called the *quality* of the judgment. But they differ in "content," or in the *matter* of the judgment. Similar distinctions between quality and matter are made for all acts.

The term "content" in the sense of matter means a component of a concrete act-experience, which this act can have in common with acts of entirely different quality. This is seen clearly when we set up a series of identities in which the act-qualities change while the matter remains identically the same. Thus *the same* content may be the content of a mere presentation, and again the content of a judgment, question, doubt, wish, etc. He who has the presentation that there are intelligent beings on Mars presents the same thing that one does when he states that there are intelligent beings on Mars, and as one does when he asks that, etc. What is meant here by the same content? It is not sufficient to say that the intentional objectivity is the same in the various acts. For the immanent phenomenological view, the objectivity itself is nothing; it is transcendent of the act. No matter in what sense and with what right one speaks of its "being," no matter whether it is real or ideal, possible or impossible, the act is "directed upon it." The non-existent or the transcendent can function as an intentional object of an act. The referring to an object is a peculiarity belonging to the essential nature of the act-experience, and the experiences which show it are called, according to definition, intentional experiences or acts. All differences in the manner of the objective reference are descriptive differences of the intentional experiences concerned.

The quality only determines whether that which is already "made presentational" as something wished, questioned, etc., is intentionally present. Accordingly the term "matter" means that feature of the act which endows it with a relation to something objective. Not only is the objective something in general which the act means determined through the matter, but also the manner in which that is meant. Hence it embraces the characters and relations that are peculiar to the phenomenological content of the act. Like matters can never have a different objective reference, but different matters can have the same objective reference.

The act-quality is an abstract factor of an act which would be unthinkable apart from all matter. There could be no judgment-quality which is not a judgment with a determinate matter, for then the judgment would lose the character of an intentional experience. The same holds for the matter, for a matter which would be neither the matter of a presentation, nor that of a judgment, and the like, would be unthinkable.

The ambiguous use of the expression "manner of objective reference," which may refer to differences of quality and of matter, must be noted, and must be met by appropriate interpretations of the terms quality and matter.

10. The Intentional Essence and the Meaning Essence

Another distinction will now be considered, by which a new concept of the "intentional content" will be determined. Quality and matter have been distinguished as two factors in the descriptive content of every act which mutually require one another. But they make up only a part and not the complete, concrete act. In fact, two acts can be alike with respect to their quality and their matter, and nevertheless be descriptively different. Since quality and matter are the essential constituents of an act, their unity may be designated as the *intentional essence* of the act. Husserl also introduces a second term. Because meaning-endowing acts which function with expressions are here in question, he speaks of the *meaning* (*bedeutungsmässig*) *essence* of the act. Its "ideating" abstraction yields the meaning in an ideal sense.

It is generally said that an individual at different times, or divers individuals at the same or at different times, can have *the same* presentation, or remembrance, or perception, can make *the same* assertion, etc. To have the same presentation means to be sure, but is not the same as, to present the same object. The presentation that I have of Greenland is certainly different from that of Nansen; but the object is the same. Similarly the ideal objects "straight line" and "shortest line" are identical, but the presentations (with the appropriate definition of straight lines) are different.

Two presentations are *the same in essence* if purely on the basis of the content of each of them, exactly the same and nothing else can be stated about the presented thing. This is also true of the other kinds of acts. Thus two judgments are essentially the same judgment, if all that holds for the judged fact according to the one judgment would also have to hold for it according to the other judgment, and nothing else. Their truth-value is the same, and that is the case when "the" judgment, the intentional essence consists of a unity of judgment-quality and judgment-matter.

But the intentional essence does not exhaust the act phenomenologically. For example, a phantasy-presentation, which is "qualified" as mere imagination, is changed non-essentially if the fullness and liveliness of the sensuous contents that enter into its construction increase or decrease; or, referring to the object: if the object appears now with greater clarity and distinctness, or dissolves into cloudy haziness, etc. With all the phenomenological changes of the phantasy-appearance, the object can stand continually before our consciousness as one and the same thing, as unchanged (identity of matter); we "mean" it as constant, and ascribe the changes to the "appearance"; and we mean it thus in the manner of mere fiction (identity of quality).

The case is similar with perception, as well as acts of all kinds. If we have "the same" perception in common or merely "repeat" a perception, the identical unity of the matter, and consequently of the intentional essence, does not exclude a change in the descriptive content of the experience. Furthermore, the *same* wish is cherished by many people if their wishing intention is the same. For one the wish may be fully explicit, and not for another; or it may be intuitively clear for one and less clear for another, etc. In every case the identity of that which is "essential" is to be found in the two factors of quality and matter, which are the same.

In support of the conception of the meaning essence (meaning *in concreto*), the identity-series by which the unity of the meaning was separated from the unity of the objectivity in the first investigation may be recalled, as well as the examples which served for the illustration of the intentional essence. The identity of "the" judgment or of "the" statement lies in the identical meaning, which is repeated as the same in many single acts and is represented in them by the meaning-essence.

11. Critique of the "Image Theory" and of the Doctrine of the "Immanent" Objects of Acts

One must guard against two fundamental errors in the phenomenological interpretation of the relationship between act and subject:

(a) Against the error of the "image theory," which accounts for the factor of presentation in every act by saying: The thing itself is or may be "outside"; in consciousness, as its representative, there is an image. This view completely overlooks the most important point, that in image-presentation, on the basis of the appearing "image-object," we mean the *copied* object (the "image-subject"). But the image is not an inner character (not a "real predicate") of the object — as though an object were also pictorial, just as it is, say, red and spherical. It must be explained how it is that we get beyond the "image" and relate it to an object foreign to consciousness. The reference to the similarity between the image and the thing is no answer. The similarity between two objects, no matter how great that may be, does not make the one to be the image of the other. The image first becomes an image through the capacity of a presenting ego, to make it to be an image-representative of something similar, and to *mean* it. The image as such is constituted in a peculiar intentional consciousness; and the *inner* character of this act, the *specific* peculiarity of this act, the *specific* peculiarity of this "manner of apperception," not only makes up that which is pictorially called presenting, but also makes up that which is called the pictorial presentation of an object. The crude talk of inner images (in contrast to outer objects) may not be tolerated in descriptive psychology, and certainly not in pure phenomenology. Phenomenologically, the relation of consciousness to its objectivity is a relation to a "transcendent" thing. This relation is a "direct" one if a simple presentation is involved, and a mediate one if a founded (e.g., a copying) presentation is in question. Accordingly one should not speak as though the so-called "image" were related to consciousness similar to the way in which a picture is to the room in which it is hung.

This discussion can be carried over *mutatis mutandis* to the theory of representation in the broader sense of the theory of signs. Being a sign is also not a real predicate; it also needs a founded act-consciousness, involving immanent, phenomenological act-characters.

All such "theories" are met with the objection that they ignore the abundance of essentially different manners of presentation, which can be shown within the sphere of intuitive presentation through pure phenomenological analysis.

(b) It is also a great error to make an immanent distinction between the "merely immanent" or "intentional" objects, on the one hand, and "real" and "transcendent" objects perhaps corresponding to them, on the other hand. This distinction may then be interpreted as one between a sign or image present immanently in consciousness and the denoted or pictured thing; or one may interpolate an immanent datum of consciousness, perhaps a meaning-giving factor. Such arguments, dragged through the centuries (one thinks of the ontological argument of Anselm), although they also have arisen out of actual difficulties, are based upon an ambiguous use of the concept of immanence. Everyone must recognize that the intentional object of a presentation is the same as its actual object, and that it is absurd to draw a distinction between the two. The transcendent object would not at all be an *object of this presentation*, if it were not its intentional object. That is an analytical statement. The object of the presentation or of the "intention" *is* the presented, the intentional object. If I present God or an angel, a physical thing or a round square, etc., then that which is here named and is transcendent is meant, and hence is an intentional object; and it does not matter whether this object exists, whether it is fictitious or absurd. That the object is "merely intentional" does not mean that it exists in the *intentio* as its immanent constituent, or that a shadow of it exists therein. It means that the intention, the meaning-the-object exists, but *not* the object. If, on the other hand, the intentional object exists, then it is not merely the intention, the intending, that exists, but also that which is meant.

Obvious though all this may appear to be, it was still misconstrued by many investigators. What has been said does not exclude the distinction between the object simply, which is intended, and the object, *just as* it is intended.

C. THE MATTER OF THE ACT AND THE PRESENTATION AT ITS BASIS

1. The Relationship between the Matter and Quality of the Act

The general investigations relating to the phenomenological structure of intentional experiences are closed with a discussion that is important for the clarification of the leading problems in the domain of meaning. What is in question is the relationship of quality and matter, as well as the sense in which every act needs a presentation as its basis. The fundamental difficulties encountered here were hardly noticed at the time of the first edition of the *Logical Investigations*.

Quality and matter have been distinguished by Husserl as two inner constituents of all acts. If, e.g., an experience is designated as a judgment, it must have an inner determination and not an externally attached mark, which distinguishes it as a judgment from wishes, hopes, and other kinds of fact. It has this determination in common with all judgments; but what distinguishes it from every other one is (apart from certain factors to be investigated later) the matter. This is not seen so well in a direct way, for one is not easily able to separate the quality and the matter in an isolated single judgment. It may be seen more readily by comparison, if we juxtapose qualitatively different acts, and then find the theoretical matter as a common factor in them, just as the same intensity or color may be found in the sensuous domain. The nature of this identical something must be determined, and also the way in which it is related to the quality-factors. This question is the more important because the matter is supposed to be that element in the act which endows it with a determinate objective reference. Because all thinking is performed in acts, this question is of fundamental epistemological interest.

2. *Matter as a Founding Act of "Mere Presentation"*

The readiest answer is given by the principle that Brentano used in the determination of his "psychical phenomena," namely, that every phenomenon, or in Husserl's language, that *every intentional experience is either a presentation, or is based upon presentations.* That is, in every act the intentional object is an object *presented* in an act of presentation; and in cases other than "mere" presentation, the presented object is there as judged, wished, etc. These new intentional characters are not to be regarded as complete and independent acts. They are not thinkable without the objectivating act of presentation, and hence are founded on it. It is not thinkable that a desired object or fact could occur without being presented. This holds as a general, essential law that is clearly evident.

The identity of the matter along with changing quality is based upon the "essential" identity of the underlying presentation. Expressed otherwise: If acts have the same "content" and are distinguished with respect to their intentional essence by the fact that the one is a judgment, the other a wish, the third a doubt, etc., they possess "essentially" the same presentation as a basis. If the presentation underlies a judgment, it is (in the present sense of "matter") the judgment-content. If it underlies a desire, it is the desire-content; etc. This does not mean that the matter and the basic presentation are really identical, since the matter is merely an abstract factor of an act. What are involved when one speaks of essentially the same presentation are presentations of one and the same matter, which can be distinguished phenomenologically through factors which are irrelevant to the matter. Since the quality is also the same, all these presentations have the same "intentional essence."

Whereas every other intentional essence is a complex of quality and matter, the intentional essence of a presentation is mere matter — or mere quality, just as one wishes to call it. It therefore follows that the distinction between quality and matter is really not a distinction between fundamentally different genera of abstract factors of acts. Considered by themselves, the matters themselves are nothing other than "qualities," namely, qualities of presentation. What has been called the intentional essence of the acts is just the total quality in them; this is what is essential in them as opposed to that which changes accidentally.

3. The Problem of the Differentiation of Quality-Genera

The judgment-character which is added to the founding presentation in a concrete judgment will now be considered. Is it entirely the same for all judgments; and is the simple species of "judgment-intention" (taken purely ideally, and not complicated with presentation) really the lowest specific difference?

All this may appear to be very simple to some readers. It might seem sufficient to point out that every act of presentation has a presentational act-character which does not admit of further differentiation; and that it is the "content" that distinguishes presentations from one another — the presentation *pope* presenting the pope, and the presentation *Kaiser* presenting the Kaiser. But such readers have not made clear the phenomenological distinctions; they have not distinguished between the content as object and the content as matter ("apprehension-sense" or meaning); and they do not recognize that the object in a real sense is nothing "in" the presentation. Such objects cannot effect a difference between presentations, and especially not the difference manifested by the very content of the presentations, with respect to *what* they present. If this *what* is regarded as the "content" which is inherent in the presentation itself, and if it is distinguished from the intended object, then its nature must be explained.

There appear to be only two possibilities, as follows: (1) Either it will be assumed that what makes up the changing intentional essence is the presentation-quality itself, which is now differentiated in one way, and again in another way. According to this view, the distinction between the presentations *pope* and *Kaiser* (not the pope and Kaiser themselves) is analogous to that between the colors red and blue. (2) Or it will be assumed that the complete intentional essence (or the complete meaning essence) that undergoes ideating abstraction when we speak of *the* (ideally one) presentation *pope* can be divided into two abstract factors — the presentation-quality, the act-character of the presentation, which is the same everywhere; and the "content" or matter. The one is related to the other as, e.g., a definite color is to the extension it requires. Every color involves a certain extension, just as every presentation involves a certain content. In both cases the connection is necessary and *a priori*.

If the first possibility is accepted, the presentation appears to be an objectionable exception in the series of intentional experiences. The distinctions of content between judgments, wishes, etc., would only be distinctions of the "underlying" presentation-qualities, complicated with the actual qualities. As for the second possibility, its acceptance would compel further changes in our view. For if the "contents" are only united through complication with the act-character of the presentation, why should the situation be different for different kinds of acts?

4. The Testimony of Direct Intuition; Perceptual Presentation and Perception

Husserl closes these arguments with that which must be first in the investigation of such controversial descriptive questions, with the "testimony of inner perception," or, as he prefers to express it, with the testimony of the immediate, intuitive, essential analysis of the intentional experiences. Its testimony, however, when it is adduced and stated conceptually, surrenders much in force and thus permits of doubt. Appealing to the same "inner perception," some come to one view, and others to an opposing view; some read one thing out of it, and others something else. This also applies to the present case. The analyses carried through enable us to distinguish the deceptions from the interpretation of what is given in phenomenological essential intuition.

In Husserl's view it is incorrect to speak of inner perception instead of immanent essential intuition, in the usual appeals to the "evidence of inner perception." For such appeals serve the establishment of facts which are either essential connections (*Wesensverhalte*) of the pure phenomenological sphere, or mere transfers of them to the sphere of psychological reality. Establishments of phenomenological facts can never have their cognitive grounds in psychological experience and especially not in inner perception in the natural sense of the term, but only in phenomenological, essential intuition. To be sure, the point of departure for the latter is inner intuition. But on the one hand, this inner intuition does not have to be actual inner perception or remembrance; any inner phantasy can serve it just as well, if it has sufficient intuitive clarity. On the other hand, the phenomenological intuition, as has been emphasized repeatedly, eliminates all psychological and natural-scientific apperception and real positing of existence, and everything transcendent of pure consciousness. The phenomenological essential intuition is an immanent ideation on the basis of inner intuitions, the ideating view being exclusively concerned with the immanent or intentional content of the seen experiences; and it is such that the specific modes of experience which are isolated in these single experiences, as well as the essential connections belonging to them, are brought to adequate intuition. It is of the greatest importance to make this clear, and to see that in epistemological discussions the source of the evidence does not lie in (natural) inner experience, or in existence-positing acts. This cardinal misunderstanding is at the basis of that variety of psychologism which has been believed to do justice to the requirements of pure logic, ethics, and theory of knowledge, and to be able to overcome extreme empiricism, by speaking of apodictic evidence and even of *a priori* insights, without really leaving the ground of inner experience and psychology.

It is indeed evident that every intentional experience has a "presentation" at its basis — that we cannot judge without the fact, about which we judge, being presented, etc. But does "presentation" mean the same here as outside of this context? Has an equivocation been incurred in the formulation of the law that every act-experience is either a "mere presentation" or has "presentations" as its basis? If we really hold to the description of the experiences, an analysis of the acts which are not "mere presentations" into the apparently constructive partial acts will not always be possible.

Let us juxtapose a case of true complexity in the intentional mode of relationship (in which there is complete identity of matter) and one of the doubtful cases. I cannot be glad about something without that something being there in the mode of being, in the mode of perception, of remembrance, judging, and the like. Here the complexity is entirely unmistakable. If I enjoy myself perceptually, then the act-character of the enjoyment is based upon the perception; this has its own act-character and its matter at the same time provides the matter for the enjoyment. The character of the enjoyment can disappear entirely, but the perception remains, unchanged in itself.

Perception provides an example of doubtful act-complexity. The quality and the matter will be distinguished here, as with all acts. The comparison with a corresponding mere presentation, say a mere phantasy, shows how the same object can be represented as the same (with the same "apprehension-sense") and yet in an entirely different "manner." In the perception the object appears to be there "bodily," whereas in phantasy it only "appears to us." That is not the distinction, however, which enters into consideration for us here; it is a distinction through factors which concern neither matter nor quality. Let us compare the perception with a "mere" presentation corresponding to it, in abstraction from such distinctions. According to Husserl's view an abstract common something, the matter, is given with a different act-quality. According to the other view, appearing doubtful to him, the matter which is basic to the perceiving is itself supposed to be an act-quality, namely, that of a founding act of mere presentation. Is anything of that to be found in the analysis? Can the perception be regarded as an act-complex, and can a mere presentation actually be detached from it as an independent act?

Perhaps the possibility of an illusion exactly corresponding to it will be pointed to, and it will be suggested that it, after the unmasking of its deception, is to be regarded as the isolated mere presentation, which had been interwoven in the perception and had provided it with matter. According to this view, the basic perceptual presentation, whose quality makes up the matter of the perception, is supplemented by a belief-character.

An example of an experience of illusion will elucidate. On the stairs in a panopticon we meet a cordially beckoning, strange lady — the well-known panopticon joke. It is a doll, which deceives us for a moment. So long as we have the illusion we have a perception, as good as any other. We see a lady, not a doll. If we have recognized the error, then the reverse is the case; we now see a doll which *presents* a lady. But the perception of the doll-thing is not the basis of a pictorial consciousness; rather, the lady merely appears as identical with the doll: two perceptual apprehensions, or two thing-appearances permeate one another, so to speak coinciding with one another with respect to a certain appearance-content. And they permeate one another in the manner of a conflict. Both (doll and lady) certainly have something in common; they are as much alike in this example as is possible between perception and corresponding presentation. Certainly both have the same matter. It is the same lady that appears in both cases, and that occurs with the same phenomenal determinations. But, on the one hand, it stands before us as a reality, and, on the other hand, as a fiction, appearing as bodily and still as nothing. The distinction lies in the qualities in both cases. The same matter is in the one case the matter of a perception, and again the matter of a mere perceptual fiction; and they cannot be united at the same time.

The descriptive analysis does not favor the view that every perception is a complex in which a factor of belief, which makes up the qualitative element of the perceiving, is built up upon a complete act of "perceptual presentation" that is endowed with its own quality.

5. The Case of Judgment

A similar situation is found in the case of judgments, acts which are of particular interest to the logician. This term is here taken in its prevailing sense, as referring to statements or predications, and as excluding perceptions, remembrances, and similar acts (despite their relatedness). In a judgment, a *fact* is intentionally objective for us. But a fact, even if it concerns something sensuously perceived, is not an object which could appear sensuously to us in the manner of a perceived thing, either "outer" or "inner." In a perception an object is given to us as bodily existent. We *name* it as something existing at present, if we, on the basis of this perception, assert the judgment *that it exists*. In this judgment, which is essentially the same even if the perception is omitted, "that which appears," that which is intentionally known, is not the existent sensuous object, but rather the matter of fact *that it exists*. In the judgment it seems to us furthermore that something is constituted in a certain way, of which we are convinced. It occurs in various forms: it is a meaning, *that S is or is not; that S is p or is not p; that either S is p or Q is r; etc.*

The "objective" of the judging meaning is called the *judged fact*; and it is distinguished in reflective knowledge from the judging itself, just as, in the case of perception, the perceived object is distinguished from perceiving as an act. The controversial question is now to be considered, whether the matter in the act of judgment, or that which determines the judgment to be a judgment of this fact, lies in a founding act of presentation. By means of this presentation the fact would be presented, and the judgmental positing would refer to that which is presented as the new act-quality built thereupon.

It will not be doubted that for every judgment there is a presentation which has the same matter. Thus corresponding to the judgment *The mass of the earth is approximately* $\dfrac{1}{325000}$ *of the mass of the sun*, as the "mere" presentation belonging to it, is the act which someone performs who hears this claim and understands it, but has no motive to make a decision judgmentally. It may now be asked: Is this same act also a constituent of the judgment and does it differ from the latter merely through the judgmental decision that is *added* to a mere presentation as a "plus"? Such a thing is not borne out in descriptive analysis; the required duality in the act-quality cannot be substantiated. One should be on his guard against verbal arguments when speaking of "mere" presentations. The "mere" refers to a deficiency; but a deficiency is not always to be removed by a supplement. When "mere" imagination is opposed to perception, the distinguishing element lies in an advantage on the side of the perception, and not in something additional. The same is true in the present case: there is a deficiency on the side of the mere presentation, and an advantage on the side of the judgment, namely, the advantage of a judgmental decision with regard to the situation that is only presented.

6. "Approbation" or "Assent" to the Mere Presentation of the Fact

Perhaps others will find that the complexity which Husserl misses appears in certain cases. They may recall the well-known experiences in which a mere presentation occurs without being decided judgmentally, and to which assent (or rejection) is later added as a new act.

This evidence will not be doubted, but it will be interpreted differently. A new act is indeed added to the "mere presentation"; it follows the latter and is then asserted in consciousness. But it is a question as to whether the new act actually comprises the old one entirely — whether the new one simply grows out of the old one in such a way that the specific judgment-quality, the character of belief, is joined with the mere presentation, and the concrete judgment-experience is completed therewith — just as the act-quality of joy is joined with an act of perception, thus completing the concrete act of joy.

Consider an example in which assent is illustrated. We assent to a judgment that another person expresses. His statement does not immediately awaken a harmonious judgment on our side. To execute a harmonious judgment, simply to take over a communication, is not to assent. We must first of all understand the statement without ourselves judging, and we must consider it. We reflect upon that which the other person means; we put it in question, and we intend a decision. Then the decision enters in, the approbation itself, and we judge in harmony with the other person. In this judgment the preceding "mere presentation" is not contained. A judgment is given that is in harmony, on the one hand, with the judgment of the speaker and, on the other hand, with the reflective question, i.e., it has the same matter; and thus the assent is executed. I assent to the judgment, namely, I judge precisely the same, I judge on the basis of the same matter. I assent to the question, namely, I hold precisely that to be true which was held to be questionable in the question. The act again occurs on the basis of the same matter.

But, more closely examined, the analysis is still incomplete; that which is specific in the assent is lacking. The succession of question and harmonious judgment, or of judgment and harmonious judgment, still does not make the whole: assenting judgment to the question, or to the judgment. The two distinguished items are mediated by or connected by a certain *transitional experience*. The considering and questioning "intention" finds its fulfillment in the harmonious decision, and in this unity of fulfillment of the *answer* (which has the phenomenological character of a factor of unity), both acts are not a mere succession, but are innerly and unifiedly related to one another. In other words, the answer *conforms* to the question.

Where the consideration is one that vacillates back and forth like a scale — where the question becomes "Is it so or not?" — there the intention is a double one, and the entire experience of deliberation finds its fulfillment through each of the two possible decisions: *It is so — It is not so.* The fulfilling answer refers especially to the half of the deliberating question corresponding to it. In more complex disjunctions, which are not restricted to Yes and No, the negative fulfillment may lie in the decision: *neither A, nor B, nor C*, etc. In this experience of fulfillment, which refers to the deliberating question, in this loosening of a kind of tension, lies the original source of the assenting judgment — assenting in relation to another judgment which is asserted by any speaker.

Assent is, accordingly, a transitional experience entirely similar to the fulfillment of a supposition, expectation, hope, wish, and other "aiming" intentions. For example, in the case of wish-fulfillment we do not have the mere succession of a wish-intention followed by that which is wished, but rather unity in a characteristic consciousness of fulfillment. Here also there is agreement with regard to the matter; but the agreement alone cannot do it, for otherwise it would bring any two acts with the same matter to the unity of fulfillment. It is the consciousness of fulfillment that coördinates the wish that *S be p* and the judgmental experience that *S is p*, and gives to the latter the relative character of the fulfilling act, just as the wish itself has the character of an intending, aiming act.

This analysis makes it completely clear that a "theory of judgment," or more appropriately expressed, that a pure phenomenological characterization of judgment which identifies the peculiar quality of judging with assent or approbation, or with the rejection of a presented fact, or object, is on the wrong track. The added assent is not an act-quality added to the act of mere presentation.

Husserl does not overlook the fact that in the deliberation preceding an assent a wish-intention is mostly interwoven, which is directed upon the judgment-decision. He points out that it would be incorrect to identify the *answering fulfillment* of the so to speak *theoretical question* (in

which the appearing-to-be-questionable is constituted) with the fulfillment of the wish-question founded on it. The term "question" is ambiguous. In the one sense a certain wish is meant, in the other an
act of a peculiar kind, which is presupposed by every such wish. A
wish is directed toward a "judgment-decision," i.e., it is directed toward
a judgment that decides the question, and where it is disjunctive, the
doubt ("two cases"). In short, the wish aims at the answer to the "question," which is therefore not itself the wish here.

In the course of his further discussion Husserl again points out that he
has not defined the concept of an act by an activity, and that the term is
simply an abbreviation of the expression *intentional experience*. By the
latter is understood every concrete experience that "refers" "intentionally"
to an objectivity in the well-known "modes of consciousness." [12]

The fifth investigation closes with a study of presentation in relationship
to judgment, in the course of which the various meanings of the terms
presentation and content are distinguished.

D. FOUNDING PRESENTATIONS, WITH PARTICULAR REGARD
TO THE THEORY OF JUDGMENT

1. The Ambiguity of the Term Presentation

In view of what has been established, two senses of the term presentation are to be distinguished. In the first sense, like judgment, wish, etc.,
it is an act (or a peculiar act-quality). This is illustrated when words
or sentences are merely understood, apart from their normal function.
Thus statements or wishes may be understood without judging or wishing. In the second sense, the term refers to the act-matter which makes up
one side of the intentional essence in a complete act, or, taken more concretely, this matter in union with the other factors which it needs for its
full concretion — that which Husserl later calls representation. "Presentation" in this sense is basic to the act of presentation in the first sense,
just as it is to every act.

The principle that every intentional experience is either a (mere) presentation, or has a presentation as a basis, turns out to be a supposed evidence, a deception which is due to the ambiguity of the term presentation.
In the first part of the principle, the term refers to a certain act-species;
and in the second, to completed act-matter, as indicated above. The second

---

[12] Husserl refers finally to the *Ideen*, § 109. The deeper knowledge of the peculiarity of
the "qualitative modification" ("neutrality-modification") required further developments of
the doctrine of the "act-quality," which leave untouched the essential content of the discussion
of the present chapter, but result in a partial reinterpretation of the results obtained.

part by itself, which states that every intentional experience has a presentation as its basis, would be a genuine evidence in so far as presentation is interpreted as completed matter. The false principle, opposed by Husserl, arises when presentation is also construed as an act.

But is there only one way of construing "presentation" as an act? May not the principle in question permit of other interpretations which remain untouched by Husserl's objections?

2. Restoration of the Principle with a New Concept of Presentation

The principle gains a new and unobjectionable sense if another concept of presentation is used, namely, one to which the consideration of *names as expressions of presentations* leads. Presentations may be taken to include every act in which something is objective for us in a certain narrow sense.

The following descriptive distinction is what Husserl has in view: If a judgment is asserted, then something appears to us to be or not to be, e.g., *S is p*. But the same being that is thereby "presented" to us is presented to us in an entirely different way, if we say: *the p-ness of the S*. Similarly the fact *S is p* comes to our consciousness in a judgment in an entirely different manner, if we simply state *S is p*, and if in the *subject-act* of another judgment we say *the circumstance that S is p*, or simply *that S is p — has as a consequence . . . , is gratifying, is doubtful, etc.* Similarly also, if in the antecedent of a hypothetical or causal proposition we say *if*, or *because S is p*; in a disjunctive consequent *or S is p*; etc. In these cases, the fact may be said to be objective, although it is no thing, and is nothing at all that could be perceived, imagined, or pictured in a real sense.

With regard to the propositions functioning as subjects, Husserl states that they are not presentations of judgments, but rather of the corresponding facts. Judgments, as concrete experiences, are, like things, objects of possible perception and imagination. They can also function as subjects in judgments. This is the case for judgments about judgments. If the judged judgments are not indirectly denoted (e.g., as *this, your judgment*), then a proposition is in the subject-place. But when a proposition is in the subject-place, it does not always have the additional function of *naming* a judgment. To judge about a judgment is different than to judge about a fact; and it is again a different matter to present a fact subjectively, or to name it. If, e.g., I say *That S is p, is gratifying*, then I do not mean that the judgment is gratifying. The actual state of affairs, the objective fact, is what is gratifying. This is also shown by expressions which are objectively equivalent, although they modify the meaning, *The p-ness of the S (the victory of the just cause) is gratifying*.

If one adopts the changed concept of presentation, and also drops the claim that a presentation as a founding act comprises the whole·matter of what is founded, then the rejected principle, that every act which is not itself a presentation must be founded on a presentation, seems to have merit. It would now have to be formulated as follows: *Every act is either itself a presentation, or it is founded on one or more presentations*. Examples for which the first half of the principle applies are provided by one-termed (one-rayed) acts of perception, remembrance, expectation, imagination, and the like. They would be the "mere" presentations. Examples of the second half of the principle are provided by judgments (predications), as well as the mere presentations (according to the earlier sense of the word) corresponding to them. A judgment has at least one presentation as a basis, just as every completely expressed statement contains at least one "name." If the prevailing view is correct, which assigns to the simple judgment the normal form *S is p*, then a minimum of two presentations, or two names, would have to be assumed. But the maximum number is unlimited, for any number of presentations are possible in a single judgment; and each compound judgment is also·*one* judgment.

The same seems to hold for all other acts, such as wishing, in so far as they are complete and whole acts. Lastly, the proposition may be added that the final founding acts in every act-complex are necessarily presentations.

3. The Concept of a Name; Positing and Non-Positing Names

The new concept of presentation is to be sure not free from difficulties. That those acts which serve for the final foundation have something in common in so far as they present something objective is unmistakable. But it is not at all easy to decide wherein the common element is to consist.

Names are usually regarded as expressions of presentations, in agreement with the present concept of a presentation; and such "presentations" form a unity, which must first be examined. Names may not be construed as mere nouns, which by themselves do not characterize a complete act. A mere noun, even with an accompanying adjectival or relative proposition, does not constitute a complete name; we must add the definite or indefinite article, which has a very important meaning-function. *The horse, a house which is built out of sandstone, the opening of the Reichstag,* and also expressions such as *that the Reichstag is opened*, are names.

Now an important distinction must be noted. In many but not in all cases, the names, or the nominal presentations, are such that they intend and name the object as something really existent, without being more than mere names; in other words, without their being complete statements. The latter is excluded, for a statement can never enter the subject-place with an unmodified meaning. Judgments can indeed function as judgment-subjects in the sense of *judged objects*, but never, without a certain change of sense, as *subject-acts* of other judgments, as "presentations." This important proposition must of course be fully established. Consider such names as *Prince Henry, the Roland statue on the market-place, the letter-carrier hurrying past*, etc. Whoever uses these names in a normal sense "knows" that Prince Henry is a real person, that a Roland statue stands on the market-place, that the letter-carrier hurries past. Even more, they do not only appear to one as existent, but they are expressed as such. The positing is performed through the factor of the act that is expressed in the definite article, and only the matter is changed. It is not stated *that S exists*, but that *S* (in a possible modification of sense) is presented attributively as *really existing*, and in addition to that is posited and therefore *named* in the form *the really existent S*; and naming is here not identical with *stating*.

If this is admitted, then two kinds of names or nominal acts are to be distinguished, those which ascribe to what is named the value of an existent, and those which do not do it. An example of the latter is provided by the nominal matter of every existential consideration which really begins without any stand concerning existence.

The distinction between positing and non-positing acts is extended over the entire domain of presentation in the present sense, which extends far beyond that of the really nominal presentations. In the sphere of the intuitive presentations belonging here, which do not themselves function nominally, but have the logical calling to fulfill nominal meaning-intentions, there are positing acts: the sensuous perception, remembrance, and expectation ascribing that which is objective in *one* ray of positing meaning. On the other hand, a perception is non-positing, if it is deprived of its existence-valuation; e.g., the illusion kept free from any stand regarding the reality of what appears, and similarly every case of mere phantasy. For every positing act there is in general a possible non-positing act of the same matter, and conversely.

This is a distinction of the *act-quality*, and thus there is a certain division in the concept of a presentation. May we still speak of a genus of presentation in a strict sense; may we assume that positing and non-positing presentations are species or differences of this unified genus? The analysis leads to the result that what is common to a positing and a non-positing act with the same content does not consist of a complete act, but merely of act-matter, which is given in the two cases with a different act-quality.

4. Nominal Positing and Judgment; Whether Judgments Can Become Parts of Nominal Acts

Let us return to the question put above, of the relationship between positing presentations and predicative judgments. It would be wrong to regard the difference between the two kinds of acts as being non-essential, so that the nominal form is a mere indication of the judgment — e.g., "the letter-carrier passing by," which contains the judgment "The letter-carrier passes by." Most logicians, including Bolzano, held the distinction between names and statements to be an essential one, and the more mature science justifies them. There can be something in common on both sides, but that the difference is merely external must be disputed. More exactly expressed, it must be made clear that nominal acts and complete judgments can never have the same intentional essence, and that therefore every transformation of the one function into the other, despite retention of a common content, introduces necessary changes in their nature.

Many names, including all attributive names, have "arisen" directly or indirectly out of judgments, and accordingly refer back to judgments. What is given in the name, as a sediment of the judgment, is a modification of the judgment that is sharply distinguished from it. The performance of the modified act no longer contains the unmodified one. If we have experienced or have the insight *that the city of Halle is on the Saale, that π is a transcendental number*, then we continue: *the Saale-city Halle, the transcendental number π*. We no longer execute the judgment therewith, or at least that is not necessary, and it makes no contribution to the act of nominal meaning. And so in every case.

The judgment itself is not an attributive function, and can never take over such a function; it merely provides the ground from which the attributive meaning arises phenomenologically. If this contribution is performed, the judgment can again fall away, and the attribute with its meaning-function remains. In exceptional cases we have to do with complexes; the attributive function is interwoven with the predicative. The usual cases of the attributive function are free from this complication.

For the understanding of this discussion, an important addition is necessary. The terms "arising from" and "modification" are not to be understood in an empirical-psychological and biological sense, but express a peculiar essential relationship based upon the phenomenological content of the experiences. It belongs to the very essential content of the nominal, attributive presentation, that its intention "refers back" to the corresponding judgment, that it presents itself as a "modification" of this judgment. If we want to "realize" the sense of presentations of the type *the S being p* (the transcendental number π), if we are interested in the fulfillment of what is "meant" by such an expression, then we must so to speak appeal to the corresponding predicative judgment, we must execute it and "originally" take from it the nominal presentation, derive the latter from it. The same holds *mutatis mutandis* for non-positing presentations. In the "actual" performance they require phenomenological predicative acts of a qualitatively modified kind (the counterparts of the real judgments), in order to be able to proceed from them originally. In the essence of attributive presentation there is a certain indirectness, which gives rise to the talk of arising, being derived, and, on the other hand, of referring back. It thus occurs that the establishment of the validity of every nominal attribution reduces *a priori* to that of the corresponding judgment; and it can also be said correlatively, that the nominal object, in its actual categorial form, is "derived" from the appurtenant fact, and that is really prior to the former.

It may now be asserted generally that differences exist between names and statements which concern the meaning essence, or which are based upon "presentations" and "judgments" as essentially different acts. Just as in the intentional essence it is not the same thing to grasp an existent perceptually, or to judge *that it is*; and it is also not the same thing to name an existent as such, or to assert *that it is*.

It is evident that a possible judgment corresponds to every positing name, or a possible predication to every attribution, and conversely. After denying the identity of the acts with respect to their essence, there only remains the assumption that ideal laws obtain here. As ideal laws they do not mean the causal issuing or the empirical coexistence of the co-ordinated acts; they mean a certain ideal belonging-together of the relevant act-essences that can be ideationally grasped,[13] which have their "being" and their lawful "order of being" in the realm of phenomenological ideality, like the pure numbers and the pure species of geometrical forms in the realm of arithmetical or geometrical idealities. There are laws such as, e.g., one cannot reasonably begin with *this S* without "poten-

---

[13] Purely logically and grammatically, there is here a certain kind of meaning modification which is based upon the pure essence of meaning.

tially" admitting *that there is S.* In other words, to assert that a proposition holds with any positing names, and to maintain that the existential judgments corresponding to these names do not hold, is an *a priori* incompatibility. It is one of that group of "analytic" ideal laws which are based upon the "mere form" of thinking, or upon the categories, as the specific Ideas which belong to the possible forms of "genuine" thinking.

5. *Whether Statements Can Function as Whole Names*

Still another important type of example must be considered, in order to preserve the present conception of the relation between nominal acts and judgments. That is, the cases in which statements seem to appear as names, as complete and whole names. For example, *That rain has finally come will gladden the farmers.* The subject-proposition is a complete statement. But consider the example more closely. The farmers are glad *about the actual fact that rain has finally fallen.* Hence the actual fact, the fact posited in the mode of being, is the object of the joy, is the subject about which a statement is made. We can speak of *the actual fact of the rain that has come,* or "that rain has come." Thus this proposition is a name; it names, and in naming it presents; and just as other names name things, properties, etc., it names (or presents) a fact, in particular an empirical fact.

What is the difference between this *naming* and the *statement of the fact* in the independent statement: *Finally rain has come?* It happens that we at first simply assent and then refer to the fact by name: *Finally rain has come — that will gladden the farmers.* The contrast can be studied here; it is unmistakable. The fact is the same in both cases, but it becomes objective in an entirely different manner. In the simple judgment we judge about the rain and its coming; both are "objective," and are "presented." We do not perform a mere succession of presentations, however, but a judgment, a peculiar "unity of consciousness" that "joins" the presentations; and in this joining the consciousness of facts is constituted for us. To execute the judgment is the same thing as to become conscious of a fact in this "synthetic" manner of "placing something upon something." A thesis is asserted, and is followed by a second dependent thesis, in such a way that the synthetic unity of the fact is constituted intentionally. This synthetic consciousness is entirely different than in the case of presentation, involving a one-rayed thesis. The intention that is directed in one ray upon a synthetically constituted fact presupposes a many-rayed intention, and refers back to it in its own sense. There is always the *a priori* possibility (as an "ideal," essential possibility) that a many-rayed mode of consciousness may be led over into a single-rayed one, in which the fact is "objective" or "presented" in a significant sense. It is now clear that the "mode of consciousness," the way in which the object becomes intentional, is in both cases a different one — which means that we have to do with "essentially" different acts, with acts of different intentional essence.

Propositions which function as names of facts and the corresponding statements of the same fact differ with respect to their intentional essence. Never can a statement function as a name or a name as a statement without a change of its essence and of the meaning itself.

Naturally the corresponding acts are not totally strange to one another descriptively. The matter of the statement is partially identical with that of the nominal act; in both cases the same fact is intended by means of the same terms, although in a different form. Hence the great relatedness of the form of expression is not accidental, but is due to the meanings themselves. If occasionally, despite the changed meaning-function, the expression is unchanged, we have to do with a particular case of equivocation. It belongs to the large class of cases in which expressions function with anomalous meaning.

Thus presentations and judgments are distinguished everywhere, and within the presentations, the positing presentations which assign existence are distinguished from those which are non-positing. Furthermore, examining the judgment-character of causal antecedents, or propositions of the kind *because S is p,* Husserl brings them into the same relationship to hypothetical antecedents, as has been recognized between positing and non-positing names. The *because* may refer back to a judgment which stated that *S is p*; but in the causal proposition itself this judgment is not performed any more. It is no longer stated that *S is p,* but a consequent-thesis is based upon (performed "on the strength of") a simply "presentational" support — which as a causal antecedent-thesis is characterized in its own sense as a modification of a judgmental synthesis. The whole is a new form of judgmental synthesis, whose meaning-content can be expressed as the being of the grounding fact *conditioning* that which follows. Only in the manner of a complex can the antecedent and consequent function as a judgment besides, as when we state *S is p, and because that is the case, Q is r.* The point is not only to establish the conclusion synthetically, but also to have and to hold these two facts, "*S is p*" and "*Q is r*," judgmentally in the relating, synthetic consciousness itself.

The extensions just made show that the nominal presentations in a narrower and real sense only represent to us a broader but firmly delimited class of "thetic," "one-rayed," positing acts. To be noted carefully is the terminology that is adopted here, according to which "judgment" is the meaning of an independently closed statement. That this meaning cannot become the meaning of a hypothetical or causal antecedent proposition without inner modification, or a nominal meaning in general, is the thesis that was established above.

6. The Concept of an Objectivating Act

The preceding discussion has not yet disposed of the question raised at the beginning of § 3. "Presentation" and "judgment" have been found to be essentially different acts. There "presentation" is used in the sense of a nominal act, and "judgment" in the sense of a statement, of the performance of a normal statement that is closed in itself. Naming and stating are therefore not "merely grammatically" different, but "essentially different." Has it been proved therewith that the acts which endow naming and stating with meaning and a fulfilling sense belong to different "fundamental classes" of intentional experiences?

The answer must be negative. There was no talk of that. The intentional essence is constructed out of *matter* and *quality,* and the distinction of "fundamental classes" of acts refers only to act-qualities. It has also not even been suggested that nominal and propositional acts are at all of different quality, let alone having to be of a different quality-genus.

The essential modification of meaning, in the transition of a statement into the nominal function (or one on a par with it), upon the proof of which weight was laid in the above, may be merely a change of matter with identity of quality or at least (according to the kind of nominal modification) of the quality-genus.

That this is correct is shown by a careful inspection of the matters themselves. The addition recognized as necessary in the examples discussed above, through the nominal article or through nominal expressions, such as *the circumstance, that . . . , the fact, that . . .* , in the case of a transfer of the propositional meaning to the subject-function, shows us places where the transformation of meaning is manifested in the identical, essential content of the matter that is carried over, and hence where functions of apprehension appear which were lacking in the original statement. The mutually agreeing essential factors undergo a different "categorial formation." Compare, e.g., the form *S is p* with its nominal modification, *S, which is p.*

On the other hand, the following considerations will make it clear, that nominal and propositional acts have a common genus with respect to the *quality.* Another concept of presentation will be defined therewith, one that is broader and more significant than the one last considered, and which will have significance for the principle of the basing of every act upon presentations. In order to keep the two present concepts of "presentation" distinguished, *nominal acts* will be spoken of with relation to the narrower concept, and *objectivating acts* with relation to the broader concept.

7. *Qualitative and Material Differentiation of Objectivating Acts*

A distinction has been made between nominal acts that are positing and those that are non-positing. The former are to a certain extent existential intentions; they are either sense-perceptions, or perceptions in the broader sense of the supposed grasping of being in general, or other acts which, without supposing to grasp the object "itself," nevertheless mean it as *existing.* The latter acts leave undecided the being of their objects: the objects may or may not exist; but they are not supposed to exist, and are "merely presented." It is a law that corresponding to every positing nominal act is a non-positing one, a "mere presentation" with the same matter, and conversely; whereby the correspondence is to be understood in the sense of an ideal possibility.

A certain modification leads every positing nominal act over into a mere presentation with the same matter. Exactly the same modification is again found with judgments. The modification occurs by means of an act which merely presents precisely that which the judgment holds to be true, i.e., has an objective without deciding about truth or falsity. Phenomenologically viewed, the modification of judgments is completely homogeneous with that of positing nominal acts. The judgments as *positing propositional acts* therefore have their correlates in mere presentations as non-positing propositional acts. The corresponding acts have the same matter, but are of different quality. Just as positing and non-positing nominal acts belong to one quality-genus, so also do judgments and their modified counterparts. As regards the transition from a positing nominal act to an act of asserting statement, there is no qualitative difference. The matter alone makes up the difference; it alone determines the unity of the nominal and again the unity of the propositional acts.

A comprehensive genus of intentional experiences is accordingly delimited, which comprises all the acts considered with respect to their *qualitative* essence and determines the broadest concept which the term *presentation* can signify within the total class of intentional experiences. This is the qualitatively unified genus of *objectivating acts.* It yields (a) through qualitative differentiation, the classification into positing and non-positing acts, and (b) through differentiation of the matter, the difference of nominal and propositional acts — but it remains to be considered, whether this difference is not merely one among a series of equally justified material differences.

In fact, if one surveys the preceding analyses, the really thoroughgoing opposition here is the one between *synthetic, many-rayed-unitary acts* and *one-rayed acts*, positing in *one thesis*. But it is to be noted that the predicative synthesis only represents a specially preferred form of synthesis (or rather a whole form-system), to which other forms, often interwoven in it, are opposed: thus conjunctive and disjunctive synthesis. For example, we have in the plural predication *A and B and C are p* a unified predication terminating in three predicative strata in the identical predicate *p*. This act of judgment is as it were divided by a "caesura" into the positing of a subject and the positing of a predicate, in such a way that the *one* subject-term on its side is a unified conjunction of three nominal terms. What was seen in the consideration of predicative syntheses (referring to the primal predicative form only, that of "categorical" synthesis) is seen again with all syntheses: with all of them the fundamental operation of nominalization is possible, of the transformation of synthetic "many-rayedness" into a "nominal" "one-rayedness" with the appurtenant matter referring back to the originally constitutive matter, or to the originally constitutive consciousness.

Accordingly we come back in the total view of ideally possible "objectivating" acts to the basic distinction of "thetic" and "synthetic," one-rayed and many-rayed acts. The one-rayed are not articulated, the many-rayed are articulated. Every part has its objectivating quality (its kind of position with regard to "existence," or the corresponding qualitative modification) and its matter. At the same time the synthetic whole has, as *one* objectivating act, its quality and a matter, which latter is, however, an articulated one. The analysis of such a whole leads, on the one hand, to parts, and, on the other hand, to synthetic, syntactic forms; and further, on the side of the parts, to simple and complex, namely, those which are themselves again articulated and therewith synthetically unified, as in the case of conjunctive subjects of plural predications; etc.

Finally we come to simple, one-rayed objectivating parts, but not necessarily to primitive ones in a final sense. For the one-rayed parts can still be nominalized syntheses, nominal presentations of facts (or of conjunctions or disjunctions) whose parts themselves may be facts, etc. If the parts cannot refer back any further, then they are simple in *this* respect; as, e.g., with presentations of proper names, or one-termed perceptions (not analyzable in explicative syntheses), phantasy-presentations, etc., such simple objectivations are free of all "categorial forms." The analysis of every (not simple) objectivating act finally leads back to such "simple" act-parts, simple with respect to *form* and *matter*.

The general view of possible systematic arrangements and synthetic formations leads to the pure-logical and grammatical laws discussed in the fourth investigation. In this context only the "matters" (the objectivating act-meanings) are really concerned, in which all forms in the structure of the objectivating syntheses are stamped. The theorem belongs here, e.g., that every unified, closed, objectivating matter (and hence every possible, independent meaning) can function as part-matter in every synthesis of every possible form; and also the theorem that every such matter is either a complete, propositional (predicative) one or a possible part of one. Having regard, on the other hand, to the qualities, the theorem can be asserted that, taken ideally, any objectivating matters can be connected with any qualities.

If the special distinction of nominal and propositional acts is considered, then this possibility of the connection of any qualities with any matters is easily confirmed. In the analyses of the preceding paragraph it did not appear all-sidedly, inasmuch as only modifications of judgment, and hence of positing propositional acts into nominal acts, were considered. But it is unmistakable that every judgment qualitatively modified to a "mere" presentation can be transformed into a corresponding nominal act, e.g., *2 × 2 is equal to 5* (in a merely understanding assertion, and without taking a position regarding it) into the name *that 2 × 2 is equal to 5*. It is well to call that modification which concerns the *qualities* (positing names or statements transformed into non-positing ones) *qualitative modification*. In so far as the matter which alone gives form or establishes form-differences remains preserved herewith (the name remains a name, the statement a statement, and that according to all inner arrangements and forms), we have also to speak of *conforming modification* of the positing act. However, if the concept of conforming modification is taken in natural generality, so that it is extended over every modification not touching the *matter* of the act, then it is, as will be discussed (§ 9), broader than the concept of qualitative modification which is here in question.

8. *Presentation in the Sense of an Objectivating Act and Its Qualitative Modification*

For the comprehension of objectivating acts under one class, it was important that this whole class be characterized by a qualitative opposition, so that just as is the case for every nominal belief, every propositional belief, or every complete judgment, also has a "mere presentation" as its counterpart. The doubt is now raised, as to whether this qualitative modification is suited to characterize a *class* of intentional experiences, and whether it does not rather have its validity in the total sphere of these experiences as an underlying motive of division. For the latter an obvious argument is offered, to the effect that to every intentional experience there corresponds a mere presentation: to the wish the mere presentation of the wish, to hate the mere presentation of it, etc. — just as there are corresponding presentations for actual naming and asserting.

Nevertheless, one may not confuse fundamentally different things here. There is a possible presentation relating to every possible act or experience, and, indeed, to every possible object, and this may be positing or non-positing in character (a "mere" presentation). Taken basically, however, there is a whole manifold of different presentations, and this holds even if we restrict ourselves (as we shall have tacitly done) to nominal presentations. This type of presentation can present its object as intuitive and intellectual, as direct or attributively mediated. But it is enough for our purposes to speak of *one* presentation, or to select any one of them, say the imaginative, since all kinds of presentations are possible everywhere in the same manner.

Hence to every object there corresponds the presentation of the object, to the house the presentation of the house, to the presentation the presentation of the presentation, to the judgment the presentation of the judgment, etc. But here it is to be noted (as seen in § 2), that the presentation of the judgment is not the presentation of the judged fact. And similarly, more generally, the presentation of an instance of positing is not the presentation of the presented (posited) object. The objects presented in both cases are different. Therefore, e.g., the will which wants to realize a fact is different from the will that wants to realize a judgment or a nominal positing of this fact. Corresponding to the positing act is its qualitative counterpart, in a totally different manner than the presentation of this act corresponds to it. The qualitative modification of an act is so to speak a totally different "operation" than the production of a presentation relating to it. The essential difference of these two operations is shown in this, that the latter, the *operation of presentational objectivation*, according to the pattern of the symbols

$$O, P(O), P[P(O)], \ldots$$

whereby O denotes an object, and $P(O)$ the presentation of O, can be iterated *in infinitum*, but the qualitative modification cannot; and again, that the presentational objectivation is applicable to all objects in general, whereas the qualitative modification has meaning only for acts. And again in this, that in the one modification-series, the "presentations" are exclusively nominal, whereas in the other series this restriction does not occur; and finally, that in the one case the quality is not in question, and hence the modification essentially concerns the matter, whereas in the other case it is the quality that is modified. To every act of belief a "mere" presentation corresponds as a counterpart, which presents the same objectivity in just the same way, i.e., on the basis of the same matter as the act of belief. But instead of positing the presented objectivity, the question of existence is left undecided. This modification cannot be iterated, any more than it would have sense for acts which do not come under the concept of belief. It therefore provides a unique connection between acts with this quality and their counterparts. For example, positing perception or remembrance has its counterpart in a corresponding act of "mere" imagination with the same matter — as in a perceptual intuition of a picture, when we allow it to affect us merely aesthetically without taking a stand on the being or non-being of that which is represented; or also in the intuition of a "phantasy-picture," when we indulge in phantasy without taking any actual stand on being. Naturally the "mere" presentation does not again have a counterpart here. If a "belief" has been transformed into "mere presentation," then we can at most *return* to the belief; but there is not, in the same sense, a modification that is repeated and continued.

It is different if we exchange the operation of qualitative modification with that of presentational objectivation. Here the possibility of iteration is evident. This can be shown most simply in the relation of acts to the ego and their distribution with respect to different time-points or persons. At one time I perceive something, at another time I have the presentation that I perceive this, at a third time I again have a presentation that I have the presentation that I perceive, etc.[14] Or another example: A is painted, a second painting represents the first pictorially, a third the second, etc. Here the differences are unmistakable. They are not mere differences of sensation-contents, but differences of the apprehending act-characters (and especially of the intentional matters), without which the talk of phantasy-picture, painting, etc., would also be meaningless. These differences are discerned immanently, and one is *phenomenologically* certain of them when he has the corresponding experiences and is reflectively turned

[14] The reader is again reminded that this is not to be understood in an empirical-psychological sense, and that what are concerned (as everywhere in the present investigation) are *a priori* possibilities and essential structures, which we grasp as such with apodictic evidence.

toward their intentional differences. This is, e.g., the case when one observes: I now have a perception of A, a phantasy-presentation of B, C is represented here, in this painting, etc. If one has made these relationships clear, he will not commit the error of maintaining that the presentations of presentations are not provable and are mere fictions. That would be to confuse the two operations distinguished here, to insert instead of the presentation *of* a mere presentation, the indeed impossible qualitative modification of this presentation.

A common generic character may be assumed with regard to the qualities that are coördinate with one another through a "conforming modification." [15] Finally, it appears obvious that the mere presentations of acts, which were distinguished above from the possible qualitative counterparts in the case of positing acts alone, are themselves, as mere presentations, such counterparts — but not of their "original" acts, which are rather their objects of presentation. The mere presentation of a wish is not the counterpart of the wish, but of some positing act referring to it, e.g., of a *perception* of the wish. *This* pair, the perception and the mere presentation of the wish, belong to the same genus, both are objectivating acts; whereas the wish itself and its perception, or also its imagination or some other presentation relating to it, belong to different genera.

9. Qualitative and Imaginative Modification

It cannot be said that all non-positing acts are imaginative, and all positing ones non-imaginative. For example, an imagined sensuous object can confront us as existent in the mode of positing, just as in the modified mode it can be an imagined object. It is sufficient that a perception can pass over into a corresponding image (hence into an act which harbors the same matter in itself, although in a different form of apprehension), without change of its positing-character.

Two kinds of conforming modifications can be distinguished here, the *qualitative* and the *imaginative*. In both the matter remains unchanged. With identity of the matter it is not merely the quality which can change in the act. Quality and matter have been regarded here as essential and inseparable from acts; but it has been pointed out from the outset that still other factors are distinguishable in acts. As the next investigation will show, it is these factors which enter into consideration for the distinction

---

[15] Cp. the interpretation of "Gattungsgemeinschaft" as a peculiar relationship of "essence and counter-essence" in the *Ideen*, p. 233. The further development of the results of the present investigation led to some essential deepenings and improvements. Cp. especially §§ 109 to 114 and § 117 on "Neutrality Modification."

between non-intuitive objectivation and intuition, and again between perception and imagination.

If the descriptive relationships are once clarified, it is merely a terminological question, whether the word judgment is restricted to the (unmodified) statement-meanings, as we do in the sense of the tradition, or whether it applies to the whole sphere of acts of belief. Since judgment is a logical term, only the logical interest and the logical tradition will decide which concept is to give it meaning. Such a fundamental concept as that of the (ideal) statement-meaning, which is the final unity to which everything logical must refer back, must retain its natural and hereditary expression. The expression "act of judgment" would therefore have to be restricted to the corresponding kinds of act, to the meaning-intentions of complete statements, and to the fulfillments adapted to them and possessing the same meaning-essence. The designation of all positing acts as judgments has the tendency to veil the essential difference which separates nominal and propositional acts despite all that they have in common qualitatively, and therewith to confuse a group of important relationships. Similar to the term judgment is the case of the term presentation. What logic is to understand by that must be decided by its own need. Certainly account must be taken of the distinction between presentation and judgment, and of the circumstance that presentation presumes to be something building up the complete judgment.

10. The Objectivating Act as the Primary Bearer of the Matter

A number of investigators have construed the term presentation so widely that it includes reference not only to the "merely presentational" acts but in effect to the entire sphere of objectivating acts. Laying down this important concept, which determines a closed quality-genus, the principle of the presentation as the basis of all acts gains a new and especially significant sense, of which the preceding one, built up on the nominal concept of presentation, is merely a secondary branch. It may be said that every intentional experience is either an objectivating act or has such an act as its "basis," i.e., in the latter case it has an objectivating act as a constituent of itself, whose total matter is at the same time *its* total matter.

The reference to objectivity is first constituted in the matter. But every matter is the matter of an objectivating act, and can only by means of such an act become the matter of a new act-quality founded on it. Primary and secondary intentions must be distinguished to a certain extent, and the latter are indebted for their intentionality to their foundation by the former. Whether the primary objectivating acts have the character of positing ("holding-to-be-true," believing) or non-positing ("merely presentational," neutral) is indifferent for this function. Some secondary acts require the character of "holding-to-be-true" (*Fürwahrhaltung*), as, e.g., joy and grief; for others mere modifications are sufficient, as, e.g., for a wish, or for an aesthetic feeling. Often the underlying objectivating act is a complex which comprises acts of both kinds.

11. Fundamental Theorems for Complex Acts

The following observations are added for further elucidation.

Every compound act is *eo ipso* qualitatively complex; it has as many qualities (whether of different or of the same species) as single acts are distinguishable in it. Furthermore, every compound act is a founded act; its total quality is not a mere sum of the qualities of partial acts, but is *one* quality, whose unity is founded on these constructive qualities, just as the unity of the total matter is not a mere sum of the matters of the partial acts, but, provided that a division of the matter with respect to the partial acts occurs at all, is founded on the partial matters. There are, however, essential differences in the way in which an act is qualitatively complex and is founded on other acts, and this with regard to the different manner in which the different qualities are related to one another and to the total unified matter and the possible partial matters, in which they gain unity through different elementary foundations.

An act can be so complex that its total complex quality can be divided into divers qualities, each of which has the same matter in common; thus, e.g., in the joy about a matter of fact the complex of the specific quality of the joy and that of the "holding-to-be-true," in which the matter of fact is presented to us. Accordingly, one might think that each of these qualities with the exception of a single one of them could fall away, while a concrete, complete act could always remain. One might also think that qualities of any genus could be connected with a single matter in a stated manner. Our law states that all that is not possible, and that in every such complex and in every act in general, an objectivating act-quality must necessarily be present, because a matter in general is not realizable, except as matter of an objectivating act.

Qualities of another genus are consequently always founded on objectivating qualities; never can they be connected immediately and by themselves with a matter. Where they appear, the entire act is necessarily a qualitatively *multiform* one, i.e., one containing qualities of various quality-genera; and more fully, such that a complete objectivating act (namely, one-sidedly), which also possesses the total matter of the total act as its total matter, is separable from it at all times. In a corresponding sense *uniform* acts do not have to be simple ones. All uniform acts are objectivating, and we may even say conversely that all objectivating acts are uniform; but objectivating acts can be complex besides. The matters of the partial acts are now mere parts of the matter of the total act; the total matter can be constituted because parts of the matter belong to the partial acts, and the unity of the total matter belongs to the unity of the total quality. The division can for the rest be an explicit arrangement of the parts; but also (in the earlier described manner of nominalization) there can be an implicit arrangement of every form within nominalized matters, which otherwise is permissible in free syntheses. Every statement, if it functions in normal meaning (as asserting) or in modified meaning, provides us with a pertinent example. To the terms there correspond underlying partial acts with partial matters; to the connecting forms, the *is* or *is not*, the *if* and *then*, the *and*, the *or*, and the like, there correspond founded act-characters, but at the same time founded factors of the total matter. With all this complexity the act is a uniform one; we also find only *one* objectivating quality, which belongs to the total matter; and more than one objectivating quality cannot refer to a single matter that is taken as a whole.

From such uniformity there arises multiformity, either by the total objectivating act connecting with new kinds of qualities that refer to the total matter, or also by the new qualities joining merely single partial acts; just as, on the basis of a unified intuition, there may be pleasure with respect to the one part and displeasure with respect to the other. Conversely, in every complex act, which as always contains act-qualities of a non-objectivating kind, whether based upon the total matter or upon its parts, these act-qualities can all so to speak be "crossed out." A complete objectivating act then remains, which still contains the total matter of the original act.

A further consequence of the laws obtaining here is that the *final founding* acts of every complex act (or the parts finally implied in the nominal parts) must be objectivating acts. These are all of the species of nominal acts, and the finally implied terms are in every respect *simple* nominal acts, simple connections of a simple quality with a simple matter. The proposition may also be asserted that all simple acts are nominal ones. Naturally the converse does not hold; not all nominal acts are simple. As soon as a matter that is divided into parts appears in an objectivating act, a categorial form is also present in it, and it is essential to all categorial forms to be constituted in founded acts, as will be more fully discussed in the sixth investigation.

In the present and the following considerations, one does not have to understand by matter the mere abstract factor of the intentional essence; one could also substitute for it the whole of the act, only with the abstraction of the quality, and hence that which is called the representation in the next investigation: everything essential would then remain.

12. *Retrospective View of the Earlier Interpretations of the Principle*

It is now understood why it was asserted above that the principle of Brentano, interpreted on the basis of the nominal concept of presentation, is a merely secondary consequence of the same principle in the new interpretation. If every act that is not itself objectivating (or not *pure*) is founded on objectivating acts, then it must also be founded finally on nominal acts. For every objectivating act is, as has been discussed, either simple, hence *eo ipso* nominal, or compound, and therefore founded on simple, i.e, again on nominal acts. The new interpretation is obviously much more significant, because only with it do the essential basic relations receive a pure formulation. In the other interpretation, although nothing that is incorrect is asserted, two fundamentally different kinds of foundation are mixed:

(a) The foundation of non-objectivating acts (such as joys and wishes) on objectivating acts (presentations, instances of "holding-to-be-true"), whereby an act-quality is primarily founded on another act-quality and only indirectly on a matter.

(b) The foundation of objectivating acts on other objectivating acts, whereby an act-matter is primarily founded on other act-matters (e.g., that of a predicative statement on those of the founding nominal acts). The circumstance that no matter is possible without an objectivating quality must then have the consequence that, where a matter is founded on other matters, an objectivating act of the first matter is also founded on just such acts of the other matters. Consequently the fact that every act is at all times founded on nominal acts has various sources. The original source, however, consists in this, that every simple matter (and hence no matter comprising a material foundation) is a nominal one, and accordingly every finally founding, objectivating act is a nominal one. But since all other kinds of act-qualities are founded on objectivating ones, the final foundation through nominal acts is carried over from the objectivating ones to all acts in general.

1. "Presentation"

The numerous meanings of the terms presentation and content of presentation constitute one of the leading sources of confusion. The various meanings must be distinguished carefully. (a) By "presentation" may be meant, first of all, the matter of the act, or the representation that underlies the act, as the complete content of the act with the exclusion of the quality. The matter indicates which object is meant in the act and the sense in which it is meant. The representation involves, in addition to that, factors that lie outside the intentional essence and determine the objects being meant perceptually, imaginatively, or non-intuitively. The sixth investigation contains a detailed analysis of this distinction. (b) "Presentation" may also be used in the sense of a "mere presentation," as a qualitative modification of any form of a "belief." Thus there may be a mere understanding of a proposition without any decision to assent or to reject, to doubt, etc. (c) By "presentation" may be meant a nominal act, as when a presentation is taken to be the subject of an act of assertion. (d) It may also be used in the sense of an objectivating act. There is a "basic class" of acts which must always be present, because every case of matter or of representation must be given as the matter or representation of such an act. This class comprises the acts of belief, both nominal and propositional, as well as their "counterparts," so that presentations in the foregoing senses also belong here. (e) The term presentation is frequently contrasted with mere thinking, a distinction which is the same as the opposition of intuition and concept. One has a presentation of an ellipsoid, but *a priori* impossibilities such as "round square" cannot be "presented." But neither can the number π be presented. In such cases, which are free of all incompatibility, "mere concepts" are given to us. More exactly, we have nominal expressions, and these, animated by meaning-intentions, are "thought." The "presenting" is distinguished from the mere thinking in that it is the fulfillment of the mere meaning-intention. (f) A common use of the term presentation is illustrated by the opposition of imagination and perception. If one sees a building, he presents it, or has an idea of it. But one can also present it by means of remembrance, or if one has it before his eyes in a painted picture. "Presentation" is thus a concrete act of the imagination. (g) The picture of the preceding illustration, as a physical thing, presents the building and is also called a presentation of it. This equivocation is also carried over to remembrance and phantasy. The appearance of that which is phantasied is naively interpreted as being an image within consciousness. That which appears, in its particular mode of appearance, is taken to be an inner picture, and serves as a "presentation" of the thing that is phantasied. (h) In those cases in which a picture-relationship is supposed, the often inadequate picture "represents" and symbolizes the thing. A photograph recalls the original act and is at the same time its representative. A sign such as an algebraic symbol can function similarly. It stimulates the presentation of that which is signified, even if that is something non-intuitive, such as an integral. A sign may also function in mathematical operations, just as though that which is symbolized were directly given. In general, a sign, whether it be a picture-sign or a name-sign, is a "presentation" of that which is signified. (i) The difference between perception and imagination is often confused with the difference between sensations and phantasms. The former is a difference between acts, and the latter between non-acts, or the experienced contents. A phantasm corresponds to phantasy-presentation; it is the complex of the representing contents of the phantasy-image. (j) Because of the confusion between an appearance, as, e.g., a concrete phantasy-experience or a "phantasy-image," and that which appears, the presented object is also called a presentation. The same applies to perceptions, etc. Thus, e.g., "The world is my presentation." (k) The contents of consciousness have also been called presentations, the supposition being that we are aware of conscious experiences by means of inner perception or some other kind of inner view. Consciousness or the ego presents the content. These are the "ideas" of British empirical philosophy since Locke. To have a presentation and to experience a content are often regarded as equivalent expressions. (l) In logic it is of the greatest importance to separate the specifically logical concepts of presentation from other concepts of presentation. In addition to what has been distinguished in the foregoing, there is Bolzano's concept of a "presentation in itself," which was interpreted by Husserl as every independent or dependent partial meaning within a complete statement. With regard to purely logical concepts of presentation it is necessary to distinguish the ideal from the real, e.g., a nominal presentation in the logical sense of the acts in which it is realized. On the other hand, the mere meaning-intentions are to be distinguished from the experiences of more or less appropriate fulfillment, i.e., from presentations in the sense of intuitions. (m) Finally, there are still other meanings which are in part less important. For example, presentation may be used in the sense of opinion, view, conception, etc.

2. "Content of a Presentation"

The expressions correlative to "presentation" are correspondingly ambiguous, as illustrated by the phrase "content of a presentation." As already shown, the distinction between content and object is not sufficient, although it is helpful to make a beginning with necessary distinctions. In the sphere of logic it is not enough to distinguish "content" in one sense of the term from the named object. First of all, by the content of a nominal presentation, e.g., the meaning as an ideal unity can be meant, which is the presentation in a purely logical sense. Corresponding to it, as an immanent factor in the immanent content of the act of presentation, is the intentional essence with its presentation-quality and matter. In the immanent content the separable constituents not belonging to the intentional essence are distinguished. Distinctions of form and content which are ambiguous also arise. Especially important is the distinction between matter, in an entirely new sense, and categorial form. Connected therewith is the expression "content of a concept," the content being the totality of the "characters" as distinguished from their form of connection.

In a final note Husserl discusses the view that there is no difference between presenting and the presented content, or that it is not provable phenomenologically. One's view here depends upon the interpretation of the terms presentation and content. If they are interpreted as the mere having of sensations and phantasms, overlooking the phenomenological factor of apprehension, then it follows that there is not a peculiar act of presentation. In that case, presenting and that which is presented are one and the same thing. The mere having of the content, as a mere experiencing of the experience, is not an intentional experience which refers to something objective; and neither is it an inner perception. Therefore Husserl also identified sensation and content of sensation. But such a concept of presentation cannot be maintained; it has arisen by the misinterpretation of the more original, intentional concept of presentation. Such a concept has no function in the critique of knowledge and logic, so that it would be merely confusing to introduce it.

Owing to that confusion von Ehrenfels [16] once held that we could not do without the assumption of an act of presentation that is different from the content of presentation. His main reason was that we would not be able otherwise to specify a psychological difference between the presentation of an object and the presentation of a presentation of it. But he was never able to convince himself directly of the existence of that phenom-

[16] *Zeit. f. Psych. u. Phys. d. Sinnesorgane*, vol. xvi (1897).

enon. In Husserl's view, an act of presentation becomes directly evident as such when we *phenomenologically* ascertain just this difference between presentation and presentation of the presentation. If no such cases occurred, there could not even be an indirect justification of such a distinction. Thus one directly ascertains the existence of an act of presentation if he makes clear the difference between a mere sound-formation and the same sound-formation as an understood name.

CHAPTER XIII

OBJECTIVATING INTENTIONS AND FULFILLMENTS

THE SIXTH INVESTIGATION,[1] entitled "Elements of a Phenomenological Elucidation of Knowledge," was regarded by Husserl as the most important phenomenologically. The preceding investigation, which seemed to be lost in remote questions of descriptive psychology, considerably furthered his knowledge-clarifying interests. All thinking, especially all theoretical thinking and knowing, occurs in certain "acts," which appear in the context of expressive speech. In these acts lies the source of all the valid unities which confront the thinker as objects of thought or knowledge, or as their explanatory grounds and laws, as their theories and sciences. In these acts lies also the source of the general and pure ideas which are involved, whose ideal-lawful connections pure logic aims to bring to light and whose clarification is the aim of the critique of knowledge. Obviously much is gained for knowledge-clarifying purposes by the determination of the phenomenological peculiarity of the acts as such, which constitute a much disputed and much misunderstood class of experiences. By the ordering of the logical experiences into this class, a first important step for the analytical understanding of the logical sphere and of the fundamental concepts of knowledge is accomplished. The progress of the investigation led to the separating out of various concepts of *content*, which usually are confusing where acts and ideal unities belonging to them are in question. Distinctions that were already recognized in the more restricted sphere of meanings and meaning-endowing acts in the first investigation returned now in the wider domain and in their

---

[1] As originally planned, the sixth investigation was published as a separate volume. Husserl soon became convinced that it would not be enough to work over the old material paragraph by paragraph. Having made much progress, he was unwilling to make any compromises. He therefore proceeded more freely and added whole series of new chapters, which greatly increased the extent of the investigation.

The war and his new Freiburg duties were mainly responsible for the long delay in publishing the new edition of this investigation. The first section was reprinted almost literally; but the important second section on "Sensibility and Understanding" was improved. The chapter on "sensuous and categorial intuition," in connection with the material of the preceding chapters, was intended to clear the way for a phenomenological elucidation of logical evidence, and for its parallels in the axiological and practical sphere. Some misunderstandings of the *Ideas* would have been obviated if this discussion had been considered. The immediacy of the seeing of general essences, which is spoken of in the *Ideas*, just like that of any

most general form. The newly gained and notable concept of content in the last investigation, that of the intentional essence, also did not lack this relation to the logical domain, for the same series of identities which served earlier for the illustration of the unity of meaning, yielded, appropriately generalized, a certain identity relating to any acts as the "intentional essence." Through this ordering of the phenomenological characters and ideal unities of the logical domain under the general characters and unities which belong in the act-domain in general, the former gained considerably in phenomenological and critical understanding.

The discussion of the distinction of act-quality and act-matter within the unified intentional essence also led deeply into the sphere of logical interests. The question of the relationship of this intentional matter to the presentation-basis essential to every act required that various important and confused concepts of presentation be separated, whereby a fundamental portion of the "theory of judgment" was worked out. But the specifically logical concepts of presentation and the concept of judgment remained without final clarification.

Even the nearer aim, to make clear the origin of the idea of meaning, was not realized. It is a valuable insight, that the meaning of expressions lies in the intentional essence of the acts concerned; but the question, what kinds of acts are capable of the function of meaning in general, or whether acts of every kind are on a par in this respect, was not considered. As soon as this question is taken up, we come upon *the relationship of meaning-intention and meaning-fulfillment,* or in the traditional but equivocal

---

other categorial intuition, is the opposite of the mediateness of non-intuitive, say of symbolic-empty thought. As opposed to that, this immediacy was construed as intuition in the usual sense, just because the fundamental distinction between sensuous and categorial intuition was not recognized.

It is no different with the chapter, also improved, on "the *a priori* laws of genuine and figurative thought." It provides at least the pattern for the refutation of psychologism in the theory of reason. In the present investigation this is restricted to formal-logical reason. How superficially this had been read was shown by the often repeated but unfounded charge, that after the rejection of psychologism in the first volume, Husserl fell back into psychologism in the second volume. Schlick, in his *Allgemeine Erkenntnislehre* (p. 121) had attributed to Husserl the assumption of a special intuition *that is not supposed to be a real psychical act,* which clearly perverted his meaning.

After twenty years of further work, Husserl naturally changed some of his views. For example, he no longer approved the doctrine of categorial representation. Nevertheless he believed that even that which is not mature, or which is even unsuccessful in this work, is worthy of full consideration. As for Section III, Husserl notes that he had changed his position regarding the problem of the phenomenological interpretation of question- and wish-propositions shortly after the first edition, which required big changes. He therefore left the text unchanged. The appendix on "outer and inner perception," which had been much used, is much improved in the new edition, while retaining the essential content of the text.

mode of expression, upon the relationship of "concept" or "thought," here understood as intuitively unfulfilled intention, and "corresponding intuition."

The class of acts in which the differences of intention and fulfillment, or disappointment, of the intention are found, extends far beyond the logical domain. The class of objectivating acts is distinguished by the circumstance that the syntheses of fulfillment belonging to its sphere have the character of knowledge, of identification, of "agreement"; and accordingly, the disappointment-syntheses have the correlative character of "separation," of "conflict." Within this widest sphere of objectivating acts Husserl proposes to study all relationships pertaining to the unity of knowledge, and not only so far as regards a fulfillment of those particular intentions which are attached to the expressions as meaning-intentions. Analogous intentions also appear independently of grammatical connection.

Husserl proposes to characterize the general concepts of *signification* and *intuition* phenomenologically by recourse to the phenomena of fulfillment, and to investigate the analysis, fundamental for the clarification of knowledge, of the various kinds of intuition, first of all, of sensuous intuition. Then he proceeds to the phenomenology of the levels of knowledge, to clarify and determine a series of basic concepts of knowledge referring to them. New concepts of content, treated only incidentally in the foregoing analyses, appear here: the concept of the *intuitive content* and the concept of the *representative* (apprehended) *content*. The previous concept of the intentional essence is followed by the *cognitive essence*, and within the latter, the intentional quality, the intentional matter as the apprehension-sense (*Auffassungssinn*), the apprehension-form, and the apprehended (apperceived, or representative) content are distinguished. The concept of *apprehension or representation*, as the unity of matter and representative content through the form of apprehension, is determined.

As regards the stages of intention and fulfillment, the differences of greater or lesser *mediateness in the intention itself*, which excludes a simple fulfillment and requires a graded succession of fulfillments, are considered, and therewith the most important and still unclarified sense of *indirect presentations* is examined. Then the differences of greater and lesser conformity of the intention to the intuitive experience fusing with it in the cognition as fulfillment are followed out, and the case of *objectively complete conformity* is determined. In connection therewith, Husserl seeks a final phenomenological clarification of the concepts of *possibility* and *impossibility* (concord, compatibility — conflict, incompatibility) and of the ideal axioms relating to them. As for the distinction relating to positing acts, of *provisional* and *final* fulfillment, the final fulfillment represents an ideal of completion in a corresponding "perception" (whereby a necessary extension of the concept of perception beyond the limits of sensibility is involved). The synthesis of fulfillment in this case is *evidence* or *knowledge* in the significant sense of the word. Here *being in the sense of truth*, of "agreement" correctly understood, of the "adaequatio rei ac intellectus," is realized, here it is itself given, it is to be directly intuited and apprehended. The various concepts of truth, which are to be constituted on the basis of one and the same phenomenological condition, are completely clarified here. The situation is analogous for the case of incompleteness, and hence of absurdity, with respect to "conflict" and to the non-being or untruth experienced therein.

In keeping with the original interest of the investigation in meaning-intentions, the simplest meanings are first considered, in abstraction from any differences of form. The supplementary investigation of the second section, taking account of these differences, leads at once to a completely new concept of matter, namely, to the fundamental contrast of sensuous "substance" (*Stoff*) and categorial form, or, to change from the objective to the phenomenological view (*Stellung*), between *sensuous* and *categorial acts*. In close connection therewith is the important distinction between real sensuous and categorial objects, determinations, or connections; and it is characteristic of the categorial that they can, in the manner of "perception," only be "given" in acts which are founded on other acts, ultimately on acts of sensibility. The intuitive, and hence also the imaginative fulfillment of categorial acts, is founded on sensuous acts. However, never can mere sensibility provide fulfillment of categorial intentions (or, more exactly, provide it for intentions containing categorial forms); rather, the sensibility is always formed through categorial acts. The original sensuous concepts, intuition and perception, are necessarily extended, so that one may speak of *categorial* and especially of *general intuition*. The distinction between sensuous and purely categorial abstraction then underlies the distinction of general concepts into sensuous concepts and categories. The old epistemological opposition between *sensibility* and *understanding* receives all desired clarity through the distinction between simple or sensuous, and founded or categorial intuition. The same holds for the opposition between *thinking* and *intuition,* which in philosophical usage confuses the relationships of signification and fulfilling-intuition with the relationships of sensuous and categorial acts. All talk of logical form concerns that which is purely categorial in meanings and meaning-fulfillments. The logical "matter," the totality of "terms," can however, by virtue of a step-like superposition of categorial intentions, itself admit of distinctions between *substance* and *form*, so that the *logical* opposition of substance and form is a relative one.

The main part of this investigation is closed with a discussion of the limits which hold in check the freedom of the actual categorial formation of a "substance." The analytical laws of genuine thought are considered, which, being based upon pure categories, are independent of the particular nature of "substances." There are parallel limits to "figurative thought," i.e., mere signification, if it is to be capable of expression in a real sense, *a priori* and independently of the "substances" to be expressed. From this requirement arises the function of the real laws of thought as norms of mere signification.

The question raised at the beginning of the investigation, of a natural delimitation of meaning-giving and meaning-fulfilling acts, is settled by their being ordered under the class of objectivating acts, and by the classification of objectivating acts into significative and intuitive acts. The clarification of the phenomenological relationships concerning fulfillment makes it possible to appraise critically the arguments for and against the Aristotelian conception of wish- and command-propositions, etc., as predications. The closing section of the investigation is devoted to the elucidation of this controversial question.

These aims are not the final and highest ones of a phenomenological elucidation of knowledge in general. The fruitful domain of mediate thought and knowledge is left almost entirely untreated by the present analyses; the essence of mediate evidence and its ideal correlates remains without sufficient clarification. However, an attempt is made to make clear the lowest and first foundations of the critique of knowledge. The problems of knowledge must first be dealt with in their simplest forms. That such a modest epistemological work has still to overcome a great mass of difficulties, in fact has still to accomplish everything, is shown by the analyses that follow.

A. MEANING-INTENTION AND MEANING-FULFILLMENT

1. The Expression of an Act; Formulation of the Theme

The investigation begins with the question whether all or only certain kinds of acts can function as bearers of meaning. All acts are indeed *expressible*. But that is not to say that all acts can also function as *bearers of meaning.* The term "express" is ambiguous, as seen in the first investigation, and it remains ambiguous if it refers to acts which are to be expressed. One can designate meaning-conferring acts as expressed, or "manifesting" acts in a narrower sense. But still other acts can be said to be expressed, although in a different sense. Very common cases are here meant, in which we name acts which we experience, and by means of the naming, *state that* we experience them. In this sense I give expression to a wish in the form *I wish that* . . . , to a question in the form *I ask whether* . . . , to a judgment in the form *I judge that* . . . , etc. Obviously we can judge about our own inner experiences just as well as we can judge about external things, and if we do this, the meanings of the propositions in question are in the judgments about these experiences and not in the experiences themselves, the wishes, questions, and the like. Similarly the meanings of statements about external things are not in these things (the horses, houses, etc.), but in the judgments which we internally assert about them, or in the presentations which help to build up these judgments. That the judged objects are in the one case transcendent of consciousness (or are presumed to be) and in the other case are immanent in consciousness does not make any essential difference here. To be sure, the wish which fills me while I state it is concretely one with the act of judgment. But it does not really contribute to the judgment. The wish is apprehended in an act of reflective perception, is comprehended under the concept *wish*, and is named by means of this concept and the determining presentation of the wish-content; and thus the conceptual *presentation* of the wish directly makes its contribution to the judgment about the wish, and the corresponding wish-*name* makes its contribution to the wish-statement, just as the presentation of a man makes its contribution to the judgment about the man (or the name man its contribution to the statement about the man). A wish-statement can be understood and reëxperienced judgmentally in the same sense by a hearer who does not at all share the wish. One can see from that, that the wish, even where it may be one with the act of judgment directed upon it, really does not belong to the judgment-meaning. A truly sense-giving experience can never be omitted if the living sense of the expression is to remain unchanged.

Three meanings of "expressed acts" may be distinguished. Either what are meant are acts in which the sense, the meaning of the expression concerned is constituted, or on the other hand the acts which the speaker wants to set up predicatively, as just experienced by him. In a *third* sense of the term what is referred to is, as in the second, a judging belonging to the acts involved, or some kind of objectivation; but not a judging *about* these acts — hence not an objectivation of them by means of presentations and names referring to them — but a judging *on the basis* of these acts, which does not require their objectivation. For example, that I *give expression to my perception*, that it has this or that content. But it can also mean that I derive my judgment from the perception, that I not only assert the matter of fact in question, but perceive it and assert it just as I perceive it. The judgment is then not asserted about the perception, but about that which is *perceived*. When one speaks simply of perceptual judgments, as a rule judgments of this class are meant. In a similar manner we can give expression to other intuitive acts, imaginations, remembrances, expectations.

It is proposed to bring to clarity the relationship between meaning and expressed intuition in this connection. Whether this intuition is itself the act constituting the meaning must be considered; and if not, their relationship must be accounted for otherwise. The more general question is first raised, whether the acts which *give* expression, and the acts which can *experience* expression, belong to essentially different kinds of act; and whether, with all that, there is a comprehensive generic unity which comprises the totality of the acts *which are capable of a meaning-function in the broader sense* — whether it be of the function of meaning itself, or that of "meaning-fulfillment" — so that the acts of all other genera of such functions remain excluded *eo ipso* and as a matter of law. The first goal of the investigation is indicated therewith. In the course of the discussion, the obvious extension of the domain of investigation will make evident the meaning of the questions raised for the understanding of knowledge in general.

2. *The Expression of a Perception* ("*Perceptual Judgment*")

Consider an example. I look out into the garden and give expression to my perception with the words *A blackbird flies up*. Which is the act here, in which the meaning lies? In accordance with the first investigation, it may be said that it is not the perception, at least not it alone. The present state of affairs cannot be described as though nothing besides the word-sound were given or were required for the significance of the expression, other than the perception with which it is connected. On the basis of the same perception, the statement could read entirely differently and have an entirely different sense. I could have said, for example: *This is black, is a black bird; This black animal flies up*, etc. And conversely, the word-sound and its sense could remain the same, while the perception changes. Every accidental change of the relative position of the perceiver changes the perception itself, and different persons who perceive the same thing at the same time never have exactly the same perception. But differences of this kind are irrelevant to the meaning of the perceptual statement. If they were to be intended, the statement would have to read entirely differently. The perception can not only change, but can be absent entirely without the expression ceasing to remain meaningful. The hearer understands my words and the whole proposition without looking into the garden; he produces the same judgment without the perception.

If, however, the statement has meaning despite the omission of the perception, and even the *same* sense as previously, then we cannot assume [2] that the perception is the act in which the sense of the perceptual statement, its expressive intending, occurs. This function of meaning must be assigned to an act which is homogeneous everywhere, which is free of the limits of perception (so often denied us) and even of phantasy, and, where the expression "expresses" in a real sense, is only united with the expressed act.

The "expressing" of a perception (or, stated objectively, of something perceived as such) is not a matter of the word-sound, but is a matter of certain expressive acts. "Expression" signifies in this context the expression animated by its entire sense, which is here placed in a certain relationship to the perception, which on its side is said to be "expressed" for the sake of this relationship. *Between* the perception and the word-sound an act (or an act-structure) is *inserted*: an *act*, because the expression-experience has, whether accompanied by perception or not, an intentional relation to something objective. It must be this mediating act which really serves as sense-giving; it is the essential constituent of the meaningfully functioning expression and provides that the sense is identically the same, whether a verifying perception may be associated with it or not. The soundness of this conception will be confirmed by the following investigation.

3. Perception as an Act Determining But Not Containing Meaning

It may be objected, however, that even if a perception never makes the complete meaning of a statement asserted on the basis of the perception, it nevertheless contributes something to the meaning. This becomes more clear if we modify our example and speak of *this blackbird* instead of *a blackbird*. *This* is an essentially "occasional" expression, which only becomes completely significant with regard to the circumstances of the utter-

[2] Also disregarding the categorial forms, which are ignored purposely in this section.

ance and the experienced perception. The perceived object, just as it is given in the perception, is meant by the *this*. The present tense in the grammatical form of the verb also expresses a relation to the actual present. Obviously the same holds for the unmodified example; for whoever says "A blackbird flies up" does not mean a blackbird in general, but a blackbird that flies up here and now.

To be sure, the intended meaning is not attached to the word-sound. Since the sense of the unitary statement is located in the total act of intention which may be basic to it, it must be admitted that a perception, when it brings a fact to intuition which the statement expresses judgmentally, makes a contribution to the meaning-content of this judgment. Of course, it is a contribution that may also be made by other acts in a manner essentially in agreement. Thus a similar understanding of the meaning may be produced by means of phantasy.

A second interpretation is possible, however. In a certain sense it is to be said that the intuition makes a contribution to the meaning of the perceptual statement, namely, in the sense that the meaning could not develop in its definite relationship to the meant objectivity without the assistance of the intuition. But that is not to say that the act of intuition is itself the bearer of the meaning, or that it really makes contributions to the meaning, contributions which then could be found present as constituent parts of the finished meaning. The essentially occasional expressions do indeed have a meaning that changes from case to case; but something common remains in all the change, which distinguishes such ambiguity from that of ordinary equivocation. It is due to intuition that this common element is directed objectively; but this contribution does not require that a part of the meaning itself must lie in the intuition.

I say *this* and mean the paper lying before me. The word owes the reference to *this* object to the perception. But the meaning is not in the perception itself. I do not merely perceive, when I say *this*; but on the basis of the perception a new act is constructed, conforming to it, the act of intending *this*. The meaning resides in this intending reference alone. Without the perception — or a corresponding functioning act — the reference would be empty, without definite differentiation, and not at all possible *in concreto*.

Hence the perception realizes the possibility of the development of the *intending-this* with its definite relation to the object, e.g., to this paper before my eyes; but it does not constitute the meaning itself, not even a part.

The meaning of the *this* remains the same, if instead of the perception we have any act from the manifold of imaginative presentations which present the same object in an identical manner. But it is changed if intuitions from other perceptual or pictorial spheres are involved. We can mean *this*, but the common character of the act of meaning which obtains here, namely, of the aiming directly at the object, has an intention toward another object.

A confirmation of this view, which regards perception as an act determining meaning but not as an act containing meaning, is provided by the circumstance that essentially occasional expressions, such as *this*, frequently can be understood and used without an appropriate basis of intuition.[3]

4. The Static Unity between Expressing Thoughts and Expressed Intuition; Recognition (Erkennen)

The relationships that obtain between intuitive acts on the one hand, and expressive acts on the other hand, will now be examined more closely. The investigation is first restricted to the simple case of nominal expressions, or meaning-intentions — in particular, nominal expressions which relate to a "corresponding" perception and other intuition in as obvious a manner as is possible.

First to be considered is the *static relationship of unity*: the meaning-endowing thought is based upon intuition, and thereby related to its object. For example, I speak of *my inkstand*, and it is before me, I see it. The name refers to the object of the perception by means of the act of meaning.

---

[3] In the first investigation, proceeding from the understanding of the hearer, the "indicating" and "indicated" meaning of an essentially occasional expression, and especially of the *this*, were distinguished.

Two things can be meant when one speaks of *indicating* and *indicated* meaning. (1) The two thoughts characterizing the successive understanding of the hearer: *first* the indeterminate presentation of something intended by the *this*, *then* the modification formed through the supplementary presentation, the act of the definitely directed reference. In the latter act would lie the indicated, in the former the indicating meaning. (2) If we hold to the finished, definitely directed reference, which is given in the speaker from the outset, then two things can be distinguished in it itself: the general character of the reference, and that which determines it, that which restricts it to the reference to *this*. The former can again be denoted as an indicating meaning, inasmuch as it is that which the hearer can grasp immediately by virtue of its expressible generality and which can serve him for the indication of what is intended. If I say *this*, then the hearer at least knows that something is referred to. On the other hand, the real goal of the language does not lie in this generality, but in the direct intention toward the object concerned. It and its fullness of content represent our aim, and those empty generalities contribute nothing or as good as nothing to its determination. In this sense, the direct intention is the primary and indicated meaning.

This second distinction was laid down as basic by the definition in the earlier dscussion of meanng, in the first investigation. The distinction made here, and the dscussion, may be regarded as contributing to a further clarification of the difficult problem.

The relation between the name and that which is named has here a certain *descriptive character*. If we go back to the experiences, we find, as described in the first investigation, the acts of word-appearance on the one hand, and on the other hand, the similar acts of thing-appearance. In the latter respect the inkstand confronts us in perception.

Phenomenologically this means that we have a certain set of sensuous experiences, sensuously unified in their togetherness, determined in a certain way and "spiritualized" by a certain act-character of "apprehension," which endows them with objective meaning. This act-character makes an *object*, this inkstand, appear in the manner of perception. And in a similar manner the appearing word is constituted in an act of perception or phantasy-presentation.

Hence not the word and the inkstand, but the described act-experiences in which they appear, although they are nothing at all "in" them, enter into relationship. But what brings the acts to unity? The answer seems clear. This relation as a *naming* one is mediated through acts not merely of meaning, but of *recognition*, and here it is acts of *classification*. The perceived object is recognized as an inkstand, and inasmuch as the meaning expression is one with the classificatory act, and this again as recognition of the perceived object is one with the act of perception, the expression appears so to speak as *laid upon* the thing as though it were its garment.

Normally we speak of knowledge and classification of the *object* of perception as though the act were concerned with the object. There is no object in the experience itself, however, but rather the perception; hence the act of knowledge in the experience is based upon the act of perception. But this is not to say that the perception is classified instead of its object. That is not what is meant. That would presuppose more complex acts, as indicated by the expression *the perception of the inkstand*. Hence a recognition which blends simply and definitely the expression on the one side with the perception concerned on the other side, constitutes the experience: recognition of this thing as *my inkstand*. It is similar in cases in which an image-presentation serves instead of the perception.

5. *Recognition as an Act-Character and the "Generality of a Word"*

We are really justified, in all cases of the naming of something intuitively given, in assuming recognition as a mediating act-character between the appearance of a word-sound, or of the entire sense-animated word, and the thing-intuition. One often hears of the generality of word-meanings, and usually understands this to mean that a word is not bound to an individual intuition, but belongs to an infinite manifold of possible intuitions.

In what sense does it "belong"? Consider the name *red* as a simple example. When it names an appearing object as red, it belongs to this object by virtue of the factor of red appearing in it. And the same name *belongs* to every object that bears a homogeneous factor, and it belongs to it by virtue of the identical sense. The word is not attached to the same kind of features of the intuitions on the basis of concealed psychical mechanisms. The mere fact that wherever such a feature appears in the intuition, the word as a mere sound-structure is associated with it, is not sufficient. The mere togetherness of these two appearances with it does not produce an inner relation between them, and certainly not an intentional one. Such a relation obviously is present as something phenomenologically peculiar. The word names the red as red. The appearing red is that which is intended by the name, in this case as red. In this manner of naming-intending, the name appears as belonging to that which is named, and as one with it.

On the other hand, the word also has its sense outside of the connection with this intuition, even without connection with a "corresponding" intuition. Since the sense is the same everywhere, it is clear that we must regard the genuine and complete word as basic for the naming relation, in place of the mere word-sound. But then the unity of the meaningful word and of the corresponding intuition may not be described as a mere togetherness.

If we think of the word as it is known outside of all actual naming, as understood merely symbolically, and add the corresponding intuition, then it may be that the two appearances are joined into a phenomenological unity due to genetic reasons; but the joining in itself is not this unity, which arises as something obviously new. It would be thinkable *a priori* that this unity might never arise, in which case the coexistent appearances would be unrelated phenomenologically: that which appears would not stand there as that which is meant in the *significant* word, as that which is named, and the word would not function as a name.

Since we are phenomenologically in the position to find the innermost intentional unity, instead of a mere sum, it may be said that the two acts, of which one constitutes for us the complete word and the other of which constitutes the thing, come together intentionally to an act-unity. One can describe what is present with the words: *The name red names the red object red*, just as well as with the words: *The red object is recognized as red and is called red by means of this recognition. To name red* — in the actual sense of naming, which presupposes the underlying intuition of what is named — and *to recognize as red*, are expressions that are fundamentally identical in meaning; only that the latter brings out more clearly that there is here no duality, but rather a unity given through an act-character.

Obviously, the act-character of the recognition, to which the word owes its meaningful relation to the object of the intuition, does not belong essentially to the word-sound, but rather belongs to the word with respect to its significant (meaning) essence. With the most different word-sounds one may think of "the same" word in different languages, the cognitive relation being identically the same.

The *generality of a word* means accordingly that one and the same word so comprises (through its unified sense) an ideally delimited manifold of possible intuitions, in such a way that each of these intuitions can function as a basis of a nominal cognitive act with the same meaning. To the word *red* there belongs, e.g., the possibility of recognizing and naming as red all red objects which may be given in possible intuitions. Connected therewith is the possibility, guaranteed *a priori*, to become aware *by the identifying synthesis* of such recognitions that they are the same in meaning, that this *A* is red and that *A* is *the same*, namely, also red; the two intuitive particulars belong under the same "concept."

What has been said holds everywhere, and not merely for the expressions which have a general meaning in the manner of general concepts. It also holds with regard to the expressions with individual meaning, such as the proper names are. That which one usually denotes as the "generality of the word-meaning" does not mean the generality attributed to generic concepts in opposition to individual concepts; on the contrary, it comprises both of them in the same manner. Accordingly, the "recognition" of which we speak in the relation of a meaningfully functioning expression to a corresponding intuition, is not to be conceived as an actual classification that occurs in the ordering of an intuitive object or of one presented in thought into a class — and hence as necessarily involving general concepts and names. Proper names also have their "generality," although there is no talk of classification for them. A name does not belong to a definite perception, or to a definite imagination. In countless possible intuitions the same person comes to appearance, and all these appearances have not merely intuitive but also cognitive unity.

The generality of a proper name and of the proper meaning corresponding to it is naturally of an entirely different character than that of a class name. In the former case, a synthesis of possible intuitions belongs to an individual object, and these are unified by a common intentional character, which, without prejudice to the other phenomenal differences between the single intuitions, endows each one with relationship to the same object. This unity is then the foundation for the cognitive unity which belongs to the "generality of the word-meaning." Thus the naming word has a cognitive relation to an unlimited manifold of intuitions, whose *one and the same object* it recognizes and thereby names.

It is entirely different with class names. Their generality comprises an *extension of objects*, to each of which, considered by and for itself, a possible proper name belongs. The general name "encompasses" this extension by being able to name every member of the extension generally, i.e., to name it, not in the manner of the proper names through proper recognition, but as "an *A*" in the manner of common names, through classification.

6. *Dynamic Fulfillment and the Consciousness of Identity*

Instead of "static" coincidence (*Deckung*) between meaning and intuition, a *dynamic* one will now be considered; to the first merely symbolically functioning expression the (more or less) corresponding intuition is now joined. If this occurs, we experience a descriptively peculiar *consciousness of fulfillment*: [4] the act of pure meaning finds its fulfillment in an envisaging act in the manner of an aiming intention. We experience how *the same* objectivity is intuitively presented, which was "merely thought" in the symbolic act. It is only another expression for it, if we say that *the intentional essence of the act of intuition is adapted* (more or less completely) *to the meaning essence of the expressing act*.

Recognition was spoken of when the static relationship between the acts of meaning and intuition was considered. This produces the significant relation of a name to that which is given in an intuition as named. But the meaning is not the same as the recognition. In the case of purely symbolic word-understanding the word means something to us, but nothing is recognized. The difference lies not in the mere co-givenness of the intuition of what is named, but in the phenomenologically peculiar *form of unity*. The latter makes clear to us the dynamic relationship. The meaning-intention is first given by itself; then the corresponding intuition enters in. At the same time the phenomenological unity is produced, which is now manifested as *conciousness of fulfillment*. The words "knowledge of the object" and "fulfillment of the meaning-intention" therefore express the same state of affairs, only from different standpoints. The former is from the standpoint of the meant object, whereas the latter

[4] Reference is made to the "Psychologische Studien" of 1894, *l. c.*, p. 176.

takes the acts on both sides as points of reference. In any case, the acts exist phenomenologically, but not always the objects. Hence the talk of fulfillment gives better expression to the *phenomenological* essence of the relation of knowledge. It is a primitive phenomenological fact that acts of signification and intuition can enter into this peculiar relationship.[5] And where they do it, where an act of meaning-intention is fulfilled in an intuition, there we also say, "The object of the intuition is recognized through its concept," or "The name in question finds application to the appearing object."

The phenomenological distinction between the static and dynamic fulfillment or recognition is easily done justice. In the dynamic relationship the terms of the relation and the cognitive act relating them are temporally distinct; they are unfolded in a time-form. In the static relationship, which remains there as a result of this temporal occurrence, they "coincide" in a temporal and material manner.

With respect to the objective side one may speak of "unity of identity." Whether the case be static or dynamic, *objective identity* can be ascertained. The object of intuition is *the same* as the object of the thought fulfilling itself in it, and in the case of exact adaptation, the object is intuited exactly the same as it was thought (or what is always the same here: meant). It is clear that the identity is not first brought in through a comparative reflection that is mediated by thought, but that it is there from the outset, that it is an experience, an unexpressed, unconceived experience. In other words: what we characterize phenomenologically, with regard to the acts, as fulfillment, is with regard to the objects *on both sides*, to the intuited object on the one side, and the thought object on the other side, to be expressed as an experience of identity, a consciousness of identity, an act of identification; the more or less complete identity corresponds objectively to the act of fulfillment, or "appears" in it. For that reason, not merely the signification and intuition may be denoted as an act, but also the adequation, i.e., the unity of fulfillment, because it has an intentional correlate peculiar to it, an objectivity toward which it is "directed." Another variant of the same state of affairs is expressed when one speaks of recognition. The circumstance that the meaning-intention is united in the manner of fulfillment with the intuition gives to the *object* appearing in the latter, where we are primarily concerned with it,

[5] The term "signification" is the same as "meaning" for Husserl. Similarly, he often speaks of *significative* or *signitive acts*, instead of acts of meaning-intention, of meaning, and the like. *Signitive* is also good as expressing opposition to *intuitive*. A synonym for *signitive* is *symbolic*.

the character of that which is recognized. Recognition as well as fulfillment — the former is only another word for the latter — may obviously be designated as an identifying act.

A doubt regarding the otherwise clear conception of the identity- or knowledge-unity appearing here as an *act* of identification or of recognition must be considered finally; and it is all the more important to consider it because it proves to be serious in the course of the investigation and to lead to fruitful discussions. With more precise analysis it occurs to us that when a name refers to an object of intuition by actually naming it, we mean the intuited and named *object*, and not the *identity* of this object, as that which is at the same time intuited and named. Shall we say that it is the preference of attention which decides here? Or should we not rather admit that the act of identification is really not entirely constituted: the main part of this act, the factor of the unification of the meaning-intention and of the corresponding intuition, is to be sure immanently present; but this unity-factor does not function as a "representative" of an objectivating "apprehension"; the experienced unity of coincidence does not establish any act of *relating identification*, no intentional consciousness of identity, in which the identity would first of all be objective for us as a meant unity. In reflecting about the unity of fulfillment we would provide the relating apprehension which the form of its unity permits *a priori*. In the most general form, related to categorial acts in general, this question is considered in the next chapter. Temporarily the designated character of unity will continue to be treated as a complete act, or it will not be separated explicitly from the complete act. The essence of the discussion will not be affected thereby, inasmuch as the transition from the experience of unity to the relating identification is at all times open, since its *a priori* possibility is guaranteed, so that it may be said with right: identifying coincidence is experienced, even if the conscious intention toward identity, the relating identification, does not take place.

7. *The Different Character of the Intention within and without the Unity of Fulfillment*

The introduction of dynamic fulfillment, taking place in the form of an articulated process, for the purpose of the interpretation of the static act of knowledge, also removes a difficulty which threatens to confuse the clear comprehension of the relationship between the meaning-intention and the complete act of knowledge. May we really assert that in the unity of knowledge four things can be distinguished: the verbal expression, the act of meaning, the act of intuition, and finally the overlapping character of the unity of the recognition, or of the fulfillment? One might be doubtful, and argue that the analysis really finds only the linguistic expression on the one side, in particular the name, and on the other side, the intuition, and both as united by the character of the recognizing nam- ing; and that it must be denied that an act of meaning is connected with the linguistic expression. That an act of meaning is connected with the linguistic expression, as something distinguishable from the knowledge- character and the fulfilling intuition, and as something identifiable with the understanding-character of the same expression outside its knowledge- function, that would have to be denied, according to this objection; at least it is regarded as a superfluous assumption.

The following must be borne in mind in considering this objection. First, the comparison of the expression standing within the knowledge- function and the one standing outside of it shows that the meaning is the same in both cases. Whether I understand the word *tree* merely sym- bolically, or whether I use it on the basis of an intuition of a tree, both times I evidently mean something by the word, and both times it is the same. Second, it is evident that in the process of the fulfillment it is the meaning-intention of the expression which is "fulfilled" and therewith "coincides" with the intuition, and that consequently the knowledge as the result of the process of coincidence is this unity of coincidence itself. In accordance with the concept of a unity of coincidence, however, what is in question here is not a divergent duality, but rather an undivided unity which is first articulated through postponement in time. It must there- fore be said that the same act of meaning-intention which made up empty symbolic presentation is also inherent in the complex act of knowledge; but the meaning-intention which was formerly a "free" one is "bound" in the stage of coincidence, is brought to "indifference." It is so peculiarly interwoven in this complex, or fused with it, that although its meaning essence does not suffer from it, its character is modified in a certain manner.

The same holds in general when contents are viewed by themselves, and again in connection with others, as interwoven parts of a whole. The connection would not connect anything, if the connected contents would not undergo anything through them. Certain changes necessarily result, and it is those which, as connection-determinations, make up the phenom- enological correlates of the *relative* objective qualities. Thus one can think of a length of a line by itself, say on an empty white background, and then the same length as a constituent of a figure. In the latter case it meets with other lines, it is touched by them, intersected, etc. These are, if we disregard the mathematical ideals and hold to empirical intuitions, phenomenological characters, which enter into the determination of the impression of the appearance of the length. The same length (the same with respect to its inner content) always appears differently to us, according to whether it enters into one or another phenomenal context; and if we insert it in a line or surface qualitatively identical with it, then it enters into this background "without distinction," it loses phenomenal separation and autonomy.

8. *Intuitions as Intentions Needing Fulfillment*

For the further characterization of the consciousness of fulfillment, a character of experience is pointed out which also plays a big part in our mental life. It is only necessary to recall the contrasts of wish-intention and wish-fulfillment, will-intention and will-fulfillment, or the fulfillment of hopes, solution of doubts, etc., to see that in various classes of intentional experiences essentially the same contrast appears, as occurs here in the contrast between meaning-intention and meaning-fulfillment. This point was touched upon in the fifth investigation, when a class of intentional experiences was delimited under the title of *intentions*, which are characterized by the peculiarity of being able to found relationships of fulfillment.

If, e.g., the beginning of a familiar melody sounds, it stimulates definite intentions which are fulfilled by the gradual playing of the melody. It is similar if the melody is strange to us. The "indefiniteness" that is intended is a descriptive peculiarity belonging to the character of the intention.

In this example we have to do with a relationship of *expectation* and *fulfillment of the expectation*. But it would be incorrect to construe every relationship of an intention to its fulfillment as a relationship of expectation. Intention is not expectation; it is not essential to it to be directed upon a future occurrence. If I see an incomplete pattern, e.g., of this carpet, which is partly covered by pieces of furniture, then the seen part is so to speak affected with intentions which refer to completions (we *feel*, so to speak, that the lines and color-forms continue in the "sense" of that which is seen); but we do not expect anything.

An infinity of examples belonging here are provided by outer perceptions. The determinations coming into the perception refer to the completing determinations, entering into the appearance in new possible perceptions. Analysis shows that every perception and every connection of perception is constructed out of components which are to be understood from both these points of view, intention and (actual or possible) fulfillment; a condition which applies at once to parallel acts of phantasy, etc. Every perception and imagination is a network of partial intentions, fused into the unity of a total intention. The correlate of the latter is the thing, whereas the correlates of the partial intentions are *thingal parts and factors*. Only thus can we understand how consciousness can reach beyond that which is truly experienced. It can so to speak "mean beyond," and the meaning can be fulfilled.

9. *Disappointment and Conflict; the Synthesis of Distinction*

In the wider sphere of acts which admit of distinctions of intention and fulfillment, disappointment must be considered, as their excluding opposite. The for the most part negative expression which is usually used here, e.g., the expression non-fulfillment, does not mean a mere privation of fulfillment, but rather a new descriptive fact, a form of synthesis just as peculiar as is fulfillment. This also holds in the narrower sphere of meaning-intentions in their relationship to intuitive intentions. The synthesis of knowledge was consciousness of a certain "agreement." But corresponding to agreement as a correlative possibility is "disagreement," "conflict." The intuition does not "agree" with the meaning-intention; it "conflicts" with it. Conflict "separates," but the experience of the conflict places into relationship and unity; it is a form of *synthesis*. The earlier synthesis was one of identification, whereas this is one of *distinction*. In the "distinction" (*Unterscheidung*) here in question, the object of the disappointing act appears as "not the same," as "different" than the object of the intending act. These expressions refer, however, to more general spheres of cases than have been selected so far. Not merely the significative but also the intuitive intentions are fulfilled in the manner of identification and are disappointed in the manner of conflict. The question of the natural delimitation of the total class of acts to which the *the same* and the *different* belong (or the *is* and *is not*), will be considered more fully (§ B, 2).

Both syntheses are not completely coördinated. Every conflict presupposes something that gives to the intention the direction toward the object of the conflicting act, and this direction can only be given to it finally by a synthesis of fulfillment. The conflict presupposes as it were a certain ground of agreement. If I mean *A is red*, whereas it turns out "in truth" to be green, then the red-intention conflicts with the green-intuition. That is only possible on the basis of the identification of the *A* in the acts of signification and intuition. Only thus can the intention reach this intuition. The total intention refers to an *A* that is red, and the intuition shows an

A that is green. While meaning and intuition correspond to each other with respect to the direction toward the same *A*, the unifiedly co-given intentional factors enter first of all into conflict, the meant red (that is meant as red of the *A*) does not agree with the intuited green. Through the relation of identity the factors that have not been brought to coincidence *correspond* to one another; instead of being "connected" through fulfillment they are "separated" through conflict, the intention is referred to that which is coördinated with it in intuition, but is nevertheless rejected by it.

What has been said here with special reference to meaning-intentions and the disappointments befalling them holds for the entire class of objectivating intentions. In general it may be said: An intention is disappointed in the manner of a conflict only by being a part of a more comprehensive intention whose complementary part is fulfilled. There can therefore be no possible talk of conflict in the case of simple or isolated acts.

The relationships until now considered between intention (in particular, meaning-intention) and fulfillment were those of total agreement and total conflict. Attention should also be called to the important cases of partial agreement and non-agreement between the intention and the act fulfilling or disappointing it. All essential findings hold for the intentions of the wider class already indicated, and are not restricted to the meaning-intentions.

All conflict reduces to the circumstance that the given disappointing intention was a part of a comprehensive intention which was partially fulfilled, i.e., with respect to the complementary parts, and at the same time is alienated with respect to the first part. In every conflict there is therefore partial agreement and partial conflict. The consideration of the objective relations could also have led to these possibilities; for where coincidence is spoken of, there exclusion, inclusion, and overlapping arise as correlative possibilities.

B. INDIRECT CHARACTERIZATION OF OBJECTIVATING INTENTIONS THROUGH DIFFERENCES OF FULFILLMENT-SYNTHESES

1. The Synthesis of Recognition as the Form of Fulfillment Characteristic of Objectivating Acts; Subsumption of Acts of Meaning under Objectivating Acts

Meaning-intentions have been included in the wider sphere of "intentions" in the significant sense of the word. To all intentions there correspond possible fulfillments (or their negative counterparts: disappointments), peculiar transition-experiences which are themselves characterized as acts, and which allow an intending act to so to speak reach its goal in a correlative act. The latter, in so far as it fulfills the intention, is called the fulfilling act, but it is called that only by virtue of the synthetic act of fulfillment. This transition-experience does not have the same character everywhere. In the case of significative and also in the case of intuitive intentions it has the character of knowledge-unity, which, with regard to the objects, is unity of identification. This does not hold, however, in the larger sphere of intentions in general. Although one can always speak of a coincidence, and can even find an identification present everywhere, this often arises by means of interwoven acts which provide a unity of identification.

An example will make this clear at once. The fulfilling of a wish occurs in an act which includes an identification as a necessary constituent. For there is a law that a wish-quality is founded on an objectivating act, on a mere presentation; and there is also a supplementary law that the wish-fulfillment is also founded on an act which "identifyingly" comprises the founding presentation: the wish-intention can only be fulfilled by trans-forming the mere presentation of that which is wished, which is basic to it, into a conforming verificatory perception (*Fürwahrnehmung*). What is present is, however, not the mere change, and hence the mere matter of fact that the imagination is replaced by the verifying perception; but both are one in the character of the identifying coincidence. In this synthetic character the *It is really and truly thus* is constituted (namely, as we had formerly merely presented and wished it); which of course does not preclude this reality from being merely supposed, especially since in most cases it is something inadequately presented. If the wish is founded on a purely signitive presentation, the identification can naturally also have the character of that more special coincidence fulfilling the sig-nification by a conforming intuition, which has been described above. It is similar with all intentions which have their basis in presentations (as objectivating acts); and that which holds for fulfillment can, *mutatis mutandis*, be applied to the case of disappointment.

It is now clear that if the wish-fulfillment, to continue with our example, is also founded on an identification and perhaps on an act of intuitive recognition, this act does not exhaust the wish-fulfillment. The satisfying of the specific wish-quality is a peculiar and different kind of act-character. It is a figure of speech if we also speak of satisfaction, or of fulfillment, outside the sphere of feeling-intentions.

Hence the special character of the fulfilling correspondence is connected with the special character of the intention. Not only that to every adumbration of the intention there corresponds a similar one of the correlative fulfillment, and at the same time a fulfillment in the sense of a synthetic act, but corresponding to the essentially different classes of intentions there are also thoroughgoing class-differences of fulfillment in the double sense that has been mentioned. Obviously the relevant terms in these parallel series always belong to *one class of acts*. The syntheses of fulfillment in the case of wish- and will-intentions are surely closely related and are sharply different from those appearing in meaning-syntheses, for example. On the other hand, the fulfillments of meaning-intentions and of intuitive acts are certainly of the same character, and thus generally for all objectivating acts. For this class, which alone interests us here, we can say that its unity of fulfillment has the character of unity of identification, and perhaps the narrower one of unity of knowledge, and consequently that of an act to which objective identity corresponds as an intentional correlate.

It was shown above that every fulfillment of a signitive intention by an intuitive one has the character of a synthesis of identification. But, conversely, the fulfillment of a meaning-intention by means of a corresponding intuition does not occur in every synthesis of identification. And still more: one can hardly speak of the fulfillment of an intention and accordingly of a recognition in every case of identification. In the widest sense, in ordinary speech every actual identification is called a recognition. In a narrower sense, however, what is in question is an approximation to a cognitive goal, in the narrowest sense of the critique of knowledge even the attainment of this cognitive goal itself. To transform the mere feeling into distinct insight and to delimit precisely the sense of this approximation, or attainment, will be the next task. Meanwhile the proposition will be adhered to that the unity of identification and therewith all unity of knowledge in the narrower and narrowest sense originates in the sphere of objectivating acts.

The peculiarity of the fulfillment can serve to characterize the unified class of acts to which it belongs essentially. Accordingly the objectivating acts could be defined as those whose synthesis of fulfillment has the character of identification, and whose synthesis of disappointment therefore has the character of distinction, or also as those acts which can function phenomenologically as members of a possible synthesis of identification or distinction; or finally, in anticipation of a law still to be formulated, as those acts which, whether as intending or fulfilling or disappointing acts, can have a possible knowledge-function. To this class there then belong the synthetic acts of identification and distinction themselves; they are themselves either a mere supposition to grasp identity or non-identity, or the corresponding *actual* grasping of the one or the other. That supposition can be "confirmed" or "refuted" in a cognition; and in the first case identity, or non-identity, is really grasped, i.e., "adequately perceived."

The analyses indicated lead to the result that the acts of meaning-intention, as well as those of meaning-fulfillment, the acts of "thought" as well as those of intuition, all belong to the class of objectivating acts. It is established therewith that other kinds of acts never can function as sense-giving, and can only "come to expression" because the significative intentions attaching to the words are fulfilled by means of perceptions or imaginations, the *objects* of which are the acts to be expressed. Whereas in the cases in which acts have the function of meaning and in this sense find expression, the signitive or intuitive relation to objects is constituted in just these acts, in the other cases *the acts are mere objects*, and other acts function as the real bearers of meaning.

But before discussing this more fully it is necessary to examine more carefully the important facts of fulfillment in the sphere of the objectivating acts.

2. Distinction between Signitive and Intuitive Intentions through Peculiarities of Fulfillment

a. Sign, picture, and self-representation

It has been noted that the generic character of a synthesis of fulfillment is innerly connected with that of the intentions, and this so much so that the class of objectivating acts may be defined through the generic character, which is presupposed as known, of the identifying synthesis of fulfillment. The question arises whether the essential distinctions of species *within* this class of objectivations can be determined through the pertinent distinctions of the modes of fulfillment. By a fundamental classification, objectivating intentions divide into the *significative* and the *intuitive*. The two kinds of acts will now be considered.

The *significative intentions* have been regarded, by virtue of our departure from expressive acts, as significations, as meanings of expressions. These signitive intentions have an intuitive support on the sensuous side of the expression, but they do not therefore have an intuitive content; they are different in kind from intuitive acts.

The difference between expressive and purely intuitive intentions readily appears when signs and pictures are compared with one another.

A sign has mostly no content in common with that which is signified; it can denote something heterogeneous just as well as something homogeneous with it. A picture, however, is related to the thing by *similarity*, and if that is lacking, there can be no more talk of a picture. The sign as an object is constituted in the act of appearing. This act is not yet denotative; it requires the connection of a new intention, of a new mode of apprehension, by which something new, the denoted object, is meant instead of that which appears intuitively. The picture, as, e.g., the marble bust, is also a thing like anything else; it is first the mode of apprehension which makes it to be a picture; it then does not merely appear as a marble thing, but on the basis of this appearance a person is meant pictorially.

The intentions that are joined on both sides are not attached externally to the appearance-content, but are essentially founded on it, in such a way that the character of the intention is determined through it. It would be a descriptively incorrect view of the situation if one were to think that the entire distinction consists in the same intention being at one time connected with the appearance of an object *similar* to the meant object, and at another time connected with the appearance of an object dissimilar to it. For the sign can also be similar to what is signified, even perfectly similar. The sign-presentation does not, however, thereby become a picture-presentation. The photograph of the sign *A* we at once apprehend as a picture of this sign. But if we use the sign *A* as a sign of the sign *A*, as when we write: *A is a written Roman character*, then despite the pictorial similarity *A* is apprehended as a sign and not as a picture.

The objective fact of similarity between that which appears and that which is meant is, however, not unimportant for the case of picture-presentation. This is shown in the possible fulfillment; and it is only this possibility which permitted bringing in the "objective" similarity here. The picture-presentation has the obvious peculiarity that wherever it achieves fulfillment, the object appearing to it as a "picture" is identified through similarity with the object *given* in the fulfilling act. To designate this as a peculiarity of picture-presentation is to say that here the fulfillment of the similar through something similar innerly determines the character of the synthesis of fulfillment as an *imaginative* one. If, on the other hand, as a result of an accidental similarity between a sign and that which is signified, there is knowledge of their mutual similarity, then this knowledge does not belong to the fulfillment of the signitive intention. In accordance with the peculiar essence of a *significative* intention, the appearing object of the intending act and that of the fulfilling act (e.g., a name and that which is named in the realized unity of both) "have nothing to do" with one another. It is clear, accordingly, that the descriptively different manner of fulfillment, which is based upon the different descriptive character of the intention, can also call attention conversely to the difference of this character and determine it definitionally.

Until now only the difference between signitive and imaginative intentions has been considered. As distinguished from the imagination, perception is characterized by the fact that the object appears to it "itself," and not merely "in the image." The imagination is fulfilled through the peculiar synthesis of image-similarity, and perception through the synthesis of the material identity; the thing is confirmed through "itself," because it is displayed from various sides and is always the same.

b. The perceptual and imaginative adumbration of the object

The following difference must, however, be noted: a perception, because it pretends to give the object "itself," really pretends not to be a mere intention, but an act which may offer fulfillment to others, and does not itself need any further fulfillment. Mostly, and, e.g., in all cases of "outer" perception, it remains with the pretension. The object is not really given; it is not completely given as that which it is itself. It appears only "from the front side," "perspectively shortened and adumbrated," and the like. If the perception were everywhere what it pretends to be, real and genuine self-representation of the object, there would be only a single perception for every object, since its peculiar essence would be exhausted in this self-representation.

On the other hand, it is to be noted that the object, as it is in itself, is not a totally different one than that which the perception incompletely realizes. It lies so to speak in the sense of the perception, to be the self-appearance of the object. Even if, to consider it phenomenologically, the common perception is constructed out of many intentions — in part perceptual, in part merely imaginative, and even signitive intentions — as a total act it apprehends the object itself, if only in the manner of adumbration. If a perception is thought of as fulfilling an adequate perception, i.e., a perception which would give the object itself to us, then it can be said: the perception intends the object in such a way that the ideal synthesis of fulfillment would have the character of a *partial coincidence* of the purely perceptual content of the intending act with that of the fulfilling act, and at the same time would have the character of a complete coincidence of the perceptual intentions on both sides. The "purely perceptual" content in "outer" perception is that which we retain after abstraction from all merely imaginative and symbolic components; it is therefore the "sensed" content in the purely perceptual apprehension immediately belonging to it, which regards all its parts and factors as self-adumbrations of corresponding parts and factors of the perceptual object, and thus gives to the entire content the character of a "perceptual image" of the perceptual adumbration of the object. In the ideal limiting case of adequate perception this sensed or self-representing content is coincident with the perceived object.

This common relation to an object in itself, and consequently to the ideal of adequation, which belongs to the sense of all perception, is also manifested in the phenomenological belonging together of the various perceptions pertaining to the one object. In the one perception the object appears from this, in the other from that side, once near, the other time far, etc. In each the one and the same object is "there"; in each it is intended just as it is known to us and present in this perception. Corresponding to it phenomenologically is the continuous flow of fulfillment or identification, in the series of perceptions "belonging to the same object." Each of them is a mixture of fulfilled and unfulfilled intentions. To the former there corresponds in the object that which was given by it in *this* single perception as a more or less complete adumbration; to the latter, that which was not yet given by it, and hence would be actually present as a fulfillment in new perceptions. All such syntheses of fulfillment are distinguished by a common character, as identifications of self-appearances of an object with self-appearances of the same object. Parallel distinctions hold also for imaginative presentation. There is also the ideal of complete representation, in which the adumbration would coincide with the complete image.

These analyses are instructive regarding the homogeneousness of perceptions and imaginations, and their common contrast to signitive intentions. A general distinction must be made between the meant — the denoted, pictured, perceived — object, and a content actually given in the appearance, but not meant: the sign-content on the one side, the imaginative and the perceptual adumbration of the object on the other side. Whereas, however, the signs and that which is signified "have nothing to do with one another," inner connections exist between the adumbrations (whether imaginative or perceptual) and the thing itself. These relationships are documented phenomenologically in the differences of the constitutive intentions, and also in differences of the syntheses of fulfillment.

This discussion does not disturb the interpretation of *every* fulfillment as an identification. The comparison referred not to the meant objects, but to signs and adumbrations in their relations to the meant objects, or to that which corresponds phenomenologically to these relations.

The distinction between intuitive and signitive acts has been characterized indirectly. A direct characterization will be provided later (§ C, 11) on the basis of the intentions viewed by themselves and without regard to the possible fulfillments.

3. Signitive Intentions outside the Meaning-Function

In the foregoing, certain components of intuitive acts have been treated as signitive intentions. But in the entire series of investigations up to this time signitive acts were regarded as acts of meaning, as sense-giving factors in expressions. The words signification and signitive intention were taken to be identical in meaning. It is now appropriate to consider the question whether the same or essentially homogeneous acts with a meaning-function can also appear outside this function, separated from all expressions.

This question is to be answered in the affirmative, as shown by certain cases of wordless recognition. For example, we recognize an object to be an ancient Roman road-stone, we recognize its furrows to be weather-beaten inscriptions, without words entering in; or we recognize a tool as being a drill, but the word does not occur to us. These cases of wordless recognition are nothing but fulfillments of meaning-intentions which have been detached phenomenologically from the signitive contents otherwise belonging to them. Again, in the case of scientific thinking, the series of thoughts which rush along are to a very large extent not bound to the words referring to them, but are excited by the flow of intuitive images or by their own associative interlacings.

Signitive intentions which appear identically, just as they are, at one time within and at another time outside the meaning-function, should not alone be considered. Countless signitive intentions are without any relation to expressions, whereas they still belong essentially to the same class as the meaning-intentions. Consider, e.g., the perceptual or imaginative running off of a melody, and the intentions as well as fulfillments (definite or indefinite) which enter in; and also the empirical order and connection of things in their phenomenal coexistence, with respect to that which gives unity to the things (and their parts) appearing in this order. Representation and recognition through analogy can only bring the image and the thing (the analogue and that which is analogized) to unity and consequently have them appear as belonging together; not what is merely given together in contiguity, but rather what appears as belonging together. Even if images appear which imagine that which is signitively represented in advance, and then are confirmed by fulfillment in their things, the unity between a contiguity-representative and that which is represented thereby cannot be given through the image-relationship, but only through the peculiar relationship of signitive representation, as one through contiguity.

Signitive intentions are accordingly included, in addition to perceptual and imaginative elements, in the complexes of primitive intentions entering into inadequate perceptions and imaginations. In general, all phenomenological differences of objectivating acts can be reduced to the elementary intentions and fulfillments building them up, and these are united through syntheses of fulfillment. On the side of the intentions there then remain, as the only final distinction, the difference between signitive intentions as intentions through contiguity, and imaginative intentions as such through analogy, each simple and pure in its kind. On the side of the fulfillment, intentions of both kinds function as components; but in some cases (as in the case of perception) also those which are no longer to be regarded as intentions, components which only fulfill and do not strive for fulfillment any more, self-representations of the object meant by them. Through the character of the elementary acts the characters of the syntheses of fulfillment which determine the homogeneous unity of the complex act are determined, and at the same time, with the aid of the power of attention, the character of the elementary acts is carried over to the unity of the total act: the entire act is imagination or signification or perception, and where two such united acts enter into relation, relationships of agreement and of conflict arise, whose character is determined by the total founding acts, and finally by their elements.

In the discussion to come, it is proposed to hold purely to the phenomenologically given unities, to the sense which they carry in themselves, and which they make known in the fulfillment. Thus the way of hypothetical construction may be avoided, with the doubts of which the clarification of knowledge does not need to be burdened.

C. THE PHENOMENOLOGY OF KNOWLEDGE-LEVELS

1. Mere Identification and Fulfillment

In the present account of the relation of meaning-intention and fulfilling intuition, which proceeded from the linguistic expression of a perception, it was said that the intentional essence of the intuitive act is adapted to or belongs to the meaning essence of the signitive act. The same holds in every case of a total identification which brings positing and positing acts, or non-positing and non-positing acts, to a synthesis; whereas with a difference of the qualities the identification is based exclusively upon the matters of the acts on both sides. This is carried over with appropriate changes to cases of partial identification, so that it may be stated that the matter is the factor that is essential for the identification (and also for the distinction) in the act-character of the acts which are synthesized.

In the case of identification the matters are the special bearers of the synthesis, but are not themselves identified. The term identification refers to the objects presented through the matter. On the other hand, the matters come to coincidence in the act of identification itself. That even if equality of the qualities is presupposed, no complete equality of the acts on both sides is obtained, is shown by every example, and that is because the intentional essence does not exhaust the act. That which remains is seen to be most significant in the careful investigation of the phenomenology of the levels of knowledge, which is the next task. If recognition admits of stages of completeness, and that with the same matter, then the matter cannot be responsible for the differences of completeness, and hence also cannot determine the peculiar essence of knowledge as opposed to any identification. The further investigation is connected with the consideration of this distinction between *mere identification* and *fulfillment*.

Fulfillment has been equated to recognition (in a narrower sense), and it has been pointed out that only certain forms of identification are denoted therewith, which bring us closer to the goal of knowledge. What that means may perhaps be made more clear in the following way: In every fulfillment there occurs a more or less complete *envisagement* (*Veranschaulichung*). What the intention means, but pictures in a more or less figurative or inadequate way, is placed directly before us by the fulfillment, i.e., the act which offers the "fullness" to the intention in the synthesis of fulfillment; or at least relatively more direct than the intention. In the fulfillment we experience as it were an *It is that itself*. This *itself* is to be sure not to be taken in a strict sense: as though a perception would have to be given, which would bring the object itself to us at the actual phenomenal present. It may be that in the progress of knowledge, in the step-like ascent from acts of less to those of richer knowledge-fullness, we must always finally attain to fulfilling perceptions; but not every level, i.e., every single identification already characterized as fulfillment, must therefore contain a perception as the fulfilling act. But the relative talk cf "more or less direct" and of "itself" indicates the main point to a certain extent: that the synthesis of fulfillment displays an inequality of the connected terms, such that the fulfilling act produces an advantage which is lacking to the mere intention, namely, that it gives to it the fullness of the "itself," and at least leads it more directly to the thing itself. And the relativity of this *direct* and *itself* again indicates that the relation of fulfillment has something of the character of a relation of increase or gradation (*Steigerung*). A concatenation of such relations accordingly appears to be possible, which rises step-like; whereby every such series of increases refers to an ideal limit or realizes it in its last term, which sets an insuperable goal to all increase: *the goal of absolute knowledge, of the adequate self-representation of the object of knowledge.*

This is a tentative treatment of fulfillments within the wider class of identifications.[6] For not in every identification is there such an approximation to a goal of knowledge, and accordingly identifications without a goal and moving on to infinity are possible. For example, there are infinitely many arithmetical expressions which have the identical number-value 2, and thus we can add identification to identification *in infinitum*. Similarly there may be infinitely many pictures of one and the same thing, and the possibility of infinite chains of identification not striving toward any goal of knowledge is determined thereby. Similarly there can be an infinite manifold of possible perceptions of one and the same thing.

If we attend to the elementary constitutive intentions in these intuitive examples, we do indeed find that factors of genuine fulfillment are also mostly interwoven in the whole of the identification. That is the case if we unite image-presentations which are not of completely the same intuitive content, so that the new image brings something to clear presentation and perhaps places it before our eyes "just as it is," which the earlier image merely indicated by adumbration, or even symbolically. If we imagine an object in phantasy as turning on all sides, the series of images is always connected through syntheses of fulfillment with respect to the partial intentions; but each new image-presentation is as a whole not a fulfillment of the preceding one, and the entire presentation-series is without a progressive approximation to a goal. It is similar with the manifold of perceptions pertaining to the same external thing. On the other hand, the entire synthesis of the series of imaginations, or perceptions, represents an increase in knowledge-fullness, in comparison with an isolated single act from such a series; the imperfection of the one-sided representation is relatively overcome in the all-sided presentation. We say "relatively overcome" because the all-sided presentation does not occur in such a synthetic manifold — as is required by the ideal of ade-

[6] Cf. § C, 9 for deeper analyses.

quation — at one stroke, as pure self-representation and without the ad-mixture of analogy and symbolism, but rather piecemeal and continually dimmed by such admixtures. Another example of an intuitive fulfillment-series is provided by the transition from a rough outline-sketch to a more exact pencil-sketch, from this to a finished picture, up to the life-like painting, for the same object.

2. The Question Concerning the Relationship between Fulfillment and Envisagement

The question is now, what role do the various genera of objectivating acts — the signitive and intuitive acts, and under the latter title, the per-ceptual and the imaginative — play in the function of knowledge? The relationship between intention and fulfillment constitutes the basis for the formation of the pair of concepts *thought* (more narrowly: *concept*) and *corresponding intuition*. But a concept of intuition oriented merely with respect to this relationship would by no means be coincident with that of an *intuitive act*, although it would presuppose it. To "make clear" a thought means, to begin with, to provide cognitive fullness to the content of the thought. But this can also be done in a certain manner by a sig-nitive presentation. To be sure if we make the requirement of evident clarity, such as "the thing itself" is clear to us, and consider its possibility and truth, we are referred to intuition in the sense of our intuitive acts. For that reason the term clarity has this narrower sense in epistemological contexts; it means going back to the fulfilling intuition, to the "origin" of the concepts and propositions in the intuition of the things themselves.

Careful analyses of examples are now necessary to confirm and continue what has been indicated here. They will help to show the role played by intuition in every fulfillment. The difference between real and figurative envisagement, or fulfillment, will be clearly drawn, and the difference between mere identification and fulfillment will receive its final clarifica-tion. The contribution of intuition is such that in real fulfillment, under the title "fullness," it imparts something new to the intending act. The "fullness" turns out to be a new factor of intuitive acts, as opposed to the quality and matter; it is new as a supplement especially belonging to the matter.

3. The Gradations of Indirect Fulfillments; Indirect Presentations

Every mathematical conception developed in a definition-chain shows the possibility of chains of fulfillment, which are constructed term for term out of signitive intentions. We make the concept $(5^3)^4$ clear by going back to the definitional presentation: "the number which arises when one forms the product $5^3 . 5^3 . 5^3 . 5^3$." If we wish to make this last presentation clear in turn we must go back to the sense of 5^3, hence to the formation 5.5.5. Going back still further, we would have to explain 5 by the chain of definitions $5 = 4 + 1, 4 = 3 + 1, 3 = 2 + 1, 2 = 1 + 1$. Corresponding not only to the final result, but also to each single step in such a process of explanation, is an act of fulfillment. In this way every simple decadic number refers to a possible chain of fulfillment, whose number of terms is determined by the number of its units less one, so that such chains of an unlimited number of terms are possible *a priori.*

A remarkable peculiarity of such examples, as well as of the class of signitive presentations which illustrate them, is the fact that in them the content of the presentations (or more distinctly expressed, the matter) predelineates in an *a priori* manner a definite gradation of fulfillment. The fulfillment which follows indirectly can never follow directly at the same time. To every signitive intention of this class there corresponds a definite fulfillment (or a definite group of fulfillments) as the nearest, to this one again a definite one as the nearest, etc. This peculiarity is also found in the case of certain intuitive intentions, as when we make a thing concrete by the picture of a picture. The matter of the presentation also prescribes a first fulfillment here, which would place the primary picture "itself" before our eyes. A new intention, however, belongs to this picture, and its fulfillment leads us to the thing itself. In all these indirect presentations, whether signitive or intuitive, the presentations do not make their objects concrete in a simple manner, but through presentations of a lower and higher level that are built upon one another; the presentations present their objects as objects of other presentations.

In this context one may speak of *indirect* intentions (or those that are built upon one another), or fulfillments, and hence also of *indirect presentations.* The proposition then holds, that *every indirect intention requires an indirect fulfillment,* which obviously ends after a finite number of steps in a direct intuition.

4. *The Distinction between Indirect Presentations and Presentations of Presentations*

The presentations of presentations, or those presentations which relate to other presentations as their objects, are to be distinguished from these indirect presentations. Although the presented presentations, to speak generally, are themselves intentions, and hence admit of fulfillment, the nature of the given, of the presenting presentation, does not require an indirect fulfillment through the fulfillment of the presented presentations. The intention of the presentation of the presentation $P_1(P_2)$ refers to P_2. This intention is therefore fulfilled if P_2 "itself" appears; it is not enriched if the intention of the P_2 is fulfilled, if its object appears in an image or even in perception. For P_1 does not mean this object, but simply its presentation P_2. Obviously nothing is changed in more complex cases, such as $P_1[P_2(P_3)]$, etc.

For example, the thought *signitive presentation* is fulfilled by the intuition of a signitive presentation, e.g., of the presentation *integral* (if we wish, of the presentation *signitive presentation* itself). Such cases should not be misunderstood to mean that the signitive presentation *integral* lays claim to the character of intuition. Not the signitive presentation *integral*, but the *inner perception* of this presentation is the fulfilling intuition for the thought *signitive presentation*; instead of functioning as a fulfilling intuition, this presentation functions as the object of the fulfilling intuition. Just as the thought of a color is fulfilled by the intuition of this color, so the thought of a thought finds its fulfillment in an act of intuition of this thought, and hence final fulfilling intuition is obtained in an adequate perception of it. Naturally the mere being of an experience is not an intuition and especially a perception of it. It should be noted that in the contrast between thought or intention and fulfilling intuition, "intuition" does not mean outer intuition, perception, or imagination of outer, physical objectivity. "Inner" perception can also function as fulfilling intuition.

5. *Genuine Envisagements in Every Fulfillment; Genuine and Figurative Envisagement*

After having clarified the difference between indirect presentations and presentations of presentations, it will be well to look at what they have in common. According to the foregoing analysis, every indirect presentation includes presentations of presentations, in that it intends its object as an object of certain presentations presented in it. Thus, e.g., if we present 1000 as 10^3, i.e., as the number which is characterized as the object of that presentation, that would arise in the carrying out of the involution indicated. From that it follows that genuine envisagements play the essential role in every fulfillment of indirect intentions, and in every step of this fulfillment. The description of an object as an object of a presented presentation (or as one standing in a certain relation to objects thus defined) presupposes, in the fulfillment, the fulfillment of the presentations of presentations, and these interwoven *intuitive* fulfillments first of all give the character of a fulfillment to the entire identification. The increase in "fullness" by steps consists in this, that gradually all presentations of presentations, whether the ones interwoven at the outset or those appearing anew in the fulfillment, are fulfilled, so that finally the dominant total intention with its over- and into-one-another of intentions appears identified with a direct intention. This identification also has, as a whole, the character of the fulfillment. This kind of fulfillment will, however, have to be included among the figurative envisagements, for an envisagement is said to be genuine if it imparts fullness to the object presented by the *total* presentation. Fundamentally this means that a merely signitive intention has no fullness at all, and that all fullness consists in the actual representation of determinations which attach to the object itself.

The distinction between genuine and figurative envisagement can also be designated as one between genuine (or "real") and figurative (or "unreal") fulfillment, inasmuch as the intention aims at its object, and fulfillment in a significant sense means that at least something of the fullness of the object is brought to the intention. But the genuine and figurative fulfillments within the syntheses of identification are distinguished by a common phenomenological character (fulfillment in a broader sense); and all figurative fulfillment implies genuine fulfillment, and hence "is indebted" to the latter for the character of fulfillment.

It will be well to describe more exactly the difference between genuine and figurative envisagements and to dispose of a class of cases in which figurative envisagements have the appearance of genuine ones. When the fulfillment of a signitive intention occurs on the basis of an intuition, the matters of the acts concerned do not always coincide, in such a way that the intuitively appearing object is itself there as that which is meant. Only where this proves to be the case, however, can one speak of illustration in the true sense; only then is the thought realized in the manner of perception, or illustrated in the manner of the imagination. It is otherwise if the fulfilling intuition allows an object to appear which has the character of an indirect representative; e.g., if with the naming of a geographical name the phantasy-presentation of a map springs up and fuses with the meaning-intention of this name; or if an assertion about certain street-connections is confirmed by the inscriptions on a map lying before one. The intuition in this case is not a fulfilling one in a true sense — its own matter does not enter into action; the actual foundation of fulfillment does not reside in it, but in a signitive intention that is interwoven with it. That the appearing object functions here as an indirect representative of the meant and named object, means phenomenologically that the intuition constituting it is the bearer of a new intention which points out beyond it, the appearing object, and characterizes it thereby as a sign. The analogy between that which appears and that which is meant, which may occur here, does not determine a simple image-presentation, but rather a sign-presentation built up upon the image-presentation. The outline of England, as the map portrays it, may copy the form of the country itself; but the phantasy-presentation of the map springing up with the talk of England does not mean England itself in a pictorial way, and also not indirectly, as that which is copied by this map; it means England in the manner of a mere sign, owing to the external relations of association, which has connected all our cognitions about the country and people with the figure on the map. Because the nominal intention is fulfilled on the basis of this phantasy-presentation, it is not the object (the map) imagined in the latter, but the object first represented by it, which is *the same* as that which is meant by the name.

6. The "Fullness" of a Presentation

It will now be necessary to examine more closely the contribution of the intuitive intentions. Because the fulfillment of indirect intentions reduces to the intuitive fulfillment of direct intentions, and the final result of the whole indirect process is a direct intention, the question of the intuitive fulfillment of direct intentions is of interest here. With regard to the intentional essences, the matter alone should be the criterion for the relationships to be determined. The qualities (positing and "mere" presentation) can therefore be assumed arbitrarily.

The following proposition may be asserted: To every intuitive intention there belongs (in the sense of an ideal possibility) a signitive intention exactly adapted to it with respect to the matter. This unity of identification necessarily possesses the character of a unity of fulfillment, in which the intuitive and not the signitive member has the character of fulfillment, and also the character of *giving* the fullness.

This last can be expressed otherwise, by saying that the signitive intentions are "empty" in themselves, and are "in need of fullness." The signitive intention merely refers to the object, whereas the intuitive intention makes it concrete in a significant sense; it brings something of the fullness of the object itself. No matter how far behind the object the image may be in the case of imagination, it has some determinations in common with it and "resembles" it. But the signitive presentation does not present through analogy, it is "really" not at all a "presentation," nothing of the object becomes living in it. The complete fullness as an ideal is therefore

the fullness of the object itself, as a totality of the determinations constituting it. But the fullness of a presentation is the totality of those determinations belonging to it itself, by means of which it represents its object
by analogy or grasps it as itself given. This fullness is, therefore, in addition to quality and matter, a characteristic factor of presentations; a positive constituent to be sure only for intuitive presentations, a deficiency for
the signitive. The "clearer" the presentation, the richer it is in fullness.
The ideal of fullness would be attained, accordingly, in a presentation
which would contain its object completely in its phenomenological content. Only perception is capable of that, and not imagination, if the individualizing determinations are included in the fullness of the object.
But if these determinations are disregarded, the ideal also applies to imagination.

In a pictorial presentation, every characteristic of its object is co-meant,
just as it is in every presentation. But not every one has in the phenomenological content of the presentation a peculiar factor which so to speak
"analogizes" it (or represents it pictorially). The totality of these innerly
fused factors, conceived as foundations of the purely intuitive (here purely
imaginative) apprehensions, which first give to them the character of representatives of the corresponding objective factors, makes up the fullness
of the imaginative presentation. The case of perceptual presentation is
similar. In addition to imaginative representations, perceptual presentations or self-representations of objective factors are also taken into consideration here. The totality of the factors of a perceptual presentation,
whether functioning imaginatively or perceptually, determines its fullness.

7. *Fullness and "Intuitive Content"*

The concept of fullness is still ambiguous. One can view the factors indicated above with respect to their own existence as contents, abstracting
from the functions of pure imagination and perception, which first give to
them the value of pictorialness or adumbration and consequently their
value for the function of fulfillment. One can, on the other hand, view
these factors *in* their apprehension, and hence not these factors alone, but
the complete images or adumbrations. The "purely intuitive" acts which
are included are what give to the acts as wholes the character of perceptions and image-presentations, and which give fullness and increase or
enrich the fullness that is present in the case of fulfillment. In view of the
ambiguity of the term fullness, the following terms are introduced:

By *representing* (*darstellenden*) or *intuitively representing contents* are
meant those contents of intuitive acts, which, by virtue of the purely imag-

inative or perceptual apprehensions whose bearers they are, uniquely refer to them definite corresponding contents of the object, represent them in the manner of imaginative or perceptual adumbrations. The act-factors characterizing them in this manner are excluded, however. Since the character of the imagination lies in the analogical copy, in the "re-presentation" in a narrower sense, and the character of the perception can also be denoted as presentation, the names *analogical* or *copying* and *presenting* or *self-representing* may serve as distinguishing names for the representing contents in the two cases in question. The expressions *imaginative* and *perceptively adumbrating* are also pertinent. The representing contents of outer perception define the concept of sensation in the usual narrow sense. The representing contents of outer phantasy are the *sensuous phantasms*.

The representing or intuitively representing contents in and with the apprehension belonging to them is called the *intuitive content of the act*, disregarding the quality of the act (whether it is positing or not), as indifferent for all distinctions here in question. Excluded from the intuitive content are, further, all signitive components of the act.

8. *The Relationship of Weight between Intuitive and Signitive Contents of the Same Act*

For the complete clarification of the concepts just defined, and for the easier definition of a series of new concepts, consider the following. In an intuitive presentation an object is meant in the manner of imagination or perception; it "comes to appearance" in it, more or less completely. Certain factors or portions of the act correspond to every part or in general to every determination of the object, as meant *hic et nunc*. That to which no meaning refers is not present for the presentation. The possibility of the following phenomenological distinction is in general given: (a) the *purely intuitive* content of the act, as that which corresponds in the act to the totality of the determinations of the object "coming to appearance"; (b) the *signitive content* of the act, likewise corresponding to the totality of the remaining determinations which are co-meant but do not come to appearance.

If the weight of the intuitive or signitive content is defined as the totality of the intuitively or signitively presented objective factors, then both weights supplement one another in every presentation to constitute the unity of the total weight, i.e., the collective totality of the objective determinations. Hence the symbolic equation that $i + s = 1$ holds always. The weights i and s can vary: the same (intentionally the same) object can become intuitive with more or with less determinations; and the sig-nitive content is also changed correspondingly — it increases or decreases.

Ideally, two limiting cases are possible: $i = 0$ and $s = 1$; and $i = 1$ and $s = 0$. In the first case the presentation would have only a signitive con-tent; no determination of its intentional object would be left which would bring it to representation in its content. The purely signitive presentations, well known to us especially as pure meaning-intentions, therefore appear here as limiting cases of the intuitive. In the second case the presentation contains no signitive content at all. Everything is fullness in it; there is no part, no side, no determination of its object, which is not intuitively represented, which is merely co-meant indirectly. Everything that is meant is represented. These presentations are defined as *pure intuitions*. This expression is used in two senses: when the complete act is included, and again in abstraction from the quality. Thus one can speak of *qualified* and *non-qualified* pure intuitions. And similarly for all related acts.

In every presentation we can abstract from the signitive components while restricting ourselves to that which actually comes to representation in their representative content. We can therefore form a *reduced* presen-tation, with an object reduced in such a way. We can also say, accord-ingly, that the intuitive content of a presentation comprises that which is pure intuition in it, just as we may also speak with regard to the object of *its* purely intuitive content, namely, a content coming to pure intuition in this presentation. This is carried over to the signitive content of the presentation; we can designate it as that which is *pure signification* in it.

The total actual act of intuition has either the character of perception or that of image-presentation. The intuitive content is then called *per-ceptual content* or *content of perception*, as well as *imaginative* or *image-content*. It is not to be confused with the perceptively or imaginatively presenting content in the sense already defined.

The perceptual content comprises presenting contents, although as a rule not exclusively; the image-content comprises only "analogizing" con-tents. That these latter contents sometimes admit of still another appre-hension, in which they function as presenting, as in the case of physical pictures, does not affect what has been said.

By virtue of the mixture of perceptual and imaginative components, which the intuitive content of a perception permits and usually displays, a separation of the content of perception into the *pure content of percep-tion* and a *supplementary image-content* can be undertaken.

In every pure intuition also, if w_r and b_r are the weights of their purely perceptive or imaginative components, then the symbolic equation

$w_r + b_r = 1$ may be set up, whereby 1 stands for the weight of the intuitive total content of the pure intuition, and hence the total content of its object. If $b_r = 0$, i.e., the pure intuition is free from all image-content, then it is a *pure perception*; for the qualitative character usually included by the sense of the term perception is disregarded here. If, however, $w_r = 0$, the intuition is a pure image-presentation (*pure imagination*). The "purity" of the pure perception therefore applies not only to signitive, but also to imaginative ingredients. The limitation of an impure perception through the exclusion of the symbolic components provides the pure intuition inherent in it, and it is a further step of the reduction, the exclusion of everything pictorial, that first provides the content of pure perception.

Is not the representing content in a pure perception identical with the object itself? The essence of pure presentation indeed consists in its being self-representation of the object, hence in its meaning the representing content directly (in the manner of the "itself") as its object. But that would be a fallacy. Perception, as presentation, grasps the representing content so that the object appears as self-given with and in it. The presentation is then pure if every part of the object is actually presented in the content and none is merely imagined or symbolized. Just as there is nothing in the object which is not presented, so there is nothing in the content which is not presentational. Despite this exact correspondence, the self-representation can have the character of a mere adumbration, even if all-sided (of a complete "perceptual picture"); it does not need to attain the ideal of adequation, for which the representing content is at the same time the represented one. The pure picture-presentation, completely picturing its object by virtue of its freedom from all signitive ingredients, possesses in its representing content a complete analogue of the object. This analogue can more or less approach the object, up to the limit of complete likeness. The same can also hold for pure perception. The difference consists only in this, that the imagination apprehends the content as an analogue, as a picture, but for perception it is the self-appearance of the object. Not merely pure imagination, but also pure perception accordingly admits of differences of fullness, while retaining its intentional object.

With regard to the gradations of fullness in intuitive content, with which the gradations of fullness run parallel *eo ipso* to the representing content, the following can be distinguished: (a) *the extent of wealth of fullness*, changing according to whether the content of the object comes to representation with greater or lesser completeness; (b) the *liveliness* of the fullness as the degree of approximation of the primitive similarities of the representation to the corresponding factors of the content of the object; (c) the reality-content of the fullness, its more or less in *presentational contents*.

In all these relations, the adequate perception represents the ideal; it has the maximum of extent, of liveliness, and of reality, precisely as the self-grasping of the complete and whole object.

9. Series of Increases of Fulfillment

The discussion of "fullness" referred to "fulfillment," that peculiar form of the synthesis of identification. Not only the concept of fullness, but also the differences of its greater or lesser completeness, liveliness, reality, and also the gradations of pictorialness and adumbration, were explained through relationships of inner factors of presentations to one another and to the intended objective factors. Corresponding to these relationships are possible series of increases, constructed out of syntheses of fulfillment, which will now be considered.

Fulfillment occurs, in this context, when an intuitive act "gives" fullness to a signitive intention. The consciousness of increase (*Steigerung*) is based upon the partial coincidence of the fullness with the correlative part of the signitive intention, whereas no share in the consciousness of increase can be ascribed to the identifying coincidence of the empty portions of the intentions on both sides which correspond to one another.

There are intervals in the increase of fulfillment, and the concatenation of the relationships is "transitive." If image 2 is "more complete" than image 1, and image 3 more so than image 2, then image 3 is more complete than image 1. It is thus at least if we take account of the three factors of fullness that were distinguished above: extent, liveliness, and reality.

To these increases and series of increases there correspond similarities and series of similarities with respect to the *representing* contents of the fullnesses. The similarity of the representatives should not be regarded without question as increase, or the concatenation of similarities as a series of increases. It is due to the fact that in the order of the fulfillment-series and of the increases obtaining among their acts, every later act appears still richer in fullness, that the representative contents of the acts also gain an ascending order; step by step they themselves appear not only as giving fullness in general, but as giving ever richer fullness. The designation of these constituent parts as fullnesses is relative, functional; it expresses a characteristic which accrues to the content through the act and through the role of this act in possible syntheses of fulfillment. The case is similar here to that of an "object." To be an object is no positive characteristic, no positive kind of a content; it refers to a content only as an intentional correlate of a presentation. For the rest, the relationships of fulfillment and of increase are based upon the phenomenological contents of the acts purely in accordance with their specific nature. What are concerned are ideal relationships, determined through the corresponding species.

In the synthesis of intuitive acts, however, the increase of fullness does not always occur, for partial fulfillment and partial "non-fulfillment" (*Entfüllung*) can go hand in hand. Finally, the distinction between mere identification and fulfillment reduces to this, that for the former either no fulfillment at all in a true sense occurs, because identity-theses of acts are involved, which are all without fullness; or fulfillment as well as enrichment of fullness occurs, but along with simultaneous non-fulfillment, along with the abandonment of already present fullness, so that no definite and pure consciousness of increase comes about. The primitive relationships referring to the elementary intentions are in any case: fulfillment of an empty, i.e., purely signitive intention, and as it were the filling-up of an already somewhat filled intention, i.e., increase and realization of an imaginative intention.

10. *Fullness and Intentional Matter*

The relationship between the new concept of the content of presentation to content in the sense of matter, which played a big role in the previous investigation, will now be considered. By matter was meant that factor of the objectivating act which makes the act present just *this* object and just in *this manner*, i.e., just in these arrangements and forms, with particular relation to these determinations or relationships.

The concept of matter is defined through the unity of the total identification, as that which serves in the acts as the foundation of the identification; and consequently the many differences of fullness, passing beyond mere identification and determining the peculiarities of fulfillment and increase of fulfillment, are not taken account of in this conception. No matter how the fullness of a presentation varies within its possible series of fulfillment, its intentional object, just as it is intended, remains the same; in other words, its matter remains the same. But, on the other hand, matter and fullness are not unrelated. If an act of intuition supplies fullness to a purely signitive act, the fullness should not be regarded as a distinct third factor that is joined to the common quality and matter.

The relationships obtaining here may be shown by means of the parallelism of signitive and intuitive acts, in the following manner: A purely signitive act would exist as a mere complex of quality and matter, if it could at all be by itself, i.e., if it could form a concrete experience-unity by itself. But it cannot do that; it is always found as an appendage to a founding intuition. This intuition has to be sure "nothing to do" with the object of the significative act, i.e., it does not enter into any relation of fulfillment to this act; but it realizes its possibility *in concreto* as that of a simply unfulfilled act. It may be said that it is not the founding intuition as a whole, but only its representative content, which essentially endows the support to the signitive act. For what goes beyond this content and determines the sign as a natural object can vary arbitrarily, without disturbing the signitive function. It is indifferent, e.g., whether the letters of a logogram are of wood, iron, printer's ink, etc. It is only the readily recognized form that enters into consideration, not as the objective form of the thing of wood, etc., but as the form really present in the representing sensuous content of the intuition.

In the parallel case of a purely intuitive act, its quality and matter (its intentional essence) are also not separable; here, too, there must be a necessary supplement. The representative content provides this content (in the case of sensuous intuition, the sensuous content), which in the present interweaving with an intentional essence takes on the character of an intuitive representative. If we note that the same (e.g., sensuous) content can once serve as the bearer of a signification, and again as the bearer of an intuition (pointing to — copying), then it is obvious that the concept of the representative content must be extended, and that *signitive* and *intuitive representative contents* (or briefly: signitive and intuitive representatives) must be distinguished.

This classification is incomplete, however. Only purely intuitive and purely signitive acts have been considered. Now the mixed acts, which are generally included under the title of intuition, must be taken up; they have a representative content which functions with regard to the one part of the presented objectivity as a copying or self-representing representative, and with regard to the supplementary part as a mere indication. The mixed representatives must be added to the purely signitive and purely intuitive representatives; they represent signitively and intuitively at the same time, and that in relation to the same intentional essence. It may now be said that every concrete, complete objectivating act has three components — the quality, the matter, and the representative content. Depending upon whether this content functions as a purely signitive or as a purely intuitive representative, or as both at the same time, the act is purely signitive, or purely intuitive, or both.

11. Representation or Apprehension

The question is now, how this functioning is to be understood, since it is an *a priori* possibility that the same content, in connection with the same quality and matter, may function in this threefold manner. It can only be the phenomenological peculiarity of the form of unity which justifies the distinction as phenomenologically present. This form connects the matter and the representative. The representative function does not suffer through the change of quality. Whether a phantasy-appearance is valid for us as the representation of an actual object, or as a mere imagination, does not alter its being an image-presentation. The phenomenological unity between the matter and the representative, in so far as it invests the latter with the character of a representative, is therefore called the form of *representation*, and the whole produced by those two factors *representation simply*. This designation expresses the relation between the representing and the represented content (the object, or part of an object, which is represented) with respect to its phenomenological ground. The object that is not given phenomenologically will be left out of play, in order to state that where the content functions as a representative of this or that kind, it always "feels" different, and we speak of a change of the apprehension. The form of the representation can therefore be designated as the form of apprehension. Since the matter so to speak specifies the sense according to which the representing content is apprehended, we can also speak of the *apprehension-sense*; if we want to hold to the old term and at the same time indicate the contrast to the form, we also speak of the *apprehension-matter*. The following would accordingly have to be distinguished phenomenologically in the case of every apprehension: apprehension-matter or apprehension-sense, apprehension-form, and apprehended content; and the latter is to be distinguished from the object of the apprehension. The expression "apperception" is not appropriate, although it is given historically, because of its false terminological contrast to perception, so that "apprehension" is preferable.

The next question concerns the distinguishing characteristic of the various manners of representation or apprehension, which, according to what has been said, can also be different along with identity of the apprehension-matter. In the preceding section the differences of representations have been characterized through the differences of the forms of fulfillment: in the present context the aim is an inner characterization which is restricted to the peculiar descriptive content of the intentions.

The *signitive representation* between the matter and the representative produces an accidental, external relation, but the intuitive representation an essential, inner one. There is no necessary connection between a sign and that which is signified. In the case of purely intuitive representation, however, there is an inner, necessary connection between the matter and the representative, determined by the specific content of both of them. A content can serve as an intuitive representative of an object only if it is similar or equal to it.

It does not seem possible to explain further how it is that the same content in the sense of the same matter can be apprehended at one time as an intuitive and at another time as a signitive representative, or wherein the different peculiarity of the form of apprehension consists. What is here in question may well be a phenomenologically irreducible distinction.

In these considerations, representation as unity of the matter and the representing content has been viewed by itself. If we again go back to complete acts, they are seen to be connections between the act-quality and the representation, whether intuitive or signitive. The entire acts are called intuitive or signitive, a distinction which is therefore determined through the interwoven representations. The study of the relationships of fulfillment had led to the concept of the intuitive content of the fullness of an act. If we compare this conception with the present one, it marks off the purely intuitive representation (= pure intuition) belonging to an act of "impure" intuition. The "fullness" was a concept which was coined especially for the comparative view of acts in their fulfilling function. The opposite limiting case to pure intuition, pure signification, is naturally the same as purely signitive representation.

12. The Relation of an Act to Its Object

Every objectivating act includes a representation in itself; and every act is, as seen in the fifth investigation, either an objectivating act, or has one as its basis. Hence the final basis of all acts is "presentations" in the sense of representations.

The essential ambiguities that have been pointed out in the discussion of the relation of an act to its object will now be summarized. They concern: (a) The *quality* of the acts, the manners of belief, of merely being left undecided, wishing, doubting, etc. (b) The basic *representation*, and that as (1) the form of apprehension — whether the object is presented merely signitively, or intuitively, or in a mixed manner — the differences between perceptual presentation, phantasy-presentation, etc., belong here; (2) the matter of apprehension — whether the object is presented in this or that "sense," e.g., significatively through different meanings, presenting this same object, but determining it differently; (3) the apprehended contents — whether the object is presented by means of these or those signs, or by means of these or those representative contents. The distinctions in this second case relate to the form even with the same matter, by virtue of the relationship of law between intuitive representatives, matter, and form.

13. Intentional Essence and Fulfilling Sense; Cognitive Essence

In the first investigation, fulfilling sense was opposed to meaning (or, the fulfilling meaning was opposed to the intending meaning); it was pointed out that in the fulfillment the object is "given" intuitively in the same manner in which it is meant by the mere meaning. That which coincides with the meaning, ideally conceived, was taken as the fulfilling sense, and it was stated that through this coincidence the mere meaning-intention, or the expression, gains relationship to the intuitive object (the expression expresses it and precisely it).

If we employ the conceptions introduced later, the fulfilling sense is taken as the intentional essence of the completely fulfilling act. This conception is correct and sufficient for the purpose of generally characterizing a situation where a signitive intention gains relationship to its intuitively presented object, and hence expresses the important insight, that the meaning essence of the signitive (expressing) act is found again in the corresponding intuitive act, despite the phenomenological difference of the acts, and that the living unity of identification realizes the coincidence itself and at the same time the relation of the expression to what is expressed. On the other hand, it is clear that by virtue of this identity the fulfilling sense does not imply anything of the fullness, that it therefore does not comprehend the entire content of the intuitive act in so far as this enters into consideration for the critique of knowledge.

It is useful to form a more comprehensive concept. The *cognitive essence* of an objectivating act may be defined (in opposition to the mere meaning essence of the same) as the total content coming in question for the function of knowledge. To it belong the three components of quality, matter, and fullness or intuitive contents; or quality, matter, and intuitive representative content, of which the latter (and with it the "fullness") drops out in the case of empty intentions. All objectivating acts with the same cognitive essence are "the same" act for the ideal interest of the critique of knowledge. If we speak of objectivating acts *in specie*, we have the corresponding idea in view.

14. Complete and Incomplete Intuitions; Conformable and Objectively Complete Envisagement; Essence

In an intuitive presentation, a different extent of intuitive fullness is possible. This refers to possible series of fulfillment; progressing in them we learn to know the object better by means of a representative content, which is ever more similar to the object, and grasps it more completely. With regard to differences of the extent of the fullness, two important possibilities are to be distinguished: (a) The intuitive presentation presents its object as *conformable*, i.e., with an intuitive content of such fullness, that to every constituent part of the object, just as it is meant in this presentation, there corresponds a representative constituent part of the intuitive content. (b) Or this is not the case; the presentation contains only an incomplete adumbration of the object, which it presents *nonconformably*.

Conformity and non-conformity of a presentation to its object are here in question. But since conformity in the context of fulfillment will also be spoken of in a broader sense, the terms *complete* and *incomplete* (*lückenhaft*) intuitions (more particularly: perceptions, or imaginations) will be used. All pure intuitions are complete. That however the converse does not hold, and the present classification does not simply coincide with the division into *pure* and *impure* intuitions, is shown by the following:

Whether the presentations are simple or complex is not presupposed in the distinction. The *intuitive presentations* can, however, be compounded in a twofold manner: (a) in such a way that the relation to the object is simple, and there are no partial acts (or no separated matters) which by themselves present the same entire object. This does not preclude the act being built up out of partial intentions, albeit homogeneously fused ones, which relate to single parts or sides of the object. One can hardly avoid assuming such composition in the case of "outer" perceptions and imaginations. On the other hand, (b) there is the kind of composition which builds up the total act out of partial acts, each of which is a complete intuitive presentation of the same object. This relates to the remarkable, continuous syntheses which join a manifold of perceptions referring to the same object, to a single "many-sided" or "all-sided" perception, continuously viewing the object in a "changing position"; and the same for the corresponding syntheses of the imagination. The identically *one* object appears only once, and not as often as single acts are distinguishable. But it appears in a continuously changing fullness of content; and at the same time the matters and likewise the qualities remain in continuous identity, at least if the object is known from every point of view and always comes to light as such without being enriched.

The distinction between conformity and non-conformity refers to these continuous syntheses. For example, a conformable presentation of an external thing with respect to the all-sided surface-formation is possible in the form of a synthesis, but is not possible in the form of a simple objective presentation.

Among the complete intuitions, the objectively simple ones, but not the objectively compounded ones, are pure intuitions. The pure intuition corresponding to an empirical thing and denied us is contained in the complete synthetic intuition of it, but so to speak in a scattered manner and frequently confused with signitive representatives. There is a continuity of intuitive contents, in which every objective factor comes not once but frequently to representation, to continually changing adumbration, and only the continuity of the "identity-fusion" makes up the phenomenon of the uniqueness of the object.

If an intuitive act functions as one giving fullness to a signitive, say an expressive meaning-intention, analogous possibilities come to light. The object, just as it is meant, can be envisaged conformably or non-conformably. In the case of complex meanings, two distinct kinds of completeness apply to the former, one referring to the completeness of the adaptation of signitive acts to corresponding intuitions, and the other to the completeness of the adaptation of signitive acts — by means of *complete* intuitions — to the object itself. Thus the expression *a green house* can be envisaged, in that a house is actually pictured to us intuitively as a green one. But another type of completeness is illustrated if there is an adequate presentation of a green house. The first case is usually meant when one speaks of the conformable envisagement of expressions. In order, however, to emphasize the distinction, *objectively complete envisagement of the signitive presentation* will be spoken of in contrast to its *conformable but objectively incomplete* envisagement.

There are similar relationships in the case of conflicting instead of fulfilling envisagement. If a signitive intention is disappointed on the basis of an intuition, e.g., if it means a green A whereas the same A (and perhaps even an A in general) is red and is just now intuited as red: then the objective completeness of the intuitive realization of the conflict requires that all constituent parts of the meaning-intention find their objectively complete envisagement. It is therefore necessary that not only the A-intention be fulfilled in the given intuition with objective completeness, but also that the green-intention be fulfilled in another intuition which is "incompatible" with the intuition *red A*. Then not the merely signitive, but the objective, completely fulfilled green-intention conflicts with the red-intuition.

When nothing is specified particularly, the term envisagement will be used in the sense of fulfilling envisagement in what follows.

The differences of fullness with the same quality and matter give rise to an important conception: Two intuitive acts possess the same essence if their pure intuitions have the same matter. Thus a perception, and the entire series of phantasy-presentations, unlimited with regard to their possibility, of which each presents the same object with the same extent of fullness, have one and the same essence. All objective, complete intuitions with one and the same matter have the same essence.

A signitive presentation has no essence. However, in a figurative sense a certain essence is ascribed to it, if it permits complete fulfillment through an intuition from the possible manifold of intuitions of this essence; or what is the same, if it has a "fulfilling sense."

The true meaning of the Scholastic term, which is concerned with the possibility of a "concept," is made clear therewith.

D. COMPATIBILITY AND INCOMPATIBILITY

1. The Ideal Distinction of Meanings into Possible (Real) and Impossible (Imaginary)

Intuitive acts cannot conform to every signitive intention in the manner of "objectively complete envisagement." [7] Accordingly, meaning-intentions are divided into *possible* (compatible in themselves) and *impossible* (incompatible in themselves, imaginary). This classification, as well as the law at its basis, does not apply to isolated acts, but to their cognitive essences and to the matters therein contained, which are to be conceived generally. The possibilities and impossibilities do not refer to the intuitions actually found in any empirical complexes of consciousness; they are not real but ideal possibilities, and are based solely upon the specific characters. The axiom in question reads therefore: The meanings (*in specie* the concepts and propositions) are divided into possible and impossible (real and imaginary).

The *possibility* (reality) of a meaning can be defined by stating that corresponding to it in the sphere of objectivating acts *in specie* is a conformable essence, namely, one whose matter is identical with its own; or

---

[7] The understanding of the analytical elucidations attempted in this and in the following sections depends upon one's keeping in mind the well-defined concepts established in the foregoing, and not taking them in their vague, popular sense.

what is the same, that it has a fulfilling sense, or also, that *there is* a complete intuition *in specie*, whose matter is identical with its own. This "there is" has here the same ideal sense as in mathematics; to reduce it to the possibility of corresponding particulars means, not to reduce it to another thing, but to express it in a merely equivalent manner. (Thus at least, if the possibility is understood to be a pure one, and not as empirical and in *this* sense as "real.")

The idea of the possibility of a meaning really expresses, examined more closely, the generalization of the relationship of fulfillment in the case of objectively complete envisagement, and the above definitions are to be regarded as the ideal necessary and sufficient criteria of the possibility. They include the particular law that, where that relationship between the matter of a meaning and the matter of an essence exists, the "possibility" also obtains; and conversely, that in every case of possibility this relationship exists.

There is, furthermore, a law that such an ideal relationship occurs, and hence is "possible," as follows: *There are "possible" meanings* (whereby it is to be noted, that "meaning" does not mean "act of meaning"). Not every empirical relationship permits such generalization. If we find this intuited paper rough then we cannot state generally *Paper is rough*, as we may state on the basis of a certain actual meaning: *This meaning is possible (real)*. For that reason the proposition *Every meaning is either possible or impossible* is not a particular case of the principle of the excluded middle, in the well-known sense, which expresses the exclusion of contradictory predicates of *individual* subjects. The exclusion of contradictory predicates in an *ideal* sphere (i.e., the arithmetical, the meaning-sphere, etc.) is not self-evident, but must be proved anew or set up axiomatically in every such sphere. Back of the classification of meanings into possible and impossible is a general law, a law that governs the phenomenological factors in an ideal manner by connecting their species in the manner of general propositions.

One must have *insight* into such an axiom; and it is certain that we have evidence in this case. If, e.g., we realize the meaning of the expression *white surface* on the basis of intuition, we experience the reality of the concept. The fulfilling intuition does not only present a white surface, but brings it to intuitive givenness through its content, as completely as the meaning-intention requires it.

Possibility is joined with impossibility as an idea entitled to the same right, which is not merely to be defined as the negation of possibility, but is to be realized as a peculiar phenomenological fact. This is the presupposition for the finding of an application of the concept of impossibility, and especially for its occurring in an axiom, including also the axiom: *There are impossible meanings.* The equivalence of the terms *impossibility* and *incompatibility* indicates that this phenomenological fact is to be sought in the domain of conflict.

2. Unifiability or Compatibility as an Ideal Relationship

Let us proceed from the concept of compatibility or unifiability holding in the widest sphere of contents in general (of objects in the widest sense). Two contents which are parts of a whole are united in it, and are compatible in the unity of a whole. But the same contents would also be compatible if they were not accidentally united. It is surely meaningful to speak of the unifiability of contents whose actual union will always be precluded. If two contents are united, however, their unity proves not only their own unifiability, but also that of an ideal, immense number of others, namely, of all pairs similar to it. It is an axiom that the unifiability does not belong to the scattered particulars, but to the content-species; that if, e.g., the factors *redness* and *roundness* are once found united, a complex species can be obtained through ideating abstraction, which comprises both species *redness* and *roundness* in their likewise specifically conceived form of connection. It is the ideal "existence" of this complex species which founds *a priori* the unifiability of redness and roundness in every thinkable single case, a unifiability which is consequently an ideal, valid relationship, whether empirical unifiability occurs in the world or not. The term unifiability always has relationship to some kind of whole.

The correlate of this unifiability in content is the "possibility" of complex meanings. This results from the above criteria of possibility. The conformable essence, or the complete envisagement of the corresponding complex content, establishes the unifiability of its parts; just as, conversely, there is an essence and a meaning corresponding to this unifiability. The reality of a meaning means the same as: the meaning is an objectively complete "expression" of an intuitive unifiability in content. In the limiting case of a simple content one may define the validity of the simple species as unifiability "with itself." That the connection between expression and that which is expressed (meaning and *corresponding*, i.e., "objectively and completely conformable" intuition) is itself a connection of unifiability, whose particular specific content was determined above, is self-evident. On the other hand, unifiability with respect to meanings ("concepts") does not merely involve their unifiability to a whole, even to a meaning-whole — that would be rather the pure-logical, grammatical

unifiability in the sense of the fourth investigation — but rather the unifiability of the meaning to a "possible" meaning, i.e., to a meaning which
can be united with a corresponding intuition to the unity of objectively
conformable knowledge. The original possibility (or reality) is the validity, the ideal existence of a species; at least it is completely guaranteed
thereby. Then the intuition of a particular corresponding to it, and again
the single thing to be intuited, is said to be possible. Finally, the meaning
fulfilled in such an intuition with objective completeness is said to be
possible. The difference between unifiability and possibility consists merely
in this, that whereas the latter designates the simple validity of a species,
the former (before the extension of the concept by the limiting case)
designates the relationship of the partial species of a unifiedly valid species
— and the same applies to partial intuitions and partial meanings.

Like the concepts of possibility and unifiability, the concept of *essence*
first gives its original sense to the domain of meaning by transfer. This
original concept of essence is expressed by the proposition: *Every valid
species is an essence.*

3. Non-Unifiability of Contents in General

Contents are *non-unifiable* if they are not consistent in the unity of a
whole. Expressed phenomenologically: a unified intuition is not possible,
which gives such a whole in complete conformity. How do we know that?
In particular empirical cases we attempt to bring contents to unity, and
sometimes succeed, and again do not — we experience an irresistible contradiction. But the *factual failure* does not prove a necessary failure.
Couldn't greater force overcome the resistance? However, in the empirical
effort to remove the competition of the contents we experience a unique
relationship of the contents that is again grounded in their specific nature,
and in its ideality is independent of all empirical effort and of anything
else of the particular case. It is the relationship of conflict.

This relationship sets definite kinds of content into connection, within
definite contexts of contents. Colors do not conflict with one another in
general, but only in definite contexts, as when they are to be related to
the same extension. A content of the species q is never simply incompatible with a content of the species p; the assertion of their incompatibility
always refers to a content-connection of a definite kind $G(\alpha, \beta, \ldots; p)$,
which contains p and which is supposed also to comprise q. What is in
question is a descriptively peculiar relationship between the q and the p
of the content-whole G, and the relationship involves nothing individual,
but is based purely upon the species G, p, q. The specific character of the

consciousness of conflict belongs to these species, i.e., the generalization of the situation is actually realizable in a unified, intuitive consciousness of generality; it yields a unified, valid ("possible") species which *unites* the *p* and *q* through *conflict* on the basis of the *G*.

4. How Conflict Also Can Found Unity; Relativity of Unifiability and Conflict

The paradox of the idea of union through conflict is clarified by noting the relativity of these expressions. The objection may be made that conflict simply excludes unity; that everything may be "united" in the form of a conflict; that where unity is lacking, conflict exists, and is to be regarded as a unity; that would be to make fluid the absolutely rigid opposition between unity and conflict and to make its genuine meaning worthless. However, conflict and unity do not "simply" exclude one another, but do so in a definitely correlated manner, changing from case to case. In this way they exclude one another as fixed opposites.

A conflict produces another kind of unity. An example will elucidate. With respect to a known phenomenal context, red and green are said to be incompatible, red and round compatible. The character of conflict determines the incompatibility in the first case; it brings about "separation" between red and green. But with respect to another kind of context, it aids in bringing about a unity, namely, the context "conflict between sensuous characters of a phenomenal object." Now the conflict between red and green is a unity, and naturally a unity with regard to the elements *conflict, red, and green*. On the other hand, "conflict of *red* and *round*" is now disunion, and that with regard to the elements *conflict, red, and round*.

5. Some Axioms

Now, after clarifying the meaning of the relations of compatibility, the primitive axioms can be formulated and clarified phenomenologically. To begin with, there is the axiom of the convertibility of the compatibility-relations (compatibility, or incompatibility).

Then there is the axiom that unity and conflict or unifiability and non-unifiability — the pairs in question being related to the same foundation of the correlation — mutually exclude one another (i.e., again, they are *not unitable* with one another). Unification and conflict are concepts that are differently founded phenomenologically; the conflicting is a positive phenomenological character. If a *p* conflicts with a *q* with regard to the unity-form G $(p, q, \ldots)$, the unification of the *p* with the *q* is not "possible" in the sense of the same *G*. And conversely, if this unification takes place, then the corresponding conflict is "impossible."

The proposition that a conflict exists and that unity does not exist among the same but optional *p*, *q*, . . . means one and the same thing. Every *not* expresses a conflict.

If *p* and *q* do not conflict, are *not* not united, then they are united (axiom of double negation). From this it follows that *one of the two takes place, either unification or conflict* — there is not a "third."

Four possibilities are to be distinguished here, which are expressed as follows: unification, or conflict, takes place; they do not take place. Non-unification is another word for conflict, and non-conflict, according to the preceding axiom, an equivalent for unification.

The final clarification of these axioms and their relation to pure logic goes beyond the present investigation's limits. What has been presented indicates only the inner relations, which must of course be developed further, and shows that we are already at work here upon the phenomenological foundation of pure logic.

6. *Non-Unifiability of Concepts as Meanings*

The concept of non-unifiability as related to intentions is a special case of the original one, but with a definite content, limited to relationships of disappointment. The analogue of what was said above with regard to unifiability or compatibility applies here. The term non-unifiability as applied to meanings ("concepts") does not refer to any ideal (e.g., purely grammatical) non-unifiability of them; it concerns only the relationship of partial meanings of a complex meaning, which is not fulfilled in an objectively complete envisagement, but disappoints, or is able to disappoint.

The ideal laws of possibility to be set up for meanings are based upon the more general concepts and axioms which have been formulated. Propositions belong here such as: that non-unifiability and unifiability of the same meanings and with relation to the same contexts exclude one another; that of a pair of contradictory meanings one is possible and the other impossible; that the negative of a negative, i.e., a meaning which presents the non-unifiability of a certain thing *M* itself as a non-unifiability, is equivalent to the corresponding positive. This positive is defined as the meaning which presents the inner harmony of the same *M* by means of the same presentation-matter (remaining after the elimination of the negations).

Obviously a real theory of meanings with regard to their logical relationships is required, so that all such propositions can be set up and proved in systematic order.

These fragmentary considerations are here broken off, their fuller treatment being left for later investigations. For logical purposes, a broader and more complete phenomenology and theory of identifications and distinctions (and particularly the partial ones) and their relations to the doctrine of unity and conflict is necessary.

E. THE IDEAL OF ADEQUATION; EVIDENCE AND TRUTH

1. Introduction: Possibility and Imagination

Nothing was presupposed concerning qualities of acts in the foregoing. Possibility and impossibility have no special relation to the qualities. It has no influence upon the possibility, e.g., of a proposition, whether we realize the proposition-matter as the matter of a positing act (as a mere act of belief), or whether it is given in a qualitatively modified manner as the matter of a mere presentation; the proposition is "possible" if the concrete act of propositional meaning permits the fulfilling identification with an objectively complete intuition of like matter. Whether this fulfilling intuition is a perception, or a mere phantasy-formation, and the like is similarly irrelevant. Since the production of phantasy-images is subject to our will to a much greater extent than that of perceptions and positings in general, we are accustomed to relate possibility to phantasy-imagery. Accordingly, anything is possible which may be realized in the manner of a conformable phantasy-image, whether we succeed in doing so or not as particular empirical individuals. But because of the ideal connection between perception and imagination, according to which a possible imagination corresponds *a priori* to every perception, this proposition is equivalent to the one here set forth, and the restriction of the concept to the imagination is unessential.

The influence of the distinctions indicated upon the relationships of fulfillment will be considered briefly, in order to bring the present considerations to a tentative close.

2. The Fulfillment-Function of Perception; the Ideal of Final Fulfillment

With regard to the way in which an objectivity is presented in presentation, differences of the completeness of fullness have been shown to be significant. The lowest level is formed by the signitive acts, which have no fullness at all. The intuitive acts have fullness, but with gradual differences of the more and less, and that also occurs within the sphere of the imagination. But no matter how great the completeness of an imagination, there is still a difference as opposed to perception: it does not give the object itself, not even in part; it gives only its image, which, so long as it is an image, is never the thing itself. For the latter we are indebted to perception. It also "gives" the object in different gradations of completeness, in different degrees of adumbration. The intentional character of perception is the presenting in opposition to the mere representing of the imagination. There is an inner difference of the acts, and a difference of the form of their representation (form of apprehension). But the presenting does not in general make a "truly being-present," but only an "appearing to be present," in which the objectivity that is present and with it the completeness of the perception displays gradations. This account is independent of genetic considerations, for we know very well that these, like all similar distinctions, have arisen associatively. The differences of adumbration have already been touched upon, and have also been found in the case of the imagination. All adumbration has a representative character; it represents through similarity, but the manner of this representation through similarity is different, depending upon whether the representation apprehends the adumbrating content as an image or as a self-representation (self-adumbration) of the object. The ideal limit which the increase of adumbration-fullness admits is, in the case of perception, the *absolute self* (just as in the imagination it is the absolutely similar image), and that for every side, for every presented element of the object.

Thus the consideration of the possible relationships of fulfillment points to a final goal of fulfillment-increase, in which the complete intention has attained its final fulfillment. The intuitive content of this final presentation is the absolute sum of possible fullness: the intuitive representative is the object itself, just as it is in itself. And where a presentation-intention has procured final fulfillment through this ideally complete perception, there the genuine *adaequatio rei et intellectus* has been provided: the objectivity is actually "present" or "given," just as it is intended; no partial intention is implied, which would be lacking in fulfillment.

The completeness of the adequation of the "thought" to the "thing" is a double one: the conformity to the intuition is, first, a complete one, for the thought does not mean anything which the fulfilling intuition does not present as belonging to it. This refers to "objective completeness." Second, there is a perfection in the complete intuition itself; there is the *final* fulfillment of the intention. Every true and pure description of an intuitive object or occurrence provides an example of the first completeness; and if the objectivity is innerly experienced and is grasped in reflective perception, just as it is, then the second completeness can be joined with it.

This point of view places the final fulfillment of all intentions in perceptions. But it may be asked, what about "general objects," for which the distinction between perception and imagination does not enter in? This objection calls attention to a lacuna in the investigation. Perception was construed, to begin with, as sensuous perception, and intuition was taken to be sensuous intuition. But the limits of these concepts have been overridden, e.g., in the context of the discussion of compatibility. The necessity of an extension of the concepts of perception and other intuition will be shown in the discussion of categorial forms. It may be remarked now that the imagination, which is the basis of generalizing abstraction, does not therefore exercise the real function of fulfillment, and hence does not represent the "corresponding" intuition. The individual particular of the appearance, as has been emphasized, is not the general and does not contain it in itself.

3. Positing Acts with the Function of Fulfillment; Evidence in a Loose and in a Rigorous Sense

Until now, positing and non-positing acts have been included under the title of intentions. However, the term intention, the aiming at a goal, seems only to apply to positing acts. Every actual identification, or distinction, is a positing act, whether it is itself founded on positings or not. With reference to the question of whether just positing or also non-positing acts can function as intending and fulfilling, distinctions must be clarified such as those between illustration (perhaps exemplification) and confirmation (proof and, in the opposite case, refutation). The concept of confirmation refers exclusively to positing acts in relationship to their positing fulfillment and finally to their fulfillment through perceptions.

Special attention must be devoted to this especially important case. In it the ideal of adequation is presented by actual *evidence*. In a looser sense we speak of evidence wherever a positing intention (especially an assertion) receives its confirmation through a corresponding and fully conformable perception, even if it be a suitable synthesis of connected single perceptions. It is then meaningful to speak of degrees and stages of evidence. In this respect, the approximations of perception to the objective completeness of their objective presentation come in question, and then, further, the progress toward the final ideal of perfection: to that of adequate perception, of the complete self-appearance of the object — in so far as it was meant in the intention to be fulfilled. The strictly epistemological sense of evidence, however, exclusively concerns this last insuperable goal, the act involving this most complete synthesis of fulfillment, which gives to the intention, e.g., the judgment-intention, absolute fullness of content, that of the object itself. It is indifferent, whether an individual or a general object is involved, or whether it be an object in a narrower sense or a fact (the correlate of an identifying or distinguishing synthesis).

The evidence itself is the act of that most complete synthesis of coincidence. Like every identification it is an objectivating act; its objective correlate is called *being in the sense of truth* or also *truth* — in case one does not prefer to assign this term to another of the series of concepts, all of which are rooted in the phenomenological state of affairs. But a more exact discussion is needed here.

4. *Evidence and Truth*

(a) If the concept of truth just indicated is held fast, then truth is, as the correlate of an identifying act, a *fact*, and as the correlate of a coinciding identification, an *identity: the complete agreement between that which is meant and that which is given as such*. This agreement is *experienced* in the evidence, in so far as the evidence is the actual performance of the adequate identification. The truth is "present" in fact. The possibility exists here *a priori* to look at all times upon the agreement and to bring it to intentional consciousness in an adequate perception.

(b) Another concept of truth concerns the ideal relationship which obtains in the unity of coincidence (defined as evidence) between the cognitive essences of the coinciding acts. Whereas the truth in the preceding sense was the objectivity corresponding to the act of evidence, the truth in the present sense is the idea belonging to the act-form, namely, the cognitive essence, conceived as an idea, of the accidental, empirical act of evidence, or *the idea of absolute adequation as such*.

(c) On the side of the act giving fullness, we furthermore experience, in evidence, the given object in the manner of the meant object: it is the fullness itself. This also can be designated as being, or truth, in so far as it is experienced as ideal fullness for an intention, as *realization*; or, as ideal fullness of the *specific* cognitive essence of the intention.

(d) Finally, from the standpoint of the intention, the conception of the relationship of evidence yields truth as *correctness of the intention* (especially, e.g., *correctness of judgment*), as its adequacy with regard to the true object; or as the correctness of the cognitive essence of the intention *in specie*. In the latter respect, e.g., there is the correctness of the judgment in the logical sense of the proposition: the proposition "conforms" to the thing itself; it says, it is thus, and it is actually thus. This expresses the ideal and hence general possibility that a proposition with such matter may be fulfilled in the sense of the strictest adequation.

It should be particularly noted that the being which (as the objective, first sense of truth) is here in question is not to be confused with the being of the copula of the "affirmative" categorical statement. In evidence a total coincidence is involved, but this being corresponds to partial identifications, if not always, then in most cases.

Even where a total identification is predicated, the one being does not coincide with the other. In the case of a judgment-evidence (judgment = predicative statement), the being in the sense of judgment-truth is experienced, but not expressed, and therefore is never coincident with the being that is meant and experienced in the "is" of the statement. This being is the synthetic factor of the existent in the sense of the true. Different kinds of agreement are here brought to a synthesis. One of them, partial, predicative, is affirmatively meant and adequately perceived, and hence is itself given. (What this means will be made more clear in the next chapter by the more general theory of categorial objectivations.) This is the agreement between subject and predicate. Second, there is the agreement which makes up the synthetic form of the act of evidence. That is the total coincidence between the meaning-intention of the statement and the perception of the fact itself, a coincidence which naturally occurs step by step. *This* agreement is obviously not stated; it is not objective in reference like the former one pertaining to the judged fact. Undoubtedly it *can* at all times be stated, and stated with evidence. It then becomes the confirming fact of a new evidence, of which the same holds, and so on. But at each step one must distinguish between the confirming fact and the fact constituting the evidence itself, between the objectivated and the non-objectivated one.

These distinctions lead to the following general discussion.

In the statement of the relationships of the concepts of evidence and truth, facts and other objects were not distinguished, on the objective side of the acts which find their strict adequation in evidence, whether in the function of intention or that of fulfillment. The concepts of truth and correctness are usually conceived more narrowly than has been done here; they are usually related to judgments and propositions, or to their objective correlates, the facts; at the same time, they deal with being mainly with relation to *absolute objects* (non-facts). But the right of the present, more general conception is indisputable. It is necessary, at least at first, that the concepts of truth and falsity be extended so widely that they comprise the total sphere of objectivating acts. The concepts of *truth* and *being* may be differentiated in such a way that the concepts of *truth* (a certain amount of play of equivocation is unavoidable, but not harmful after clarification of the concepts) are related to the side of the acts themselves and of their ideally conceived factors, and the concepts of *being* (truly-being) to the relevant *objective correlates*. Hence truth according to (b) and (d) would be defined as the idea of adequation, or as correctness of objectivating positing and meaning. *Being* in the sense of truth would be determined according to (a) and (c) as the identity of the meant and given object in the adequation, or as that which is adequately perceivable in an indeterminate relation to any intention thereby to be made true (to be fulfilled adequately).

With regard to the distinction of relating and non-relating acts (predications — absolute positions), narrower concepts of truth and being can be defined. The narrower concept of truth would then be limited to the ideal adequation of a relating act to the relevant adequate perception of the fact; and the narrower concept of being would concern the being of absolute objects and separate that from the "existence" of the facts.

The following is accordingly clear: If judgment is defined as a positing act in general, then, subjectively put, the sphere of judgment coincides with the united spheres of the concepts of truth and falsity in the widest sense. If one defines it through a statement and its possible fulfillments, and if by judgment therefore only the sphere of relating positings is meant, then the same coincidence exists again, whereby only the narrower concepts of truth and falsity are laid down.

Until now the case of evidence has been treated one-sidedly as the act described as total coincidence. Corresponding to evidence, with regard to the correlative case of conflict, is *absurdity*, as the experience of complete conflict between intention and quasi-fulfillment. There then correspond to the concepts of truth and being the correlative concepts of falsity and non-being. The phenomenological clarification of these concepts is now easily accomplished. The negative ideal of *final disappointment* would first have to be determined.

With the strict formulation of the concept of evidence that has here been laid down, doubts such as have been expressed in recent times are absurd: namely, whether with the same matter A, there could be evidence in the case of one experience, and absurdity in the case of another. Such doubts were only possible so long as evidence and absurdity were construed as peculiar (positive or negative) *feelings*, which, attached accidentally to the act of judgment, distinguish it as true or false. If someone experiences the evidence *A*, then it is *evident* that no other person can experience the absurdity of the same *A*; for, that *A* is evident, means: *A* is not merely meant, but is also truly given in accordance therewith; it is in the strictest sense itself present. How should this same *A* be meant in the case of a second person, but the meaning, that it is *A*, be truly excluded by a truly given non-*A*? What is involved is the same essential state of affairs which the principle of contradiction brings to expression.

From these analyses it follows that being and non-being are not concepts which express, with respect to their origin, an opposition of judgment-*qualities*. As viewed phenomenologically, *every* judgment is a positing one, and positing is not a character of the *is*, the qualitative counterpart of which is found in the *is not*. The qualitative counterpart to judgment is the mere presentation of the same matter. The differences between the *is* and the *is not* are differences of the intentional matter. Just as the *is* expresses predicative agreement in the manner of meaning-intention, so the *is not* expresses predicative conflict.

CHAPTER XIV

SENSIBILITY AND UNDERSTANDING

1. The Problem of the Fulfillment of Categorial Meaning-Forms

UNTIL NOW, a big lacuna has been felt in the investigation. It concerns the objective categorial forms, or the "synthetic" functions in the sphere of the objectivating acts through which these objective forms are constituted, through which they come to "intuition" and also, in accordance therewith, to "knowledge." This gap will now be filled to some extent, and this will be connected with the beginning of the investigation, in which the goal in the clarification of knowledge was limited to the relationship of an expressive meaning-intention and the expressed sensuous intuition.

In the case of a perceptual statement it is not only the interlaced nominal presentations that are fulfilled; the statement-meaning is fulfilled as a whole by means of the underlying perception. It is likewise said of an entire statement that it gives expression to a perception. We do not say merely, *I see this paper*, e.g., but also *I see that this paper is described*, etc. If the fulfillment of nominal meanings is sufficiently clear, then the question may be raised as to how the fulfillment of entire statements is to be understood, and especially concerning that which reaches beyond their "matter," i.e., beyond the nominal terms. What is it that can provide fulfillment to the meaning-factors (the factors of "categorial form") which make up the proposition-form as such, to which the copula belongs for example?

This question applies also to nominal meanings, unless they are formless like proper (or non-attributive) meanings (*Eigenbedeutungen*). Like a statement, a name has its "matter" and its "form." If it is divided into words, the form lies in part in the manner of the arrangement side by side, in part in peculiar form-words, and also in the manner of formation of the single word, which then permits the distinction of factors of "matter" and of "form" in itself. Such grammatical distinctions refer back to distinctions of meaning; at least in the rough, the grammatical arrangements and forms express the arrangements and forms based upon the essence of the meaning; in the meanings, parts of very different character are found, and those which are expressed by form-words are especially striking, such as *the, an, some, many, few, two, is, not, which, and, or,* etc. Furthermore, there are the substantival and adjectival forms, singular and plural forms of words, etc.

Having regard to the ideal of complete fulfillment, it will be asked whether there are parts and forms of perception corresponding to all parts and forms of meaning. In that case a parallelism would obtain between the meaning and the fulfilling intuition. The expression would be a pictorial counterpart of the perception (namely, with respect to all its parts or forms, which are supposed to be expressed), although produced out of a new substance — an "ex-pression" in the substance of the meaning.

The prototype for the interpretation of the relationship between meaning and intuition would therefore be the relationship of a proper meaning to the corresponding perception. He who knows *Cologne* itself and accordingly has the true proper meaning of the word *Cologne,* possesses in the actual meaning-experience something which corresponds precisely to the future confirming perception. It is not a genuine counterpart of the perception, like the corresponding phantasy; but just as in the perception the city (supposedly) is present, so the proper name *Cologne* means the same city "directly" — it itself, just as it is. The simple perception brings the object to appearance which the meaning-intention means, and just as it means it, without the aid of acts built upon the perception. The meaning-intention therefore finds in the mere perception the act in which it is fulfilled with complete conformity.

If instead of considering directly naming, formless expressions, we take formed and articulated expressions, the situation appears to be similar at first. *I see* white paper and *say* white paper, and so express only what I see. The same holds for whole judgments. *I see, that* this paper is white, and I express just this; I state: This paper is white. The word *white* does indeed mean something in the white paper itself, and consequently in the state of fulfillment this meaning coincides with the partial perception referring to the white factor of the object. But the assumption of a mere coincidence with this partial perception will not suffice. It is usually said here that the appearing *white* is recognized *as white* and named. However, the term recognition normally signifies the object as that which is "recognized." In *this* recognition there is obviously another act, which perhaps includes the former, but is in any case different from it. The *paper* is recognized as white when we, expressing the perception, say *white paper.* The intention of the word *white* coincides only partially with the color-factor of the appearing object; a surplus remains in the meaning, a form which finds nothing in the appearance itself to confirm it (white, i.e., paper that *is* white). This form is repeated, although remaining more concealed, with the noun paper. Simple perception can obviously not attain to such forms in its function of fulfillment.

We need only to ask what corresponds on the side of the perception to the distinction, made on the basis of the same perception, between *this white paper* and *This paper is white* — hence to the distinction between the attributive and the predicative statement-form — and we note the same difficulty. It is seen that the situation is not as simple for a formed meaning as for a proper meaning with its simple relation of coincidence with the perception.

Extending the field of examples, judgments are included which have no definite relation to an individual particular, but in a general manner express relations between ideal unities. The general meanings of such judgments can also be executed on the basis of "corresponding" intuition, just as their origin lies directly or indirectly in the intuition. But the intuitively single thing is not what is meant; it functons at best as a single case, as an example, or only as a raw analogue of an example of the general, which alone is what is in view. Thus, e.g., if we speak generally of *color* or of *redness*, the appearance of a single red thing provides the supporting intuition.

Occasionally it happens that a general statement is designated as the expression of an intuition. That is the case if one says, e.g., that an arithmetical axiom expresses what lies in an intuition; or if one regards a geometer as merely expressing what he sees in the figure instead of deducing formally. But the intention is not directed toward the intuitively given appearance and its intuitive properties or relationships: the figure in the geometrical sense is an ideal limit which cannot be exhibited intuitively *in concreto* at all. However, the intuition has here an essential relation to the expression and to its meaning; these therefore form an experience of general knowledge related to intuition — no mere togetherness, but a homogeneous unity. Concept and proposition are here also oriented with respect to the intuition, and only thereby does evidence, the value of knowledge, arise. On the other hand, it is readily seen that the meaning of the expressions belonging here does not at all reside in the intuition. The great majority of general statements, especially scientific ones, function significantly without any clarifying intuition, and only a very few may be completely illuminated intuitively.

Just as is the case in the domain of the individual, the term knowledge refers in the domain of the general to intuitively founded acts of thought.

If the intuition drops out entirely, the judgment to be sure recognizes nothing, but it still means in its purely intellectual way exactly that which would come to knowledge through the aid of the intuition — if the judgment is at all a true one. The cognition has, however, like every other cognition, the character of fulfillment and identification. But how is identification to take place, if there are no elements corresponding to the form of the general proposition, especially the form of generality, in the individual intuition? For the solution of this difficulty, there is the possibility of founded acts which would be formed as follows:

When general thoughts find their fulfillment in intuition, new acts are built up upon the perceptions and other appearances of the same order — acts which relate to the appearing object in an entirely different manner than the intuitions that actually constitute it. Here the intuitive object does not stand as that which is meant itself, but functions only as a clarifying example for the real, general meaning. When the new intention is fulfilled adequately by intuition, it proves its objective possibility, or the possibility (or "reality") of the general.

2. The Difference between Sensuous and Categorial Form in the Total Sphere of Objectivating Acts

After these preliminary considerations, in which the difficulty and its possible solution were indicated, its real elaboration will be undertaken. It was pointed out that the concept of a pictorial expression cannot be used to describe the relationship obtaining between expressive meanings and expressed intuitions in the case of formed expressions. This will now be determined more precisely. It will be noted that there is something in intuition that corresponds only to certain parts of statements, whereas nothing at all can correspond to other parts.

Certain types of perceptual statements can be distinguished readily, such as *E is p* (where *E* may refer to a proper name), *An S is p*, *This S is p*, *All S are p*, etc. Numerous complications arise through negation, conjunction, etc.; and sharp distinctions of meaning are seen in the difference of these types. The distinction between "substance" and "form" is repeated with "terms." There are ultimate elements present in the terms, the "substantial" (*stofflichen*) elements, which find direct fulfillment (perception, imagination, and the like) in intuition; but although the supplementary *forms*, as meaning-forms, also demand fulfillment, there is nothing immediately in the perception and the coördinated acts which could ever conform to them.

This fundamental categorial distinction, which extends over the whole sphere of objectivating presentation, is denoted as the categorial and absolute distinction between the form and substance of a presentation, and this is separated from the relative or functional distinction, innerly connected with it, which was indicated in the above.

The terms matter or substance as contrasted with categorial form have nothing to do with the term matter as opposed to the act-quality (matter, which tells us how the objectivity is meant in the meaning). To separate it more easily, it is desirable to speak here of "substance," and where the matter is meant in the preceding sense to speak of *intentional matter* or of "apprehension-sense."

3. The Objective Correlates of the Categorial Forms No "Real" Factors

The point is now to clarify the distinction just indicated. The form-giving inflection, the being in the attributive, predicative function, is not fulfilled in any perception, as has been said. The Kantian proposition is recalled here: *Being is not a real predicate.* I can see the color, but not the colored *being.* I can feel the smoothness, but not the smooth *being.* The being is nothing *in* the object, no part of it, no factor inherent in it; no quality or intensity, but also no figure, no inner form in general. But the being is also nothing *at* an object; it is not a real inner or a real outer character, and therefore in a *real* sense no "character" at all. For it also does not concern the *material* forms of unity, which connect objects to more comprehensive objects, colors to color-forms, tones to harmonies, things to more comprehensive things or thing-orders (garden, street, phenomenal external world). It is upon these material forms of unity that the external characters of the objects are based, the right and left, the high and low, the loud and soft, etc., among which nothing like the *is* is found.

Thus, nothing corresponding to *being* is to be found among the *objects.* It follows that *being* is not perceptible, inasmuch as the objects exhaust the extension of possible perceptions.

This must be clarified, however. Perception and object are most intimately connected concepts whose meanings mutually refer to one another, enlarging and narrowing them together. But a very narrow concept of perception or of object has been used here. One also speaks of perception and especially of seeing in a very extended sense, which includes the grasping of entire facts and even the *a priori* evidence of laws (as "insight"). In a narrower sense, and expressed popularly and roughly, that which we can see with our eyes, hear with our ears, or grasp with any "outer" sense is said to be perceived. Therefore if the "inner sense" is introduced the concept of sense perception would have to be enlarged appropriately, so that all "inner" perception and the correlative sphere of "inner objects" — hence the ego and its inner experiences — would be included.

In the sphere of sense perception thus understood, and corresponding to sense intuition in general, a meaning such as that of the word *being* has no possible objective correlate, and therefore no possible fulfillment in the acts of such perception. What holds for being, holds also for the other categorial forms in statements, whether they connect constituent parts of the terms among themselves or connect the terms themselves to the unity of the proposition. The *a* and the *the*, the *and* and the *or*, the *if* and the *then*, the *all* and the *none*, the *something* and the *nothing*, the *forms of quantity* and the *determinations of number*, etc. — are all significant propositional elements, but we seek in vain for their objective correlates (in case we may at all ascribe such to them) in the sphere of real objects, which means nothing other than objects of possible sense perception.

4. The Origin of the Concept of Being and of the Remaining Categories As Not in the Domain of Inner Perception

This holds, however, for the sphere of the "outer" senses as well as for that of the "inner" sense. It is a fundamentally erroneous doctrine, generally held since Locke, that the meanings in question, as well as the meanings corresponding to them which are nominally rendered independent — the *logical categories*, such as being and non-being, unity, plurality, totality, number, ground, consequence, etc. — arise through reflection upon certain psychical acts, and hence in the domain of the inner sense, of "inner perception." In such a way, concepts such as perception, judgment, affirmation, denial, collection and counting, presupposing and deducing arise — which are therefore all "sensuous" concepts, namely, belonging to the sphere of the "inner sense" — but never the concepts of the first group, which are certainly not concepts of psychical acts or their real constituent parts. The thought *judgment* is fulfilled in the inner intuition of an actual judgment; but the thought of the *is* is not fulfilled therein. The being is not a judgment, and not a real constituent part of a judgment. No more than being is a real constituent part of any outer object, is it a real constituent part of any inner one; and hence not of a judgment. In a judgment — a predicative statement — the *is* occurs as a meaning-factor, just as *gold* and *yellow* do, although in a different position and function. *Gold-is-yellow* appears; judgment and judgment-intuition are unified into an evident judgment, in a favorable case, evident in the sense of an ideal limit.

If one understands by judgments not only the meaning-intentions belonging to the actual statements, but also the fulfillments that may be completely adapted to them, then it is surely correct that a being can only be grasped in a judgment; but that is by no means to say that the concept of being must be or can ever be gained "in reflection" upon certain judgments.

The relating being that brings the predication to expression, e.g., as "is," "are," and the like, is something dependent; if we elaborate it to the complete *concretum*, the actual *fact* arises, the objective correlate of the complete judgment. We can then say: just as the sensuous object is related to sense perception, so is the fact related to the act of awareness "giving" it (one may feel impelled to say simply: so is the fact related to the fact-perception). Just as the concept *sensuous object* ("real object") cannot arise through "reflection" upon perception, because then the concept of perception, or a concept of certain real constituent parts of perceptions would arise, so also the concept *fact* cannot arise out of reflection upon judgments, because only concepts of judgments or of real constituent parts of judgments could be received thereby.

That in the one case perceptions and in the other case judgments or judgment-intuitions (fact-perceptions) must be *experienced* in order that the actual abstraction may occur, is obvious. To be experienced is not to be objective. The "reflection" means, however, that that upon which we reflect, the phenomenological experience, becomes objective for us (is perceived innerly by us), and that out of this objective content the determinations to be generalized are really yielded.

Not in reflection upon judgments, or upon judgment-fulfillments, but in the judgment-fulfillments themselves does the origin of the concepts fact and being (in the sense of the copula) lie; not in these acts as objects, but in the objects of these acts do we find the foundation of abstraction for the realization of these concepts. Just as another concept (an idea, a specific unity) can only "arise," that is, can itself be given to us only on the basis of an act which places some particular corresponding to it before our eyes, so the concept of being can arise only if some being, real or imaginative, is placed before our eyes. In the case of predicative being, some fact must be given to us, and that through a giving act — the analogue of the common sensuous intuition.

The same holds for all categorial forms, or for all categories. A totality, e.g., is given and can only be given in an actual comprehending-together, hence in an act that comes to expression in the form of the conjunctive connection *A and B and C*. But the concept of a totality does not arise through reflection upon this act; instead of attending to the giving act, we have rather to attend to that which it gives, to the totality which it brings to appearance *in concreto*, and to elevate its general form to general conceptual consciousness.

5. *Enlargement of the Concept of Intuition; Sensuous and Categorial Intuition*

If the question is now put: Wherein do the categorial forms of the meanings find their fulfillment, if not through perception or intuition in the narrower sense of "sensibility"? — then the answer is already indicated.

First of all, it is readily shown by any example of a true perceptual statement that the forms are really fulfilled (i.e., the entire meaning-forms, and not merely the "substantial" meaning-factors). That is why the entire perceptual statement is called an expression of the perception and, in an extended sense, an expression of that which is intuited and itself given in the perception. There must be an act which performs the same service for the categorial elements of meaning as the merely sensuous perception does for the "substantial" elements of meaning. To say that categorially formed meanings find fulfillment simply means that they are related to the object itself in its categorial formation. The object with these categorial forms is not merely meant, as in the case of the purely symbolic function of meanings, but is placed before our eyes in just these forms; in other words, it is not merely thought, but is intuited, or perceived. We cannot avoid using the terms "intuition," "perception," and "object," although in an extended sense, when we speak of fulfillment in this context. Thus totalities, indeterminate pluralities, numbers, disjunctives, predicates (*the being-just*), and facts become "objects," and the acts through which they appear as given become "perceptions."

It is also seen that the concept of the imagination is correspondingly extended. We could not speak of the supersensuously or categorially perceived if the possibility did not exist of imagining that also "in the same manner" (hence not merely sensuously).

The enlarged concept of perception admits also of a narrower and a wider interpretation. In the widest sense, general facts are also said to be perceived; we have "insight" into them; they are "seen" in evidence. In the narrower sense, perception is concerned only with individual, hence temporal being.

6. *Phenomenological Analysis of the Distinction between Sensuous and Categorial Perception*

The separation between "senuous" and "supersensuous" perceptions was only superficially indicated in the above. The antiquated talk of outer and inner senses, the origin of which may be traced to everyday life with its naive metaphysics and anthropology, was useful in order to point out the domain which must be excluded; but the real determination of the sphere of sensibility is not accomplished therewith, and thus the concept of categorial perception still lacks a descriptive basis. The clarification of the distinction in question is all the more important because such fundamental distinctions as the one between categorial form and the sensuously founded matter of knowledge, and similarly the distinction between categories and all other concepts, are entirely dependent upon it. The point is, then, to seek more deeply lying descriptive characteristics which afford insight into the essentially distinguished constitution of sensuous and categorial perceptions, or intuitions.

Every perception grasps its object *itself* or directly. But this direct grasping has a different sense and character, depending upon whether a perception in a narrower or in a wider sense is involved, or whether the "directly" grasped objectivity is sensuous or categorial; or, expressed otherwise: depending upon whether it is a real or an ideal object. The sensuous or real objects may be characterized as objects of the lowest level of possible intuition, the categorial or ideal ones as objects of the higher levels.

In the sense of the narrower "sensuous" perception, an object which is constituted in the act of perception in a *simple* (*schlicht*) manner is directly grasped or is itself present. This means that the object is perceived as a directly given object, and is not constituted in relating, connecting acts. Sensuous objects do not have to be constituted in a many-rayed manner in acts of a higher level, which constitute their objects by means of other objects already constituted in other acts.

Every simple act of perception can, however, whether by itself or together with other acts, function as a basic act for new acts which either include or only presuppose it. Because of new acts of conjunction, disjunction, generalization, etc., not only do subjective experiences arise, or acts which are connected with the original ones, but acts which constitute new objectivities; acts arise in which something appears as itself given, in such a way that it could not be given in the founding acts alone. On the other hand, the new objectivity is based upon the old one; it has an objective relation to the objectivity appearing in the basic acts. Its mode of appearance is essentially determined by this relation. What is in question here is a sphere of objectivities which can "themselves" come to appearance only in such founded acts.

That which is categorial in intuition and recognition lies in such founded acts; an asserting thought, where it functions as an expression, is fulfilled by them, and the possibility of perfect conformity to such acts determines the truth of the statement as its correctness. Thus far only the sphere of perception and in it only the simplest cases have been considered. It is seen at once that the distinction between simple and founded acts can be carried over from perceptions to all intuitions. The possibility of complex acts that are based in a mixed manner, in part upon simple perceptions and in part upon simple imaginations, may be noted; and furthermore the possibility that new foundations are constituted upon founded intuitions, and hence that a whole series of foundations can be built one upon the other; etc. But the clarification of the simple cases is the immediate problem.

7. Characterization of Sense Perception as "Simple" Perception

Consider first the acts in which concrete sensuous things and their sensuous constituent parts are represented as given; and then, in contrast to them, the entirely different acts through which concretely determined facts, conjunctions and disjunctions are given as complex "objects of thought," as "objects of a higher order," which immanently contain their founding objects in themselves; and again, acts of generalization or of indeterminate single apprehension, whose objects are to be sure of a higher level, but do not include their founding objects in themselves.

In sense perception the "outer" thing appears to us at one stroke, as soon as we look at it. It does not need the apparatus of founding or founded acts. Out of what and out of how complicated psychical processes it may have arisen genetically, is of no importance here.

Just as the thing does not appear as a mere sum of the countless single determinations which subsequent analysis may distinguish, but rather as a unified thing, so also is the act of perception always a homogeneous unity, which makes the object be present in a simple and direct manner. The unity of perception therefore does not arise through peculiar synthetic acts, as though only the form of the synthesis could provide the unity of the objective relation to the partial intentions through founded acts. It does not need articulation and consequently actual connection. The unity of perception comes about as a simple unity, as an immediate fusion of the partial intentions, and without any new act-intentions being added.

It may further be that instead of at "one glance," we view the thing from all sides in a continuous process of perception. But every single perception of this process is already a perception of this thing. Whether I look at this book from above or from below, from the inside or the outside, I always see *this book*. It is always the one and the same thing, the same not in the mere physical sense, but with respect to the intention of the perceptions themselves. The continuous process of perception is also shown by more exact analysis to be a fusion of partial acts to one act, and not as a peculiar act founded on the partial acts.

With regard to the sameness, it may be said that the unity is the unity of identification. This is correct, but unity of identification is not the same as unity of an *act* of identification. An act means something; the act of identification means identity, presents it. In the present case, identification is performed, but no identity is meant. The object meant in the various acts of the continuous process of perception is always the same, and the acts are united through "coincidence"; but what is perceived in this process, what is objective in it, is only the sensuous object, never its identity with itself. It is only when we make the process of perception to be the foundation of a new act, when we articulate the single perceptions and place their objects in relation, that the unity of the continuity obtaining between the single perceptions (i.e., fusion through coincidence of the intentions) serves as a support for a consciousness of identity.

The identity then becomes objective itself; the factor of the coincidence connecting the act-characters now serves as a representative content of a new perception which is founded on the articulated single perceptions, and brings to our intentional consciousness: the now and the previously perceived thing are one and the same. The act of identification is in fact a new consciousness of objectivity which brings a new "object" to appearance for us, an object which can only be "itself grasped" or "given" in a founded act of this kind.

The concept of a sensuous or real object (real in the most original sense) is clarified if the sense of simple or sensuous perception may be regarded as now clarified. It may be defined as a possible object of a simple perception. By virtue of the necessary parallelism between perception and imagination, according to which to every possible perception a possible imagination (or, more exactly, a whole series of imaginations) of the same essence corresponds, a simple imagination is coördinated with every single perception. The sensuous objects can be defined as the possible objects of sensuous imagination and sensuous intuition in general, but that is no essential generalization of the foregoing definition. On the basis of the parallelism just emphasized, both definitions are equivalent.

Through the concept of a real object the concept of a real part, or, more particularly, the concepts "real portion," "real factor" ("real character"), "real form" are determined. Every part of a real object is a real part.

In a simple perception the entire object is said to be "explicitly" given, and each of its parts (part in the broadest sense), "implicitly" given. The totality of objects which can be given in simple perceptions "explicitly" or "implicitly" makes up the widest sphere of sensuous objects.

Every concrete, sensuous object is simply perceivable in the manner of an explicit object; and the same holds for every portion of such an object. But what about the abstract factors? Their nature is such that they cannot be by themselves. It is therefore evident that their perception and imagination is something dependent, inasmuch as the representative content, even where mere representation through analogy occurs, cannot be experienced by itself, but only in a more comprehensive *concretum*. But that is not to say that the intuition must be a founded act. It would have to be that if the grasping of an abstract factor would necessarily have to be preceded by the grasping of the concrete whole; and this is not self-evident. On the other hand, it is certain that the grasping of a factor and in general of a part as a part of a given whole, and hence also the grasping of a sensuous character as a character, of a sensuous form as a form, refers to nothing but founded acts, of the species of relating acts. The sphere of "sensibility" would be left therewith and that of the "understanding" entered. The group of founded acts just indicated will now be submitted to a closer examination.

8. *Characterization of Categorial Acts as Founded Acts*

A sensuous object can be apprehended in different ways — first of all in a simple way. This possibility, which like all possibilities in question is to be interpreted as an ideal one, characterizes it as a sensuous object. Thus apprehended it stands before us as it were simply: the parts which constitute it are in it to be sure, but they do not become explicit objects for us in the simple act. We can, however, also apprehend the same object in an "explicating" manner: we "lift out" the parts in articulating acts, and by means of relating acts we place these parts in relationship, whether to one another or to the whole. It is first through these new modes of apprehension that the connected and related terms obtain the character of "parts," or of "wholes."

Let us first consider the relationships between part and whole, and, restricting ourselves to the simplest cases, the relationships *A is (has) a* and a *is an* A. To point out the founded acts in which these typical facts are constituted as given, and to clarify the forms of categorical statements that have just been used (i.e., to go back to their intuitive origin, to their adequate fulfillment) are the same. It is not the act-qualities that are here in question, however, but only the constitution of the forms of apprehension, and to that extent the present analysis, regarded as an analysis of judgment, will be incomplete.

A perceptual act grasps A as a whole at one stroke and in a simple manner. A second perceptual act is directed toward the a, the part or the dependent factor, which constitutively belongs to the A. These two acts are connected into a single act, in whose synthesis the A is first given as having the a in itself. With an inverse "direction" of the relating "perception," the a can similarly come to self-givenness as belonging to the A.

Let us go into this more deeply. The total intuitive meaning of the object implicitly includes the intention toward the a. The perception means to grasp the object itself, and thus its "grasping" must meet with all the constituent parts in the entire object. What are in question here are only the constituent parts of the object just as it appears in perception, and not those which belong to the object existing in "objective reality," which subsequent experiences, cognitions, and sciences first show.

All the relationships between a whole and its parts are of a categorial and hence of an ideal nature. It would be wrong to place them in the simple whole and to want to find them in it through analysis. The placing of the part-relationships into the whole would signify a confusion of fundamentally different things: of sensuous, or real forms of connection, and categorial, ideal ones. The sensuous connections are factors of the real object, actual factors of it, present in it, if only implicitly, and are lifted out of it through an abstractive perception. On the other hand, the forms of categorial connection are forms belonging to the mode of the act-synthesis, and hence forms which are objectively constituted in the synthetic acts built up upon a sensory basis. In the formation of external relations the sensuous form may give the foundation for the constitution of a categorial form corresponding to it; as when we apprehend or express the sensuous adjoining of the contents A and B, given in the intuition of a comprehensive G, in the synthetic forms A *adjoins* B, or B *adjoins* A. But with the constitution of the latter forms, new objects have arisen, belonging to the class fact, which comprises only "objects of a higher order." In the sensuous whole the parts A and B are united through the factor of contiguity, which connects them sensuously. The lifting out of these parts and factors, the formation of the intuition of A, B, and of contiguity, still does not provide the presentation *A adjoins B*. This requires a new act, appropriately forming and connecting these presentations.

9. Conjunctions and Disjunctions

Only some of the most simple fact-forms have been considered as examples of categorial and synthetic object-forms, namely, total and partial identity-relations and single external relations. Two synthetic forms will now be considered, which, while not themselves facts, play a large role in the context of facts: *collectiva* and *disjunctiva*. It is the acts in which they are constituted as something given which provide the fulfilling intuition for the meanings of the relations *and* and *or*.

I can paint *A* and paint *B*, but I cannot paint the *both*, the *A and B*. There is only the possibility, open at all times, that we perform the new act of conjunction (collection) on the basis of the two single intuitive acts, and thereby mean the *togetherness* of the objects *A and B*.

That an act which unites these perceptions is here spoken of, rather than some kind of connection or togetherness of these perceptions in consciousness, is due to a unified intentional relation being given, and corresponding to it a unified object which can only be constituted in this act-connection, just as a fact can only be constituted in the relating connection of presentations. One recognizes here the essential error of certain modern logicians, who regarded a mere co-consciousness of the nominal and propositional acts as being basic to the conjunctive connection of names, or statements, and consequently ascribed an objective logical form to the *and* (reference is here made to Sigwart). One should also be careful not to confuse the simple perceptions of unified sensuous aggregates, series, swarms, etc., with conjunctive perceptions, in which alone the consciousness of plurality is really constituted.[1] As already seen, Husserl had tried to show in his *Philosophy of Arithmetic* how the sensuous characters of unity (which are there called figural or quasi-qualitative factors of sensuous intuitions) serve as sensuous signs of multiplicity; i.e., as sensuous points of support for the recognition (signitively mediated through them) of multiplicity as such and as multiplicity of the kind in question. This recognition no longer needs an articulating single apprehension and single cognition, but also does not have the character of a genuine intuition of the collection.

---

[1] Just this question: how estimates of plurality and of number are possible at one glance, and hence in simple instead of in founded acts, whereas actual collection and counting presuppose articulated acts of a higher level, had itself called Husserl's attention to the intuitive characters of unity.

10. General Objects Constituted in General Intuitions

The simple synthetic acts which have been dealt with so far were founded on simple perceptions in such a way that the synthetic intention was also directed toward the objects of the founding perceptions, because it brought them together ideally or to a relating unity. This is a general character of synthetic acts. Now examples from another group of categorial acts will be considered, in which the objects of the founding acts do not also enter into the intention of that which is founded. The domain of *general intuition* belongs here, an expression which will sound no better to some than would "wooden iron."

Abstraction occurs on the basis of primary intuitions, and a new categorial act-character appears therewith, in which a new kind of objectivity comes to appearance. Abstraction in the mere sense of the emphasis upon some dependent factor in a sensuous object is not meant, but rather *ideating abstraction*, in which instead of the dependent factor, its "Idea," its generality comes to consciousness and is actually given. This act is presupposed, so that as opposed to the manifold of single factors of one and the same kind, this kind *itself*, as one and the same, can stand before our eyes. For we become conscious of the identity of the general in the repeated performance of such an act on the basis of several individual intuitions, and that occurs in an act of identification which brings all single acts of abstraction to synthesis. That which is general is itself given to us in the act of abstraction, which does not necessarily have to be performed with the aid of naming; we do not think it in a merely significative manner, as in the case of the mere understanding of general names; we grasp it, we see it. It is certainly justifiable to speak here of intuition, and more exactly, of perception of the general.

It might be objected, however, that the talk of perception presupposes a corresponding imagination, and the separation between them belongs, as has been pointed out, to the natural meaning of the term intuition. It is precisely this distinction which we miss here. The reason for this appears to be that the abstracting acts are not differentiated according to the character of the simple founding intuitions, that they are completely indifferent to whether these founding acts are positing or non-positing, whether they are perceptual or imaginative acts. The red or the triangle of mere phantasy are specifically the same as the red or the triangle of perception. The consciousness of generality is built up equally well on the basis of perception and of the conformable imagination, and if it is built up at all, then that which is general, the Idea *red*, the Idea *triangle*, is itself grasped;

it is intuited in the one way which admits of no differences between a picture and the original.

It is to be noted, however, that the examples adduced were examples of adequate perception of the general. The general was actually grasped and given on the basis of actually corresponding single cases. Where this is the case, a parallel imagination with the same intuitive content seems to be lacking — as in every case of adequate perception. The case is different, however, if we indirectly conceive curves of a third order, e.g., without a curve of this genus ever having been intuited by us. An intuitive figure, whether drawn or imagined, may nevertheless serve as an intuitive picture, as an analogue of the intended generality: i.e., the consciousness of generality is built up upon the individual intuition as intuitive and yet analogical. An ordinary rough drawing, which is analogical in comparison wth the ideal figure, also conditions the imaginative character of the *general* presentation. Similarly we intuit the idea of a steam-engine on the basis of the model of a steam-engine, whereby there can be no talk of an adequate abstraction, or conception. In such cases we do not have to do with mere significations, but rather with general representations through analogy, and hence with general imaginations. If, however, the consciousness of mere analogy is lacking, which, e.g., may occur with the intuition of a model, then a case of perception of the general, although of inadequate perception, is before us.

The distinction between a positing consciousness of generality and one that is left undecided may similarly be found. Where we conceive a general object merely through analogy, imaginatively, we can intend it in a positing manner, and this act can, like every positing intention, be confirmed by a future conformable perception, or be refuted. The former is the case if the general intention is constituted in an adequate perception, i.e., fulfilled in a new consciousness of generality, which is constituted on the basis of a "real" abstraction of the corresponding single case. The general object is then not merely presented and posited, but is itself given. We can again present the general in an analogical manner, but without positing it. We conceive it, but leave it undecided. The intention toward the general, built up on an intuitive basis, now does not decide regarding "being" or "non-being," but does decide as to whether the general and its being-given is possible in the manner of adequate abstraction, or not.

1. Complication to Ever New Forms; the Pure Form-Theory of Possible Intuitions

The various forms of founded acts, in which categorially formed and synthetically connected objects are constituted instead of simple, sensuous-intuitive objects, permit many complications to new forms, inasmuch as categorial unities can again and again (on the basis of certain categorial laws of an *a priori* kind) become objects of new relating or ideating acts. Thus one can, e.g., collectively connect general objects, and again connect such collections of the same or of different kinds, and so on *ad infinitum*. Similarly one can, although within determinate limits, unite facts to make new facts; one can seek out the inner and outer relations between all possible unities, again use these results as objects of new relations, etc. The complication occurs in founded acts of an ever higher level. The laws obtaining here are the intuitive counterpart of the pure-logical, grammatical laws. Here, too, laws are not in question which judge the true being of the presented objects of different levels. In any case these laws say nothing directly about ideal conditions of the possibility of adequate fulfillment. Corresponding to the pure form-theory of meanings is a pure form-theory of intentions, in which the primitive types of simple and complex intuitions are shown through intuitive generalization to be possible; and the laws of their successive complication to ever new and more complicated intuitions would have to be determined. Inasmuch as adequate intuition itself represents a type of intuition, the pure form-theory of intuitions in general comprises all the laws which concern the forms of adequate intuitions, and these have their particular relation to the laws of the adequate fulfillment of significative or already intuitive intentions.

2. The Relative or Functional Distinction between Matter and Form; Sensuous Concepts and Categories

The relative, merely functional distinction of "substance" and form is connected with the possibility of making categorial intuitions themselves again to be foundations of new categorial intuitions, and then of expressing them in corresponding expressions or meanings, as already indicated. In an absolute sense, a founding sense perception provides the substance for the acts of categorial form built thereupon. In a relative sense, the objects of the founding acts form the substance, namely, relative to the categorial forms newly arising from them in the founded acts. If we place two categorial objects, e.g., two facts, in a relation, then these facts are the substance, relative to the relation-form positing both in union. The traditional distinction between matter and form as applied to statements corresponds exactly to this determination of the concepts of substance and form.

The acts of simple intuition were called *sensuous*, and the founded acts, directly or indirectly leading back to sense perception, *categorial*. Within the sphere of categorial acts, however, it is important to distinguish between pure categorial acts, acts of the "pure understanding," and mixed acts of the understanding, "dealing" with sense perception. Ultimately everything categorial is based upon sensuous intuitions; a categorial intuition, and hence an insight of the understanding, thinking in the highest sense, is absurd without a founding sensory experience. The idea of a "pure intellect," interpreted as a "faculty" of pure thought (here: of categorial action) and completely detached from every "faculty of sensibility," could only be conceived *before* an elementary analysis of knowledge. Nevertheless, the concept of a purely categorial act, and hence the concept of a pure understanding, has its legitimate sense. If we consider the peculiarity of ideating abstraction, to be based upon individual intuition, but not therefore to mean that which is individual in this intuition; if we observe that it is rather a new mode of apprehension, which constitutes generality instead of individuality: then the possibility of *general intuitions* arises, which exclude not only everything individual, but everything sensuous from their intentional content. In other words, *sensuous abstraction*, which gives us *sensuous concepts* — either purely sensuous or mixed with categorial forms — is distinguished from *pure categorial abstraction*, which gives us *pure categorial concepts. Color, house, judgment, wish* are pure sensuous concepts; *quality of being colored, virtue, parallel-axiom* and the like are categorially mixed; *unity, plurality, relation, concept* are purely categorial. When categorial concepts are spoken of, pure categorial ones are always meant. The sensuous concepts have their immediate basis in what is given in sensuous intuition, and the categorial in what is given in categorial intuition. If there is a relational intuition at the basis of the abstraction, then the consciousness of abstraction may be directed upon the relation-form *in specie*, in such a way that everything sensuous of the relation-foundations remains out of play. Thus arise the categories, or the primitive concepts belonging here.

Concept and species have just been identified. If, however, one understands concepts to be general presentations instead of general objects, whether it be general intuitions or the general meanings corresponding to them, then the distinction applies to them; likewise to presentations of the form *an A*, namely, with regard to the species *A* being able to contain something sensuous or to exclude it. All logical forms are accordingly purely categorial, such as *all S are p*, etc.; for the letters *S, p*, etc., are merely indirect indications for "certain" indeterminate and "optional" concepts, and hence corresponding to them in the total meaning of the formula is a complex thought, built entirely out of categorial elements. Like all pure logic, the whole of pure arithmetic, set theory, in short the *pure mathesis* in the widest sense, is pure in the sense that it does not contain any sensuous concept in its entire theoretical nature.

3. The Categorial Formation No Real Transformation of the Object

The expression *categorial form* is ambiguous, but harmlessly so. On the one hand, it may mean the founded act-characters which give form to the acts of simple or even of already founded intuition and transform them into new objectivations. The latter constitute an objectivity which is modified in a peculiar way. The original objects are presented in certain forms which connect them in a new manner, and these are the categorial forms in a second, *objective* sense. The conjunctive connection *A and B*, which as a unified act means a categorial unity of objects (the totality, the "both"), can serve as an example.

The expression *A and B* illustrates, particularly with regard to the "*and*," still another sense of the expression "categorial form," according to which the *significative forms* that have possible fulfillment in the founded act-characters are designated as categorial forms in a figurative sense.

It should now be emphasized that although the categorial functions "form" the sensuous object, they leave it untouched in its real essence. The object is intellectually grasped through the intellect, and especially through cognition (which is itself a categorial function), but it is not falsified. To make this clear, recall the distinction between the categorial unities understood in an objective sense, and the real unities, such as, e.g., the unity of the parts of a thing, of the trees of an avenue, etc. The unity of the immanent, constituent parts of a psychical experience and similarly of all coexistent experiences in an individual consciousness is also a real unity. These unities, regarded as wholes, are, like their parts, objects in the primary and simple sense; they can be experienced in possible simple intuitions. They are not merely categorially united, and are not constituted by being viewed together through conjunction, disjunction, etc.; they are unified "in themselves" and have a form of unity which is perceivable in the whole as a real unity-factor, and hence as a real determination — perceivable in the same sense as are any of the connected elements and *their* inner determinations.

It is entirely different with the categorial forms. The new objects which they produce are not objects in the primary and original sense. The categorial forms do not glue or connect the parts together, so that a real, sensuously perceivable whole would come about. They do not form in the sense in which the potter forms something. Otherwise that which is originally given in sense perception would be modified, and relational thought would not be thought of that which is, but rather a falsifying transformation into something else. But the categorial forms leave the primary objects untouched; they cannot change them in their own being, because the result would then be a new object in a primary and real sense, whereas the result of a categorial act (e.g., an act of relation) consists in an objective formulation of that which is primarily intuited, which can only be given in such a founded act, so that the thought of a simple perception of what is formed, or of its givenness in another simple intuition, is absurd.

4. The Freedom in the Categorial Formation of Pre-Given Substance and Its Limits; the Purely Categorial Laws (Laws of "Genuine" Thought)

Real outer or inner sensuous forms of unity are determined by law through the essential nature of the parts to be connected, and are absolutely determined with the complete individuation of these parts. All unity refers to law, real unity to real law. That which is really one must also be really unified. When we speak of the freedom to unite or not to unite, we do not take the contents in their complete reality, to which the spatio-temporal determinations also belong. Whereas the consciousness, and especially the simple intuition of real contents, is *eo ipso* consciousness of their real connections or forms, the case is entirely different with regard to the categorial forms. In the case of real contents no categorial forms which are to be adapted to them are necessarily given; there is abundant freedom here in the connecting and relating, in the generalizing and subsuming, and the like. We can divide a sensuously unified group arbitrarily and in many ways in partial groups; and these can be ordered and connected arbitrarily, or collections of a second, third . . . level can be built upon one another. Thus many possibilities of collective formation on the basis of the same sensuous substance arise. Similarly we can compare every element of one and the same sensuous complex with any of the other elements, or distinguish it from them; we can make each one to be the subject-term, or by an arbitrary conversion of the relationships in question, to be the object-term; we can then connect these relationships, classify them, etc.

Despite the great freedom of categorial unity and formation, it has its determinate limits. Unity and law are also inseparable from one another here. Because the categorial forms are constituted in founded act-characters, and only in them, they contain a certain necessary connection. How could one speak of categorial perception and intuition, if any substance at all could be brought into any form, and hence the founding simple intuitions could be connected at will with the categorial characters. Thus it would be impossible to intuit a part as a whole and the whole as a part, with the content unchanged. We are also not free to conceive this relationship as one of total identity or of total exclusion, etc. To be sure we can "think" of every kind of relationship between all kinds of relative points, and of every kind of form upon the basis of every substance, namely, thinking in the sense of mere signification. But we cannot intuit the sensuous substance in every categorial form, and especially not perceive it, or adequately perceive it.

There is a certain element of constraint in the extended concept of perception, *eo ipso*. Not as though the character of perception were immanently bound to the sensuous content. It is never that; for that would mean that there is nothing which is not perceived and which *must* not be perceived. But there is nothing which *can* not be perceived. That means, however, that the actual performance of the actual acts on the basis of these substances, or more exactly, on the basis of just these simple intuitions, is possible in an ideal sense. These possibilities are, like ideal possibilities in general, limited by law.

The ideal laws which regulate the connection of these possibilities and impossibilities belong to the categorial forms *in specie*, and hence to the categories in an objective sense. They determine which variations of any pre-given categorial forms are possible, with presupposed identity of the determinate but optional substance; they delimit the ideally closed manifold of reorderings and transformations of categorial forms on the basis of the identical substance. The substance comes in question here only in so far as it must be held intentionally in identity with itself. But in so far as the species of the substances are variable with complete freedom and are only subject to the obvious condition that they, as bearers of the forms assumed, are capable of functioning, the laws in question have the character of completely pure and analytic laws; they are completely independent of the particular nature of the substances. Only algebraic symbols are used in expressing the laws, as bearers of indeterminate general presentations, of certain optional substances in general, which are to be maintained as identical with themselves.

For insight into these laws, the actual performance of a categorial intuition which makes its substances actually intuitive is not needed; any categorial intuition suffices, which places before one's eyes the possibility of the categorial formation in question. In the generalizing abstraction of the entire possibility, the unitary intuitive "insight" into the law is achieved, and this insight has the character of adequate, general perception. The general object, which is given in it itself, is the categorial law. It may be said that the ideal conditions of the possibility of categorial intuition in general are correlatively the conditions of the possibility of the objects of categorial intuition, and of the possibility of categorial objects themselves. That an objectivity formed categorially in a certain way is possible is essentially correlated with the possibility that a categorial intuition — a mere imagination — can place such a completely conformable objectivity before our eyes; in other words, that the categorial syntheses in question and the other categorial acts are actually performable on the basis of the founding intuitions concerned (even if they are imaginations).

The ideal conditions under consideration, the analytical laws, do not specify *which* categorial formation any particular perceptually or imaginatively pre-given substance permits *de facto*. That one cannot do as he pleases without limit, and that the "actual" performableness has the character, not of empirical reality, but of ideal possibility, is shown by the above examples. And they also show that it is the particular nature of the substance which delimits the possibilities, so that we can say, e.g., G is really a whole of g, or γ is really a property of G — whereby the categorial form, unlike the real, is not restricted to the genera of the G, g, γ, and the like. On the contrary, it is evident that contents of all genera can be formed through all categories. The categorial forms are not founded on the substantial contents, as seen above. Therefore those pure laws cannot prescribe which form a given substance can assume. They merely state that if a given substance, or any substance in general, has assumed a certain form or is capable of assuming it, a definite sphere of further forms is at the disposal of the same substance; or, that there is an ideally closed sphere of possible transformations of the form in question into ever new forms. The ideal possibility of the new forms on the basis of the same substance is assured *a priori* by the "analytic" laws.

These are the pure laws of "genuine thought," understood as laws of categorial intuitions with respect to their pure categorial forms. The categorial intuitions function in theoretical thought as actual or possible meaning-fulfillments, or disappointments, and according to their function, invest the statements with the logical value of truth or untruth. The normative regulation of thought, whether purely signitive or signitively obscure (*getrübt*), depends upon the laws just discussed.

The sphere of meanings or meaning-intentions will now be examined more closely.

5. The New Laws of Validity of Signitive and Signitively Obscure Acts (Laws of Figurative Thought)

Categorial acts have been conceived as being free from all significative contribution in the foregoing discussions, and hence not as founding any kind of acts of recognition and naming. It will surely be admitted by every unprejudiced analyst that we can intuit, e.g., totalities or divers primitive facts, without bringing them to nominal or propositional expression. Now let us oppose the case of mere signification to the case of mere intuition, and consider that pure significative acts can correspond to all the acts of categorial intuition with their categorially formed objects. This is obviously an *a priori* possibility. There is no act-form belonging here, to which a possible meaning-form would not correspond; and every meaning can be thought as performed without a correlated intuition. The ideal of a logically conformable language is that of a language which would provide unique expression to all possible substances and all possible categorial forms. Certain significative intentions then uniquely belong to the words, and these intentions can also come to life in the absence of the "corresponding" (fulfilling) intuition. Parallel to all possible primary and founded intuitions is the system of the primary and founded meanings expressing them (possibly).

But the domain of meaning is much more comprehensive than that of intuition, i.e., than the total domain of possible fulfillments. There is the unlimited manifold of complex meanings which lack "reality" or "possibility"; they are structures of meanings, which do indeed form unified meanings, but such that no possible unitary fulfillment-correlate can correspond to them.

Accordingly, no complete parallelism exists between the categorial types, or the types of categorial intuition, and the types of meaning. To every categorial type of a lower or higher level there corresponds a meaning-type: but, with our freedom to connect the types significatively and to form complex types, a type of categorial objectivity does not correspond to every type thus arising. One can cite the types of analytic contradictions, such as *an A which is not A, all A are B and some A are not B*; etc. Only with respect to the primitive types can and must the parallelism exist, since all primitive meanings have their "origin" in the fullness of correlated intuition. Whereas *a something that is at the same time A and not A* is impossible, *an A and B* is possible; the and-form has, as a simple form, a "real" sense.

If we apply the term *categorial* to the domain of meaning, it is seen that to every genuine categorial form, whether it be one in the objective sense, or the relevant categorial form of intuition (in which the categorial objectivity is constituted perceptually or imaginatively), there corresponds a peculiar significative form, or also a peculiar meaning-form *in specie*. In this form of signification the significative intending of a conjunction or disjunction, of an identity or non-identity, and the like occurs. If one speaks of the contrast between real and figurative presentation, one usually has the opposition between *intuitive* and *significative* in view (unless, which also occurs on occasion, the other opposition between adequate and inadequate is intended). Accordingly, the present cases would be cases of "formative" conjunction, disjunction, identification, abstraction, etc.

If all the categorial acts, through which the judgments (as predicative significations) acquire their fullness and finally their entire cognitive value, are comprised under the title *acts of thought*, then the distinction must be drawn between genuine and figurative acts of thought. The figurative acts of thought would be the meaning-intentions of statements and, more broadly, all the significative acts which can possibly serve as parts of such predicative intentions (and all significative acts can serve thus). The genuine acts of thought would be the corresponding fulfillments, and consequently the fact-intuitions and all intuitions which can function as possible parts of fact-intuitions; but all intuitions can do that, and there is no categorial form which could not become a constituent of a fact-form. The general doctrine of the forms of symbolic judgments (of statement-meanings) comprehends that of meaning-forms in general (the pure logical-grammatical forms); similarly the general doctrine of pure forms of fact-intuitions (or of fact-forms) comprehends that of the categorial forms of intuitions (or of the objective categorial forms) in general.

If, as often happens, thought and judgment are identified, then genuine and figurative judgment ought to be distinguished. The concept of a judgment would then be determined through that which is common to a statement-intention and the statement-fulfillment, hence through the intentional essence as the unity of quality and of intentional matter. Not merely the acts of judgment, but all possible partial acts of judgments, would have to be valid as thought-acts in a wider sense.

In the sphere of figurative thought, of mere signification, we are free of all limits of categorial laws. Everything and anything can be brought to unity in it. But this freedom is also subject to certain limitations. As seen in the fourth investigation, the "pure logical-grammatical" laws, as laws of complication and modification, separate the spheres of sense and nonsense. We are free in the figurative categorial formation and trans-formation, in so far as we do not conglomerate the meanings nonsensically. If formal and real absurdity is to be avoided, however, the widest sphere of figurative thought, or that which can be connected significatively, must be restricted. The point in question is the objective possibility of the com-plex meanings, and hence the possibility of their intuitive fulfillment as wholes. The pure laws of the validity of meanings, of the ideal possibility of their envisagement, run parallel to the pure laws which regulate the connection and transformation of the *genuine* categorial forms.

In the pure laws of the validity of meaning the point in question is not laws in which the validity of pre-given meanings could be read off, but rather the purely categorially determined possibilities of the connection of meaning and the transformation of meaning, which may be under-taken in any pre-given case *salva veritate*, i.e., without the possibility of meaning-fulfillment. If, e.g., the statement that *g is a part of G* is valid, then a statement of the form *G is a whole of g* is also valid. If it is true *that there is an α which is β*, then it is also true *that a certain α is β*, or *that not all α are not β*, etc. In such propositions all "substantial" mean-ings are replaced by indirect and completely indeterminate algebraic signs. These propositions are in this way characterized as *analytic*. The point is not whether the substance is constituted in perceptions or imaginations. The possibilities and impossibilities relate to the production of envisaging acts, conformable to the meaning-form, on any kind of substantial basis; in short, the pure conditions of the possibility of completely conformable signification in general are in question, which on their part refer back to the pure conditions of the possibility of categorial intuition in general. Naturally these laws of the validity of meanings are not themselves the genuine categorial laws, but they follow them truly, on the basis of the laws which regulate the connections of meaning-intention and meaning-fulfillment.

The entire discussion that has just been carried through requires a nat-ural and obvious extension. The discussion has been simplified by con-sidering only two extremes. The entirely intuitive, and hence actually performed categorial act-structure, has been contrasted with the purely signitive, and hence really not at all performed act-structure, which is to be realized in processes of possible fulfillment. The usual cases are mixtures, however; the thinking occurs intuitively to some extent, and to some extent signitively. Such complex acts have, taken as wholes, the character of figurative categorial intuitions; their total objective correlate is not really presented, but only "figuratively"; their "possibility," or the objectivity of their correlate, is not guaranteed. The sphere of "figurative thinking" must accordingly be conceived so widely that it also comprises these mixed act-structures. Everything that has been stated holds then *mutatis mutandis* with this extension. Instead of laws of the validity of mere meanings, of merely symbolic judgments, etc., we then have to speak of laws of the validity of signitively obscure presentations or judgments. When one speaks of merely symbolic thinking he has these mixtures mostly in view.

6. The Pure Logical-Grammatical Laws: Their Psychological Significance and Their Normative Function with Respect to Inadequate Thought

Both kinds of laws are obviously ideal in character. That a sensuous material can only be contained in certain forms and connected only in accordance with certain forms, and that the possible transformation of them is subject to pure laws in which the material elements are freely variable; that consequently the expressive meanings can only take on certain forms, or be transformed according to prescribed types, if they are not to forfeit their real capacity for expression: these are not matters pertaining to empirical accidents of the stream of consciousness, and also not of our human intellectual organization. They pertain rather to the specific nature of sensibility and understanding in general. An understanding with other than the pure logical laws would be an understanding without understanding; if we define the understanding in contrast to sensibility as the faculty of categorial acts and of "correct" expression or meaning, then the general laws based upon the species of these acts belong to the definitional essence of the understanding. Other beings may look into other "worlds," they may be equipped with different "faculties" than we have; but if they are at all psychical beings and possess intentional experiences, they have both sensibility and understanding, and are "subject" to the laws belonging thereto.

Naturally the laws of genuine thinking also pertain to the nature of human consciousness, to our general human "psychical organization." On the other hand, they are not peculiar to this organization. The laws are based, as has been said, upon the purely specific nature of certain acts, and as such they pertain to all possible organizations which can be built up out of acts of that kind, and not merely to the human type.

The relation to "our" psychical organization or to "consciousness in general" (understood as the general human element of consciousness) does not define the pure and genuine *a priori*, but a falsfied one. The concept of a general psychical organization has, like that of a physical organization, a merely "empirical" meaning, the meaning of a mere matter of fact. The pure laws are, however, pure of any matter of fact; what they refer to is removed from the sphere of reality. Thus the genuine logical *a priori* deals with all that belongs to the ideal essence of the understanding in general, with the essences of its act-species and act-forms, and hence with that which cannot be suspended so long as the understanding, or the acts defining it, are what they are, of a definite kind and retaining their identical conceptual essence.

To what extent the logical laws, and above all the ideal laws of "real" thought, are also psychologically significant, and to what extent they also regulate the course of factual psychical happening, is at once clear. Every genuine "pure" law that expresses a unifiability or non-unifiability based upon the nature of certain species, restricts, if it relates to species of psychically realizable contents, the empirical possibilities of psychological (phenomenological) coexistence and succession. What is seen as incompatible *in specie*, cannot be united and hence be compatible in a single empirical case. Therefore the *a priori* laws of genuine thought and of genuine expression become norms of the merely supposing and figurative thought, or expression. Or expressed somewhat differently: based upon the "genuine" laws of thought are new laws which may also be formulated as practical norms, and which are ascribed to the sphere of signitive or signitively obscure presentation, and express the ideal conditions of possible truth (= correctness), namely, the ideal conditions of "logical" (because they refer to possible adequation) compatibility within this sphere of signitively obscure supposition. Psychologically the laws of "figurative" thinking do not amount to empirical laws of the becoming and change of such thinking, but rather to ideally founded possibilities or impossibilities of the adequation of variously formed acts of figurative thinking to corresponding acts of real thinking.

7. *The Absurd Problem of "the Real Meaning of the Logical"*

It is now completely understood, why the thought is absurd that the course of the world could ever go contrary to the logical laws — those analytic laws of genuine thought, or the norms of figurative thought built thereupon — or that the experience of any sensuous matter of fact would have to and could first of all establish these laws and prescribe the limits of their validity. The point is to recognize that the so to speak factual aspect of an empirical fact belongs to sensibility, and that the thought of establishing pure categorial laws with the aid of sensibility — laws which exclude all sensibility and factuality, and merely make pure essential statements about categorial forms as forms of possible correctness, or truth in general — represents the clearest metabasis ($\mu\epsilon\tau\acute{\alpha}\beta\alpha\sigma\iota\varsigma$ $\epsilon\grave{\iota}\varsigma$ $\mathring{\alpha}\lambda\lambda o$ $\gamma\acute{\epsilon}\nu o\varsigma$). Laws which do not mean any empirical fact cannot be verified or refuted by any empirical fact. The problem, treated so earnestly and profoundly by great philosophers, of the "real or formal meaning of the logical," is therefore an absurd problem. No metaphysical or other theories are needed to explain the agreement of the course of nature and of the lawfulness "innate" in the "understanding"; what is needed is the phenomenological elucidation of meaning, thinking, knowing, and the ideas and laws arising therein.

The world is constituted as a sensuous unity; in accordance with its sense, it is a unity of actual and possible simple perceptions. In its true being it is never adequately given in any perceptual process, however. It is for us at all times only an inadequate unity of theoretical investigation, meant partially through simple and categorial intuition, and partially through signification. The more our knowledge advances, the better and richer is our idea of the world, and the more are incompatibilities separated out from it. Doubts as to whether the world is really such as it appears to us, or such as it is supposed in the existing theoretical science, has its legitimate sense; for inductive science can never adequately form the idea of the world, no matter how far it may bring it. But it is also absurd to doubt whether the real course of the world, the real connection of the world in itself, could conflict with the forms of thought. For that would imply that a determinate, hypothetically supposed sensibility would bring the world in itself to an adequate self-representation and would be capable of assuming the categorial forms, but would force unifications upon these forms which are excluded by the general essence of the same forms. But, that the laws of the categories are valid as pure laws which abstract from all sensuous substance, and hence cannot be affected by its unlimited variation, is not merely meant by us; we have insight into it, it is given to us with the most complete adequation. The insight naturally occurs subjectively on the basis of an accidental empirical intuition; but it is a general insight, related purely to the form.

It is absurd, if one supposes the possibility of an antilogical course of the world in signitive thought, and makes the claim that this possibility takes place, and if one, so to speak in the same breath, suspends the laws which invest this as well as every possibility in general with validity. It could be pointed out further, that the correlation to being-able-to-be-perceived, -to-be-intuited, -to-be-meant, -to-be-recognized, is inseparable from the sense of being in general, and that consequently the ideal laws which belong to these possibilities *in specie* can never be suspended by the accidental content of an actual existent itself. But all these arguments are only versions of one and the same state of affairs which was discussed in the *Prolegomena*.

8. Distinctions Confused in the Usual Contrast of "Intuition" and "Thought"

The relationship between thought and intuition has been made clear. The following distinctions, whose confusion has affected epistemological investigation to a large extent, will now be summarized.

(a) The distinction between intuition and signification: Intuition as perception or imagination (regardless of whether it be categorial or sensuous, whether it be adequate or inadequate) is contrasted with mere thinking, as merely significative intending. The distinctions placed in parentheses are usually overlooked, but the greatest importance is attached to them here.

(b) The distinction between sensuous and categorial intuition: Sensuous intuition, or intuition in the common, simple sense, and categorial intuition, or intuition in an extended sense, are contrasted. The founded acts which characterize it are now regarded as the "thinking" which intellectualizes the sensuous intuition.

(c) The contrast between inadequate and adequate, or more generally between adequate and inadequate presentation, taking together intuitive and significative presentation: In an inadequate presentation we imagine that such is the case (it appears so), in an adequate one we see the state of affairs itself and intuit it completely.

(d) The contrast between individual intuition (usually conceived narrowly as sensuous intuition) and general intuition: According to this contrast a new concept of intuition is determined; it is opposed to generalization, and to the categorial acts which imply generalizations, and in unclear confusion therewith, also to the significative counterparts of these acts. An "intuition," it is now said, merely gives a particular, whereas "thinking" deals with the general and occurs by means of "concepts." Usually one speaks here of the contrast between "intuition and concept."

How great the inclination is to make these contrasts flow into one another, would be made clear by a critique of the theory of knowledge of Kant, which illustrates the lack of a firm separation of these antitheses. Of course the categorial (logical) functions played a big role in Kant's thought, but he did not attain to the fundamental extension of the concepts of perception and intuition over the categorial domain; and that because he did not appreciate the great distinction between intuition and signification, in their possible separation and usual fusing, and therefore did not analyze the distinction between the inadequate and adequate adaptation of meaning to intuition. He therefore also failed to distinguish between concepts as general word-meanings and concepts as species of really general presentation, and again, concepts as general objects, namely, as the intentional correlates of general presentations. From the outset Kant was restricted by a metaphysical theory of knowledge because he aimed at the critical "rescue" of mathematics, natural science, and metaphysics, before he had prepared the ground for it. It is necessary first to subject knowledge as such, the total sphere of the acts in which pre-logical objectivation and logical thinking are performed, to a clarifying essential analysis and critique, and to trace back the primitive logical concepts and laws to their phenomenological origin. It was fateful that Kant held the purely logical domain in the narrowest sense to be disposed of with the observation that it is subject to the principle of contradiction. Not only that he never noted how little the logical laws possess the character of analytic propositions in the sense which he himself had fixed definitionally; he did not see how little is gained for an explanation of the contribution of analytic thinking by the reference to an evident principle of analytic propositions.

It may be added that all the fundamental unclearnesses of the Kantian critique of reason are connected with the fact that Kant had never made clear the peculiarity of pure "ideation," of the adequate "seeing" of conceptual essences and of universally valid essential laws, and that he therefore lacked the genuine phenomenological concept of the *a priori*. Hence he could not set up the only possible goal of a rigorously scientific critique of reason, namely, the goal of investigating the pure essential laws which govern the acts as *intentional* experiences according to all their modes of objectivating sense-giving and of the fulfilling constitution of "true being." It is Husserl's thesis that it is only through the evident knowledge of these essential laws that all questions which can be meaningfully asked about the "possibility of knowledge" can find a satisfactory answer.

9. *That Not Every Meaning Involves Recognition*

The difficult questions which were raised at the beginning of this investigation have now been clarified, and above all the view that the meaning of expressions must be regarded as recognition, and even as classification. It is said: An expression must "give expression" to some act of a speaker; but in order that this act find the appropriate mode of expression, it must be apperceived or recognized in a pertinent manner — a presentation as a presentation, an attribution as an attribution, a negation as a negation, etc.

To this it may be answered that the term knowledge refers to a relationship between an act of thought and fulfilling intuition. Acts of thought, however, do not come to expression in a statement or in parts of a statement, e.g., in names, by again being thought and known. Otherwise these new acts of thought would be the bearers of meaning; they would be expressed to begin with, and would therefore again need new acts of thought, and thus *in infinitum*. If I call this intuitive object *watch*, then in the naming I perform an act of thought and knowledge, but I recognize the watch, and not the recognition. This is naturally the case with all meaning-endowing acts. If I say *or* in the context of expressive speech, I perform a disjunction, but the thinking (of which the disjunction is a part) does not relate to the act of disjunction, but rather to the *disjunctivum*, just as it belongs to the unity of the fact. This *disjunctivum* is recognized and denoted objectively. The particle *or* is not a name, and merely manifests the act of disjunction. This also holds for whole judgments. If I state something, I think of the things (*Sachen*); that the matters stand in such and such a way (*dass sich die Sachen so und so verhalten*). That is what I express, and perhaps I also recognize it; but I do not think and recognize the judging.

But does not the grammatical adaptation of the expression to the act that is to be expressed refer to an act of recognition, in which this adaptation occurs? In a certain manner surely, or in certain cases, namely, wherever expressions are considered in the sense in which they were discussed at the beginning of the present investigation. But not where the expression involves mere manifestation, according to which all kinds of meaning-giving acts are then valid as expressed through the words (the word-sounds); and again not where expression is equivalent to meaning, and that which is expressed is the identical meaning. In the latter double sense every statement, whether merely significative or intuitively fulfilled, expresses something, namely, the judgment (the conviction) or the "judgment-content" (the identical proposition-meaning). In the sense first indicated, however, only the statement that is intuitively fulfilled or is to be fulfilled expresses something, whereby not the word-sound, but the already sense-animated language represents the "expression" for the corresponding intuition. In every case the meaning-endowing function effects the unified complication of the signitive intentions attached to the words. These make up the merely signitive judging, where every fulfilling intuition is wanting; the synthesis of agreement or non-agreement, which the total signitive intention "expresses" (or pretends to express), is not "really" performed here, but is only meant signitively. If, on the other hand, this real performance of the indicated synthesis occurs, then the "genuine" synthesis coincides with the figurative one (the synthesis in the signification): they are unified in the identical intentional essence which represents one and the same meaning, one and the same judgment (whether judged intuitively or merely signitively). This holds analogously for the cases in which only individual word-intentions are provided with intuitive fullness. The signitive acts comprehend the same intention as the intuitive ones, without their fullness; they merely "express" them, and the simile is all the more fitting because after the dropping off of the intuitive acts they also preserve for us the sense of the intuition, as an empty cover without the intuitive core. The unity of coincidence is indeed, in the case of intuitive judgment, really unity of knowledge (even if not unity of the relating recognition), but we know that in the unity of knowledge it is not at all the fulfilling act, and hence here the "real" judgment-synthesis that is the known, but rather its objective correlate, the fact. In the intuition of the things we perform a judging synthesis, an intuitive *It is thus* or *It is not thus*; in that the expressing intention with the associated word-sounds (hence the grammatical expression) fits this act of the intuition of the fact, the recognition of the intuited fact takes place.

C. SUPPLEMENT: OUTER AND INNER PERCEPTION; PHYSICAL AND PSYCHICAL PHENOMENA

1. The Traditional Distinction

After Descartes had roughly separated *mens* and *corpus*, Locke introduced the two corresponding classes of perception into modern philosophy under the title of *sensation* and *reflection*. This division has remained until the present. Outer perception is according to Locke our perception of bodies, and inner perception is the perception which our "mind" or the "soul" possesses of its own activities (they are the *cogitationes* in the

Cartesian sense). Thus a separation of the perceptions is determined through the separation of the perceptual objects. A distinction in the kind of origin is at the same time coördinated with it. In the one case the perception arises out of the effects which the physical things exert by means of the sense-organs upon the mind; in the other case, out of the reflection upon the activities which the mind performs upon the basis of the "ideas" already obtained through sensation. In recent times the effort has been made to modify and deepen the rough and vague determinations of Locke.

The traditional estimate of the relative cognitive value of the two kinds of perception will be recalled: outer perception is deceptive; inner perception is evident. Upon this evidence is based one of the pillars of knowledge, which skepticism cannot undermine. Inner perception is also the only one in which the object truly corresponds to the perceptual act, and in fact is inherent in it. It is therefore the only perception which deserves the name. — In the interest of the theory of perception the essence of inner in distinction from outer perception had to be investigated more exactly.

On the other hand, psychological interests were taken into consideration. The much disputed fixing of the domain of empirical psychology was in question, as opposed to the sciences of nature, through the delimitation of a domain of phenomena peculiar to it. To classify perceptions on the basis of an assumed dualism could not be satisfactory. The point was to establish purely descriptive characteristics for the separation of the types of perception, or the bodily and mental phenomena corresponding to them.

The Cartesian method of doubt appeared to open up a practicable way, by showing that we have "evidence" of the existence of the objects of inner perception, but not in the case of outer perception. Hence only phenomenal or "intentional" existence may be claimed for the latter. If the concept of perception is understood to require the actual being of the perceived object, then outer perception, in this rigorous sense, is not perception at all. In any case the *character of the evidence* provides us with a *descriptive characteristic* which distinguishes the two kinds of perception and is free from all presuppositions about metaphysical realities. It is a character which is given with the perceptual experience itself, or is lacking, and this alone determines the separation.

The phenomena which are offered in the two kinds of perception are also seen to constitute essentially different classes. That is not to say that the objects in themselves which we suppose, whether with right or wrong

— the minds and bodies — are essentially different; but rather, regarded purely descriptively, and disregarding all transcendence, an insuperable distinction between the phenomena is to be ascertained. On the one side are the sense-qualities, which form a closed unity by themselves, whether there are such things as senses and sense-organs or not. Entire propositions enter into consideration here, e.g., that there is nothing spatial in intuition without quality; and according to some the converse also holds, that there is no quality without something spatial. Others admit only certain particularizations: that there is no color, no tactual quality, without something spatial, and the like. Other propositions belonging here would be: There is no tone-quality without intensity, etc.[2] On the other side are phenomena such as presentation, judgment, supposing, wishing, hoping, etc. We are here so to speak in another world. The phenomena may have relationship to something sensuous, but they are themselves "incomparable" with the sensuous, and do not belong to the same genus. They have the character of "intentional inexistence."

Naturally the above descriptive distinction of inner and outer perceptions can also serve to distinguish both classes of phenomena. It is now a good definition to say: The psychical phenomena are the phenomena of inner, and the physical of outer perception. Thus Brentano[3] regarded it to be a "distinguishing characteristic" of all psychical phenomena "that they are only perceived in inner consciousness, whereas in the case of physical phenomena only outer perception is possible." He believed this to be a sufficient characterization of psychical phenomena. Inner consciousness is merely another expression for inner perception. In that way a more exact consideration of both kinds of perceptions appears to lead not only to a descriptive and epistemologically significant characterization of them, but also to a fundamental, descriptive separation of the phenomena into the two classes of physical and psychical phenomena.

This appears to provide psychology and natural science with a definition that is determined by the phenomena themselves. The physical phenomena are now no longer defined as the appearances which result from the action of bodies upon our minds by means of sense-organs; and the psychical phenomena no longer as the appearances which we find in the perception of the activities of our minds. In both cases the descriptive character of the phenomena, just as we experience them, is alone our criterion. Accordingly, psychology can now be defined as the science of psychical

[2] Husserl observes that it is striking that the attempt had never been made to base a positive determination for "physical phenomena' upon these intuitive connections.

[3] *Psychologic*, vol. 1, pp. 118 f.

appearances, and natural science as the science of physical appearances. These definitions need certain restrictions, however, in order actually to correspond to the nature of the given sciences, restrictions which refer to the explanatory metaphysical hypotheses.

2. *Inner and Outer Perception, and Their Relation to Apperception*

Inner perception plays a significant role in the psychology of Brentano, to whose theory of inner consciousness reference is here made. According to Brentano, inner is distinguished from outer perception (a) by the evidence and certainty, and (b) by the essentially different phenomena. In inner perception we exclusively experience the psychical, in outer perception the physical phenomena.

In opposition to that it appears to Husserl that inner and outer perception have the same epistemological character. There is to be sure a justifiable distinction between *evident* and *non-evident*, unerring and deceptive perception. If one construes (as Brentano does) outer perception to be the perception of physical things, events, etc., and takes inner perception to include all other perceptions, then this division does not at all coincide with the preceding one. Thus every perception of the ego, or every perception of a psychical condition that is connected with the ego, is certainly not evident, if one understands the ego to mean one's own empirical personality. It is also clear that most perceptions of psychical conditions cannot be evident, since they are perceived as localized bodily. That *fear makes a lump rise in my throat*, that *the pain bores in my tooth*, etc., I perceive in precisely the same sense as that *the wind shakes the trees*. Outer perceptions are indeed also present here along with the inner: that does not alter the fact that the perceived psychical phenomena, *just as they are perceived*, do not exist. Is it not clear that psychical phenomena can also be perceived transcendently? In fact, all psychical phenomena viewed with the natural and empirical-scientific attitude are apperceived transcendently. Pure experience-givenness, on the other hand, requires the purely phenomenological attitude, which prohibits all transcendent positings.

It will be objected here that the distinction between perception and apperception has been missed; for inner perception means the simple conscious experience of psychical acts, which are taken here as that which they *are*, and not as that which they are apprehended or apperceived to be. One would think, however, that what is correct for inner perception must also apply in the case of outer perception. But if perception is not essentially apperception, then all talk of perception in relation to something external, to mountains, forests, houses, etc., is wrong, and the normal sense of the word perception would be given up. Outer perception is apperception, and the same must be true of inner perception. It is essential to perception that something appears in it; but the apperception makes up what we call *appearing*, whether it be incorrect or not. The *house* appears to me, in that I apperceive the actually experienced sense-contents in a certain manner. I hear a hand-organ, and I interpret the sensed tones as *hand-organ-tones*. Similarly I "apperceivingly" perceive my psychical appearances, the blessedness filling "me" with awe, the sorrow in my heart, etc. They are called "appearances," or, better, appearing contents of the apperception.

3. The Meaning of "Appearance"

The ambiguity of the term "appearance" is especially harmful here, so that it will be well to summarize its various meanings, which have already been touched upon in the course of the investigations. It may mean:

(a) The concrete experience of intuition (the having-intuitively-present of a certain object); e.g., the concrete experience when we perceive the lamp before us. The appearance coincides here with what is defined as representation in the sixth investigation; whether we hold the object to be existent or not does not matter.

(b) The intuited (appearing) object, as that which appears *hic et nunc*; e.g., this lamp as that which it is for the perception which just took place.

(c) But in a misleading way the immanent constituent parts of the appearance in the first sense are also called appearances. Especially the presenting sensations are called appearances — the *experienced* factors of color, form, etc., which are not distinguished from the *properties* of the (colored, formed) *object* corresponding to them and *appearing* in the act of their "interpretation." But it is important to distinguish them. The appearing properties of things are not themselves sensations, but only appear as analogous to the sensations. No matter how the question of the existence or non-existence of the phenomenal outer things may be decided, the reality of the perceived thing cannot be held to be the reality of a perceived sensation-complex in the perceiving consciousness. For it is shown by phenomenological analysis that the thing of perception, this apparent sensation-complex (with respect to the single properties and also as a whole) is different under all circumstances from the sensation-complex factually experienced in a given perception, whose objective apperception first intentionally constitutes the appearing thing.

The original concept of appearance is the second one enumerated above, i.e., that which appears, or that which possibly appears, or that which is intuitive as such. All kinds of experiences can become objects of reflective, inner intuitions (including the experiences of outer intuitions, whose objects are then called outer appearances); hence all experiences are called "phenomena" in the experience-unity of an ego. *Phenomenology* means, accordingly, the doctrine of experiences in general, including all that can be shown to be given in the experiences — not only immanently, but also intentionally given. Pure phenomenology is then the theory of the essence of the "pure phenomena," of the "pure consciousness" of a "pure ego," which means freedom from transcendent apperceptions and existential assumptions relating to objects transcendent of consciousness. It therefore does not establish any truths about physical and psychical realities of nature. All the apperceptions and judgment-positings which go beyond that which is given in adequate, immanent intuition (or beyond the pure stream of experience) are taken as the experiences which they are in themselves, and they are subjected to a purely immanent, "descriptive" investigation of essence. Its investigation of essence is pure in a second sense, in the sense of "ideation," so that it is *a priori* investigation in a genuine sense. Thus understood, all investigations of the present work — in so far as they did not have ontological themes, as in the third and sixth investigations, and seek *a priori* determinations for *objects* of possible consciousness — were purely phenomenological. They spoke of no psychological facts and laws of an "objective" nature, but rather of pure possibilities and necessities which belong to some form of the pure "cogito"; with respect to their immanent and intentional contents or to their *a priori* possible connections with other such forms in an ideally possible context of consciousness in general.

Like the term appearance, the term perception is also ambiguous. *Perceived* means, e.g., what "appears" in the perception, and hence its object (the house), and, again, the sensation-content experienced in it, i.e., the totality of the presenting contents which are "apprehended" in their complex as the house and singly as its properties.

4. *Physical and Psychical Phenomena; Adequate and Inadequate Perception*

How deceptive these ambiguities prove to be is shown by Brentano's theory, with its separation of inner and outer perception with respect to their evidence-character, and its distinct groups of phenomena. Thus it is pointed out that outer perception is not evident and is even deceptive.

This is true if "physical phenomena" are understood to be physical things, or their properties, changes, etc. But Brentano confuses this genuine sense of the word *perceived* with the figurative one, which refers to the presenting contents immanently belonging to the perception, instead of to the outer objects; and he designates not only outer objects but also these immanent contents as "physical phenomena." The latter would therefore also appear to be affected by the deceitfulness of outer perception. One must distinguish more exactly here. If an outer object is perceived (the house), then *in this* perception the presenting sensations are experienced, but not perceived. While we are deceived concerning the existence of the house, we are not deceived concerning the existence of the experienced contents because we do not at all judge about them, or do not perceive them in this perception. If we attend subsequently to these contents and abstract from that which we just meant by them, and if we take them simply as that which they are, then we *perceive them*, to be sure, but not the outer object *through* them. This new perception has the same claim to be unerring as any "inner" perception. To doubt that which *is* immanent, and is meant thus, would be unreasonable. I may doubt whether an outer object ever exists, and whether any perception referring to such objects is correct: but I cannot doubt the *experienced sensuous content* of the perception — naturally whenever I "reflect" upon it and simply intuit it, *just as it is*. There are therefore evident perceptions of "physical" contents, just as there are of "psychical" contents. — An ambiguity analogous to that of the concept of a *physical* phenomenon is found also in the concept of a psychical phenomenon, if that is treated consistently. That is not the case for Brentano.

The pairs of concepts *inner* and *outer, evident* and *non-evident* perception, do not coincide. The first pair is determined by the concepts of the physical and psychical, no matter how they may be separated. The second involves the epistemologically fundamental opposition between *adequate* perception (or intuition in the narrowest sense), whose perceptual intention is exclusively directed toward a content actually present, and the merely supposed *inadequate* perception, whose intention does not find its fulfillment in the present content, but rather constitutes through it the bodily givenness of something transcendent, as continually one-sided and presumptive. In the first case the sensed content is at the same time the object of the perception. The content does not mean anything else; it stands for itself. In the second case, content and object move apart. The content represents what does not lie in itself, but is "represented" in it, and is therefore analogous to it in a certain sense (if we hold to what is directly intuitive), as, e.g., the color of the thing is to the sensed color.

The essence of the epistemological difference between inner and outer perception lies in this distinction. It is involved in the Cartesian method of doubt. I can doubt the truth of inadequate, merely adumbrating perception; the intended or intentional object is not immanent in the appearing act; the intention is there, but the object itself which is finally to fulfill it is not identical with it. How could it be evident to me that the object exists? But I cannot doubt the adequate, purely immanent perception, because no residue of intention remains in it which seeks fulfillment. The intention is fulfilled with respect to all its factors. If it belongs to the essence of adequate perception that the intuited object itself actually inheres in it, then it is merely another expression to say: Only the perception of one's own actual experiences is indubitable or evident. Not every such perception is evident, however. Thus in the perception of a toothache the pain may appear as boring in a healthy tooth. The perceived object is not the pain as it is experienced, but the pain as it is transcendently interpreted, as ascribed to the tooth. But it belongs to an adequate perception, that the perceived, just as it is perceived (just as the perception intends, apprehends it), is experienced in it. We obviously only have an evident perception of our experiences in so far as we take them purely, and do not go beyond them apperceptively.

One could object, however, that an experience is surely the same as a psychical phenomenon, so that the dispute is pointless. The reply is: If one understands by *psychical phenomena* the real constituent parts of our consciousness, the experiences themselves which are there from time to time; and if one furthermore understands *perceptions of psychical phenomena,* or inner perceptions, to be adequate perceptions whose intention finds immanent fulfillment in the experiences in question: then the range of inner perception does indeed coincide with that of adequate perception. It is important to note, however, that

(a) The psychical phenomena in this sense are not identical with those in the sense of Brentano, and also not with the *cogitationes* of Descartes and with the *acts or operations of mind* of Locke; for all the sense-contents, the sensations, also belong in the sphere of experiences in general.

(b) The *non-inner* perceptions (the complementary class) do not coincide, then, with outer perceptions in the normal sense of the word; but rather with the much wider range of *transcendent, inadequate* perceptions. If a sensory content, a sensory complex, or a process of sensory contents is apprehended as a thing standing there, or as an outer occurrence, then we have an outer perception in the usual sense. A non-sensory content can, however, also belong to the representative content of a transcendent perception, especially in connection with sensory contents. As a perceived object, an *outer* object can just as well stand there with perceived *psychical* determinations (in the apprehension of one's own or another body as a "man") or (likewise in psychophysical apperception) an *inner* object, a subjective experience, with *physical* determinations perceived in it.

(c) If we understand by perceptions of psychical phenomena, or by *inner* perceptions, within the frame of psychology as an objective science of animal mental life, the perceptions of one's own experiences, which the perceiver apprehends as his, then there is an obvious distinction between inner perceptions and the outer perceptions involving transcendent apperception. Even if it is conceded that they include *adequate* perceptions (i.e., in so far as they take the experiences in question as they are in themselves), they are affected with a certain inadequacy because of the relationship to the knowing organism and the objective world. On the other hand, there are inner, just as there are outer, perceptions, for which the perceived object does not exist, in the sense assigned to it in the perception. The distinction between adequate and inadequate perception, which is also fundamental for psychology — whereby the psychological adequacy is to be understood as indicated above — intersects the distinction of inner and outer perception and also goes through the sphere of the former.

5. *The Classification of Phenomena; Brentano's Confusion*

The use of the term "phenomenon" to designate the appearing objects and properties at one time, or at another time the experiences constituting the act of appearance (especially contents in the sense of sensations), and finally all experiences in general, as phenomena, explains the temptation to jumble together two essentially different psychological kinds of division of "phenomena":

(a) Divisions of the *experiences*; e.g., the division of them into *acts* and *non-acts*. Such divisions naturally fall entirely in the sphere of psychology, which deals with experiences that are apperceived transcendently as experiences of animal natural beings.

(b) Division of the *phenomenal objects*; e.g., into those that appear as belonging to one *ego-consciousness*, and those that do not; in other words, the division into psychical and physical objects (contents, properties, relations, and the like).

The two divisions are confused by Brentano. He simply contrasts physical and psychical phenomena, and defines them as a division of the *experiences* into acts and non-acts. But under the title of physical phenomenon he soon confuses the sensed contents [4] and the appearing outer objects, or their phenomenal properties, so that the division is at the same time a division of the phenomenal objects into physical and psychical.

In close connection with this confusion is the erroneous determination, also used by Brentano for the separation of the two classes of phenomena, that the physical phenomena exist "only phenomenally and intentionally," whereas the psychical phenomena have "an actual existence besides the intentional." If we understand the physical phenomena to be the phenomenal things, it is certain that they at least do not have to exist. The creation of productive phantasy, most objects of artistic representation in paintings, statues, poems, etc., hallucinatory and illusory objects exist phenomenally and intentionally, i.e., they really do not exist at all, but rather only the *acts of appearance* in question, with their immanent and intentional contents. The matter is entirely different with regard to the physical phenomena, understood in the sense of the sensed contents. The sensed (experienced) color-contents, shape-contents, etc., which we have in continuous change in the picture-intuition of Böcklin's "Fields of the Blessed," and which, animated by the act-character of the pictorializing, develop to the consciousness of picture-objects, are immanent constituent parts of this consciousness. They do not exist merely phenomenally or intentionally (as appearing and merely supposed contents), but actually. Naturally one may not overlook the fact that "actually" does not mean "existing outside of consciousness," but rather "not merely supposedly."

---

[4] Brentano understands sensations to mean *acts* of sensation and contrasts the sensed contents with them. In phenomenology there is no such distinction. By sensation (*Empfinden*) is meant the mere fact that a sensory content or a non-act is present in the experience-complex. In relation or in opposition to the appearing, the talk of sensing could in any case serve to indicate the apperceptive function of such contents (namely, that they function as bearers of the apprehension, in which the appearing in question takes place as a perception or imagination).

/

CHAPTER XV

THE PHENOMENOLOGICAL PHILOSOPHY OF LOGIC

A. THE PHENOMENOLOGICAL SIGNIFICANCE OF THE "LOGICAL INVESTIGATIONS"

As seen from the perspective of transcendental phenomenology, the *Logical Investigations* did much to inaugurate a new style of philosophizing. It was a predominantly preparatory work, abounding in distinctions and the fixing of concepts. It will always remain an indispensable aid in understanding the later phenomenological philosophy, both because it settles accounts with the then prevailing and traditional theories of knowledge and philosophies of logic, and because it provides the initial methodological steps and conceptual groundwork of the new philosophy. Historically, it was the refutation of psychologism which overshadowed the investigations themselves. That was the only portion of the work which was generally read, although the work as a whole came to be much admired.

Judging the *Logical Investigations* from his later point of view, Husserl declared it to be only on the way to the truly philosophical level of analysis. The radical revision of the second edition, the elaborate attempt to bring it up to the level of the *Ideas,* is sufficient evidence of Husserl's own opinion of the lower, "pre-transcendental" level of the "neutral" descriptions of the earlier work. But instead of hastening to the conclusion that Husserl was not yet a phenomenological philosopher, one should consider two things: (1) the merit of his descriptive work, and of his original ideas, even if only partially developed, which were preserved and extended in the later writings; (2) the merit and level of his thought as represented in the first edition, in comparison with the general state of philosophy at the time. The only justifiable conclusion would be the recognition of his great achievement in the initial formulation of a pure phenomenology. The subsequent transition to transcendental phenomenology represents a great methodological development, with a resultant reinterpretation of descriptive results already achieved. The continuation of descriptive analysis after the *Logical Investigations* never invalidated work already performed, except in a few instances, which have been indicated. However, the change in method was from a relatively simple stage of reflection to one of much greater thoroughness, the ideal being an adequate account of all the constitutive activities of thought and experience. The soundness of the descriptive analyses of the simpler stage is no more to be impugned than are the findings of experimental investigators in the field of the natural sciences.

One of the obstacles in the way of an understanding appreciation was the style in which it was written. Only the *Prolegomena* was really readable as a whole, although here and there throughout the work one did encounter passages that could be said to be well written. The use of a large number of new terms, or of familiar terms in new or special senses, made for difficult reading; and this was not improved by the elaborate additions and interdigitations in the revised edition. Sentences were sometimes long and occasionally difficult to understand, obviously in need of being rewritten. In the course of the investigations the anchorage of the work to the generally known stream of scholarship is gradually broken off, and the practice of dealing almost solely with principles and problems as such, so characteristic of Husserl's later works, becomes more and more evident. Not everything that is contained in it is indispensable from the point of view of the phenomenological philosophy, and some of it could readily be deleted as no longer of interest (Husserl himself said as much in connection with his retention of the passages relating to the "ego," for example). To be a "purist" in defending the lasting importance of everything in the work would therefore be absurd. On the other hand, on the positive side, is the striking feature of the truly philosophical earnestness which pervades it, and the fact that the work exhibits the best features of phenomenological inquiry. If it is true that one cannot learn philosophy, but can only learn to philosophize, then the merit of the *Logical Investigations* in this respect should not be underestimated. It is moreover a series of investigations in which some conspicuous lines of cumulative progress are evident, so that it has general philosophical significance.

The original point of view represented was that of a "neutral" phenomenology. Neither idealism nor realism could be said to profit by it, for it was purely descriptive. It might be said that the strict rejection of subjective idealism implied a realistic point of view. But it is obvious that care was taken to avoid metaphysical commitments. On the other hand, the logical point of view could be said to be "realistic" as opposed to constructionalism in the sense of such logicians as Brouwer.[1] This is seen in the draft of a pure logic, and particularly in the conception of a definite manifold. When validity is declared to be independent of the

[1] Cf. M. Farber, "Logical Systems and the System of Logic," *Philosophy of Science*, vol. IX (1942), pp. 40–54.

judgment of the scientist, that may also be said to be "realistic." But, methodologically, phenomenology is neither realistic nor idealistic in any traditional sense.

It is noteworthy that the term "idealism" is used here in a non-metaphysical sense, and that it merely means the point of view that the ideal is a condition of the possibility of objective knowledge. For Husserl, the term "real" applies to what is "within" consciousness as well as "outside," temporality being a sufficient characteristic of reality. The "being" of the ideal, on the other hand, is "non-temporal." The term "real" is also used to suggest a relationship to things, as distinguished from the term "reell," or "immanent"; and real objects are defined as objects of possible sense perception. It is misleading, however, to state that ideal objects "exist truly," for existence should also be regarded as coextensive with temporality. It is sufficiently clear that metaphysical hypostasis is to be avoided in any case. In keeping with his subjective approach to philosophy, Husserl assumes that everything that exists is valid as existent by virtue of the evidence with which it is grasped in thought as being, and he concludes that "ideal being" in this sense cannot be denied. This is the unassailable form which his idealism takes in the *Logical Investigations*. On the other hand, when Husserl speaks of the founding intuition which "gives" the object, or of perception as "giving" its object, he uses a potentially dangerous type of expression, more suited to idealism in a non-phenomenological sense. The same may be said of the term "objectivation." Although the emphasis placed upon the ideality of meaning, and of pure logical forms, was of no metaphysical significance at that time, the later development of phenomenological idealism makes this emphasis significant in a new way, which was not originally intended.

In characterizing the point of view of the *Logical Investigations*, it is perhaps best to describe it as an attempt to realize the ideal of a true analysis of experience. Its aim is to be a true empiricism and not an empiricism that is subject to any passing psychological or scientific dogmas. Thus Husserl remarks in the course of the sixth investigation that when one speaks of "the object itself," its only intelligible meaning is that it is the realization of an intention. In other words, being can only be meaningfully considered as known or experienced being. The technique that is necessary for such a philosophy of experience requires the elaboration of the phenomenological (transcendental) reduction, one of the themes of the *Ideas* and the *Cartesian Meditations*.

Husserl's thoroughgoing rationalism and faith in the boundlessness of objective reason is shown in his contention that everything that is, is knowable "in itself" and is documented in "truths in themselves." He again takes the opportunity to affirm his faith in reason when he observes in another context that the object of knowledge is not falsified because of the use of intellectual forms. This confidence in reason is reflected in his view that what we cannot think, cannot be, and what cannot be, we cannot think. If this is taken to include reference to material objects of the physical-real order, as well as to general objects of the ideal sphere, it must be clear that actual thinking is not in question. The correlation between thinking and being is itself an "ideal" one; every instance of being may be conceived as "possibly" given as an object of thought.

When Husserl argues that an understanding with other than the pure logical laws would be an understanding without understanding, he has really injected the required meaning into the concept of the understanding. He says, as a matter of fact, "If we define the understanding . . ." and what he means by categorial acts is the basis for his contention. It can only be concluded that the contention is more modest than one might at first suppose.

Obviously concerned about the problem of the cogency of phenomenological findings, Husserl again considers the objection that different people could react differently with respect to "evidence." His reply can only be expressed hypothetically, for if one person has the evidence in question, then it is impossible that another person have the evidence of its absurdity, that being ruled out by the meaning of evidence. For the rest, it may be observed that the ultimate reference of confirmation to fulfillment through perceptions indicates how phenomenology does justice to the claims of positivism; and that the concluding discussion of the investigation of wholes and parts shows Husserl's early interest in the problem of "the world" in phenomenology, despite the fact that it was necessary to separate phenomenological and causal analysis on principle.

B. CONTRIBUTIONS TOWARD A PHILOSOPHY OF LOGIC

In addition to an enormous amount of material belonging to the theory of knowledge proper, and bearing upon traditional issues, material which remains a valuable descriptive portion of phenomenology as a philosophy, the *Logical Investigations* makes a number of important contributions toward a philosophy of logic. The autonomy of pure or formal logic is first of all safeguarded; pure logic is emancipated from naturalistic psychology (but, as has been seen, that did not mean that the value of the various devices of logic conceived as an "art" was denied). The subsequent history of formal logic has shown the desirability of effecting as complete as possible an emancipation from philosophy in general. But it has also been shown that there are philosophical aspects to formal logic which cannot be ignored. Difficulties occurring within the frame of formal reasoning have indicated the need for searching "foundational" studies which would aid in obviating them through more careful constructive work. Added to that is the need to conduct studies which trace the way from thought-processes to the pure forms. The epistemic self-sufficiency assumed by formal logic must be examined and justified, if that finality of understanding is to be achieved which is the aim of philosophy. The "clarifying" studies of the *Logical Investigations* contributed toward that end.

The epistemological studies of the second volume of the *Logical Investigations* did not, and could not, represent a return to the psychologism which was refuted in the first volume. There was a difference of principle between the naturalistic psychologism that had been found unsuitable for the purposes of pure logic, and the "presuppositionless" investigations of the nature of meaning and logical forms. The rejection of "naturalistic psychologism" did not imply the rejection of all subjective analysis, especially in the form of "phenomenological psychology." [2]

The expression "foundation of logic" is ambiguous. There is really a fourfold "foundation of logic," which calls attention to the various meanings of the term. From different points of view, and for different purposes, each foundation or approach is valuable. The four types of foundation are as follows: (1) the psychological and epistemological, (2) the inductive, (3) the formal, and (4) the ontological. As for (1), the naturalistic type of psychology cannot be meant, as is now clear. A "pure psychological" investigation is called for which clarifies the very subject-matter, the very "substance" of logic — the ideal meanings — as well as the fundamental concepts of logic in terms of their "origin" in the rudimentary features of experience. Such concepts as truth, evidence, proposition, etc., are examined in their "essential" nature, and not in a factual setting. This type of clarification is continued in Husserl's later logical writings, the *Formal and Transcendental Logic* and the posthumously published *Experience and Judgment*. (2) The inductive basis of knowledge, and of logic, is necessary from the naturalistic point of view, from the point of view of practical living and its problems. Husserl did not consider the problem of induction in this sense, if only for the reason that he was interested in essential structures. As a matter of fact, he regarded it as an insoluble

[2] Cf. Husserl's article on "Phenomenology" in *Encyclopaedia Britannica* for a discussion of phenomenological psychology and its relationship to transcendental phenomenology.

problem, observing that one should only raise questions that can be answered; and his mode of construing it was in terms of the association of ideas, etc. (3) The formal foundation of logic must face the problem of circularity, and of relativity in logic. According to the logical absolutist, it is possible to designate a select group of principles as certain, and as justified by "insight." Such are the "gilt-edged" principles of the traditional logic, as represented by the laws of identity, excluded middle, and non-contradiction. As seen in recent formal logic, such principles appear as theorems, and are no more "necessary" than any other logical principles. Among the problems making necessary a philosophy of logic are the paradoxes, which indicate unclearness in basic concepts and the need for criteria of meaning; the decision problem, involving the concepts of definiteness and constructibility; the need for a theory of logical knowledge, which will serve to order logic within the total structure of a theory of knowledge; the relationship between truth-logic and consistency-logic; and the relationship between logical form and reality. (4) The ontological foundation of logic is indicated therewith. A general theory of objects and of wholes is required in order to meet all logical needs.

In the *Logical Investigations,* there are discussions which bear upon three of the four approaches named. The inductive, naturalistic approach is dismissed, but not without due acknowledgement of its value and importance for practical purposes. The greatest emphasis is placed upon the cognitive approach, which is defined as pre-metaphysical. The very concept of "being" is questioned, and objects are considered as correlates of thought-processes, or of meaningful experiences. Had the work been written as a unified treatise, the discussion of the theory of objects and wholes, as well as the consideration of formal principles, would have been reserved for the end, and all the material on meaning would have been organized in one part, probably following the historical studies. The caution which Husserl observed in treating logic as an ideal structure was shown in his emphatic treatment of the alleged problem of the "real" meaning of logical forms, which was declared to be absurd. That was in accordance with the "neutrality" of that work; but it also presaged a tendency toward the ultimate foundation of all knowledge upon pure consciousness, construed as "transcendental."

The investigation of the "origin" of the concept of meaning requires the examination of the psychical experiences involved, naturally under the clearly defined conditions of phenomenological analysis. This concept, as well as the concept of "constitution," is repeatedly illustrated in the last two investigations, so that their meaning is unmistakable. Attention is again called to the *essential* interest of phenomenology, and it is only the use of ordinary language that suggests empirical-psychological procedures.

The distinction between the identical meaning and the psychical character of the act of meaning is of the first importance for the understanding of logic, for the locus of logic is defined as the sphere of ideal meanings. The nature of the phenomenological foundation of logic is seen further in connection with the question of abstraction; and care is taken to distinguish the process by which meanings arise as "species" from empirical procedures. Husserl indicates the sense in which one can speak of "logical presentation," and he shows that he never loses sight of the fact that there is a "noetic" side to logic. The purely formal logician may profess not to be interested in it, but *qua* philosopher he cannot avoid being interested in it. Special interest attaches to the axioms which are formulated in connection with the account of the relations of compatibility, as an illustration of the type of analysis provided by the phenomenological foundation of logic, which is not devoted alone to the analysis of judgment and meaning.

The pure form-theory of meanings, which is defined as a "lower" logical domain, is restricted in its application; there is no reference to questions of truth and objectivity. This "founding domain" of pure logic is called "pure-logical grammar." Husserl's reply to those who find this discipline lacking in utility is pertinent: the philosopher is surely one who should not be influenced by considerations of utility.

The gradually unfolding program of the *Logical Investigations*, and its continuation in the later logical studies, shows Husserl to be the philosopher who really realized Kant's transcendental method and aims. Husserl's complete philosophy of logic, with its theory of knowledge, may be regarded as a positive, constructive answer to Kant's difficulties, as an accomplished fact of transcendental analysis. The Kantian pattern is there, only immeasurably clearer and more consistent — a really "pure" theory of knowledge, which Kant had required but had been unable to achieve.

C. THE CRITIQUE OF FORMAL LOGIC AND THE PROGRAM OF
TRANSCENDENTAL LOGIC

1. Levels of Logical Analysis

Husserl's mature conception of logic is presented in his *Formal and Transcendental Logic*, an exceedingly difficult work to read, but one which deserves careful study by all students of the philosophy of logic. Because it completes and evaluates the earlier logical studies, and brings the logical-epistemological type of analysis illustrated in the *Experience and Judgment* into connection with the traditional and prevailing conceptions of logic, it is now pertinent to consider its critique of formal logic.

Logic is treated by Husserl as a *theory of science* whose task it is to make clear and explain the genuine meaning of science. His goal is an "intentional explication" of the real meaning of formal logic. The method consists in taking traditional logical forms and carrying them back to the living intention of the logicians, from which they arose as forms of meaning. The procedure also involves going back to the intentionality of the scientists in order to consider objective examples of concrete scientific theory. Thus the logician is oriented with respect to the "pre-given" sciences. This implies, of course, that all methods in use in the various sciences would also have to be considered in a complete critique of the theory of science, so that logic must be given a wider scope than is usually allotted it either by formalists or transcendentalists.

Fundamentally logic must be considered as *transcendental*, in Husserl's view. The positive sciences are used as guides or clues for transcendental investigations, which are designed to create genuine sciences for the first time. It is only a transcendental logic, it is maintained, that can answer the requirement of a final theory of science, providing the deepest and most universal theory of the principles and norms of all sciences. This fundamental logic has been lacking to modern science. Its function is to deal in a unified way with the problems of science, and to illuminate the way for the sciences with the deepest self-knowledge of knowledge. This logic is thus not a pure and formal logic, nor is it a mere empirical art, interested in the practical success of science. As the highest expression of the purely theoretical interest it aims to present the system of transcendental principles which are essential to genuine science.

Husserl indicates the distinction between logical forms in science and logic in general. The forms that are created and expressed linguistically in science have the specific "logical" connection of a theory, and on a higher level, of a "system." As a theory of science, logic has to set up "pure," "a priori" generalities. In Husserl's view, logic is not to follow the pre-given "so-called" sciences empirically, and abstract empirical types from them. Free from all ties to the factual world, which merely constitutes its point of departure, it aims to bring to light the essential forms of genuine knowledge and science in all their basic forms, and their essential presuppositions, as well as the essential forms of the correct methods which lead to them.

The double nature of logic is now apparent. It is an *a priori* science of science in general, and at the same time it is itself a science. Logic is accordingly defined as the self-inspection (*Auslegung*) of pure reason, or, expressed ideally, as the science in which pure theoretical reason carries through complete self-reflection and objectifies itself in a system of principles. Pure reason, or logic, is thus referred back to itself; the self-inspection of pure reason is itself a purely rational activity and is subject to the principles which are investigated.

That Husserl retained his broad view of logic as a practical discipline is shown by his discussion of the normative function of logic. Every *a priori* science provides norms for the factual sciences coming under it. Logic is normative in this sense, but is unique in being a universal norm. The genuineness of science and of its methods is determined by means of the general norms of pure reason. Logic also enters into functions of the practical formation of science, and is thus a practical logical art, with possible empirical-anthropological connections. In this respect it is subject to its own canons.

Logic may be viewed from two sides: the side of the contributions of reason, of contributive *activities*, and also the side of that which is contributed, the *results* which remain. In the latter respect, the theme of logic consists of the various structures of knowledge which develop for knowers during the performance of their activities of thought. In the unity of science, all such structures, and the whole field of productions which have arisen in the unity of a theoretical interest, are united in the form of a universal theory.

In the *Logical Investigations* Husserl defined (he asserts that he was the first to do so) the pure form-theory of judgments, or pure-logical grammar, which he regarded as the first formal-logical discipline. Disregarding all questions such as the distinction between truth and freedom from contradiction, the aim was to make a descriptive classification of judgments entirely from the point of view of form. This pure form-theory of judgments was present in a rudimentary form in the traditional logic. It concerns, according to Husserl, the mere possibility of judgments as judgments, without regard to whether they are true or false, or whether they are compatible or contradictory judgments.

There are "basic forms" from which new and more differentiated forms can be engendered constructively by virtue of their own essential laws, culminating in the system of all thinkable forms of judgment. Husserl notes that it is strange that this was never recognized, and adds that it would have been necessary to point out first that every judgment-form is a generic unity. Thus it could be seen that the form S_p *is q* is ordered under the form S *is* p, and that $(S_p)_q$ *is* r is ordered under the former, etc. The form S *is* p, where p is a property and S its substrate, is a "primal form" within the highest genus (or form) "apophansis" of the apophantic logic. Since only judgment-certainties come under this genus, the modalities of judgment must be transformed into certainties about possibilities, probabilities, etc., in order to be brought under it.

In so far as they indicate basic kinds of "operations" which can be undertaken with any pair of judgments or judgment-forms, conjunction and the hypothetical form are also designated as basic forms. The concept of an operation is a guiding concept in the investigation. It is construed so widely that the basic form S *is* p is regarded as the operation of determining the substrate S. Similarly every modalization is viewed as a form-constructing and meaning-transforming operation, with the form of "apophansis" (asserting certainty) characterized as a primal form. There is a law for every construction of forms, and every law of operation allows for iteration. This general "law of iterable operation" pervades the whole domain of judgment, and makes possible the construction of an infinity of judgment-forms.

The logic of consistency or of freedom from contradiction is represented as a second level of formal logic. The traditional logic was not a pure logic of non-contradiction, and it was necessary to establish it as such. That requires the investigation of the essential laws which determine the analytical inclusion or exclusion of judgments, apart from the consideration of truth. The problem of non-contradiction applies also to the compossibility of collections of judgments that are set up in any manner whatsoever, so long as they are united into one collective judgment.

Husserl thus arrives at the closed concept of a "pure apophantic analytic," which comprises not only syllogistic reasoning but also formal-mathematical analysis. Analytic consistency and contradiction are accordingly the basic normative concepts on this level.

Remaining on the level of the pure apophantic analytic, Husserl turns to the evidential distinctions at the basis of the separation of the apophantic into levels, and considers the evidence of clarity and of distinctness. In describing the "modes of execution" of a judgment, it is seen that a judgment can be given evidently as the same judgment in many subjective ways. It could appear as a vague fancy, for example. The descriptive treatment of the process of "making distinct" is worth noting. No criterion of distinctness is given, for it is sufficient in an "eidetic" investigation to determine the essential relationship (thus "distinct judging" is the evidence for a "distinct judgment"), without regard to the question of their achievement in any particular cases. The latter question presents a practical problem, and is of a different order.

Since logic is an *a priori* science, the pure analytic does not deal with actual judgments that are asserted at a given time or place, but deals with *a priori* possibilities, under which all corresponding realities are ordered. The pure analytic logician begins with examples and by means of "essential intuition" gains essential generality. He can thus use his own actual judgments, or those of others, or he can live in a world of phantasy, etc. The essential genus of *distinct judgment*, with its range of possible judgments, is his domain. The basic question is then: Under what conditions are judgments, considered merely with respect to their form, possible in a unity of judgment, and in which relations are they possible? The answer is that they are possible only in consistency. From the side of the judging person, "non-contradiction" means the possibility of being able to judge distinct judgments in the unity of a judgment that is to be executed with distinctness. The mere judging-together is itself a unity of judgment, a unity of "being valid together."

The question of the formal laws of possible truth and its modalities appears to be a logical question of a higher order. How can a logic that is concerned only with forms of the meaning of statements become a real logic of truth? For Husserl it is at once apparent that non-contradiction is an essential condition of possible truth; and it is by means of an essential connection of these concepts that the analytic is transformed into a formal truth-logic. The concept of truth is introduced if questions are raised concerning the "adequation" of distinct judgments that are concerned as distinct with respect to the things themselves. The predicate "truth" is taken to refer to judgments, whether in the narrower sense of a judgment-concept (*apophansis*) or in the wider sense. So long as we hold to the evidence of distinctness, every contradiction is indeed excluded, but factual absurdity and other types of untruth remain open. There is therefore no reference to factual possibility, or to the question of verification.

The aim to have essential insight concerning possible judgmental truth requires that possible judgments be conceived in possible verification or adequation. In accordance with the now familiar analysis of judgments, judgments are viewed as permeated by a cognitive striving, as meanings which are to be fulfilled, or as a way to the desired "truths." If one adopts the cognitive attitude toward judgments in the place of the theoretical attitude, it appears to be a matter of essential insight, that what is incompatible in the unity of a distinct judgment is also incompatible in truth, or that a contradiction in the judgments excludes the possibility of adequation. In other words, truth and falsity are predicates which can be attached only to a judgment that is distinct (one that can be actually executed), or can be made to be distinct.

In Husserl's view this concept of truth is at the basis of the old principle, that truth and falsity are predicates of judgments. The pure analytic is therewith shown to be a basic part of the formal logic of truth. Every case of the consistency of judgments becomes, if it is to be performed intuitively, a case of the consistency of truths or of "material" possibilities. But every contradiction excludes the possibility of adequation, and is *a limine* a case of falsity. Thus the pure analytic is portrayed as the basis of the formal logic of truth, and non-contradiction as a condition of possible truth.

The question as to why "truth" may not occur despite contradiction requires much more attention than is given it by Husserl. The subordination of the facts of reality to logical forms by way of a "predicate" theory of truth is a formal method of meeting the question. But it requires a more thorough discussion and justification. Is one to infer the impossibility of being from an impossibility of thought? And is there to be no criterion of the latter? The answer to these questions will again depend upon one's recalling the nature of all phenomenological questions as relating to essential structures. It is not possible to determine the order of matters of fact by any cognitive principles without invoking the idealistic principle of the priority of thought to being. The danger of circularity if non-contradiction is taken to define the range of possibility should also be considered.

2. *The Principles of Logic and the System of Forms*

Husserl's treatment of the basic logical principles is of particular interest, all the more so because of the present controversy and doubts concerning their nature and validity. It may well be that Husserl has found the proper way out of a perplexing situation. Difficulties arising in the use of logical methods and principles should be better understood, if not obviated by recourse to the process of knowledge. It has already been abundantly shown that the essential analysis of abstract thinking is indispensable for the understanding of logic and its problems.

Husserl adopts the following formulation of the double principle of contradiction and of excluded middle: "If a judgment is true, then its contradictory opposite is false" and "of two contradictory judgments one is necessarily true"; and both taken together: "Every judgment is one of the two, true or false." The analogue of these propositions in the logic of consistency is a principle that belongs to the essence of judgments that are given with the evidence of distinctness. It reads: Contradictory judgments are not possible as actual judgments, both cannot be brought to the evidence of distinctness; but one of them is to be made distinct. This parallelism of statement is in keeping with the double aspect of logic.

Husserl uses the expression "system of forms" when he asserts that all forms of contradictory judgments belong to the system of forms. The concept of a system of forms is an important one.[3] The term "system" is thus used in a loose sense, as a collection. There is a collection of all possible combinations of forms, or of permutations, for that matter. But the statement is ambiguous. It may be taken to mean all possible combinations of *possible forms*, or of specialized forms, such as grammatical forms, etc., in a restricted domain. The question arises, whether a contradictory totality underlies every well-defined system, just as Husserl's apophantic "system of forms" is the basis of the apophantic. If that is the case, then all deductive systems represent problems of definition and construction. The difficulties met with in reflexive judgments which incur contradictions are then but a small part of the pre-deductive possible contradictions. This view has the advantage of indicating clearly that all deductive systems are matters of careful selection and construction, the fundamental principles of logic being regulative and determinative in character, so that there is nothing inherently wrong with logic as such if contradictions occur. The latter merely indicate technical errors.

3. The Formal Apophantic and Formal Ontology

The "threefold stratification" of formal logic in the sense in which it has been described in the foregoing was not recognized by past logic. Even though the words were used, Husserl's claim that the distinction between the formal logic of contradiction and of truth is essentially new appears to be justified. The terms in question meant something quite different in the past; they referred to the difference between formal logic and the knowledge of matters of fact, with its interest in truths about the real world. This shows how clearly Husserl conceived his method of procedure to be purely cognitive in character. The knower with his forms of knowledge constitutes the point of departure; and this predetermines a theory of truth as conditioned in terms of the activity of knowing.

The complete formal theory of science is obviously broader than the

---

[3] Cf. Jørgensen's remarks on this in his *Treatise of Formal Logic*, vol. III, pp. 267 ff.

pure analytic of non-contradiction. Husserl's interest in the unity of logic and mathematics is not due to formal reasons. His is the philosophical interest, which is concerned with questions of principle, beginning with the meaning of the theory of science. With regard to the question of the unity of logic and mathematics, it is of interest to note that Husserl maintains that disciplines like pure geometry, pure mechanics, and also "analytic" geometry and mechanics are excluded, so long as they really refer to *space* and *forces*. This philosophical objection will naturally not deny the purely formal procedure of effecting the conceptual unity of all formal science, which is now an accomplished fact. The formal unity is only partial unity, of course.

The new mathematics, which combines syllogistic algebra with "analysis" is spoken of as "unclear" by Husserl. The extended formal mathematics is apparently already here, and still not here. That is explained by the lack of the defining idea for a unified science, according to which the theoretical and technical unity is construed as a necessary belonging-together of meaning. The problem of a formal ontology is encountered therewith.

In considering the problem of a unified formal science, one sees that, as distinguished from the formal apophantic type of "mathematics," which operates with propositional forms as the basic concepts, there are the various types of non-apophantic mathematics — set theory, theory of numbers, etc. — which refer to "object in general" or "something in general" rather than to predicative propositions. The idea of a comprehensive formal mathematics is then defined as comprising the extension of "something in general" and all its derivations, the latter including set or aggregate, finite and infinite number, combination, relation, whole and part, etc. This entire mathematics is called an ontology, or *a priori* theory of objects; and it is a formal discipline, referring to the pure modi of something in general.

Since judging means judging about objects, formal ontology and the formal apophantic belong together. Although the thesis concerning their unity is here rendered plausible, further investigation is admittedly needed.

The reason why this problem first appeared in phenomenology in its present significance is the lack of the necessary concepts in the tradition. The recognition of the problem in its complete form requires the idea of a formal ontology, and the understanding of the ideality of apophantic structures.

It is Husserl's thesis that logical structures are exclusively given from within, through spontaneous activities and in them; whereas things are originally pre-given as ego-strange, from without. Instead of being satisfied, as mathematicians had been, with a unity of theoretical technique, or as most philosophers had been, with an apparent separation between the fields in question, Husserl undertakes to examine the "inborn" meaning of both disciplines and thus to gain an understanding of their unity.

Husserl's use of "something in general" in connection with the unity of formal mathematics may be questioned. "Something" is a *material* notion, and in formal mathematics there are clearly non-material notions, if not "impossible" ones. "Something" is hardly the common denominator for that reason. It is the common denominator for all real entities. A term to indicate correlates of judgment as such, *noema*, e.g., is preferable. Instead of "formal ontology," one would then speak of "noematic regions." Strictly speaking, "being" has no meaning apart from space and time.

The idea of an *a priori* ontology had been introduced in the *Logical Investigations*, despite its having been tabooed by Kantianism and empiricism. But the problem of the relationship of apophantic logic and formal logic was not raised there. The "theory of deductive systems" sketched by Husserl represented a high-point of his earlier logical studies.

These remarks may serve as an indication of the development and significance of Husserl's conception of formal logic, and of the direction in which the work of its philosophical clarification had to proceed.

D. ORIGIN–ANALYSIS AND THE CONSTITUTION OF LOGICAL FORMS

The developed technique of the phenomenological method is needed for the thoroughgoing foundation of logic. The examination of logical reason is an integral part of the examination of reason and experience in general, although it may well be its most important and instructive illustration. Although the technique for phenomenological analysis must be presupposed in such an account, a more detailed consideration of it will be reserved for the next chapter.

The need for clarifying studies of logic is apparent, if there is to be a complete understanding of that discipline. Formal logic treats the structures with which it is concerned as disengaged, "pure" entities. How can they be embraced by a philosophy of experience? The class of experiences to which logical judgments belong must be determined. An analysis of the essential structures of the acts involved must be carried through. Indeed, the very material of formal logic must be provided by the analysis.

One of the functions [4] assigned to phenomenology in the *Logical In-*

---

[4] The other function was the preparation of psychology as an empirical science, by investigating the essential structures of experiences of presentation, judgment, and knowledge.

vestigations was to reveal the "sources" out of which the fundamental concepts and the ideal laws of pure logic "arise," and to which they must be traced back in order to provide the clarity and distinctness that is necessary for a critical understanding of pure logic. The general thesis was that logical concepts must originate in intuition, and must arise through abstraction on the basis of certain experiences. It was necessary to investigate the "pure categories of meaning," which were described as the primitive concepts that "make possible" the objective nexus of knowledge. There are also concepts of a second order, or concepts of concepts and other ideal unities, such as concept, proposition, truth, etc. Correlative to the categories of meaning are the pure or formal categories of objects, such as object, fact, relation, etc. The problem was to investigate the "origin" of such concepts. It was not the psychological question of the genesis of conceptual ideas that was involved, but rather their "phenomenological origin." [5] What was in question was *insight* into the essence of the concepts, and, as a matter of method, the determination of unique, sharply distinguished meanings of words. In the case of complex concepts, an analysis of the elementary concepts inherent in them and of their forms of connection was required. Thus we are able to "understand" them. The psychology of judgment cannot be a final explanation, for it presupposes the analysis of such concepts as sign, expression, meaning, conception, proposition, object, fact, perception, etc.

The locus of logic is the sphere of "ideal meanings." The concepts, judgments, and inferences of logic are ideal unities in this sense. Logic may be defined [6] as the science of meanings as such, of their essential kinds and distinctions, as well as of the ideal laws grounding in them. Because identity or sameness is necessary for all knowledge, and for logic in particular, the description of the experience and factor of sameness is called for.

The necessity for thought of the ideal meanings will not be denied. But the question of their status must be determined carefully. As already seen, the problem is to avoid Platonic realism [7] and nominalism, as well as the psychological hypostasis of the general.

The task and scope of phenomenological analysis as originally conceived has now been indicated. Questions such as the following are of interest

[5] In the *Logical Investigations*, Husserl pointed out that the term "origin" was inappropriate and unclear. But he retained it in later writings.

[6] Cf. *Log. Unt.*, first investigation, § 29.

[7] As Husserl stated it in *Erfahrung und Urteil*, the ideality of the general should not be understood Platonically and hence metaphysically as though there were a being-in-itself unrelated to all that is subjective.

for it: what we intend in general when we make a statement; what constitutes the intending as such, with respect to its sense; how it is essentially constructed out of partial intentions; which essential forms are exhibited by it; and so on. What interests phenomenology *qua* theory of knowledge must be shown exclusively in the content of the experience of meaning and fulfillment itself, as something essential. On the other hand, every thought-experience has, viewed *empirically*, its descriptive content and its causes and effects; it enters into the bustle of life and exercises its genetic functions. As originally conceived, only essence and meaning belong in the sphere of phenomenology, whose function is the clarification of the ideal unities of thought and knowledge. This meant investigating the "subjective sources" of logical structures. If all logical distinctions are viewed as constituted in logical acts in the sense of intentions, the study of the nature of acts as such is necessary for the understanding of the general ideas of logic.

The appeal to direct insight and intuitive experience raises the difficult problem of evidence, which presents the real goal of the critique of knowledge.[8] The logical structures and their general forms are given to begin with in a "direct" evidence. It is then necessary to reflect upon this evidence, that is, upon the formative activity that had been performed directly and naively. The process of clarification requires that an account be given of every kind of doing and its contribution. The method "which creates judgments and forms of judgment as logical" is held to be the most primitive or "original." The leading idea to be noted is that, corresponding to every law of the theory of forms is a law of the constituting subjectivity, a formal law referring to every thinkable judger and his subjective possibilities of forming new judgments out of judgments. The formation of the basic or primitive logical concepts represents a first critique of the "direct" logic.

How much remains to be done toward the clarification of formal logic is indicated by the presuppositions which had been simply taken over as self-evidences. For example, formal logic refers to an infinity of possible judgments, whose ideal identity it assumes. The *same* judgment must be constituted as an identical objectivity. It is also assumed that one can at all times become certain of the identity of any judgment-intentions, and can become insightfully certain of them as lasting possessions. The ques-

---

[8] In the *Formale und Transzendentale Logik*, § 59, evidence is defined as the intentional contribution of self-giving. It is the primal consciousness: I grasp "it itself," *originaliter*. The *primal modus* of self-giving is perception. Clear remembrance is an intentionally modified and complexly constructed *modus* of self-giving.

tion for the critique of logic is, then: How is the establishment of the ideal being of the judgments (as meanings identifiable at all times) possible?

The critique of logic requires nothing less than a detailed account of the part played by the mind in experience. This is attempted in the work on *Experience and Judgment*, which, by means of "origin-analyses," shows more thoroughly than had heretofore been achieved, how the basic concepts of logic may be clarified. Formal logic is held to be in need of a process of clarification which traces back all ideas and forms encountered on higher levels of knowledge to their "origin." Logical "performance" is found to be present on all levels of experience and knowledge, and not only on the comparatively high level of linguistic statements, with which the traditional logic begins. Formal logic does not inquire into the conditions of the evident givenness of the objects of judgment, and neither has psychology done so with its type of subjective examination. But the phenomenological elucidation of the genesis of judgment is interested primarily in the evident givenness of the objects of judgment as the presupposition of all judgment-evidence. The simplest case of object-evidence is that of the givenness of individuals, or of "final substrates." The theory of pre-predicative experience, which "pre-gives" the most primitive substrates in object-evidence, represents the first portion of the phenomenological theory of judgment.

In the course of the analysis, the ideas of negation, possibility, and of modalities in general are traced out to their "origin" in pre-predicative experience. The origin of negation may serve as an example.[9] Instead of the fulfillment of an intention of expectation, a disappointment may enter in. Thus it may be found that the perceived red color on a sphere is not spread over the whole object, which turns out to be green in part, instead of the expected red. There is then a conflict between the living intentions, and the new objective sense "green" has a force of certainty which overwhelms the certainty of the expectation of the being red. The latter is still known, although as "null." The descriptive analysis of the original phenomenon of negation, of nullity, or of "annulment" is typical. It is intended to show that negation is not first of all a matter of predicative judgment, but that it already occurs in its primal form in the pre-predicative sphere of receptive experience, which is the lowest stage of the activity of the ego. Negation is essentially a modification of consciousness. It is always a partial cancellation on the basis of a certainty of belief that is maintained therewith, ultimately on the basis of a universal world-belief.

The various modalities of judgment have their origin and basis in occur-

[9] Cf. *Erfahrung und Urteil*, pp. 94 ff.

rences of pre-predicative experience. The consciousness of doubt and of possibility may thus be described on this basis. Problematical possibility arises out of a situation of doubt, and is contrasted with open possibility, which is founded on the uninhibited course of perception. Abstracting from all modalizations, various stages of "perceptual performances" are described, including inner determinations of objects, or "explicatives," and "relative" determinations, referring to other objects. The attempt is also made to analyze the experience of relations on this rudimentary level. This leads to the consideration of time, which is regarded as the first and basic form, and as the presupposition of all connections which establish unity.

It is necessary to pass beyond the domain of receptivity if the goal of cognitive activity is to be attained. The will to knowledge aims at more than the complete intuitive givenness of an object; it wants to hold fast the known once and for all. Objectivating performances of a new kind are required in order to constitute the categorial objectivities or logical structures; and since judgment is a performance of the understanding, these are called objectivities of the understanding. This higher level of activity is characterized as a creative spontaneity which produces objects, and these are the objects which logicians have used without inquiring into the manner of their original production. Knowledge is sedimented in these structures in such a way that it can be a lasting possession which is not only identical for me, but for others as well. So closely related are receptive experience and predicative spontaneity, that every step of predication presupposes a step of receptive experience. At every stage of judgment, not only is there a further determination of the pre-given substrate, but a new kind of objectivity, the fact "S is p," to mention the simplest form, is produced in creative spontaneity. Corresponding to such facts on the level of receptivity are relationships or "states of affairs" (*Sachlagen*), such as relationships of larger and smaller, etc.; and these are *founded objects* which finally refer to elementary objects. A state of affairs which is founded on a pair — e.g., the "magnitude state of affairs" a-b — comprises the two facts, $a > b$ and $b < a$.

Every relation is an example of an objectivity of the understanding. These objectivities are described as "irreal" and timeless. Their timelessness, their "everywhere and nowhere," distinguishes them from individual objectivities. Whereas something individual has its time-place and time-duration, such an irreality as a proposition has the temporal being of supertemporality or all-temporality. By an irreality is meant an identical, and not merely similar, determination which can occur in various realities. The objectivities of the understanding are objective in the sense that facts, e.g., can be "discovered" and then thought again at will. But they were really valid before they were discovered. Whether they are "realized" in individual acts of judgment as truths is another question. A judgment can cease to be true. Thus the judgment "The auto is the quickest means of transportation" is no longer true. Nevertheless, as a supposal it has its "supertemporal" (it would be preferable to say "timeless") identity, which is what is in question. The irreality of the irreal objectivities is explained by construing them as sense-objectivities which are essentially "meaning-of. . . ." It is essential to a sense-objectivity not to be otherwise than in real embodiments, whose meaning they make up: e.g., *Faust*, the ideally one *Faust*. The irreal objectivities are, like all objects from the phenomenological point of view, identical poles of a manifold of supposals relating to them.

The constitution of general objectivities and the forms of general judgments presents the final problem in this analysis. The problem is now the grasping of generalities. Such new, spontaneously produced objectivities can enter into judgments as general cores. Husserl's procedure is to ascend from the lowest and simplest empirical generalities to the highest and purest, seeking out all forms in the originalness of their production. Pure generalities are obtained by means of "essential seeing" (*Wesenserschauung*). It is indeed meaningful, as has already been shown, to speak of the "seeing" of generalities. Of course, sensuous seeing is not in question here. One cannot see the general red as he can see an individual red. What is meant is that something common to any number of individually seen cases is directly "seen," analogous to the seeing of particular things. This must be considered in connection with the "method of variation" for determining essences. By means of this method, reality becomes a matter of indifference and the particular point of departure is merely an example. By freely varying a thing, an invariant remains as the necessary general form without which the thing, as an example of a species, would be unthinkable. In order to obtain a generality in a really pure form there must be no positing of reality. The necessity of eliminating all positings of being thus indicates the importance of a preliminary "reduction" as a stage of the constitutive procedure. The general truths which refer to essential generalities are held by Husserl to be prior to all truths of matters of fact in validity. Every reality that is given in experience must accordingly correspond to the *a priori* "conditions of possible experience."

The talk of "priority" and of "*a priori* conditions of possible experience" may be misleading, even to phenomenologists. An ideally complete set of possible forms is really presupposed if one is to speak of such "conditions of possible experience." But even so, how can one hope to legislate for the factual realm, unless the customary assumption of uniformity is made? It may be asked whether an illicit metabasis is incurred even in speaking of "possible experience" in this way, i.e., if one means the possible *real* experience of actual beings. The problem of the relationship of essences and their laws to the factual world remains the most serious difficulty of all — for pure phenomenology, as well as for all pure, formal science. The line of pragmatic relativism taken by the latter was unavoidable in view of the plurality of "alternative" formal systems, including logical systems. The issue of the intuitive, phenomenological philosophy of logic as opposed to pragmatic relativism is therefore of crucial importance. It would be naive to defend an "absolute" conception of logic without doing justice to the full truth of pragmatic relativism.

The phenomenological philosophy of logic, by virtue of its program of clarification, applies to every relational structure, to every type of "logical system" which is designed to serve as "a" logic. If there are any basic principles and concepts which are required by any type of discourse whatsoever (even though they may be applied or construed differently, with different ranges of application), then Husserl is in principle right in his point of view, and his findings may be reconciled with the work of the formalists. The latter must in any case be accepted, just as is the valid work in any department of pure mathematics. But the technical elaboration of a formal system should not be identified with the philosophy of logic. In other words, the epistemic (phenomenological) level of logical analysis underlies all work on the formal level. That is because thought is truly creative and constitutive.

Problems which arise on a higher constitutive level, such as the paradoxes, show that there are defects in the construction of logic. One cannot speak of a system as genuinely scientific if paradoxes occur. Bertrand Russell has remarked that the value of the paradoxes consists in their being warnings of defects to be uncovered, so that they are indirectly useful. Instead of resorting to technical devices to meet technical difficulties, Husserl proposes that a correct construction of logical forms be attempted from the simplest possible beginning. That is the most radical possible "constructional" point of view. Everything not *given* sensuously is in the constitutive realm, the origin and construction of which must be accounted for. The constitutive realm is not "free," but has essential laws of its own. The logic of the tradition is "bracketed," in order to make its construction subject to the canons of phenomenological procedure. The pure science of logic, as an ideal discipline, is shown to belong to the

THE FOUNDATION OF PHENOMENOLOGY

domain of ideal meanings, which makes the account of the process of idealization, which "gives" the elements of logic, to be of the first importance.

An *understanding* philosophy of logical reason cannot avoid such an account. But is this not psychology, it will be asked? The answer is emphatically in the negative if naturalistic psychology is meant. A science of transcendental subjectivity, or phenomenology in its most critical and radical form, is required for the foundation of logic in the present sense.

The constitutive activity is most readily seen in the realm of logic. The discussion of the constitution of an ideal objectivity on the basis of subjectivity appears to be entirely in place there. That explains why, in addition to the motivation derived from the original problem of logical psychologism and the objective validity of formal principles, the course of the development of phenomenology should have been from the consideration of the ideality of logical structures to their subjective constitution, and from there to constitution as a general program for philosophy.

CHAPTER XVI

THE TECHNIQUE FOR A PRESUPPOSITIONLESS
PHILOSOPHY

A. THE DESCRIPTIVE ANALYSIS OF TIME–CONSCIOUSNESS

THE *Logical Investigations*, and particularly the analysis of "intentional" or meaningful experience, were extended by studies of inner time-consciousness.[1] The central theme of the latter is "the temporal constitution of pure sense-data and the self-constitution of the 'phenomenological time' which is basic to such constitution." Following these studies a definite transition to idealism was made, as seen in the *Ideas*, in which work much attention is devoted to method. The final period of Husserl's development has led to the formulation of an absolute system of philosophy, his "First Philosophy." The diversity of standpoints and interests among his disciples is due largely to their failure or refusal to develop along with him; and even before his retirement from active teaching some of the younger phenomenologists showed evidence of independence in starting out on new paths.

In keeping with the pretensions of a system of philosophy Husserl sought to establish the phenomenological method as an absolute or presuppositionless and certain method, which he introduces into his studies of time-consciousness. Whether this is a later addition is not stated, but that might well be the case, since the requirements of the later system are not involved on the purely descriptive level of consciousness. As already pointed out, there are at least two senses in which the term "phenomenology" has been used: (1) In a narrower sense, as pure "eidetic" or essential psychology, a discipline which is basic to empirical psychology; (2) in a wider sense, as transcendental phenomenology or First Philosophy, which is supposed to serve as the ultimate ground of all science. The lectures on inner time-consciousness obviously belong to the former, although the peculiarly fundamental nature of phenomenological time and Husserl's insistent use of his method of the "elimination of transcendences" give them direct significance for his conception of a general philosophy. The achievement of such detailed studies protects Husserl against the

[1] *Vorlesungen zur Phänomenologie des inneren Zeitbewusstseins* (1905–1910), ed. by M. Heidegger (Halle, 1928).

charge of excessive preoccupation with empty methodological questions. Not only are the knives sharpened in phenomenology — that is important in itself — but there turns out to be a good deal that is cut.

In the introduction to the work on time-consciousness Husserl defines the problem of time as viewed phenomenologically. That requires the abandonment of the "natural attitude," in which one's view is directed at or to the object as an independently existing thing. Although time is probably the best known of all things, he observes, its adequate understanding is very difficult, and must include placing objective time and subjective time-consciousness in their proper relationship to one another, and the explanation of how temporal objectivity, and hence individual objectivity in general, can be "constituted" in subjective time-consciousness. Husserl's purpose is the phenomenological analysis of time-consciousness, which requires the complete exclusion of all assumptions and convictions concerning objective time or transcendent existence. "Objectively" every experience, as well as every real being, may have its place in the one and only objective time, which therefore includes the experience of the perception of time and the idea of time itself. It might be of interest to determine the objective time of an experience, or to compare the estimates of time-intervals with real time-intervals. But these are no problems for phenomenology. The real thing, the real world, is no phenomenological datum, and neither is world time, nor the time of nature in the sense of natural science and also of psychology as the natural science of the psychical. Now it might appear to the reader, when Husserl speaks of the analysis of time-consciousness or of the temporal character of objects of perception, memory, and anticipation, as if he had already assumed objective time and then only studied the subjective conditions of the possibility of time perception and of real knowledge of time. But what he professes to take over is not the existence of a world time, the existence of a thingal duration, and the like, but rather *appearing* time and appearing duration *as such*. These are regarded as being absolutely given, since doubting them would be meaningless: the external objects may or may not exist in truth, but the appearances themselves are indubitable. An existing time is assumed in the realm of appearances, but that is not the time of the experiential world; it is the immanent time of the stream of consciousness. Thus there is an essential change from the contingent realm of transcendence to the "certain" realm of immanence. The evidence that we have for the fact that the consciousness of a tone or melody exhibits a succession is given as an example of such inner certainty; it is such that all doubt or denial would appear meaningless. This is the basic distinguishing character of the phenomenological field of description, to which Husserl attains by means of a systematic elaboration of the Cartesian method of doubt, which requires the elimination of all transcendent existence. Objective space and time, and with them the world of real things and occurrences, are all examples of transcendent entities which must be "eliminated" and "bracketed" if a descriptive science of pure immanence is to be realized.[2]

Beginning with the field of cognition as such, it is then the task of the phenomenologist to describe its content and trace the "constitution" of objectivity in it. Suppose that we look at a piece of chalk; we close and open our eyes. Then we have two perceptions, although we say that we see the same chalk twice. The contents of our experience are separated temporally, but there is no separation in the object, which persists as the same. Thus there is duration on the side of the object, and change in the phenomenon. The experienced content is "objectivated," and then "the object is constituted out of the material of the experienced contents through meaningful apprehension." But the object is not merely the sum or complex of these "contents," which do not enter into it at all; it is more than content and other than it. The objectivity belongs to "experience" and in fact to the unity of experience; expressed phenomenologically, "the objectivity is not constituted in the 'primary' contents (i.e., sensed contents), but rather in the characters of meaningful apprehension and in the laws which belong to the essence of these characters." It is thus clear that the ultimate purpose of the phenomenology of knowledge is to construct a theory of objectivity on the basis of cognitive immanence. That this is a setting particularly favorable for idealism is shown by Husserl's later writings, although the particular form of the idealism is distinctive.

Husserl insists upon the distinction between the phenomenological (or epistemological) approach to the problem of time and the psychological approach. The epistemological question concerning the possibility of experience is answered by a study of the essence of experience; and similarly the problem of time leads back to a study of the "origin" of time, i.e., the primitive formations of time-consciousness. He is not interested in the psychological problem of the origin of time, or in the manner in which objective space and time perception arise in the human individual or species. For him the question of the empirical origin of time is indifferent; he is interested only in pure experiences with respect to their descrip-

[2] Thus Husserl states (p. 482): "The phenomenology which I had in mind in the *Logical Investigations* was the phenomenology of experiences in the sense of what is given in inner consciousness, and that is a closed domain in any case."

tive content and objective meaning. The phenomenologist does not fit the experiences into any "reality." He is concerned with reality only in so far as it is meant, perceived, or conceived. With regard to the problem of time this means that the *temporal experiences* interest the phenomenologist. That they are in turn contained in a world of things in which they have their empirical being and origin does not interest him; he knows nothing of that. On the other hand, it is important for him that "objective temporal" data are *meant* in these experiences. The description of the way in which cognitive acts mean this or that "objectivity," or, more specifically, the determination of the "*a priori* truths," which govern the "constitutive factors of objectivity," belong to the task of phenomenology. Husserl endeavors to delineate this *a priori* nature of time by investigating time-consciousness and determining its essential structure, an investigation which takes account of the specific contents of temporal experience as well as the acts through which they arise. By the essential structure of time he means laws such as the following: that the fixed temporal order is a two-dimensional infinite series, that two different times can never be at the same time, that the relational nature of time is insymmetrical, that it is transitive, that to every time there belongs an earlier and a later stage, etc. What distinguishes these laws from the usual analyses of time is the context of pure consciousness in which they are elaborated, and what is here called "*a priori*" would ordinarily go by the name of "formal properties."

One of the most interesting and instructive features of the studies of time-consciousness is the exposition and critique of Brentano's theory of the origin of time. It not only has intrinsic value, but is useful as an illustration of the descriptive side of phenomenology. Husserl's thoroughgoing and constructive critique of Brentano's theory shows his genius for making distinctions and adhering to them; and he is revealed at his best when he proceeds to concrete descriptive studies. Brentano believed that he had found an explanation of the origin of time in the occurrence of the "original associations" which are attached to all perceptions. That is to say, in any act of perception what is perceived remains present for a time, but not without modifying itself; in addition to changes in intensity and content, there is also the peculiar modification of being pushed back temporally. Thus every sensation of a tone, after the passing of the stimulus, awakens out of itself an idea which is similar and is determined temporally, and this makes possible the idea of a melody. This principle is then stated as a general law: a continuous series of ideas is naturally connected with every given idea, and in this series every idea reproduces the content of its predecessor, i.e., every new idea acquires the property of being past. Phantasy is therewith regarded as being productive, for it is held to create the factor of time in ideas. The origin of temporal ideas is thus referred to the domain of phantasy. The present sense-content of a given experience is caused by a stimulus, and if the stimulus disappears the sensation also disappears. But the sensation then becomes creative: it begets a phantasy-idea which is similar or nearly similar with respect to content, and is enriched by the temporal character. This idea awakens a new idea which is attached to it, and so on. The continuous series of such modifications is what Brentano means by "primitive" or "original" associations. In consistency with his theory he denies the perception of succession; we believe that we hear a melody and hence that we hear something past, but that is only an appearance which is due to the liveliness of the original association. The modifying temporal predicates he holds to be "unreal," only the determination of the "now" being real, and the real "now" becomes unreal in turn through a series of infinitesimal differences.

In his critique of Brentano's theory Husserl points out, as he never tires of doing, that it does not meet the requirements of a phenomenological analysis of time-consciousness. For although it deals with the immanent side of consciousness, it still operates with transcendent presuppositions, with existing temporal objects which "stimulate" us and "cause" sensations. He therefore regards it as another theory of the psychological origin of time. But Husserl recognizes that it contains parts of an epistemological theory of the conditions of the possibility of time-consciousness, for duration, succession, and change are spoken of as "appearing." A "now" appears in a succession, and united with it is a "past." The unity of the consciousness comprising the present and past is a phenomenological datum. The question arises, whether the past really appears in consciousness by means of phantasy. Inspection shows that a distinction must be drawn between time as perceived and time as phantasied; the difference between the perception of a succession and the remembrance or phantasy of a perceived succession must be explained. Insisting upon an examination of all the factors involved in experience, Husserl finds still further defects in Brentano's analysis, for the latter does not distinguish between act and content, or between act, content of apprehension, and the apprehended object. To which of these factors is the element of time to be attributed? As a matter of fact, we do not merely discern the element of time in connection with the primary or sensed contents of experience, but also in connection with cognitive objects and acts. An analysis of time which is limited to one level of "constitution" is not adequate and fails to grasp the essence of time as a real succession.

A complete descriptive analysis of the process of experience and particularly of the acts of knowledge through which objects are given must therefore be undertaken for the foundation of an adequate theory of time. Husserl asks: How are we to explain the apprehension of transcendent time-objects, whether changing or changeless, and which are extended over a duration? Such objects are "constituted" in a manifold of immanent data and views, which occur as a succession. Is it possible to unite these successively occurring representative data in a present experience? An entirely new question arises therewith: How, along with the temporal objects, both immanent and transcendent, is time itself constituted, how are the duration and succession of objects constituted? These various avenues of description, which are here indicated briefly, and which require still further analysis, must be kept in view in the investigation, although all of these questions are closely related. It is evident that the perception of a temporal object has time, that the perception of duration presupposes the duration of perception, and that the perception of any time-form has its own time-form; and if we abstract from all transcendences, then only phenomenological time remains, which belongs to the irrefragable essence of perception. Husserl goes beyond description and reveals his metaphysical tendency when he states that "objective time is actually constituted phenomenologically" and that "it is there for us as an objectivity and as an element of an objectivity only through this constitution." [3] It follows that a phenomenological analysis must take account of the constitution of time-objects.

A typical example of Husserl's descriptive analysis will serve to show why his procedure may be justified on grounds of description alone; stripped of some of its vocabulary there would be no suggestion of metaphysical implications. Suppose that a time-object, a tone, e.g., is viewed as a pure sense-datum. It begins and stops, and the unity of the entire occurrence recedes into the ever more remote past. In the recession I still have a "hold" on it, I have it in retention; and as long as the retention lasts the tone has its own time, it is the same, its duration is the same. I can attend to its aspect of givenness. It and the duration which it fills are known in a continuity of "modes," in a "continuous stream"; one point, or one phase of this stream, is called "consciousness of the beginning tone," and in that the first time-point of the duration of the tone is known in the mode of the now. The tone is given, i.e., it is known now; and it is known as now as long as any one of its phases is known as now. But if any phase of time, with the exception of the beginning phase, is a

[3] Page 384.

present now, then a continuity of phases is known as "before," and the entire stretch of the time-duration from the beginning-point until the now-point is known as a past duration; but the remaining stretch of the duration is not yet known. At the close the end-point is itself known as a now-point, and the entire duration is known as past. "During" this whole stream of consciousness the one and the same tone is known as enduring, as enduring now. It was not known "before," in case it had not been expected; and it is "still known" for a time "afterwards" in retention, in which it can be fixated and remain as past. The entire stretch of the duration of the tone or "the" tone in its extension remains then as something "dead," with no creative point of the now to animate it; but it is continually modified and lapses back into "emptiness."

What has been described is the whole in which the immanent temporal object "appears" in a continuous stream, in which it is "given." However, to describe this mode is not the same as to describe the appearing time-duration itself. For the same tone with the duration belonging to it was not described but rather presupposed in the description. The same duration is a duration now being built up, and then becomes a "past" duration: it is still known and is formed anew "as it were" in memory. The tone which now sounds is the same tone which is viewed as past in a later stream of consciousness. The points of a time-duration remove themselves from my consciousness analogous to the way in which the points of a resting object in space are removed from me when "I remove myself from the object." The object keeps its place, and similarly the tone keeps its time; every time-point is changeless, but it flees to the remotenesses of consciousness, the distance from the creative now becomes ever greater. The tone itself is the same, but the tone "in the mode now" appears always as a different one.

There is much of a descriptive nature in Husserl's work which shows how the theory of knowledge may be enriched by the adoption of the phenomenological method in the narrower sense of pure descriptive psychology. The discussion of the difference between retention and reproduction, or between primary and secondary memory or phantasy,[4] completes the correction of Brentano's theory of time as based on phantasy, and again illustrates Husserl's skill in finding great complexity where others see only simplicity. In this respect phenomenology does extend the vision of philosophy. There is a difference, e.g., between the modification of consciousness which transforms an original now into a reproduced now, and the modification which transforms either an original or reproduced now into

[4] Page 404.

a past now. The latter passes by continuous gradations into the past; whereas there can be no talk of a continuous transition from perception to phantasy, or from impression to reproduction. Perception is built up on the basis of sensation, and sensation, which functions in the presentation of an object, forms a continuum. Similarly, the phantasms form a continuum for the representation of a phantasy-object. From the standpoint of reflective consciousness we apperceive when we view the contents of sensation, even though we may abstract from all transcendent apperception; the "flow of time" or duration is presented as a kind of objectivity. An instance of Husserl's readiness to pass from the order of knowledge to that of reality is seen when he states that "objectivity presupposes the consciousness of unity or identity." [5] In strict keeping with the method of description he should have said that our knowledge or experience of objectivity presupposes the consciousness of unity or identity. The same tendency is illustrated in his discussion of the stages of the constitution of time and of temporal objects.[6]

Husserl finally divides the sphere of time-consciousness into three levels, which are called "stages of constitution": (1) The first stage is the perception of empirical objects in the usual sense, including the thing of the experience of an individual subject, the intersubjective identical thing and the thing of physics. (2) From the phenomenological point of view the object is taken as a phenomenon and attention is directed to the process of perception. All appearances and forms of consciousness have the properties of being now and receding into the past, properties which characterize all "subjective" time. Perception, memory, anticipation, phantasy, judgment, feeling, the will — in short everything that may be the object of reflection — appears in the same reflective time, and in fact in the same time in which the perceptual objects appear. The appearances are viewed as immanent unities in a "pre-empirical" time. (3) The third and last stage is that of the absolute stream of consciousness, which constitutes time. Subjective time is regarded as being constituted in an absolute "timeless" consciousness, which cannot be an object of cognition. This absolute consciousness is supposed to be prior to all constitution. In other words, the phenomena which constitute time are different in principle from those which are formed in time. They are not individual objects or events, and therefore it cannot be said that they are present or past. Nevertheless, the absolute consciousness comes to givenness. Consider, e.g., the appearance of a tone, and attend to the appearance as such. The tone-appearance has

[5] Page 324.
[6] Pages 427 ff.

its duration, and presents itself as an immanent object. But that is not the ultimate consciousness. The immanent tone is a constituted phenomenon, for with each tonal now there is a series of tone-nuances, in which each now recedes as a past. The perception of the present and the memory of the past may be apprehended in a comprehensive now. In the ordinary experience of the consciousness of objects one regards the past from the point of view of the present. But it is possible to grasp the entire consciousness of objects as a now, or to view it in its togetherness as "at once." Time-consciousness of this kind cannot in turn be made to be an object of consciousness, for that would assign to it a position in a process of subjective time. The flow of absolute time-consciousness has a permanent formal structure. This structure is determined by the law that a now is constituted by means of an impression, to which a series of retentions and a horizon of protentions or anticipations are attached. A continuity of appearances belonging to the stream of consciousness is ingredient in a now, but this stream is not something temporally "objective." It is, in short, "absolute subjectivity," [7] which as the most fundamental principle of experience defines at the same time a necessary condition for *objects* of experience.

On the basis of this principle, the emergence of all objects, including transcendent objects and things, is to be explained. The principle that all possible objects are by themselves as they are for knowledge is a reasonable assumption for philosophy; but Husserl goes a step further when he implies that objects can only be "in" the system of knowledge, and are in fact conditioned and formed by an absolute consciousness. There can be no doubt that he had this goal in view as soon as phenomenology was conceived as a universal philosophy. The term "constitute" is ambiguous, if one considers its ordinary connotation. It may be taken to mean "create" — literally — or it may be construed as applying to the realm of meaningful experience, in which complex meaning-structures may be viewed as being formed out of simpler elements. Any inclination to combine the two meanings while disregarding the purely methodological nature of the phenomenological point of view would be unfortunate, and would violate the strict use of that method. That temporal things are constituted and are as such dependent upon an absolute subjectivity, and that, furthermore, spatial things are constituted similarly, since they are held to presuppose temporal constitution,[8] clearly indicate a standpoint of genetic, transcendental idealism. That standpoint may

[7] Page 429.
[8] Page 446.

be rendered self-consistent on a purely descriptive basis which says no more than it has a right to say — descriptively; or it may succumb to the temptation to express the only "conceivable" meaning of reality, in terms of experienced reality, and thus convert itself into a metaphysical view.

The studies of time-consciousness illustrate the strength of the phenomenological method with respect to descriptive results; but they also reveal a danger which persists from that point on in the literature of phenomenology. While granting all the advantages claimed for this method, namely, that it furnishes a certain or indubitable realm for investigation, and that it makes possible the exact delineation of the facts of knowledge as such, thus deepening our understanding of the problem of knowledge, it must be admitted that there are pitfalls in the use of the method. Husserl's very language betrays his predisposition to treat the transcendent realm of existence, in which belief was suspended as a matter of method, as something reducible to pure consciousness. The formulation of the problem of the constitution of objectivity in subjectivity need not commit one to a metaphysical position, but it does indicate Husserl's leaning. That the stream of experiences occurs in configurations, that cognitive contents are formed as unities amid multiplicity, may be taken as simply true, whether empirically or phenomenologically. Furthermore, that they refer to objects "of" which they are appearances is recognized by Husserl: but the objects themselves are not "constituted" phenomenologically. The constitution occurs only on the cognitive side, and it would be sheer dogmatism to inject such a condition into the essence of objectivity.

In performing the "reduction," the phenomenologist is well aware that it is impossible to get ouside of the field of nature. He knows furthermore, that the material realm of existence must be assumed for the world of experience, and that no theory of reality can afford to dispense with it. But there should be no talk of "leaving" the natural world; it is the "natural attitude" that is changed. When the reduction is performed in the only justifiable sense in which it may be considered, as a methodological expedient, it becomes clear that assumptions which are similar in principle to those of the natural attitude must be made on the phenomenological level. For one thing there is the concept of consciousness in general, with a fixed essential structure. Strictly speaking, if certainty in the sense of indubitability is to be achieved, Husserl must begin with solipsism in the use of his method, for the only indubitable sphere is that of individual consciousness — the "egological" sphere. But even then it is at once apparent that only the actual experience of the present moment is "certain." It would be better to speak of the present experience as *unavoidable*; and nothing of any significance follows from it without special assumptions. Husserl's transition to intersubjectivity presents a serious difficulty which is by no means completely solved in the writings made available thus far. It depends in the last analysis upon the assumption of a consciousness in general. The trust in memory introduces another group of assumptions of the "essential" uniformity of phenomenological "substances," whose character of being assumed cannot be obviated by an appeal to "essential insight" into the structure of knowledge. That logical principles must be employed in the ordering of phenomenological data, even before the "constitution" of logical forms has been achieved, presents no difficulty so long as that fact is explicitly pointed out.

It must be admitted that the phenomenological procedure is not "presuppositionless" in every sense. In attempting to examine all presuppositions naively accepted, even in theoretical reasoning, it is found necessary to assume a "stratum of being" which is placed beyond reach of the inquiry, as Husserl has expressed it. On its assumed basis, and with its carefully defined method, which is restricted to essential structures as viewed reflectively in the realm of pure consciousness, the transcendent world can only be reinstated as a "constituted" world. This procedure is both innocuous and valuable for purposes of philosophical understanding if care is taken to use the concept of constitution in its proper sense, and to avoid the tacit assumption of a subject-object limitation applied to all reality. If that is done, the phenomenological method will enable us to extend the descriptive method to include all regions of pure consciousness, and the traditional error of supposing that pure consciousness may be the adequate source of all science and reality will not be committed. Care must be taken lest by incautious procedure the desired system may tend to smother the method.

B. THE PHENOMENOLOGICAL METHOD

The two decisive steps in Husserl's development, which he regarded as being of fundamental importance, were the adoption of the *eidetic* point of view, and the recognition of categorial intuition, or "general seeing." The *Ideas* contains extensive pertinent materials, in addition to the *Logical Investigations*. The importance attached to the eidetic point of view is indicated by the expression "eidetic reduction," which is paired with "transcendental reduction" in the complete phenomenological reduction. The eidetic point of view was intended to realize the classical interest in a realm of essences, or of ideal forms, although in a non-metaphysical manner. In addition to a discussion of "Fact and Essence" in the *Ideas*,[9] there is a helpful explanation of essence and the method of variation for determining essences in *Experience and Judgment*.[10] This type of "reduction" has not occasioned anything like the controversy brought on by the "transcendental reduction." In view of the great care taken in the *Logical Investigations* to avoid all semblance of Platonic hypostasis of the general, it would indeed be a perverse misunderstanding which would lead one to read dogmatic metaphysics into what is in effect merely the recognition of the structure of scientific (and hence philosophical) knowledge and its objects. It is unavoidable that "sciences of essence" be constructed independently of empirical facts, which are at best approximations to the ideal structures, as in the case of geometry. It may well be that the term "reduction" is poorly chosen in this context. But its meaning is clear.

1. The Natural Attitude and Phenomenological Reflection

The transcendental reduction is given its first elaborate statement in the *Ideas*, in which the "natural attitude" toward the world is examined, and its thesis of existence is "eliminated." That is a response to the motive for completeness of understanding, which forbids the acceptance of any assumptions, and requires the suspension of all beliefs. According to the standpoint of natural experience, I am conscious of a world infinitely extended in space and becoming in time. This is the immediate fact which I intuitively have. Through the medium of sense-perception bodily things are *simply there for me* in some kind of spatial presentation; they are "present" whether I am concerned with them cognitively or not. Other men are also included in my immediately given field of experience, and I understand what they think and wish. They, too, are present as realities even when I do not attend to them. The perceptual world is as such essentially incomplete, and there is a dark horizon of indefinite reality which fringes it. This holds for both the spatial and temporal orders of being. The world which is present to me in this "now" has its two-sided infinite temporal horizon, its known and unknown, immediately vivid and faint past and future. In the free exercise of experience I can follow the connections of the world, can change my standpoint in space and time, can direct my view temporally backwards and forwards, etc. So I find myself at all times in conscious life, without being able to change it, related to the one and same world, although with respect to its contents it is engrossed in a process of change. It is constantly "present" for me, and

---

[9] Cf. *Ideas*, ch. 1.
[10] Cf. *Erfahrung und Urteil*, § III.

I myself am a member of it. Besides, the world is no mere world of things for me; but it is there (in the same immediacy) as the world of values, or goods, or as the practical world. Things are there as beautiful and ugly, as useful objects (the "table" with its "books," etc.). These valuational and practical attributes belong constitutively to the "present" objects as such, whether I attend to them at all or not. This world, including in its scope physical nature and human society, constitutes the substrate of our experience and scientific thinking. With this attitude we live *in* the experiencing, in the theorizing and activities of all kinds. To live in this manner is to have consciousness of *something*, of various things, changes, and connections of nature; and in the higher cognitive life to have consciousness of propositions, theories, etc.

The natural attitude has its justification and is the point of departure for all other attitudes, just as the material thing is the foundation for all other objects. It is "naive" because the world is presupposed as existent, and the problem of transcendence does not enter into consideration at all. The theoretical view of natural science is not entirely "radical" because of its assumptions; its analysis goes far beyond the unquestioning view of natural experience, but it does not "question" natural existence as a whole. The general theoretical attitude is to be further distinguished from that of reflection. As Husserl viewed it, the theoretical subject as an "objectivating" subject apprehends and posits objectivity as existent, and determines it through judgment; and the objectivity in question is "constituted" *before* these theoretical acts by means of certain intentional experiences. It is only by a redirection or turning of the theoretical view (through a change in the theoretical interest) that one comes to the stage of pre-theoretical constitution, to the pre-given objects. This is accomplished by means of the *reflective* attitude. "Reflection" in this wide sense refers not only to the apprehension of acts, but to every "retrospection" or turning away from the natural direction of view to the object. This would also include attending to what Husserl calls the "noemata" (in the *Ideas*), or the correlates of the experiences, which are judged, remembered, etc., as such, and whose manifolds brings the identical thing to appearance. It is peculiar to the theoretical attitude and its acts that the objects "lie before" it in a certain manner. On the other hand, such "pre-given" objects can also arise through constitution by means of the theoretical acts, although the specifically theoretical objects are on a higher constitutive level. The lower level of intentionally constituted objects is included in the phenomenological sphere. The elaboration of this view is provided in constitutive phenomenology, in which the various levels of objectivity are traced, from the level of sensibility to that of the ideal objectivities of the understanding.

Husserl frequently indicated the parallelism of structure of the various types of acts, including wishing, willing, etc., when discussing the nature of judgment. This parallelism is again seen when the axiological and practical attitudes are juxtaposed with the theoretical attitude. Valuational acts, including all sorts of acts of pleasing and displeasing, or affective acts in general, can also refer to a pre-given objectivity. Such "intentional" acts are also constitutive of objects of a higher level. Suppose, e.g., that you perceive the blue sky, and live in the rapture you have concerning it. You therewith leave the theoretical or cognitive attitude for the affective attitude. There is no abrupt transition, since certain ontological characteristics remain in both cases, which must be carefully described. The scientist who is theoretically directed to the same object may indeed have pleasure in the view, but he does not "live in" the pleasure. The phenomenological modification incurred in passing from the one attitude to the other is an essential one, and is ideally possible for all acts. It is of importance to the idea of a universal science that all acts which are not theoretical to begin with may be transformed into theoretical acts by means of the change of attitude. You can view a painting with enjoyment (or "enjoyingly"); you then live in the "performance" of aesthetic pleasure, in the "pleasing" attitude. You can, again, judge the painting to be beautiful from the standpoint of the critic or historian of art. You then live in the performance of the theoretical or judging attitude, and not that of the valuational, pleasing attitude. Husserl here uses the term "valuational" in the sense of the general affective attitude (whereas if one judges *about* a value, the attitude is theoretical). In the aesthetic enjoyment the object is there as an object of enjoyment; but in the aesthetic judgment the object is that which is perceived with the aesthetic predicate. In the theoretical attitude which involves only the sense-perception of the lowest level you have a mere thing. Going over to the aesthetic apprehension and judgment of value, you have more than a mere thing; you have the thing with the predicate of value. This value-object is the correlate of the theoretical apprehension of value, and is therefore a theoretical object of a higher level. The same holds for the sphere of volition. There is a difference between actual willing or performing the will, and, in the theoretical attitude, judging that which is practically willed. You can live in the act of "making up your mind"; or change your attitude when you theoretically apprehend or judge your decision.

Objects can, then, be known differently in accordance with the different kinds of acts involved, as the objects of judgment, of value, or of will.

With the theoretical attitude, which is always possible, the objects become theoretical objects, objects of an actual positing of *being*, in which the ego apprehends them as *existent*. This makes possible a comprehensive and systematic view of *all* objects, as possible substrates of the theoretical attitude. An element of reflection is involved in this extended theoretical view, which must be pointed out.

The transition to the theoretical attitude must, as has already been stated, be distinguished from the transition to reflection, which every act permits on principle. The extended theoretical attitude also includes the immanent perception or retention which may be directed upon any act, and where the retention of a past act is also a case of objectivation. This is, however, a kind of immanent reflection upon the acts, which, in Husserl's view, is still included within the scope of the theoretical attitude. When you have aesthetic enjoyment and live in it, the situation is simple. But you can reflect upon your enjoyment and say, "I have pleasure in it." The judgment is indeed about your act of enjoyment; but it is entirely different to direct your view upon the object and its beauty. You perceive the beauty "at" the object, although not as you perceive its color or form in simple sense-perception: you find the beauty "at" the object itself. "Beautiful" is then a predicate of reflection. It is not a relational predicate referred to the act, but arises by means of your change of attitude, the acts in question being presupposed. Instead of living in the acts, you direct your view to the object as the correlate of your affective acts; the object has not only a stratum of sensuous predicates, but also of such predicates as "beautiful," "sad," "joyful," etc. This is the extended theoretical attitude of reflection, where one does not find objective predicates, but only *predicates of consciousness*. This distinguishes the attitude of reflection, which posits nothing, from the sheerly theoretical attitude, which refers to objective existent entities and posits nature as reality.

In short, there is a social-historical and cultural context for the "natural attitude." The natural world in which we take our start, originally as well as cognitively, is one the independent existence of which is taken for granted "naively." There is always some theory in this view, as there must be in a "common-sense" view of the world. The theoretical view is also directed upon an independent objectivity, with the conscious use of principles of interpretation of the world, the Aristotelian, Ptolemaic, and Newtonian theories being special illustrations. Furthermore, there is reflection within the universal theoretical view; and the distinction must be drawn between "natural" reflection and pure reflection, with the performance of the phenomenological reduction.

The phenomenological attitude involves a "reduction" to pure consciousness, really carrying out the attempt made by Descartes (who, to be sure, had a very fragmentary idea of the goal envisaged by phenomenology). The world and I as a body and empirical subject are "put out of play," eliminated (*ausgeschaltet*) and bracketed (*eingeklammert*). The pure sphere of transcendental subjectivity can only be attained by means of the phenomenological attitude, which requires the performance of an "epoché" (ἐποχή). The stream of my *cogitationes* is immediately and apodictically given; and the world is there as a *cogitatum*, or as the corresponding object of experience. The objects of experience are then not limited to the factual world, but include all possible objects (as *cogitata*), such as ideal objects, so-called impossible objects, etc. That is the gain, since this attitude is then directly useful for epistemology, logic, and metaphysics. It is necessary to define the domain of possible objects of possible thought, to begin with.

On the basis of the phenomenological attitude one can speak of absolute givenness ("absolute" in the sense that nothing is presupposed or posited as existent; and also as "evident" and indubitable). This applies to the *noetic* side ("I think," "I experience," etc.) as well as to the *noematic* side (referring to what is correlatively involved, as "that which is experienced, thought, etc."). The latter has the character of "intentional being as such," of being in quotation-marks. Pure consciousness, with "that which it means as such," is absolutely given in phenomenological reflection. This is purely immanent, as distinguished from the inner experience of psychology. Everything natural is given in a certain sense, but is always *relatively* given. It is always and necessarily given with certain reservations. Every natural experience, no matter how apparently certain it may be, leaves open the possibility of doubt and negation. It is always possible that grounds for doubt or negation might arise. This applies to all *natural experiences*, i.e., those referring to "nature." But this does not hold for the "original" consciousness we have in pure reflection. In this sphere there can be no reservation; that which is intended in it is absolutely given. Pure consciousness is our theme with this attitude: we investigate it without positing as real, possible, valuable, etc., that which is the theme of consciousness itself; but *that* this consciousness has such and such contents and posits in this or that manner, values, etc. — that belongs essentially to our theme.

The instrument for the "purification" of consciousness is the transcendental "reduction." It was stated above in connection with the natural view, that a "World-All" is *simply there*, is *present*; and that it is there not only as posited through an existential judgment, but also as the substrate of a "potential" thesis, i.e., a thesis not expressed. Husserl states that this potential thesis can also be suspended, just as has been done in the case of the actually expressed thesis (as a judgment).[11] The phenomenological "suspension" is an entirely peculiar operation. It does not mean that a thesis is abandoned which was laid down, or that a conviction has been altered. The thesis in question is as it were "placed out of action," "eliminated," "bracketed." It remains in this bracketed form; it is still an experience, but we "make no use of it." This peculiar epoché can be examined with regard to every thesis; it involves a certain abstention from judgment, which is compatible with an unshaken conviction of truth. The judgment becomes a "bracketed judgment." In the case of phantasied objects one eliminates the judgment or assumption "I think it as being such and such." Instead of the universal doubt of Descartes, then, Husserl proposes this universal "epoché." A new scientific domain is thus determined. All the sciences which refer to the natural world are also eliminated: no use is made of their propositions and results. They may only be "assumed" in brackets, and not as propositions presuming validity. That which remains when the entire world is eliminated (including us with all "cogitare") is "pure" or "transcendental" consciousness. That is the phenomenological residuum.[12]

The field for investigation is not limited to such consciousness as I really have and which I later view in reflection, i.e., not to the accidental real acts which I find in immanence as a momentary "this." We have the freedom of phantasy, and therewith goes the freedom to form a manifold of "possible" consciousness, which is a phantasied consciousness. Phantasy may be characterized as being a modification of "original" consciousness. It is *as it were* an experiencing consciousness, which can be seen in reflection. Its objects are not real objects, but are "as it were" real objects, e.g., the often phantasied centaur, which is there in the *modus* of reality "as if." And further: not only can we reflect *upon* the phantasy-consciousness as actual experience, but we can also reflect *in* phantasy. Just as the reflection upon the perceived table leads us back to the perceptual experience of the table, so the reflection "in" phantasy of the "as it were" perceived centaur leads back to its as-it-were-perceiving; this is not a real consciousness, but an "as if." The same holds for modified presentation, e.g., a memory. It

[11] Cf. *l. c.*, pp. 53 ff.
[12] Husserl states (*op. cit.*, p. 58), however, that the elimination does not apply to the world as "eidos," not to an *essential* sphere. The elimination of the world does not signify the elimination of, e.g., the number series and arithmetic.

THE FOUNDATION OF PHENOMENOLOGY

is similar to phantasy in that what is given or remembered is known in the "as if," namely, as if it were present. But the modification of the "as if" does not affect the thesis of reality as it does in the case of phantasy. The memory *posits*; the "as it were" perceptual object, as represented, is real; it is not present, but past (or future, in the case of anticipation). "Now to be remembered" means the same as "to have been perceived." Further cases may be noted, as when one remembers a phantasy-experience, etc.

It is thus seen that phantasy and the consciousness of possibility are essentially related to one another. Possibilities can also be or not be, can be meant falsely, be given "originally," etc. Phantasy "gives" possibilities originally. Reflection in phantasy yields possibilities of consciousness originally, and these are indubitable. The phenomenological reduction can thus be made in the infinite domain of phantasy. This extends the region of absolute givenness over the entire field of possible consciousness (as a sphere of "transcendentally purified" possibilities). In the example of the centaur, there is a kind of quasi-perception, which refers to what is perceived, the quasi-sense-data (the phantasm), the corresponding modified conceptions, etc. This is a possibility of consciousness which is absolutely given in phenomenological reflection, and that as "reduced." There is, then, on the one hand, the universe of pure ego-experiences which are really given through phenomenological perception, remembrance, etc.; and, on the other hand, the universe of the possibilities of pure ego-experiences. This is the field of investigation which is determined by phenomenology as the science of *transcendental phenomena*.[13]

2. *The Radicalization of Reflection and the Constructive Program*

This methodological procedure was deepened and worked out in greater detail in the *Cartesian Meditations*, a work which merits much more attention than it has received, despite the serious difficulties which it faces. The breach caused by the *Ideas* between Husserl and his non-idealistic adherents could only be widened by this later work.

Beginning with a generous expression of indebtedness to Descartes, Husserl portrays phenomenology as the historical completion of the subjective movement inaugurated by Descartes' *Meditations*. The central idea of Descartes, judged from Husserl's point of view, was the return to the self, or to the stream of experiences, by means of the method of doubt. The reform of the sciences and the establishment of their essential unity

[13] Cf. Dorion Cairns, "An Approach to Phenomenology," in *Philosophical Essays in Memory of Edmund Husserl*.

on a philosophical basis are themes which are prominent in both thinkers. That Husserl sees more in Descartes in some respects than is warranted is due to his own interest in exploiting the method of doubt for purposes of transcendental phenomenology. That explains his painstaking elaboration of Descartes' "beginning." That which has historical significance for Descartes as a reaction against a tradition harboring obscurity, dogma, and authoritarianism is appropriated by Husserl as an essential part of the technique for developing a philosophy out of pure consciousness.

Voicing his discontent with the state of philosophy, Husserl proposes to begin with Descartes' starting-point, the pure *ego cogito*, and to lead the way from there to transcendental phenomenology, which is submitted as the proper basis for unity in philosophy. Like Descartes, Husserl holds that the evidence of the existence of the world is not apodictic, for it is capable of being doubted without contradiction. The *ego cogito* indicates the province of transcendental subjectivity, which is the domain of certain and first being. But Descartes failed to make any philosophical capital out of his discovery of certainty. This error is rectified by Husserl, who proceeds to sketch the field of transcendental experience and its general structures. The indubitable data of self-consciousness form a stream of experiences, which may be regarded from the side of the act of experience (the *cogito*), or as its correlate, that which is thought (the *cogitatum*). The already well-known distinction between natural reflection and transcendental reflection, the "intentional" nature of experience and its basic characteristics, such as identification and the element of time, indicate leading stages of the investigation.

The "way in" to consciousness having been outlined, the interest now turns to the "way out," or to the consideration of the "constitutive problem of truth and reality." The idea of constitution is of the first importance in Husserl's philosophy. Since the point of departure is the experiences themselves, reality is construed as the correlate of real experience; and it has to be accounted for on that basis, and not assumed in any sense. "Reality" corresponds to one of the modes of consciousness, other modes being consciousness of probable, doubtful, or null being. Husserl's statement that the terms truth and reality have a meaning for us because of the structure of consciousness indicates his method of procedure. He holds that we could not be assured of "real being" except by the synthesis of verification in experience, which alone presents true reality. Thus his emphasis is epistemological as a matter of method; like Hume, he does not, at least to begin with, raise objective metaphysical questions, but investigates our beliefs in an external or independent order. However, his language suggests that a setting is prepared for a metaphysical theory. He asserts that all adequate evidence for reality is due to a synthesis that belongs to us, and it is in us that reality has its transcendental foundation. The being of the world is admittedly "transcendent" of consciousness, but it is maintained that all transcendence is uniquely constituted in the life of consciousness, and is inseparably bound to this life. Consciousness, taken particularly as consciousness of the world, is held to carry in itself not only the unity of the meaning constituting this "world," but also "this world really existing." "Being an object really existing" means "being an identical object of actual or potential intentions in the unity of consciousness." The "real object" belongs to the world surely enough, but the world itself is an "infinite idea," which involves infinities of harmonious experiences and is correlative to the idea of a complete synthesis of possible experiences. The subject-object limitation of reality is thus prominently displayed in Husserl's construction as a matter of method. The programmatic aim of his philosophy is indicated by the various provinces of "constitution," which include physical nature, human society, culture, etc. Husserl at this point professes to be interested in examining the side of intentional experience; he states that the question is each time to disclose the intentionality implied in the experience itself.

In the interest of "radicalism" of understanding, the phenomenological method requires a "reduction" to individual consciousness first of all; and it must then face the problem of establishing the reality of other subjects. The method may be said to be "radical" in the sense that all possible beliefs are suspended, and only the most certain data are admitted as a beginning. In carrying out the method, the world and all human beings except myself are "bracketed." But this first reduction must be carried a step further, in conformity to the ideal of the method. If I as an individual ego "eliminate" other human beings, I must also suspend all judgments based upon them or involving them. The phenomenological residuum becomes correspondingly narrower. What does it comprise? This is answered by a more precise application of the phenomenological method. With the natural attitude I find myself in the world, along with other human beings. If I abstract from the others, I am "alone." That which is peculiar to my ego is my concrete being as a "monad." For the purposes of method it is important to begin by extruding from the field of investigation not only the reality of others for me, but all modes of consciousness referring to what is strange to me, i.e., everything referring to "others," such as predicates expressing cultural values.

Thus Husserl attempts to achieve the determination of a completely individual sphere of consciousness, proceeding with what is given in intuitive experience. This is not to say that cultural values are not a part of the immediately given "intuitive" field of experience. For the natural view of the world, and for the theoretical view of modern science, values are immediately given, are "there" in a social context. The cultural anthropologist reflects (with a theoretical attitude) and performs a partial epoché when investigating the values. But the universal epoché of the phenomenologist must go much further; and it cannot stop before it reaches the "rock bottom" of an individual (solitary) ego, as here indicated. Not that *all* questioning comes to an end there — all regressive questioning *of this kind* comes to an end in that way.[14]

Having eliminated all strange elements, there remains "the phenomenon of the world," as the transcendental correlate of the experience of the world. The sphere which comprises my own world represents the extreme limit which is attainable by phenomenological reduction. This is "first," and it must be attained in order to constitute the experience of "an other ego distinct from me"; and without having the latter idea I am not able to have the experience of an "objective world." But I do not need the experience of an objective world or of another ego in order to have "my own world." How non-temporal (in the naturalistic sense) is Husserl's mode of thought is seen by the extension of his method. To be sure, "my own world," and the very conditions of my meaningful experience, presuppose other selves and an objective world, which can as a matter of fact never be suspended; that fact is genetically and causally prior to the level of the phenomenological method, and is not altered by the adoption of that method. Husserl distinguishes the "nature" which remains after the "reduction" from the nature of the sciences, which abstract all psychical elements. In my own reduced world, or "nature," I find my body, distinguished from all other things by the fact that it is organic. If I reduce another me to "my sphere," I obtain material bodies; but if I reduce myself as a man, I arrive at my organism and mind, or at myself as a psychophysical unity, and at the me-personality. This is what belongs to me in an exclusive manner, and it intuitively forms a coherent unity.

It now becomes imperative to demonstrate the reality of other minds. A direct experience of another ego is ruled out because it would then be nothing but a part of my being to me. It is therefore held to be necessary

---

[14] The studies in *Experience and Judgment* show how the constructive procedure, beginning with an individual experience of an individual object, becomes the starting-point for analyses of more complex types of objectivity and experience. It should be clear that "the social" is not neglected, and that all that can be ascertained by means of any other attitude or method remains valid — on its own grounds — and is not denied in phenomenology.

to use a kind of mediate intentionality, and although this appears to leave
the deep level of the "primordial world," the latter nevertheless remains
fundamental. The new intentionality represents a "coexistence" which
can never be present "in person." The type of experience which meets the
need is an act which makes others "co-present," an act of apperception
by analogy which Husserl calls "appresentation." The other body resembles my own and leads me to conceive "by analogy" that it is another
organism. A sharp distinction is drawn between apperceptions which
pertain to the primordial sphere and those which appear with the meaning
of another ego, thus adding new meaning.

There still remains the constitution of humanity or of the community.
When Husserl speaks of intentional analysis of the community, he has in
mind the possibility of acts of the ego which penetrate into other egos by
means of experience of appresentation of other egos. Such acts "go from
me to you," and are the social acts which are necessary to establish the possibility of communication between human persons. He holds it to be an
important problem to study these acts in their different forms and to clarify
the essence of the social from the transcendental point of view. His point
of view shows the Kantian influence. He is concerned with pointing out
the necessary presuppositions or conditions of an ordered process of experience, including social experience. This method of approach carries
with it the idealistic postulate that the conditions of experience are also the
conditions of a world of experience, the world being interpreted in terms
of such experience. The different types of social community are portrayed
as being constituted in the interior of the objective world, as spiritual objectivities *sui generis*. These communities are constituted in their various
possible gradations, including personalities of a higher order. Every one
lives in the same nature, which is common to all; and due to the essential
community of all individual lives, nature is transformed into a world of
culture, which assumes value for man no matter how primitive it may be.

The objective world is "pre-given" in the sense that it was already present for all egos; and it is constantly constituting itself in accordance with
an *a priori* structural form of meaningful acts. The non-evolutionary point
of view of Husserl is shown again in his belief that the general empirical
structure of the given objective world, including nature and culture, is to
a great extent an "essential necessity." The problem of an *a priori* ontology
of the real world, which is intended to make clear its universal structure
as conforming to intuitively given essential laws, is not truly philosophical
in Husserl's sense. Phenomenology aims to clarify the essential laws which
determine the manner in which the objective world sinks its roots into

transcendental subjectivity, i.e., the laws which make comprehensible the world as a constituted meaning. The temptation to use the terms "existence" and "meaning of existence" interchangeably in this context is clearly great. But this temptation must be resisted if a fallacy of confusion (in this case "the constitutive fallacy") is to be avoided.

Phenomenology is anti-metaphysical only with respect to the tradition. It attempts the construction of *a priori* sciences on the basis of concrete intuition — such sciences as pure grammar, pure logic, pure law, the eidetic science of the world intuitively apprehended, etc., and the elaboration of a general ontology of the objective world which embraces everything. This is metaphysics, says Husserl, if it is true that the ultimate knowledge of being may be called metaphysics. Rejecting the traditional metaphysics because of its speculative excesses, he sets up his own "apodictic" theory. Eidetic descriptions of constitutive experiences take the place of physical reality. The objection will be raised that "pure" subjectivity can yield nothing but itself, no matter how it may be multiplied. That is true enough with regard to matters of fact, but it constitutes an objection only if the purely cognitive and the natural orders are confused. Despite Husserl's inclination to construe reality in subjective terms, it must always be borne in mind that one is concerned with meaningful experiences in phenomenology.

One is by no means to be confined to his egological sphere. Husserl argues that although one's ego is alone absolutely certain, it cannot have experience of the world without being in intercourse with other egos. It must be a member of a "society of monads." It follows that a world in which communication is possible must be arranged spatially and temporally. Furthermore, this is the only (if not the best) possible world. Not more than one world could be constituted, for it follows from the egological premise that a second world would not be compossible. Husserl adds that it is necessary that this one unique nature exist, if it is true that I carry in me structures that imply the coexistence of other monads. The fact that "I am" determines in advance which monads are "others" for me; and the same may be said from the point of view of pure possibility. The tacit assumption that being depends upon thought, as also the proposition that what cannot be thought cannot be, condition the validity of the argument. The statement that other persons can only be found and not created can hardly be reconciled with the assertion that the objective world is "innate" in the monadological world. What is true of persons ought to be true of things in general.

An important function of phenomenology as Husserl sees it is the great task of giving to science a new and higher form. His sketch of investigations concerning "the transcendental constitution of the world" begins the clarification of the meaning and origin of such concepts as world, nature, space, time, animal being, man, spirit, organism, social community, culture, etc. These concepts, without being analyzed and clarified, serve as fundamental concepts in the positive sciences. But in phenomenology they are to be engendered with a clearness and distinctness that does not admit of possible doubt. All the *a priori* sciences are regarded as branches of the transcendental tree, the universal *a priori* being innate in transcendental subjectivity. Transcendental phenomenology, systematically and fully developed, is *eo ipso* a "universal ontology"; not a merely formal ontology, but one which contains all the possibilities of existence. Thus is constituted an absolute foundation for the sciences.

Phenomenological psychology, which excludes everything touching psycho-physiology, amounts to transcendental metaphysics. Husserl states his purpose of explaining the intentionality of the being of a spirit in general, and in projecting investigations which explain the intentionality constituted in this spirit. "First being," which sets the foundation for all that is objective in the world, is transcendental intersubjectivity, or the totality of the monads. Husserl makes the interesting statement that within this subjective sphere all the problems of contingent reality appear, such as death, destiny, the "meaning" of history, and so on. It is his purpose to place such ethical and religious problems on grounds where every question must be placed which can have a possible meaning for us. Were he speaking of experience in the ordinary sense, this contention would hardly be surprising, and would have merit. But the sense in which historical problems may be treated by means of the phenomenological method remains to be shown. In the form in which the method has been introduced up to this point, concrete historical problems are as foreign to it as is death, whether actual or eidetic. The treatment of historical knowledge as a problem of *intentional analysis* may indeed be fitted into the framework of phenomenology; but its properly limited function must then be recognized.

The *Cartesian Meditations* is fittingly concluded with an expression of reverence toward the subjective tradition. Stating that positive science is a science of being which is lost in the world, Husserl adds that it is necessary first to lose the world by the method of reduction in order to find it later in the field of universal self-consciousness. The words of Saint Augustine, to the effect that truth is to be found in the self, express the dominant idea of the *Meditations*. It follows then either that objective or "outer" truth is inaccessible, in which case we are committed to agnosticism; or that an absolute consciousness (whatever that may *be*, as one may observe with the natural attitude) conditions and constitutes reality itself, and not only our meaningful experience of reality. It is the latter alternative which is accepted by transcendental phenomenology as an idealistic philosophy.

Husserl has increased "seeing," or the field for description, offering a method for treating all types of experience. To attempt to use the phenomenological method exclusively, with an artificial conception of experience as divorced from its natural status in the world and its cultural conditions, would be to fail to do justice to experience itself in the complete sense of the term. That would be to substitute metaphors for reality, and to miss the descriptive role of phenomenology. In that case, the advantage gained by adopting the attitude of phenomenological reflection would be incomparably outweighed by the loss of the natural world (i.e., if the phenomenological method were intended to be used exclusively — which it is not), which can never be *really* constituted out of pure consciousness. It is not a question of choosing either the phenomenological method or the natural view of the world. The method has its usefulness in the theory of knowledge or in descriptive psychology, as well as in general philosophy, and it thus supplements our knowledge. In a systematic, analytic sense it may be said to provide the foundation of all ordered knowledge. Its clarification of basic concepts and structures extends to all fields of knowledge, including the social sciences.[15] Just as "pure logic" was not intended to displace logic as an art, so there can be no thought of making an eidetic and transcendental discipline legislate for or substitute for the factual sciences. The universal scope of phenomenology is seen in this clarifying function, on the one hand; but it also consists in the very nature of its descriptive procedure, which begins by defining an all-comprehensive, infinite realm for investigation, a realm which includes all the data of the sciences (in a "reduced" form). In this way nothing should be lost by the reduction, for all findings of positive science are retained in it. One must be careful to avoid metaphysical dogma, as well as seemingly persuasive epistemological arguments leading to such dogma, and to see the phenomenological method as retaining all knowledge from its detached point of view, while making its own addition to knowledge in providing answers to its own peculiar questions.

Husserl's philosophy is non-evolutionary even when he introduces the

[15] Cf. Alfred Schuetz, "Phenomenology and the Social Sciences," in *Philosophical Essays in Memory of Edmund Husserl.*

time-form. That follows from the placing in abeyance of the entire "naively" posited realm of natural existence. He is interested in determining the necessary conditions for any concrete experience or objects of experience. But what *can* the phenomenological mode of approach contribute, if it does not go the way of temporal evolutionism, or of genetic psychology? It attempts to go the way of *evidence* (= self-givenness), and to see how far it can proceed constructively in that way. All concepts, of whatever field of knowledge, and of whatever degree of complexity, must then be referred to the bar of intuitive experience and must there justify themselves. This is of course no violation of the findings of genetic psychology, or of any other scientific discipline. It is rather an attempt to provide all disciplines, and all concepts, with a final foundation in direct experience or evidence. But, it may be asked, why go to the trouble of doing that? The cogency of the reply will depend upon one's interest in achieving completeness of understanding and rigor of knowledge — in short, upon one's insight into the ideal of philosophy. More may be said positively, however, for the constitutive process cannot but be of aid in separating the genuine from the spurious in knowledge. The phenomenological philosophy of logic is one illustration in point, particularly in its answer to relativism.

It is essential that the phenomenological reduction be viewed as a purely methodological device, without any pretense to metaphysics. It is radical in the sense of helping us to make clear the ultimate presuppositions of experience. As such a quest for presuppositions it cannot fail to exercise a freeing influence on the mind. But it must never forget its own "mother-earth," its own actual ("naturalistic") genetic foundation, if it is to constitute a world which will satisfy experience. To do so, and to go the way of cognitive idealism, would mean that the phenomenological quest would have to rest content with the pale shadow of reality, depending upon a hypostatized *logos* in an ethereal absolute consciousness. In short, phenomenology is not metaphysics in the traditional or current sense of the term. The phenomenological investigation of intentional experience, taken *as such*, may indeed illuminate metaphysical questions and even result in dissolving pseudo-questions, but it may not be construed metaphysically as idealism or realism within the frame of the method. The door is not closed therewith for proceeding "beyond phenomenology" (to use Koehler's expression),[16] as has already been made sufficiently clear.

[16] Cf. W. Koehler, *The Place of Value in a World of Facts* (New York, 1938).

CHAPTER XVII

THE SIGNIFICANCE OF PHENOMENOLOGY

A. THE GOAL OF AN ABSOLUTELY FOUNDED PHILOSOPHY

T HE "REDUCTION" is intended to provide an "absolute" ground for philosophy, and the restriction to essential analysis frees the philosophic quest from the vicissitudes of the empirical order. Husserl's conception of absolute knowledge and its relationship to the concept of essence was made clear in his *Logos* essay on "Philosophy as a Rigorous Science." [1] Every judgment which brings to adequate expression what lies in essences, how essences of a certain genus are connected with certain others, as, e.g., "intuition" and "empty meaning," how "phantasy" and "perception," how "concept" and "intuition," etc., are united with one another, are necessarily "unitable" on the basis of certain components of essence, are perhaps related to one another as "intention" and "fulfillment," or conversely are non-unitable and found a "consciousness of disappointment," etc.: every such judgment is in his view an absolute, generally valid cognition, is an essential judgment of a kind that it would be absurd to want to establish, verify, or refute by experience. It is of interest to note the description of absolute knowledge as "generally valid," and also the insistence upon the complete independence from experience, whether as proof or refutation. The special sense in which the term "absolute" is used shows that the traditional problem of universals and *a priori* knowledge has been raised anew in the setting of phenomenology; and it is also apparent that the attempt is made to bring the *a priori* within the field of intuitive observation. "Essences" are regarded as being directly experienceable. Thus one can "see" an essence just as directly as one can hear a tone — e.g., the essence "tone" itself, or "judgment," etc.; and it is maintained that one can assert judgments of essence while "seeing." The term "essence" as here used refers to conceptual forms or types. Essences constitute the theme of pure phenomenology as conceived in the *Logos* essay, and not existence or "self-observation." No individual *is* an essence; an individual "has" an essence which can be asserted about it. The question of the effective relationship between essential structures and matters of fact must then be faced by phenomenology. If, as is maintained, the

[1] *L. c.*, p. 316.

knowledge of essences provides the clarification of empirical knowledge, it follows that the essential knowledge of the psychical is presupposed by all psychological knowledge.

The program of phenomenology that is presented in the *Ideas* includes the insights of the *Logos* essay, but construes them within the frame of a transcendental philosophy. That it was an early attempt to state the nature and method of phenomenology, in view of the still more subtle and thoroughgoing elaboration of the method which is presented in later publications, has been seen; and the orientation with respect to Descartes has been pointed out. The latter was a favorite device of Husserl's for introducing his conception of transcendental subjectivity. Descartes was perhaps the most important philosopher in the tradition from the point of view of anticipating transcendental phenomenology. Husserl regarded him as the great beginner of the science of pure consciousness, even though he did not discern the real nature of his discovery. Descartes' method of doubt, designed to establish certainty in knowledge, lends itself readily to use for an absolute beginning for philosophy. As a reflexive method, the process of systematic doubt is directed internally. It is not concerned with the evidence for propositions in the ordinary sense, for it is unable to accept the reality of anything of which it is possible to doubt. That means that one should practice doubt as far as it is possible to do so without incurring a contradiction. Thus it was held to be "possible" to doubt the existence of the "external" world and of other human beings, and finally of one's own body, without contradiction (i.e., self-contradiction).

This procedure may be questioned, however. The meaning of "contradiction" need not be accepted as it must be employed in the Cartesian sense, as a momentary affair. The plane of experience is bigger, comprising a series of co-occurring and related experiences, which continually justify themselves. But to this one might reply with Descartes that our whole experience may be illusory or false. This suggestion is met adequately by applying the reflexive method to it, for the assertion of the general falsity of experience necessarily suspends itself; and also by appealing to the success of practical experience, for which everything speaks, as over against the empty class of arguments in favor of illusion or falsity. Is it "possible" that we could be consistently deceived in our experience, or indeed that we be deceived at all? Possibility in an empty sense stands in contrast to possibility as based upon experience. If we consider anything to be possible which does not incur a contradiction, either inherently or in the course of experience, the evidential support of such a possibility is null at any rate. A weightier objection to the thesis of doubt is directed against the troublesome distinction between the bodily and mental realms, with their respective assumptions. Descartes' process of doubting ended when he reached the experience of doubting itself, for it appeared to be certain that the experience itself could not be doubted. That led him to conclude certainty for the realm of thought, certainty meaning indubitability. The remainder of the attempt scarcely deserves mention. The logically unworthy demonstration of the existence of an omnipotent being whose benevolence would not permit of deceit brings Descartes back to his starting-point.

The entire attempt is nugatory and would be devoid of value except for the one virtue of promoting a challenging attitude of mind. As employed in phenomenology, it is of aid in leading one to search for the basic presuppositions of knowledge, especially those which are usually overlooked, and also in aiding in the definition of a universal realm of knowledge and experience. That these ends cannot be achieved without various assumptions is merely evidence of the inescapableness of the logic-centric predicament. The historical utility of the procedure will not be denied. But inspection shows that it is only the actually occurring "I doubt" that is indubitable; or, rather, it cannot be doubted as a matter of fact, which is different from being "indubitable," as well it might be, for how could the two doubts be simultaneous? It is really an already past doubt which is reaffirmed as indubitable, and this involves reliance upon memory, which is admittedly faulty. The speedy generalization concerning the primacy of mind is indicative of a haste born of desire. It should be observed, finally, that the Cartesian questioning of the validity of our experience of reality is an indication of acute consciousness of the failure of the traditional system of knowledge, and is not to be construed as a kind of pathological distrust.

Husserl has credited Descartes with providing a "beginning" for transcendental idealism in his sense of the term. From the logical point of view, however, Descartes' contribution to the development of deductive method in philosophy is more noteworthy and anticipated the Leibnizian-Husserlian ideal of a *mathesis universalis*. Despite his radicalism, he retained much of the tradition, as shown by the ideas of substance and the self, and by the doctrine of innate ideas and principles. The significance of his use of method is both historical and systematic in character: (1) historically, he adopted a *modus vivendi* for the times in the form of a dualistic theory, which made possible (2) an expansion of the spirit and to some extent the principles of the mathematical method to philosophy and scientific knowledge in general.

The phenomenological method is designed to be monistic in the sense that the "reduction" to pure consciousness, which is accomplished by means of the "elimination" of all beliefs and of existential positings of any kind, results in the delimitation of a unified sphere for reflective analysis; and this is to serve as an adequate basis for the constitution of all knowledge and reality. By means of the phenomenological method it is possible to get "back of" the natural attitude or the theoretical attitude, etc. It is finally necessary, in order to appraise this method, to ascertain whether it at any point oversteps its due limits or exceeds its promise, *to include it in our universal reflective scope*, i.e., to "reduce" the phenomenological method itself. This is of course methodological criticism, which is analogous in its way to transcendental reduction. If one can speak of the attitude that is directed toward theory-forms, e.g., then one can also analyze the attitude which considers possible methods, including the phenomenological method. This is maintained in opposition to the contention that the phenomenological method may not be juxtaposed with other methods, all of them being subsumed under the genus of method. It would seem that such an admission would forfeit the claim to absoluteness of the phenomenological method, for the criticism of methodological criteria would be the most fundamental of all studies. But that fear would really be unfounded. The method is capable of being self-critical, and must in fact be self-justifying; and it is also undeniable that it may be judged from another point of view, in the light of methodology in general. By means of the reflective criticism of the method of phenomenology, it will be apparent whether at any point there is an illicit introduction of metaphysical dogma, or whether there are any presuppositions in its use, in any of the various senses of the term "presupposition."

It is difficult to understand Husserl when he asserts that the transcendental sphere has an infinite amount of knowledge preceding deduction.[2] When the reduction is performed, the knower is posited as real, not as a member of a world of existence, but rather as a subject "for which the world is not considered." The cardinal principle of idealism is indicated clearly in the passage which follows, and which may be cited as characteristic of the later Husserl, namely, "If, in this (i.e., transcendental) description, the transcendental ego exists absolutely in and for itself prior to all cosmic being, which first obtains in and through it existential validity. . . ." It cannot be meant that this "priority" obtains only as a matter of transcendental description. That would be possible as a device, while incorrect in fact. But that would not be what is desired. The transcen-

[2] Cf. the author's preface to the English edition of the *Ideas*, p. 12.

dental approach is not pointless if the claim to metaphysical truth is abandoned. Truth on the phenomenological plane does not mean the denial of truth in a naturalistic setting, or in any other sense. Its purely descriptive character is of value in two senses: (1) the "origin" of the concept of truth in experience is clarified, as has been seen; (2) the reflective attitude which makes that possible is at the same time presupposed by the examination of truth and its criteria in any universe of discourse, or with any other attitude.

This may be considered in connection with another passage, which bears out the present interpretation. "I now become aware that my own phenomenologically self-contained essence can be posited in an *absolute* sense, as I am the ego who invests the being of the world . . . with existential validity. . . . I myself as this individual essence, posited absolutely as the open infinite field of phenomenological data and their inseparable unity, am the 'transcendental ego,' the *absolute positing*[3] means that the world is no longer 'given to me in advance' . . . but that henceforth it is exclusively my ego that is given (i.e., from my new standpoint) . . . as that which has being in itself, in itself experiences a world, confirms the same, and so forth."[4] Husserl speaks of his transcendental-phenomenological idealism and of its alleged solipsism as a means devised in the interest of the *problem of a possible objective knowledge*. He holds that the very meaning of that problem refers back to the ego that is in and for itself; "and that this ego, *as the presupposition of the knowledge of the world*, cannot be and remain presupposed as having the existence of a world, and must therefore, in respect of the world's being, be brought to its pure state through phenomenological reduction, that is, through epoché." Such passages show how Husserl shifts from conditions of knowledge to conditions of being. This is done in accordance with the cardinal principle of idealism, which is none the less in need of justification in its present form.

In view of the assumptions so patently present in the foregoing passages, it is now clear that one kind of presupposition has been substituted for another, which is perfectly legitimate if recognized as such, as Husserl does elsewhere. Unquestionably much is gained by the reflective procedure. When Husserl[5] contrasts the positive sciences and philosophy, maintaining that philosophy cannot begin in a naive, direct manner, he must also acknowledge the assumptive nature of the general field of subjectivity. If the positive sciences are based upon "the previously given ground of our

[3] Cp. with Fichte's use of "positing" in his *Wissenschaftslehre*.
[4] *Ideas*, pp. 17 f.
[5] *Ibid.*, p. 27.

experience of a world, presupposed as something that exists as a matter of course," may not the same be said in an analogous sense of the realm of pure consciousness? If the "naive" assumptions made by the positive sciences "cause them all to have problems in respect to their foundations, and paradoxes of their own, a condition which a subsequent and belated theory of knowledge first seeks to remedy," what is one to think of the difficulties which beset phenomenology in the course of its methodological procedure, and not only its expression? These questions should be faced squarely by all who are interested in phenomenology, including its convinced adherents. Subjectivity cannot be said to have a being of its own, independently of the natural conditions of existence. It, too, has a locus in the physical world, if by being *actual existence* in the natural sense is meant. It can — and must for philosophical purposes — however, be *treated* as autonomous, as disengaged from its natural setting.

It will be agreed that philosophy requires radical (i.e., thoroughgoing) reflection about the meaning and possibility of its own scheme. When considering the belief that such reflection takes possession of the absolute ground of pure preconceptual experience, one must ascertain the exact meaning of the term in that sense alone. The same holds for the next stage in the scheme of philosophy, in which original concepts are to be *created* and adjusted to the absolute ground. Correctly understood, the ideal of an "absolutely (meaning 'thoroughly') transparent method" is precisely what is the aim of a genuinely logical-constructive philosophy.

The ultimate presuppositions of phenomenology must in turn be judged by logical means. Not that it is fallacious to make use of presuppositions in phenomenology: it is sufficient that they be pointed out explicitly, and that they differ from presuppositions in the usual sense, as used in other, non-transcendental contexts. Furthermore even though logic is bracketed in the epoché, its canons may not be violated in any reasoning undertaken by the phenomenologist, any more than may be the case with arithmetical operations. If it is true that methodology is enriched by the addition of the phenomenological method, it is also true that the principles of methodology must be invoked to judge the phenomenological procedure. In addition to accurate, painstaking descriptions, there is much reasoning and argumentation in the literature of phenomenology. Hence "external" as well as "internal" criticism must be undertaken. That is the sense in which phenomenology is subject to logical criticism. "Transcendental intersubjectivity" was regarded by Husserl [6] as "the con-

---

[6] Cf. *Encyclopaedia Britannica*, article on "Phenomenology" by Husserl, 14th ed., vol. XVII, pp. 701 f.

crete ultimate ground, whence all that transcends consciousness, including all that is real in the world, derives the *sense* of its existence." The dual nature of the argument is seen in the interchangeable use of knowledge and being, for "sense" belongs to the order of knowledge. Interpreted as a statement with cognitive reference, no exception will be taken to the assertion. But one may not therefore attach the condition of knowing to the order of being. That the cardinal principle of idealism is again used in this favorite argument of Husserl, which is so characteristic of idealism, is shown by his next assertion, that "all objective existence is essentially 'relative,' and owes its nature to a unity of intention," which is established according to transcendental laws. The "non-dogmatic" phenomenological method thus seems to stand in need of some of its own purification in this respect. Its program, expressed in non-assumptive terms, is laudable and in fact necessary for philosophy. But it must be adhered to strictly.

B. PHENOMENOLOGY AND ITS PARADOXES

One of the most striking and at the same time disconcerting expressions of the aims of phenomenology is presented by Fink in an essay which is endorsed completely by Husserl as representing his own views.[7] In this way Husserl finally published a much-needed reply to some of the critics of his mature philosophy. This is a significant publication, possessing all the more interest because of its attempt to meet certain objections to phenomenology of long standing. It is a revealing discussion in the sense that helpful light is shed on the real meaning of transcendental phenomenology, and also because of the way in which the question of the proper reaches of phenomenological analysis is raised. It undertakes the very difficult task of preserving the continuity and validity of Husserl's past work, of the phenomenological era at any rate, while admitting shortcomings and inadequacies. A frank recognition of the growth of his thought, right up to the end, makes it possible to criticize past partial states of "pure" phenomenology. The disputed question whether he made progress in all ways in his last period can only be answered with finality when all the pertinent material has been made available. It is true that his conception of a pure philosophy was brought to a high degree of internal consistency. The account of phenomenology in Fink's essay attempts to

---

[7] Cf. Eugen Fink, "Die phänomenologische Philosophie Edmund Husserls in der gegenwärtigen Kritik," with a preface by Edmund Husserl, *Kant-Studien* (Berlin, 1933), pp. 319–383. Husserl states that he agrees with every statement in the essay. Dr. Fink was his private assistant at the time.

justify the various stages of its development, and emphasizes the basic unity of Husserl's thought almost to the extent of minimizing his epochal changes, and gives the impression at times of apologetic writing. Its value as a portrayal of the latest phase of phenomenology is, however, undiminished thereby.

Husserl has been one of the most misunderstood men in the history of philosophy. Thus his *Logical Investigations* was not understood, as he had the occasion to point out in reply to some of its critics. Külpe misunderstood him, and so did Schlick,[8] to cite only a few cases. In the preface to the present essay, he states that all critiques that were known to him missed the fundamental meaning of his phenomenology so badly that it was not touched at all, despite the quotation of his words. If his critics fare badly, his adherents are not much better off, for the founder of phenomenology regarded himself as being merely a beginner, and only Fink was accepted as orthodox among his associates at the close of his career.

The objections to phenomenology advanced by Rickert and his "criticistic" school [9] constitute the initial theme of the discussion. Although Zocher and Kreis, who are selected as representative and responsible critics, had carefully and intensively studied the published writings of Husserl, insufficient attention had been devoted to the *Formal and Transcendental Logic*. Husserl is led by their failure to raise the basic question, whether the essential content of phenomenology can be understood at all in terms of a mundane philosophy, which means by one not performing the phenomenological reduction.

The method of transcendental reduction is declared to be the sole fundamental method of phenomenology, and the reduction is described as the way to the "thematic" domain of philosophy which must be undertaken for the beginning of philosophical thought. It is the "approach" to transcendental subjectivity, and contained in it are all the problems of phenomenology, as well as the special methods referring to them. The reader is warned against the error of using the "pre-reduction" method of the *Logical Investigations*, and is informed that the real understanding of that work presupposes insight into the meaning of transcendental phenomenology. The earlier work was on the way to phenomenology, and

[8] Cf. M. Schlick, *Allgemeine Erkenntnislehre* (Berlin, 1918), pp. 119 ff., and also the second edition (1925), pp. 127 f., in which Schlick withdrew his criticism.

[9] In his "System of Philosophy" Rickert characterized his philosophy as Kantian in the sense of critical subjectivism. Cf. also R. Zocher, *Husserls Phänomenologie und Schuppes Logik* (1932), and F. Kreis, *Phänomenologie und Kritizismus* (1930).

that trend can only be understood adequately from the point of view of the *Ideas*.

It is a simple matter to meet the charge of the critics in question that the method of the *Logical Investigations* was dogmatic. Much more serious is the charge that there was a turning to "criticism" in the *Ideas*. Both claims are declared to be incorrect assumptions. Husserl admits that the transition from the earlier to the later work is formally similar to the transition from the naive, empirical knowledge of existence to the "criticistic" knowledge of the possibility of experience. The *Ideas* accordingly signifies the overcoming of dogmatism and the growth of the really philosophical attitude. Phenomenology and criticism (or critical philosophy) are held to differ fundamentally nevertheless. The basic transcendental question of the possibility of objective knowledge is admittedly not put in the *Logical Investigations*, and hence is not answered. But neither is the criticistic question in the horizon of the *Ideas*. The "cardinal insinuation" that the criticistic and the phenomenological ideas of transcendental philosophy are the same is rejected, although it is admitted that there is an apparent basis for such a misunderstanding in the *Ideas*, which is "the first literary objectification of the fundamental ideas of phenomenology." A far-reaching similarity of terms is employed in the two philosophies, "which conceals the abysmal difference of meaning"; thus, e.g., "transcendental," "transcendental ego," "constitution," "transcendental idealism," etc., have radically different meanings in the different contexts of the criticistic and the phenomenological philosophy.

Characteristic of this version of phenomenology is the assertion that all positive sciences begin in a dogmatic situation, i.e., they are based upon presuppositions which they can themselves no longer know. In so far as philosophy refers to the sphere of presuppositions, it is supposed to make transparent the ground upon which the positive sciences are based, and to found them in a sense which they themselves cannot realize in their "bases." Philosophy thus functions as a transcendental theory of science. It is not made clear why logical criticism would not be adequate to "know" such presuppositions, or why the phenomenological technique for seeking out all presuppositions may not be added to the usual means for logical analysis. Only harm can come from an expression of disdain for the alleged failure to comprehend the true nature of phenomenological analysis, if this point is ignored. It is suggested herewith that the best interests of phenomenology will be served by a frank recognition of the principle of the *coöperation of methods*; and, indeed, this is amply justified by the development of phenomenology as a whole. This proposal indicates a way to appropriate the contributions of the phenomenological method without falling prey to a peculiar type of agnosticism.

Husserl is in agreement with the criticists concerning the transcendental problem of knowledge. Thus there is the ontological thesis of transcendental idealism, that *existence is in principle the result of "constitution."* Both hold that the "empirical reality" of existence is founded upon its transcendental ideality, and that it is only understandable upon that basis. Furthermore, the principle of the *priority of meaning to being* is contained in the "idealistic" thesis that existence is constituted. It would be strange, in the context of phenomenology, to construe this thesis literally, without recognizing that it is an assumption. Due to long usage the cardinal principle of idealism appears to be self-evident to philosophers deriving from or influenced by Kant, and it tends to be tacitly accepted. If "transparency" is to be achieved in the process of examining presuppositions, then the idealistic machinery must also be made evident or transparent. In phenomenology the problem of constitution is formulated as the "endowment of meaning" (*Sinngebung*), which calls attention to its cognitive character. The criticistic contention that meaning and theoretical validity lie before the real object of knowledge, and that their recognition in the pure judgment-functions of "transcendental apperception" first makes possible the objective givenness of the real, is cited as a point of agreement with phenomenology. But in phenomenology the professedly non-metaphysical procedure requires the elimination of the dogma of idealism, and the constitutive procedure, in keeping with the "radical" method, allows the metaphysical question to remain open and unanswered, or, at best, it is merely a partial answer, going as far as the analysis of experience will allow.

The difference between the criticistic examination of the conditions of existence and the thoroughgoing phenomenological analysis of all presuppositions whatsoever is shown by means of the "problem of the world." "Criticism" explains existence by going back to the meaning which lies before all existence, but its interpretation of the problem of the world remains world-immanent, i.e., on the ground of the world. The fundamental problem of phenomenology, in the present version, is formulated as the question of the origin of the world.[10] ·One's surprise is not lessened, and the

---

[10] Cf. the searching formulation in *Erfahrung und Urteil*, §§ 10–11, where the "pre-given" world is said to be permeated by the sediment of logical contributions and where the process of penetrating back to the transcendental subjectivity constituting it is described as occurring in two stages: (1) proceeding from the pre-given world with all its meaning-sediments, with its scientific determinations, to the original life-world; and (2) proceeding further from the

hope that this is merely a generous extension of the term "origin" is destroyed, when this question is described as the eternal human question of the beginning, which has been answered by myth, theology, and philosophical speculation. It is argued that the question of the origin of the world cannot be formulated by one who naively regards the world as the totality of things existing in themselves, since one would in that case necessarily be led to a dogmatic metaphysics, explaining being by means of being. Unfortunately, it is not satisfactorily pointed out why this should be objectionable. This argument appears to be but another form of the old argument from the infinite regress. One must avoid treating "being" as a finished totality, and care should be observed in the use of the term "explain." By means of descriptive analysis and the determination of laws we are able to "explain" being on the basis of being, or, finally, with the performance of the complete epoché. There are various degrees of escape from "naïveté," depending upon the extent of the analysis of being, or whether it is assumed at all; and only in the latter case can being be completely "placed in question." As Husserl sees it, the basic problem of dogmatic metaphysics is the question of the origin of existence, whereas phenomenology investigates the origin of the world, i.e., it places in question the unity of being and the form of the world. It is thus possible to outflank the "criticistic critique" by getting back of its own construction. This treatment of the criticists is particularly effective, and is successful in setting phenomenology off as a unique discipline.

The aim of phenomenology is said to be the achievement of an "absolute knowledge of the world," which it attempts to accomplish by going beyond all "worldly" forms of explanation. The explanation of the world by means of the "ultimate ground of its being" is not regarded as a speculative undertaking, but is advanced in the form of a rigorous science. Instead of "being," the phrase "experiential unity" might be used, in order to free the statement from its assumptive and misleading connotation. This means that the "ground of the world" is made the object of theoretical examination, which results in the clarification of a customary assumption. The statement that phenomenology lives in the "pathos" of investigation can hardly be reconciled with a method of procedure which purports to be rational throughout. Along with some other elements in Fink's account it suggests a danger of mysticism which has no proper place in phenomenology, although examples of mysticism are prominent in the

---

life-world to the subjective contributions out of which it itself "arises." It is evident that this procedure could be expressed in purely phenomenological terms. Cf. also L. Landgrebe, "The World as a Phenomenological Problem," *l. c.*

literature of the larger movement. The knowledge of the "origin" is held to be prior to all knowledge of the world and is therefore not subsumed under the heading of science in general as a mere addition to the mundane sciences. The absolute "ground" of the positive sciences as well as the "construction" of the criticistic transcendental philosophy are subjected to analysis by means of the phenomenological method. The radical foundation of the mundane sciences is held to be fundamentally different from the relations of foundation illustrated among the sciences themselves. The role of phenomenology thus appears to be one of clarifying the relation between the knowledge of the origin of the world and all mundane knowledge in general, the former functioning as the foundation of the latter. That the term "mundane" is construed in such a way as to preclude the possibility of a "radical" examination of the mundane in its own terms is apparent. The method of phenomenological reduction provides the means of "transcending" the world, and is intended to lead one back to the "world-transcendent origin." The relation of the origin of the world to the world is transcendental in the sense that the process of transcending the world which occurs in the performance of the reduction does not lead to an origin that is separate from the world. The world is retained in the "universe of absolute being" which is laid free by means of the reduction. Thus the world remains immanent in the absolute; it is discovered as "lying in the absolute," where it lay "concealed" before the reduction. It follows that the transcendental problem of the world cannot be formulated before the reduction has been made, for it is concealed from the natural attitude. This is taken to be the reason for detaching the phenomenological philosophy from any mundane problems as the motivating sources.

This formulation of the phenomenological program, with its pictorial language suggesting the extravagant claims of the traditional German idealism, should be restated in strict methodological terms, restricting the statement to what is actually accomplished. The performance of the reduction is then seen to be a simple operation (logically simple, even if it is rarely understood), with no suggestion of entering a hitherto unconceived "realm"; there is also to be no talk of "concealment" from the natural view; and expressions such as "retaining the world," "laying free a universe of absolute being," etc., are to be avoided. The suspicion grows in the critical reader that it is not merely a matter of the use of a tradition-laden, assumptive terminology, but rather that there is at times a suggestion of an ineffable element which violates the strictly experiential and descriptive character of the method. There is unfortunately ample evidence in support of this impression.

In accordance with the aim of making sure that the phenomenological philosophy is "pure," motives, as one kind of presupposition, are eliminated, or at least only phenomenological motives are allowed. It is therewith placed beyond the reach of most criticism. If not even the motivation comes from the natural world, how can one judge it? One must make the reduction in order to see the problems and motives, and then one has no right to make "natural" objections. Does that include logic? It does, in accordance with the sweeping requirements of the method of reduction. In the present writer's conception of logic as methodology, there is no such "agnostic" gap between the perceptual and conceptual orders, whether "pure" or "natural," and all phenomenological statements (one is tempted to say "significant statements," except that Husserl distinguishes significance according to "attitudes") are capable of logical formulation. This has bearing upon the entire question of the foundation of philosophy. Without in the least denying or detracting from the force of the reduction, or questioning its uniqueness in its philosophical form, it is nevertheless possible, as will be shown, to judge one type of method from the point of view of another.

The very connection with mundane problems is taken by Husserl to be an indication that the phenomenological realm has not been reached. Such mundane problems as are represented by the theory of knowledge and of science, ontology, and universal self-reflection must therefore be transformed by means of the reduction. Not even the mundane problems from which phenomenology proceeds are recognized as philosophical, for phenomenology begins with the performance of the reduction. Its own presuppositions will then be entirely infra-phenomenological, or that is at least the intention. As has been pointed out, phenomenology is not only held to be presuppositionless, but is also to be unmotivated, both terms being understood in their "natural" meanings. But, it will be asked, does not the formulation of the basic problem of phenomenology as the question of the origin of the world contradict the statement that phenomenology is unmotivated? Can a motive for the reduction be effective in advance, namely, the problem of the origin of the world? It is denied that a pre-given mundane problem can motivate us if we really go the cognitive way of phenomenology. The mundane forms of the real problem of the origin of the world are rejected, and are regarded as being merely "symbolic anticipations." Even though the basic problem of phenomenology does not "exist" before the reduction, in talking vaguely about phenomenology it can be provisionally indicated in advance. It is claimed that no "metaphysical" character is involved by the conception of a world-origin. It has been seen, however, that we and the world are supposed to be immersed in an "absolute," which means the region of transcendental subjectivity. Although that is not intended to be metaphysical in the usual dogmatic sense, it is none the less effective in promoting the idealistic thesis. The mischievous term "absolute" is fully equipped with connotations which may deceive the phenomenologist into thinking that he has uncovered a real (in a non-phenomenological sense) region of being by means of his method. The expression "picture-book phenomenology" has been used to describe an earlier type of phenomenology which was pursued at a time when the central interest was the determination of essences. The present type, if it gets into the wrong hands, may come to be characterized similarly because of its use of metaphors which threaten to become fixed and hypostatized structures. It will be granted, in any case, that phenomenology is a distinct kind of idealism; and although human ingenuity may well be illimitable, the small number of possible forms suggests that it may be the last stronghold of idealism.

One learns from the present essay that not only is the reduction unknown as a matter of fact, but its possibility is also unknown. A discussion of the reduction appears to engender a paradoxical situation indeed; it requires a process which seemingly takes us beyond or "transcends" the horizon of our own possibilities. The reduction must be unknown, it is argued, because it cannot appear within the limits of the "natural attitude," and only when the world is transcended does it itself become knowable in its "transcendental motivation." This is a curious argument. Why cannot one provide all the meanings necessary for the suspension of the natural attitude on the basis of the natural attitude? There is also no reason why the phenomenological program cannot be translated into natural terms. This may be maintained while admitting that the very awareness of the natural attitude as such presupposes a corresponding reflective point of view. The term "attitude" (*Einstellung*) has become solidified through long usage. What Husserl means is that the reduction presupposes itself in such a way that it first opens up the dimension of problems, with respect to which it establishes the theoretical possibility of knowledge. This is a special kind of assumption, which operates simultaneously and reflexively. The "strange paradox of the beginning of philosophy" which results from the attempt to expound the reduction is illustrated in the case of logic, which presupposes itself similarly. Logic also presupposes phenomenology, but the converse would be denied by Husserl, who maintains the self-sufficiency of phenomenology as the science that is concerned with "origins" and which proceeds intuitively.

Because the possibility of the reduction is held to be unknown, and the procedure unmotivated, it is believed to follow that every exposition of it must be false in a certain sense. That is due to the necessity of presenting a mundane exposition in terms of the natural attitude, which must be suspended in the process of the reduction. How we *know* the falsity in this case is not clear. Husserl assumes that knowledge of the reduction must be "reduced" knowledge. He has not proved that there can be no "natural" logical knowledge of the reduction. Why cannot there be such knowledge, as well as reduced knowledge of the natural attitude? If we can only know one attitude by having recourse to another, then we cannot know the phenomenological attitude except by means of some other attitude. To be consistent, Husserl must mean that each attitude is limited to its own terms and problems. In that case how can the phenomenological attitude help us with the natural attitude and its problems? How can it establish the unity of scientific knowledge? The answer is not difficult to find. Every finding in the phenomenological realm of essence has general validity as a possible form or pattern which may be exemplified in the actual world of experience. Furthermore, it is simply incorrect and untenable to cut loose the phenomenological point of view so violently from other points of view. It should rather be regarded as a necessary extension of hitherto known methods.

"Reduced" knowledge is knowledge which involves "bracketing," as distinguished from "natural" knowledge, for which the epoché is not performed. Really, what is in question is the nature of the meaningful questions that apply to each "attitude." The statements pertaining to other attitudes may be referred to, with the required bracketing, in phenomenology. Phenomenological statements involving such objects are merely more complicated structures, adding in each case the "purifying" requirements. There must also be a more inclusive point of view, which allows for inter-methodological judgments. This is provided for by *logical pluralism*, which recognizes the autonomy of the various domains of knowledge, and their methods, while not denying the underlying unity of the cognitive enterprise, a unity which may be established purely cognitively, along phenomenological lines, or bio-pragmatically, taking man the knower in his natural setting, or by the "logic of questions," as based upon a universal methodology.

The idealistic thesis, which as Hartmann [11] says lies in the blood of so

---

[11] Cf. N. Hartmann, *Grundzüge einer Metaphysik der Erkenntnis* (Berlin, 1921), p. 131. Hartmann states that phenomenology becomes idealistic instead of remaining with descriptive method, which is inconsistent with the method. In his view phenomenology can essentially never be an interpretation of the phenomena, can never be a theory. He holds that an idealistic or immanence-philosophical interpretation is here nothing other than an atavism of stand-

many philosophers, including Husserl, leads the latter to assign a greater role than is appropriate for the phenomenological attitude, by means of the process of "constitution." The procedures of reduction and constitution, which represent the negative or preparatory and the positive or constructive aspects of the method, prove to be the means for the instatement of idealism as a philosophy.

The reader is warned by Husserl that the theory of the reduction must be gone over thoroughly because of the unavoidable falsity of the initial exposition. Neither can the concept of the natural attitude be developed fully at the beginning, for it is regarded as a transcendental concept rather than as a pre-given mundane concept. It would be preferable to use another term in the place of "transcendental." One ought to speak of "trans-natural" characteristics or of trans-natural judgments, meaning thereby the characterization of the natural attitude as a whole. Granting that we are caught "in" the natural attitude, and that for philosophical purposes it is necessary to "break through" it by means of the phenomenological reduction, it does not follow that we have entered a totally different realm. The use of such pictorial terms as "breaking through" is likely to be misleading. The positive elements in the reduction can and must be expressed in "natural" terms as an extension of logical method in its customary form. That is not to say that all propositions, real and ideal, can be expressed in physical terms. The term "natural" is ambiguous. It may refer to the naive view of the world, or to the world of scientific thinking. It may also be taken to comprise the realm of theoretical thinking which, employing ideal entities and fictions, is an extension of the thought related to the natural world. All of these types of thought involve assumptions. The phenomenological realm is supposed to be free from all assumptions of being and validity. Its clearly expressed aim, to "recreate" or constitute all scientific knowledge as an organization of meaning-structures on the basis of a first science of pure consciousness, is seriously obscured by the recent element of "unmotivated agnosticism."

In order to judge the phenomenological method it is necessary to reflect upon the reduced realm as well as the natural attitude. One then sees how knowledge of being is confused with being, and why "riddles" arise. An

---

point-prejudgments, which unconsciously lie in the blood of the phenomenologist just as they do in everyone else's (in Germany), and that the neutral method of phenomenology ought to master such prejudgments if any method is to do so. Cf. also p. 132 for the charge that phenomenology neglects the freedom of the understanding, i.e., the independence of thought, in the interest of "intuition," a charge which could not be sustained in the face of Husserl's later publications, the *Experience and Judgment*, e.g., in which work the "freedom of the understanding" is done full justice.

idealistic riddle is indeed suggested by the statement that our human existence implicates world-being in itself, just as world-being implicates human
existence. That is clearly an expression of the subject-object limitation of
idealism. It becomes increasingly apparent that the phenomenological
epoché is being used as a means to establish transcendental idealism. The
epoché eliminates the belief in the world, and at the same time discovers
the world as a "transcendental dogma." The "true subject" of the belief
is thus discovered, the transcendental ego, for which the world is a universe of transcendental validities (*Geltungen*). This is advanced within
the frame of a radical method "which is not to be surpassed." Phenomenology refers the being of the world back to the transcendental subjectivity
in whose life the world is "valid." The question for a presuppositionless
philosophy, as viewed in phenomenology, is one of questioning the world
about itself. The leading question of philosophy is described as world-
knowledge, but the nature of that knowledge is difficult to determine.
The present context forbids interpreting it as involving relationships to
the sciences. The question concerning the being of the world is transformed into the question of the essence of transcendental subjectivity, for
which the "world" is valid ultimately. To speak of the belief in a world
in relationship with the unity of a universal apperception in the life of
the transcendental subjectivity would not accomplish anything for Husserl's purposes without the postulation of a general consciousness, or the
positing of a general region of subjectivity.

It is asked clearly enough in the present essay whether the phenomenological world-question is really a transformation of the basic cosmological
question of philosophy. Is not the being of the world eliminated? This
question is not answered satisfactorily. Furthermore, the "question of the
being of the world" must be examined for its legitimacy. The logic of
questions, or the discipline which seeks to ascertain which questions are
meaningful in any particular field of knowledge, is in its way prior to
all fields, including phenomenology. Phenomenology cannot escape the
"predicament" of other organizations of knowledge on this point. If it
is to be of any use, or even of significance for us, naturally and otherwise,
its proper sphere of questions must be delimited. The possibility of establishing some kind of common denominator for all systems of knowledge,
including phenomenology, must therefore be granted. In other words, the
claim to uniqueness need not imply total difference.

Special problems arise due to the mechanism of the method of reduction.
Thus the "identity" of the world-believing and world-belief-eliminating
ego is made to be a problem. In fact, the three egos involved in the re-

duction are supposed to possess a peculiar identity. The ego of natural reflection reflects upon man within the limits of the natural attitude. In the process of transcendental reflection the human ego is eliminated and is replaced by an "outside" ego as reflecting agent. An enumeration of the various "egos" will be helpful for the determination of the assumptions of the phenomenological analysis. The three egos belonging to the structure of the process of reduction are: (1) the world-immersed ego, or I the man; (2) the transcendental ego; and (3) the epoché-performing "observer." What is at issue, in this distinction, is the *degree* of reflection: the transcendental ego, which ought to be taken in this sense and not involve the cardinal principle of idealism, does not interfere with the "world-belief," thus allowing the world-immersed ego to remain valid. The transcendental theoretical "observer," however, makes no use of any positing of the world, whether theoretical or atheoretical. Because it does not participate in the belief, the world is not valid for it simply, but only as a phenomenon, as the correlate of the transcendental belief which is thematized by this ego. It is indeed fortunate that this phenomenological trinity has not been exploited for theological purposes by those on the fringe of the movement. There is danger that the urge to give this situation a dramatic turn may prove to be stronger than the rational ideal to which the phenomenologist is formally committed. The reader learns of the "tension" belonging essentially to the performance of the reduction, the tension of the egos, which determines the "pathos" of phenomenology.

Husserl's idealism, although non-Berkeleyan in character, nevertheless makes use of the cardinal principle of idealism. His idealism is not psychological, for the world-experience of psychology is impotent as far as accounting for being is concerned. The distinction between being-in-itself and being-for-us is essential to the natural attitude. But what happens to "being-in-itself" or to the "world" on a deeper phenomenological stratum is another matter. It has already been seen how it has been placed in the universe of the absolute. If this is merely a metaphor, it may, as is the way with metaphors, gradually come to be structuralized and endowed with a reality of its own. "Life" is also a metaphor that soon comes to life, as illustrated by the concept of the "world" or of the whole of being as a valid unity "lying in the life" of the transcendental subjectivity.

In the course of the epoché the world-belief is bracketed. The correlate of this belief, or its "noema," is determined transcendentally. The transcendental noema is described as being the world itself as the valid unity lying in the belief of the streaming world-apperception of the transcendental subjectivity. One is led to ask at this point concerning the proper

reaches of this subjectivity. It is necessary to observe carefully what is involved here, lest the price paid for the discovery of the transcendental
problem of the world may prove to be too great. As distinguished from
the psychological noema, which is the meaning of an actual intentional
experience and is different from the being to which it refers, the transcendental noema is the being itself. Therewith we have arrived, to stay, in
the realm of subjectivity. Husserl would reply that we have merely discovered where we were to begin with. The contention that the method
of reduction leads the philosophical subject, in the most extreme radicalism
of self-inspection, through itself to the transcendental life of belief, whose
correlate the world "is," must be judged in the light of the dangers that
have been pointed out. If the epoché is defined as the cognitive way to
the absolute, it is necessary to clarify the concept of "the absolute." That
is not done satisfactorily in the present context, nor is it usually made clear
in the literature of phenomenology. The two meanings assigned by Kant,[12]
independence of being and general validity, do not cover the meaning of
the concept as employed in phenomenology. The knowledge made possible
by phenomenology is "intuitive," meaning by that actual "self-giving,"
and not intuition as opposed to discursive thinking. One proceeds absolutely as a matter of method by abstaining from existential positings, and
by abstaining from dependence upon formal principles. The "ego" is
analyzed while using the "phenomenon of the world" as a guide. What
really happens in the process of using the "guidance" of natural experience
and science is a reinterpretation of the latter in terms of a constitutive
consciousness. The "world" is referred to in assumptive terms as a "totality
of validity." The expression "validity" suggests dependence upon a "life,"
as seen in the statement that the phenomenological observer inquires concerning the life in which the validities arise.

The criticism, made earlier, that knowledge of being is confused with
being is again illustrated by the statement that the mundane and the transcendental are different *in the manner of their being*. To regard the mundane as a predicative concept of "is," which is to be reduced, is to predeter-
mine the analysis. It is easy to argue in such a way as to protect phenomenology against all criticism. Thus in answer to the charge that
phenomenology is "ontologistic" it is asked whether the mundane concept
of being has been injected into it by its critics. This is unwarranted, how-

---

[12] Bannes, in his *Versuch einer Darstellung und Beurteilung der Grundlagen der Philosophie Edmund Husserls* (Breslau, 1930), cites two meanings of the term "absolute" according to Kant: (1) it might mean, metaphysically, freedom from all dependence, or (2)
logically, unlimited validity.

ever, for it cannot be maintained that one can only use the terms of a theory for a theory. It has not been proved that one cannot judge phenomenology from another perspective, on other grounds. The opposite is true, for one must do so. There is an ultimate circularity in the theory of systems of knowledge, which include systems of philosophy of the natural and transcendental varieties. Each one can be judged from the point of view of the others. The "principle of duality" as regards theory and practice indicates one way to break the circle, and to provide an objective basis for the evaluation of theoretical systems.

We have been accustomed in the past to regard Husserl as a staunch upholder of rationalism and the unlimited power of reason. The elements of obscurantism and mystery in the present essay are somewhat reminiscent of the later Schelling. An intensive examination of intentionality is believed to provide a methodical approach to the innermost "hidden" essence of the transcendental processes of contribution. There are "secrets" to be revealed as well, as one learns from the plan of gaining insight into the secret nature of actual being in "validities" that are built up in the streaming transcendental life. It is again not clear whether belief and knowledge are being built up, or the reality itself. This observation, for which there is an occasion repeatedly, is only too appropriate. The description of the reduction as a procedure which de-objectivizes and de-mundanizes the intentional life by removing the self-apperceptions that place it in the world can be construed in terms of belief and knowledge. Expressed epistemically, the method is, or can be, thoroughly radical. The metaphysical implications which are introduced are in part the result of metaphysical language, and in part the effect of the latent idealistic principle.

The transcendental life which is attained by means of the phenomenological method is described as "creation," in contradistinction to the receptivity of the natural psychical life. "Creation" is another assumptive term that is capable of being seriously misleading. "Constituting" is, however, neither receptive nor productive, but is regarded as something that cannot be handled by means of ontic concepts; it is a relationship that can only be shown by the performance of constitutive investigations. It follows that such investigations can neither be defended nor impugned from the outside, which means that they are neither true nor false in any "real" sense. The epistemic interpretation of the concept of constitution has undoubted merit if it is defined carefully. Phenomenology aims to get back of both the formal or *a priori* and the material presuppositions of knowledge, and thus to constitute everything. As distinguished from the traditional idealism, it is not concerned with the constitution of the objects of knowledge by means of subjective judgment-functions of an epistemological ego, but rather with the "constitution of the world." Construed epistemically, in the sense of method alone, this indicates a far-reaching stage of analysis. It turns out to be a way to idealism, phenomenological idealism being described as the discipline which traces the world back to its constitutive origin. The independent existence of the natural world is not ignored, nor are man's insignificant status in the cosmos and the receptivity of human knowing. The unreflective realism of the natural attitude is allowed to stand despite the transition to a new dimension of investigation. The "primal phenomena" of the natural attitude are now treated as the subject of an analysis which is constitutive in the sense that all such phenomena are to be accounted for on the basis of immediately given data of experience, beginning with the simplest elements which analysis can reveal. The question that has already been raised, whether it is possible to proceed further and judge the phenomenological philosophy, can be answered by means of an extension of the method of reduction to include all types of method.

In the method of reduction the world as a whole is viewed as being the result of a transcendental constitution, and it is "taken back" into the life of the absolute subjectivity. It is readily understandable that the whole procedure can afford to be innocent so far as ontic significance and assumptions are concerned, provided that the absolute is the source of it all; and that well-seasoned term is laden with misleading connotations.

The recognition of the "relative truth" of the natural attitude occurs in the interest of the absolute phenomenological view. Reminiscent of Hegel is the statement that phenomenological "subjectivism" is not opposed to the immediate truths of the natural attitude, such as the independence of being from the inner-worldly spirit. It is alleged to receive all such truths in itself, but preserves (Hegel's term "aufheben" is used) them in the full transcendental truth which contains the mundane as a factor. What Husserl opposes is thus the "absolutizing" of a relative situation. The world is interpreted idealistically, in a sense different from the subjectivism of the natural attitude. It is interpreted as the scientific proof and systematic development of the constitutive ideality of the world. This "proof," to which Husserl finally appeals, must be "seeing" in the last analysis. Husserl once remarked that he who would attempt to establish (*begründen*) seeing would be a fool. Not that there is any guarantee that in the event of a disagreement one person could compel another to "see" things the same way: there is no empirical guarantee. But the *possibility* of adequate seeing must be allowed. Whatever occurs as a matter of fact, or fails to occur, will not alter the fact that seeing is the final test.

The world is portrayed by Husserl as being a "stratum" in the transcendental life, as the level of the termination of all constitutive processes, and as related to the surface of the transcendental life which permits the world to arise. This pictorial language cannot be ascribed to the necessity of talking in terms of the natural attitude. When it is said that the reduction brings the world back to the origin in knowing (whereby it must be determined whether an origin for knowing is meant) and that it discovers the transcendental ideality of the world, as the final objectification of the absolute spirit, one cannot fail to recognize the Hegelian pattern.

The essay closes with a formulation of what is called the threefold paradox besetting the phenomenologist. The paradoxes are instructive and helpful in calling attention to the difficulties encountered in the method of reduction. (1) There is first of all the paradox of the communication of knowledge from the "transcendental observer" to the "dogmatist" with the natural attitude. Does not that presuppose a common ground between them? This problem is solved readily. The phenomenologist does not have to leave the transcendental attitude (one ought to say "give up" rather than "leave," but the metaphorical language persists) and return to a state of naïveté; he places himself rather "in" the natural attitude as a transcendental situation that is seen through by him. All that the phenomenologist can accomplish in his communication is to supply enough knowledge to lead the naive person to make the reduction himself. This paradox also serves to show why it is impossible to present the entire reduction from the beginning, which presumably exonerates the "incompleteness" of the account in the *Ideas*. (2) The second fundamental paradox, concerning the "phenomenological proposition," which is based upon the first, relates to the mundane word-concepts and language which are alone at the disposal of the communicating phenomenologist. Expressing his belief that the mundane meaning of all available words cannot be entirely eliminated, Husserl concludes that no phenomenological analysis, above all of the deep constitutive strata of transcendental subjectivity, can be presented adequately. In short, all phenomenological reports are inadequate because of the attempt to give a mundane expression to a non-worldly meaning. It is denied that this difficulty could be met by the invention of an artificial language, on the ground that such a language would be without meaning, and the problem is mainly one of communication to the dogmatist. Husserl has not proved his case in this paradox. Inadequacies in language can be met by means of well-defined terms. Language as a whole can be examined without incurring a vicious circle. Specially introduced technical terms really function as "artificial language," and Husserl himself has made ample use of that device. The "paradox of communication" opens the door to the danger of mysticism, to the ineffable, and if it has the advantage of eluding criticism of every "natural" kind, there is also the danger that all sorts of muddled individuals will stake claims in the new territory, or that it may even become institutionalized. There is no "inner conflict" between mundane word-meaning and the indicated transcendental meaning in itself. What is feared is the danger that the dogmatist may only grasp the mundane meaning of the words used, and disregard the transcendental meaning. It follows that one may even quote the text of Husserl correctly, and still have a wrong interpretation. Thus it appears that if phenomenology has presuppositions, they cannot be expressed (i.e., "naturally"). (3) The third paradox is called "the logical paradox of transcendental determinations," and is intended to show that logic is not equal to the task of solving the problems arising in the determination of basic transcendental relations. This does not mean that no logic holds in the realm of transcendental subjectivity; it is rather an objection to the world-relatedness of logic, even when it is formalized. There is perhaps a sense in which the paradox is justified after all. Thus, for example, there is the question as to how the identity of the transcendental ego and of the human ego is to be determined. Are they the same ego, or two separate egos? It is contended that all *ontic* forms of identity are incapable on principle of "logically" determining the *constitutive identity* of the transcendental ego and of man. One should ask whether there is any identity at all. It turns out, as the expression "constitutive identity" indicates, that one of them constitutes the other. The identity in question is so conceived that it cannot be determined within the horizon of the mundane idea of being. But the separation of the two egos is just as false as the equating of them. The solution of this problem proves to be transcendental in character, and is accomplished with the aid of "the infinite essence of the spirit."

The paradoxes are reminiscent of Gorgias, whom Husserl is inclined to take seriously, and to credit with the discovery of the problem of transcendence. Indeed, the first paradox states that the phenomenological realm cannot be "known," i.e., in natural terms; and the second informs us that it cannot be "communicated," i.e., in natural language, or in any language for that matter. The third paradox, in effect, removes the realm of phenomenology beyond proof or disproof in their customary sense, in that it declares for the inadequacy of "mundane" logic. The formulation of the paradoxes, especially the third one, shows that one may not hope for a satisfactory answer, or in fact for any answer at all, on the basis of the natural attitude concerning matters pertaining to the transcendental sphere. One can therefore never be convinced of phenomenology in natural terms, but must adopt the phenomenological attitude. This situation may be compared to the "tension" of the three egos. The proved claims of reason and radicalism, which are so conspicuous in the movement, are compelled here to give way to the "pathos" of nescience.

The third paradox must be carefully considered because of its characterization of logic as "world-bound." The phenomenologist aims to rise "above" it by means of another *method* which puts logic out of play, as Husserl describes it elsewhere. But it is pure logic that is eliminated. Logic as a universal methodology must be effable,[13] and only that philosophy which is statable in its terms, or conforms to it, can be considered. This is not to imply that Husserl has not made a contribution which will enforce the widening of the field of logic. On the contrary, it does so in a double sense: first, the region of the application of logic is extended because of the new devices and insights illustrated in phenomenology; and second, Husserl has added to the methods of knowledge. He has developed a phenomenological conception of logic which provides the equivalent of an epistemological and "pure" psychological foundation of logic, and his technique for a presuppositionless procedure in philosophy is of lasting value as a methodological device. His work has served to deepen the meaning of presuppositions in philosophy. It is really a generalization of the deductive method of defining assumptions. One is not necessarily committed thereby to any dogma; the careful handling of the phenomenological method will guard against that failing. To gain an adequate understanding of the bases of philosophy, it was necessary to construct a method which would make universal reflection possible. The phenomenological method aids toward that end. If it is assimilated to a critically founded and complete methodology, it is an indispensable aid in assuring universal reflection and objective knowledge.

C. THE PROPER FUNCTION OF PHENOMENOLOGICAL ANALYSIS

It cannot be denied that when the frequently occurring passages relating to phenomenological idealism are considered, including the direct attempts to justify the idealistic thesis in the *Formal and Transcendental Logic*, e.g., that Husserl has exceeded the limits of a purely descriptive philosophy. It is unavoidable that all his work be judged in the light

---

[13] Cp. H. M. Sheffer, "Ineffable Philosophies," *Journal of Philosophy*, vol. VI (1909), pp. 123–129.

of the severe canons of his avowed method. The following consideration of the requirements and proper function of phenomenological analysis, which will include a summary recapitulation of the principal stages of that philosophy, will endeavor to represent phenomenology as a consistently realized discipline, so that its general significance for philosophy will be unmistakable. In this way the positive nature of phenomenology will be seen all the better, after the various doubts that have been considered.

1. The Interpretation of the Given and Its Analysis

As has been seen, phenomenology was originally conceived as "descriptive psychology"; and the original problem confronting Husserl, presented by logical psychologism, became for him the problem of reconciling the objective validity of logic and mathematics with the subjective processes of experiencing. The goal then became the achievement of a complete analysis of experience, which meant the inclusion of the "a priori" in its descriptive sphere and the extension of the concept of intuition to include "categorial" intuition.[14]

The descriptive preparation and clarification of logic was the first task of phenomenology. The next step was the definition of the ideal of a science of philosophy. "Unity of science" was to be achieved on a basis of final clarity and understanding. That meant the examination of all presuppositions and motives, on the one hand, and completeness of descriptive analysis — a really complete "radical empiricism" — on the other hand. The attainment of this ideal required a method which would define the *universal* field for philosophical investigation and provide the technique for a "radical" descriptive procedure. That could only be accomplished by means of a purely subjective mode of approach. The starting-point had to be "mind," and not the "world," for the latter had to become a problem, like everything else. Mind may make itself to be a problem, in the same way that it makes all other things to be problems. If philosophy is to begin with a maximum of problems and a minimum of assumptions, the self-reflection of the meditating ego must constitute the beginning. This "ego" is no construction, and not at all a metaphysical principle. The "Cartesian reduction" by which its scope is defined shows it to comprise the stream of experiences of an individual, experiencing being, taken with their intended objects *as such*, which means that all judgments of transcendent existence are suspended. That is done *for methodological purposes alone.*

[14] Cf. Scheler's remarks concerning his first meeting with Husserl, in his "Deutsche Philosophie der Gegenwart," *Deutsches Leben der Gegenwart*, ed. by Philipp Witkop (Berlin, 1922), p. 198.

There is no thought of "eliminating" *the world itself* (of the "natural attitude") or of "bracketing" the world itself. The reduction is an affair of knowledge, and only an incautious or confused use of language would permit this matter to remain in doubt. The real purpose of the method is seen when one recognizes that the experience of individual objects on the part of a single knower provides the simplest possible beginning for the critique of knowledge.

The desired "final clarity" can be obtained only by reaching back to the "simplest elements" of experience; only by an analysis which gives an account of the part played by mind (or subjectivity) in its relationship with that which is "given" in experience. Husserl has formulated the method which is implicit in all attempts, from Kant to Lewis, to determine the *a priori* aspect of experience. The technique required by such analysis must be explicitly determined. If there is to be final understanding, it is necessary to reflect upon all interpretations by mind, and to question and justify all assumptions. At least, that is the ideal. In order to inspect all elements of interpretation, abstracting from the sheerly given in experience (in the analytical sense in which the term "given" is here intended, in contradistinction to the "given" complex natural and cultural world of which the knower is a part), the universal "pure" reflective method of phenomenology is required. The suspension of all positings of transcendent existence results in the determination of a realm of pure or "transcendental" subjectivity.

Just as the "reflexive predicament" (i.e., the necessity of using the mechanism of knowledge in investigating cognition) cannot be avoided in fact, but can be met in principle by a systematic procedure of descriptive clarification, so the general difficulty of using "conceptual interpretations" may be met. This difficulty is faced by all epistemological analyses, no matter what the method may be. Whether the ideal of inspecting all elements of interpretation can actually be realized in an analysis may perhaps not be answered in the affirmative with confidence, but that does not affect the value of epistemological inquiry. The already known elements may be accounted for descriptively, and our knowledge of hitherto unrecognized elements may be increased by the greater thoroughness made possible by practiced reflection. The explicit use of the phenomenological epoché is a great aid in this procedure; and it should be rendered explicit in any case, if it is used.

It is a familiar argument, to hold that the attempt to inspect all interpretations by mind is as hopeless as attempting to lift oneself by his bootstraps, for it is tantamount to attempting to avoid the mind while using it.

To express the "predicament" in that way is to load the term "mind" to start with, in such a way as to cut off access to the truth. It is particularly important in this case to avoid metaphors when stating the question. Because many "interpretations" (concepts, hypotheses, idealizations) of the past had to be modified, or discarded and superseded by others, is no reason why *some* interpretations may not be true, and "final" in that sense.

That the problem is as difficult as it is fundamental is shown by an analysis of the "given." [15] It may mean: (a) not contributed by mind, in the sense of "raw material," or of a "sensuous residuum," or of physical objectivity; (b) sensuous content, due to organic interaction and reaction to stimuli; (c) interpretative (meaningful) experience, on the non-reflective level; and (d) reflective experience. The "given" is historical throughout, in all the senses indicated, although at a different tempo: (c) and (d) have a history; but so has (b), even though it changes more slowly; and (a) is slowest of all in its history, or evolution. The problem of reconciling this fact with the idea of a fixed, "timeless," *a priori* structure of knowledge and reality (with the *a priori* of knowledge as conditioning the structure of reality) is more serious and pertinent than any epistemological predicament could be.

2. *The Purely Cognitive Level of Analysis*

In accordance with the phenomenological method, everything that can have the validity of being must be viewed as constituted in my ego, and hence everything existent appears to be a mere factor of what is called my "transcendental being." [16] The entire investigation is guided by the precept that nothing is to be "postulated" and "interpreted appropriately," but that everything is to be *exhibited*. This method of procedure is intended to achieve that final understanding of the world beyond which it is not meaningful to inquire.

As a matter of method, I choose to regard the world and all its realities "as a universe of constituted transcendences." It is regarded as "constituted in experiences and powers of my ego," which "precedes this constituted world as the final constitutive subjectivity." This can be stated in simple, innocuous language, or it can be construed (wrongly, to be sure) as implying some kind of actual precedence of the constitutive subjectivity. The precedence is purely logical, of course. The methodological procedure that has been proposed results in the "priority" of the

---

[15] Cp. J. Wild, "The Concept of *the Given* in Contemporary Philosophy," *Phil. and Phen. Research*, vol. 1 (1940), pp. 70 ff.

[16] Cf. *Formale und Transzendentale Logik*, § 96.

mind, and the individual mind to begin with. That is why Husserl could state that "the transcendence of the world is a transcendence in relation to this ego," and could refer the real world to the continually predelineated presumption that experience will continue to go on in the same constitutive style. When he, furthermore, stated that all objective being, and all truth, have their ground of being and of knowledge in transcendental subjectivity, he could defensibly mean only *known* objective being, i.e., as known. That which is objective is, in accordance with the method adopted, based upon "a synthetic unity of actual and potential intentionality belonging to transcendental subjectivity." In this way the final foundation of all truth is ascribed to the "universal self-reflection of phenomenology." In accordance with the "radicalism" of this process of self-reflection, every "pre-given existent" becomes "an intentional index for a system of constitutive contributions." There may be no prejudgments, and hence nothing may be taken as pre-given: not the world, or a realm of numbers, etc. In short, no pre-given realms, whether real or ideal, may be admitted (i.e., given phenomenological status) if absolutely founded knowledge is to be achieved. That is the prime requirement for a transcendental critique of knowledge.

By no means does this mean that mind actually creates the real world of our natural experience. No principle of spirit may be injected into the procedure. It will be agreed that the phenomenological method insures that there are "no objects in advance" for the immanent "innerness" of the knower. When Husserl stated that the evidences as functions constituting the existent perform the contribution whose result is then called "existent object," he can only be interpreted as restricting himself to the level of pure description. Since there is no hypostatized ego or metaphysical principle, there can be no reified objects. Phenomenologically, one can indeed only account for what is "called" the existent object. Nothing further may be implied. In general, such pictorial terms as "creative," "arises," etc., are dubious and only too easily lead to misunderstandings.

All that is true or valid for the natural attitude remains true for any other attitude, including phenomenological reflection, even though it may be "put out of play" for reasons of method. The abandonment of the natural attitude does not result in the surrender of any meanings. They are transformed through being reduced and constituted. The first step is to transform all experiences into reduced experiences. The experience obtained with the natural attitude serves as a guide or clue for the pure reflective procedure. But no use is made of it in that form. If reduced and non-reduced elements are confused, pseudo-problems result.

In comparison with the use of the formal-logical method in philosophy, this is seen to be a deeper level of analysis. The symbols themselves must be "constituted," as well as all meanings. All presuppositions on the level of language-systems must be questioned and analyzed, if they are to be retained at all. The device of transforming "thing-language" into "word-language" [17] helps to show that the ideal of a *mathesis universalis* can be realized. It is also of aid in eliminating pseudo-problems by referring all terms to their systems of knowledge. Useful and important though that method is, it is not adequate for general philosophical purposes, if the leading aim is "final understanding." The formal unity of science — which can only be partial — must itself be founded by means of more searching studies. The latter, as phenomenological, establish a basis for the unity of science by means of an investigation of the basic concepts and idealities used in formal science, and in science in general. The formal-logical method, as used for philosophy, is partially naive, in that it does not bring with it a complete or adequate critique of knowledge. Although its departure from "thing-language" detaches philosophy from the special sciences and metaphysics, it does not carry the critique far enough. The point is, to carry it as far as is possible, which requires the use of the phenomenological reduction. Furthermore, the proposed linguistic transformation of philosophical statements may not neglect the sources of the significance of those statements, a requirement which phenomenological analysis seeks to meet by means of its treatment of meaning.[18]

3. Phenomenological Questions and Intermethodological Judgments

The phenomenological method aims to be autonomous, and, for its purpose, it is self-contained; but such autonomy is always relative. Unless one were completely to deny the validity of the various systems of knowledge, he must admit the possibility of judging phenomenology, as a whole or in part, on the basis of some other system or method. That is a consequence of the objective validity of methods which cannot be denied. It amounts to the recognition of the relative autonomy of systems of knowledge, with the right to frame questions involving meanings from any and all spheres, so long as such questions are permitted by the basic concepts and principles of the system in question.

This applies directly to the case of the phenomenological philosophy. Questions of existence apart from phenomena are meaningless for it; and

[17] Cf. R. Carnap, *Philosophy and Logical Syntax.*
[18] Cf. Felix Kaufmann, "Phenomenology and Logical Empiricism," in *Philosophical Essays in Memory of Edmund Husserl.*

there should be no talk of existence (i.e., natural existence) in connection with the essential structures or generalities that are described.[19] "Pure" phenomenology has *its* proper questions, just as is the case with any formal system; and there are "system-strange" questions with respect to it (i.e., questions which are irrelevant to the system concerned). Furthermore, it is meaningful to judge it as a whole on the basis of another system; or, besides, to judge any one or set of its statements with respect to the factual content of another system. Thus the activity of phenomenological analysis itself may be made to be the subject of historical, sociological, or psychological judgments by being projected upon the historical plane. Such inter-methodological judgments may be interesting and instructive. In this case, the contribution of the phenomenologist is considered as a whole in the light of human needs and historical antecedents. Although the naturalistic, evolutionary method of explanation is judged to be "naive" [20] (this is a technical term with no valuational implication), the phenomenologist must concede the value of viewing himself and his efforts as cultural, evolutionary products. He may do this even if he follows Husserl in holding that "all evolution in the usual sense belongs in the constituted world." The two types of method are simply concerned with different questions and patterns of explanation. To utilize the one is not to repudiate the other. On the contrary, it may be said that one of the acid tests of a philosophy is its ability to integrate its methodology with methodology in general.

4. Some Prominent Misunderstandings of Phenomenology

In view of the numerous misunderstandings of phenomenology, it will be well to summarize some of the chief errors which are even now current in the literature of philosophy and psychology.

(a) It should be noted that Husserl's opposition to logical psychologism was *not* an opposition to psychology. He denied that his critique of psychologism was in any way an opposition to the psychological foundation of logical methodology, or to the descriptive-psychological explanation of the

[19] In the second of the *Logical Investigations*, Husserl maintained that the general is not a thought-content in the sense of a real constituent of a thought-experience, and that it is an *object* that is thought. But he did not place the being of the ideal upon the same level as the being thought of the fictive or the absurd. The latter does not exist at all, and nothing can be stated categorically about it in a real sense. To speak of them as having their own kind of being, the "merely intentional" kind, is really to use figurative language. In his view ideal objects exist truly, on the other hand.

[20] The same term is applied to Marxism by Husserl, again with no valuational implication. Cf. M. Farber, "Phenomenology," in *The Twentieth Century Philosophy*, ed. by D. Runes (Philosophical Library, New York, 1943).

origin of logical concepts. It was advanced rather against an epistemological position that had unfavorably influenced the mode of treatment of logic, and not against the methodological type of logic of such writers as Mill, Sigwart, and Wundt: and he did not dispute the basing of that type of logic upon empirical psychology. The point was, however, that psychology was not its only basis, but also "pure logic," an *a priori* discipline whose laws are applied and made fruitful under the empirical conditions of scientific thinking. It was unfortunate that this misunderstanding was added to by Husserl's own repeated efforts to distinguish phenomenology from psychology, and his use of such terms as "naive" to describe non-phenomenological points of view. But phenomenology is intended to serve psychology, as well as all other sciences. In part, also, it may be considered as a department or extension of psychology, as illustrated by its descriptive analyses of meaning and time-consciousness.

(b) One may define the conditions which must be fulfilled if evidence is to be realized, without raising the question of its actual realization. Important though the latter be, it is an independent question. An essential analysis may be valid even if the structures are never actually illustrated in experience, just as the propositions of arithmetic are valid independently of our reckoning, or of our actual thought-processes. Obviously, if the structures were not illustrated in experience, there would be little interest in them. *Approximations* are what we have, as a matter of fact, and these may differ from case to case. The general, the "eidos," on the other hand, is an object of thought, a "contribution of the understanding." That locates it properly.

(c) There are a number of things which phenomenology conspicuously does not do or mean: (1) It does not "tear the meaning loose from the act." [21] (2) It does not deny or reject the external world.[22] (3) It does not try to answer *all* questions, and is not intended to be an all-inclusive method for all purposes. (4) It is also not intended to be a substitute for other methods, and above all for those involving factual and hypothetical elements. (5) It does not deny inductive truth, nor does it fail to distinguish between different types of "truth." (6) It is not a trap for metaphysical purposes. As a descriptive, preliminary discipline, its findings may be used for metaphysical (or dialectical) purposes, just as are the results of logical analysis. But it is not a short-cut to spiritualism in metaphysics, for one thing.

(d) In contrast to these misunderstandings, there are a number of things

[21] Cf. Husserl's reply to Palagyi, already referred to.

[22] The term "discard" as used by W. Koehler in his *The Place of Value in a World of*

that phenomenology does do or mean: (1) It is the *first* method of knowledge because it begins with "the things themselves," which are the final court of appeal for all knowledge, and also in a logical, explanatory sense, because it seeks to point out all presuppositions. (2) It views everything factual as an exemplification of essential structures, and is not concerned with matters of fact as such. (3) It deals not only with "real" essences, but also with "possible" essences. (4) Direct insight, evidence in the sense of the self-givenness of the objectivity is the ultimate test for it. (5) Despite the "reduction," the phenomenologist still has a brain (an "evolutionary" brain), in the same sense that he breathes. That statement is as true as it is irrelevant to the method.[23]

As a peculiarly philosophical method, the method of phenomenological analysis is of significance for all knowledge. It does on a universal scale, and in a thoroughgoing manner, what is only partly done by other methods. Its complete epoché and technique for philosophical. analysis represents an ideal of methodological rigor that cannot but be generally helpful. But it must be strictly limited to description. Perry's warning concerning the ego-centric predicament applies here: no metaphysical capital is to be made out of an attempt that aims at an understanding of knowledge and experience in their essential forms and accomplishments.[24] It should be possible to keep the method free from all dogmas, which either involve special assumptions or are due to fallacious inference, and thus make it generally acceptable for philosophy. Whoever discusses or uses this method must be fully aware of the responsibility involved, for there is danger that the invalidation of abuses of the method may lead one to suppose that the method as a whole has been invalidated. Such an unfortunate conclusion would prevent the recognition of one of the most important advances in recent philosophy, one which offers promise of a unified basis

Facts is also unfortunate, for the "convictions about existence" are simply "suspended," and continue to be of interest phenomenologically.

[23] The present conception of phenomenology in its relationship to other methods may also serve to indicate the direction of a reply to the interesting line of argument of V. J. McGill ("A Materialist's Approach to Husserl's Philosophy") and Charles Hartshorne ("Husserl and the Social Structure of Immediacy") in *Philosophical Essays in Memory of Edmund Husserl*. Other essays in the same volume, not mentioned thus far but pertinent for the present subject, include the following: Herbert Spiegelberg, "The 'Reality-Phenomenon' and Reality," Helmut Kuhn, "The Phenomenological Concept of 'Horizon,' " Jacob Klein, "Phenomenology and the History of Science," Fritz Kaufmann, "Art and Phenomenology," Louis O. Kattsoff, "The Relation of Science and Philosophy in the Light of Husserl's Thought." Of interest also are the essays by William E. Hocking ("Outline-Sketch of a System of Metaphysics"), Gerhart Husserl ("Men and the Law"), and Hermann Weyl ("The Ghost of Modality").

[24] Cf. R. B. Perry, *Present Philosophical Tendencies* (New York, 1916), pp. 128 ff.; and p. 114 for the formulation of the "cardinal principle of idealism."

for philosophical activity because it aspires to be truly self-critical and self-justifying, making use of no preconceived ideas and constructions.

D. HISTORICAL MEANING AND THE APPROACH TO PHILOSOPHY

As Husserl recognized, phenomenology cannot complete its task without allowing for its self-examination, which is done according to its own intuitive standard. This leads to the final question to be raised, namely, to the consideration of the phenomenological philosophy with respect to the problem of historical meaning. The principle of the coöperation of methods will receive added emphasis therewith.

1. Method as a Response to Problems

When the stage of the conscious use of method in philosophy has been reached, it is important to make clear the conception of a goal and the leading problems in the mind of the philosopher. The aim of a philosophy may be well defined; or, again, it may be due to motives that are unconscious and represent needs or prejudices of the age. Because the approach to philosophy is conditioned by different motives, the choice and application of methods are also predetermined to a large extent. No one method may be expected to solve all problems. As Russell has pointed out, "Every philosophy has been invented to solve some one problem, and is incapable of dealing with many others." [25] The same may be said of methods. Every method is a response to a need, to solve problems or to answer questions. A philosophy which raises no distinctive questions is either superfluous or useless; and if it does ask meaningful questions of its own, it must be interested in questions of method. "By their questions shall they be known" may be said to be especially true for philosophy.

No charge could be more severe than to accuse a philosopher of having no method. But it is also an error to hold that one "method" must be used exclusively, with a resolute disregard of the problems and aims that may be set up. To conceive the function of philosophy as a logical method in the restricted sense of giving rules for the formation and transformation of sentences is to miss much of method itself. The formal-logical method, as an exact method, is of value on its own account, for it leads to a science of pure forms. The emptiness, relativism, or nihilism into which it eventuates if used exclusively merely indicates its essential limitations in philosophy.

[25] Cf. B. Russell's article on Dewey's *Essays in Experimental Logic, Journal of Philosophy,* vol. XVI (1919), p. 22.

The various methods of knowledge are at the disposal of the philosopher, the formal-logical among others. The question then arises, whether there is a peculiarly philosophical method. The phenomenological method may be said to be distinctively philosophical, and — which is characteristic of everything philosophical — its results turn out to be significant for all other methods, as well as all knowledge.

2. *Historical and Sedimented Meaning*

The conception of a logical-historical constructive philosophy provides a necessary completion of the phenomenological method. The exclusive preoccupation with a "pure" systematic method is apt to lead in time to the neglect of subject-matter, the historical basis and nature of the field, and the motives that guide or prompt thought. To be faithful to its subject-matter, which includes reference to the special sciences, a philosopher should take account of such historical factors. The sciences themselves have their historical aspect, and are historically conditioned in an important respect. That is especially the case in social science, but is also true at least of the motivation of the natural sciences. Only by considering their historical significance will it be possible to determine the real significance of philosophical problems.

The philosopher should adopt a reflective attitude toward his own historical period, or toward any historical period, and also toward their interpretations, in keeping with the general reflexive nature of philosophy. Philosophy must include itself in its subject-matter. If it is to be a universal critic, it must criticize itself. This is a situation more general than that of the circularity of logic, which must assume at least a part of itself in order to make possible its own foundation. That really means the assumption of the whole of logic, as the basic principles imply the remaining propositions. The necessary amount of assumption is greater in philosophy as a whole. This problem is faced in phenomenology by means of the recognition of a "pre-given" realm which is antecedent to reflective analysis, and by using all pertinent examples of "naturally" established knowledge as a guide for the "constitutive" method.

There are two major stages in the complete use of philosophical method: first, the systematic treatment, as a matter of logical analysis and generalization, of the special sciences, of real experience, and of possible experience, whether real or phantasy experience; and second, all of these must be regarded as historically conditioned. The historical fact is of course practically irrelevant to many propositions and theories. But in the larger sense of their total significance, they are seen to be organizations of historical meanings. All meaning is historical in a sense. When Husserl undertook, in his last period, to do justice to the element of history within the frame of the phenomenological method,[26] he spoke of the "sedimentation" of meanings. In seeking to take account of the element of history, two courses are open: to adopt the customary naturalistic genetic method; or to undertake the phenomenological "genetic" method, which is devoted to "intentional" analysis, and is concerned with essential structures here, as elsewhere. The latter is illustrated in Husserl's study of the "origin" of geometry as an intentional-historical problem.

This type of analysis, for which the eidetic reduction is performed, so that actual events and their dates are irrelevant, however important they may be from another point of view, is not intended to displace the naturalistic type of genetic investigation. They are not rivals in any sense, but cooperate as necessary types of method, each with its own proper function.

3. The Problem of Objective Truth

The projection of all knowledge and experience upon the plane of historical events is indispensable for complete philosophical understanding, and cannot fail to have a salutary effect upon the philosopher. The transcendental phenomenologist is himself projected, with all his contributions, upon the plane of history. His contributions are considered as a whole in the light of human needs, historical antecedents, and reality in general. It may be desirable to "project" the method of reduction in this way. Whether avowedly or not, every theory serves interests, and that aspect should be examined in each case. Should it turn out that a method which withdraws from all reference to the factual world is (even if in the wrong hands) in effect a way of condoning dislocations in that world, that fact should be considered seriously in the self-criticism of philosophy. The reflective process involved in the "historical projection" must in turn be examined, because all reflection occurs in a historical setting. There is no endless regress, however, because the requirements of an objective analysis are met when the reflecting observer is considered in his relationship to his field of inquiry. Further stages of reflection would yield nothing more. The fact that all philosophizing occurs in a definite social-historical context, and involves sedimented historical meanings, presents no essential obstacle to an objective analysis.

A philosophy may be objectively true while representing a response to actual historical needs. Much knowledge, including philosophy, is ob-

---

[26] Cf. Fritz Kaufmann, "The Phenomenological Approach to History," *Phil. and Phen. Research*, vol. ii (1941), pp. 159–172.

jective in the sense of being verified as true under stated conditions, or as valid independently of particular historical conditions. The latter is the case for mathematics and formal logic, for example. The propositions and theories which have no other basis than that they appeal to social interests at a particular time are readily appraised by considering them in their significance for such contexts. All limitations of traditional or one-sided points of view are embraced in the subject-matter of the propositions that are asserted, in the required objective restatement of them. Constant historical needs present no problem in this connection. It is the difficulty of reflectively transcending the changing particular interests of a given period which is a cause for concern. The "reduction" is essential for that end. Applied to historical meanings, it is seen in its most complete form as serving the program for an objective philosophy which comprises cultural as well as abstract meanings.

4. *The Priority of Phenomenology and the Coöperation of Methods*

Since concrete, factual propositions belong to the special sciences, the goal as expressed in phenomenology is the intuitive foundation and clarification of the essential structures which underlie knowledge and (known or experienced) reality. When used strictly in accordance with its proper function, it will not be adversely criticized because it fails to achieve what is accomplished by means of the deductive method, or by means of a naturalistic, inductive philosophy of change which generalizes on the basis of the special sciences.

There are obviously other approaches to philosophy than the pure reflective beginning adopted by phenomenology. One may begin with the world of natural existence, for example. But if one's purpose is "final understanding" — or at least the greatest possible approach to it — and the elaboration of a "First Philosophy" which in a systematic sense is "prior" to all concrete knowledge, then he is committed to the use of the phenomenological method. The most important elements of this method have been in partial use, at least — that is true of the "epoché," for example, which is imposed upon all beliefs bearing upon a given subject-matter — so that it may be regarded as a natural extension of generally accepted procedures. Reflection is used in all regions of discourse; and essences or universals are indispensable to thought. Their thoroughgoing analysis is therefore antecedent to all special regions of discourse. So long as the phenomenologist recognizes that his procedure is one type of method which is to be subsumed under methods in general, so that he does not disparage the "naive" theorizing of those who use naturalistic methods and the various explanatory devices that are so valuable practically, he may take his place, coöperatively, among thinkers concerned with problems that are of real and lasting significance. Having regard to the work already performed, that place may in truth be said to be an honored one

INDEX

INDEX

I. References to Husserl's Writings (*other than the* LOGICAL INVESTIGATIONS)

II. Proper Names (*other than Husserl*)

III. Subjects and Terms

Date Due

SEP 20			
	PRINTED	IN U. S. A.	